THE HAMLYN PHOTOGRAPHIC GUIDE TO THE WILD FLOWERS OF BRITAIN & NORTHERN EUROPE

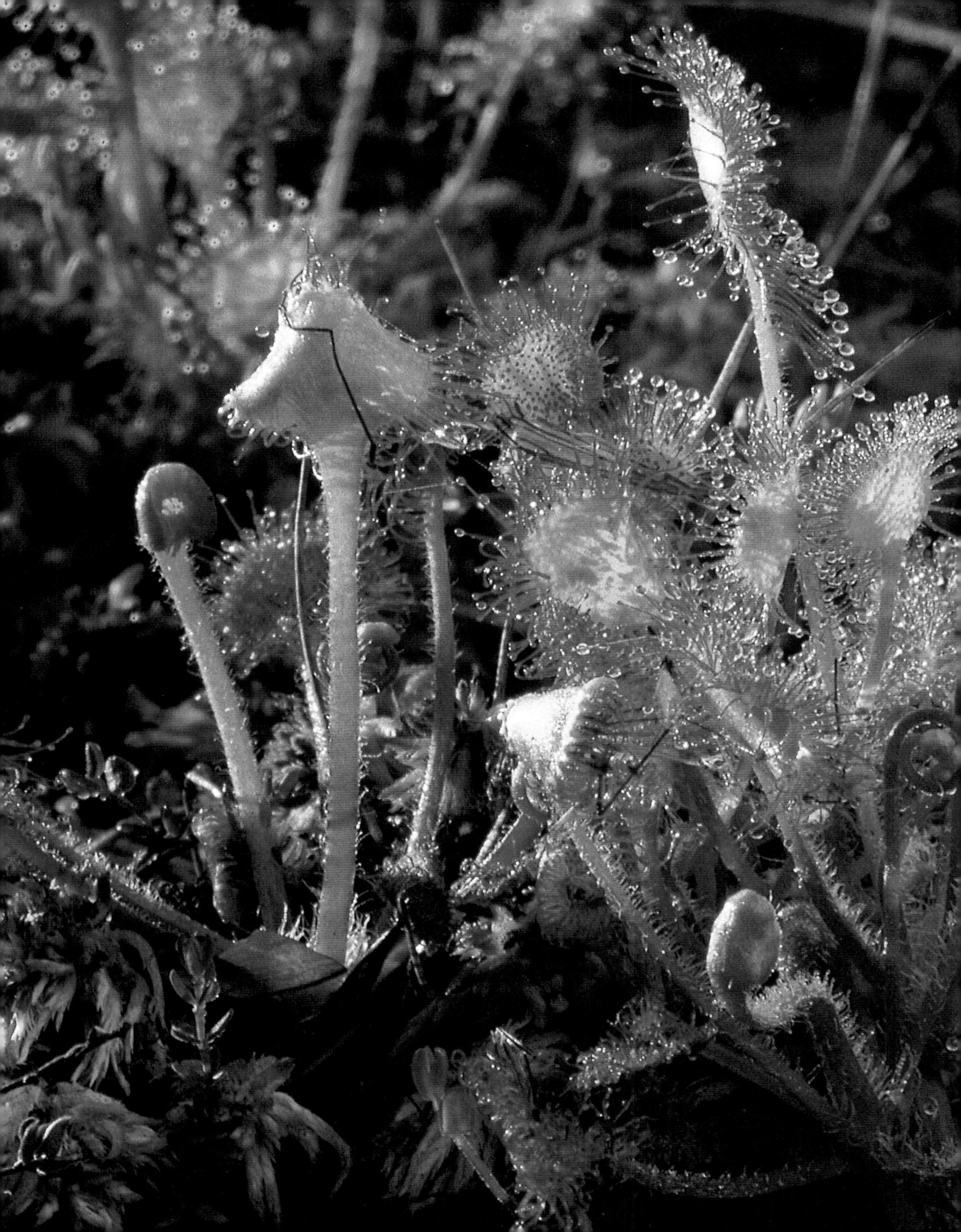

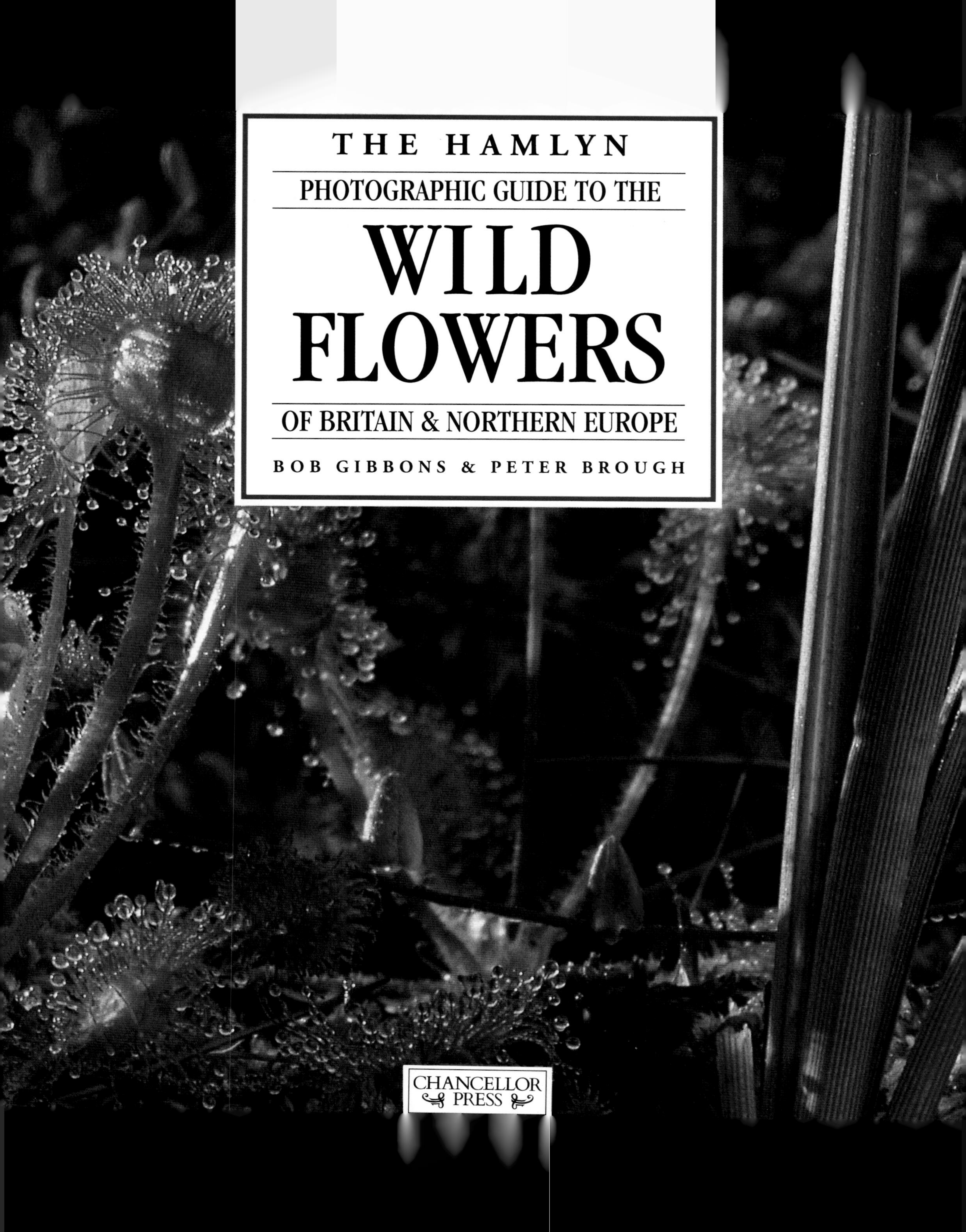
THE HAMLYN
PHOTOGRAPHIC GUIDE TO THE
WILD FLOWERS
OF BRITAIN & NORTHERN EUROPE
BOB GIBBONS & PETER BROUGH
CHANCELLOR PRESS

Acknowledgements

The high standard of the maps are due to the knowledge and toils of Martin Walters and John Akeroyd, to whom we are extremely grateful.

We also thank the artists, Chris Orr, Robin Somes and Tiffany Passmore for their splendid line drawings.

Many people have helped with the production of this book, and it may seem invidious to mention some and not others. However, with this risk in mind, we must specifically express our deep gratitude to those people who have worked long hours and played such an essential part in making the different parts of the book come together into a whole, a process which gives a new meaning to being on night duty! Without Andrew and Anne Branson of British Wildlife Publishing, the final product might not have seen the light of day. Thanks also go to David Goodfellow, Paul Sterry of Nature Photographers and Andrew Gagg of Photo Flora.

Many friends have helped us by providing information on locations of scarce or rare species for photography, and we are grateful to them all.

Finally we would like to thank our families for their patience and forbearance during the long hours of field work and writing which have been put into the book.

Peter Brough, Bob Gibbons

Bibliography

Blamey, M, Grey-Wilson, C 1989 *Illustrated Flora of Britain and northern Europe*. Hodder & Stoughton
Clapham, A R, Tutin, T G and Moore, E F 1987 *Flora of the British Isles* (third edition). CUP
Clapham, A R, Tutin, T G and Warburg, E F 1981 *Excursion Flora of the British Isles* (third edition). CUP
Dony, J G, Rob, C M, and Perring, F H 1986 *English Names of Wild Flowers* (second edition). BSBI
Edees, E S and Newton, A N 1988 *Brambles of the British Isles*. Ray Society
Fitter, R, Fitter, A and Blamey, M 1985 *The Wild Flowers of Britain and Northern Europe* (fourth edition). Collins
Garrard, I and Streeter, D 1983 *The Wild Flowers of the British Isles*. Macmillan
Lousley, J E and Kent, D H 1981 *Docks and Knotweeds of the British Isles*. BSBI
Meikle, R D 1984 *Willows and Poplars of Great Britain and Ireland*. BSBI
Mitchell, A 1982 *The Trees of Britain and Northern Europe*. Collins
Rich, T C G 1991 *Crucifers of Great Britain and Ireland*. BSBI
Richards, A J 1972 The *Taraxacum* Flora of the British Isles *Watsonia 9* supplement
Rose, F 1991 *The Wild Flower Key* (second edition) Warne
Stace, C A 1991 *New Flora of the British Isles*. CUP
Tutin, T G *et al*. (editors) 1964-80 *Flora Europea 1-5*. CUP
Tutin, T G 1980 *Umbellifers of the British Isles*. BSBI
Yeo, P F 1978 A taxonomic revision of *Euphrasia* in Europe *Bot J. Linn. Soc. 77*:223-334

Photographic research, editing and typesetting by
British Wildlife Publishing, Basingstoke Hampshire
Maps produced by Carte Blanche

First published in 1992 by Hamlyn

This edition published in 1998 by Chancellor Press
an imprint of Reed Consumer Books Limited
Michelin House, 81 Fulham Road
London SW3 6RB

A catalogue record for this book is available from the British Library

ISBN 0 75370 011 5

Printed in Spain

Photograph previous page Round-leaved Sundews

CONTENTS

INTRODUCTION

As far as we are aware, this is the first reasonably comprehensive photographic flora to cover the whole of North Europe. Although photographs have some disadvantages when compared to colour artwork, they also have a number of advantages, especially in the way that they can show the habit of a plant, often making a species easily recognisable, where detailed botanical drawings may fail. They come closer to the subconscious process in which experienced botanists identify plants at a glance by their 'jizz', rather than by precise botanical characteristics. In general, we have tried to select photographs that do give more information on the habit of the plant, except where close-ups are essential, and have supplemented the information in the photographs with line artwork where appropriate. It is rarely possible to show all the desired features of a plant in a single photograph, but the combination of photograph, artwork and text is ample in most cases.

The area covered by the book comprises northern Europe, including Scandinavia, and as far south as central France and southern Germany. In practice, the useful coverage extends more widely since the vegetation tends to change gradually as you move to different areas, and many of the flowers to be found further south and east are in the book. However, the further away one is from this core area, the less comprehensive the book becomes.

Within the primary area of the book, we cover virtually all the species that are likely to be encountered. The main exceptions to this are: a few species that only occur in isolated pockets on the fringes of the area, such as in Iceland or Spitzbergen; a proportion of genera which have a large number of similar species that are difficult to identify without a detailed text and good material, such as the hawkweeds *(Hieracium)* and the eyebrights (*Euphrasia*); and some introduced species. Because so many non-native species have become established to a greater or lesser degree within this huge area, we have selectively included those that are most naturalised and/or most likely to be encountered.

The order of the species and families within the book in general follows that adopted in *Flora Europaea*, a major international work on the flora of Europe. With a few minor exceptions, the scientific nomenclature also follows that of *Flora Europaea* as no other single system caters for the large geographical range covered here. Whilst the English names, where they exist, mainly follow those of *English Names of Wild Flowers*.

North Europe, as defined in the book, covers a considerable area of land. The diversity of its flora is further increased, however, by the wide range of conditions to be found within the area. Climatically, it encompasses extreme arctic conditions in the north, highly oceanic areas along the western coasts, and near-Mediterranean conditions in the south, as well as a gradual change to central Asian weather towards the east of the area. The diversity is further enhanced by the wide altitudinal range to be found in the region, from sea-level to alpine conditions, and everything in between. When combined with the highly varied geology, this altitudinal and climatic diversity allows an extremely wide range of habitats to develop. As a direct consequence, the number of flowering plants to be found in the area is very large.

An unimproved hay meadow in the Yorkshire Dales , England.

A dense mass of fruiting Dwarf Cornel by a fjord in northern Norway.

Using the book

The primary source of information for many users will be the photographs. A quick scan through these will often quickly show what a plant is, or at least in what group or family it is to be found. Some species, such as Motherwort (*Leonurus cardiaca*), stand out instantly as being different from almost everything else; other species will be much more difficult. For instance, it is unlikely that one could identify a species of forget-me-not from the photographs alone. To achieve accurate identification, the text provides general introductions to the characteristics of each family, introductions to main groupings, and descriptions of each species. The species descriptions are written to emphasise the differences between closely-related or similar-looking species, with the key features highlighted where appropriate. The format of the book does not allow for the provision of dichotomous keys to difficult groups, but, where appropriate, we have divided larger groups into sub-groups sharing distinctive characteristics.

The species descriptions themselves have been written in a standardised way, to make it easier to find facts and to compare species. However, it is not possible, nor useful, to describe all species in exactly the same way. For example, the colour of the hairs on the filaments is of key importance in identifying mullein species, but not for many other groups.

In addition to the straightforward anatomical information on leaf shape, height, flower colour, etc., which is largely self-explanatory, there is also information on the distribution, abundance and flowering time of each species. Following the **Br** symbol, there is also more information on the distribution within Britain and Ireland, if the species occurs there. When trying to identify a species, all this information should be taken into account. It is, for example, very unlikely that a species will be found well outside the range indicated on the maps or in the text, though some species are extending their range, and others are occasionally discovered in new localities.

The precise distribution of many species throughout Europe is still uncertain and therefore maps have only been included for those where this reasonably accurate information is available. Also, we have in most cases only mapped those species not found throughout the region.

The **colour codes on the maps** are as follows: **blue** indicates the main area of distribution; **tint of blue** indicates where the plant has a scattered distribution or where it is compartively rare; **grey** indicates where it is widely naturalised.

Flowering time (**Fl**) must be taken as a guide only. Apart from variations from year to year according to the weather, there is also a wide variation in flowering time over such a large range of altitude and latitude as is found in northern Europe. In a few cases, flowering time is one of the first aids to identification, such as in distinguishing Early Gentian *(Gentianella anglica)* from Felwort *(G. amarella)*, though this is relatively rare.

The habitat in which a plant occurs is often important. Unfortunately, over such a large area, the chosen preferences of plants may vary, so it is difficult to be precise for any given area. Nevertheless, it is worth taking this information into account when trying to identify a species; for example, it is highly unlikely that a plant recorded as occurring on heaths and heathy woods will be found on a saltmarsh or a chalk downland.

Whenever possible, take the book to the plant when attempting an identification. If necessary, collect a small sample (unless there are very few individuals present) without uprooting it, concentrating on obtaining the full range of its features from basal leaf to fruit, as well as flowers. This will make later identification much easier. Plants are under threat everywhere throughout Europe, mainly from habitat loss, and we should not add to this stress by unnecessary collecting. In addition, there are laws in many countries that outlaw collecting of plants by uprooting, or even by picking with rarer species and in certain protected areas.

GLOSSARY

Achene 1-seeded dry fruit, not splitting
Acuminate Gradually drawn out to a fine point
Acute Sharply pointed
Adpressed See appressed
Alien Introduced by man and naturalised
Alluvial Describing soils deposited by rivers
Alternate Not opposite each other, eg. leaves
Annual Life-cycle complete within 12 months
Anther Pollen-bearing tip of stamen
Apex Tip (of leaf or stem)
Appressed Pressed closely to another part eg. hairs to stem
Ascending Curving upwards
Auricle Rounded lobe projecting backwards at leaf-base
Awn Stiff, bristle-shaped projection
Axil Angle between upper surface of leaf base, or its stalk, and stem
Axillary In axil
Basal-leaves Leaves at base of stem
Berry Fleshy fruit with several seeds without a stony outer layer
Biennial Taking 2 years to complete life-cycle: usually germinating and forming leaves in first year; then flowering, bearing seeds and dying in second year
Bract Modified leaf at base of flower stalk or stalks
Bracteole Small bract at base of each individual flower-stalk
Bulb Swollen underground structure comprising short stem, leaf-bases and next year's bud
Bulbil Small bulb-like structure developing asexually on a plant and after falling being capable of growing into a new plant
Calcareous Containing calcium, eg. chalk or limestone
Calyx Outer part of flower, often divided into sepals
Carpel Division of female reproductive part of flower, consisting of ovary, stigma and style
Casual Introduced plant, neither planted nor permanently established
Cell Cavity in ovary or fruit
Cladode Leaf-like green lateral shoot
Clasping Leaf-base stalkless with backward-projecting lobes around stem
Compound leaf Having a number of separate leaflets
Compressed Flattened
Cordate Heart-shaped at base
Corm Swollen underground-stem of 1 year's duration, the new one growing on top of old
Corolla Collective term for petals
Corona Trumpet-like outgrowth, between the petals and the stamens, particularly applied to Daffodil flowers
Corymb Flat-topped raceme
Crenate With blunt rounded teeth
Cuneate Wedge-shaped
Cyme Repeatedly-divided inflorescence, with succession of lateral flowers on either one side or both sides
Decumbent Lying on ground and rising towards the tip
Decurrent Referring to base of leaf running down stem
Dehiscent Opening to shed seeds
Dentate Toothed
Dicotyledon Division of plants with 2 first leaves on germinating seedling
Digitate Having more than 3 finger-shaped leaves arising from the same point
Dioecious With male and female flowers on separate plants
Divergent Leaning away from another structure
Elliptic Leaf shape like an ellipse
Endemic Native in only one country or small area
Entire Not toothed
Epicalyx Outer calyx additional to the true (inner) calyx
Epichile Front part of flower lip of some orchids, e.g. helleborines
Epiphyte Plant growing on another plant but not parasitic
Escape Plant which has spread from cultivated stock
Fen Plant community on wet alkaline peat
Flexuous Wavy
Floret Small flower
Free Not joined together
Fruit Seeds with surrounding structures
Glabrous Without hairs
Gland Either (1) small globular sticky structure at tip of hair, or (2) in spurges, the fleshy, yellowish bracts which alternate with the leafy bracts at the base of flower-clusters
Glandular With glands
Glaucous With greyish-blue lustre
Globose Rounded like a globe
Halberd-shaped Shaped like a medieval pike-head
Hastate Leaf shape with a flat base
Herb Non-woody vascular plant
Herbaceous Green with soft, leaf-like texture
Hermaphrodite Male and female organs in same flower
Hybrid Plant derived from cross-fertilisation between 2 different species
Hypochile Rear part of flower lip of some orchids, e.g. helleborines
Hypogynous Of flowers with stamens beside or beneath ovary
Inflorescence Combination of flowers, bracts and their branches
Internode Portion of stem between 2 nodes
Introduced Not native
Involucre Ring of bracts surrounding 1 or more flowers
Irregular flower One which is not radially symmetrical with equal petals, but is only symmetrical in one plane
Keel In pea family, the 2 lower petals which join together
Labellum Lip of orchid flower, usually on the lower side but occasionally the upper
Lanceolate Lance-shaped
Latex Milky juice in stem or leaf
Lax Not dense (see loose)
Leaflet Separate segment of a leaf which often resembles a leaf but has no associated bud or stipule
Linear Long, narrow and parallel-sided
Lip Part of corolla of irregular flower, usually the lower part but occasionally the upper
Lobe Projection or division of leaf
Loose Not dense or tightly packed
Lyrate Shaped roughly like a lyre
Membrane Thin structure, not green but either opaque or transparent
Membranous With membrane
Midrib Central vein of leaf
Monocotyledon Division of plants with 1 first leaf on germinating seedling
Monoecious With male and female flowers on same plant
Mucronate Bearing a short, often sharp, point at tip
Native Not known to have been introduced
Nectary Organ secreting nectar
Nerve Line of conducting or reinforcing tissue on a leaf or seed
Node Part of stem where a leaf or leaves arise
Notch Small indentation at tip of leaf
Notched With notch
Oblong Leaf shape, central part parallel-sided
Obovate Leaf shape, with broadest part above middle
Obtuse Blunt
Ochrea (plural ochreae) Membranous stipules forming a tubular sheath around stem, in dock family
Opposite Arising in pairs at same level
Oval Leaf shape, about twice as long as broad
Ovary Central part of the flower containing the ovules which later develop into seeds
Ovate Leaf shape, like an egg
Ovoid 3-dimensional equivalent of ovate, ie. ovate in cross-section
Palmate With 3 or more lobes arising from the same point
Panicle Branched inflorescence
Pappus Tuft of hairs on a fruit, eg. Dandelion

Parasite Plant deriving all its nourishment from another living organism, to which it is attached
Peduncle Stalk of an inflorescence, or partial inflorescence
Perianth Collective name for sepals and petals
Perennial Plant which lives for more than two years, usually flowering each year
Petals Inner whorl of perianth segments, often brightly coloured
Petaloid Petal-like, usually brightly-coloured
Petiole Leaf stalk
Pinnate Leaf composed of more than 3 leaflets arranged in 2 rows on opposite side of main axis
Pinnatifid Pinnately cut, but not as deeply as pinnate
Pollen Tiny grains produced by anthers, containing male sex cells
Pollinia Pollen grains aggregated into substantial masses
Procumbent Lying loosely along the ground surface
Prostrate Lying tightly along the ground surface
Pubescent Shortly and softly hairy
Raceme Spike-like inflorescence, with flowers distantly stalked
Ray One of the stalks of an umbel
Ray-floret Outer florets of a composite flower, with part elongated into a strap-like structure
Receptacle Part of the stem from which the floral organs arise
Reflexed Curled or bent abruptly at more than a right angle
Rhizome Underground or ground-level stem, lasting more than one season, often swollen
Rosette Radiating cluster of leaves, usually lying close to the ground
Runner Above-ground stem that roots at the nodes to form new plants
Saltmarsh Vegetation growing in the intertidal zone, usually in muddy sheltered areas; also inland in suitable habitats
Saprophyte Plant which lacks chlorophyll and lives by absorbing food from decaying organic matter

Figure 1 Leaves and inflorescences simplified **a** ovate **b** lanceolate, tip acute **c** spoon-shaped or obovate, tip obtuse **d** orbicular **e** linear, tip notched **f** tip acuminate, margin double toothed **g** margin lobed, base auriculate **h** margin dentate, base cordate **i** palmate **j** pinnate, leaflets elliptic **k** twice-pinnate **l** leaves diamond-shaped, appressed **m** arrangement whorled **n** raceme **o** panicle **p** cyme (pendant) **q** umbel.

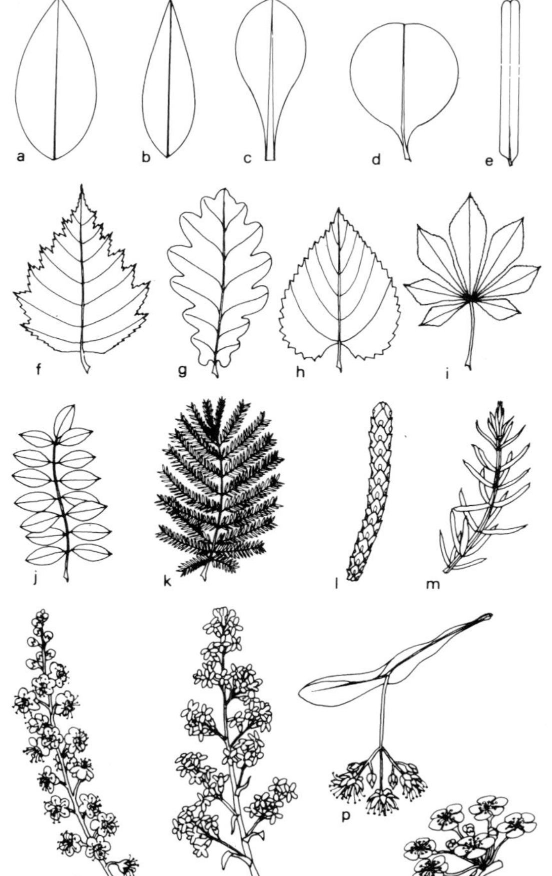

Sepal See calyx
Silicula Fruit of Cruciferae that is less than 3 times as long as wide
Siliqua Fruit of Cruciferae that is more than 3 times as long as wide
Simple Leaves that are not compound, or unbranched stems
Spadix Erect tightly-packed spike of florets in the arum family
Spathe Large bract (or pair of bracts) sometimes surrounding inflorescence eg. in arum family
Speculum Shiny, shield-like patch, eg. on the lip of *Ophrys* species
Spike Simple elongated inflorescence with individual flowers unstalked
Spur Hollow cylindrical projection from petal or sepal, usually containing nectar
Stamen Male parts of a flower, made up of a stalk (filament) and pollen-containing anther
Staminode Modified infertile stamen
Standard Uppermost petal of a pea-family flower
Stellate Star-shaped
Sterile Not producing fertile seeds or variable pollen
Stigma Receptive surface of a style, to which pollen grains adhere
Stipule Leaf-like or scale-like appendage at the base of a leaf stalk
Stolon Short-lived creeping stem from the base of a rosette plant, usually above ground
Style Part of the female organ linking the stigma to the ovary
Sucker Shoot arising from the roots of trees or shrubs
Tendril Slender climbing structure, usually coiling
Thallus Plant body, if not clearly separated into leaf, stem etc.
Tomentose Densely covered with short cottony hairs
Trifoliate Leaf with 3 separate leaflets
Tuber Swollen portion of stem or root, lasting less than 1 year
Tubercle Wart-like swellings
Umbel Umbrella-shaped inflorescence
Undulate Wavy
Vesicle Sack-like swelling
Whorled 3 or more organs (eg. flowers or leaves) arising at the same point on the stem
Wing Lateral petals of flower, especially in pea family
Winged stem Stem with longitudinal narrow outgrowths

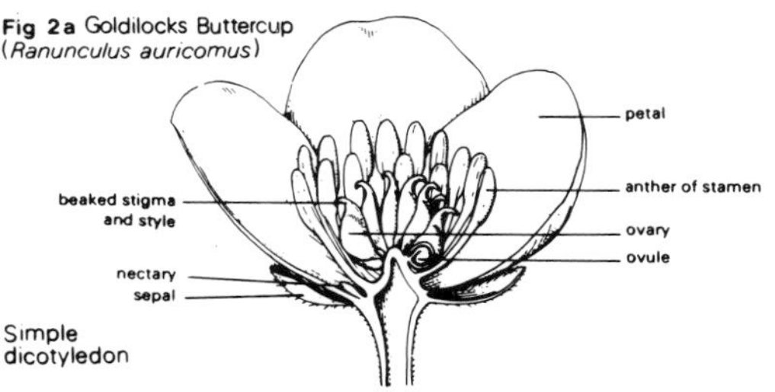

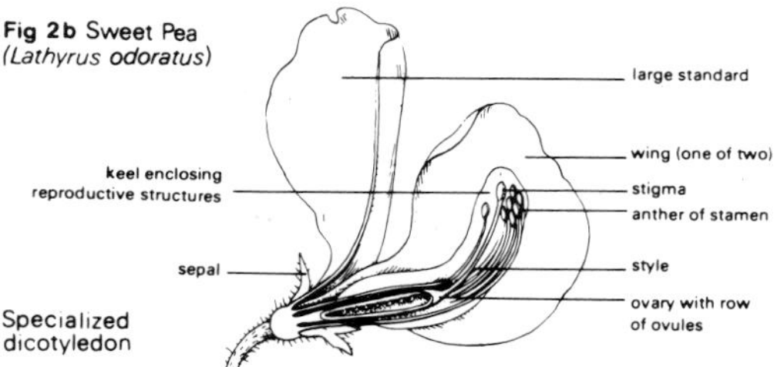

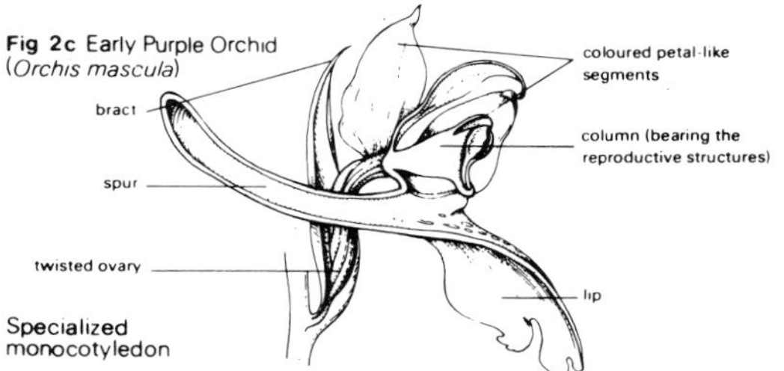

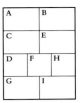

A
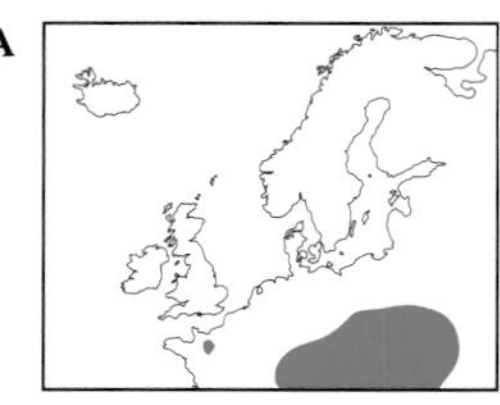

B

C

E
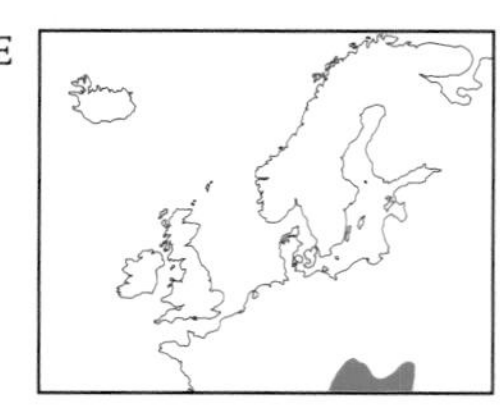

F

I
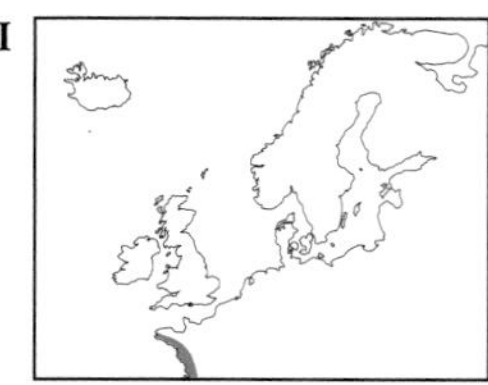

GYMNOSPERMS

Mostly evergreen trees and shrubs with naked ovules.

Pine Family Pinaceae

Trees (rarely shrubs), including some of the tallest species known. Evergreen except for *Larix*, and usually resinous. Leaves stiff, linear, narrow, entire and spirally arranged to varying degrees. Male and female flowers borne in separate conical clusters on the same tree. Winged seeds are carried in large woody cones.

A **Silver Fir** *Abies alba* Pyramidal evergreen tree to 50m, with regularly whorled branches. Bark smooth, light grey, becoming scaly with age. Leaves to 30mm, dark shining green above, with *2 pale bands of stomata beneath*. After leaf falls or when pulled off, a *neat oval scar* remains on twig. Each side of the branch has 2 flattened rows of leaves, the upper row forward-pointing. Cones erect, to 18cm with prominent downward-pointing bracts amongst the scales (**a**). Native in mountains of central Europe where it often forms extensive forests to 2,000m altitude. **Fl** 4-5. **Br** Planted widely, but cultivation difficult due to attack by gall aphids.

B **Norway Spruce** *Picea abies* Pyramidal evergreen tree to 60m, with regularly whorled branches. Bark rough-surfaced, reddish-brown. Leaves to 25mm, *4-sided*, light to dark green. Each *leaf has a woody peg at its base*, remaining after leaf-fall and giving the twigs a rough character. Cones hanging, to 15cm, without bracts between scales. Widely planted and naturalised outside its native range. **Fl** 5-6. **Br** Often planted, rarely naturalised.

C **Larch** *Larix decidua* Deciduous pyramidal tree to 50m, with irregularly whorled branches. Bark brown and fissured, shed in small plates. Leaves to 30mm, light green, keeled and pointed, *in whorled clusters*. Cones barrel-shaped, small (to 35mm) with bracts mostly concealed behind scales. Widespread and locally frequent as a native in mountains on well-drained soils; also widely planted in the lowlands. **Fl** 3-4. **Br** Introduced, widely planted, occasionally naturalised.

There are a number of closely related species and hybrids which differ, amongst other characters, in their cone shapes and sizes.

PINES *Pinus* Distinguished by having long, needle-like leaves in clusters of 2-5.

D **Scots Pine** *Pinus sylvestris* Evergreen tree to 40m, with dome-shaped crown. Bark reddish- or greyish-brown, fissured into longitudinal plates. Buds sticky and resinous. Leaves glaucous, in pairs, rigid and twisted, to 10cm. Cones hanging, ovoid, to 7cm long. Widespread and often frequent on acid or sandy soils in a variety of habitats. **Fl** 5-6. **Br** Native and forming forests in Scottish Highlands; planted or naturalised elsewhere, e.g. lowland heaths.

E **Austrian Pine** *Pinus nigra* Similar to Scots Pine but more pyramidal in outline and with longer, *dark green* leaves (8-15cm). A native of S Europe, but widely planted elsewhere and naturalised. **Br** Naturalised in the south, e.g. New Forest.

F **Maritime Pine** *Pinus pinaster* Similar to Scots Pine, but when mature devoid of branches for most of its height; leaves long, 10-25cm, more than 2mm broad. Buds not resinous. Widely planted, especially in coastal areas, and often naturalised. **Br** Introduced and naturalised on sandy soils in Dorset.

Cypress Family Cupressaceae

Evergreen shrubs or trees. Leaves either needle-like or scaly, opposite or in whorls, often completely covering the stem. Seeds usually borne in cones with woody scales, with the exception of junipers which have a fleshy berry-like fruit.

G **Juniper** *Juniperus communis* Variable evergreen shrub to 7m. Bark reddish-brown, shredding readily. Leaves spiny in whorls of 3, green and keeled beneath but with a single white longitudinal band above. Fruit fleshy and berry-like, green in the 1st year but remaining on the plant until the 2nd year when it turns blue-black. Widespread and locally frequent on well-drained soils to 1,200m altitude. **Fl** 5-6. **Br** Local and decreasing on chalk downs, limestone grassland, heaths and moors.
A number of subspecies are recognised, showing differences in habit and preferences for certain habitats:
Ssp *communis* has leaves up to 20mm long and is widespread on a variety of well-drained soils.
Ssp *nana* has leaves up to 15mm long and is spreading and mat-forming, on mountains, or even at low altitudes in the north.

Yew Family Taxaceae

Evergreen shrubs or trees. Leaves narrow, linear and spirally arranged. Fruit fleshy.

H **Yew** *Taxus baccata* Tree to 20m with spreading branches and stout trunk. Bark rusty-brown, thin and scaling. Trunk irregular, ribbed and fluted. Leaves dark green, flattened into more or less 2 ranks. Flowers green, male and female on separate trees. Fruit a poisonous scarlet berry. Widespread and common throughout on a range of soils. **Fl** 3-4. **Br** Rather local as a native, and most common on chalk and limestone, where it occasionally forms extensive woods, e.g. Kingley Vale in Sussex. Often found as a planted tree in churchyards.

Joint Pine Family Ephedraceae

Shrubs or undershrubs with opposite or whorled scale-like leaves and long internodes. Dioecious.

I **Joint Pine** *Ephedra distachya* Distinctive low shrub or undershrub to only 50cm, often only a few centimetres, with underground rhizome. Stem woody and jointed with pale green shoots. Leaves tiny at stem joints, brown above and green below with basal sheath surrounding stem. Fruit fleshy to 7mm, scarlet red, lobulated. Very local in dry, sandy or stony habitats, usually near the coast. **Fl** 5-6. **Br** Absent.

A	B
C	E
D / F	H
G	I

A **Silver Fir** showing male cones

B **Norway Spruce** showing ripened female cones

C **Larch** showing young and mature female cones

F **Maritime Pine** showing mature female cone

D **Scots Pine** showing mature female cone

E **Austrian Pine** showing mature female cones

H **Yew** female tree with ripe fruit

G **Juniper** with ripe fruit

I **Joint Pine** with ripe fruit

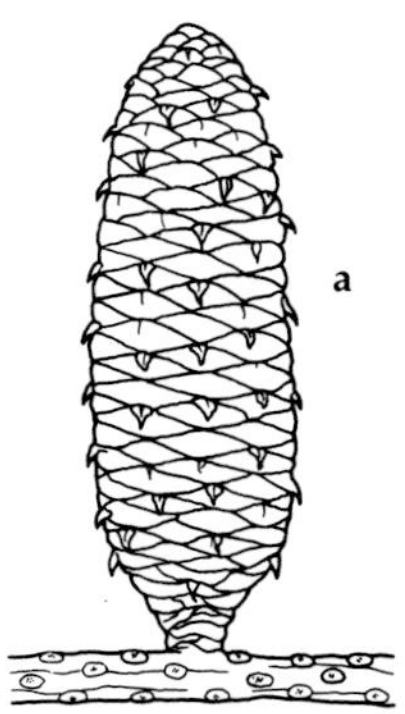

A

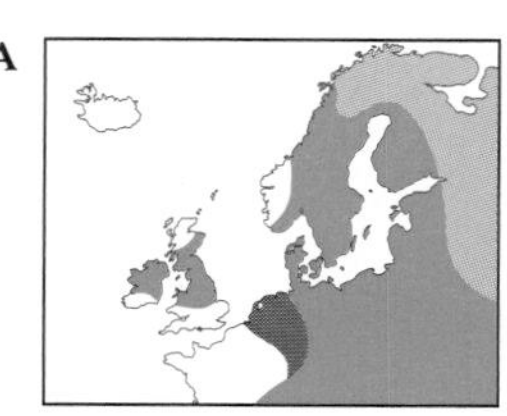

E

F

G

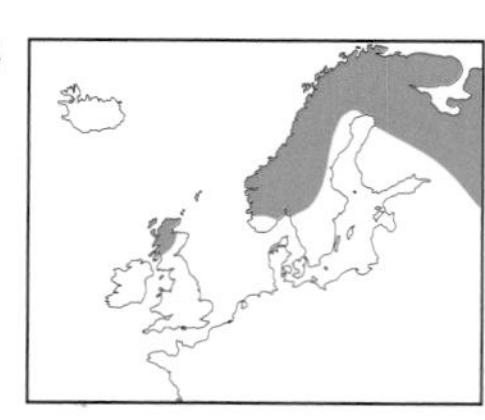

J

L

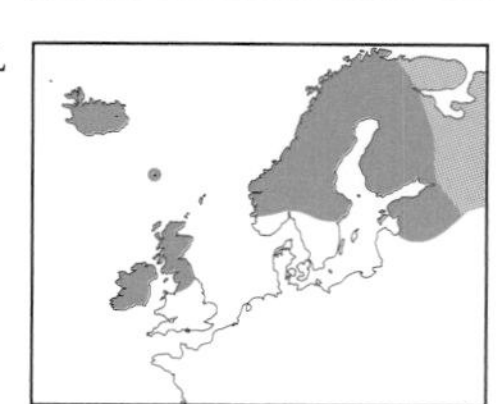

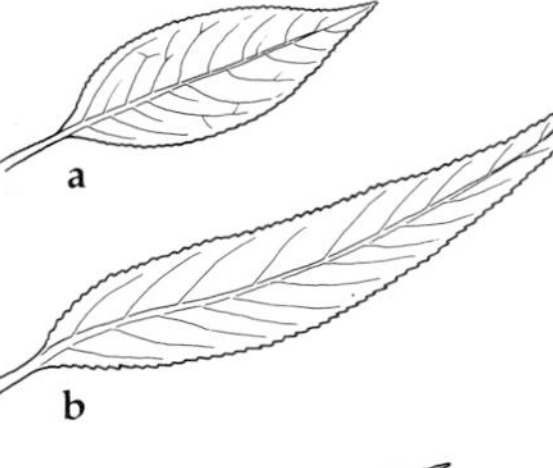

a

b

c

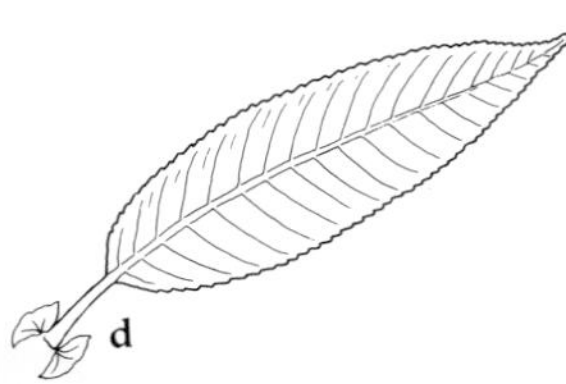

d

ANGIOSPERMS

Plants with ovules enclosed in an ovary

Dicotyledons

Major division of the angiosperms having two first leaves on the germinating seedling. Dicotyledons usually have net veined leaves and flower parts in fours or fives.

Willow Family Salicaceae

Deciduous trees or shrubs. Leaves simple and usually alternate. Flowers in catkins, male and female on different plants. Seeds surrounded by long silky hairs, aiding wind dispersal.

WILLOWS *Salices* A difficult genus varying from small creeping undershrubs to large trees, usually growing in damp situations. Buds covered by single scale and catkins usually erect (contrast these characters with the poplars). Male catkins usually have 2 stamens unless stated, and often ripen before the leaves. Although silky white at first, stamens are usually yellow, unless stated. Female catkins are usually grey-green and less noticeable.

Species hybridise readily, often making identification even more difficult.

A **Bay Willow** *Salix pentandra* Shrub or small tree to 7m. Hairless, shiny twigs. Leaves elliptical, toothed (**a**), shiny, dark green above but paler beneath. *The only non-hybrid willow with 5 (or more) stamens.* Frequent by freshwater or other damp habitats. **Fl** 5-6.
Br Frequent from N Wales and Derbyshire northwards.

B **Crack Willow** *Salix fragilis* Tall, spreading tree to 25m. Bark fissured. Twigs hairless, breaking off easily. Leaves long (to 15cm), narrow, toothed, *asymmetrical at tip* (**b**); bright shiny green above, paler beneath. Widespread and common in damp places. **Fl** 4-5.
Br Frequent, but less common northwards; native only up to mid-Scotland.

C **White Willow** *Salix alba* Tall, spreading tree to 25m. Similar to Crack Willow, but twigs not fragile; leaves to 10cm, *not or hardly asymmetrical at tip* (**c**), covered beneath (sometimes also above) with silky white hairs. Widespread and common in damp places. **Fl** 4-5. **Br** Rather less common than Crack Willow, but similar distribution.

D **Almond Willow** *Salix triandra* Shrub or small tree to 10m. Bark smooth, flaking. Leaves shaped like those of Almond tree: lanceolate, toothed (**d**), shiny dark green above, paler and glaucous beneath. The *only non-hybrid willow with 3 stamens.* Widespread and locally common by fresh water. **Fl** 4-5. **Br** Native and frequent by rivers and ponds; often planted.

E **Net-leaved Willow** *Salix reticulata* Dwarf undershrub, prostrate and mat-forming. Leaves oval, to 5cm, *untoothed* (**e**), dark green and wrinkled above, whitish below with *veins beautifully netted.* Stamens reddish or purple at first. Local or rare on rocky mountain-ledges to 2,500m, preferring basic rocks. **Fl** 6-7. **Br** Rare in the Scottish Highlands.

F **Dwarf Willow** *Salix herbacea* Dwarf undershrub, prostrate and patch-forming to a few centimetres high with underground stems. Leaves rounded to 2cm, *toothed* (**f**), shiny green above, slightly paler beneath and with *veins prominent on both sides.* Locally frequent on mountains and tundra. **Fl** 6-7. **Br** Frequent on the higher mountains from N Wales northwards, down to 100m in N Scotland.

G **Whortle-leaved Willow** *Salix myrsinites* Low undershrub to 50cm. Branches ascending, stout and crooked when mature, brown and shining. Leaves oval, to 5cm, toothed (**g**) and *shiny green on both sides* with *prominent veins;* dead leaves often remain until following year. *Stamens reddish or purple at first.* Local in mountains on wet basic rocks to 1,800m. **Fl** 5-6. **Br** Local and rare on Scottish mountains.

H *Salix glauca* Shrub to 2m. Branches dark brown, shiny, knotty and covered with long hairs. Leaves ovate, to 5cm, untoothed (**h**), bright green above and bluish-green beneath; both sides hairy. Stipules absent (*see S. stipulifera*). Locally frequent within its range in damp stony places on tundra and mountains. **Fl** 5-6. **Br** Absent.

I *Salix stipulifera* As *S. glauca*, but lanceolate stipules present. Very local in Arctic tundra. **Fl** 5-6. **Br** Absent.

J **Woolly Willow** *Salix lanata* Shrub to 3m. Young shoots, buds and leaves all woolly. Leaves broadly oval, to 65mm, untoothed with *distinctive acuminate apex* (**j**). Young leaves have yellow hairs, *older leaves are white and woolly beneath.* Stipules blunt, untoothed (*see S. glandulifera*). Male catkins broad and beautifully golden yellow, to 50mm. A mainly Arctic and sub-Arctic species occurring locally on tundra and damp stony places in mountains. **Fl** 5-7. **Br** Rare in basic mountain flushes and on mountain-ledges in E Scottish Highlands.

K *Salix glandulifera* Similar to Woolly Willow, but leaves oblong-lanceolate, *broadest above middle,* and margin very glandular. Stipules pointed, toothed. Habitats and range similar to above but more local. **Fl** 5-7. **Br** Absent.

L **Tea-leaved Willow** *Salix phylicifolia* Shrub to 4m. Young shoots slightly hairy, but mature *branches shiny reddish-brown.* Leaves ovate-lanceolate to 8cm, toothed, hairless, pointed (**l**), *rather leathery in texture,* shiny green above, dull greyish-green beneath, *stipules small or absent.* Locally frequent in a variety of wet habitats to 1,700m. **Fl** 4-5. **Br** Local in hills and mountains from the mid-Pennines northwards.

M *Salix bicolor* Similar to Tea-leaved Willow, but *leaves obviously silky hairy when young* (**m**). Locally frequent in damp stony places in mountains. **Fl** 4-5. **Br** Absent.

N **Irish Willow** *Salix hibernica* Similar to Tea-leaved Willow but *leaves untoothed.* **Br** Only 1 known locality, near Sligo in NW Ireland.

O **Dark-leaved Willow** *Salix nigricans* Shrub to 4m. Twigs *dull,* slender and hairy. Leaves to 10cm, variable ovate to lanceolate, toothed, *thin,* deep green above and rather glaucous beneath except at the tip, the undersurface slightly pubescent at least on the veins or frequently almost hairless. *Stipules large* (**o**). Widespread and locally common in damp places in hills and mountains, tundra. **Fl** 4-5. **Br** Local from Lancashire and Yorkshire northwards.

P *Salix borealis* Similar to Dark-leaved Willow, but twigs stout and leaves covered on both sides with whitish down. Local in Arctic and sub-Arctic tundra. **Fl** 5-6. **Br** Absent.

A B
C E
J D F
G L

A **Bay Willow** with male catkins

B **Crack Willow** with male catkins

C **White Willow** with female catkins

E **Net-leaved Willow** with male catkins

J **Woolly Willow** with male catkins

D **Almond Willow**

F **Dwarf Willow** with male catkins

G **Whortle-leaved Willow**

L **Tea-leaved Willow** with male catkins

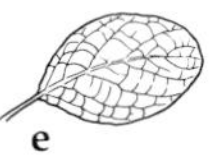

e

f

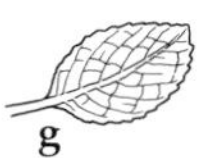

g

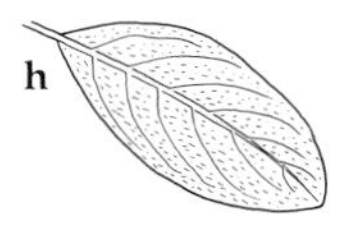

h

j

l

m

B

E

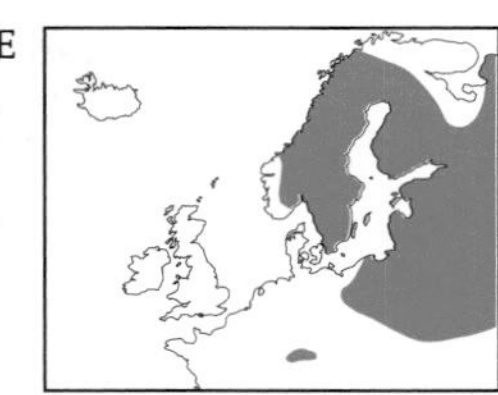

G

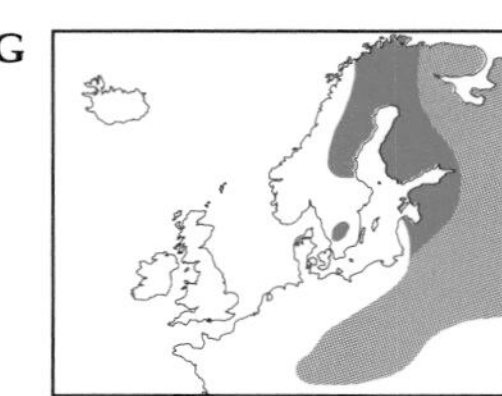

K

L

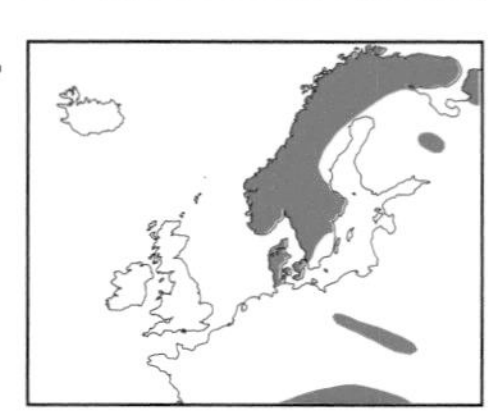

M

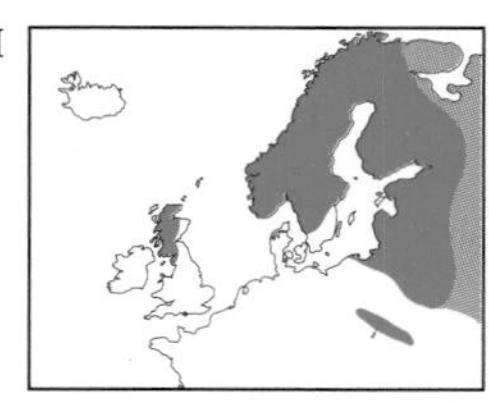

N

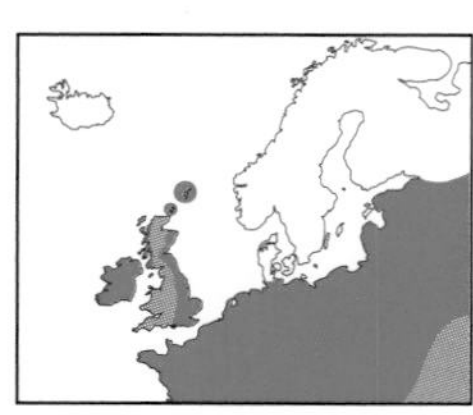

O

P

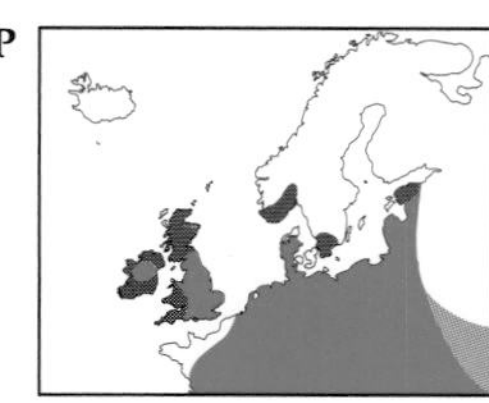

A Grey Willow *Salix cinerea* Shrub to 6m. Shoots ridged, downy. Leaves to 10cm, soft, ovoid-lanceolate (narrowed towards base), often toothed towards tip (**a**), greyish-green above, persistently grey downy beneath with *no rusty hairs* (*see S. atrocinerea*). *Stamens red-tinged*. Widespread almost throughout; in wet lowland habitats. **Fl** 3-4. **Br** Most frequent in fens of E Anglia, where it sometimes dominates; rare or local elsewhere (often confused with following species).

B *Salix atrocinerea* Shrub or small tree to 10m, similar to previous species. Shoots downy, ridged under the bark (peel off to see). Leaves (**b**) not soft to touch, buff-coloured above when young, hairy beneath with *some or all hairs rust-coloured*. Widespread and common. **Fl** 3-4. **Br** Common throughout.

C Eared Willow *Salix aurita* Small shrub to 2m. Twigs slender, branches wide-angled. *Leaves markedly wrinkled* with wavy edges and twisted apex, oblong or ovate, toothed and with *large leafy stipules* (the 'ears') at the base of each leaf (**c**). Widespread and locally common; in a variety of damp places on a range of different soils. **Fl** 4-6. **Br** Common throughout.

D Goat Willow *Salix caprea* Shrub or small tree to 10m. Bark fissured. *Twigs thick*, downy when young and not ridged. Leaves soft, broadly oblong or ovate (to 10cm), acuminate, untoothed or sometimes crenate (**d**), dark green, hairless above, *grey and downy beneath*. Catkins silvery white in bud. Widespread and common in a variety of habitats, ranging from freshwater margins to damp woodland and scrub. **Fl** 3-4. **Br** Common throughout, ascending to 900m.

E *Salix starkeana* Low undershrub to 1m. Leaves thin, toothed, broadly lanceolate to ovate (**e**), reddish and downy when young, shiny bright green and *hairless when mature* but greyish beneath. Local in damp stony places and tundra. **Fl** 4-6. **Br** Absent.

F *Salix xerophila* Similar to *S. starkeana*, but twigs and *leaves downy*, leaf margin untoothed. Local in N Scandinavia. **Fl** 4-6. **Br** Absent.

G *Salix myrtilloides* Low undershrub to 50cm, with underground creeping stems and ascending branches. *Leaves untoothed* (**g**) (*see* Dwarf Willow, which it resembles in habit), dull green above and paler beneath, with margins often rolled over. Local in peatbogs and other very wet places. **Fl** 4-6. **Br** Absent.

H Creeping Willow *Salix repens* Low *creeping* shrub to 1.5m. Branches slender and procumbent. Leaves elliptical to 5cm, untoothed or occasionally slightly toothed, hairless above when mature, silky beneath, *4-6 pairs of lateral veins* (**h**). Widespread in damp open habitats, e.g. dune-slacks, heaths, fens, etc. **Fl** 4-5. **Br** Throughout, but local.

I *Salix rosmarinifolia* Similar to Creeping Willow, but *leaves longer (to 7cm)*, erect, almost linear and with *10-12 pairs of lateral veins*. Local in similar habitats to Creeping Willow. **Fl** 4-5. **Br** Absent.

J *Salix arenaria* Similar to Creeping Willow, but leaves somewhat toothed (**j**) and *densely silky hairy on both sides*. Treated as a subspecies (*argentea*) of Creeping Willow by some authorities. Local in damp sandy places near the coast. **Fl** 4-5. **Br** Very local in dune-slacks.

K Mountain Willow *Salix arbuscula* Shrub to 1.5m. Twigs dark brown and shining. Leaves ovate or ovate-lanceolate to 4cm, pointed, variably toothed (**k**), shiny green above, grey downy below. *Male catkins have noticeably reddish anthers at first*. Flushed mountain- ledges to 1,000m. **Fl** 5-6. **Br** Very local in Scottish Highlands.

L *Salix hastata* Erect shrub to 1.5m. Twigs shiny and hairless. Leaves to 4cm, very variable in shape from round or ovate to lanceolate (**l**), dull green above, paler below. Margin finely toothed or entire. Stipules usually well developed and persistent. Male catkins long and narrow, to 6cm. Local on mountains. **Fl** 5-6. A variable species, sometimes divided into separate subspecies depending on leaf shape and length of petiole. **Br** Absent.

M Downy Willow *Salix lapponum* Compact shrub to 1.5m. Branches dark brown and shining at maturity. Leaves elliptical, to 5cm, untoothed (**m**), grey-green with *silky hairs above and below*, both surfaces being almost concolorous. *Leaves rather crowded towards tips of twigs*. Catkins stalkless or almost so, with *stamens reddish or purple at first*. Wet heaths, tundra and streamsides in mountains to 1,500m. **Fl** 5-6. **Br** Local on wet mountain rocks, Cumbria and Scottish Highlands.

N Common Osier *Salix viminalis* Shrub or small tree to 7m. Branches long, straight and flexible. Shoots downy only at first, later shiny yellowish brown. *Leaves long (to 25cm), untoothed* or almost so, linear-lanceolate (**n**), shiny dark green above, grey hairy below. *Leaf margin wavy and turned over* when young. Catkins to 3cm, almost stalkless and crowded towards shoot tips. Widespread and common in lowland wet places; scarce in the hills. **Fl** 3-4. **Br** Status uncertain; locally common throughout lowlands, and often planted for basket-making.

O *Salix eleagnos* Similar to Common Osier, but *leaves toothed towards apex* and catkins to 6cm. Freshwater margins, occasionally planted. Native of central Europe, but naturalised elsewhere. **Fl** 3-4. **Br** Planted, and very rarely naturalised.

P Purple Willow *Salix purpurea* Slender shrub to 5m. *Shoots purplish at first*, slender and hairless; later yellowish green. Leaves almost opposite, to 12cm, obovate or lanceolate, hairless, finely toothed (**p**), dull bluish green above, paler beneath. Male catkins a beautiful golden yellow with *purplish-red anthers* when young. Stamens 2 but united as 1. Widespread in similar habitats to Common Osier. **Fl** 3-4. **Br** Locally frequent especially in fens, and occasionally planted for basket-making.

Q *Salix daphnoides* Shrub or tree to 10m. Shoots have *purplish-blue waxy appearance*. Leaves to 10cm, oblong-lanceolate, finely toothed (**q**), hairless when mature, shiny dark green above, greyer below. Stipules large. Local in fens and lake-margins. **Fl** 4-5. **Br** Absent.

a

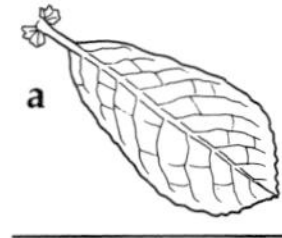

b

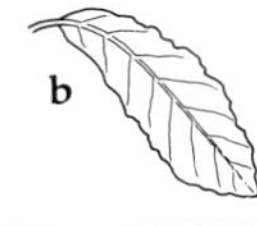

c

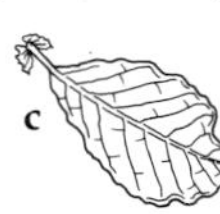

d

e

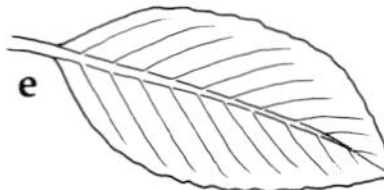

g

A		B	
C	D1	D2	
G	H	N	
		Q	

A Grey Willow

B *Salix atrocinerea* male catkins

C Eared Sallow male catkins

D Goat Willow showing leaves

D Goat Willow male catkins

G *Salix myrtilloides*

H Creeping Willow showing habit and ripe female catkins

N Common Osier

Q *Salix daphnoides* showing shoots and leaves

h

i

j

k

l

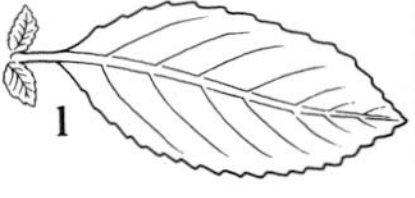

m

n

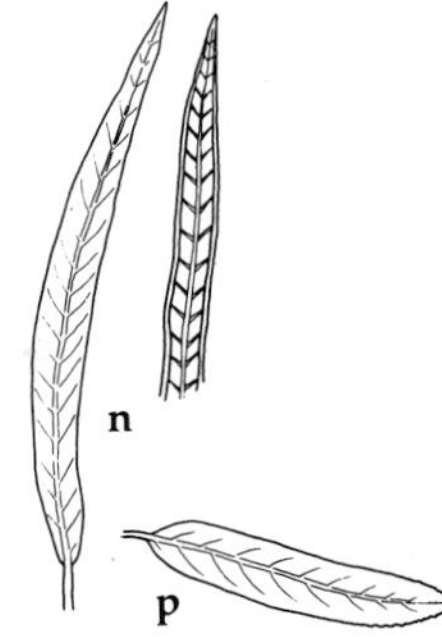

p

q

A
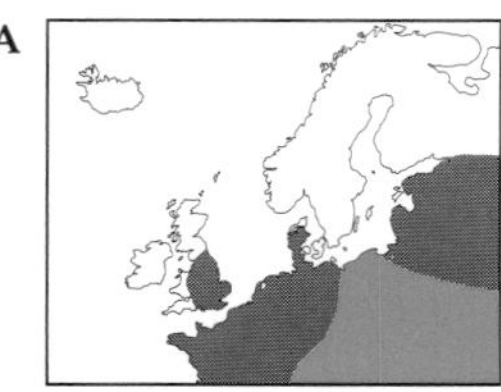
D
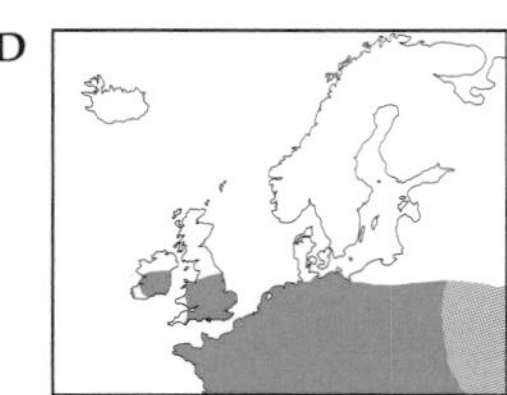
F

G
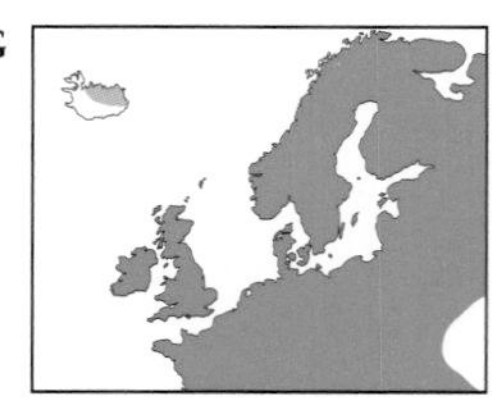
H
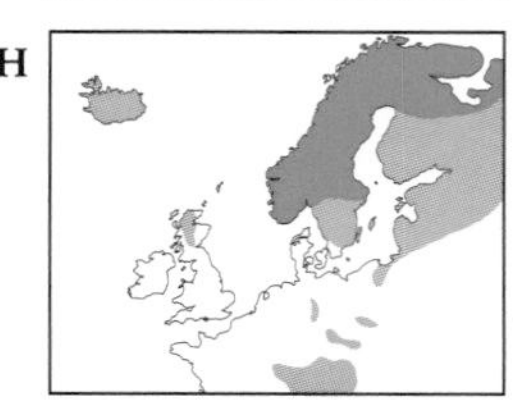
I
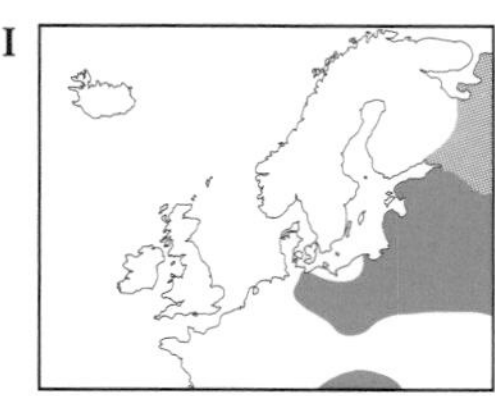
K
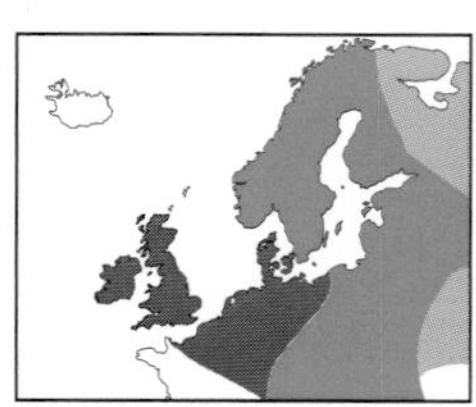
L

M
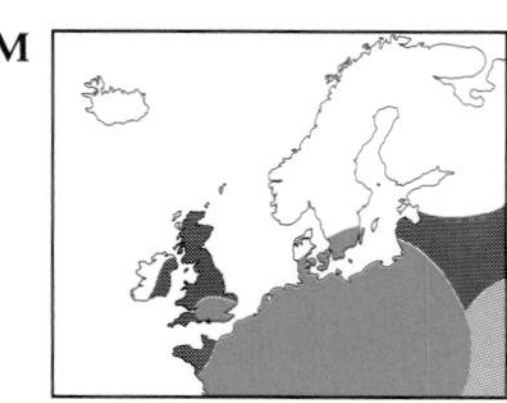

POPLARS *Populus* Deciduous trees. Buds with several outer scales, catkins pendent and stamens 4 or more (contrast these characters with willows).

A **White Poplar** *Populus alba* Tree to 30m with wide crown. Bark smooth and white at first, becoming rugged and grey. *Shoots and buds white downy*. Leaves variable in shape; 5-lobed on vigorous shoots, but otherwise often ovate with irregularly lobed margins (**a**), *dark green above but white cottony below*. Widely planted, but also native in damp woodlands. **Fl** 3. **Br** Introduced and planted, often near the sea as a shelter-belt.

B **Grey Poplar** *Populus canescens* Tall, vigorous tree to 35m, often suckering. Bark greyish green and smooth at first with horizontal lines, later pitted with diamond-shaped hollows and then becoming coarse and rugged. Buds thinly downy. Leaves variable, ovate and dentate (**b**), dull green above, grey downy beneath when young but soon becoming almost hairless. Sucker leaves larger, more coarsely toothed and remaining downy beneath. Locally common in damp woodlands and streamsides but widely planted also. **Fl** 2-3. **Br** Status uncertain; locally frequent and probably native in S, E and central England, but often planted elsewhere.

C **Aspen** *Populus tremula* Medium-sized tree, to 20m. Suckers freely, so that lone trees rarely found. Bark smooth, grey-green with small diamond-shaped hollows. *Leaves soon hairless, ovate* with rounded teeth (**c**); leaf stalk thin and flattened so that leaf trembles in the breeze. Sucker leaves more deeply lobed and with greyish down beneath. Catkin scales deeply divided at the base of each flower. Frequent in damp woods, heaths and moors. **Fl** 2-3. **Br** Throughout, commonest in the north and west, more local in the south and east.

D **Black Poplar** *Populus nigra* Spreading tree to 30m. No suckers. Bark rugged, blackish with clarge bosses. *Leaves triangular- shaped*, toothed and *hairless*. Wet woodland and river valleys on rich soils; widely planted outside its native range. **Fl** 3-4. **Br** Possibly native in E and central England; planted elsewhere.

Bog-myrtle Family
Myricaceae

Shrubs or trees, deciduous or evergreen. Leaves alternate, simple and aromatic. Flowers usually dioecious and in catkins. Fruit fleshy or a nut.

E **Bog Myrtle** *Myrica gale* Deciduous shrub to 2.5m, suckering. Twigs red-brown. Leaves oblong-lanceolate, producing strong resinous smell when bruised. Male catkins reddish-brown, oblong; female catkins green, oval. Plants usually dioecious, but sometimes monoecious or hermaphrodite, and can change sex from year to year. Widely scattered in bogs, wet heaths and fens. **Fl** 4-5. **Br** Widespread throughout, locally common in Ireland and from N Wales and N England to N Scotland, but rare or absent in many parts of S and central England and SE Scotland.

Birch Family Betulaceae

Deciduous shrubs or trees. Leaves alternate and simple. Male flowers in tight catkins, erect when young but drooping when mature; 3 flowers per bract. Female flowers in erect oval catkins (alders) or cylindrical catkins (birches). Catkin scales 3-lobed at the base of each flower. Fruit winged for wind dispersal.

F **Silver Birch** *Betula pendula* Erect tree to 30m with pendulous branches. Bark reddish-brown on young tree, later silvery white and peeling, rugged and dark at the base. Shoots hairless with *rough, raised warts*. Leaves ovoid-triangular, *hairless* and doubly toothed. Common in woods and heaths, often on poor soils. **Fl** 4-5. **Br** Throughout,.

G **Downy Birch** *Betula pubescens* Erect shrub or tree to 20m with spreading branches. Bark grey or brown, not rugged or dark at the base. Young shoots hairy, either with or without warts, *not rough* if warts present. *Leaves downy on veins beneath*, more evenly toothed. Common in woods, heaths and bogs. Often on wetter ground than Silver Birch. **Fl** 4-5. **Br** Throughout, but more common in the north.

H **Dwarf Birch** *Betula nana* Low prostrate undershrub to 1m (usually much less), with hairy twigs and rounded coarsely toothed leaves, downy when young. Tundra, moorland and bogs, to 2,000m, most frequent in the far north. **Fl** 5-7. **Br** Very local on Scottish mountains; very rare in Teesdale.

I *Betula humilis* Differs from Dwarf Birch in being much branched and having acute leaves longer than broad. Local in bogs and fens in hills or mountains. **Fl** 5-7. **Br** Absent.

J **Alder** *Alnus glutinosa* Tree or tall shrub to 20m, with dark-brown fissured bark and hairless twigs. Buds purplish, short- stalked. *Leaves ovoid* but with truncated tip, irregularly toothed, dark green and *mostly hairless*. Widespread and common in a wide range of wet places, often forming small woods. **Fl** 2-4. **Br** Common almost throughout.

K **Grey Alder** *Alnus incana* Tree or tall shrub to 20m, with pale grey, smooth bark and downy twigs. *Buds shortly stalked*. *Leaves oval-lanceolate*, pointed and coarsely toothed, *downy beneath*. Widespread and locally common in damp, mixed deciduous woodlands. **Fl** 2-4. **Br** Planted, more frequent in Scotland, and sometimes naturalised.

L **Green Alder** *Alnus viridis* Shrub to 3m with oval or elliptical, irregularly toothed leaves, sticky when young. *Buds unstalked*. Catkins with 2-3 leaves at base. Woods and scrub in mountains. **Fl** 4-5. **Br** Absent.

Hazel Family Corylaceae

Deciduous trees or shrubs. Leaves simple, alternate. Male flowers in hanging catkins, female either in erect clusters (*Corylus*) or hanging catkins (*Carpinus*).

M **Hornbeam** *Carpinus betulus* Tree to 30m but usually shorter. Trunk fluted with ribs, bark beech-like, smooth and grey. *Buds point inwards towards downy stem* (*see* Beech, page 18). Leaves oval and toothed. Green female catkins ripen to produce hanging clusters of 3-lobed bracts with nut at the base of each. Locally frequent in hedgerows, woods and sometimes in large stands. Often planted. **Fl** 4-5. **Br** Native in SE England (west to Hampshire) and E Anglia; planted elsewhere.

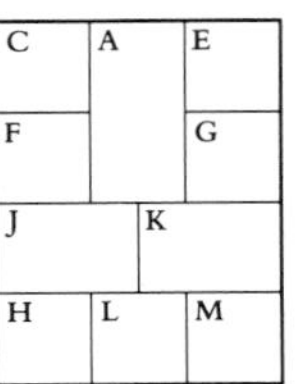

C **Aspen**

A **White Poplar**

E **Bog Myrtle**

F **Silver Birch**

G **Downy Birch**

J **Alder** with leaves and catkins

K **Grey Alder** with leaves and catkins

H **Dwarf Birch**

L **Green Alder** showing catkins

M **Hornbeam** showing leaves and bracts

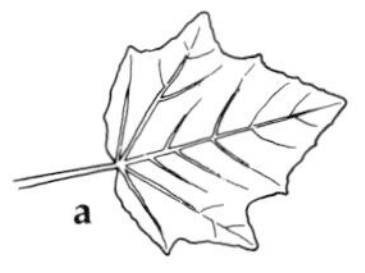
a

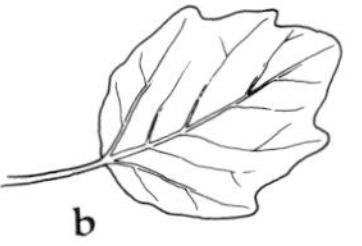
b

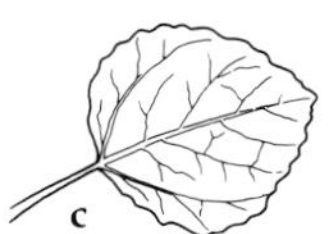
c

B
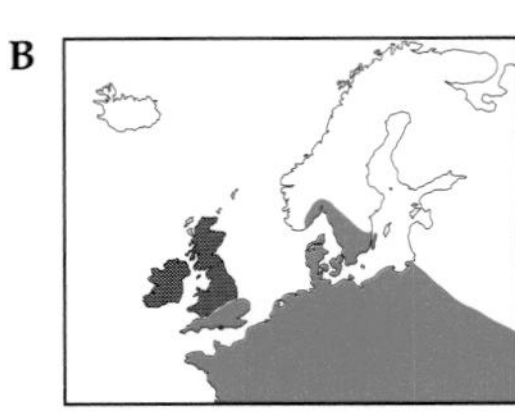

D
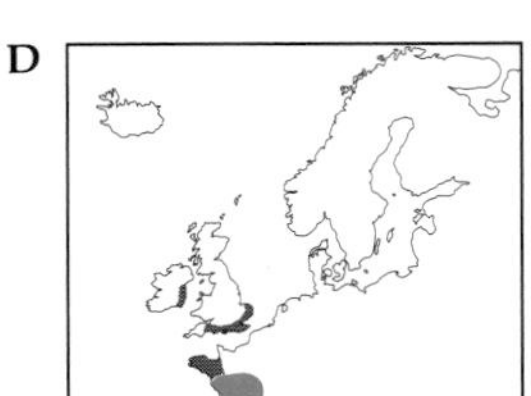

E
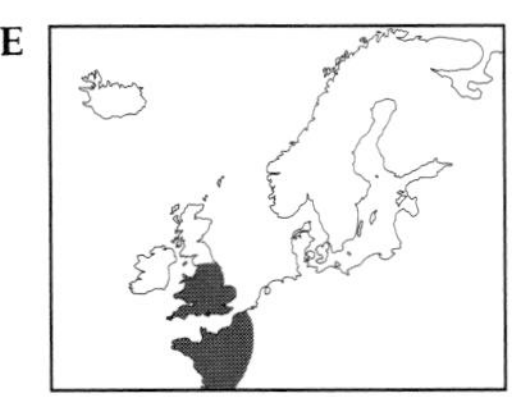

H

J
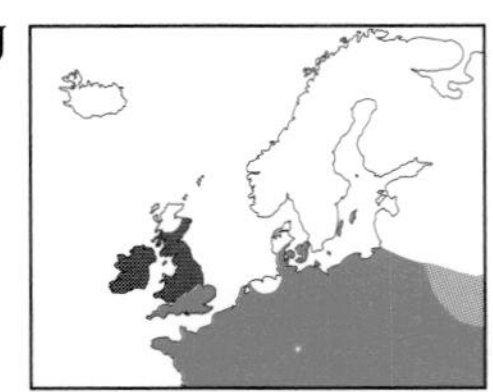

L

A Hazel *Corylus avellana* Straggling or many-stemmed shrub to 8m. Bark brown or grey mottled, smooth with prominent pores. Leaves oval or rounded with irregular sharply toothed edge and acuminate tip. Male catkins yellow, female flowers at tips of shoots, bud-shaped with tufts of protruding bright red stigmas when ripe. Fruit a nut, in clusters surrounded by jaggedly toothed involucre. Common in woods, hedgerows and scrub. **Fl** 1-3. **Br** Common throughout. Often coppiced, but most coppices are now neglected.

Beech Family Fagaceae

Trees or shrubs with alternate, simple leaves. Monoecious. Male flowers in catkins with 4- to 6-lobed perianth. Stamens double the number of lobes. Female flowers in spikes of 1-3 with involucre of bracts which later forms a woody cup around the fruit (a 1-seeded nut).

B Beech *Fagus sylvatica* Tall, stout deciduous tree to 30m. Bark smooth and grey. Buds pointed and spindle-shaped, reddish-brown and *pointing away from twigs* (*see* Hornbeam, page 16). Leaves oval-elliptical, pointed, untoothed but with a wavy margin. Veins silky hairy. Male flowers in long-stalked tassels, female in less conspicuous scaly cup which develops into the fruit, known as mast. Widespread as a woodland tree, usually on well-drained soils to 1,800m. **Fl** 4-5. **Br** Native and frequent in S England and S Wales; widely planted and naturalised elsewhere.

C Sweet Chestnut *Castanea sativa* Deciduous tree to 30m. Bark greyish-brown, strongly fissured in a characteristic spiral pattern. Leaves large (to 25cm), oblong with saw-tooth edges. Catkins long, yellow and spreading, with green female flowers at the base and male flowers along most of length. Fruit an edible nut, 1-3 enclosed in a spiny green husk. Widespread and frequent on mainly neutral or acid soils, planted and long naturalised. **Fl** 7. **Br** Possibly introduced by the Romans; now most common in S England (often as coppice); planted elsewhere.

D Evergreen Oak *Quercus ilex* *Evergreen tree* to 25m. Bark blackish-brown and scaly. Leaves variable in shape but usually oblong, entire or toothed towards apex, dark green above but *grey downy beneath*. A mainly Mediterranean species, extending to W France. Widely planted and naturalised. **Fl** 5-6. **Br** Widely planted, sometimes naturalised.

E Turkey Oak *Quercus cerris* Tall deciduous tree to 35m. Bark dark grey and fissured. Buds surrounded by stringy stipules. Young shoots downy. Leaves long, with narrow, pointed lobes; leaf stalks 8-15mm. Acorn to 40mm long, short-stalked, ripening in second autumn after fertilisation; cup distinctive, with dense covering of long downy scales. Scattered in woodland and hedges. **Fl** 5-6. **Br** Widely planted and naturalised.

F Pedunculate Oak *Quercus robur* Large deciduous tree to 45m. Bark rugged with deep fissures. Shoots hairless. *Leaves short-stalked (5mm or less)*, oblong with rounded side-lobes and *2 auricles at the base*. Separate male and female greenish-yellow catkins. Fruit (acorn) in scaly cup, 1-3 together on common stalk. Widespread and often dominating in woods on a variety of soils, to 1,500m. **Fl** 4-5. **Br** Common throughout. Dominant oak on heavier soils from Midlands southwards.

G Sessile Oak *Quercus petraea* Very similar to Pedunculate Oak, but *leaves without basal auricles* and *tapering into long stalk (18-25mm)*. Downy in axils of leaf veins beneath. Acorns almost stalkless. Widespread and often dominant in woods on poorer soils. **Fl** 4-5. **Br** Dominant oak in N and W Britain, but also locally frequent on sandy soils in the south.

H White Oak *Quercus pubescens* Deciduous tree to 25m. Shoots and leaf stalks very downy. Leaves similar to Pedunculate Oak, but *deeply lobed* and *lobes often further divided*; leaf stalks longer, 5-12mm. Woodlands and hedges on well-drained soils, to 1200m. **Fl** 4-5. **Br** Absent.

Elm Family Ulmaceae

Trees or shrubs, all deciduous in Europe. Leaves alternate, usually asymmetrical at the base, irregularly toothed. Flowers in small lateral clusters, either hermaphrodite or male, and appearing before the leaves. Fruit is a winged, flattened nut.

I Wych Elm *Ulmus glabra* Rounded, spreading tree to 40m, rarely suckering. Bark rough. Young twigs stout and hairy. Leaves to 16cm with *12-18 pairs of lateral veins*, rounded-oval with very asymmetrical bases, one 'ear' overlapping the base of the short stalk; roughly hairy above with longer hairs beneath. Green fruit sometimes abundant, like premature leaves. Widespread but rather local in woodlands, hedges and streamsides. **Fl** 2-4. **Br** Widespread and locally frequent, but more frequent in the north and west, especially on calcareous soils.

J English Elm *Ulmus procera* Tall, erect tree to 35m, suckering freely from trunk base. Bark deeply furrowed. Young twigs stout and hairy. Leaves to 9cm with *10-12 pairs of lateral veins*, broadly ovate and acute, asymmetric 'ear' at leaf base not reaching stalk base; *roughly hairy above* with hair tufts in vein axils below. Fruit uncommon, often sterile. Hedgerows and roadsides in lowlands. **Fl** 2-4. **Br** Common in the south; rare in Scotland and Ireland.

K Smooth-leaved Elm *Ulmus minor* Spreading tree to 30m. Bark grey-brown and deeply fissured. Twigs hairless. Leaves elliptical, *smooth and hairless or only slightly rough above; lateral veins 7-12 pairs*. Fruit rare. Widespread and often common in hedgerows and woodland margins. **Fl** 2-4. **Br** Locally frequent from the Midlands southwards. Varieties include: Cornish Elm var. *cornubiensis* Tall and slender with arched, fan-shaped branching. **Br** Cornwall and Devon. Lock Elm var. *lockii* Sparsely branched crown, with main stem curving over laterally at the top. **Br** Midlands.

L *Ulmus laevis* Tree to 35m. Bark grey-brown, shallowly fissured with network of broad, smooth ridges and burrs. Twigs softly downy. Leaves not rough, but hairless or softly hairy beneath; lateral veins 12-19 pairs; leaf base extremely asymmetrical (much more so than other European elms) with 1 side about 3 veins longer than the other. Finely hairy on both sides. Local in woodland, hedgerows and field-borders. **Fl** 2-4. **Br** Absent.

A	B	C
D	J1	E
F		G
I	J2	K

A **Hazel** showing leaves and nuts

B **Beech** showing leaves and mast

C **Sweet Chestnut** showing leaves and fruit

D **Evergreen Oak** showing leaves and acorns

J **1 English Elm**

E **Turkey Oak** showing leaves and acorn

F **Pedunculate Oak** showing leaves and acorns

G **Sessile Oak** showing leaves and acorns

I **Wych Elm** showing leaves and fruit

J **2 English Elm** showing leaves and fruit

K **Smooth-leaved Elm** showing leaves and fruit

D
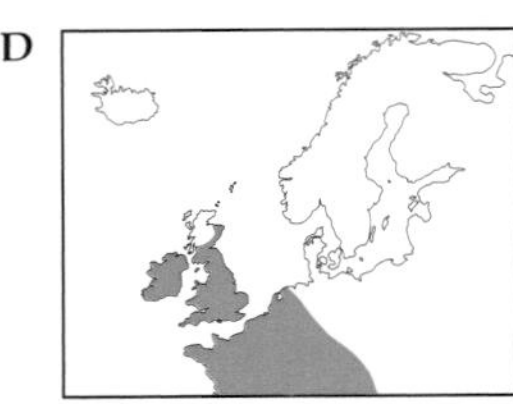
E
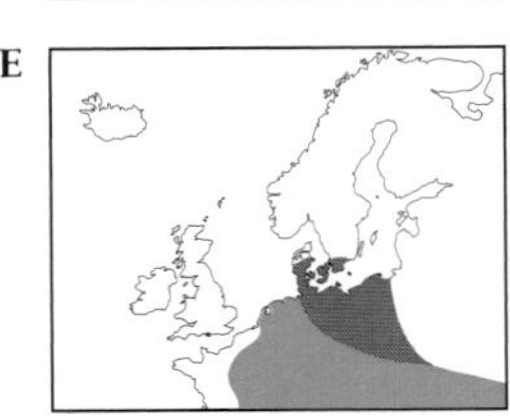
F
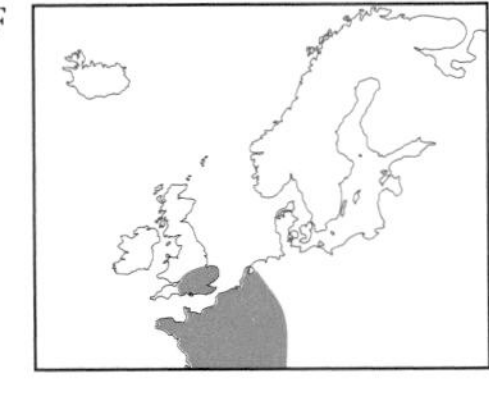
H
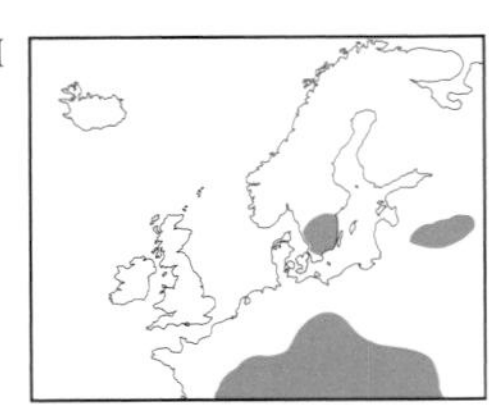
I
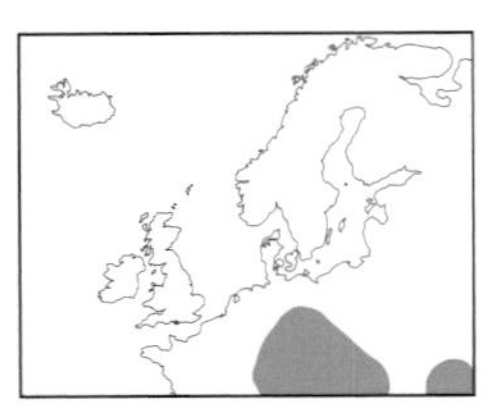
J
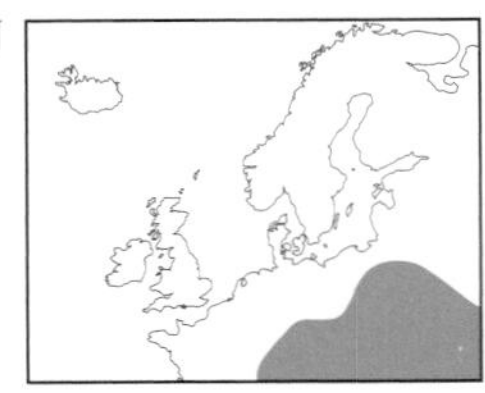
K
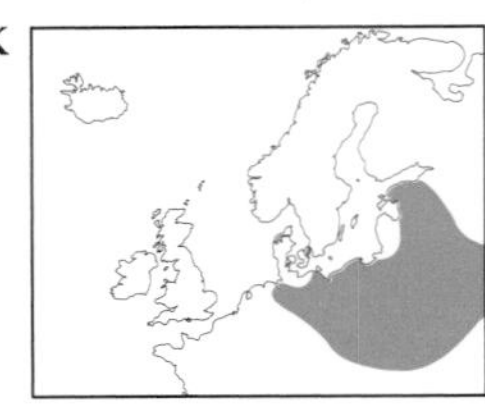
L

M
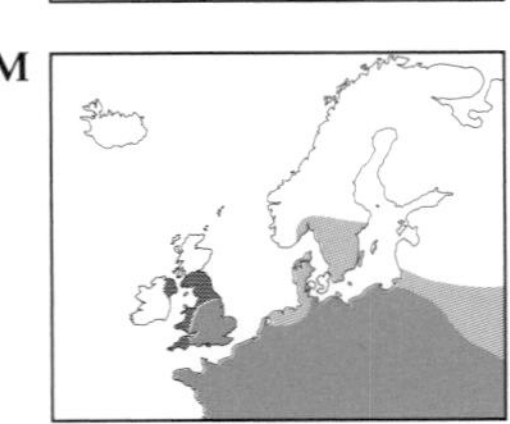

Hemp Family Cannabaceae

Dioecious herbs with leaves usually lobed. Female flowers unstalked with perianth undivided; male flowers stalked with perianth in 5 parts. Fruit an achene.

A **Hop** *Humulus lupulus* Roughly hairy, climbing perennial, with annual square aerial stems twining in a clockwise direction. Leaves long-stalked and deeply palmately divided into 3-5 coarsely toothed lobes. Male flowers greenish-yellow in panicles, female flowers (on separate plants) pale green and in cone-shaped catkins. Widespread and common in woods, scrub and hedgerows. **Fl** 7-8. **Br** Common. Introduced in Scotland and Ireland, but native in England and Wales; often an escape from cultivation where it is grown for brewing beer.

Nettle Family Urticaceae

Herbs with simple leaves, opposite or alternate, often with stinging hairs and stipules. Flowers unisexual, male and female on same or separate plants. Perianth with 4-5 parts. Fruit an achene.

B **Stinging Nettle** *Urtica dioica* Coarsely hairy perennial with square stems and creeping rhizomatous yellow roots. Leaves to 8cm, pointed, toothed and in opposite pairs with sharp hairs which sting by releasing formic acid and histamine-like substances. *All leaves longer than their stalks* (*see* Annual Nettle). Dioecious; male flowers in long drooping catkins, female in shorter heads. Widespread, common and often abundant. Prefers disturbed or enriched soils. **Fl** 6-10. **Br** Common throughout.

C **Annual Nettle** *Urtica urens* Similar to Stinging Nettle, except that it is annual; the leaves are shorter to 4cm, but more deeply toothed, the *lower leaves shorter than their stalks;* the male and female flowers are on same plant. Widespread and common in gardens, waste areas and arable land. **Fl** 6-10. **Br** Widespread and locally common; rare in W Scotland.

D **Pellitory-of-the-wall** *Parietaria diffusa* Spreading and *much-branched* perennial herb, softly hairy and with reddish stems. *Leaves to 5cm*, ovate, untoothed and alternate. Flowers in clusters on stems and leaf stalks, male and female separate within each cluster. Widespread and frequent near coasts, locally common inland on walls and hedgebanks; a predominantly western species, absent from Scandinavia and the east. **Fl** 6-10. **Br** Locally common; absent in N Scotland.

E *Parietaria officinalis* Similar to Pellitory-of-the-wall, but *stems hardly branched* and *leaves to 12cm*. Local on stony banks and well-drained soils, mainly inland. **Br** Absent.

Sandalwood Family Santalaceae

Represented in the area covered here only by *Thesium*.

BASTARD TOADFLAXES *Thesium* Perennial herbs with alternate untoothed lanceolate leaves and woody rootstock, usually semi-parasitic on roots of various other herbs. Flowers hermaphrodite, small (about 3mm in diameter) and in a panicle; petal tube 4- to 5-lobed, not divided into both sepals and petals, white inside and yellowish-green outside.

Single bract present and often a pair of bracteoles, the presence or absence of which helps to separate species.

(1) Bracteoles present.

(a) All leaves with 1 vein.

F **Bastard Toadflax** *Thesium humifusum* Short, usually prostrate, sparsely branched and woody at the base. *Bract equalling flower*, bracteole shorter (**f**). Leaves linear, 5-15mm. Fruit at least 3 times as long as perianth. Local in calcareous grassland or dunes; in the west only. **Fl** 6-8. **Br** Very local or rare from Lincolnshire southwards.

G *Thesium pyrenaicum* Erect to 20cm, sparingly branched. *Stem wavy*. Bracteole equalling flower, *bract at least twice as long*. Flowers in a wavy spike; petal tube equals fruit. Rare in dry grassy or stony habitats, in central hilly or mountainous areas, to 2,200m. **Fl** 5-9. **Br** Absent.

H *Thesium alpinum* Erect stems, usually unbranched. *Flowers in 1-sided raceme*, petal tube 4-lobed. Bracteoles equalling flower, bract 2-3 times longer. Perianth 2-3 times as long as fruit. Local in dry grassy areas in central hilly or mountainous areas and extending into Scandinavia, to 2,500m. **Fl** 5-8. **Br** Absent.

(b) Leaves mostly 3- to 5-veined.

I *Thesium bavarum* Much more robust than other species. Erect to 60cm, usually unbranched. Leaves 3- to 5-veined, dark green and rather flaccid. Fruit 3-4 times as long as perianth. Local in dry grassy areas and scrub, to 1,200m; in the Alps and central Europe. **Fl** 6-8. **Br** Absent.

J *Thesium linophyllon* Similar to *T. bavarum* but stoloniferous, to 30cm. Leaves stiff, yellowish-green, mostly 3-veined but some 1-veined. Local on sandy soils, to 1,200m, in the east. **Fl** 6-8. **Br** Absent.

(2) Bracteoles absent.

K *Thesium ebracteatum* *Stoloniferous*, slender rootstock with erect unbranched stems. Bract 3 times longer than flower. *Fruit twice as long as perianth*. Rare in dry habitats on calcareous soils; E and central Europe, extending to NW and E Germany. **Fl** 6-8. **Br** Absent.

L *Thesium rostratum* Similar to *T. ebracteatum*, but rootstock stout and *not stoloniferous*. Bract up to 4 times as long as flower. *Perianth at least twice as long as fruit*. Very local on dry calcareous soils; mainly a central European species. **Fl** 6-8. **Br** Absent.

Mistletoe Family Loranthaceae

Semi-parasitic small shrubs with opposite leaves and sticky berries.

M **Mistletoe** *Viscum album* Rather woody, parasitic shrub to 1m, forming roundish clumps on tree branches when mature. Leaves leathery and in pairs, widest towards tip. Flowers dioecious. Fruit is a sticky white berry, ripening long after flowers. Locally common, becoming rarer in the north and absent from most of Scandinavia. Parasitic on a variety of deciduous trees, especially Apple, Poplar and Lime. **Fl** 2-4. **Br** Locally frequent fom Yorkshire southwards; most frequent in the south.

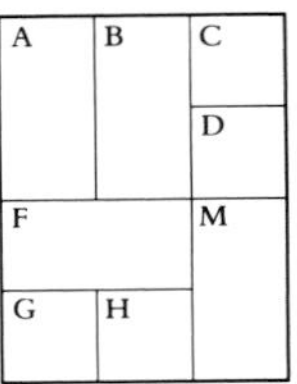

A **Hop** showing leaves and female catkins

B **Stinging Nettle**

C **Annual Nettle**

D **Pellitory-of-the-wall**

F **Bastard Toadflax**

G *Thesium pyrenaicum*

H *Thesium alpinum*

M **Mistletoe** showing fruit

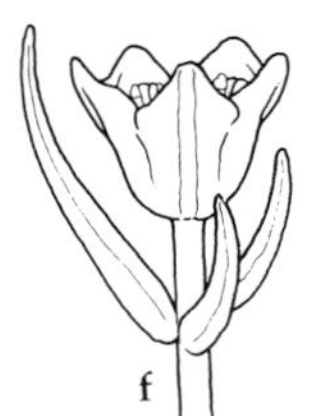

A
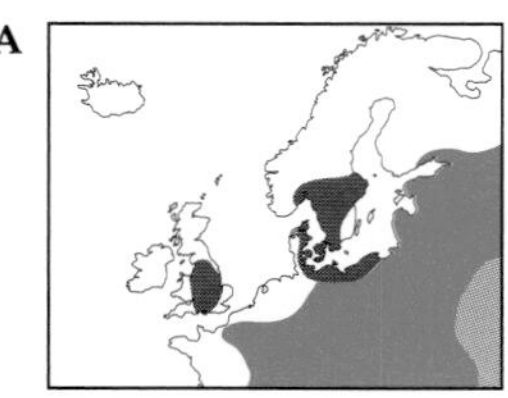
C

F
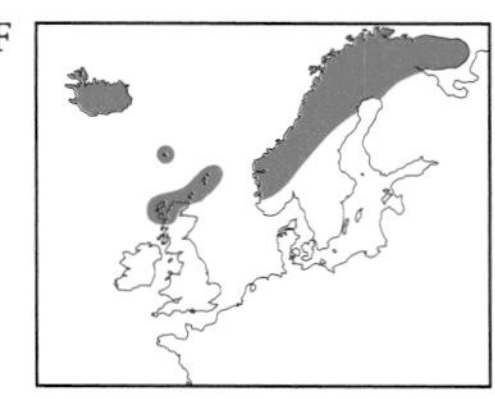
G
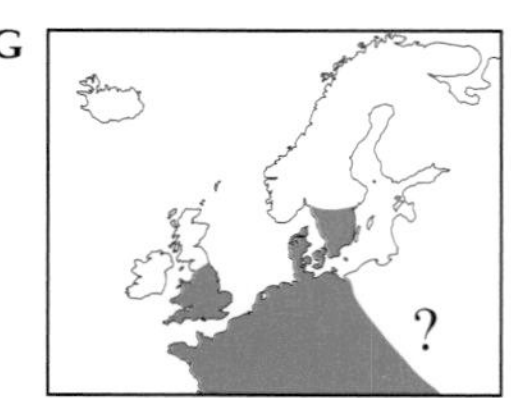

H

I
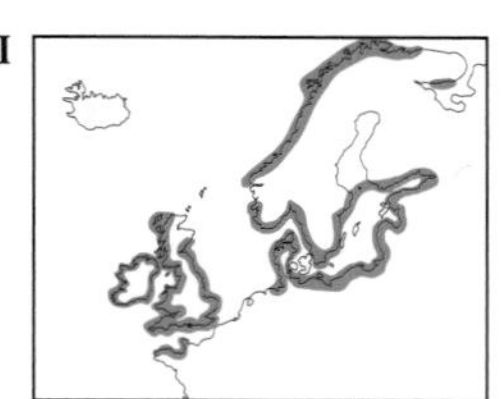
K
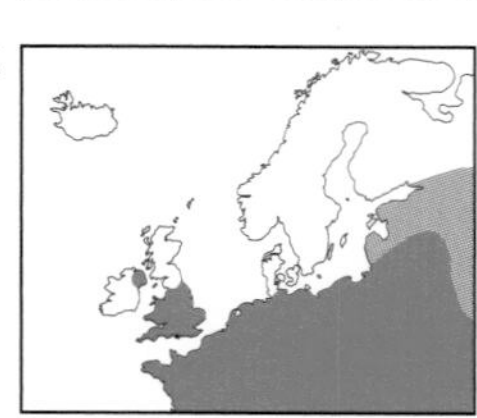
L
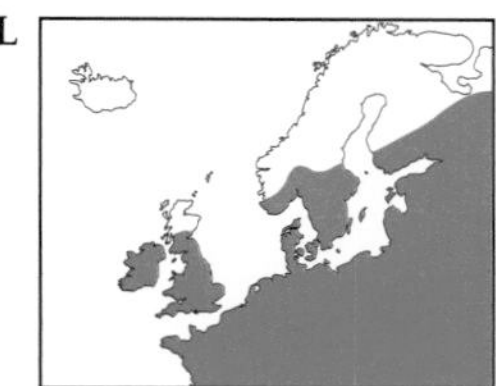

Birthwort Family
Aristolochiaceae

Herbs with alternate untoothed leaves, no stipules, and flowers tubular due to tripartite perianth being united below. Fruit a capsule.

A **Asarabacca** *Asarum europaeum* Distinctive evergreen perennial with a creeping, hairy stem. Dark green, kidney-shaped leaves, with a prominent network of veins; bell-shaped, purplish-red flowers, about 15mm long, ending in 3 pointed petaloid lobes. Locally common in woodland margins, grassy banks and scrub. **Fl** 5-8. **Br** Native but rare and decreasing, with localities to S Scotland; also naturalised.

B **Birthwort** *Aristolochia clematitis* Erect perennial to 80cm, tufted with unbranched stems. Leaves heart-shaped and deeply veined. Flowers in clusters at base of leaves, yellowish and tubular, 20-30mm long, with a smell of carrion and shape reminiscent of tiny Arum Lilies. Globose swelling at base of flower traps insects which aid pollination. Fruit pear-shaped. Formerly cultivated for medicinal aid in midwifery, and long naturalised in scattered localities; possibly native towards the south. **Fl** 6-9. **Br** Rare and declining in widely scattered spots from S England to S Scotland.

Dock Family Polygonaceae

Herbs with stipules usually united into a tubular membranous sheath (ochrea) around stem at base of leaf stalk; leaves usually alternate and flowers small with 3-6 petals or sepals and 6-9 stamens. Fruit a 3-angled or rounded nut.

C **Iceland Purslane** *Koenigia islandica* Tiny prostrate annual with reddish stems, opposite rounded leaves to 5mm and insignificant white flowers in clusters at tips of stem. Perianth divided into 3. Plant resembles Blinks (*see* page 32) which, however, has narrow leaves and perianth in 5 parts. Open, damp bare ground, frequent in the north of its range, rare in the south. **Fl** 6-9. **Br** Rare, confined to mountains on Skye and Mull.

Polygonum Prostrate or erect herbs with unbranched inflorescences in terminal spikes or leaf axils, and with perianth in 5 segments, but no separate petals and sepals.

D **Knotgrass** *Polygonum aviculare* Spreading or erect, hairless annual with wiry stems and alternate lanceolate leaves. Can be to 2m tall but is usually much less. Leaves over 5mm wide, those on main stem obviously larger than those on branches (*see* Equal-leaved Knotgrass). Ochreae silvery (brown below), about 5mm long, with few unbranched veins, *surrounding the leaf stalks.* Flowers pink and greenish, solitary or in clusters in leaf axils giving stem a knotted effect. Fruit completely covered by perianth. Widespread and common throughout; in a variety of open habitats. **Fl** 6-11. **Br** Common throughout.

E **Equal-leaved Knotgrass** *Polygonum arenastrum* Similar to Knotgrass, but forms dense, prostrate mats, and leaves on main stem are the same size as those on the branches. Widespread and common in similar habitats. **Fl** 7-9. **Br** Common almost throughout, though less so than Knotgrass.

F **Northern Knotgrass** *Polygonum boreale* Similar to Knotgrass, but *leaf stalks obviously emerging beyond ochreae* (**f**). Flowering time and habitats similar, though prefers coastal areas. **Fl** 6-11. **Br** Confined to N Scotland and the Northern Isles.

G **Cornfield Knotgrass** *Polygonum rurivagum* Similar to Knotgrass, but stem leaves 1-4mm broad, ochreae long (7-8mm) and reddish-brown below (**g**). Very local on arable calcareous soils. **Fl** 6-9. **Br** Rare in S England, and decreasing.

H **Sea Knotgrass** *Polygonum maritimum* Similar to Knotgrass, but a compact perennial, woody at the base. Leaves dark greyish green with markedly rolled-back edges beneath; ochreae silvery, often as long as upper internodes and with *6-12 conspicuous branched veins* (**h1**). Fruit much longer than the perianth (**h2**). Very local or rare on coastal sand or shingly beaches; mainly Mediterranean. **Fl** 5-10. **Br** Very rare and decreasing in SW England.

I **Ray's Knotgrass** *Polygonum oxyspermum* Similar to Sea Knotgrass, but annual with leaf margins slightly or not downturned; ochreae shorter than upper internodes and having only *4-6 unbranched veins* (**i1**). Fruit protruding beyond perianth (**i2**). Similar habitats; local. **Br** Very local on S and W coast of Britain, north to Hebrides, and coasts of Ireland.

J **Water-pepper** *Polygonum hydropiper* Erect, branched annual to 80cm, with narrow lanceolate leaves (10-25mm wide) and greenish or pinkish flowers arranged in slender spikes, nodding at the tip. Ochreae not fringed. Lower flowers in leaf axils and never opening. *Perianth segments covered in yellow glands* when viewed under lens (**j**). Fruit dull. Plant notably peppery when chewed. Widespread and common almost throughout, but absent from the far north; in damp habitats or shallow water. **Fl** 7-9. **Br** Common except in the far north.

K **Tasteless Water-pepper** *Polygonum mite* Very close to Water-pepper, with *leaves 10-25mm wide* and abruptly narrowed at base, but it is not peppery, has fringed ochreae and *no yellow glands on perianth.* Flowerheads not, or hardly, drooping. Fruit glossy, 3-4.5mm. Very local in ditches and pond-margins. **Fl** 7-9. **Br** Rare and declining, north to Durham.

L **Small Water-pepper** *Polygonum minus* Also similar to Water-pepper, but has *leaves only 5-8mm wide,* is not peppery, has very slender and *rather prostrate habit* with erect flowering stems to 40cm, and *no yellow glands* on perianth. Flowerheads not, or hardly, drooping. Fruit glossy, 1-3mm. Very local and declining in pond-margins and bare wet places. **Fl** 7-9. **Br** Rare; north to Perth and Argyll.

M **Redshank** *Polygonum persicaria* Erect or somewhat sprawling *hairless annual* to 70cm, branched and with stems reddish below and swollen at the leaf nodes. Leaves lanceolate, tapering to the base and usually with a dark central blotch. *Flowers pink* and in dense terminal or axillary spikes. Widespread and common in waste areas, arable or bare ground, damp places. **Fl** 6-10. **Br** Common throughout.

N **Pale Persicaria** *Polygonum lapathifolium* Similar to Redshank, but *rather hairy,* stems greenish, flower stalk with scattered yellowish glands and *flowers usually greenish-white* (rarely pink). **Fl** 6-10. **Br** Common throughout.

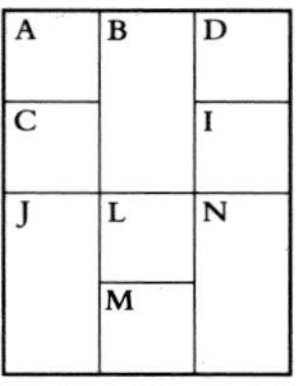

A **Asarabacca**
B **Birthwort** showing fruit
D **Knotgrass**
C **Iceland Purslane**
I **Ray's Knotgrass**
J **Water-pepper**
L **Small Water-pepper**
M **Redshank** (erect pink flower spikes) with Water-pepper (nodding flower spikes)
N **Pale Persicaria**

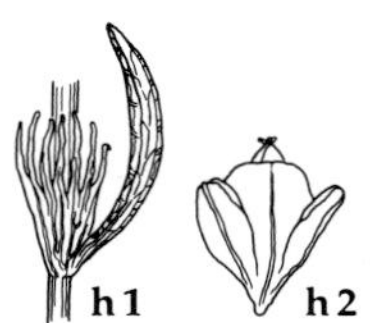

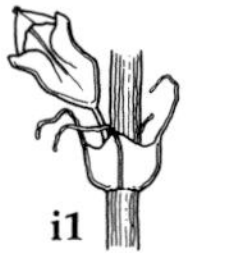

C

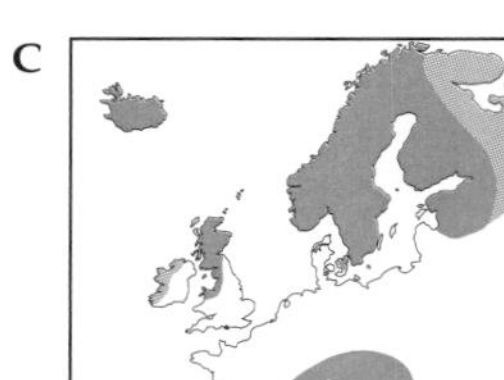

H

K

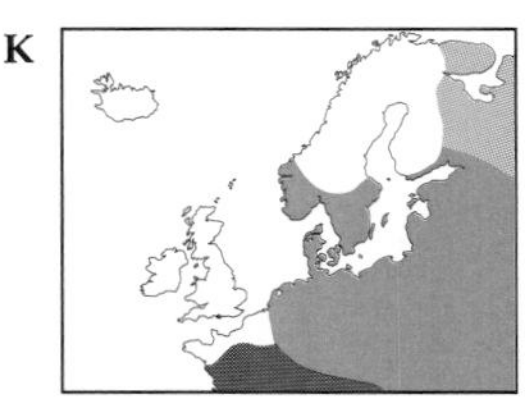

L

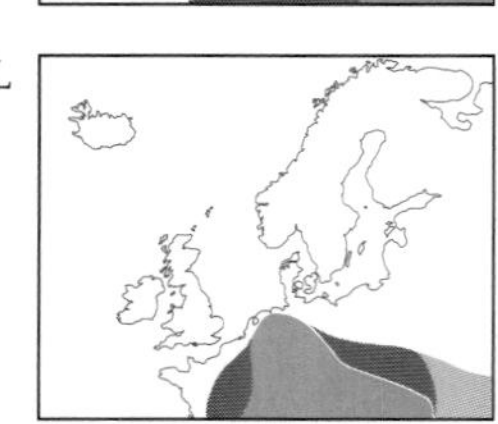

A Bistort *Polygonum bistorta* Erect and often patch-forming, unbranched, almost hairless perennial to 1m. Leaves triangular, the lower ones abruptly contracted into the long-winged leaf stalk; upper leaves almost stalkless and often arrow-shaped. Flowers pink in a dense cylindrical terminal spike. Widespread, common in some areas, rare in others; in damp grassland and meadows. **Fl** 6-10. **Br** Locally common in the north, rare in the south.

B Amphibious Bistort *Polygonum amphibium* Perennial to 75cm with 2 distinct forms: (1) aquatic form hairless with floating stem and leaves, the latter truncate at the base; (2) land form with erect stem and roughly hairy leaves narrowed and rounded at the base. Both forms have deep pink flowers in dense oval terminal spike. Widespread and frequent; aquatic form in ponds and ditches, land form on riverbanks, in damp grassland and sometimes arable or waste areas. **Fl** 7-9. **Br** Widespread and locally frequent.

C Alpine Bistort *Polygonum viviparum* Erect unbranched hairless perennial to 30cm. Leaves narrow lanceolate, lower ones tapering at the base into unwinged stalk, the upper ones unstalked; leaf margin downturned. Flowers white or pale pink, in terminal slender spikes, but flowers in the lower part of the spike replaced by purplish bulbils which are a means of vegetative propagation. Locally frequent in mountain grassland, to 2,000m. **Fl** 6-8. **Br** Locally frequent from N Wales northwards; rare in W Ireland.

D Himalayan Knotweed *Polygonum polystachyum* Tall patch-forming perennial to 1.2m with oblong or *lanceolate red-veined leaves*. Similar to Japanese Knotweed (*see* below) but leaf shape different. Numerous white flowers, in loose terminal branched clusters (panicles) with red stems. Widely naturalised on streambanks and damp waste areas. **Fl** 7-10. **Br** Increasingly frequent, especially in SW England and W Ireland.

E Black-bindweed *Bilderdykia comvolvulus* Annual, clockwise-twining plant, prostrate or climbing to 1.2m. Stem angular. Leaves heart- or arrow-shaped, pointed and rather mealy beneath. Flowers greenish-white or greenish-pink in loose spikes arising from leaf axils. Fruit a dull black triangular nut on *short stalk to 3mm*. Differs from the true bindweeds (*see* page 202) in twining clockwise and having angular stems. Widespread and common throughout; in arable and waste areas. **Fl** 7-10. **Br** Common throughout.

F Copse-bindweed *Bilderdykia dumetorum* Similar to Black-bindweed, but can be much taller climber to 2m. Stems usually more rounded and *fruit stalk 4-8mm*. Nut shiny. Sepals in fruit with broad wings running down onto stalk. Widespread but local in hedges, managed copses and open scrub. **Fl** 7-10. **Br** Rare and decreasing in S and SE England; erratic in appearance.

G Japanese Knotweed *Reynoutria japonica* Tall, rampant perennial to 2m, often forming extensive thickets. Stems reddish or bluish-green, rather zig-zag. *Leaves broadly triangular*, pointed and abruptly truncated at the base. Flowers whitish in loose branched spikes from axils of upper leaves. Introduced to Europe as a garden plant in the 19th century. Now widely naturalised and a serious pest on riverbanks, roadsides, railway embankments, etc. **Fl** 9-10. **Br** Common throughout.

H Mountain Sorrel *Oxyria digyna* Erect hairless stout perennial to 30cm. Stem almost leafless. Basal *leaves rounded and kidney-shaped*. Flowers greenish with red edges in loose branched spikes. Outer perianth segments 4. Fruit flat and broadly winged. Locally common in damp rocky places or streamsides in mountains, descending to low altitudes in Arctic and sub-Arctic areas. **Fl** 7-8. **Br** Locally common in Scottish mountains; rare in N Wales, Cumbria and W Ireland.

DOCKS *Rumex* These differ from *Polygonum* in having branched spikes of flowers with 6 (as opposed to 5) outer perianth segments in 2 whorls, the outer tiny and thin, the inner enlarging and hardening to form the so-called 'valves' which envelop the fruit. Features of the valves, notably the presence or absence of teeth and tubercles, are an important part of identification, for which a hand lens is needed.

I Common Sorrel *Rumex acetosa* Variable erect perennial to 1m (usually less). Leaves lanceolate, *arrow-shaped at the base*; basal leaves long-stalked, upper leaves unstalked and clasping the stem. Flowers dioecious and reddish. Widespread and common in grassy places. **Fl** 5-6. **Br** Common throughout.

J Sheep's Sorrel *Rumex acetosella* Variable erect perennial, differing from Common Sorrel in being shorter, to 30cm. Differs also in having *basal lobes of leaves spreading or forward-pointing*, and upper leaves stalked and not clasping the stem. Flowers greenish in loose panicles. Widespread and common on well-drained acid soils, heaths and sand-dunes. **Fl** 5-8. **Br** Common throughout. 2 subspecies are recognised: ssp *acetosella* Perianth segments form a loose covering around fruit, and are easily separated by rolling between fingers. Ssp *pyrenaicus* Perianth segments not easily separated from fruit.

K *Rumex thyrsiflorus* Tall, erect perennial to 1.2m. Similar to Common Sorrel, but *leaves with spreading basal lobes* and stem leaves becoming progressively narrower, *up to 12 times as long as broad*. Flowers greenish in much-branched dense panicles. Occasional to common in dry grasslands and on roadsides. **Fl** 6-9. **Br** Absent.

L French Sorrel *Rumex scutatus* A tufted perennial to 70cm, branched from the base with characteristic *helmet-shaped leaves*. Flowers greenish in few-flowered branched spikes. Local on old walls, stony places and screes in hills and mountains. **Fl** 6-7. **Br** Naturalised in a few places in N England and Scotland.

A	B	C
D	F	
E	G	H
I	J	L

A **Bistort**
B **Amphibious Bistort**
C **Alpine Bistort**
D **Himalayan Knotweed**
F **Copse-bindweed**
E **Black-bindweed**
G **Japanese Knotweed**
H **Mountain Sorrel**
I **Common Sorrel**
J **Sheep's Sorrel**
L **French Sorrel**

A

C
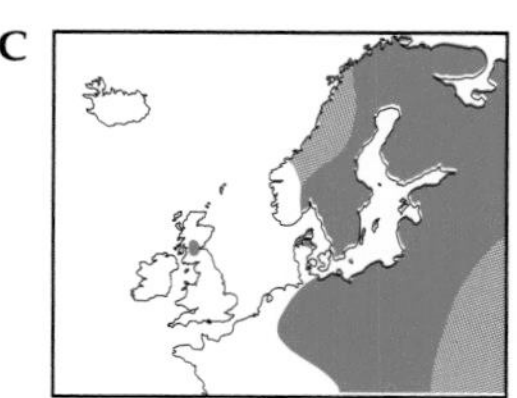

E
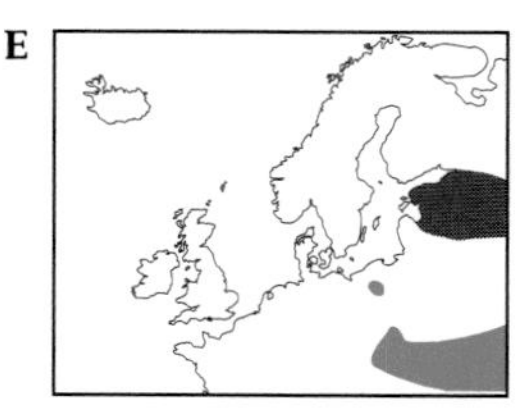

F
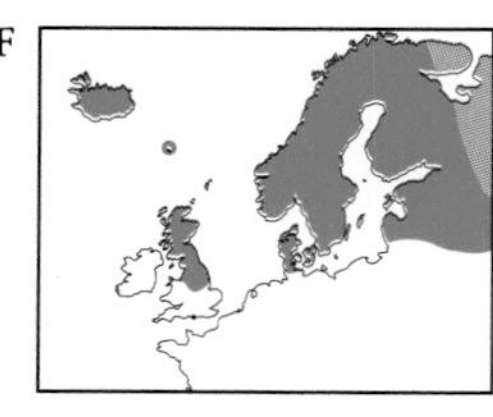

I
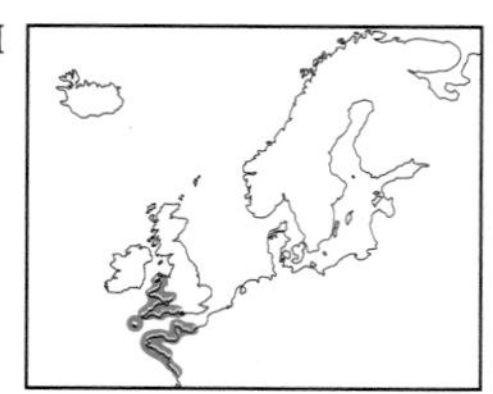

J
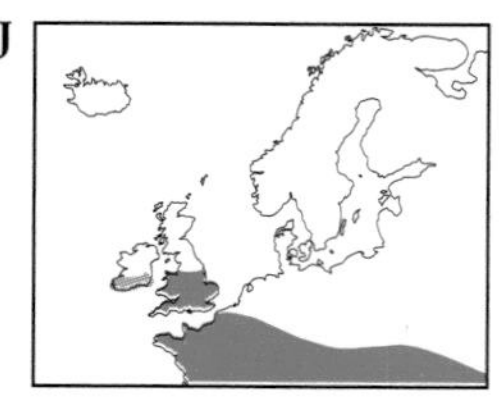

L
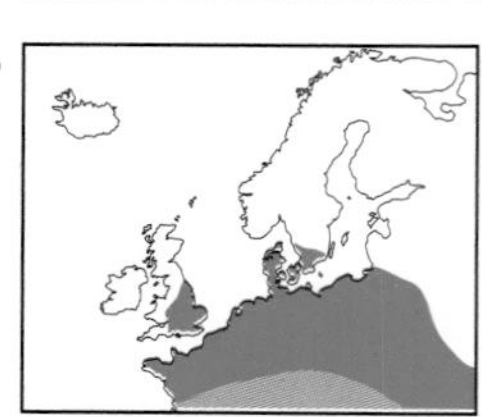

A Monk's-rhubarb *Rumex alpinus* Stout erect perennial to 1m or more, with a creeping rhizome. *Leaves large and roundish, to 40cm, wavy-edged and heart-shaped at base*. Flowers greenish-yellow in much-branched densely flowered panicles. Local in upland meadows, often near buildings; absent from much of NW Europe and from Scandinavia. **Fl** 6-8. **Br** Naturalised in widely scattered localities from the Midlands northwards.

B Water Dock *Rumex hydrolapathum* Very tall erect perennial to 2m. Basal leaves leathery and lanceolate, *very long* to 1m and tapering to *short stalk*. Flowers in dense whorls in much-branched inflorescence, leafy below. Fruit perianth segments with an elongated tubercle on each side (**b**). Frequent in wet habitats: marshes, ditches, rivers, streams, canals, etc.; absent from the far north. **Fl** 7-9. **Br** Locally frequent; rare in Scotland.

C Scottish Dock *Rumex aquaticus* Similar to Water Dock, but basal leaves *long-stalked* and *triangular with a broad base*, and fruit has *no tubercles* (**c**). Local by lake and streamsides; mainly in the east. **Fl** 7-8. **Br** Found only by Loch Lomond.

D Curled Dock *Rumex crispus* Variable erect perennial to 1m. Leaves to 30cm, oblong-lanceolate with *markedly wavy edges*. Flower spikes branched and dense. Valves untoothed and *each with a tubercle*, often 1 larger than the others on plants by the sea. Ubiquitous as a common weed of waste areas, arable land and roadsides. **Fl** 6-10. **Br** Very common throughout.

E *Rumex stenophyllus* Differs in having *fruit valves with small teeth*. Coastal marshes in Germany. **Fl** 6-10. **Br** Absent.

F Northern Dock *Rumex longifolius* Like Curled Dock, but leaves to 80cm and *fruit valves without tubercles* (**f**). Locally frequent in damp grassland, ditches and freshwater margins; mainly from Denmark northwards. **Fl** 6-7. **Br** Locally common from Lancashire and Yorkshire northwards.

G Clustered Dock *Rumex conglomeratus* Erect perennial to 1m. Stems zig-zag and branches spreading (30°-90°). Leaves oblong with a rounded base, often waisted, the lower ones long-stalked. Flower spikes leafy almost to the top. *Fruit valves untoothed, each with a tubercle* (**g**). Widespread and common in a variety of grassy habitats and woodland margins; absent from most of Scandinavia. **Fl** 6-10. **Br** Common except in Scotland, where it is rare.

H Wood Dock *Rumex sanguineus* Like Clustered Dock, but stem straighter, branches more erect (to 45°), basal leaves never waisted but sometimes red-veined. Flower spikes not leafy except lower down, and *only 1 fruit valve possessing a swollen tubercle* (**h**). Widespread and often common in grassy places and woodland margins; absent from most of Scandinavia. **Fl** 6-10. **Br** Common northwards to mid-Scotland.

I Shore Dock *Rumex rupestris* Like Clustered Dock, but recognisable by its *blunt greyish leaves*, erect branches and *inflorescence leafy only at the base*. Local in a variety of coastal habitats, from rocky shores to dune-slacks. **Fl** 6-8. **Br** Very local in SW England and S Wales.

J Fiddle Dock *Rumex pulcher* Low, *spreading* perennial plant to 50cm, *branches making a wide angle with the main stem* to give a characteristic appearance. Lower leaves small, to 10cm (but usually less), and *waisted* to give a violin shape (**j1**). Branches often tangled in fruit. Fruit valves toothed and all with tubercles (**j2**). Very local on well-drained soils in open grassy places, often near the coast; absent from the north and east. **Fl** 6-8. **Br** Local by the coast in S and SE England and Wales.

K Broad-leaved Dock *Rumex obtusifolius* Stout erect perennial to 1m, with large lower leaves to 25cm, *heart-shaped at the base* and often with a slightly wavy edge. Branched flower spikes leafy below. *Fruit valves with several long teeth*, and at least 1 with a tubercle. Widespread and very common in a variety of habitats, particularly farmed areas where there is nitrogen enrichment. **Fl** 6-10. **Br** Very common throughout.

L Marsh Dock *Rumex palustris* Erect branched annual or biennial to 70cm, with spreading branches and lanceolate pointed leaves. Flower spikes consist of dense whorls of flowers, leafy throughout. Plant a characteristic yellow-brown colour in fruit, and *fruit valves have long bristle-like teeth* in addition to a tubercle, *the teeth shorter than the valves* (**l**). Local on the bare mud of lakesides and rivers. **Fl** 6-9. **Br** Very local in the south, otherwise rare northwards to Yorkshire.

M Golden Dock *Rumex maritimus* Erect annual similar to Marsh Dock, but *golden yellow in fruit* and *bristle-like teeth on fruit valves longer than the valves* (**m**). Widespread but local in similar habitats to Marsh Dock; not only near the sea but also far inland. **Fl** 6-9. **Br** Local in central and S England; rare elsewhere and extending northwards to S Scotland. Very local in Ireland.

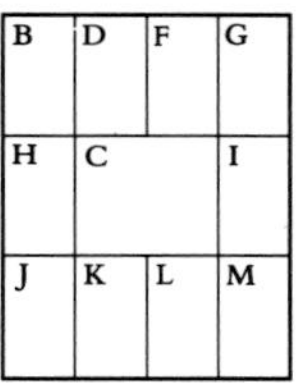

B Water Dock
D Curled Dock
F Northern Dock
G Clustered Dock
H Wood Dock
C Scottish Dock
I Shore Dock
J Fiddle Dock
K Broad-leaved Dock
L Marsh Dock
M Golden Dock

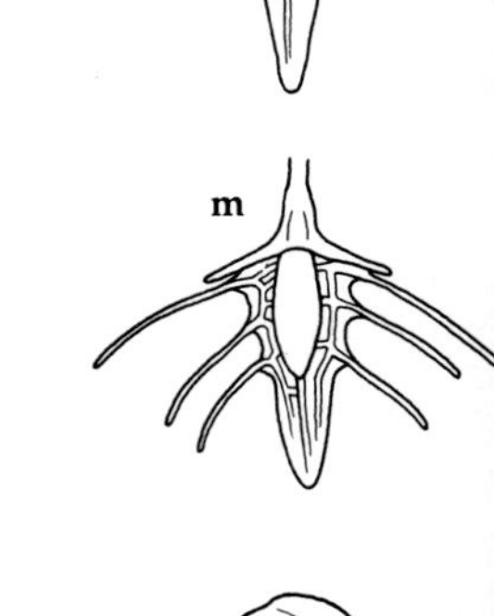

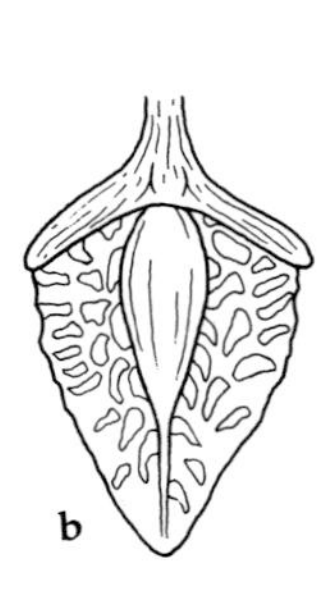

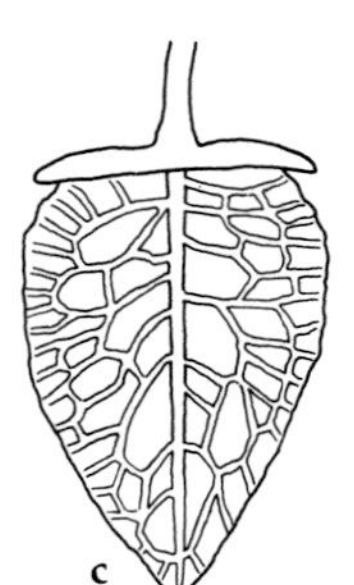

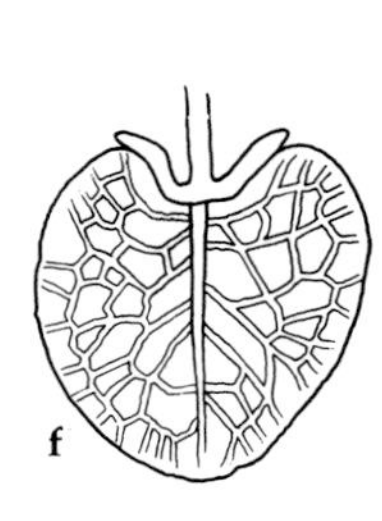

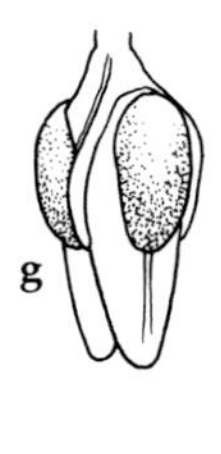

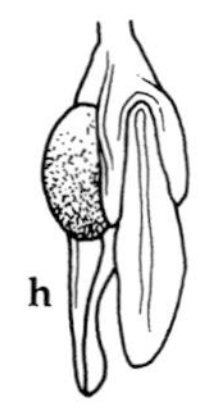

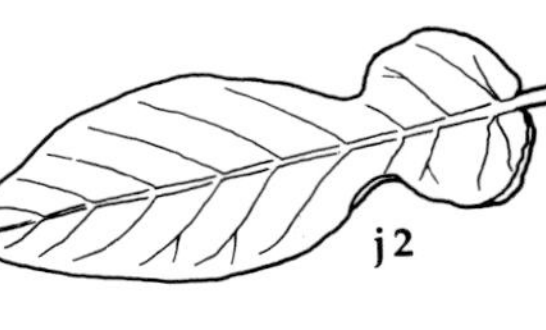

A

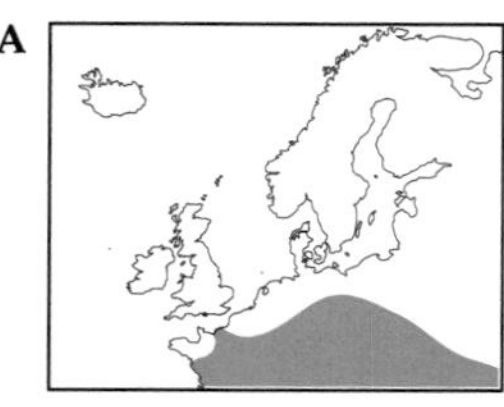

C

G

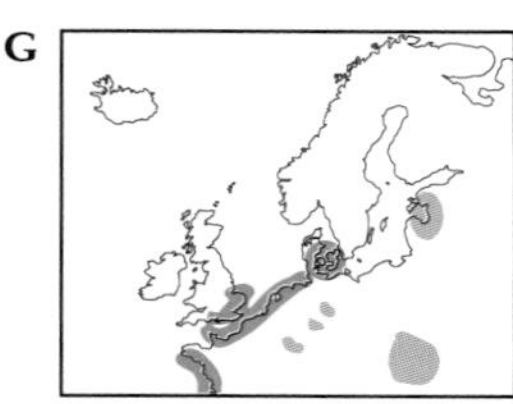

H

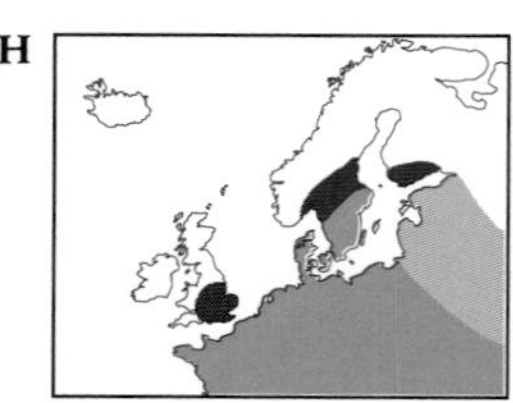

J

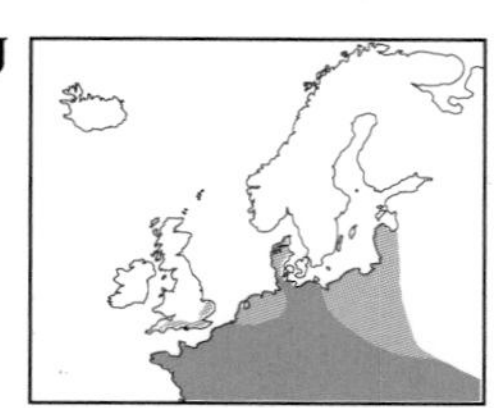

K

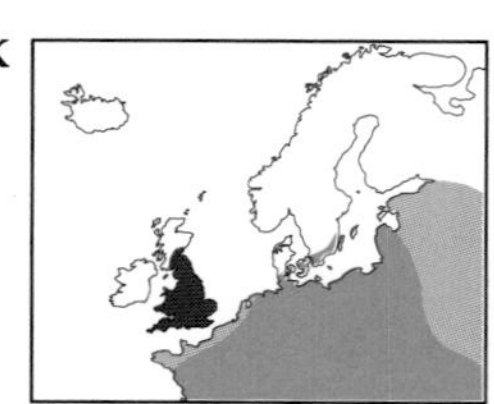

L

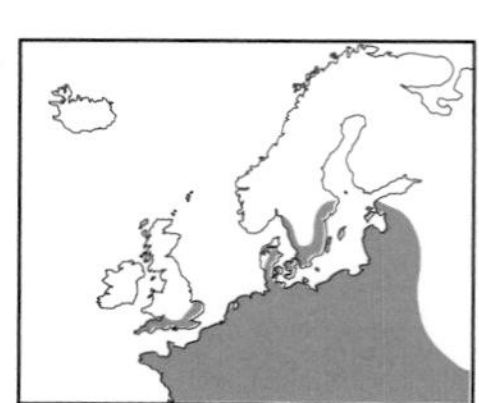

M

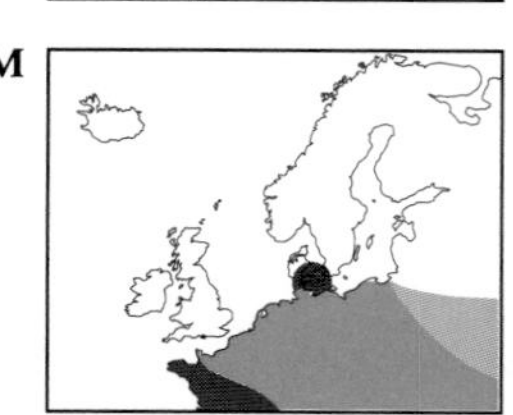

P

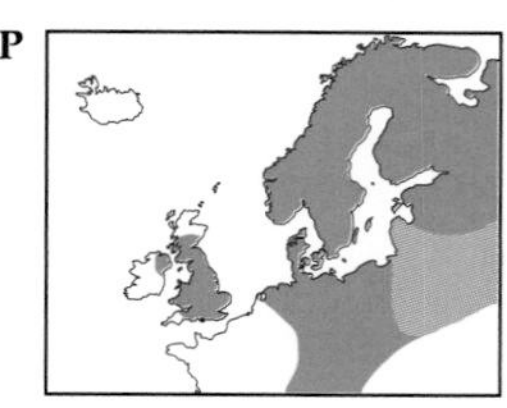

Goosefoot Family
Chenopodiaceae

A variable family of herbs usually growing on open ground, with the common features of tiny, usually greenish, 3- to 5-lobed flowers. Goosefoots (*Chenopodium*) and oraches (*Atriplex*) are usually annuals with alternate, often mealy, leaves. Oraches have male and female flowers on separate plants. In goosefoots they occur on the same plant. Oraches have fruits surrounded by 2 swollen bracts, goosefoots by 3-5 sepals. Glassworts (*Salicornia*) are succulent with indistinct leaves.

A *Polycnemum majus* A short sprawling or erect annual to 30cm with characteristic *sharply pointed, linear, needle-like leaves, to 2cm long,* triangular in cross-section. Greenish flowers tiny in the axils of the leaves. Often abundant in dry, bare ground or arable land; mainly in central and S Europe but extending north-west to Belgium. **Fl** 7-10. **Br** Absent.

B *Polycnemum arvense* Very similar to *P. majus,* but taller to 50cm and *stems obviously spirally twisted* with *leaves softly spiny, to 12mm long.* Similar habitats and range, but not reaching Belgium. **Fl** 7-10. **Br** Absent.

C **Sea Beet** *Beta vulgaris* Erect or sprawling perennial to 1m with red-striped stems and shiny dark green leaves, untoothed and leathery. Basal leaves triangular and wavy, upper stem leaves oblong. Flowers green, in dense, leafy and often branched spikes. Perianth often becomes prickly in fruit, several fruits sticking together as a result. Locally common on sea-cliffs, shingle and edges of salt-marshes. **Fl** 6-9. **Br** Frequent on coasts in the south, much more local in the north.

GOOSEFOOTS *Chenopodium* Recognised by their alternate often mealy leaves and perianth with 2-5 segments. Annuals except for Good-King-Henry. Flowers small, in clusters. Lower leaf shapes (illustrated) help separate species.

D **Good-King-Henry** *Chenopodium bonus-henricus* Erect branched perennial with stiff *stems often streaked red.* Leaves mealy at first, later *dark green. Lower leaves triangular,* to 10cm (**d**). Frequent in waste areas, arable land, on old walls and hedgebanks. **Fl** 5-8. **Br** Introduced and naturalised; locally frequent.

E **Oak-leaved Goosefoot** *Chenopodium glaucum* Erect or prostrate to 40cm, *leaves mealy beneath,* sinuately and regularly toothed (**e**). Locally frequent in waste areas, arable land and seashores. **Fl** 6-9. **Br** Rare.

F **Red Goosefoot** *Chenopodium rubrum* A variable fleshy plant, erect or sprawling to 60cm and often tinged red. Leaves to 6cm, *not mealy but shiny,* variably diamond-shaped and coarsely toothed (**f**). Locally common in waste areas, arable land, dried pond-margins and marshes. **Fl** 7-9. **Br** Common in S England; rare in the north, Wales and Ireland.

G **Salt-marsh, Small Red, Goosefoot** *Chenopodium botryodes* Similar to Red Goosefoot, but smaller (to 30cm), *branches spreading* from the base. *Leaves always red below* when mature, and hardly toothed (**g**). Very locally frequent; in salt-marshes and bare coastal mud. **Fl** 7-9. **Br** Rare in SE England.

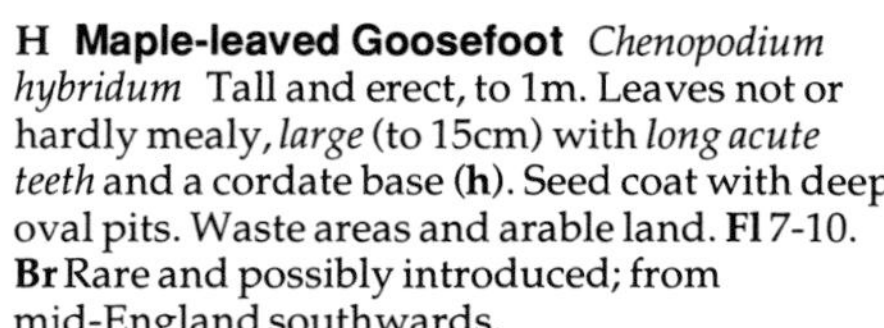

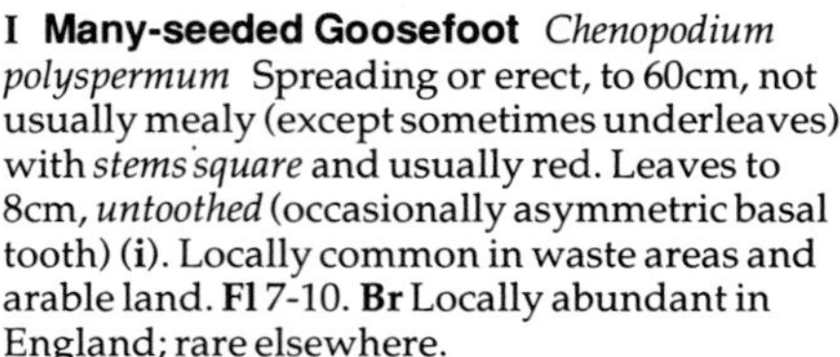

H **Maple-leaved Goosefoot** *Chenopodium hybridum* Tall and erect, to 1m. Leaves not or hardly mealy, *large* (to 15cm) with *long acute teeth* and a cordate base (**h**). Seed coat with deep oval pits. Waste areas and arable land. **Fl** 7-10. **Br** Rare and possibly introduced; from mid-England southwards.

I **Many-seeded Goosefoot** *Chenopodium polyspermum* Spreading or erect, to 60cm, not usually mealy (except sometimes underleaves) with *stems square* and usually red. Leaves to 8cm, *untoothed* (occasionally asymmetric basal tooth) (**i**). Locally common in waste areas and arable land. **Fl** 7-10. **Br** Locally abundant in England; rare elsewhere.

J **Stinking Goosefoot** *Chenopodium vulvaria* Erect or prostrate, branched, grey and mealy plant to 30cm. Leaves diamond-shaped, to 3cm, with a pair of basal lobes (**j**). *Plant smells strongly of rotten fish when bruised.* Very local in waste areas, coastal bare places. **Fl** 7-9. **Br** S England, very rare.

K **Upright Goosefoot** *Chenopodium urbicum* Always erect to 60cm and *not mealy, stems ridged* but not square. Leaves to 11cm, triangular, tapered to base and coarsely toothed, teeth often hooked (**k**). Local in waste areas. **Fl** 7-9. **Br** England, formerly widespread but now rare; possibly not native.

L **Nettle-leaved Goosefoot** *Chenopodium murale* Erect, *slightly mealy plant* to 70cm. *Leaves rarely turn red* and have coarse irregular forward-pointing teeth, reminiscent of nettle leaves (**l**). Inflorescence spreading with flower spikes leafy at the top, and short branches (compare with Fat Hen and Grey Goosefoot, which can have similar leaves). Locally frequent in waste areas, sand-dunes, arable on sandy soils. **Fl** 7-10. **Br** Scattered and local in England and Wales; casual elsewhere.

M **Fig-leaved Goosefoot** *Chenopodium ficifolium* Erect or spreading mealy plant to 90cm. Lower leaves to 8cm, *long and narrow* with 3 lobes, the middle lobe much longer than the 2 laterals (**m**). Seed coat with deep elongated pits. Rather local in waste areas, arable on clay. **Fl** 7-9. **Br** Local in central and S England.

N **Grey Goosefoot** *Chenopodium opulifolium* Variable erect or spreading mealy plant to 80cm. Basal leaves as broad as long, often 3-lobed and coarsely toothed (**n**). Inflorescence branches long and flower spikes not usually leafy to top (compare with Nettle-leaved Gossefoot). Waste areas. **Fl** 7-10. **Br** Local in S England.

O **Fat Hen** *Chenopodium album* Tall, erect, *deep green* and rather *mealy plant* to 1m. Stems stiff and *often streaked red.* Leaves ovate or *diamond-shaped,* to 8cm, coarsely and bluntly toothed (**o**). Common in arable and waste areas. **Fl** 7-10. **Br** Common throughout.

P **Green Goosefoot** *Chenopodium suecicum* Like Fat Hen, but *leaves bright blue-green,* only mealy when young. Basal leaves ovate, sometimes 3-lobed, with several forward-pointing sharp teeth (**p**). Local on rubbish tips and waste areas. **Fl** 7-10. **Br** Rare but widely scattered.

p o n m

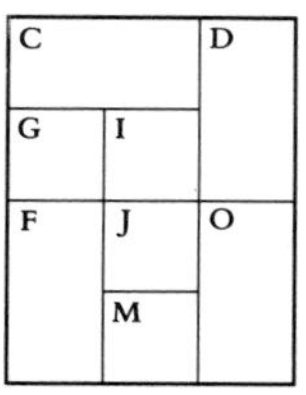

C **Sea Beet**

D **Good-King-Henry**

G **Salt-marsh Goosefoot**

I **Many-seeded Goosefoot**

F **Red Goosefoot**

J **Stinking Goosefoot**

M **Fig-leaved Goosefoot**

O **Fat Hen**

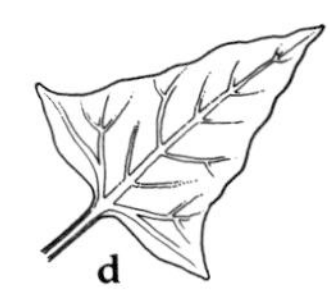

d

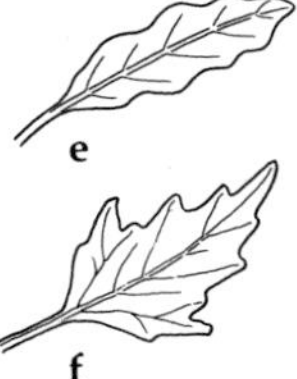

e

f

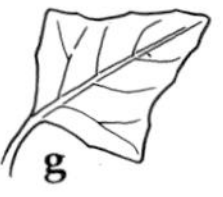

g

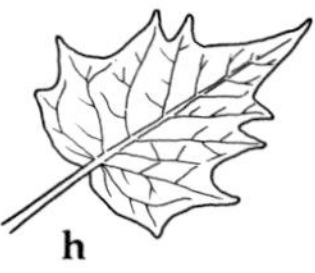

h

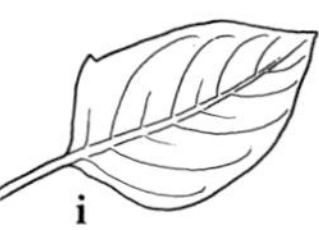

i

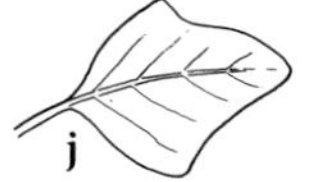

j

k

l

E

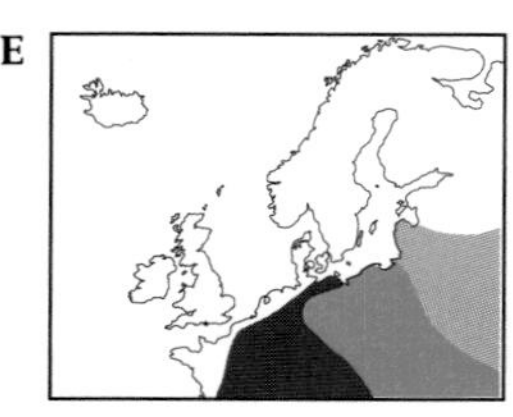

I

J

L

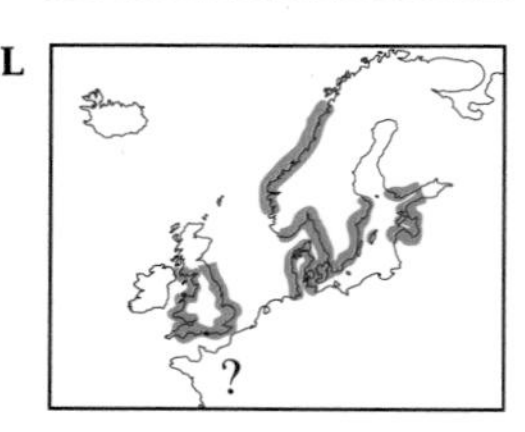

M

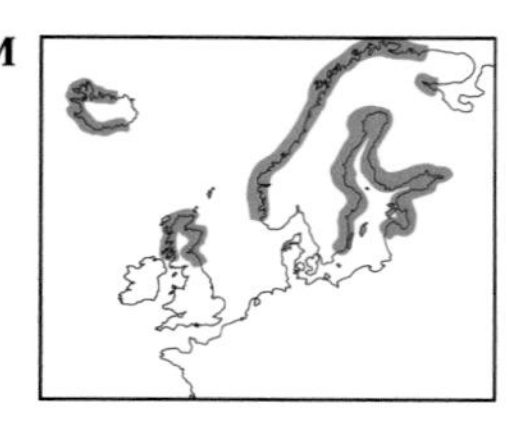

O

P

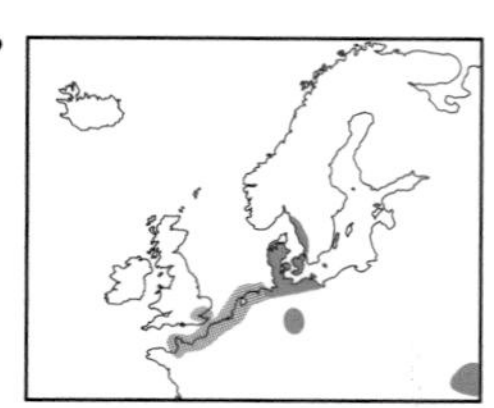

Q

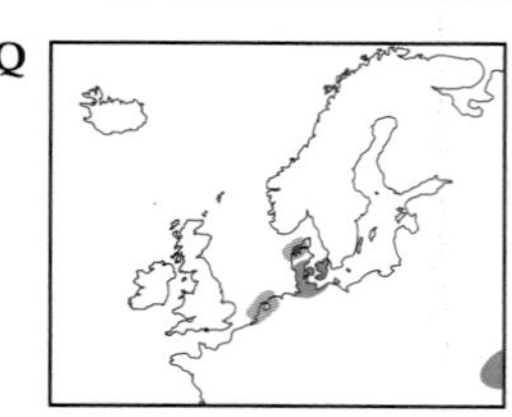

R

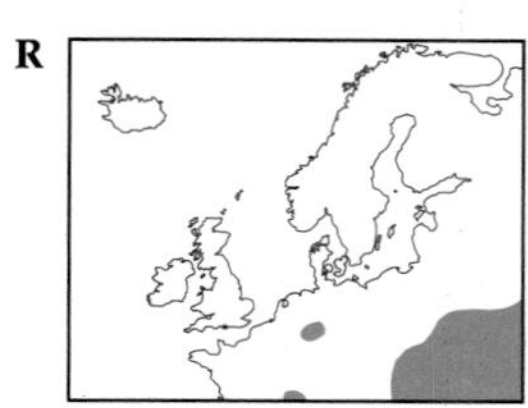

ORACHES *Atriplex* Annuals similar to goosefoots with alternate leaves and inconspicuous flowers in spikes; male and female flowers separate, with female flowers surrounded by a pair of bracts which swell in fruit. Leaves have strong lateral veins. Diagrams are of lower leaves

A **Orache** *Atriplex hortensis* Tall erect green plant to 2.5m, often flushed purplish. Lower leaves triangular or rather halberd-shaped, only slightly toothed (**a1**) and mealy only when young. Flowers in terminal spikes. Bracts a distinct oval or rounded shape, untoothed (**a2**). Casual in waste and disturbed areas. **Fl** 7-10. **Br** Uncommon escape from cultivation.

B *Atriplex nitens* Differs from Orache in having leaves grey mealy beneath, and bracts oblong or heart-shaped. Roadsides and waste areas; E and central Europe. **Fl** 7-10. **Br** Absent.

C *Atriplex heterosperma* Differs from Orache in having lower leaves arrow-shaped. Roadsides and waste areas; uncommon casual from Russia. **Fl** 7-10. **Br** Absent.

D **Frosted Orache** *Atriplex laciniata* Prostrate plant to 30cm, more silvery grey than other oraches, with a yellowish or reddish stem and wavy-edged mealy leaves (**d1**). Flowers in dense lateral leafy clusters towards top of plant. Bract hardened in lower half (**d2**). Locally common on sandy or gravelly shores. **Fl** 7-10. **Br** Local all round the coast of Great Britain; local on S and E coasts of Ireland.

E *Atriplex rosea* Differs from Frosted Orache in being erect with lateral leafy flower spikes all along stem and with large appendages on back of bracts. Leaf (**e**). Uncommon in waste and disturbed areas. **Fl** 7-9. **Br** Uncommon casual.

F *Atriplex tatarica* As Frosted Orache but flower spikes only terminal, not lateral. Leaf irregularly lobed (**f**). Uncommon in waste areas. **Fl** 7-10. **Br** Absent.

G **Grass-leaved Orache** *Atriplex littoralis* Erect plant to 1m, with ridged stems and linear leaves 20-30 times longer than broad, untoothed or slightly toothed (**g1**). Bract triangular, entire or toothed (**g2**). Common on bare muddy ground near the sea. **Fl** 7-10. **Br** Locally common on the coast of England and Wales; local in Scotland and Ireland.

H **Common Orache** *Atriplex patula* Very variable much-branched plant, erect or more often prostrate, to 60cm. Stems ridged and often reddish. Leaves mealy, the lower ones usually diamond-shaped or arrow-shaped and coarsely toothed (**h1**), the upper ones narrow-linear and slightly toothed. Lower leaves have *basal teeth forward-pointing*. Greenish flowers in long spikes from leaf axils or terminal. *Bracts diamond-shaped, not, or slightly, toothed* (**h2**). Common in waste areas inland or by the sea. **Fl** 7-9. **Br** Common throughout.

I *Atriplex oblongifolia* Differs from Common Orache in having lower leaves less lobed (**i**) and *rounded bracts*; flower spikes broken into many clusters. Uncommon in waste areas; mainly in the south-east. **Fl** 7-9. **Br** Absent.

J *Atriplex calotheca* Differs from Common Orache in its distinctive *toothed* bracts (**j2**). Leaves irregularly toothed (**j1**). Local in waste areas. **Fl** 7-10. **Br** Absent.

K **Halberd-leaved Orache** *Atriplex hastata* Usually erect, sometimes reddish, plant to 1mm with triangular or halberd-shaped lower leaves, the largest *lower teeth of which are at right angles* (**k1**) to the leaf stalk. *Bracts toothed and unstalked* (**k2**) (compare with Long-stalked Orache and Early Orache, *see* below), *staying green* even when fruit is ripe. Very common in a variety of habitats from waste areas inland to sea walls and salt-marshes. **Fl** 7-10. **Br** Throughout, but mainly coastal in the north.

L **Long-stalked Orache** *Atriplex longipes* Differs from Halberd-leaved Orache in having *untoothed stalked bracts (stalks over 5mm)*, silvery white in fruit. Leaves narrower (**l**). Local in salt-marshes. **Fl** 7-10. **Br** Scattered, very local.

M **Early Orache** *Atriplex praecox* Only up to 10cm tall, with untoothed bracts and *bract stalks 3mm or less*. Very local in salt-marshes, just above drift-line. **Fl** 7-10. **Br** Rare in NW Scotland only.

N **Babington's Orache** *Atriplex glabriuscula* Usually prostrate mealy plant, very similar to Halberd-leaved Orache, with reddish stems, but plant to only 20cm long, leaves less toothed (**n1**) and bracts thick, more diamond-shaped (**n2**) and united to half-way up, *silvery white when fruit is ripe*. Widespread on coastal shingle. **Fl** 7-10. **Br** Frequent throughout on the coast.

Halimione These differ from oraches in that the bracts do not swell in fruit, are united almost totally and leaves have lateral veins less obvious than central vein.

O **Sea Purslane** *Halimione portulacoides* Mealy spreading perennial undershrub to 1m, with woody brown stems and lower leaves opposite, untoothed. Flowers are yellowish-green, in interrupted branched spike; fruit unstalked. Widespread and frequent on the drier parts of coastal salt-marshes; absent from the far north. **Fl** 7-10. **Br** Common in England and Wales; rare in Scotland and Ireland.

P **Pedunculate Sea Purslane** *Halimione pedunculata* An erect mealy annual to 30cm, with similar leaves to Sea Purslane, but differing in that the lower leaves are alternate, flowers are greyish-green and *fruits are long-stalked*. Similar habitat to previous species, but much more local or rare. **Fl** 7-10. **Br** Very rare in SE England (Essex).

Q *Bassia hirsuta* Short spreading or ascending annual to 40cm, with slightly hairy branches. Leaves dark green, short, linear and fleshy. Flowers green and tiny in leaf axils. Very local in saline habitats near the sea. **Fl** 7-10. **Br** Absent.

R *Kochia laniflora* Similar to *B. hirsuta*, but more erect to 80cm, with soft 1-veined leaves to 25mm. Flowers green and tiny in leaf axils. Very local in dry sandy habitats inland. **Fl** 8-10. **Br** Absent.

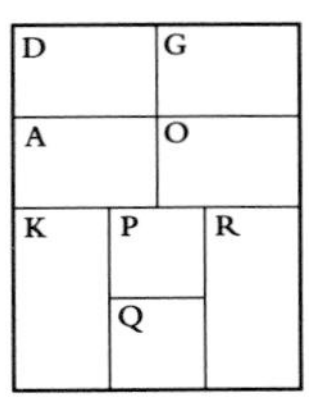

D **Frosted Orache**

G **Grass-leaved Orache**

A **Orache**

O **Sea Purslane**

K **Halberd-leaved Orache**

P **Pedunculate Sea Purslane** showing fruit

Q *Bassia hirsuta*

R *Kochia laniflora*

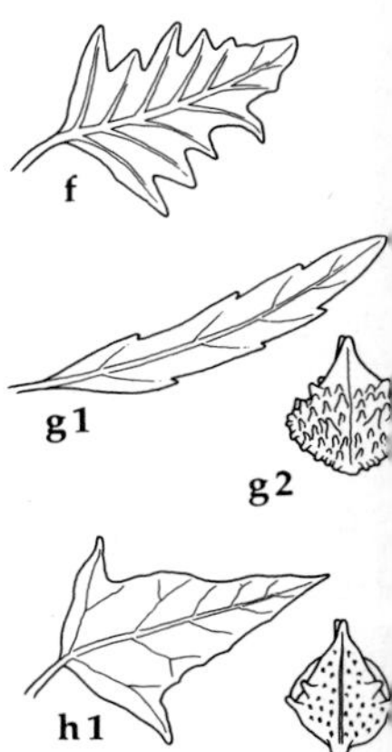

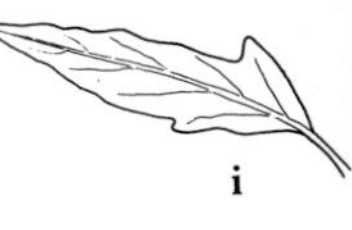

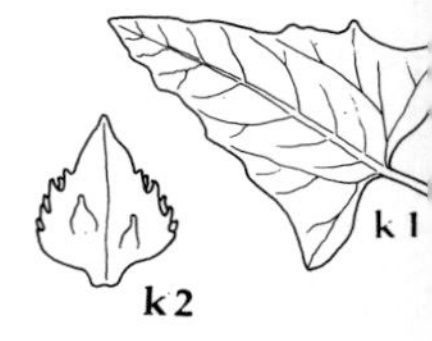

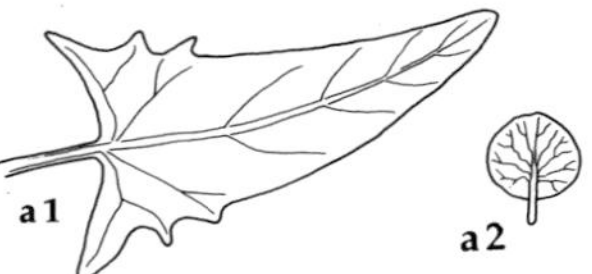

A

B

C

J

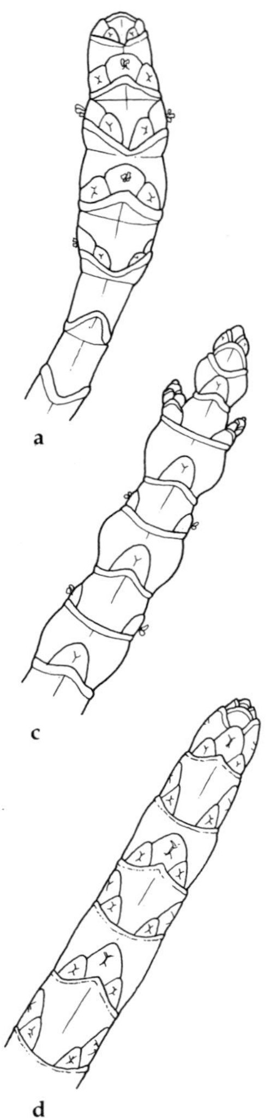

GLASSWORTS *Anthrocnemum and Salicornia*
A very distinctive group of succulent herbs with slender finger-like segmented branches and stems, with indistinct leaves and flowers.

Anthrocnemum

A **Perennial Glasswort** *Anthrocnemum perennis* Patch-forming perennial to 30cm with *creeping subterranean woody stems* and ascending slender stems, both flowering and non-flowering; dark green at first, the stems later become orange-brown. Flowers about equal in size, in 3s and almost reaching the top of each segment. Occasional or locally abundant in upper reaches of salt-marshes. **Fl** 8-10. **Br** Local in England and Wales; 1 locality in SE Ireland.

B *Anthrocnemum fruticosum* Perennial undershrub with stout, procumbent or ascending *stems to 1m long*, characteristically bluish-green. Flowers in 3s, not reaching near the top of the segments. Very local and uncommon; salt-marshes or wet coastal sand. **Fl** 7-10. **Br** Absent.

Salicornia Annual herbs, without a woody base. Flower number and size help to distinguish species. The taxonomy of the *Salicornia* species is in a state of flux, and separation of species can be difficult.

(1) Plants with solitary flowers.

C *Salicornia pusilla* Much-branched yellowish green plant (later brownish) to 25cm, and *the only Salicornia with solitary flowers*. Rather local in the upper reaches of salt-marshes. **Fl** 8-9. **Br** Local from E Anglia around the S coast to S Wales, and in S Ireland.

(2) Plants with flowers in 3s, the lateral 2 considerably smaller than the central.

D **Glasswort, Marsh Samphire** *Salicornia europaea* To 40cm, bright green but flushed red when flowering. *Fruiting segments only slightly swollen*, joints not waisted. Scarious margin at apex of segment fairly inconspicuous. Coastal mud or sand; upper salt-marshes. **Fl** 8-9. **Br** Locally common. Glaucous, matt-green plants are sometimes called *Salicornia obscura*.

E *Salicornia ramosissima* To 40cm, dark shining green becoming purplish red, much-branched and bushy. *Fruiting segments strongly beaded*, prominent waisted joints. Scarious margin of segment conspicuous. Middle and upper parts of salt-marshes. **Fl** 8-9. **Br** Locally common in S and E England, S Wales and S Ireland.

(3) Plants with flowers in 3s, almost equal in size, the lateral 2 only slightly smaller.

F *Salicornia nitens* To 25cm, green or yellowish green becoming purplish brown or orange-brown. Primary branches only. *Terminal spike with 4-9 fertile segments*. Local in upper and middle parts of salt-marshes. **Fl** 8-9. **Br** Locally common in S England and E Anglia.

G *Salicornia fragilis* To 30cm, dull green or yellowish green, not becoming brownish. Primary branches only. *Terminal spike with (4)8-16(20) fertile segments*. Local in lower parts of salt-marshes. **Fl** 8-9. **Br** Locally abundant in S and E England and S Ireland.

H *Salicornia dolichostachya* To 40cm, dark green becoming paler and then brownish when fully mature. *Much-branched and bushy*. Terminal spike with 12-25 fertile segments. Local in lower limits of salt-marshes. **Fl** 7-8. **Br** Widespread round most coasts.

I **Annual Sea-blite** *Suaeda maritima*
Succulent annual to 50cm with prostrate or ascending stems, and distinct, rather *pointed, alternate, fleshy leaves* ranging from bluish green to purplish red; leaves slightly *concave above in cross-section*. Flowers tiny, green, 1-3 together in axils of upper leaves. Common in muddy salt-mashes. **Fl** 7-10. **Br** Common on coasts.

J **Shrubby Sea-blite** *Suaeda vera* Perennial undershrub to 1.2m, much-branched with ascending stems bearing *densely crowded, blunt, fleshy leaves*, bluish green and rather *flat above in cross-section*. Flowers tiny, yellowish green, 1-3 together in axils of upper leaves. Local on coastal shingle and upper edges of salt-marshes. **Fl** 6-10. **Br** Local on coasts from Dorset east to Lincolnshire.

K **Prickly Saltwort** *Salsola kali*
Semi-prostrate prickly annual to 60cm. Stems markedly branched with pale green or reddish stripes, often rough to touch. Leaves succulent, rather flattened and abruptly narrowed at the tip into a short spine. Flowers solitary in leaf axils. Widespread and frequent on sandy shores near drift-line; occasionally inland on waste areas and sides of regularly salted roads. **Fl** 7-9. **Br** Frequent all round the coasts.

Purslane Family
Portulacaceae

Annual or perennial herbs, sometimes rather fleshy. Flowers are hermaphrodite, always with only 2 opposite sepals (in contrast to Caryophylaceae, *see* page 34) and 3-6 petals (usually 5). Fruit is a capsule.

L **Blinks** *Montia fontana* Very variable but often inconspicuous, tiny pale green plant (often patch-forming) with stems often reddish, and narrow oval opposite leaves. Flowers tiny, white and in small loose clusters with stalks lengthening when in fruit. Widespread and frequent on bare or damp ground, or submerged in water. **Fl** 5-10. **Br** Frequent throughout. Several subspecies described.

M **Springbeauty** *Montia perfoliata* Short hairless annual, 10-30cm, characterised by rather fleshy stem leaves being fused in a pair surrounding the stem, and with small white flowers in a cluster just above them. Flowers 5-8mm with 5 white petals, not, or hardly, notched. Introduced from N America, and now widespread on bare sandy soils. **Fl** 5-7. **Br** Scattered and often abundant throughout.

N **Pink Purslane** *Montia sibirica* Annual or perennial to 15-40cm, with opposite unstalked and distinctly veined stem leaves and long-stalked basal leaves. Flowers 15-20mm in diameter, 5 notched petals, pink with darker veins. Introduced from N America, very widespread; often abundant in damp shady places. **Fl** 4-7. **Br** Naturalised almost throughout.

O **Purslane** *Portulaca oleracea* Annual fleshy plant with prostrate or ascending stems 10-30cm long. Leaves 10-20mm, spoon-shaped, spirally arranged or almost opposite, most densely crowded beneath the flowers. Flowers 8-12mm in diameter, yellow, the 4-6 petals soon falling leaving the blunt sepals. Introduced and widely naturalised in waste areas. **Fl** 6-9. **Br** Scattered throughout.

A	G	D
E	H	I
J	K	L
M	N	O

A **Perennial Glasswort**
G *Salicornia fragilis*
D **Glasswort**
E *Salicornia ramosissima*
H *Salicornia dolichostachya*
I **Annual Sea-blite**
J **Shrubby Sea-blite**
K **Prickly Saltwort**
L **Blinks**
M **Springbeauty**
N **Pink Purslane**
O **Purslane**

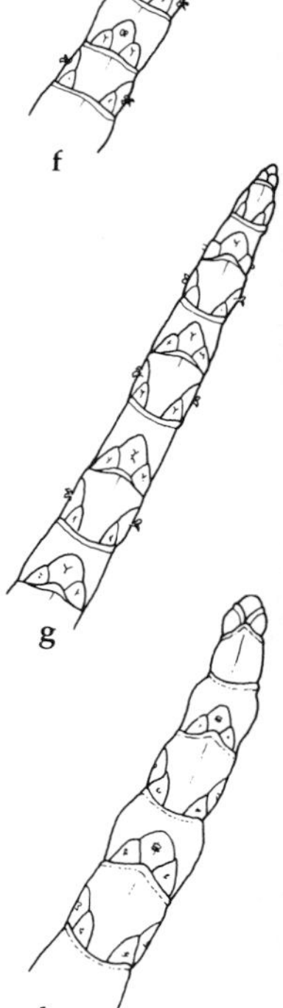

A

B

H

I

J

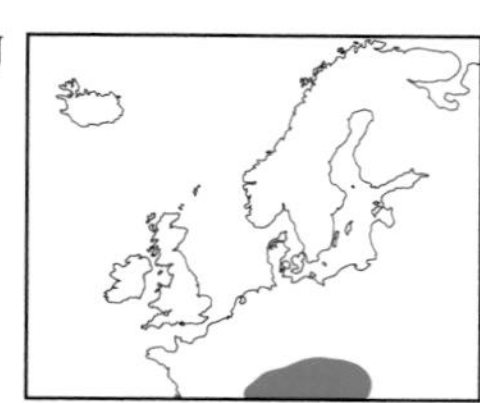

K

L

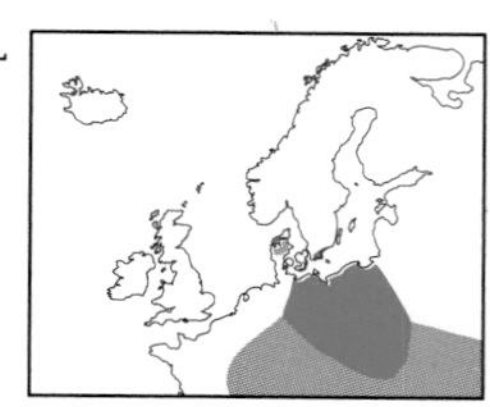

M

N

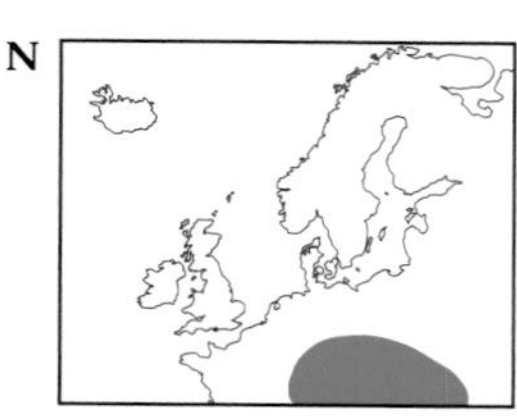

Pink Family Caryophylaceae

A large and diverse family of plants, all characterised by having flowering shoots repeatedly forked, 4-5 pink or whitish petals and, unlike purslanes, 4-5 sepals which may be free or fused into a tube. Stems have a characteristic swelling at their junction with the usually opposite and untoothed leaves. Fruit is usually a capsule, rarely a berry (*see* Berry Catchfly, page 44).

SANDWORTS These are often small or slender plants. Most have white flowers with 5 unnotched petals, ununited sepals and 3 styles, the exceptions being Mossy Cyphel and Sea Sandwort which have greenish-white flowers, and *Moehringia muscosa* which has 4 petals. There are four main genera: *Arenaria, Moehringia, Minuartia* and *Honkenya*.

Arenaria Leaves small, usually 1-veined, oblong or oval and not exceeding 10mm.

A **Arctic Sandwort** *Arenaria norvegica* Low tufted perennial with fleshy oval leaves, 3-5mm long, *not markedly veined*, and (compared to most sandworts) relatively *large white flowers* to 12mm with yellowish anthers; sepals hairless. Very local in bare, stony and gravelly places; most frequent in the north of its range. **Fl** 6-8. **Br** Rare in W Highlands and Islands, and 1 locality in Ireland. Ssp *anglica* (English Sandwort) is annual or biennial, with slightly hairy sepals; rare, on limestone pavement in N England.

B **Fringed Sandwort** *Arenaria ciliata* Similar to Arctic Sandwort, but stems rough to the touch, and prostrate then ascending. *Leaves very obviously single-veined*, and with hairs on the lower margins. Flowers to 16mm with white anthers; sepals hairy. Very local to rare on calcareous soils in mountains. **Fl** 7-8. **Br** Found in 1 locality at Ben Bulben in Ireland.

C *Arenaria gothica* Very similar to Fringed Sandwort, but annual or biennial, and taller (to 12cm) with flowers less than 12mm in diameter. Rare, on limestone pavement in S Sweden. **Br** Absent.

D *Arenaria humifusa* Mat-forming, up to only 30mm tall, with smooth hairless stems and with solitary flowers, 5-6mm in diameter, on very short stalks. Sepals usually hairless. Very rare, on moist basic soils in Scandinavian mountains. **Fl** 6-8. **Br** Absent.

E **Thyme-leaved Sandwort** *Arenaria serpyllifolia* Rather *downy*, greyish-green, prostrate or ascending annual, reminiscent of Common Chickweed but with unnotched petals and unstalked, ovate leaves. Flowers 5-8mm in diameter, petals more than half the length of the pointed sepals (**e1**). *Capsule with obviously curved sides* (**e2**). Widespread and frequent in dry places. **Fl** 4-9. **Br** Common throughout.

F *Arenaria leptoclados* Similar to Thyme-leaved Sandwort, but flowers 3-5mm in diameter and petals half the length of sepals (**f1**). *Upper half of capsule straight-sided* (**f2**). Widespread and common in similar habitats to Thyme-leaved Sandwort. **Fl** 5-8. **Br** Common throughout.

Moehringia Leaves 10-25mm, 3-veined (or more).

G **Three-nerved Sandwort** *Moehringia trinervia* Weak often straggling annual to 40cm with *petals shorter than sepals* like Common Chickweed, but unlike that plant it has *stems hairy all round, leaves 3- to 5-veined* and petals undivided. Flowers about 6mm in diameter. Widespread and frequent in woods and hedgebanks. **Fl** 4-7. **Br** Frequent throughout, especially in ancient semi-natural woodlands on rich soils.

H *Moehringia lateriflora* Similar to Three-nerved Sandwort, but perennial, *leaves 1- to 3-veined* and *petals longer than sepals*. Local in damp woodlands. **Fl** 5-7. **Br** Absent.

I *Moehringia muscosa* Very variable, short, straggling or creeping perennial with fine linear leaves and flowers 5-8mm with *only 4 white petals, which are longer than sepals*. Local in shady montane habitats. **Fl** 5-9. **Br** Absent.

J *Moehringia ciliata* Similar to *M. muscosa*, but has flowers 4-5mm, with *5 petals*. Local on limestone in mountains. **Fl** 5-8. **Br** Absent.

Minuartia A difficult genus of closely related species. They can be confused with the pearlworts (*see* page 40) but differ in that their flowers usually have 3 styles, whereas the pearlworts have the same number of styles as sepals (4-5). Leaves awl-shaped or bristle-like, to 15mm. For identification purposes it helps to separate the *Minuartia* into 3 groups.

(1) Petals much shorter than sepals (less than two-thirds); plants not tufted.

K **Fine-leaved Sandwort** *Minuartia hybrida* Slender, usually *hairless, annual*, branched at the base and also from above the middle. Habit rather like Thyme-leaved Sandwort, but more upright with narrow leaves, 3-veined at the broadened base. Flowers 5-6mm in diameter; *flower stalks longer than sepals*. Petals about half the length of sepals. Capsule longer than sepals. Local in dry sandy and stony areas, and on old walls. **Fl** 5-6. **Br** Very local or rare in England and Wales; very rare in Ireland.

L *Minuartia viscosa* As Fine-leaved Sandwort, but branched from above middle only, petals much shorter and capsule shorter than sepals. Local in dry sandy areas. **Fl** 5-9. **Br** Absent.

M *Minuartia mediterranea* As Fine-leaved Sandwort, but inflorescence densely crowded and *flower stalks shorter than sepals*, which are 3-veined (*see M. rubra*). Petals a third to half the length of sepals and sometimes absent. Rare in coastal sandy areas. **Fl** 5-8. **Br** Absent.

N *Minuartia rubra* As Fine-leaved Sandwort, but inflorescence dense like *M. mediterranea* and *flower stalks about equal to sepals*. Sepals 1-veined. Petals a third of the length of sepals. Local in dry sandy areas and arable land. **Fl** 6-9. **Br** Absent.

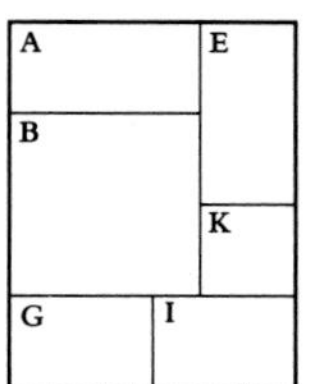

A **Arctic Sandwort**

E **Thyme-leaved Sandwort**

B **Fringed Sandwort**

K **Fine-leaved Sandwort**

G **Three-nerved Sandwort**

I *Moehringia muscosa*

e1

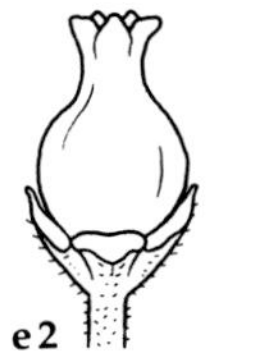

e2

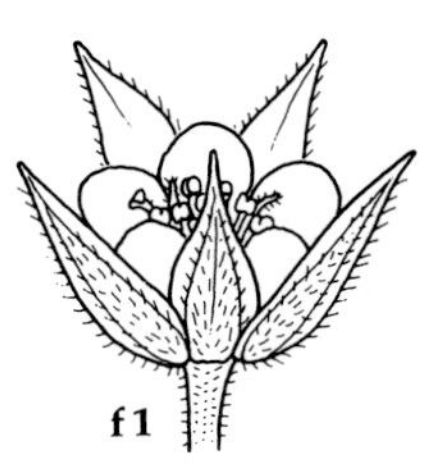

f1

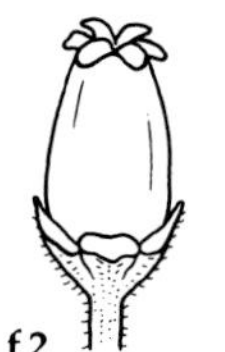

f2

A

B

D

G

I

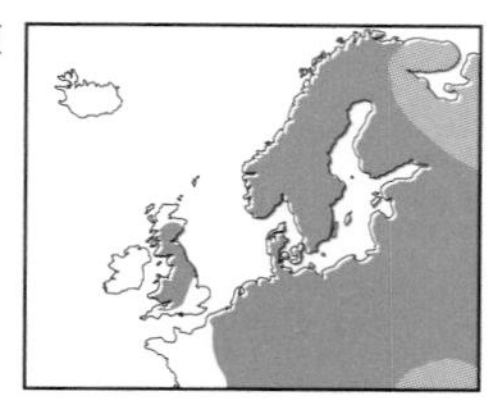

K

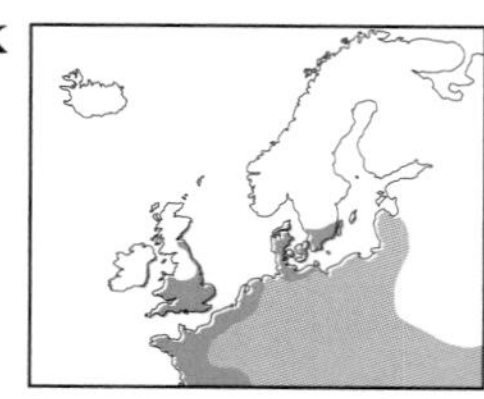

L

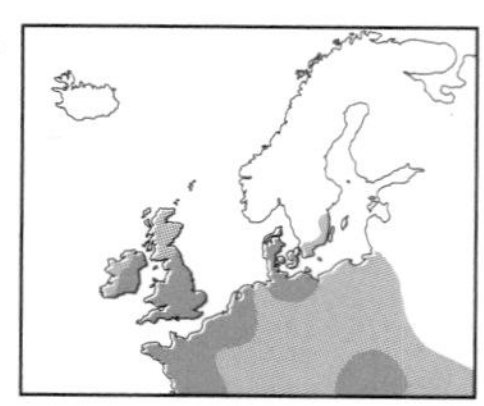

O

Q

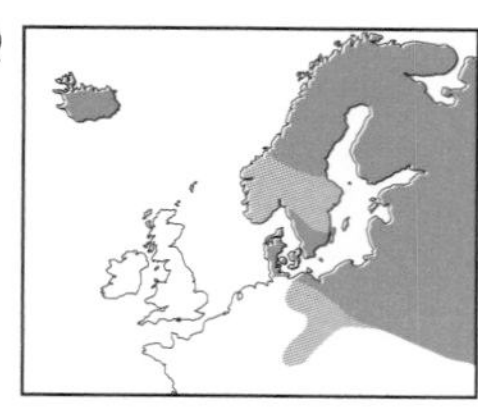

(2) Petals equal to or shorter than sepals but at least two-thirds of their length; plants tufted.

A **Mountain Sandwort** *Minuartia rubella* Low, tufted perennial 2-6cm tall with both vegetative and flowering shoots, leaves densely crowded below but distant above on flowering shoots. Leaves 3-veined. Flowers 5-9mm in diameter; petals about two-thirds the length of sepals. Similar in form to Alpine Pearlwort (*see* page 40) but flowers have 3 styles, not 5. Rocky ledges in mountains. **Fl** 7-8. **Br** Very rare; in Scottish Highlands.

B **Teesdale Sandwort** *Minuartia stricta* Tufted perennial 5-10cm tall, with similar structure to Mountain Sandwort, but flowering shoots taller, leaves 1-veined or obscurely veined and petals equal or almost equal to sepals. Wet flushes, screes and damp places in mountains. **Fl** 6-7. **Br** Teesdale only.

C *Minuartia rossii* Like Teesdale Sandwort, but flowering shoots very leafy, and vegetative shoots produced in the axils of the upper leaves. Flowers rarely produced and always solitary. Rocky places. **Fl** 7-8. **Br** Absent.

(3) Petals longer than sepals.

D **Spring Sandwort** *Minuartia verna* Low, loose, cushion-forming perennial 5-15cm tall. Leaves 3-veined, flowers 6-8mm with purplish anthers and petals slightly longer than sepals. Similar to Knotted Pearlwort (*see* page 40), but the latter has petals twice as long as sepals and 5 styles. Very local in dry grassy or rocky places, especially on limestone or spoil from old lead workings. **Fl** 5-10. **Br** Very local scattered localities in W and N Britain, with a few localities in Ireland.

E *Minuartia setacea* Like Spring Sandwort, but flowers 4-5mm and anthers yellowish. Rather local in dry bare areas. **Fl** 6-9. **Br** Absent.

F *Minuartia biflora* Tufted perennial similar to Spring Sandwort, but not cushion-forming, leaves blunt and flowers 7-12mm. Local in damp places in mountains, often near snow patches. **Fl** 7-8. **Br** Absent.

G **Mossy Cyphel** *Minuartia sedoides* Dense and compact, cushion-forming perennial with crowded fleshy leaves, to 15mm, and greenish yellow flowers, 4-5mm in diameter, which often lack petals. Local on damp mountain-ledges. **Fl** 6-8. **Br** Local in Scottish Highlands and Islands.

Honkenya Leaves fleshy, flower greenish white.

H **Sea Sandwort** *Honkenya peploides* Distinctive prostrate perennial differing from other sandworts in having oval fleshy yellow-green leaves, to 20mm, with rather wavy translucent margins; greenish-white flowers, 6-10mm in diameter, with petals slightly shorter than sepals. Flowers solitary in the forks of stems and axils of leaves. Locally common on sand and fine shingle by the sea. **Fl** 5-8. **Br** Locally common all around the coast.

STITCHWORTS and CHICKWEEDS *Stellaria* Annual or perennial herbs with white flowers possessing deeply cleft petals so that there appears to be twice the number of petals, 5 sepals, and 3 styles. Capsules oval. (Mouse-ears usually have 5 styles and cylindrical capsules.)

I **Wood Stitchwort** *Stellaria nemorum* Perennial to 60cm, with *stems hairy all round*, lower leaves cordate and long-stalked, upper leaves ovate-acuminate and almost sessile. Flowers 15-20mm in diameter, *petals twice as long as sepals*. Widespread but often very local in damp woodland. **Fl** 5-7. **Br** Locally frequent in the north and west; absent from Ireland.

J **Common Chickweed** *Stellaria media* Prostrate or semi-prostrate annual to 40cm with *stems hairy on alternate sides between leaf nodes*. Lower leaves long-stalked, upper almost sessile. Flowers 5-10mm in diameter, petals equalling sepals and with *3-8 red-violet stamens*. Widespread, very common and often abundant on disturbed or waste ground. **Fl** 1-12. **Br** Very common throughout.

K **Lesser Chickweed** *Stellaria pallida* Similar to Common Chickweed, but flowers 4-5mm in diameter, either with *minute petals or none at all* and 1-3 grey-violet stamens. Locally frequent on sandy, often disturbed, soils. **Fl** 3-5. **Br** Local, mainly in the south.

L **Greater Chickweed** *Stellaria neglecta* Overwintering annual or perennial like a large version of Common Chickweed with a similarly *hairy stem in alternate lines*. Flowers 10-12mm in diameter, with *10 stamens* which are often reddish. Local in damp shady places, often by streamsides. **Fl** 4-7. **Br** Local throughout, most frequent in the west.

M **Greater Stitchwort** *Stellaria holostea* Perennial to 60cm, with weak square stems, rough at the angles; leaves rigid with a characteristic lanceolate shape tapering from a broadish base to a fine point. *Leaf edges and midrib very rough*. Flowers 18-30mm in diameter, petals divided to half-way and twice as long as sepals. Widespread and common in woodlands and hedgerows on all except very acid soils. **Fl** 4-6. **Br** Common throughout.

N **Lesser Stitchwort** *Stellaria graminea* Similar to Greater Stitchwort, but has smooth stems, *leaves with smooth edges* and flowers only 5-18mm in diameter, with petals divided to more than half-way, and stamens often grey-violet. Widespread and common on acid soils, heathy grassland and open woods. **Fl** 5-8. **Br** Common throughout.

O **Marsh Stitchwort** *Stellaria palustris* Similar to Greater Stitchwort but stems smooth at the angles, *leaves greyish green* and smooth-edged, and *bracts with a broad membranous margin*. Flowers terminal, 12-20mm in diameter, and stamens often blackish violet or reddish. Local to locally frequent in marshes and fens, often supported by tall vegetation. **Fl** 5-8. **Br** Local and decreasing; scattered throughout except N Scotland.

P **Bog Stitchwort** *Stellaria alsine* Weak, often sprawling perennial to 40cm but usually shorter. *Stems angled and smooth*, leaves much more ovate than the previous 2 species, and flowers 5-7mm in diameter with deeply divided *petals much shorter than sepals*. Widespread and locally common in a variety of damp or wet habitats. **Fl** 5-6. **Br** Fairly common throughout, except in the extreme north.

Q *Stellaria crassifolia* Differs from Bog Stitchwort in that its petals are longer than sepals (flowers 5-8mm in diameter). Local in wet sandy or stony places. **Fl** 6-8. **Br** Absent.

R *Stellaria longifolia* Petals equal to sepals, flowers 5-8mm and leaves linear-lanceolate. Local in damp wooded places **Fl** 6-7. **Br** Absent.

A	D	G
H	I	J
K	L	M
N	O	P

A **Mountain Sandwort**
D **Spring Sandwort**
G **Mossy Cyphel**
H **Sea Sandwort**
I **Wood Stitchwort**
J **Common Chickweed**
K **Lesser Chickweed**
L **Greater Chickweed**
M **Greater Stitchwort**
N **Lesser Stitchwort**
O **Marsh Stitchwort**
P **Bog Stitchwort**

A

B

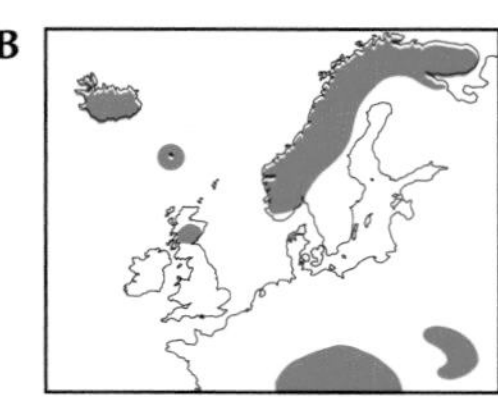

C

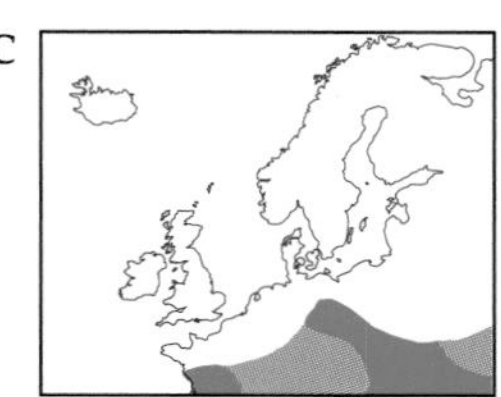

K

L

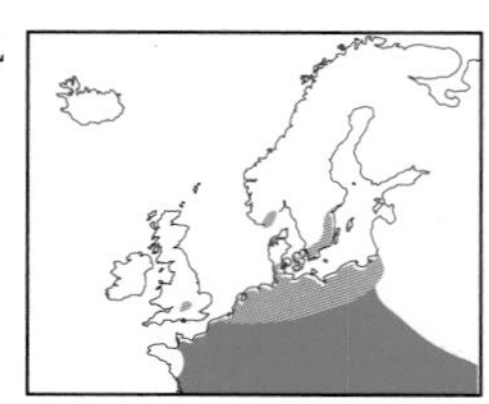

M

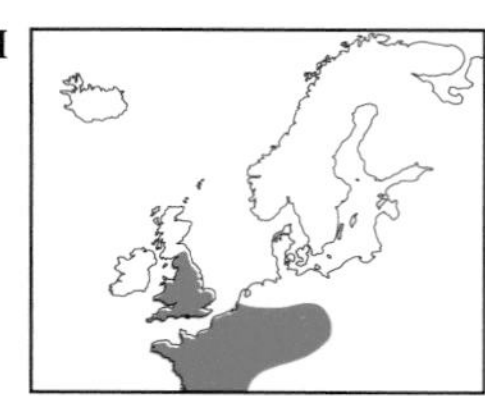

A **Umbellate Chickweed** *Holosteum umbellatum* Distinct erect annual to 20cm, with grey lanceolate leaves. Easily distinguished by its *umbel of radiating flowers* each with an equal stalk. Much decreased and now very local or rare on old walls, roofs or sandy soils. **Fl** 3-5. **Br** Extinct. Formerly in Surrey, Norfolk and Suffolk.

MOUSE-EARS *Cerastium* Similar plants to stitchworts and chickweeds but usually much more hairy, and flowers usually have 5 instead of 3 styles (exceptions are Starwort Mouse-ear and *C. dubium*). Leaves always sessile. Also, capsules are cylindrical, not ovoid. Petal length in relation to sepals helps to separate species.

(1) Petals at least 1½ times longer than sepals.

B **Starwort Mouse-ear** *Cerastium cerastoides* Low perennial to 15cm with creeping woody stems and ascending flowering shoots but prostrate non-flowering shoots. Leaves linear or oblong and rather fleshy. Flowers 9-12mm in diameter. Distinct from other *Cerastium* species in being *hairless except for alternate lines of hairs between each internode* (compare with Common Chickweed). Also unusual in having flowers with 3 styles. Mainly an Arctic and sub-Arctic plant of damp grassy habitats or streamsides, but also found in mountains on siliceous rocks. **Fl** 6-8. **Br** Very rare in Scottish Highlands and NW England.

C *Cerastium dubium* Similar to Starwort Mouse-ear, but annual and taller, to 40cm. Stem hairless and usually with sticky glands. Flowers 11-15mm in diameter. Very local in damp grassy places; mainly in SE and central Europe but extending to W France. **Fl** 5-7.

D **Field Mouse-ear** *Cerastium arvense* Rather variable perennial to 30cm, slightly hairy and with flowers 12-20mm in diameter. The only lowland *Cerastium* species with such large flowers and relatively tall height.Widespread but often very local in dry grassland, especially on calacareous soils. **Fl** 4-8. **Br** Locally common in E England; much more local or rare elsewhere.

E **Alpine Mouse-ear** *Cerastium alpinum* Low, mat-forming, greyish-green perennial, noticeable for the *long white hairs on leaves and stem*, and large white flowers 18-25mm in diameter. Leaves broadest above middle, *bracts with narrow membranous margins* and petals deeply cleft. On rock-ledges in mountains, to 2,500m. **Fl** 6-8. Ssp *lanatum* is white woolly due to a dense cover of hairs; occurs throughout the range of Alpine Mouse-ear in Europe. **Br** Local in N Wales, NW England and Scottish Highlands.

F **Arctic Mouse-ear** *Cerastium arcticum* Similar to Alpine Mouse-ear, but distinguished by its yellowish-green leaves, *short white hairs, bracts without membranous margins* and petals shallowly cleft. Local on mountain rock-ledges; to 1,700m, in north-west of area only. **Fl** 6-8. **Br** Very local in N Wales and Scottish Highlands and Islands. Ssp *edmondstonii* has purplish-green leaves; only found in Shetlands.

(2) Petals about equalling or slightly longer than sepals.

G **Common Mouse-ear** *Cerastium fontanum* Very variable hairy green or greyish-green perennial, at first glance similar to Common Chickweed but stiffer and with *longer petals in relation to sepals.* Both non-flowering and longer flowering shoots present, the latter to 45cm tall but usually much shorter. Leaves to 25mm, densely covered with whitish non-glandular hairs. Flowers small, in loose clusters, with petals deeply cleft. Widespread and common in a variety of grassy places and disturbed ground, with several different varieties described for certain habitats. **Fl** 4-11. **Br** Common throughout.

H **Sticky Mouse-ear** *Cerastium glomeratum* Short yellowish-green rather *glandular-hairy* and sticky annual to 45cm, with characteristic *compact heads of flowers.* Sepals hairy to tip (**h1**); bract with hairy margin (**h2**). Upper stem leaves rather broadly ovate. Flower stalks remain short in fruit, not exceeding sepals. Fruit stalk never drooping. Widespread almost throughout, and common in a variety of dry or bare places. **Fl** 4-10. **Br** Common throughout.

I **Dwarf Mouse-ear** *Cerastium pumilum* Low-growing often tiny annual, 2-12cm tall, *glandular-hairy* and greyish green above and purplish-red below. Sepals not hairy to tip (**i1**); *bracts with narrow transparent margins* (**i2**). Flowers with 5 stamens and styles, and petals deeply cleft. Fruit stalks drooping initially, then erect, exceeding sepals. Local in grassland on calcareous soils. **Fl** 4-6. **Br** Rare in S England.

(3) Petals shorter than sepals.

J **Little Mouse-ear** *Cerastium semidecandrum* Low, *glandular*, hairy and sticky annual 1-20cm tall. *Bracts with broad transparent margins* (**j**). Flowers 5-7mm in diameter, with 5 stamens and styles, and petals only slightly notched. Fruit stalks drooping initially, then erect, exceeding sepals. Locally common on dry or bare sandy ground. **Fl** 4-6. **Br** Locally common throughout, but mainly coastal in Ireland.

K **Sea Mouse-ear** *Cerastium diffusum* Densely *glandular* and sticky annual with prostrate or ascending stems 5-30cm tall. Upper leaves and *bracts dark green, the latter without transparent margins.* Flowers 3-6mm in diameter, usually with *parts in 4s* or occasionally 5s and with petals cleft to no more than a quarter of their length. Fruit stalk drooping initially, then erect, exceeding sepals. Locally common in dry places usually near the coast, but occasionally inland especially on old railway tracks. **Fl** 4-7. **Br** Locally common all around the coast, much more local inland.

L **Grey Mouse-ear** *Cerastium brachypetalum* Annual with *spreading, non-glandular hairs* giving the plant a shaggy appearance. Bracts without membranous margins. Petals deeply cleft to more than a quarter of their length, usually shorter than sepals, occasionally longer. Sepals have long hairs projecting well beyond their tips. Locally frequent in dry habitats, usually on calcareous soils. **Fl** 4-7. **Br** Only 1 locality in a Bedfordshire railway cutting.

M **Upright Chickweed** *Moenchia erecta* Usually tiny annual but sometimes to 12cm tall, with a characteristic waxy grey colour to the leaves. *Flowers with 4 white petals, not cleft* or divided, and only opening in very sunny conditions. Sepals white-edged, slightly longer than petals. Rare or locally common in dry grasslands, often on sandy or gravelly soils. **Fl** 4-6. **Br** Very local in S England and S Wales.

A	B	D
E	F	G
H	I	J
K	L	M

A **Umbellate Chickweed**
B **Starwort Chickweed**
D **Field Mouse-ear**
E **Alpine Mouse-ear**
F **Arctic Mouse-ear**
G **Common Mouse-ear**
H **Sticky Mouse-ear**
I **Dwarf Mouse-ear**
J **Little Mouse-ear**
K **Sea Mouse-ear**
L **Grey Mouse-ear**
M **Upright Chickweed**

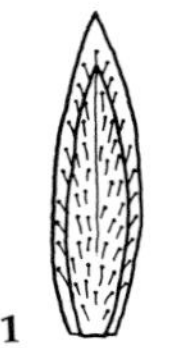

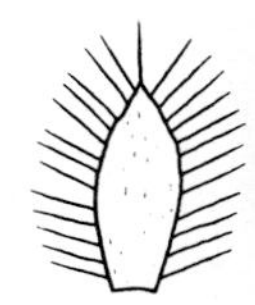

h1

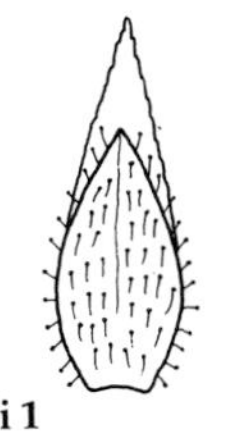

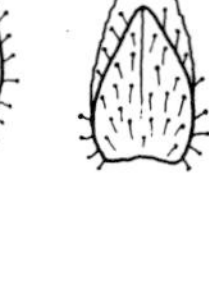

i1

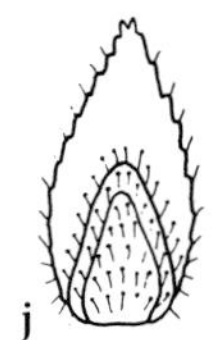

j

A

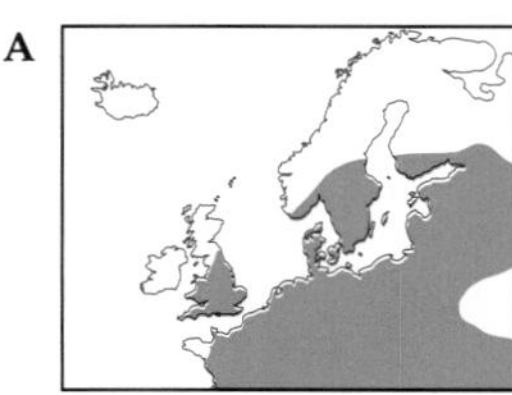

C

D

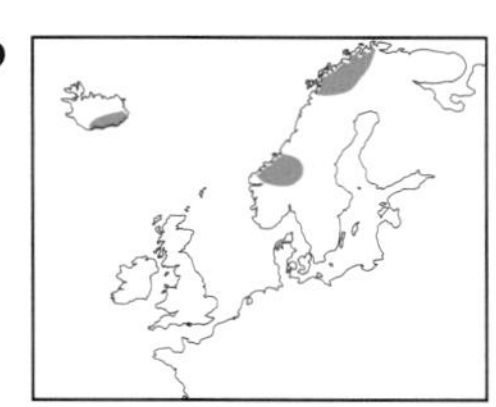

J

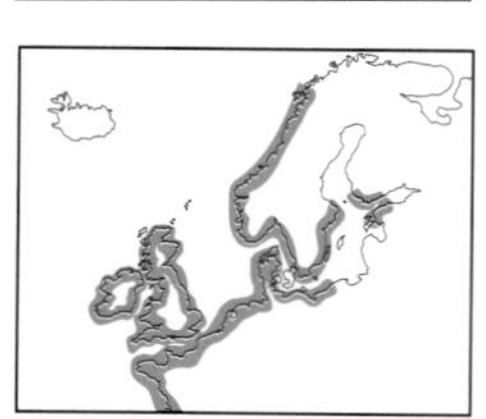

M

A Water Chickweed *Myosoton aquaticum* Rather straggling perennial with prostrate overwintering stems from which arise the flowering shoots to 1m tall. Leaves characteristic, *broadly heart-shaped and opposite*, the upper ones unstalked and somewhat wavy-edged. Flowers in loose clusters, white with *petals cleft to base and much longer than sepals* (contrast this with Greater Chickweed with which it is sometimes confused). Widespread in damp grassy places by streamsides, ditches, woodland margins, marshes and similar habitats. **Fl** 6-10. **Br** Locally frequent in England and Wales, especially in the south.

PEARLWORTS *Sagina* Characterised by small size, short awl-shaped fleshy leaves without stipules, entire white petals (minute in some species, absent in others) and 4-5 styles.

For identification purposes, pearlworts can be divided into 2 groups depending upon the number of petals and their size in relation to the sepals. Remember that in some species the white petals fall or are minute, leaving the green sepals as the obvious flower structures.

(1) Petals about equal to or longer than sepals, flowers 4- to 5-parted.

B Knotted Pearlwort *Sagina nodosa* Perennial to 15cm, and characterised by a *knotted feel to the stem* caused by tufts of shorter leaves at the leaf junctions. The largest-flowered pearlwort (flowers to 10mm in diameter) and *the only one with petals twice as long as sepals*. Can be confused with Spring Sandwort (*see* page 36) but distinguished by knotted feel to stems and 5 styles, not 3. Locally frequent in damp sandy ground, heaths or mountain habitats. **Fl** 7-9. **Br** Local but most frequent in the west and north.

C Snow, Lesser Alpine, Pearlwort *Sagina intermedia* Tiny, tufted and compact perennial, 1-3cm tall, one of the smallest pearlworts and easily overlooked. Basal leaf rosettes withering after 1st year. *Leaves 3-6mm*, with a *short point*. Flower stems bear tiny solitary flowers hardly projecting beyond top of tuft, with *petals equalling violet-edged sepals*. Petals and sepals 4- to 5-parted. Mainly an Arctic and sub-Arctic plant; on rock-ledges and screes in mountains. **Fl** 6-9. **Br** Very rare, high up on a few Scottish mountains.

D *Sagina caespitosa* Very similar to Snow Pearlwort, but basal tufts persist and flowers always 5-parted with petals slightly longer than sepals. Arctic and sub-Arctic rock-ledges and screes, but much more local than Snow Pearlwort. **Fl** 6-9. **Br** Absent.

E Heath Pearlwort *Sagina subulata* Densely tufted, mat-forming perennial with central non-flowering leaf rosette, from beneath which arise numerous lateral stickily hairy flowering stems which soon become erect, to 10cm. *Leaves long-awned* and slightly hairy, 3-12mm. Flowers solitary on long stalks projecting well above tufts. *Petals 5, about equalling glandular sepals*, or slightly shorter. Stamens 10, styles 5. Widespread but local in sandy or gravelly places. **Fl** 5-8. **Br** Very local; absent from the extreme north.

F Alpine Pearlwort *Sagina saginoides* Hairless loosely tufted perennial to 7cm tall with central leaf rosette which always bears a flowering stem from its centre. Other flowering stems arise below the rosette. *Leaves of rosette to 20mm long, stem leaves long-awned and 5-10mm long*. Petals equalling *hairless* sepals; stamens 10. Mainly an Arctic or sub-Arctic plant where it grows in damp places, often in mountains. **Fl** 6-9. **Br** Very rare, in Scottish Highlands and Skye.

G *Sagina × normaniana* A hybrid between Alpine Pearlwort and Procumbent Pearlwort, producing plants intermediate between the 2 and having *central rosette leaves to 3cm* and prostrate rooting stems. Often has fewer than 10 stamens. Grows in the same mountain habitats as Alpine Pearlwort, on wet rocks or sub-Alpine pasture. **Fl** 7-10. **Br** Very rare, in Scottish Highlands and Skye.

(2) Petals minute or absent, flowers always 4-parted.

H Procumbent Pearlwort *Sagina procumbens* Low mat-forming perennial with *central non-flowering leaf rosette* from which arise *numerous creeping stems* rooting at intervals and from which ascend the erect flowering stalks. Leaves long-awned, with non-hairy edges (**h**). Widespread and very common in a variety of damp bare places, ranging from lawns to walls. **Fl** 5-9. **Br** Common Throughout.

I Annual Pearlwort *Sagina apetala* Annual with usually *no central leaf rosette* (withers early) and erect main flowering stem with several surrounding branches which do not root and are *usually ascending* rather than creeping. Leaves long-awned with hairy edges (**i**). Widespread and common on bare ground, dry grassland and sandy habitats. **Fl** 4-8. **Br** Throughout; common in the south-east, less frequent in the north and west.

J Sea Pearlwort *Sagina maritima* Annual similar to Annual Pearlwort, but with *fleshy blunt leaves* (**j**). Sepals purple-edged, not spreading in fruit. Locally common in bare open habitats such as dune-slacks and cliffs, usually near the sea but occasionally inland. **Fl** 5-9. **Br** Local on the coast; rare in Scottish Highlands.

K Annual Knawel *Scleranthus annuus* Small, rather wiry or spiky-looking greyish annual or biennial, to 10cm high. Leaves linear and pointed, united in opposite pairs around stem. Flowers minute, in terminal or axillary clusters and with 5 *pointed green sepals* with *very narrow white border*, but no petals. Widespread and locally frequent in dry sandy or arable areas. **Fl** 5-10. **Br** Local to locally frequent throughout.

L Perennial Knawel *Scleranthus perennis* Similar to Annual Knawel, but perennial, woody at the base and with *blunt sepals* which have a noticeable *broad white border*. (NB Biennial form of Annual Knawel can be woody at the base.) Very local or rare on dry sandy soils. **Fl** 5-10. **Br** Very rare, in E Anglia and central Wales. Sometimes separated into ssp *prostratus* (prostrate and ascending stems) in E Anglia, and ssp *perenris* (more erect) in Wales.

M Strapwort *Corrigiola litoralis* Low, prostrate annual, rather greyish with stems sometimes red, and blunt leaves alternate with narrow chaffy stipules at their base. Flowers minute but made obvious in their clusters; 5 white or red-tipped petals soon fall to leave 5 green sepals with white edges. Very local to rare in damp, seasonally flooded, sandy or gravelly ground. **Fl** 6-10. **Br** Very rare in S Devon, varying in quantity from year to year.

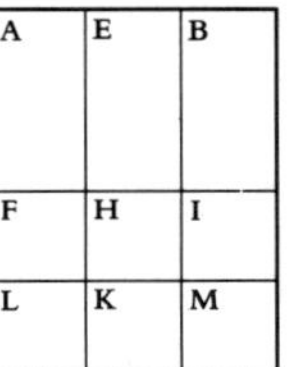

A Water Chickweed
B Knotted Pearlwort
E Heath Pearlwort
F Alpine Pearlwort
H Procumbent Pearlwort
I Annual Pearlwort
L Perennial Knawel
K Annual Knawel
M Strapwort

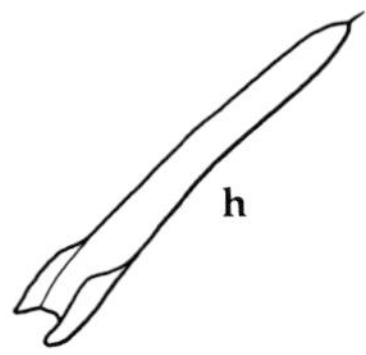

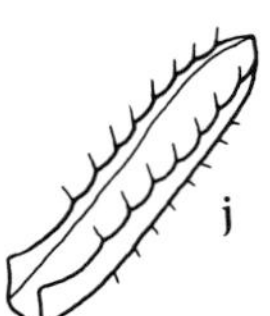

B

D

E

G
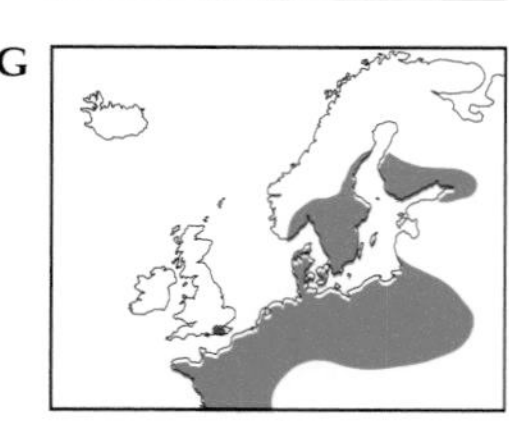

H
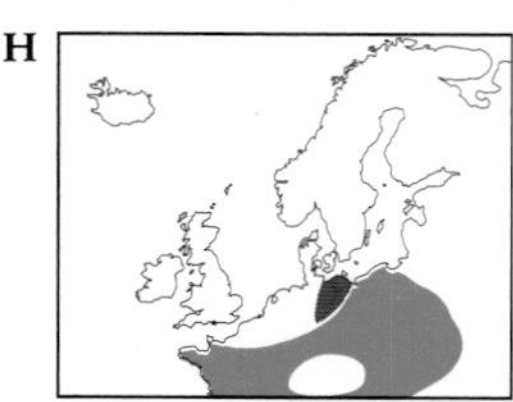

I

M
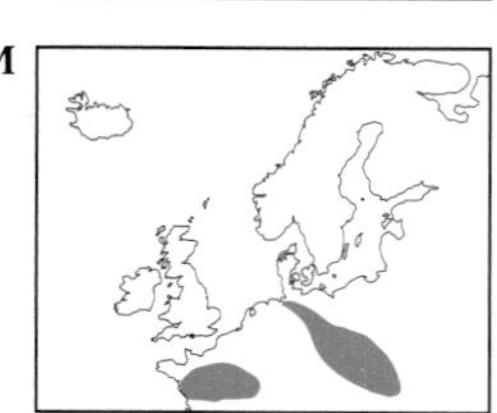

N
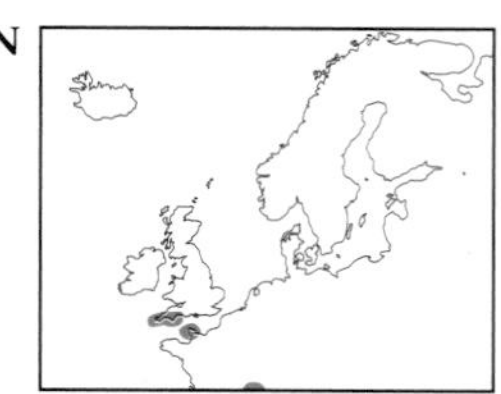

O
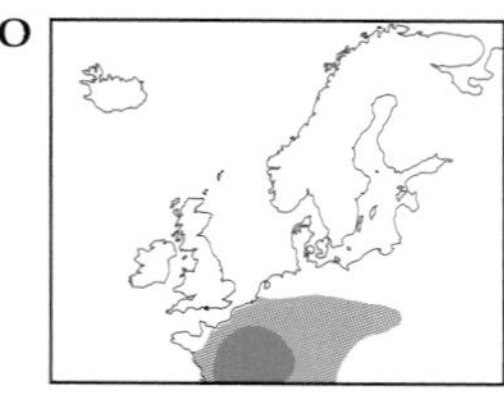

A Smooth Rupturewort *Herniaria glabra* Low, prostrate, bright green annual or biennial, with shoots to 20cm long, *hairless or slightly hairy all round*. Leaves to 10mm, elliptical and usually hairless. Flowers about 2mm in diameter, with 5 minute green petals, shorter than sepals. Sepals not hairy. Fruit pointed, much longer than sepals. Local to locally frequent in bare chalky or sandy soils . **Fl** 5-9. **Br** Rare in Breckland and in E England.

B Fringed Rupturewort *Herniaria ciliolata* Differs from previous species in being perennial with a woody base, *stems hairy on only 1 side;* sepals hairy and fruit blunt, only slightly longer than sepals. Very local in sandy or rocky habitats by the sea. **Fl** 6-8. **Br** Very rare in Cornwall and Channel Isles.

C Hairy Rupturewort *Herniaria hirsuta* Annual, differing from previous 2 species in being grey or whitish due to shoots having *dense, straight, spreading hairs.* Very local in sandy ground; absent from the north. **Fl** 6-8. **Br** Introduced and very rare.

D Coral-necklace *Illecebrum verticillatum* Low, prostrate, hairless annual with square pinkish stems up to 20cm long, bearing bright green, oval, opposite leaves which have basal clusters of tiny, bright white flowers. Sepals 5, thick corky and hooded; petals minute. Very local on damp sandy or gravelly soils, especially if seasonally flooded, and sometimes on sandy margins of ponds. **Fl** 6-10. **Br** Very rare in S and SW England.

E Four-leaved Allseed *Polycarpon tetraphyllum* Small much-branched annual to 15cm with oval leaves stalked and grouped in 4s and 2s. Flowers in branched heads, tiny, whitish and with 5 white petals which soon fall and 5 longer white-edged sepals. Local in sandy ground, often by the sea. **Fl** 6-8. **Br** Very rare in SW England and local in Channel Isles.

SPURREYS *Spergula* Characterised by being much-branched at base and having cylindrical fleshy leaves which appear to be in whorls (they are actually in pairs with the rest in axillary tufts). Stipules white and chaffy; flowers with 5 unnotched petals. 5 styles.

F Corn Spurrey *Spergula arvensis* Rather straggling annual to 30cm with stems stickily hairy above and *leaves furrowed beneath,* blunt-tipped. Flowers 4-7mm in diameter, with white petals slightly longer than sepals. Common weed of arable ground, especially on sandy soils. **Fl** 5-9. **Br** Frequent throughout; much less common than formerly, due to herbicide usage.

G Pearlwort Spurrey *Spergula morisonii* Very similar to Corn Spurrey, but *leaves not furrowed* beneath, *petals slightly overlapping and equalling sepals*. Similar habitats to above. **Fl** 4-6. **Br** Introduced in Sussex.

H *Spergula pentandra* Very similar to Corn Spurrey, but *leaves not furrowed*, flowers have *narrow acute petals, longer than sepals, not overlapping*. Local; similar habitats. **Fl** 5-7. **Br** Absent.

SEA-SPURREYS *Spergularia* Annual or perennial plants with narrow opposite leaves and leafy tufts on 1 side at each node. Leaves fleshy or not. Stipules chaffy. Petals white or pink, unnotched; 3 styles.

I Rock Sea-spurrey *Spergularia rupicola* Perennial, robust with a woody rootstock and *densely stickily hairy* throughout. Stems often purplish. Leaves fleshy and rather flattened with a mucronate point. Flowers 8-10mm in diameter, pink, with *petals equalling sepals.* Stamens 10. Seeds unwinged. Locally common on sea-cliffs. **Fl** 5-9. **Br** Common only on W coast; rare in the south and east.

J Greater Sea-spurrey *Spergularia media* Perennial, robust and hairless. Leaves fleshy, bright green, flattened above but rounded beneath and with an awned tip. Flowers 7-12mm in diameter, white or pink, *petals longer than sepals.* Seeds mostly with a winged border. Stamens 10. Widespread and common in salt-marshes, occasionally spreading inland along salted roads; absent from the far north. **Fl** 5-9. **Br** Common all round the coasts.

K Lesser Sea-spurrey *Spergularia marina* Annual, sometimes slightly stickily hairy above. *Leaves fleshy, bright yellowish-green,* awned and similar to those of Greater Sea-spurrey. Flowers 6-8mm in diameter, *petals deep pink and shorter than sepals.* Stamens 4-8. Seeds mostly unwinged. Frequent throughout the drier zones of coastal salt-marshes and occasionally near saline springs inland or along heavily salted roads. **Fl** 5-9. **Br** Common all round the coasts; occasional inland.

L Sand Spurrey *Spergularia rubra* Annual or biennial, stickily hairy above. *Leaves not fleshy, grey-green,* awned. Stipules lanceolate and silvery. Flowers 3-5mm in diameter, *pink petals shorter than sepals.* Stamens 10. Seeds unwinged. Local to locally common in open, dry, sandy ground, acid grasslands, heathlands and clifftops. **Fl** 5-9. **Br** Mostly locally common, but rare in Scotland and Ireland.

M *Spergularia echinosperma* Very similar to Sand Spurrey, but flowers have 2-5 stamens and seeds are black when ripe (brown in other *Spergularia* species). Very local in sandy ground along freshwater margins in the east. **Fl** 5-9. **Br** Absent.

N Greek Sea-spurrey *Spergularia bocconii* Annual or biennial, densely stickily hairy throughout. Leaves not fleshy, shortly awned. Stipules triangular, not silvery. Flowers 2-3mm in diameter, white or pink and very numerous in characteristic 1-sided curved spikes. Petals shorter than sepals. Very rare in dry coastal sands and gravelly areas. **Fl** 5-9. **Br** Very rare in SW England, Scillies and Channel Islands.

O *Spergularia segetalis* Annual with non-fleshy awned leaves. Like Greek Sea-spurrey, it has tiny white flowers 2-3mm in diameter, but in loose branched heads and not in 1-sided spikes. Flowers never pink. Local or locally common in arable fields or disturbed soils. **Fl** 5-7. **Br** Absent.

LYCHNIS *Lychnis* Erect perennials with upper leaves opposite and 5-parted flowers. Petals narrowed at the base into a long claw, often with scales at the base of the limb. Sepals united into a tube with 10 veins. 5 styles.

P Ragged Robin *Lychnis flos-cuculi* Distinctive perennial to 70cm, often branched. Leaves narrow-lanceolate, rough to the touch. Flowers pink, petals divided into 4 narrow lobes with a ragged appearance. Widespread throughout and common in moist grassland, fens, wet woodlands, etc. **Fl** 5-8. **Br** Frequent throughout but decreasing along with other plants of damp grassland due to agricultural 'improvement'.

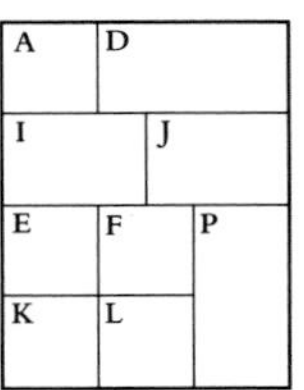

A **Smooth Rupturewort**
D **Coral-necklace**
I **Rock sea-spurrey**
J **Greater Sea-spurrey**
E **Four-leaved Allseed**
F **Corn Spurrey**
K **Lesser Sea-spurrey**
L **Sand Spurrey**
P **Ragged Robin**

A

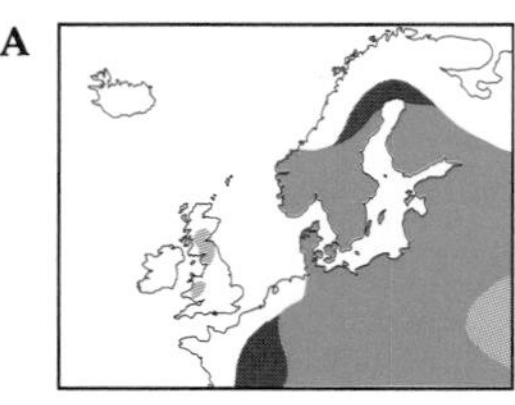

B

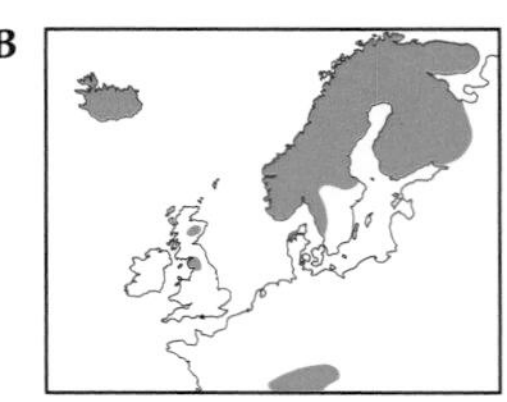

E

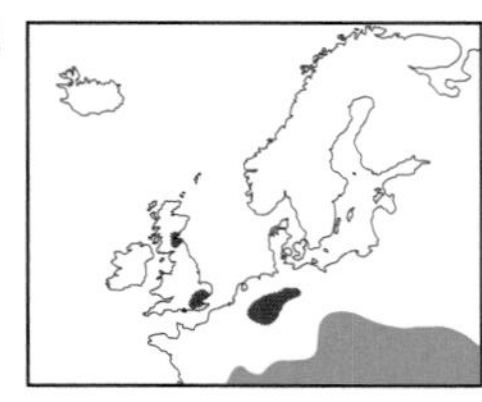

F

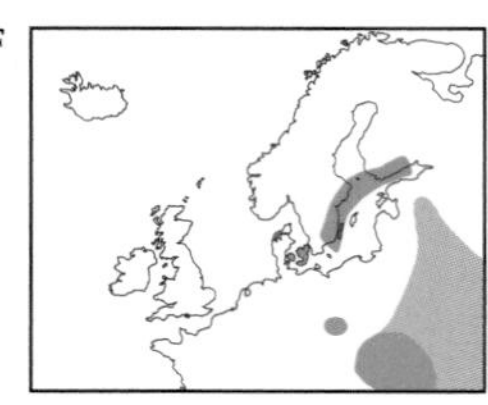

G

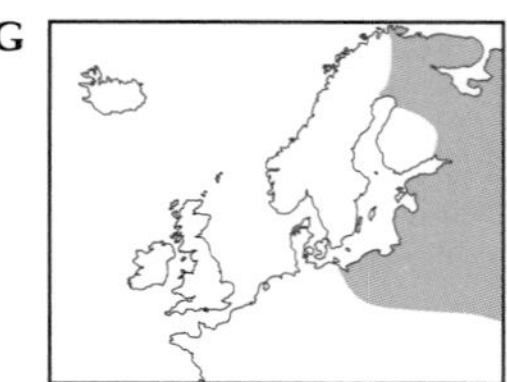

H

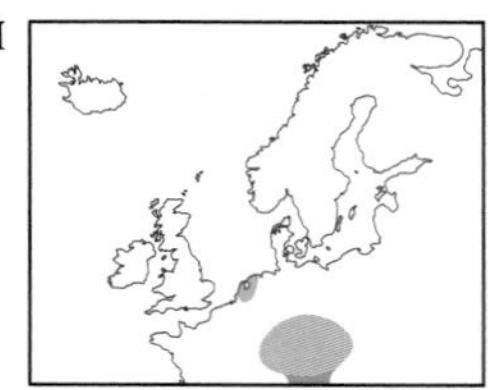

K

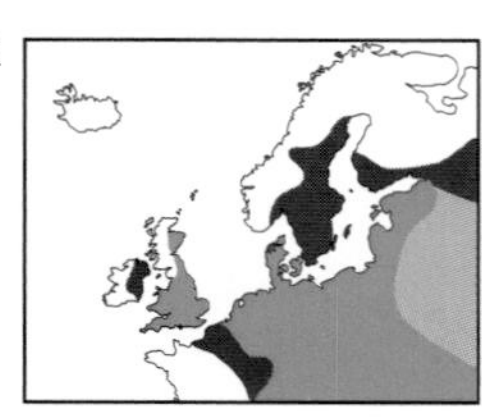

O

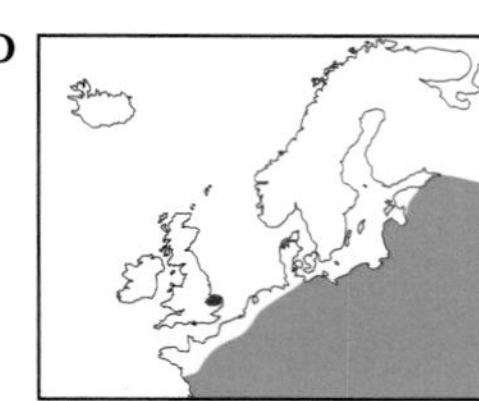

A **Sticky Catchfly** *Lychnis viscaria* Perennial to 60cm, with stems often purplish and very sticky below leaf nodes. Leaves almost hairless and lanceolate. Flowers 18-20mm in dense spikes, with petals red or purplish red, slightly notched. Locally frequent in dry sandy grasslands or rocky places. **Fl** 5-8. **Br** Very rare, on volcanic rock in Wales and Scotland.

B **Alpine Catchfly** *Lychnis alpina* Tufted perennial to 15cm, with most leaves in dense basal rosettes some of which bear the erect flowering stems; leaves narrow and spoon-shaped. Flowers 6-12mm in diameter, in dense rounded terminal clusters, petals rose-red and deeply notched. Local in rocky places, usually metal-rich, in mountains. **Fl** 6-7. **Br** Very rare; in Cumbria and Scottish Highlands.

C **Corncockle** *Agrostemma githago* Annual to 1m, covered with appressed greyish hairs. Leaves narrow-lanceolate and pointed. Flowers pale reddish-purple, with shallowly notched petals shorter than the linear sepals. Formerly locally abundant as an arable weed, but rapidly decreasing with the use of herbicides. **Fl** 5-8. **Br** Rare and sporadic in a number of counties; sometimes introduced or naturalised.

Silene and *Cucubalus* Annuals or perennials with similar characters to Lychnis (above), but flowers usually have 3 styles (rarely 5) and calyx tube has up to 30 veins. *Cucubalus* differs in that its fruit is a berry.

(1) Petals deeply cleft.

D **Nottingham Catchfly** *Silene nutans* Perennial to 80cm, stems downy below and sticky above. Basal leaves spoon-shaped and stalked; stem leaves oblong, pointed and unstalked. *Flowers drooping*, 18mm in diameter, in 1-sided panicle. Petals whitish, sometimes slightly pinkish or greenish beneath, *deeply cleft into narrow lobes which are rolled inwards during the day*, but roll back during evening when flower is fragrant. Calyx 9-12mm long with 10 purplish veins. Widespread throughout; in dry, often bare, calcareous habitats such as chalk grassland, shingle beaches and limestone cliffs. **Fl** 5-8. **Br** Very local, north to Angus.

E **Italian Catchfly** *Silene italica* Similar to Nottingham Catchfly, but *leaves have wavy margins*; flowers about 18mm in diameter, erect and not in 1-sided panicles. Petals only roll in or back slightly. Calyx 14-21mm long. Local in similar habitats. **Fl** 5-7. **Br** Introduced and very rare in quarries.

F *Silene viscosa* Biennial, more robust than previous 2 species, *densely stickily hairy* throughout. Leaves lanceolate, pointed, the lower ones with wavy margins. *Flowers large* (to 22mm in diameter), arranged in whorls in a dense panicle. Petals white and deeply cleft. Calyx green, 14-24mm long. Very local in dry, grassy places. **Fl** 6-7. **Br** Absent.

G *Silene tatarica* Differs from *S. viscosa* in that it is almost hairless and has smaller flowers with calyx 10-13mm. Very local in dry grassy places. **Fl** 7-8. **Br** Absent.

H *Silene linicola* Rough-stemmed, branched annual to 70cm, with narrow lanceolate leaves. Flowers in loose branched head. Petals deeply cleft, pink with purplish-red veins. Rapidly declining weed of flaxfields. **Fl** 6-8. **Br** Absent.

I **Bladder Campion** *Silene vulgaris* Greyish, generally hairless perennial to 90cm. Leaves pointed-oval, sometimes wavy-edged with a hairy margin. *Flowers drooping*, 16-18mm, with deeply cleft white petals, not overlapping. *Calyx very inflated* like a bladder. Widespread and often common in dry grassy places, preferring sandy or calcareous soils. **Fl** 5-9. **Br** Widespread throughout, but more common in the south and absent from much of the north.

J **Sea Campion** *Silene vulgaris* ssp *maritima* Differs from Bladder Campion in being *cushion-forming* with ascending flowering shoots to 25cm. *Leaves waxy-looking* and rather fleshy. Flowers erect, 20-25mm, petals over-lapping. Locally abundant on sea-cliffs and shingle, and occasionally on mountains and inland lakes. **Fl** 6-8. **Br** Frequent on coasts; rarely inland.

K **Night-flowering Catchfly** *Silene noctiflora* Softly hairy annual to 60cm, sticky above. Lower leaves ovate-lanceolate and stalked; upper leaves narrower and stalked. Flowers similar to White Campion in shape (*see* below) but petals yellowish beneath and pink above. *3 styles are present*, and unlike White Campion, the *flowers are hermaphrodite*. Like Nottingham Catchfly and Italian Catchfly, petals roll inwards during the day, and only roll back in the evening when the flowers become heavily fragrant to attract pollinating moths. Locally frequent, but decreasing, in arable fields, especially on chalk or sandy soils. **Fl** 7-9. **Br** Local and decreasing as a result of herbicide usage; mainly in the south.

L **White Campion** *Silene alba* Softly hairy short-lived perennial (occasionally annual) to 1m, rather sticky above. Leaves ovate-lanceolate, lower ones stalked and upper ones unstalked. Flowers few, 25-30mm in diameter, in branched clusters. Petals white, deeply notched; *flowers dioecious*, male smaller and with calyces 10-veined, female larger and 20-veined with 5 styles. Female flowers drop readily if not pollinated early. Fragrant in the evening. Widespread and common in hedgerows, roadsides, arable land and waste areas. **Fl** 5-10. **Br** Common throughout.

M **Red Campion** *Silene dioica* Similar to White Campion, with which it often hybridises. Biennial or perennial, softly hairy, sometimes sticky above. Flowers numerous, dioecious, unscented with deep rose-pink petals; male flowers smaller than female. Widespread throughout; in shady places, hedgerows, woodlands and roadsides, especially on basic soils. **Fl** 3-10. **Br** Mostly common except in some parts of E England, N Scotland and Ireland.

N **Forked Catchfly** *Silene dichotoma* Distinctive annual to 1m, sparsely hairy, branched above and with numerous horizontal flowers in characteristic *1-sided forked spikes*. Flowers 15-18mm in diameter, petals white (rarely pink), deeply notched. Arable weed; native in Poland, introduced elsewhere. **Fl** 5-9. **Br** Introduced and casual.

O **Berry Catchfly** *Cucubalus baccifer* Downy perennial to 1m, straggling amongst surrounding vegetation, the habit and ovate leaves reminiscent of Water Chickweed. Flowers about 18mm in diameter, distinctive in appearance, drooping; petals greenish white, deeply cleft. Fruit is a round black berry. Locally frequent in damp shady places. **Fl** 7-9. **Br** Status doubtful; very rare and naturalised in a few places, mainly in Norfolk.

A	B	C	D
E	I	J / K	
L	M	N	O

A **Sticky Catchfly**
B **Alpine Catchfly**
C **Corncockle**
D **Nottingham Catchfly**
E **Italian Catchfly**
I **Bladder Campion**
J **Sea Campion**
K **Night-flowering Catchfly**
L **White Campion**
M **Red Campion**
N **Forked Catchfly** (with Rampion Bellflower on left)
O **Berry Catchfly**

A
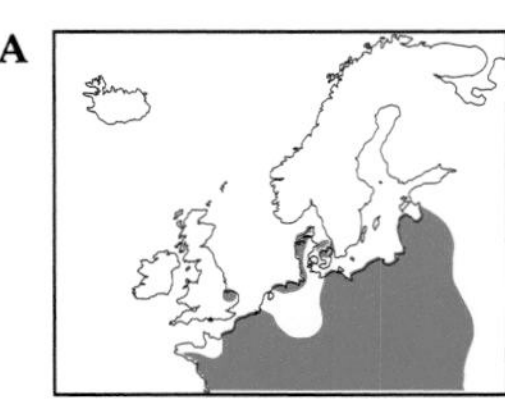
D
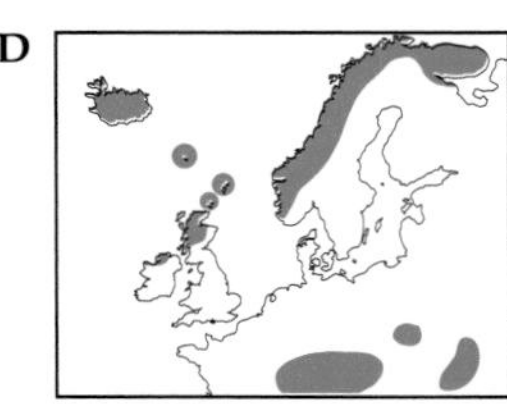
E
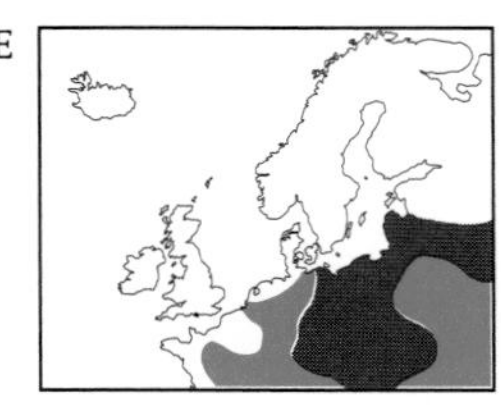
G
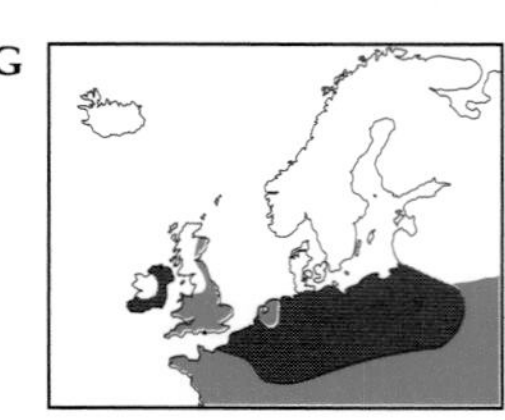
H
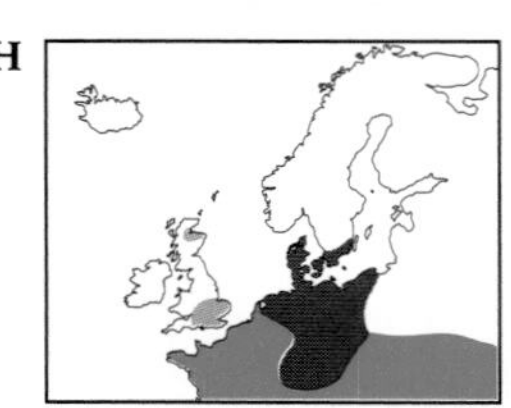
I
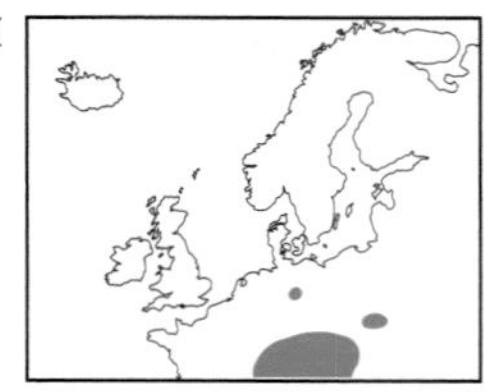
J
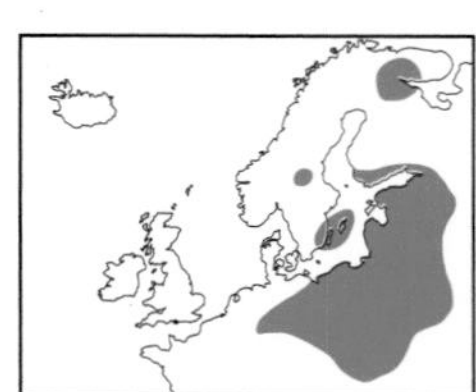
K
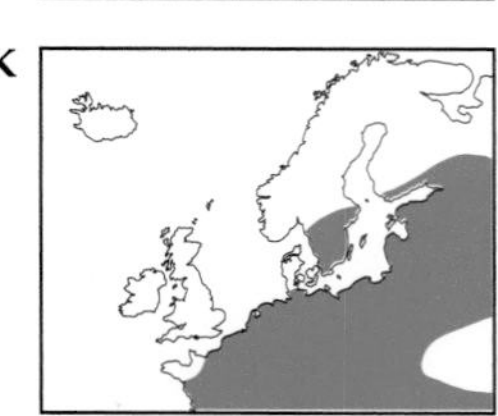
M
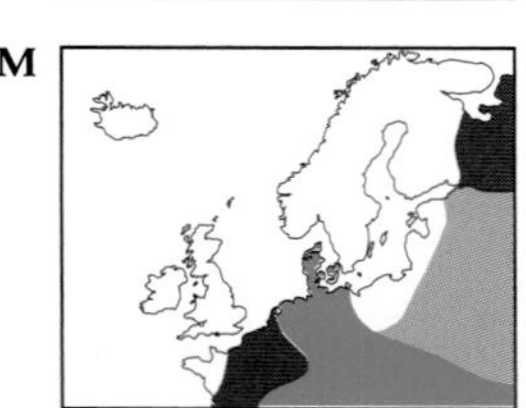

(2) Petals shallowly notched.

A **Spanish Catchfly** *Silene otites* Distinctive biennial or short-lived perennial to 90cm, stickily hairy near the base. Basal leaves spoon-shaped and stalked; upper stem leaves oblong and stalked. Flower heads unlike any other catchfly: loose, branched clusters of tiny greenish-yellow flowers, 3-4mm in diameter, with undivided narrow petals. Local on dry sandy soils and heaths. **Fl** 6-9. **Br** Very local and rare in Breckland.

B *Silene wahlbergella* Very distinctive but rather inconspicuous, *slightly hairy, unbranched perennial* to 25cm. Flowers solitary and nodding at first. Calyx tube 14-18mm, inflated and almost completely concealing the purplish petals which only just become visible at the calyceal opening. Damp meadows to 1,900m; in Scandinavia. **Fl** 6-8. Br Absent.

C *Silene furcata* Very similar to the previous species, but differs in having *branched, stickily hairy stems*, erect flowers, and uninflated calyx tube 10-12mm. Similar habitats and flowering time; Arctic meadows. **Fl** 6-8. **Br** Absent.

D **Moss Campion** *Silene acaulis* Distinctive cushion-forming perennial with moss-like habit. Leaves bright green, linear and pointed. Flowers pale or deep pink, 9-12mm in diameter, solitary on short stalks and often covering the cushions, the petals notched. Locally frequent on damp rocks, screes and short turf in mountains, to 2,500m, descending to low altitudes in Arctic and sub-Arctic areas. **Fl** 6-8. **Br** Locally frequent in mountains from N Wales to N Scotland, and in W Ireland.

E **Sweet-William Catchfly** *Silene armeria* Distinctive hairless annual or biennial to 30cm, with stems sticky above. Leaves lanceolate and greyish with upper leaves clasping the stem. Flowers 14-16mm in diameter in loose branched heads. Petals bright pink and shallowly notched; calyx reddish with 10 veins. Dry, shady places, often a garden escape. **Fl** 6-9. **Br** Introduced in S England.

F *Silene rupestris* Distinctive, hairless, erect, greyish perennial to 30cm, with lanceolate leaves and small (7-9mm) white or pale pink flowers with shallowly notched petals. Dry screes and rocky places in mountains; locally frequent in Scandinavia; absent from the north-west of the range. **Fl** 6-9. **Br** Absent.

G **Small-flowered Catchfly** *Silene gallica* Stickily hairy, rather greyish annual to 45cm. Lower leaves spoon-shaped, stalked and hairy; upper leaves narrowly lanceolate to 50mm Flowers erect in mostly 1-sided spikes, 10-12mm in diameter; petals shallowly notched, white or pink and sometimes with a basal deep-red spot. Widespread but local on arable or waste areas, mainly on sandy soils. **Fl** 6-10. **Br** Local and decreasing.

H **Sand Catchfly** *Silene conica* Stickily hairy, greyish annual to 35cm. Leaves narrow and downy. Flowers only 4-5mm in diameter, in loose clusters, and distinctive; petals deep pink or whitish, shallowly notched; calyx strongly ribbed, at first cylindrical but soon swelling below to become markedly flask-shaped. Widespread but rather local in dry, sandy areas. **Fl** 5-8. **Br** Local, mainly on the S and E coasts of England and Scotland; often casual and introduced elsewhere.

I *Gypsophila repens* *Sprawling* hairless perennial to 30cm, with greyish-green linear-lanceolate leaves to 30mm long. Flowers 8-10mm in diameter, in loose clusters, petals pink or white and slightly notched. Rocky places in mountains of central Europe, on limestone. **Fl** 5-9. **Br** Absent.

J *Gypsophila fastigiata* *Erect* perennial to 1m, *stickily hairy above*. Leaves linear, greyish green, to 80mm long. Flowers 5-8mm in diameter, in *dense flat-topped heads*. Petals lilac or white and slightly notched. Dry stony or rocky areas; mainly in the east; very local elsewhere and not extending further west than Germany or Sweden. **Fl** 6-9. **Br** Absent.

K *Gypsophila muralis* Annual to 30cm, *hairless above* and with linear greyish-green leaves to 25mm long. Flowers 4mm in diameter in loose much-branched clusters arising from axils of leaves. Petals pink or white, slightly notched. Locally frequent in damp woods and meadows; mainly a central and E European plant, becoming much more local westwards towards France and Sweden. **Fl** 6-10. **Br** Rare casual.

L **Soapwort** *Saponaria officinalis* Hairless perennial to 1m, often rather straggling. Leaves ovate, pointed and strongly veined. Flowers large, 25-38mm in diameter; petals pink, unnotched and limbs standing well clear of the reddish calyx. Widespread throughout; by roadsides, hedges, waste areas and damp woods; possibly only native in the south of its range where it grows in damp woodlands; naturalised elsewhere. **Fl** 6-9. **Br** Possibly native in parts, or long naturalised; locally frequent, but rare in Scotland.

M **Cow Basil** *Vaccaria pyramidata* Distinctive annual to 60cm, with grey-green, ovate, pointed leaves, about 50mm long. Flowers 10-15mm in diameter with pink notched petals and a characteristic calyx tube which is sharply winged on 5 angles. Uncommon arable weed on calcareous soils. **Fl** 6-7. **Br** Occasional as a casual.

A	B	G	H
D	E	F	
I	L	J	
K		M	

A **Spanish Catchfly**
B *Silene wahlbergella*
G **Small-flowered Catchfly**
H **Sand Catchfly**
D **Moss Campion**
E **Sweet-William Catchfly**
F *Silene rupestris*
I *Gypsophila repens*
L **Soapwort**
J *Gypsophila fastigiata*
K *Gypsophila muralis*
M **Cow Basil**

A
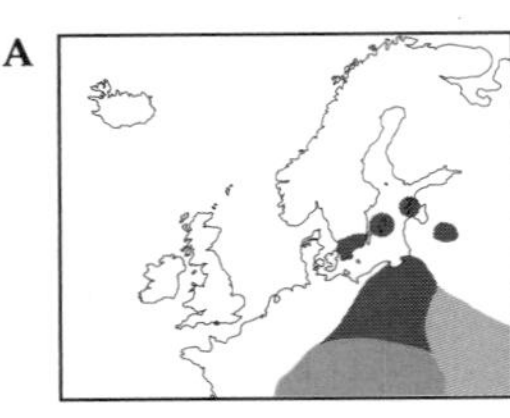

B
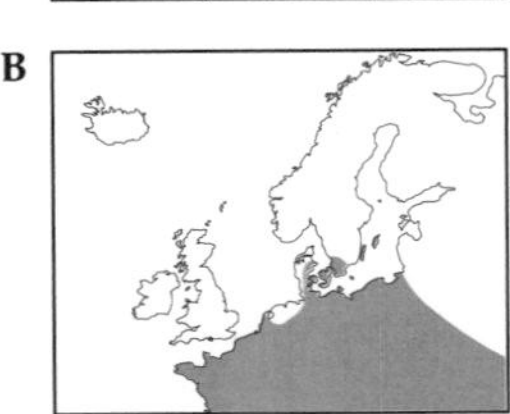

C

E

G
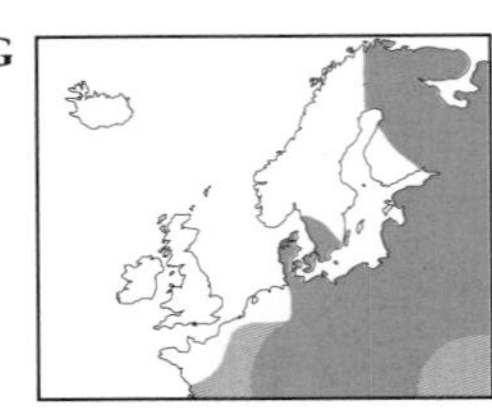

H
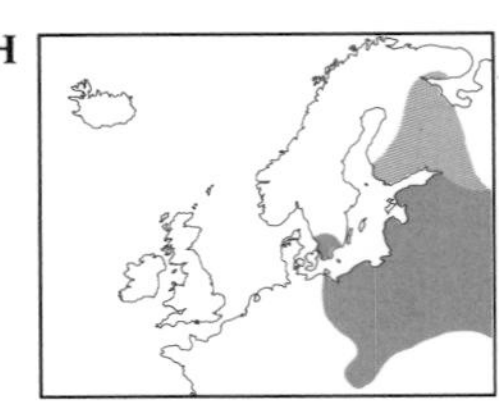

I

L

PINKS *Petrorhagia* and *Dianthus*
Characterised by being annual or perennial, with 5, usually pink, petals and base of calyx surrounded by an epicalyx of paired bracts; flowers have 10 stamens and 2 styles. *Petrorhagia* species differ from *Dianthus* species in having a scarious membrane in the gaps between the calyx teeth.

A **Tunic Flower** *Petrorhagia saxifraga*
Hairless mat-forming perennial to 35cm with decumbent, then ascending, flowering shoots. Leaves linear, pointed and rough-edged. *Flowers solitary* on long stalks, petals notched and pale pink or white. Local in dry, sandy habitats. **Fl** 6-8. **Br** Introduced, rare.

B **Proliferous Pink** *Petrorhagia prolifera*
Hairless annual to 50cm. Leaves linear, greyish and rough-edged. *Leaf sheaths about as long as wide* (*see* Childling Pink, below). Flowers 6-7mm in diameter, pink or white in a *close cluster* surrounded by brown chaffy bracts. Locally frequent in dry open places on calcareous soils. **Fl** 5-9. **Br** Absent.

C **Childling Pink** *Petrorhagia nanteulii* Very like previous species, but *stems hairy in the middle* and *leaf sheaths twice as long as wide.* Local or rare in sandy or gravelly habitats, often near the sea. **Fl** 7-9. **Br** Rare in S England.

(1) Flowers in dense clusters.

D **Deptford Pink** *Dianthus armeria* The only annual *Dianthus* in this list, to 60cm tall and hairy. Characterised by its dark green leaves, clusters of bright reddish-pink flowers, 8-13mm in diameter, subtended by *long leafy green bracts,* and with *rather pointed toothed petals,* the epicalyx having a pair of long scales equalling the sepals. Widespread throughout on dry sandy or calcareous soils; more frequent towards the south. **Fl** 6-8. **Br** Local and rare; absent from Ireland.

E **Carthusian Pink** *Dianthus carthusianorum*
Hairless perennial to 60cm. Leaves green, leaf sheaths 4 times longer than diameter of stem. Flowers 18-20mm in diameter bright pink or red in dense clusters subtended by *short brownish-green bracts, petals blunt* and toothed; epicalyx scales half as long as sepal tube. More frequent towards the south and east of its range; local elsewhere in dry grassy places. **Fl** 5-8. **Br** Occasional garden escape.

F **Sweet-william** *Dianthus barbatus* Very similar to Carthusian Pink, but has *broad flat heads* of larger flowers, 20-30mm in diameter and epicalyx scales longer than sepal tube. Widely naturalised as a garden escape. **Fl** 6-8. **Br** Occasional garden escape.

(2) Flowers not in dense clusters.

(a) Epicalyx scales less than half the length of calyx.

G **Large Pink** *Dianthus superbus* Hairless branched perennial to 90cm with narrow-lanceolate green leaves. *Flowers large,* 30-50mm in diameter, in loose branched clusters, with distinctive pink petals divided almost to the base into multiple, long, narrow, pointed segments. Widespread in dry, shady places. **Fl** 6-9. **Br** Absent.

H *Dianthus arenarius* Very similar to Large Pink, but has white petals, often with purplish margins. Locally frequent in open, grassy and stony places. **Fl** 7-8. **Br** Absent.

I **Cheddar Pink** *Dianthus gratianopolitanus*
Hairless tufted perennial to 20cm, with long creeping runners. Erect flowering stems have greyish *rough-edged linear leaves,* 20-60mm long. Flowers solitary, 20-30mm in diameter with toothed pink petals, *the teeth not more than a sixth the length of petal limb;* epicalyx scales about a quarter the length of calyx. Very local on open limestone grassland and rocks. **Fl** 5-7. **Br** Restricted to the Cheddar Gorge; occasionally naturalised elsewhere.

J **Clove Pink** *Dianthus caryophyllus* Similar to Cheddar Pink, but taller (to 50cm), with *smooth-edged leaves* and larger flowers, 35-40mm in diameter. Widely naturalised, from S Europe, on old walls and dry banks. **Fl** 7-8. **Br** Rare, on old walls.

K **Pink, Wild Pink** *Dianthus plumarius* Differs from Cheddar Pink in having white or pink petals, with *teeth almost half their limb length.* Widely naturalised from S Europe, on old walls and dry banks. **Fl** 6-8. **Br** Rare on old walls.

L **Jersey Pink** *Dianthus gallicus* Differs from Cheddar Pink in being often loosely tufted, hairy towards the base, with leaves to only 15mm long and *petals toothed to a third of their limb length.* Very local on coastal sand-dunes. **Fl** 6-8. **Br** Jersey only.

(b) Epicalyx scales at least half the length of calyx.

M *Dianthus seguieri* *Hairless,* tufted perennial to 60cm with green leaves up to 4mm wide. Flowers in loose clusters, 18-22mm in diameter; petals toothed, *deep pink or magenta* and often with pale spots at the base. Epicalyx scales very variable in length, sometimes exceeding the calyx. Local in dry, often stony places; in E France and S Germany. **Fl** 6-9. **Br** Absent.

N **Maiden Pink** *Dianthus deltoides* *Roughly hairy perennial* with short creeping runners from which arise the erect flowering stems to 20cm. Leaves greyish green with rough edges. Flowers solitary or up to 3 in a group, 17-20mm in diameter; petals toothed, deep pink (occasionally pale pink) with *pale basal spots above a dark band.* Epicalyx scales half the length of calyx. Plants occasionally grow in tufted clumps. Widespread and locally frequent throughout, especially in the south of its range; in dry, often sandy places. **Fl** 6-9. **Br** Widely scattered and varying from local to rare. Absent from the extreme north.

A	C	D
E	F	G
I	J	L
K	N	

A **Tunic Flower**
C **Childling Pink**
D **Deptford Pink**
E **Carthusian Pink**
F **Sweet-william**
G **Large Pink**
I **Cheddar Pink**
J **Clove Pink**
L **Jersey Pink**
K **Pink**
N **Maiden Pink**

B

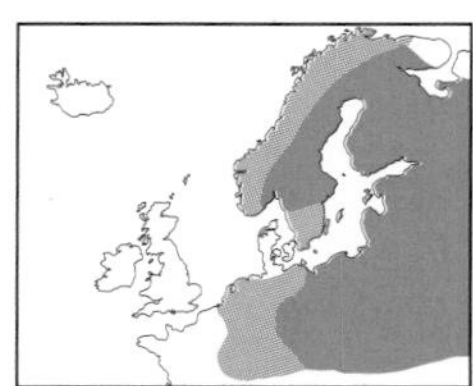

Water-lily Family
Nymphaeaceae

Aquatic perennials of either still or moving fresh water. Stems root in basal mud, leaves float or remain submerged and are oval or circular in outline. Flowers are terminal with 3 to many petals and 3-6 sepals (the 2 main genera can be separated by sepal numbers: *Nymphaea* has 4 sepals, *Nuphar* 5-6). The terminal flowers separate the Nymphaeaceae from other aquatic plants with floating leaves, such as Fringed Water-lily (*see* page 196) which has flowers in axillary fascicles. Frogbit (*see* page 290) differs by not having roots buried in mud.

The upper surface of the leaves of water-lilies is such that rainwater forms into droplets, as it would on a waxy surface, and the slight undulations in the leaf direct the droplets to the small depressions. In this way, transpiration can still occur through the pores (stomata) on the upper leaf surface.

A **White Water-lily** *Nymphaea alba* Conspicuous for its large rounded leaves, 10-30cm in diameter and its large white flowers 10-20cm in diameter only opening in bright sunshine. Basal lobes of leaves are parallel or diverging. Flowers have 20 or more petals. Widespread throughout and often common; in still or slow-moving fresh water. **Fl** 6-9. **Br** Common throughout.

B *Nymphaea candida* Very like White Water-lily, but basal lobes of leaves touch or overlap and flowers are smaller, 7-14cm, with up to 18 petals. Locally common in similar habitats, but absent from large areas. **Fl** 7-9.

C **Yellow Water-lily** *Nuphar lutea* Like White Water-lily, has conspicuous large leathery floating leaves to 40cm in diameter, but also has thinner submerged leaves. *Flowers yellow*, 6cm in diameter, held on stalks above water level. *Stigma disc not wavy when viewed from above*. Petals partially concealed by the much longer yellow sepals, which markedly overlap each other. Widespread and generally common in similar habitats to previous species, often in more nutrient-rich water. **Fl** 6-9. **Br** Throughout, mostly common, but rare in N Scotland.

D **Least Water-lily** *Nuphar pumila* Very like previous species, but smaller in all parts: floating leaves to 14cm in diameter, *flowers to 4cm in diameter*, sepals less markedly overlapping. *Margin of stigma disc wavy when viewed from above*. Local in acid lakes. **Fl** 6-8. **Br** Very local in N and central Scotland; very rare in England and Wales.

Hornwort Family
Ceratophyllaceae

Aquatic perennials, submerged and with whorled leaves divided into multiple narrow linear segments. Male and female flowers are separate on the same plant, alternating at the leaf nodes. The stems of hornworts often become encrusted with calcium during the summer, and these deposits fall to the bottom of the water as the stems and leaves decay.

E **Rigid Hornwort** *Ceratophyllum demersum* Stems flexuous, up to 1.5m long, bearing whorls of dark green, rigid, minutely toothed *leaves, forked once or twice*. Flowers tiny at leaf nodes. Fruit has 2 basal spines. Widespread throughout, but often local in freshwater habitats or occasionally brackish water; can colonise or spread very rapidly. **Fl** 7-9. **Br** Local in England; rare in Wales and Scotland.

F **Soft Hornwort** *Ceratophyllum submersum* Like rigid Hornwort, but leaves bright green, softer and *forked 3-4 times*. Fruit spineless but warty. Widespread, but very local or rare, especially inland, in fresh or brackish water. Absent from the extreme north. **Fl** 7-9. **Br** Very local in S England and S Wales, near the coast.

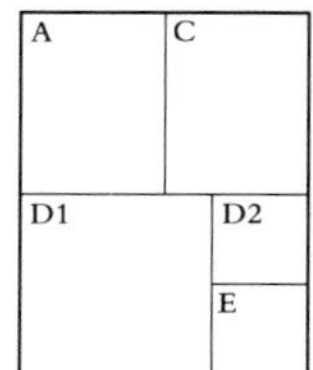

A **White Water-lily**

C **Yellow Water-lily**

D **1 Least Water-lily** showing habit and habitat

D **2 Least Water-lily** close-up of flower

E **Rigid Hornwort**

A

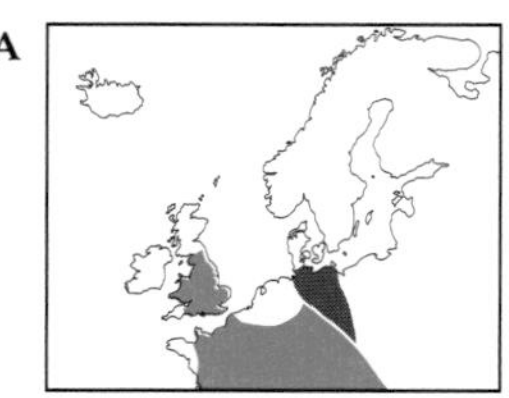

B

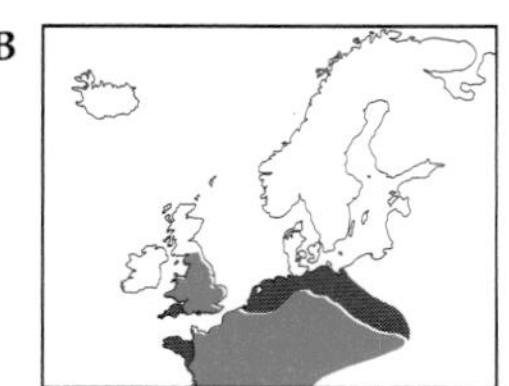

F

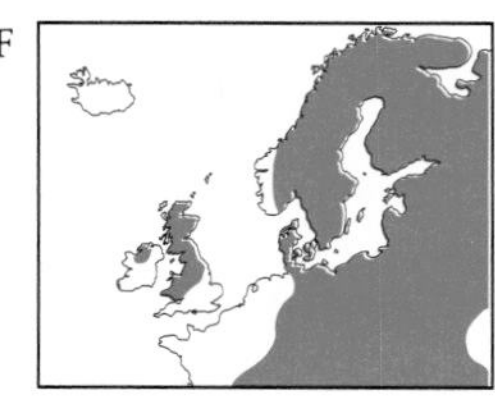

G

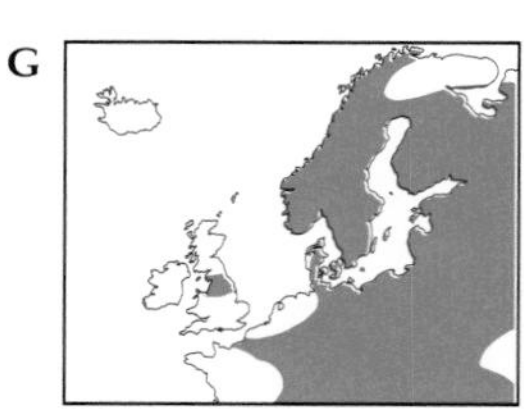

J

K

L

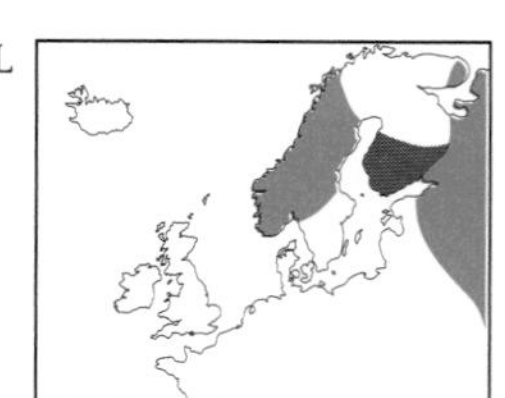

M

Buttercup Family
Ranunculaceae

A very large, primitive and variable family with a broad range of characters, but virtually all members can be recognised by their very numerous, free hypogynous stamens and their distinct carpels. Most are perennial herbs with alternate leaves and 5-6 sepals (except *Clematis* species, *see* page 54, which are woody climbers with opposite leaves and 4 sepals). Leaves usually divided or palmately lobed (but linear in Mousetail, *see* page 62, and unlobed in some *Ranunculus* species, *see* page 60,) and stipules absent. Although many members of the Rose family have numerous free stamens, there is always a gap between the ovary and the insertion of the other flower parts (*see* page 94), and stipules are usually present.

A **Stinking Hellebore** *Helleborus foetidus* Rather robust, fetid bushy perennial to 80cm, with dark green, overwintering basal leaves. All leaves palmately divided into numerous narrow toothed lobes, *arising from 2 or 3 arched stalks* and not from the same point at the top of the leaf stalk. Flowers cup-shaped, 10-30mm in diameter; sepals blunt, bright yellowish green with purplish edges; petals small, hidden by sepals. Local in open woods on calcareous soils. **Fl** 1-5. **Br** Very local in S England and Wales; sometimes naturalised further north.

B **Green Hellebore** *Helleborus viridis* Similar to Stinking Hellebore, but does not have evergreen leaves; *leaf lobes arise from a single point* and are often further lobed; flowers have spreading pointed sepals without purplish margins. Widespread but only locally frequent in moist calcareous woods. **Fl** 2-5. **Br** Local in S England, rare in the north and sometimes naturalised.

C **Winter Aconite** *Eranthis hyemalis* Very distinctive low perennial to 12cm with erect stems bearing a single, cup-shaped, bright yellow flower, to 15mm in diameter, subtended by a collar of 3 palmately divided leaves which protect the growing flower in bud. Flower has 6 conspicuous yellow sepals, whilst the petals are reduced to horn-like structures from which nectar is secreted. Widely naturalised in woodlands, churchyards and roadsides, etc. **Fl** 1-4. **Br** Naturalised widely as far north as S Scotland.

D **Nigella** *Nigella arvensis* Erect annual to 30cm, with very finely divided leaves and solitary flowers bearing 5 bluish sepals with green veins. Widespread but decreasing in arable fields. **Fl** 6-9. **Br** Uncommon casual.

E **Love-in-a-mist** *Nigella damascena* Very similar to Nigella, but has a *ruff of leaves just below the flower*. Widespread as a garden escape, and often naturalised. **Fl** 6-7. **Br** Very occasional casual.

F **Globeflower** *Trollius europaeus* Perennial to 60cm, with palmately divided, toothed leaves and distinctive lemon-yellow, globe-shaped flowers. The 10-15 sepals overlap and curve inwards, producing the orbicular shape and concealing the diminutive nectar-bearing petals. Widespread in damp upland meadows, ditches and by upland streams. **Fl** 5-8. **Br** Locally frequent From Wales to N Scotland, and in NW Ireland.

G **Baneberry** *Actaea spicata* Perennial, almost hairless, fetid herb to 70cm. Basal leaves large, like an umbellifer, the leaf stalk divided into pinnately arranged branches, with the leaflets coarsely toothed and often 3-lobed. Flowers in spikes, with 4-6 white petals and sepals and numerous long white stamens which give the flower spikes a feathery appearance. Fruit a shining berry, green at first then black when ripe, 12-13mm in diameter. Local to locally frequent; in woodlands on limestone and on limestone pavements. **Fl** 5-6. **Br** Very local in N England.

H *Actaea erythrocarpa* Almost identical to Baneberry, but has smaller red berries up to 10mm in diameter. NE Scandinavia. Very local, in woods and shady rocky places. **Fl** 5-7. **Br** Absent.

I **Marsh-marigold** *Caltha palustris* Hairless perennial with stout hollow stems, and broad heart-shaped or kidney-shaped leaves to 10cm. Distinctive when flowering, with its large bright yellow, buttercup-like flowers, to 50mm in diameter. As with many of the buttercup family, petals are absent so that the 5 sepals provide the splash of colour. Widespread throughout and common; in a variety of wetlands ranging from calcareous fens to wet woodlands. **Fl** 3-8. **Br** Still common throughout, but decreased in the lowlands along with other wetland plants due to agricultural drainage.

MONK'S-HOODS *Aconitum* Distinctive genus of herbs with spirally arranged, much-divided leaves and flowers with 5 coloured sepals, the 2 upper ones forming a prominent helmet-like hood.

J **Monk's-hood** *Aconitum napellus* Minutely downy perennial to 1m with lower stem leaves deeply divided into 3-5 lobes, each segment further divided into narrow, linear segments. Flowers blue or violet, to 20mm, with rounded *helmets equally broad as tall*. Often confused with the garden escapes which have much less narrowly divided leaves. A local plant of damp woodlands or by shady streams. **Fl** 5-9. **Br** Rare in the south and south-west.

K *Aconitum variegatum* Similar to previous species, but flowers blue with white streaks (or, rarely, completely white) and *helmets twice as tall as broad*. Woodland edges and meadows in mountains in south and east. **Fl** 7-9. **Br** Absent.

L *Aconitum septentrionale* Differs from Monk's-hood in that the violet (rarely yellow) flowers have a characteristic hood shape, tapering rapidly from the broad base into a long tip. *Lower stem leaves divided into 4-6 lobes*. Locally frequent in moist, shady grassland and woodland margins. **Fl** 7-8. Br Absent.

M **Wolf's-bane** *Aconitum vulparia* Similar to previous species, but *flowers always pale yellow*, and *lower stem leaves divided into 7-8 lobes*. Local in damp shady habitats, such as streamsides and scrub. **Fl** 6-8. **Br** Absent.

N **Forking Larkspur** *Consolida regalis* Distinctive downy annual to 30cm with leaves much divided as with the Monk's-hoods, but the blue flowers are in loose spikes, not hooded, and possess 5 perianth segments and a backward-pointing spur. Flower stalks much longer than bracts. Widespread as a casual of arable fields. **Fl** 6-8. **Br** Introduced and a rare casual.

B		C	
A	D		F
G	I		K
J	L	M	N

B **Green Hellebore**
C **Winter Aconite**
A **Stinking Hellebore**
D **Nigella**
F **Globeflower**
G **Baneberry**
I **Marsh-marigold**
K *Aconitum variegatum*
J **Monk's-hood**
L *Aconitum septentrionale*
M **Wolf's-bane**
N **Forking Larkspur**

C

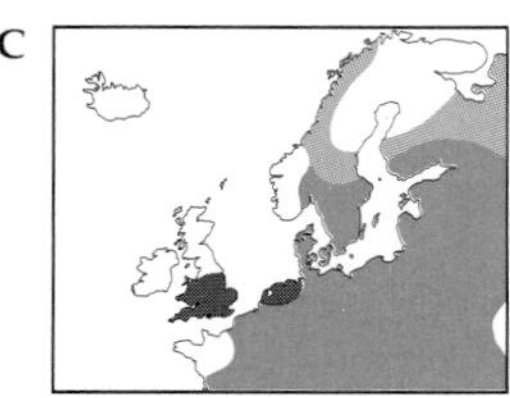

E

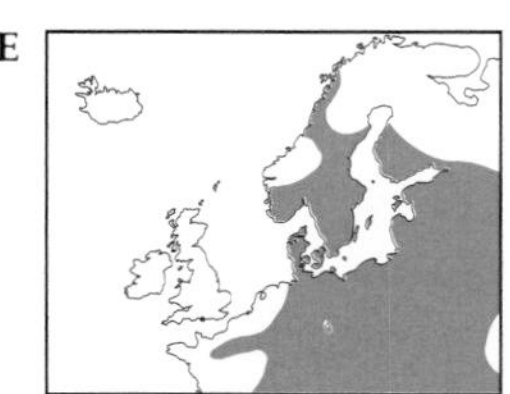

F

G

I

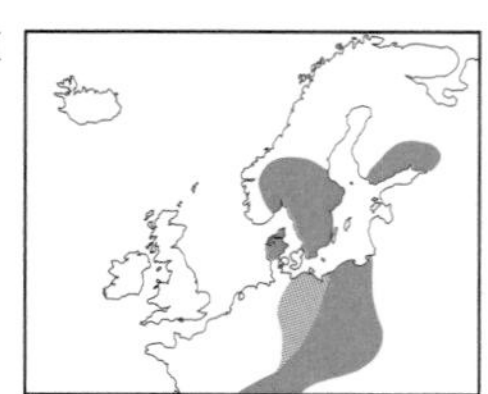

L

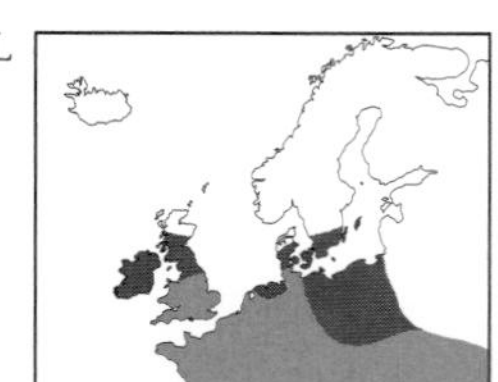

N

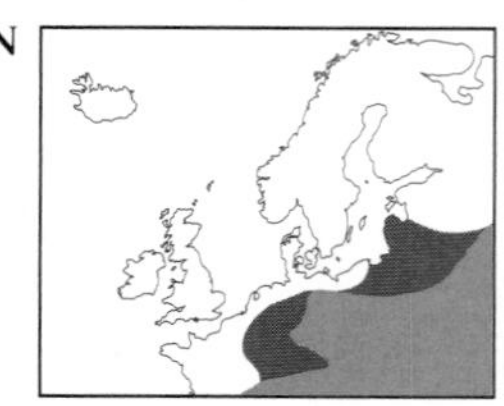

O

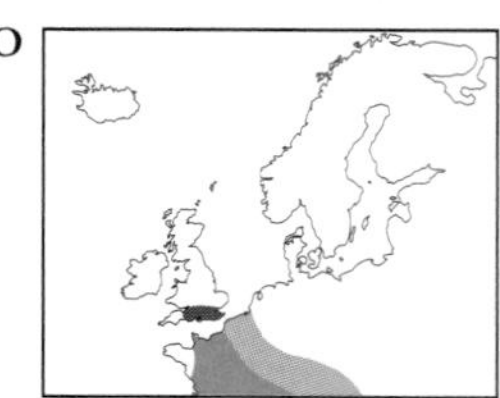

Q

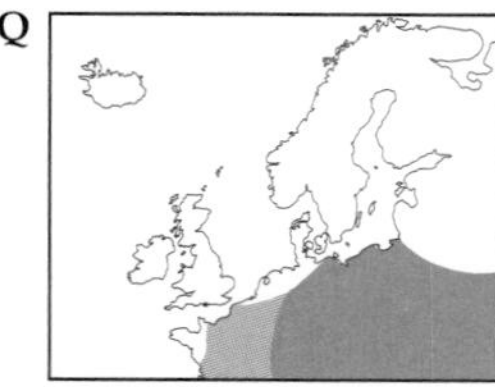

ANEMONES *Anemone* Perennials with 3 palmately lobed stem leaves in a whorl beneath the flower, the fruit a cluster of achenes.

A **Wood Anemone** *Anemone nemorosa* Perennial to 30cm with erect slightly hairy flowering stems. Stem leaves long-stalked in a whorl below flower, palmately divided into 3 lobes further divided into pointed toothed segments. Basal leaves appear after flowering. Flowers 2-4cm in diameter, terminal, *solitary* with 6-12 white or pink-tinged petaloid sepals. Fruit a globular cluster of beaked achenes. Widespread almost throughout, and common in woodlands, old hedgerows and sometimes meadows. **Fl** 3-5. **Br** Common throughout, but absent from some of the Scottish Islands.

B *Anemone narcissiflora* Very similar to Wood Anemone, but differs in having *3-8 flowers together* in an umbel. Local in woodlands and grassland, in mountains in the south and east, usually on limestone. **Fl** 6-7. **Br** Absent.

C **Yellow Anemone** *Anemone ranunculoides* Differs from Wood Anemone in having stem leaves only very short-stalked, and flowers with 5-8 bright yellow petaloid sepals. Widespread and locally frequent in deciduous woodlands. **Fl** 3-5. **Br** Rarely naturalised.

D *Anemone sylvestris* Differs from Wood Anemone in being hairy and having large white flowers, 4-7cm, and only 5 petaloid sepals; fruit woolly, elongated and strawberry-shaped. Widely scattered in dry woodlands and scrub; absent from Scandinavia and NW France. **Fl** 4-6. **Br** Absent.

E **Hepatica** *Hepatica nobilis* Hairless or slightly hairy perennial to 20cm with very distinctive 3-lobed evergreen fleshy leaves, untoothed, dark green (often mottled), purplish below. Flowers bluish violet (occasionally pink or white) with 6-9 petaloid sepals and 3 sepal-like bracts beneath. Locally frequent in woods on calcareous soils. **Fl** 3-5. **Br** Absent.

PASQUE FLOWERS *Pulsatilla* Leaves pinnately divided and fruits with elongated feathery styles. The coloured petal-like segments of the flower are really sepals.

F **Pasqueflower** *Pulsatilla vulgaris* Hairy with erect flowering stem to 30cm, usually much less. Basal leaves silky when young, twice-pinnately divided into long linear segments. Stem leaves 3, unstalked and divided into narrow segments. Flowers 5-8cm in diameter, *erect at first*, later drooping. Petaloid sepals 6, purple-violet; anthers bright yellow. Local and declining on dry calcareous grasslands. **Fl** 4-5. **Br** Very local in S and E England.

G **Small Pasqueflower** *Pulsatilla pratensis* Very like Pasqueflower, but differs in having smaller bell-shaped flowers, 3-4cm, *always drooping* and with sepals recurved at the tips, often greyish violet or yellow. Local to locally frequent; in turf on sandy soils, and in mountains. **Fl** 4-6. **Br** Absent.

H *Pulsatilla patens* Differs from Pasqueflower in having *broadly lobed basal leaves*, and flowers 5-8cm, bluish violet, with widely spreading sepals. Lowland meadows; in the east of the area. **Fl** 4-5. **Br** Absent.

I *Pulsatilla vernalis* Like *P. patens*, has basal leaves broadly lobed, but is *evergreen*, and has flowers 4-6cm with *sepals white inside* and tinged pinkish or purplish on the outside, often with a downy covering of yellow hairs. *Stem leaves unstalked*, like Pasqueflower. Local in mountain grassland or hills, often on sandy soils and near melting snow. **Fl** 4-6. **Br** Absent.

J *Pulsatilla alba* Differs from previous species in having *outside of sepals also white*, basal leaves finely divided and *stem leaves stalked*. Mountain grassland; in the south and east of the region. **Fl** 5-7. **Br** Absent.

K *Pulsatilla alpina* ssp *alpina* Flowers very like *P. vernalis*, but *finely divided stem leaves are stalked*. Mountain grassland, on calcareous soils; mainly a central and S European species. **Fl** 5-7. **Br** Absent.

CLEMATIS *Clematis* Perennial woody climbers or herbs with opposite leaves and 4 petaloid sepals. Fruits conspicuous bearded structures formed by clusters of 1-seeded achenes with persistent feathery styles.

L **Traveller's Joy, Old Man's Beard** *Clematis vitalba* *Woody climber* to 30m with pinnate leaves divided into pointed leaflets. Flowers creamy or greenish white, fragrant, in terminal or lateral loose clusters. Widespread and common; in hedgerows, woodland margins and scrub, on calcareous soils. **Fl** 7-9. **Br** Common from Lancashire and Yorkshire southwards. Introduced in Ireland.

M *Clematis alpina* Woody climber much shorter than previous species, to 1-2m with twice-pinnate leaves having more finely toothed leaflets, and large, nodding flowers to 4cm, and showy with bluish-violet sepals. Local in shady and rocky places or scrub in mountains. **Fl** 5-7. **Br** Absent.

N *Clematis recta* Differs from previous 2 species in being an erect herb to 1.5m, *neither woody nor twining*. Leaves pinnate with leaflets untoothed. Flowers whitish, in terminal umbel-like clusters. In open dry woodlands and scrub. **Fl** 5-6. **Br** Absent.

PHEASANT'S-EYES *Adonis* Annuals or perennials with feathery pinnate leaves like the pasqueflowers but pheasant's-eyes have both petals and sepals, with fruits as elongated heads of non-feathery wrinkled achenes. Petals do not have a basal nectary.

O **Pheasant's-eye** *Adonis annua* Erect hairless annual to 40cm, with stems often branched. Leaves 3-pinnate with very narrow segments, the *lower leaves unstalked*. Flowers terminal and erect with 5-8 bright scarlet petals, blackish at the base. Sepals spreading, *hairless*. Widespread, but decreasing; on arable and disturbed, calcareous soils. **Fl** 6-8. **Br** Rare and decreasing on arable land in S England.

P *Adonis flammea* Differs from Pheasant's-eye in having *hairy sepals* adpressed to petals. Very local in similar habitats; N France and central Germany southwards. **Fl** 6-8. **Br** Absent.

Q *Adonis aestivalis* Like *A. flammea*, has adpressed sepals, but in this case they are *hairless* and *lower leaves are stalked*. On arable land. **Fl** 6-9. **Br** Absent.

R *Adonis vernalis* Erect perennial to 30cm with typical *Adonis* 2- to 3-pinnate feathery leaves but with large showy *yellow flowers* 4-8cm in diameter, with 10-20 long shiny petals. Local or rare in dry grassland, and occasionally open woodland; absent from the north and north-west. **Fl** 4-5. **Br** Absent.

A	B	C
D	E	F
I	K	L
M	O	R

A **Wood Anemone**
B *Anemone narcissiflora*
C **Yellow Anemone**
D *Anemone sylvestris*
E **Hepatica**
F **Pasqueflower**
I *Pulsatilla vernalis*
K *Pulsatilla alpina*
L **Traveller's Joy**
M *Clematis alpina*
O **Pheasant's-eye**
R *Adonis vernalis*

B
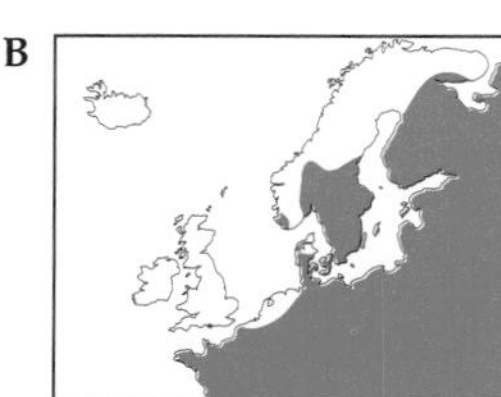
D
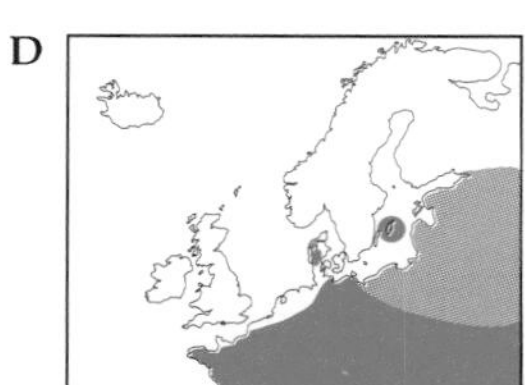
E
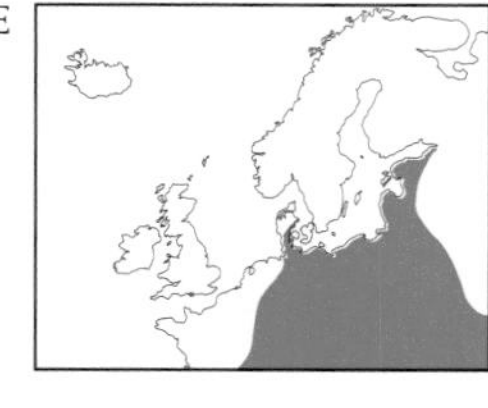
F

G
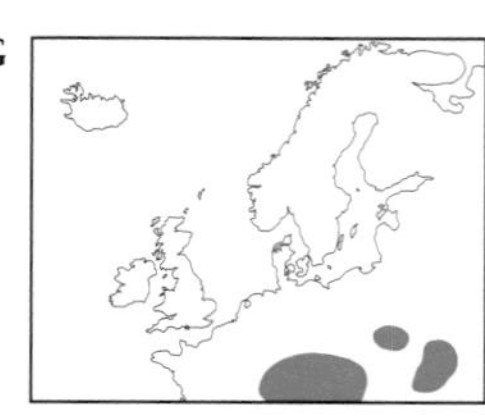
H

BUTTERCUPS AND CROW-FOOTS

Ranunculus Annuals or perennials, sometimes aquatic. Leaves entire or divided. Flowers yellow or white. Petals 5 or more, sepals 3-5. Each petal has a basal nectary.

(1) Palmately divided leaves with coarsely toothed lobes; erect or spreading sepals. Flowers yellow.

A **Meadow Buttercup** *Ranunculus acris* Softly hairy perennial to 1m, often much less. Basal leaves long-stalked and rather rounded in outline, divided into 3-7 unstalked and wedge-shaped coarsely toothed lobes (**a1**). Lower stem leaves similar, but upper stem leaves unstalked and more deeply cut into narrower linear lobes. Flowers bright golden yellow, 18-25mm in diameter, *on long unfurrowed stalks*. Achene with a hooked beak (**a2**). Very common throughout; in grassland of roadsides, meadows and ditches. **Fl** 4-9. **Br** Throughout.

B *Ranunculus polyanthemos* Very similar to Meadow Buttercup and easily misidentified, but has *basal leaves deeply cut into 5 narrow linear lobes* (**b**), and receptacle hairy (hairless in Meadow Buttercup). Achene with a curved beak. Widespread and locally frequent; in similar habitats, but often on calcareous soils. **Fl** 5-9. **Br** Absent.

C **Creeping Buttercup** *Ranunculus repens* Variable hairy perennial to 60cm with creeping runners above ground, rooting at the nodes. Basal and lower stem leaves stalked, rather triangular in outline and 3-lobed, the *middle lobe stalked* (**c**). Upper stem leaves unstalked with narrower lobes. *Flower stalks furrowed*. Very common throughout in grassy places, especially on heavier clay soils. **Fl** 5-9. **Br** Very common throughout.

D *Ranunculus nemorosus* Very similar to Creeping Buttercup in terms of leaf shape and flower stalks, but it is not creeping and the *middle lobe of the basal and lower stem leaves is not stalked* (**d**). Widespread and often common in most of the mainland, but absent from the far north and north-west; in grassy places and open woodlands. **Fl** 5-9. **Br** Absent.

E *Ranunculus lanuginosus* *Very hairy* perennial to 70cm with leaves broadly lobed into 3 lobes, not even upper stem leaves deeply divided (**e1**). Flowers with petals orange-yellow towards the base. Achenes with a revolute beak (**e2**). Meadows and damp woodlands, ascending to 1,600m. **Fl** 5-8. **Br** Absent.

F *Ranunculus montanus* Slightly hairy perennial to only 20cm. Basal leaves with 3-5 oval, toothed lobes (**f**); stem leaves similar but smaller, *partially clasping the stem*. Flowers with hairless receptacles. Local in mountain grassland, woodland and screes; in central Europe, to 2,500m. **Fl** 5-8. **Br** Absent.

G *Ranunculus oreophilus* Very similar to *R. montanus*, but stem leaves have *linear lobes* and receptacles of flowers are hairy near insertion of stamens. Local in similar habitats in central Europe. **Fl** 5-8. **Br** Absent.

H **Corn Buttercup** *Ranunculus arvensis* Annual to 60cm. Leaves stalked and pale green, *basal leaves with paddle-shaped lobes*, stem leaves with numerous narrow linear lobes. Flowers a characteristic pale lemon yellow. *Fruits very distinctive large spiny achenes*. Arable weed, now much decreased due to herbicides. **Fl** 5-7. **Br** Now very local or rare, and found mainly in the south.

I **Jersey Buttercup** *Ranunculus paludosus* Hairy perennial to 50cm, with distinctly shaped 3-lobed basal leaves (**i**), and 3-lobed stem leaves, the lobes of which are narrow with the *central lobe stalked*. Flowers distinctly large, 2-3cm in diameter. Achenes in an elongated head, like Celery-leaved Buttercup (*see* page 58). Local in wet places which dry out in the summer; in W and NW France. **Fl** 5-7. **Br** Jersey only.

J **Goldilocks Buttercup** *Ranunculus auricomus* Slightly hairy perennial to 30cm with basal leaves rounded, kidney-shaped, or deeply 3-lobed; *stem leaves with 3-6 very narrow segments*. Flowers distinctive, 15-25mm in diameter usually *with 1 or more petals absent or imperfectly developed*. *Achenes slightly hairy*. Widespread throughout; in damp woodlands or grasslands, often on rather basic soils. **Fl** 4-6. **Br** Rather local throughout, decreasing northwards.

K *Ranunculus affinis* Separated from Goldilocks Buttercup by its *hairless achenes*. Local in sub-Arctic. **Fl** 6-7. **Br** Absent.

L *Ranunculus pygmaeus* Tiny perennial to 5cm, with *flowers 5-10mm in diameter*, petals not deformed or absent. *Basal leaves kidney-shaped and 3-lobed*. Frequent in damp turf in Arctic and sub-Arctic. **Fl** 7-8. **Br** Absent.

M *Ranunculus nivalis* Similar to *R. pygmaeus*, but to 15cm tall with *flowers 12-15mm in diameter*. Frequent near snow patches in Arctic and sub-Arctic. **Fl** 7-8. **Br** Absent.

N *Ranunculus sulphureus* Has flowers like *R. nivalis*, but *basal leaves only shallowly lobed* and sepals with dense brown hairs. Very local, in Arctic tundra. **Fl** 6-8. **Br** Absent.

O *Ranunculus hyperboreus* Very distinctive in that it is creeping and has deeply cut, 5-lobed leaves and 5mm flowers with only 3 petals and sepals. Local in wet places in Arctic. **Fl** 7-8. **Br** Absent.

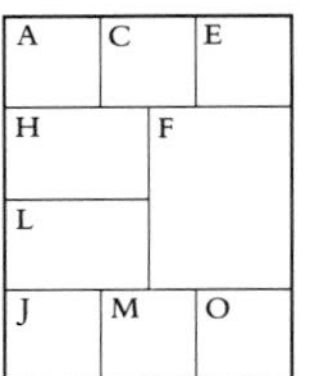

A **Meadow Buttercup**

C **Creeping Buttercup**

E *Ranunculus lanuginosus*

H **Corn Buttercup**

L *Ranunuculus pygmaeus*

F *Ranunculus montanus*

J **Goldilocks Buttercup**

M *Ranunculus nivalis*

O *Ranunculus hyperboreus*

A

D

K

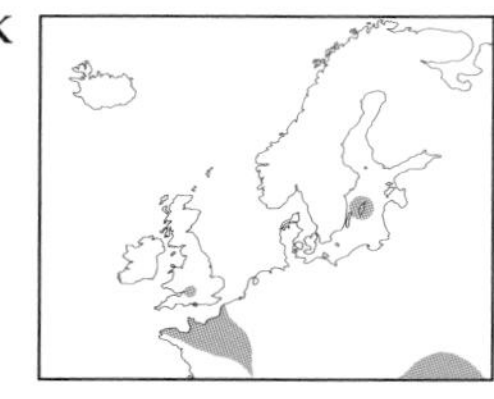

L

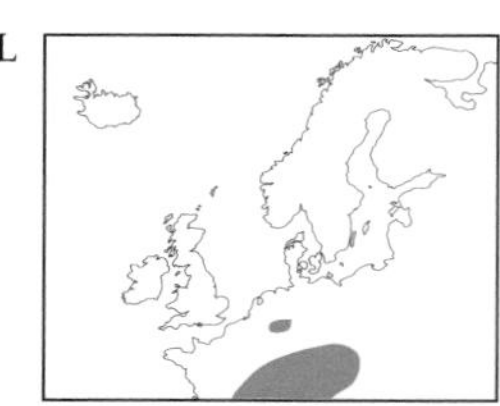

M

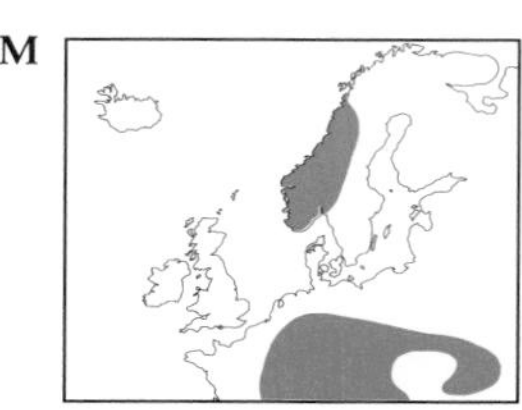

N

(2) Palmately divided leaves; sepals downturned. Flowers yellow.

A Small-flowered Buttercup *Ranunculus parviflorus* Hairy annual to 30cm, usually much less and often very short, with several decumbent branches. Very distinctive in form and habit, but easily missed as a *Ranunculus* species. Basal leaves yellowish green, stalked and rather rounded in outline with 3-5 broadly wedge-shaped lobes; stem leaves with narrower lobes. *Flowers very distinctive*: tiny (3-5mm in diameter), *with 1-5 narrow oval petals, occasionally absent altogether*. Flowers borne opposite a leaf or in the fork of a branch. Stamens 1-8, fewer if there are a large number of petals and vice-versa. Local on bare often sandy soils and grassy banks. **Fl** 4-7. **Br** Local in England and Wales.

B Celery-leaved Buttercup *Ranunculus sceleratus* Pale green hairless or slightly hairy annual to 60cm. Basal leaves stalked, deeply 3-lobed with the lobes further divided into narrow segments; lower stem leaves often shiny, short-stalked and divided into 2-3 narrow segments. *Flowers pale yellow*, 5-10mm in diameter, numerous in branched clusters. *Fruit heads distinctly elongated*. Widespread throughout, and varying from local to common; in wet places, streamsides and ditches. **Fl** 5-9. **Br** Locally common, mainly in the south; absent from parts of the north.

C Bulbous Buttercup *Ranunculus bulbosus* Hairy *perennial* to 40cm with markedly swollen stem-base underground. *Hairs are appressed above, spreading below*. Basal leaves stalked and 3-lobed. Flower stalks furrowed; flowers 20-30mm in diameter, *bright yellow*. After flowering, vegetative parts often disappear for a short period during the summer. Widespread and often very common; in dry grassland, often on calcareous soils. Absent from the far north. **Fl** 3-7. **Br** Common throughout, but more so in the south.

D Hairy Buttercup *Ranunculus sardous* Similar to previous species, but hairy *annual* with stem base not very swollen underground; *hairs all spreading*. Basal leaves 3-lobed, often shiny. Flowers 12-25mm, *pale yellow*; sepals often have dark marginal lines beneath (most easily seen in bud). Achenes with a row of tiny tubercles within a green border. Widespread in grassy places, often near the coast; occasionally in arable land on clay. Absent from the far north. **Fl** 5-10. **Br** Rather local, most frequent in the south near the coast.

E *Ranunculus illyricus* Hairy perennial to 40cm with *distinctive basal leaves divided into 3 long narrow segments*. Flowers 20-35mm. Fruit head elongated. Local in dry grassland; in S Germany and Poland, mainly a S European species. **Fl** 5-7. **Br** Absent.

F *Ranunculus lapponicus* Creeping perennial rooting at nodes and with erect flowering shoots to 15cm. Leaves 3-lobed (**f**) and flowers 8-12mm in diameter with 6-8 petals. Mountain grassland; in Arctic and sub-Arctic areas. **Fl** 7-8. **Br** Absent.

(3) Leaves heart-shaped or lanceolate, undivided. Sepals erect. Flowers yellow.

G Lesser Celandine *Ranunculus ficaria* Hairless perennial to 25cm with fleshy triangular or heart-shaped leaves having wavy margins. Sometimes has bulbils in axils of leaf stalks. Flowers bright yellow, paling with age and 20-30mm in diameter, with 8-12 petals and 3 sepals. Widespread and very common in bare damp ground; absent from much of Scandinavia and also Iceland. **Fl** 2-5. **Br** Common throughout.

H Lesser Spearwort *Ranunculus flammula* Variable perennial to 50cm, erect or decumbent with lower stems often reddish. Basal leaves oblong, often sparsely toothed; stem leaves lanceolate. Flowers few, bright yellow and *7-18mm in diameter*, on furrowed and *slightly hairy* stalks. Widespread and common, but absent from much of Scandinavia and also Iceland; in a variety of damp or wet places. **Fl** 5-9. **Br** Common throughout.

I Creeping Spearwort *Ranunculus reptans* Creeping perennial with *stem rooting at every node* from which arise tufts of long-stalked elliptical leaves to 20mm long. Flowers 5-10mm and solitary. Local in damp sandy or gravelly ground by lakes and ponds; most frequent in Scandinavia. **Fl** 6-8. **Br** Probably extinct; all existing plants in Cumbria and Scotland seem to be hybrids with Lesser Spearwort. Such plants can be identified by their longer leaves, and by not rooting at every node.

J Greater Spearwort *Ranunculus lingua* Robust perennial to 1.2m, with stems creeping at first then ascending and hollow. Stem leaves lanceolate, to 25cm long and usually untoothed. Flowers bright yellow, *30-50mm in diameter*, on unfurrowed stalks. Widespread and locally common in marshes, fens and ponds; absent from the far north. **Fl** 6-9. **Br** Local throughout.

K Adder's-tongue Spearwort *Ranunculus ophioglossifolius* Erect annual to 40cm, with stalked *heart-shaped basal leaves* and elliptical short-stalked or unstalked stem leaves. Flowers 6-9mm in diameter, their stalks rather furrowed but *hairless*. Very local or rare in marshy areas or pond-edges where surrounding vegetation is not too dense. **Fl** 5-7. **Br** Now confined to 2 sites in Gloucestershire.

(4) Flowers white.

L *Ranunculus aconitifolius* Erect tufted perennial to 60cm. Basal leaves stalked with 3-5 lanceolate toothed lobes, *the central lobe free to the base*; stem leaves similar with narrower lobes and unstalked. Flowers 10-20mm in diameter, in branched clusters. Sepals purplish-red, shedding as flowers open. In damp grassland in mountains, to 2,500m. **Fl** 5-8. **Br** Absent.

M *Ranunculus platanifolius* Differs in being taller, to 1.3m, having 5- to 7-lobed leaves, *the central lobe not free to the base*. Widespread in marshes and damp woodland, usually at lower altitudes than previous species; in southern central part of area and W Scandinavia. **Fl** 5-8. **Br** Absent.

N *Ranunculus glacialis* Hairless perennial to 20cm. Distinctive with its thick 3- to 5-lobed basal leaves, upper unstalked leaves with narrow lanceolate lobes and *large flowers 25-40mm in diameter*, pink-tinged with age. Local in rocky or stony places in mountains, often near snow patches. **Fl** 7-10. **Br** Absent.

A	B	C
G	H	
D	I	J
K	L	N

A Small-flowered Buttercup
B Celery-leaved Buttercup
C Bulbous Buttercup
G Lesser Celandine
H Lesser Spearwort
D Hairy Buttercup
I Creeping Spearwort
J Greater Spearwort
K Adder's-tongue Spearwort
L *Ranunculus aconitifolius*
N *Ranunculus glacialis*

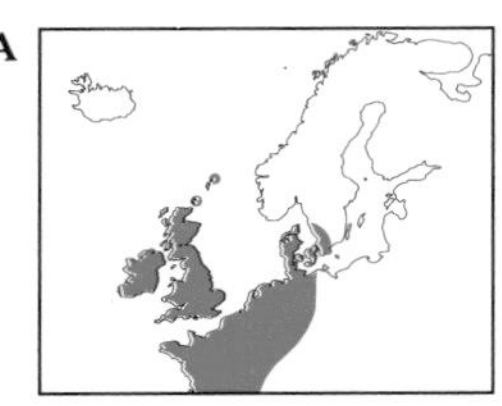
A

B

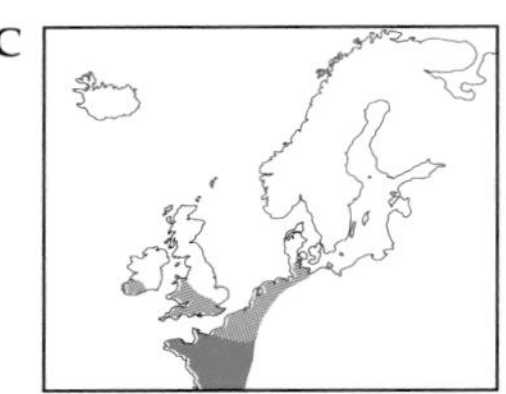
C

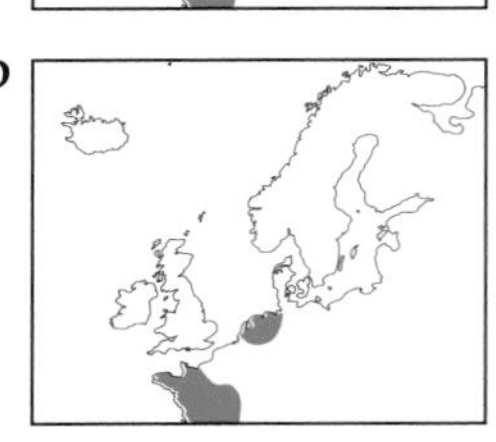
D

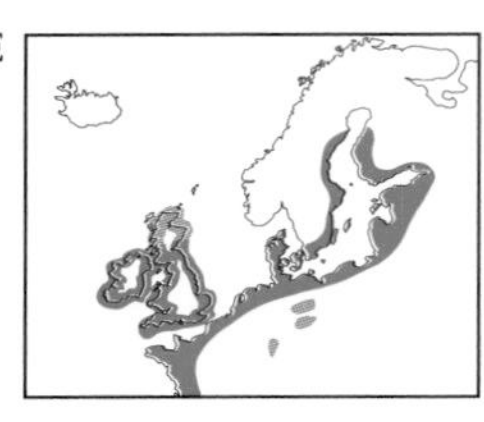
E

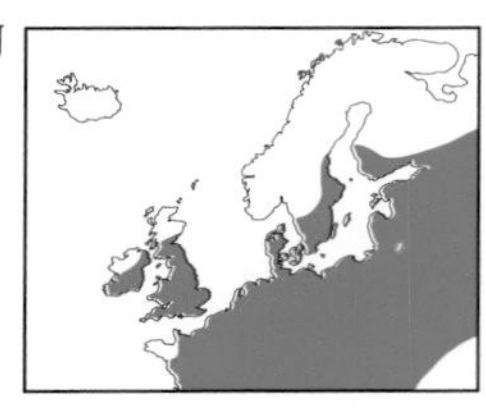
J

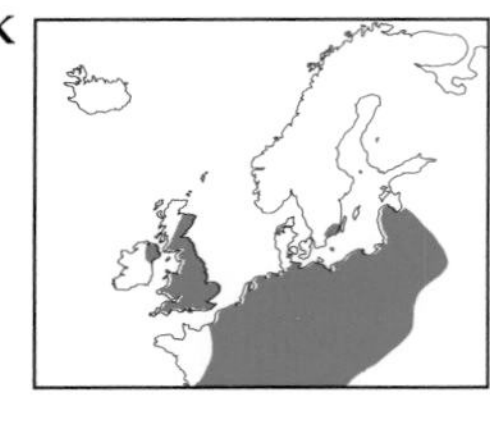
K

CROWFOOTS AND WATER-CROWFOOTS

A group of mainly aquatic plants, or sometimes growing on bare mud, all with white petals usually having a yellow base. In aquatic species, 2 types of leaves can be present: floating ones which are palmately lobed, and submerged ones which are very finely divided, or sometimes just the latter can be present especially in species which grow in fast-moving water.

The following subdivisions to aid identification apply only where the plant is found in water; on land the finely divided leaves will usually be absent anyway.

(1) Submerged leaves always absent.

A **Ivy-leaved Crowfoot** *Ranunculus hederaceus* Creeping annual or biennial with numerous leaves, all kidney- or heart-shaped and shallowly lobed (**a**). Flowers 3-6mm in diameter, *petals equal to or slightly longer than sepals*. Locally common in bare muddy places or sometimes ditches. **Fl** 5-9. **Br** Rather local throughout.

B **Round-leaved Crowfoot** *Ranunculus omiophyllus* Very similar to Ivy-leaved Water-crowfoot, but leaves more deeply lobed with lobes almost touching (**b**) and flowers 8-12mm in diameter with *petals twice the length of sepals*. Rather local in shallow non-calcareous water or bare mud. **Fl** 5-8. **Br** More local than previous species; most frequent in the south and west, scarce elsewhere.

(2) Both submerged and floating leaves usually present; floating leaves occasionally absent.

C **Three-lobed Crowfoot** *Ranunculus tripartitus* Aquatic annual or perennial, usually with both floating and submerged leaves but the latter absent in plants growing on bare mud. Floating leaves deeply 3-lobed, roundish in outline (**c1**); submerged leaves with very slender segments, *weak and collapsing out of water* (**c2**). Flowers 3-10mm in diameter; petals 6mm or less, not touching and *not more than twice as long as sepals*. Very local in muddy pools, ditches and shallow ponds; generally declining. **Fl** 4-6. **Br** Rare, in S England and Wales.

D *Ranunculus ololeucos* Differs from Three-lobed Water-crowfoot in having petals 6mm or more, touching each other and *more than twice as long as sepals*. In muddy pools, ponds and ditches; local in the north and west of mainland Europe. **Fl** 4-6. **Br** Absent.

E **Brackish Water-crowfoot** *Ranunculus baudotii* Aquatic annual or perennial with floating leaves deeply 3-lobed (occasionally absent), similar to Three-leaved Water-crowfoot, but kidney-shaped in outline (**e1**). Also differs in having *non-collapsing submerged leaves* (**e2**), and *flowers 12-18mm in diameter*. Widespread in brackish water of pools and ditches, usually near the coast. **Fl** 5-9. **Br** Local round the coasts.

F **Common Water-crowfoot** *Ranunculus aquatilis* Annual or perennial aquatic usually with both floating (**f1**) and submerged (**f2**) leaves, the latter occasionally absent. *Floating leaves deeply divided into 3-7 straight-sided segments with teeth at the tips. Flowers 12-18mm in diameter*, petals 5-10mm; fruit stalk up to 50mm. Widespread and often common in still or slow-moving shallow water. **Fl** 4-8. **Br** Frequent throughout.

G **Pond Water-crowfoot** *Ranunculus peltatus* Annual or perennial aquatic with similar floating leaves (**g1**) to Common Water-crowfoot, but the segments have rounded sides. Also, *flowers larger, 15-30mm in diameter*, with petals 8-15mm and fruit stalk 50-150mm. NB *Submerged leaves not collapsing out of water, and shorter than stem internodes* (**g2**) (compare with *R. penicillatus*.) Widespread and frequent almost throughout; in ponds, lakes and ditches. **Fl** 5-8. **Br** Frequent throughout.

H *Ranunculus penicillatus* Floating leaves (**h1**) like Pond Water-crowfoot. *Submerged leaves collapsing, longer than internodes* (**h2**). Widespread in faster-flowing streams and rivers, often in calcareous areas. **Fl** 5-7. **Br** Locally frequent; absent from N Scotland.

(3) Floating leaves always absent.

I **Thread-leaved Water-crowfoot** *Ranunculus trichophyllus* Perennial with only submerged leaves to 40mm long, with *segments not all lying in 1 plane* (**i**). Flowers 6-12mm in diameter; fruit stalk under 40mm. Widespread throughout; in ponds, ditches, canals and streams. **Fl** 5-7. **Br** Throughout, but local in Scotland and Wales.

J **Fan-leaved Water-crowfoot** *Ranunculus circinatus* Perennial with only submerged leaves to 30mm, circular in outline with the *segments rigid and all lying in 1 plane* (**j**). Flowers 8-18mm in diameter; fruit stalk 30-80mm. Widespread, but often local; in ditches, canals and slow streams. **Fl** 6-8. **Br** Locally common, but more scarce in N Scotland and Ireland.

K **River Water-crowfoot** *Ranunculus fluitans* Robust perennial with only submerged leaves *10-30cm long* (**k**), the segments greenish black and almost parallel. Flowers 20-30mm in diameter; petals 5-10, overlapping. Stems to 6m long. Widespread and locally frequent in fast-flowing streams and rivers; absent from most of Scandinavia. **Fl** 5-8. **Br** Locally frequent north to S Scotland, but rare in Wales and Ireland.

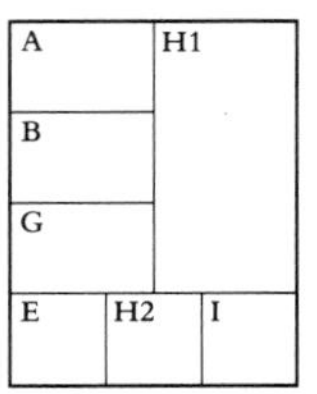

A **Ivy-leaved Crowfoot**

B **Round-leaved Crowfoot**

H **1** *Ranunculus penicillatus* showing the long submerged leaves

G **Pond Water-crowfoot** showing a dense mass of flowers, typical of water-crowfoots

E **Brackish Water-crowfoot**

H **2** *Ranunculus penicillatus* showing flowers

I **Thread-leaved Water-crowfoot**

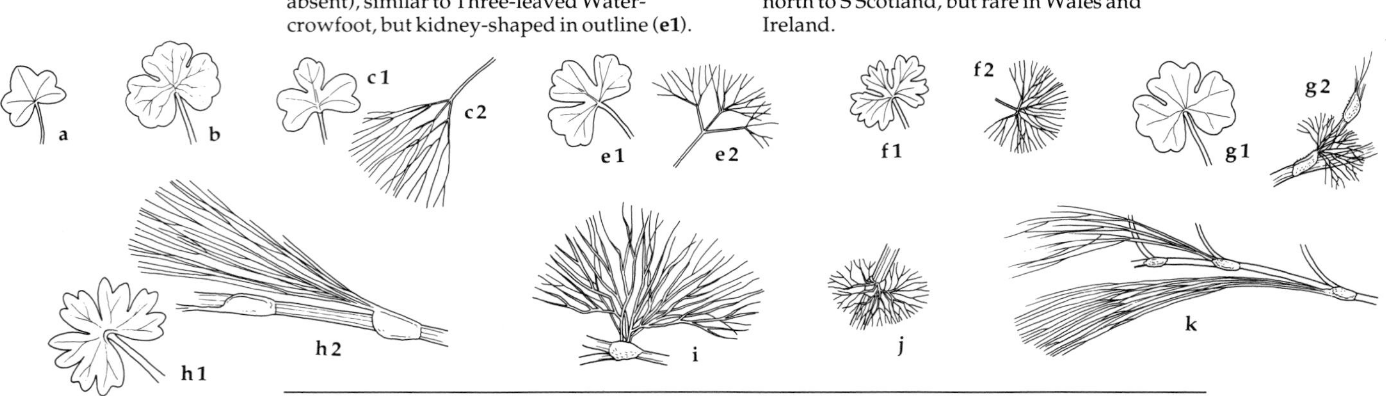

C

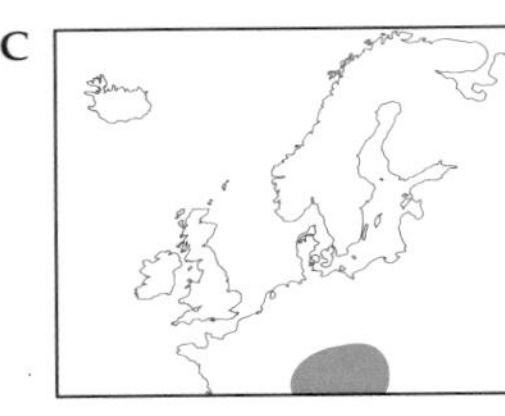

D

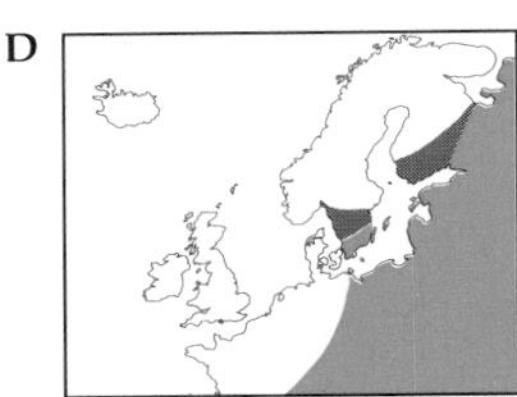

E

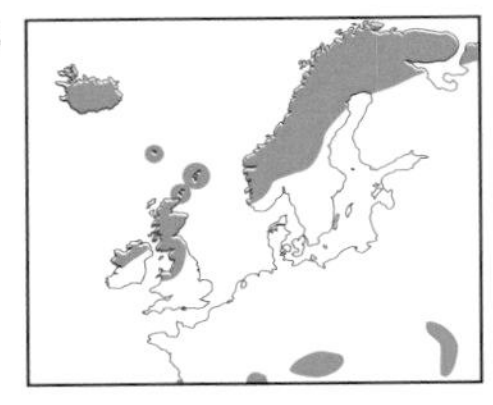

G

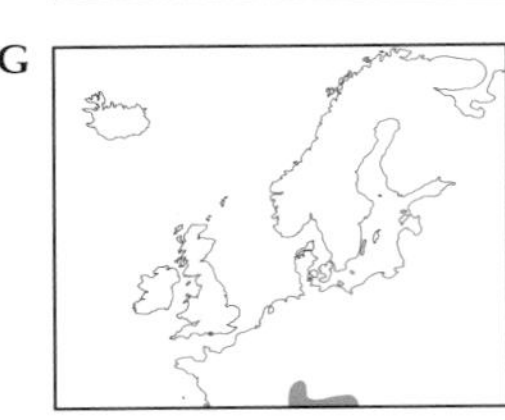

J

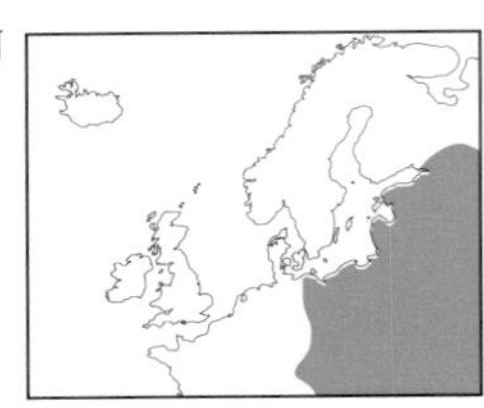

K

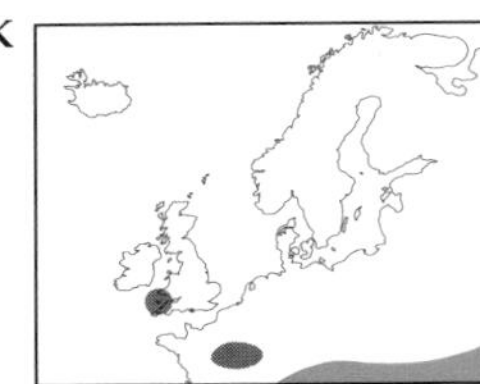

A **Mousetail** *Myosurus minimus* Distinctive, but easily overlooked, low annual from 5-12cm. Leaves rather fleshy, linear and in a basal tuft. Flowers tiny, to 5mm in diameter, pale greenish yellow and solitary on long stalks; petals and sepals 5-7. Fruit a characteristic elongated, to 7cm, head of tiny achenes, resembling a 'tail'. Widespread but decreasing in bare, often sandy, soils and arable field- margins; absent from the far north. **Fl** 3-7.
Br Increasingly rare, now mainly in S England.

B **Columbine** *Aquilegia vulgaris* Hairless erect perennial to 1m, with twice-trifoliate basal leaves on long stalks and nodding flowers, 30-50mm long, usually blue but rarely white or bluish red. Petals 5, with distinctive long hooked spurs bearing nectaries; *stamens not or hardly protruding beyond petals*. Widespread, but local or absent in the north; in a variety of habitats, including damp open woods, scrub and fens. **Fl** 5-7. **Br** Rather local northwards to S Scotland; very local in Ireland.

C *Aquilegia atrata* Similar to Columbine, but has dark violet flowers with *stamens protruding well beyond the petals*. Local, in open mountain woodlands on limestone; in E France and S Germany. **Fl** 5-7. **Br** Absent..

MEADOW-RUES *Thalictrum* Perennials with rather fern-like compound leaves and flowers having 4-5 petaloid sepals and a feathery appearance as a result of the multiple protruding stamens.

D *Thalictrum aquilegifolium* Tall, to 1.5m, with twice- trifoliate leaves and rather broad toothed leaflets. Flowers in a dense branched head with distinctive lilac stamens. Fruit with 3 wings. Woods and scrub, especially in hills and mountains. **Fl** 6-7. **Br** Absent.

E **Alpine Meadow-rue** *Thalictrum alpinum Slender*, easily overlooked, plant *to only 15cm tall*, with twice-trifoliate dark green leaves and tiny rounded leaflets. Flowers in a terminal raceme, the lower flowers drooping, all with purplish sepals and stamens and yellow anthers. Local in damp mountain-ledges and turf. **Fl** 5-7. **Br** Very local from N Wales to N Scotland; rare in W Ireland.

F **Common Meadow-rue** *Thalictrum flavum* To 1m tall with leaves 2- to 3-pinnate, *the end-leaflet being longer than broad* and *toothed. Stems not shiny (see T. morisonii)*. Flowers erect in dense clusters, and appearing yellowish despite white sepals because of the feathery, protruding, erect stamens. Widespread and frequent in damp meadows, fens or by streams and lakes, especially on basic soils, but absent from mountainous areas. **Fl** 6-8. **Br** Frequent throughout, except extreme N Scotland.

G *Thalictrum morisonii* Differs in being taller, to 1. 8m, having *stems shiny* and *end-leaflets of upper leaves untoothed*. Very local in meadows; in E France and SW Germany. **Fl** 6-7. **Br** Absent.

H **Lesser Meadow-rue** *Thalictrum minus* Very variable species and despite its name, to 1.5m tall (less tall in drier places). Leaves 3- to 4-pinnate, with *end-leaflets as broad as long*. Flowers not densely clustered, *drooping at first then erect*; stamens pendulous. Widespread and locally frequent in a variety of habitats, ranging from dry grassland, dunes and rocky places to streamsides, but generally on base-rich soils. **Fl** 6-8. **Br** Local throughout, but absent from most of central S England.

I *Thalictrum simplex* Another very variable species to 1.2m tall, with 2- 3-pinnate leaves like Common Meadow-rue, end-leaflets longer than wide, but with flowers like Lesser Meadow-rue – *drooping* at first with pendulous stamens. Local in damp grassland and stream-margins; in the east of the region. **Fl** 6-8. **Br** Absent.

J *Thalictrum lucidum* Differs from *T. simplex* in having unstalked leaves and dense rounded clusters of flowers. Local in meadows and grassy places in the south-east of the region. **Fl** 6-7. **Br** Absent.

Peony Family Paeoniaceae

Perennial herbs or shrubs with alternate leaves, solitary flowers with 5-10 petals, 5 sepals, numerous stamens, and fruits consisting of a group of up to 8 follicles, each follicle bearing several seeds.

K **Peony** *Paeonia mascula* Stout perennial herb to 50cm, with twice-trifoliate leaves, dark green and shiny. Flowers solitary, 8-12cm in diameter with up to 10 shiny petals. Follicles 3-5, recurved and with seeds first red, then blue and finally black. Mainly a S European species, in rocky places and cliffs; in N central France; introduced elsewhere. **Br** Introduced and well established on Steep Holm in Bristol Channel.

Barberry Family Berberidaceae

Herbs or shrubs with alternate leaves, hermaphrodite flowers with 6-9 perianth segments in several whorls, and 4-6 stamens opposite a similar number of nectar-bearing petals. Fruit a berry or capsule.

L **Barberry** *Berberis vulgaris* Deciduous shrub to 3m with long ribbed shoots bearing 3-spined prickles, from the axils of which arise very short shoots bearing tufts of sharply toothed oval leaves. Flowers yellow in pendulous racemes, perianth segments 15 in 5 whorls. Fruit an orange-red elliptical berry. Widespread in hedgerows and scrub, often on calcareous soils; most frequent in central Europe. **Fl** 5-6. **Br** Very local throughout. Possibly native in some localities, although introduced in many. Not native in Ireland.

M **Oregon-grape** *Mahonia aquifolium* Evergreen shrub to 2m, with holly-like dark green glossy leaves, pinnately divided into identical leaflets, and yellow flowers in dense spikes. Fruit globose, blue-black like a small grape. Introduced from N America and widely naturalised in hedges and scrub. **Fl** 1-5. **Br** Locally naturalised and widely scattered, mainly in central and E England.

A	B	D
E		F
H	M	K
L		

A **Mousetail**
B **Columbine**
D *Thalictrum aquilegifolium*
E **Alpine Meadow-rue**
F **Common Meadow-rue**
H **Lesser Meadow-rue**
M **Oregon-grape**
L **Barberry**
K **Peony**

B

G

I

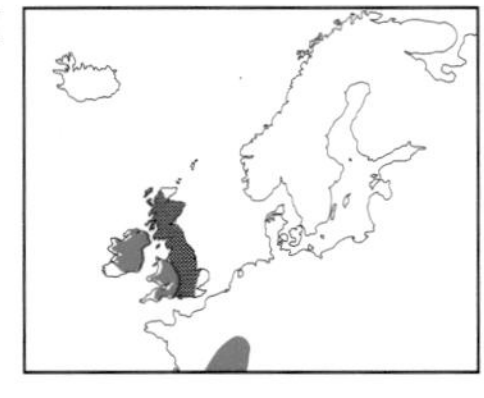

J

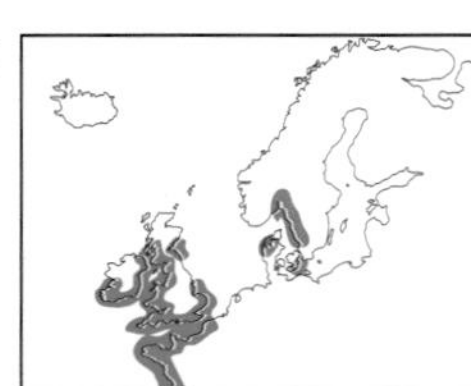

Poppy Family Papaveraceae

Herbs with milky or slightly coloured latex and leaves usually deeply divided. Flowers with 4 petals and 2 sepals which fall early; stamens numerous. Fruit a capsule opening by pores or splitting into valves.

(1) Flowers red with petals overlapping at base when flowers open wide.

A **Common Poppy** *Papaver rhoeas* Annual to 60cm, often with *spreading hairs*. Leaves deeply divided into narrow segments, the lower leaves stalked and the upper ones sessile. Flowers 7-10cm with 4 overlapping scarlet *petals often having a dark blotch at the base*. Capsule ovoid (**a**). Common in arable and waste areas; absent from the far north. **Fl** 6-9. **Br** Common but declining in England; local in N Scotland, Wales and W Ireland.

B **Long-headed Poppy** *Papaver dubium* Similar to Common Poppy, but has *appressed hairs;* flowers 3-7cm in diameter with orange-red overlapping *petals which do not have a dark blotch at the base*; anthers purplish-tinged (compare with Yellow-juiced Poppy, below). Capsule more than twice as long as wide, gradually narrowing downwards from the top (**b**). Locally common in arable and waste areas. **Fl** 6-8. **Br** Locally common throughout.

C **Rough Poppy** *Papaver hybridum* Similar to previous 2 species, but leaves bristle-pointed, flowers 2-5cm with crimson overlapping *petals that have a dark blotch at the base*. Capsule rounded with *dense yellowish bristles* (**c**). Local to rare, in arable and waste areas, often on calcareous soils; absent from the north. **Fl** 6-8. **Br** Rare, mainly in S England.

(2) Flowers red with petals not usually overlapping at base when flowers open wide.

D **Yellow-juiced, or Babington's, Poppy** *Papaver lecoqii* Annual with *latex turning yellow on exposure*. Flowers 3-8cm in diameter with red petals not usually overlapping and *not having a dark blotch at the base;* anthers yellow (compare with Long-headed Poppy). Capsule more than twice as long as wide (**d**). Local in arable and waste areas, mainly on calcareous soils; absent from the east and north. **Fl** 6-8. **Br** Scattered localities in S and E England.

E **Prickly Poppy** *Papaver argemone* Annual with bristle-pointed leaves. Flowers 2-6cm in diameter with pale red petals not usually overlapping at base but having *a dark blotch*. Capsule narrowly oblong and *ribbed with erect bristles* (**e**). Local in arable and waste areas, usually on sandy soils; absent from the north. **Fl** 5-9. **Br** Local, mainly in the south.

(3) Flowers not red.

F **Opium Poppy** *Papaver somniferum* *Greyish-green waxy* annual to 1m. Leaves oblong and coarsely toothed. Flowers large, to 18cm; *petals pale lilac* or sometimes white, with a dark blotch at the base. Capsule ovoid. Widely naturalised or casual, on cultivated and disturbed ground. **Fl** 6-8. **Br** Introduced throughout.

G *Papaver radicatum* Extremely variable, tufted perennial to 25cm, with yellow latex and *leaves acutely pinnately lobed*. Flowers 3-5cm in diameter, usually yellow but occasionally pinkish or white. Capsule elliptical, widest about the middle. Gravelly or bare rocky places, screes to 1,800m; in Scandinavia. **Fl** 6-8. **Br** Absent.

H *Papaver lapponicum* Like *P. radicatum*, tufted with yellow flowers 3-6cm, but has *leaves with narrow blunt lobes;* capsule pear-shaped, widest towards the top. Gravelly places or tundra. **Fl** 7-8. **Br** Absent.

I **Welsh Poppy** *Meconopsis cambrica* Perennial to 60cm, with pinnate *long-stalked basal leaves*, the *segments coarsely toothed*. Flowers 5-8cm in diameter with overlapping petals orange-yellow on opening but soon changing to yellow. Capsule 4- to 6-ribbed and splitting above to form 4-6 valves. Atlantic distribution in moist, semi-shaded, often rocky, places. **Fl** 6-8. **Br** Locally frequent in Wales, SW England and Ireland.

J **Yellow Horned-poppy** *Glaucium flavum* Greyish biennial or perennial with waxy leaves. Basal leaves long-stalked, deeply pinnately lobed, the lobes progressively longer towards the tip. Flowers 6-9cm in diameter with overlapping yellow petals. *Capsule very distinctive, greatly elongated, slender and curved* to 30cm. Rather local plant in coastal shingle and dunes. **Fl** 6-9. **Br** Locally common round most of the coasts.

K **Greater Celandine** *Chelidonium majus* Perennial to 90cm with brittle stems. Leaves irregularly pinnate with ovate, blunt, coarsely toothed segments. Flowers 2-3cm in diameter with 4 bright yellow petals not overlapping. Fruit a narrow elongated capsule to 5cm, splitting on 2 sides from below. Frequent in hedgebanks, open woods and waste areas, often near habitation; native in most areas but also widely introduced; absent from the far north. **Fl** 4-10. **Br** Throughout, but most frequent in the south.

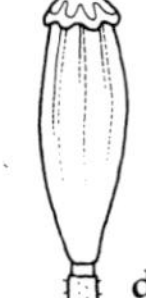

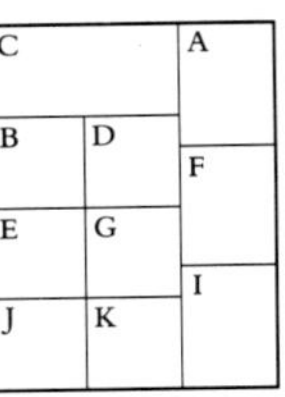

C **Rough Poppy**
A **Common Poppy**
B **Long-headed Poppy**
D **Yellow-juiced Poppy**
E **Prickly Poppy**
F **Opium Poppy**
G *Papaver radicatum*
J **Yellow Horned-poppy**
K **Greater Celandine**
I **Welsh Poppy**

A

F

H

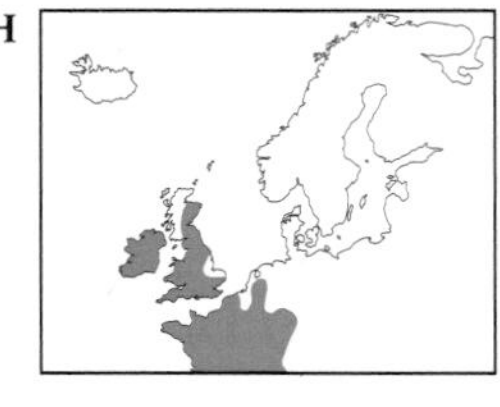

I

K

Fumitory Family Fumariaceae

Delicate herbs with much-divided leaves, and spikes or racemes of 2-lipped flowers which have 2 small sepals, 2 outer petals (1 or both spurred) and 2 inner narrower petals. Fruit an oblong many-seeded capsule in *Corydalis* species or a rounded 1-seeded nutlet in *Fumaria* species.

A **Climbing Corydalis** *Corydalis claviculata* Delicate pale green climbing annual to 80cm, with twice-pinnate leaves ending in a branched tendril. Flowers 5-6mm long, pale creamy white, in racemes opposite leaves. Fruit a 2- to 3-seeded capsule. Local in woodlands, rocky areas or heaths, usually on acid soils or peat. **Fl** 5-9. **Br** Locally common, especially in W Britain, but rare in Ireland.

B **Yellow Corydalis** *Corydalis lutea* Perennial to 30cm, with 2- to 3-pinnate leaves and bright yellow flowers, 12-18mm long, in racemes opposite leaves. Naturalised on old walls and rocky places. **Fl** 5-9. **Br** Scattered throughout.

C *Corydalis solida* Perennial to 20cm with *stem bearing an oval scale near the base*. Leaves twice- or thrice-trifoliate and flowers purplish, 15-30mm long, in dense racemes. Lower *flower stalks more than 5mm. Bracts large and toothed*. Widespread, but local, in open woods, hedgerows and disturbed ground; absent from the north. **Fl** 3-5. **Br** Introduced and naturalised in a few places.

D *Corydalis bulbosa* Very similar to previous species, but differs in *not having an oval scale at the stem base*, in having *untoothed bracts* and in having markedly down-curved spurs to flowers. Similar habitats; from E France eastwards. **Fl** 3-5. **Br** Absent.

E *Corydalis intermedia* Like *C. solida*, but *bracts untoothed* and *flowers 10-15mm long*. Similar habitats. **Fl** 3-5. **Br** Absent.

F *Corydalis pumila* Like *C. solida*, but *flowers 10-15mm long* and lower *flower stalks less than 5mm*. Similar habitats, but much more local. **Fl** 3-5. **Br** Absent.

FUMITORIES *Fumaria* A difficult genus of very closely related annuals.

(1) Flowers 9mm long or more, lower petal not markedly paddle-shaped so that sides are parallel for most of their length.

(a) Upper petal laterally compressed.

G **Western Ramping-fumitory** *Fumaria occidentalis* Robust and sometimes climbing. Inflorescence loose (12-20 flowers), equalling its stalk. *Flowers 12-14mm*, first white then bright pink with dark purple tips (**g1**). Upper petal compressed with *upturned margins concealing the central keel*; lower petal with broad spreading margins (**g2**). Arable and waste areas; in SW England and Scilly Isles only. **Fl** 5-10. **Br** Endemic to Cornwall and Scilly Isles.

H **White Ramping-fumitory** *Fumaria capreolata* Robust and climbing, up to 1m. Inflorescence dense (12-20 flowers), shorter than its stalk. *Flowers 10-14mm*, creamy white with dark purple tips (**h1**). Upper petal compressed but *upturned margins not concealing keel*; lower petal with erect narrow margins (**h2**). *Fruit stalk strongly curved* (**h3**). Local in hedgebanks, scrub and arable land, mainly in the west. **Fl** 5-9. **Br** Scattered throughout, but mostly in the south and west.

I **Tall Ramping-fumitory** *Fumaria bastardii* Robust but not usually climbing. Inflorescence loose (15-25 flowers), *longer than its stalk. Flowers 9-11mm*, pink with a dark purple tip (**i1**). Upper petal laterally compressed, the wings not concealing keel; lower petal with narrow spreading margins (**i2**). Rare to locally frequent, in arable and waste areas; confined to the west. **Fl** 4-10. **Br** Locally frequent in W Britain and Ireland.

(b) Upper petal not laterally compressed.

J **Purple Ramping-fumitory** *Fumaria purpurea* Robust and climbing. Inflorescence loose (15-25 flowers), about equalling its stalk. Flowers 10-13mm, pinkish purple with dark tips (**j1**). Upper petals with broad wings concealing keel; lower petal with narrow spreading margins (**j2**). *Fruit stalk slightly curved*. In hedgebanks and arable areas; British Isles only. **Fl** 7-10. **Br** Endemic. Scattered throughout but very local, or rare, in Scotland, Ireland and E England.

K **Common Ramping-fumitory** *Fumaria muralis* Rather variable: slender and spreading or robust and climbing. Inflorescence loose (12-15 flowers), about equalling its stalk. Flowers (**k1**) either 9-10mm (ssp *muralis*) or 10-20mm (ssp *boraei*), pink with dark tip. Upper petal flattened and spoon-shaped with broad wings concealing keel; *lower petal with narrow erect margins* (**k2**). In hedgebanks, on walls and arable land. **Fl** 4-10. **Br** Ssp *muralis* is rare in SW England and Wales; ssp *boraei* is locally frequent almost throughout.

L **Martin's Ramping-fumitory** *Fumaria martinii* Robust, often climbing. Inflorescence loose (15-20 flowers), *longer than its stalk*. Flowers 11-13mm, pink with dark tips (**l1**). Upper petal with broad wings concealing keel; *lower petal with narrow spreading margins* (**l2**). Rare, in arable areas. **Fl** 5-10. **Br** Very rare in S and SW England.

(2) Flowers not more than 8mm long; lower petal distinctly paddle-shaped, broadening markedly towards tip.

(a) Leaf segments linear, channelled.

M **Dense-flowered Fumitory** *Fumaria densiflora* Rather robust. Inflorescence very dense (20-25 flowers), *much longer than its stalk*. Flowers 6-7mm, pink with dark tips (**m1**); upper petal laterally compressed with erect wings not concealing keel. Lower petal (**m2**). *Bracts longer than fruit stalks*. Locally frequent in arable areas. **Fl** 6-10. **Br** Locally frequent in S England, Scotland and Ireland.

N **Fine-leaved Fumitory** *Fumaria parviflora* Robust, spreading or climbing. Inflorescence dense in flower, (about 20 flowers) but loose in fruit, *almost stalkless*. Flowers 5-6mm, white or pale pink with dark tips (**n1**). Lower petal (**n2**). Sepals a fifth or less the length of flower. *Bracts equal to fruit stalks*. Local in arable land, usually on calcareous soils. **Fl** 6-9. **Br** Local in S and E England; rare elsewhere.

(b) Leaf segments not channelled.

O **Common Fumitory** *Fumaria officinalis* Weak or robust, spreading or climbing. Inflorescence dense first then loose (*20-40 flowers*), longer than its stalk. Flowers 7-8mm, pink with dark tips (**o1**). Lower petal (**o2**). Upper petal flattened, with wings concealing keel.Sepals at least a quarter the length of flower. Bracts shorter than fruit stalks. Fruit (**o3**). Widespread and often common in arable areas. **Fl** 5-10. **Br** Common generally but less so in the west.

P *Fumaria caroliana* Weak or robust. Inflorescence dense (*10-15 flowers*), longer than its short stalk. Flowers 6-7mm, pink with dark tips and similar to Common Fumitory. Sepals at least a quarter the length of flower. Fruit (**p1**). Very local and rare on arable land in NE France. **Fl** 4-9. **Br** Absent.

Q *Fumaria vaillantii* Slender and markedly branched, *with very grey leaves*. Inflorescence loose (*5-16 flowers*), longer than short stalk. Flowers 5-6mm, pale pink with dark tips (**q1**) on *2.5mm stalks*. Upper petal flattened. Lower petal (**q2**). Sepals no more then a fifth the length of flower. Local in arable areas on calcareous soils. **Fl** 6-9. **Br** Very local in S and E England.

R *Fumaria schleicheri* Like *F. vaillantii* but inflorescence with up to 20 flowers and *flower stalk 4mm*. Local in arable areas, south-east of the region. **Fl** 5-9. **Br** Absent.

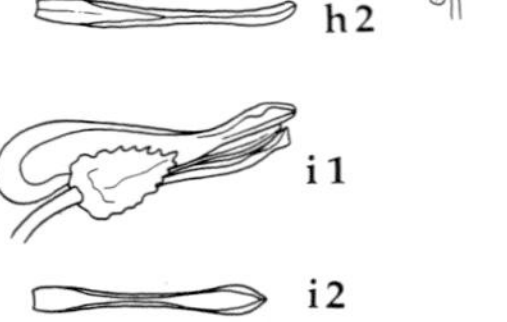

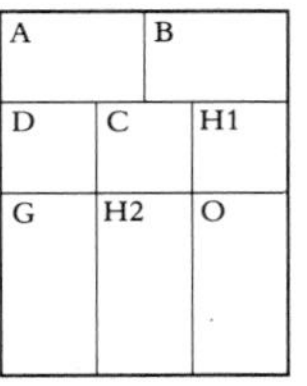

A **Climbing Corydalis**

B **Yellow Corydalis**

D *Corydalis bulbosa*

C *Corydalis solida*

H **1 White Ramping-fumitory** showing broad leaf segments

G **Western Ramping-fumitory**

H **2 White Ramping-fumitory** showing flowers

O **Common Fumitory**

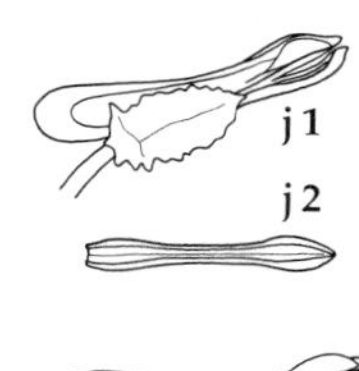

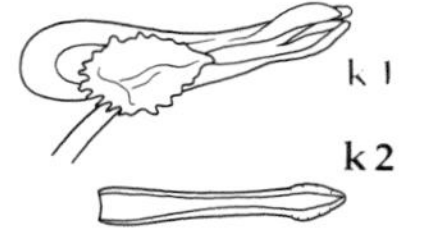

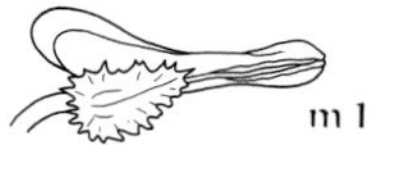

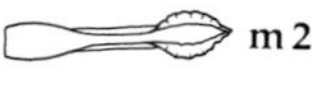

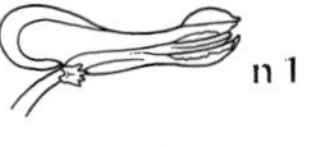

C

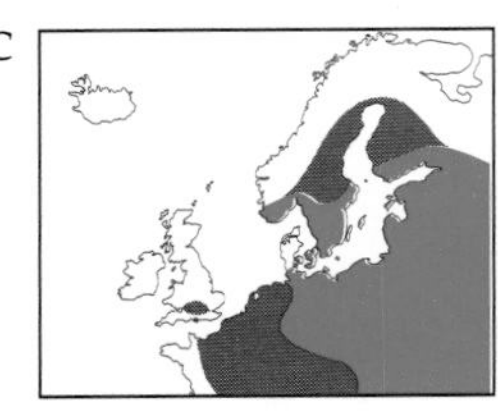

D

H

N

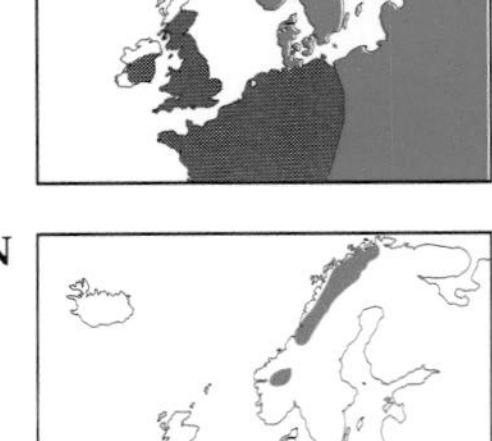

O

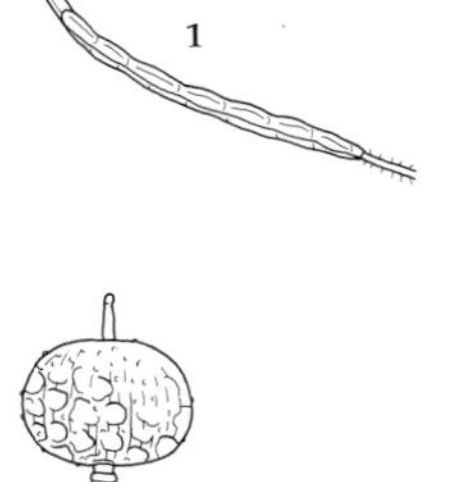

Crucifer Family Cruciferae

A large family of distinctive herbs with 4 free sepals, 4 free petals, 6 stamens and a superior ovary with 2 carpels. The family name is derived from the appearance of the flowers which have the 4 usually equal petals separated and in the form of a cross. The fruit is in the form of a pod, called a siliqua when long and linear (**1**), or a silicula when less than 3 times as long as broad (**2**). The presence or absence of a beak at the top of the pod helps to separate genera.

SISYMBRIUMS *Sisymbrium* Distinguished by having slender fruit (siliqua) not beaked (compare with *Sinapis* and *Coincya*) and valves of pod 3- to 7-veined (veins often indistinct); seeds never extend beyond ends of valves. Stem leaves often have a halberd-shaped larger end-lobe.

A **Hedge Mustard** *Sisimbryum officinale* Stiff, erect annual or biennial to 90cm. *Upper part characteristically branched*. Basal leaves deeply pinnatifid (**a**); stem leaves with halberd-shaped, longer end-lobe. Flowers yellow, 3mm in diameter, in terminal rounded clusters, overtopping the *short fruits (10-20mm) which are closely pressed to the stem*. Widespread and common on waste ground or roadsides. **Fl** 5-10. **Br** Common throughout.

B **London-rocket** *Sisimbryum irio* Erect annual to 60cm, leaves deeply pinnately lobed with the end-lobe larger and halberd-shaped (**b**). *Flowers 3-4mm*, with petals longer than, or equal to, sepals. Fruit 30-50mm long, *overtopping the open flowers*. Introduced and naturalised in waste places and docks. **Fl** 6-8. **Br** Rare, mainly around London and Dublin.

C **False London-rocket** *Sisymbrium loeselii* Differs from preceding species in having flowers 4-6mm, with petals about twice as long as sepals; fruit 20-40mm long, *not overtopping flowers*. Leaves (**c**). Rather local in similar habitats. **Fl** 6-8. **Br** Rare casual, more scattered in England than previous species.

D *Sisymbrium austriacum* Similar to False London-rocket, but biennial or perennial, *flowers 7-10mm and fruit with a persistent 1-2mm style*. Leaves (**d**). Casual in waste areas and docks. **Fl** 6-8. **Br** Very rare casual.

E *Sisymbrium volgense* Similar flowers to *S. austriacum*, but *upper leaves linear-lanceolate* (**e**) *and unlobed except at base*. Fruit to only 45mm. Rare in similar habitats. **Fl** 6-8. **Br** Rare casual.

F *Sisymbrium strictissimum* *All leaves unlobed*, the lower ones ovate (**f**) and the upper ones linear-lanceolate. Flowers 4-6mm. Fruit 50-70mm. Rare in similar habitats. **Fl** 6-8. **Br** Rare casual.

G **Eastern Rocket** *Sisymbrium orientale* Erect annual to 90cm, hairy with downward-pointing hairs. Leaves lobed, *stem leaves stalked and with only a few lateral lobes* and a halberd-shaped, longer end-lobe, or even unlobed (**g**). Basal leaves die before plant flowers. Flowers 7mm in diameter, petals twice length of sepals. Fruit 4-10cm long and *characteristically spreading*. Naturalised or casual in waste areas. **Fl** 6-8. **Br** Most frequent in S England.

H **Tall Rocket** *Sisymbrium altissimum* Erect annual to 1m, hairy only below. Leaves deeply pinnatifid with narrow lobes (**h**); *stem leaves unstalked with long narrow linear or filiform lobes*. Basal leaves dying before plant flowers. Flowers about 11mm in diameter, petals twice length of sepals. Fruit to 10cm long. Naturalised or casual, widespread in waste areas. **Fl** 6-8. **Br** A casual, most frequent in S England; rare in Scotland, Wales and Ireland.

I *Sisymbrium supinum* Annual to 25cm. Leaves pinnately lobed with a longer halberd-shaped end-lobe (**i**). *Flowers white*, 5-7mm in diameter. Fruit 10-30mm. Differs from other white-flowered crucifers in that the pods are not flattened. Very local in arable and waste areas. **Fl** 6-8. **Br** Absent.

J **Flixweed** *Descurainia sophia* Hairy grey-green annual or biennial to 80cm. Leaves 2- to 3-pinnatifid, the segments narrow and linear. Flowers 3mm in diameter, pale yellow; *petals equal sepals, or slightly shorter*. Fruit to 50mm. Widespread on waste areas and roadsides, often on sandy soils. NB Amongst yellow crucifers, only this species, *Sisymbrium irio* (sometimes) and *Rorippa* species have petals equal to sepals. **Fl** 6-8. **Br** Native or long-introduced casual, locally frequent in E England; uncommon elsewhere.

K **Garlic Mustard** *Alliaria petiolata* Biennial to 1.2m. Leaves thin, pale green, heart-shaped and toothed; *smelling strongly of garlic when crushed*. Flowers white, 6mm in diameter, petals twice length of sepals. Widespread in hedgerows, roadsides and woodland margins. **Fl** 4-6. **Br** Common almost throughout, less so in N Scotland and Ireland.

L **Thale Cress** *Arabidopsis thaliana* Annual or biennial to 50cm, roughly hairy below and with a *basal rosette of elliptical, toothed or untoothed leaves*. Flowers 3mm in diameter, white. Fruit a *siliqua to 20mm long*, not flattened (compare with *Arabis* and *Cardaminopsis*, species *see* page 74), and obliquely erect on long stalks; valves 1-veined. Widespread and common in disturbed places on dry sandy soils, or on old walls. **Fl** 3-10. **Br** Fairly common except in upland areas, and uncommon in Ireland.

M *Arabidopsis suecica* Differs from Thale Cress in having *strongly toothed or pinnatifid basal lobes*, flowers 4-5mm and *fruit to 40mm*. Very local in gravelly places; in Scandinavia. **Fl** 5-10. **Br** Absent.

N *Braya linearis* Differs from *A. suecica* in being perennial, having leaves narrow-linear and fruit to 15mm. Very local on calcareous screes. **Fl** 7-8. **Br** Absent.

O **Woad** *Isatis tinctoria* Biennial or perennial to 1.2m, with downy lanceolate basal leaves in a rosette. Stem leaves greyish, arrow-shaped, clasping the stem, yielding a blue dye when dried and crushed. Flowers yellow, 4mm in branched panicle. *Fruit distinctive, broadly winged, purplish brown and pendulous.* Naturalised in dry, often rocky or chalky places. **Fl** 6-8. **Br** Rare and established in a few places in Gloucestershire and Surrey.

P **Warty-cabbage** *Bunias orientalis* Perennial to 1m with most leaves (except the upper) pinnately lobed, and flowers yellow, 15mm in diameter. *Fruit distinctive: ovoid, shiny, long-stalked and warty.* Native in Poland; introduced and established in waste areas and disturbed ground elsewhere. **Fl** 5-8. **Br** Locally established, especially in SE England.

A	B	C
F	K	G
H	O	J
L		P

A **Hedge Mustard**
B **London-rocket**
C **False London-rocket**
F *Sisymbrium strictissimum*
K **Garlic Mustard**
G **Eastern Rocket**
H **Tall Rocket**
J **Flixweed**
L **Thale Cress**
O **Woad**
P **Warty-cabbage**

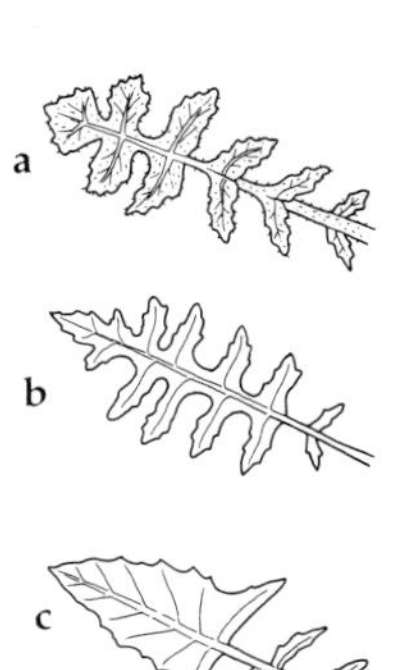

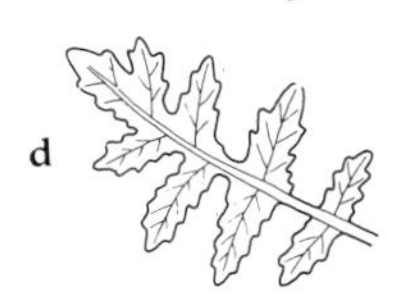

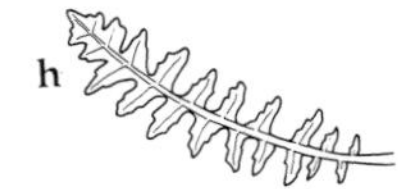

B

C

D

E

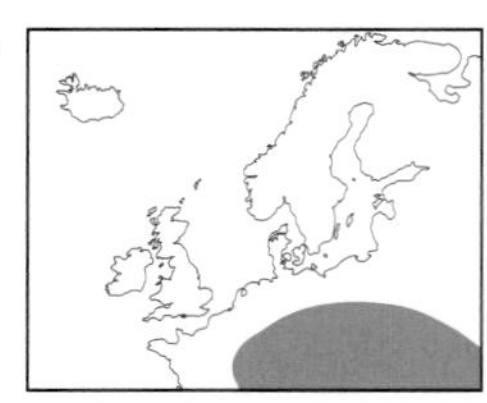

H

I

L

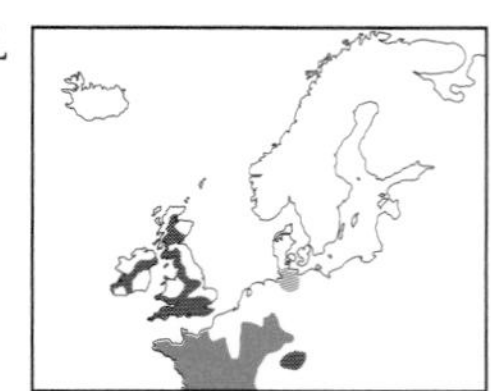

R

TREACLE MUSTARDS *Erysimum* Difficult genus of plants characterised by being hairy with branched hairs; leaves usually simple or only shallowly lobed; flowers yellow; sepals erect; fruit a 4-angled siliqua, less than 3mm wide with each valve usually strongly 1-veined.

A **Treacle Mustard** *Erysimum cheiranthoides* Annual to 90cm, with angled stem. Basal leaves simple, shallowly toothed, short-stalked (**a**), in a rosette, withering before flowering; stem leaves similar, often unstalked. Flowers 6-10mm in diameter. Flower stalks 4-8mm, longer than sepals. Fruit to 25mm. In waste and arable areas. **Fl** 6-9. **Br** Possibly introduced but long naturalised, most frequent in SE England.

B *Erysimum repandum* Differs from Treacle Mustard in having petals twice length of sepals and fruits 45-100mm long. Leaves (**b**). Very local in waste areas. **Fl** 6-8. **Br** Rare casual.

C *Erysimum hieracifolium* Biennial or perennial with flower stalk 2-5mm when in flower, equalling sepals. Local in waste areas and rocky places. **Fl** 6-9. **Br** Absent.

D *Erysimum crepidifolium* Biennial or perennial with flowers 16-18mm, and fruit strongly compressed in cross-section. Very local on dry calcareous soils. **Fl** 6-9. **Br** Absent.

E *Erysimum odoratum* Biennial with flowers 18-20mm, and fruit square in cross-section. Leaves (**e**). Local in dry places. **Fl** 6-9. **Br** Absent.

F **Dame's-violet** *Hesperis matronalis* Hairy biennial or perennial to 90cm, with toothed, shortly stalked lanceolate pointed leaves. Flowers 17-20mm, violet or white and fragrant in dense racemes. Fruit a siliqua, to 10cm long. Native in Poland, but widely naturalised in grassy areas and roadsides, often as a garden escape. **Fl** 5-8. **Br** Naturalised throughout.

G **Wallflower** *Cheiranthus cheiri* Perennial to 60cm, with woody stem base and branched hairs. Leaves narrow-lanceolate, untoothed. Flowers 2-3cm in diameter, orange-yellow, in racemes; erect sepals half the length of petals. Fruit a flattened siliqua to 7cm. Introduced and widely naturalised on old walls and cliffs. **Fl** 3-6. **Br** Locally common throughout.

H **Hoary Stock** *Matthiola incana* Erect grey downy annual or perennial to 80cm, with woody stem base. Leaves lanceolate, untoothed. Flowers 25-50mm, fragrant and ranging from white through to purple. Fruit to 13cm, without glands. Very local on sea-cliffs. **Fl** 4-7. **Br** Status doubtful; rare and possibly native on S coasts of England and Wales; very rare and naturalised in Scotland and Ireland.

I **Sea Stock** *Matthiola sinuata* Similar to Hoary Stock, but without woody stem base; lower leaves wavy-edged and toothed or lobed; fruit with obvious glands. Very local on sea-cliffs and dunes. **Fl** 6-8. **Br** Very rare in SW England, S Wales and Channel Islands.

WINTER-CRESSES *Barbarea* Biennials or perennials with angled stems, yellow flowers and clasping leaves. Fruit a 4-angled siliqua with convex valves having strong midrib.

J **Winter-cress** *Barbarea vulgaris* Hairless biennial or perennial to 90cm. Lower stem leaves shiny and lobed with characteristic *large end-lobe which is shorter than rest of leaf*; upper leaves clasping, progressively less lobed and uppermost leaves undivided. Flowers 6-9mm in diameter, in dense racemes. Fruit a 4-angled siliqua to 30mm. Widespread and common in a variety of damp habitats. **Fl** 4-8. **Br** Common in the south, decreasing further north.

K **Small-flowered Winter-cress** *Barbarea stricta* Similar to Winter-cress, but flower spikes are more upright in habit (**k1**), flowers only 5-6mm with petals more upright (**k2**), flower buds sparsely hairy and *end-lobe of lower leaves longer than rest of leaf* (**k3**). Local on river and canal banks, ditches, marshes and waste areas. **Fl** 5-9. **Br** Scattered sites in England; rare in Wales and Scotland; rare casual in Ireland.

L **Medium-flowered Winter-cress** *Barbarea intermedia* Differs from both the previous species in that all leaves are lobed (**l**) and basal leaves have 3-5 pairs of lateral lobes. Flowers 5-6mm. Fruit to 30mm. Increasingly frequent by roadsides, in waste areas and arable land. **Fl** 3-8. **Br** Introduced and now a frequent casual.

M **American Winter-cress** *Barbarea verna* Has all leaves lobed as in Medium-flowered Winter-cress, but basal leaves with 5-10 pairs of lateral lobes (**m**), flowers 7-10mm in diameter. Fruit to 60mm. Similar habitats; native in W France. **Fl** 3-8. **Br** Introduced and infrequent casual, especially in S and W England.

YELLOW-CRESSES *Rorippa* Annual to perennial herbs with yellow flowers and fruit valves always convex, without a strong midrib. Seeds usually in 2 rows in each cell.

N **Great Yellow-cress** *Rorippa amphibia* Perennial to 1.2m, with runners and stout, erect, *hollow stems*. Lower leaves short-stalked and sometimes lobed, upper ones unstalked and never lobed. Flowers 5-7mm in diameter, petals twice length of sepals. Fruit elliptical, 3-6mm long, on spreading stalks. Widespread and often common in wet habitats; absent from the far north. **Fl** 6-9. **Br** Locally common in England; rare in S Scotland and E Wales; scattered localities in Ireland.

O **Creeping Yellow-cress** *Rorippa sylvestris* Perennial to 50cm, with *stem not hollow* and leaves pinnately lobed or pinnatifid. Flowers 5mm in diameter, petals twice the length of sepals. Fruit 8-18mm, curving upwards. Widespread, often common in damp, bare habitats; absent from the far north. **Fl** 6-10. **Br** Frequent in England and Wales; local in S Scotland; occasional in Ireland.

P **Marsh Yellow-cress** *Rorippa palustris* Annual to 60cm, with erect hollow angular stems. Leaves pinnatifid with narrow lateral lobes. Flowers about 3mm in diameter, *petals about equalling sepals*. Fruit elliptical, 4-7mm long. Widespread in moist places, particularly where water stands in winter. **Fl** 6-10. **Br** Throughout, but rare in N Scotland.

Q **Northern Yellow-cress** *Rorippa islandica* Differs from Marsh Yellow-cress in having semi-prostrate stems and fruit 2-3 times longer than stalk (up to 2 times in Marsh Yellowcress). Rare on bare sandy margins of pools. **Fl** 7-10. **Br** Very rare in W Scotland and W Ireland.

R *Rorippa austriaca* Perennial to 90cm, with irregularly toothed *simple leaves, the upper ones clasping*. Flowers 3mm in diameter, petals slightly longer than sepals. Fruit rare, spherical, about 3mm in diameter. Native in central Europe; naturalised elsewhere. **Fl** 6-8. **Br** Rare casual in England and S Wales.

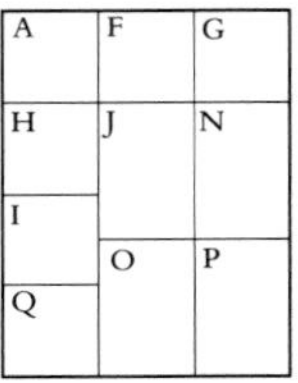

A **Treacle Mustard**
F **Dame's-violet**
G **Wallflower**
H **Hoary Stock**
J **Winter-cress**
N **Great Yellow-cress**
I **Sea Stock**
Q **Northern Yellow-cress**
O **Creeping Yellow-cress**
P **Marsh Yellow-cress**

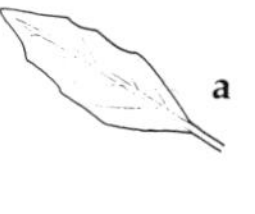

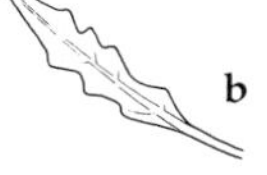

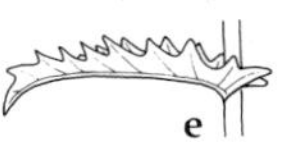

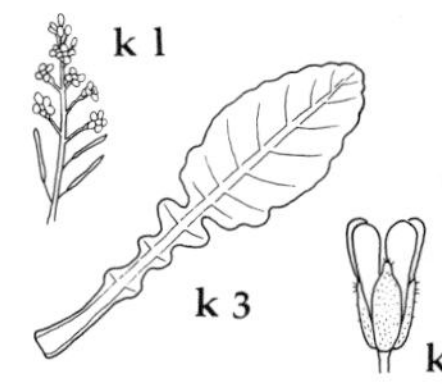

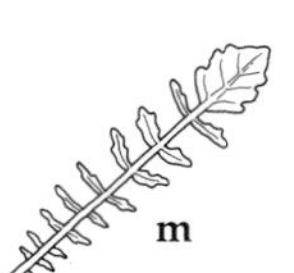

A

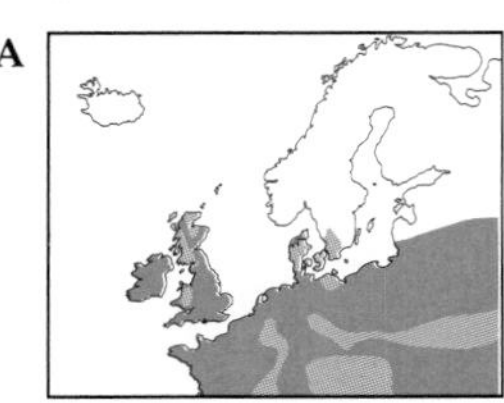

C

D

E

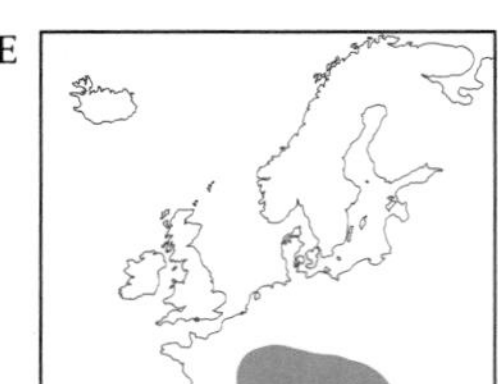

G

M

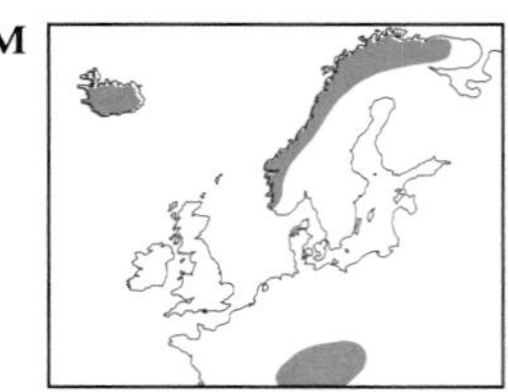

N

O

A Water-cress *Nasturtium officinale* Perennial with hollow creeping or floating stems, rooting below. Leaves pinnate with rounded lobes untoothed or sinuate-toothed, persisting green over winter (*see* Narrow-fruited Water-cress). Flowers 4-6mm in diameter in dense racemes. Fruit a siliqua 14-18mm, spreading or ascending on stalks 8-12mm; *seeds in 2 rows per cell* (**a**). Widespread and often common, in freshwater habitats such as ditches and streams. **Fl** 5-10. **Br** Common except in mountains. NB Fool's Water-cress (*see* page 170) has finely toothed leaves, flowers in umbels and leaf stalks sheathing the stems.

B Narrow-fruited, or Brown, Water-cress *Nasturtium microphyllum* Very similar to Water-cress, but fruit 16-22mm and curved, stalk 11-15mm and *seeds usually in 1 row per cell* (**b**), *except at base*. Similar habitats, but flowers slightly later. **Br** Widespread, but less frequent than Water-cress; more frequent in N Britain.

BITTER-CRESSES *Cardamine* Leaves pinnate or trifoliate, and, if pinnate, the basal leaves have the lateral leaflets stalked (unlike other crucifers). Pods long with veinless valves which coil spirally from the base when ripe, often releasing the seeds explosively.

C Coralroot *Cardamine bulbifera* Perennial to 70cm with no root leaves and pinnate stem leaves having 1-3 pairs of leaflets; upper leaves simple, and characteristically *bearing purplish-brown reproductive bulbils in their axils*. Flowers 12-18mm in diameter, pale rose-pink, in short terminal racemes. Fruit to 35mm, but often not ripening, especially in the north of its range. Locally frequent in semi-shaded woods on calcareous or sandy soils, but absent in many areas. **Fl** 4-5. **Br** Very local or rare; SE England only.

D *Cardamine heptaphylla* Perennial to 70cm, with *all leaves pinnate*, the lowest having 3-5 pairs of toothed lanceolate leaflets. Flowers 18-21mm in diameter, varying from white to purplish. Fruit to 80mm. No bulbils. Very local in mountain woods; in France and SW Germany. **Fl** 5-7. **Br** Rare garden escape.

E *Cardamine pentaphyllos* Differs from *C. heptaphylla* in having leaflets of leaves all arising from same point, palm-like. Similar habitat and distribution. **Fl** 5-7. **Br** Absent.

F *Cardamine enneaphyllos* Perennial to 70cm, with *twice-trifoliate leaves* and lanceolate, toothed leaflets, together with distinctive *drooping heads of pale yellow flowers*, 12-18mm in diameter. Fruit to 80mm. In mountain woods in the south-east. **Fl** 4-7. **Br** Absent.

G *Cardamine trifolia* Perennial to 40cm, with distinctive *trifoliate basal leaves, broadly and apiculately toothed*, and *purplish beneath*. Flowers white or pale pink, 10-15mm in diameter. Fruit to 25mm. Local in mountain woods. **Fl** 3-6. **Br** Rarely naturalised.

H Large Bitter-cress *Cardamine amara* Perennial to 60cm, with pinnate leaves not in a basal rosette, leaflets obscurely toothed and elliptical; end-lobe longer than broad. *Flowers white*, 12mm in diameter, *violet anthers*. Fruit to 40mm. Widespread and locally abundant; in wet woodlands, flushes, marshes and streamsides. **Fl** 4-6. **Br** Locally abundant, especially in SE, N and central England, and S and E Scotland.

I Cuckooflower, Lady's Smock *Cardamine pratensis* Variable perennial to 60cm, with basal leaves pinnate and in a rosette, leaflets rounded but end-lobe kidney-shaped; upper stem leaves with *very narrow unstalked* linear leaflets. *Flowers lilac or white*, 12-18mm in diameter, *with yellow anthers*. Fruit to 40mm. Widespread and common in a variety of damp, open or semi-shaded habitats. **Fl** 4-6. **Br** Common throughout.

J *Cardamine palustris* Differs from Cuckooflower in having *leaflets of upper stem leaves elliptical and distinctly stalked*; flowers 18-26mm; fruit to 55mm. Widespread in similar habitats. **Fl** 4-6. **Br** Mainly in the west. Distribution imperfectly known because previously this has been treated as a variant of Cuckooflower.

K *Cardamine nymanii* Similar to Cuckooflower, but tufted to 30cm, with *thick leaves* having *markedly impressed veins*. Fruit to only 18mm. Very local in damp grassland and streamsides in the far north. **Fl** 5-7. **Br** Absent.

L *Cardamine matthiolii* Similar to Cuckooflower, but has *stems much-branched from the base* and with lateral flower spikes from axils of stem leaves. Flowers white, 9-13mm in diameter. Very local in damp grassland; Germany. **Fl** 4-6. **Br** Absent.

M *Cardamine bellidifolia* Perennial to 25cm, with thick, elongated, spoon-shaped leaves in a basal rosette; stem leaves often absent. Flowers white, 5-10mm, in terminal clusters. Fruit to 25mm. Damp or gravelly places in mountains. **Fl** 6-8. **Br** Absent.

N *Cardamine resedifolia* Differs from *C. bellidifolia* in being taller, to 30cm, and having upper stem leaves with 3-7 lobes. Very local in damp rocky or stony places. **Fl** 6-8. **Br** Absent.

O *Cardamine parviflora* Annual to 30cm, with pinnate leaves with narrow linear lobes, upper leaves 5-8 pairs and the lower 3-5 pairs. Flowers white, *2-4mm*. Fruit erect, to 20mm. Very local in damp, often shady, places. **Fl** 5-8. **Br** Absent.

P Narrow-leaved Bitter-cress *Cardamine impatiens* Annual or biennial to 60cm, with a furrowed stem and distinctive pinnate leaves having 3-lobed leaflets; *conspicuous auricles clasping stem at leaf base*. Flowers 3-4mm, white or pale greenish, made more inconspicuous by absence of petals. Fruit 20-30mm, spreading. Local in damp, shady woodland, usually on calcareous soils or scree. **Fl** 5-8. **Br** Very local; mainly in the west; very rare in S Scotland and Ireland; annual population fluctuations.

Q Hairy Bitter-cress *Cardamine hirsuta* Annual to 30cm, with *straight*, erect, *hairless* stems. Leaves pinnate, mainly in basal rosette; leaflets rounded or oval, terminal leaflet kidney-shaped. *Stem leaves 1-4* on main stem (compare with Wavy Bitter-cress). Flowers white, 3-4mm in diameter, petals often absent. fruit to 25mm, curving upwards and markedly overtopping flower heads. Widespread in a variety of damp, often disturbed, places and old walls. **Fl** 2-11. **Br** Common throughout.

R Wavy Bitter-cress *Cardamine flexuosa* Similar to Hairy Bitter-cress, but taller, to 50cm; *stem wavy, hairy*, often branched above. *Stem leaves 4-10* on main stem. Fruit only slightly overtopping flower head. Widespread in damp or wet habitats and waste areas. **Fl** 3-9. **Br** Common throughout.

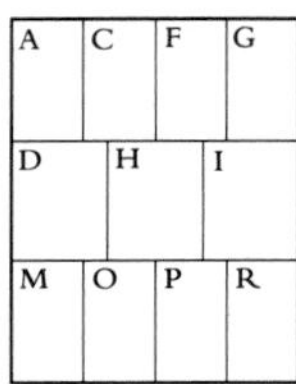

A Water-cress
C Coralroot
F *Cardamine enneaphyllos*
G *Cardamine trifolia*
D *Cardamine heptaphylla*
H Large Bitter-cress
I Cuckooflower
M *Cardamine bellidifolia*
O *Cardamine parviflora*
P Narrow-leaved Bitter-cress
R Wavy Bitter-cress

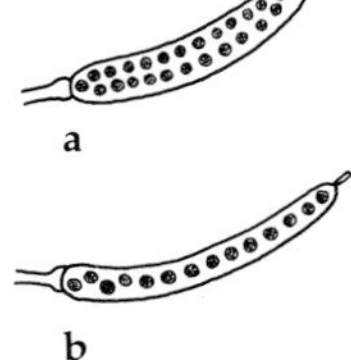

A
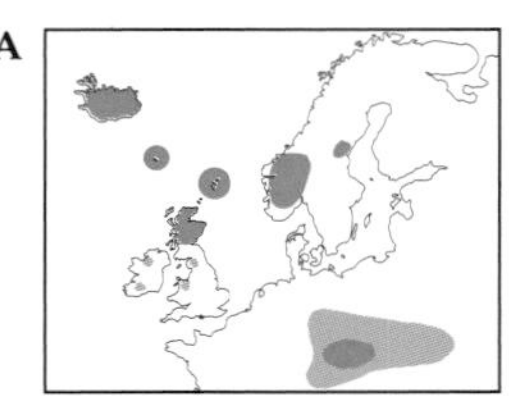

C
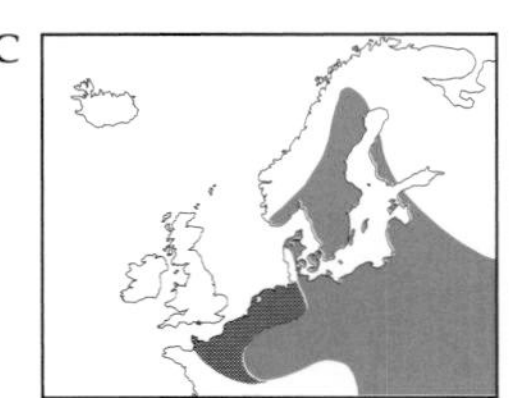

D
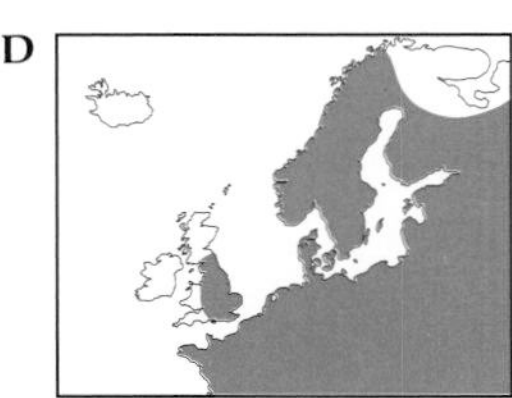

E

F
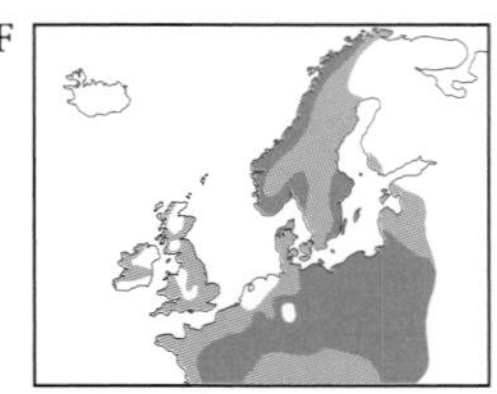

J
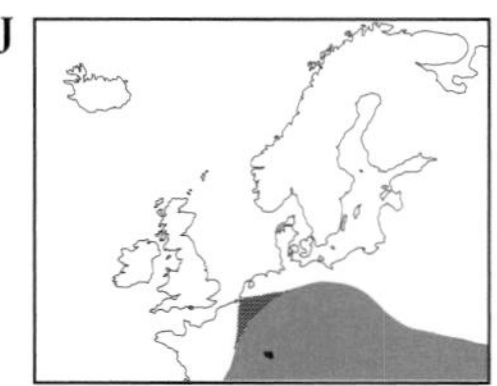

K

L
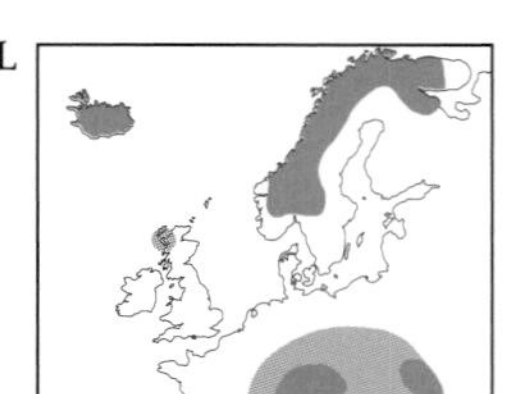

O
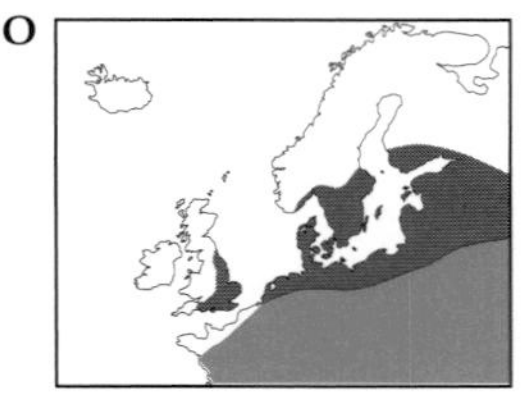

Cardaminopsis These differ from Bitter-cresses in that fruit valves have a strong midrib, and do not open spirally from below (**1**). Seeds make prominent bulges in the pod, whereas this is not usually the case with *Arabis* (*see* below), or if so then the valves do not have a distinct midrib.

A Northern Rock-cress *Cardaminopsis petraea* Variable perennial to 30cm, hairy below. *Basal leaves lanceolate,* lyrate-pinnatifid, in a rosette; stem leaves narrow-oblong, only slightly toothed or untoothed, *not clasping*. Flowers few, white to purplish, 5-7mm in diameter. Fruit to 45mm, curving upwards. Valve 3-veined, with distinct midrib. Local in mountain rocks and screes. **Fl** 6-8. **Br** Local in Scotland; rare in Wales and W Ireland.

B *Cardaminopsis halleri* Differs from Northern Rock-cress in having *basal leaves rounded*, or if lobed then with rounded end-leaflet. Local in rocky habitats in hills and mountains; absent from the north. **Fl** 4-5. **Br** Absent.

C Tall Rock-cress *Cardaminopsis arenosa* Annual or perennial, variable in height from 10-70cm. Differs otherwise from Northern Rock-cress in being *much-branched,* and in having *many flowers,* white or lilac, 7-9mm in diameter. Fruit to 45mm, curving upwards. Widespread and often common; on calcareous rocks or sandy soils. **Fl** 4-6. **Br** Absent.

Arabis Characterised by having numerous unstalked stem leaves and a strongly flattened siliqua with indistinct midribs on valves.

D Tower Mustard *Arabis glabra* Biennial to 1m. *Basal leaves downy*, oblong, long-stalked and sinuate-toothed; stem leaves hairless, grey-green and distinctively *arrow-shaped*, 30-50mm, irregularly toothed and *clasping stem. Flowers creamy yellow or greenish*, 6mm in diameter in terminal raceme. Fruit to 60mm, erect, dense and *closely pressed to stem*. Local on dry, often sandy, banks, heaths and shady rocks. **Fl** 5-7. **Br** Very local, decreasing and mainly in SE England.

E *Arabis pauciflora* Differs from Tower Mustard in having *basal leaves hairless*; stem leaves narrowed in middle; fruit to 80mm. Local in dry calcareous grassland in hills and mountains. **Fl** 5-7. **Br** Absent.

F Hairy Rock-cress *Arabis hirsuta* Extremely variable biennial or short-lived perennial to 60cm. *Stems and leaves markedly hairy*. Basal leaves ovate, scarcely toothed, in a rosette; stem leaves untoothed (sometimes with a few teeth), *half-clasping*, erect and close to stem. Flowers many, white, 3-5mm in diameter, in compact inflorescence. Fruit to 35mm, erect. Widespread and locally frequent in calcareous grasslands. **Fl** 5-8. **Br** Local throughout. Ssp *brownii* is *hairless except for leaf margins*. **Fl** 5-8. **Br** Endemic to W Ireland, in sand-dunes.

G *Arabis planisiliqua* Differs from Hairy Rock-cress in having *stems usually reddish* and *stem leaves arrow-shaped with clasping bases*. Fruit pod constricted between seeds. Widespread in fens and calcareous areas, but absent from Scandinavia. **Fl** 5-7. **Br** Absent.

H *Arabis sagittata* Differs from *A. planisiliqua* in having basal lobes of stem leaves spreading. Similar habitats. **Fl** 5-7. **Br** Absent.

I Tower Cress *Arabis turrita* Hairy biennial or perennial to 70cm, with *stems often reddish below*. Basal leaves oblong, sinuate-toothed in rosette; stem leaves 30-50mm, irregularly toothed and *clasping with rounded bases. Flowers pale yellow*, 7-9mm in diameter. *Fruits very distinctive, to 15cm long and all arching over to 1 side* (**i**). Local in rocky places and on old walls. **Fl** 4-7. **Br** Introduced and rarely established on old walls, as at Cambridge.

J *Arabis recta* Hairy annual to 30cm. Basal leaves oblong, *untoothed and soon withering;* stem leaves bluntly arrow-shaped, *clasping at the base with rounded lobes.* Flowers white, to 5mm in diameter. Fruit to 35mm and spreading. Local on mountain rocks and screes. **Fl** 4-6. **Br** Absent.

K Bristol Rock-cress *Arabis stricta* Roughly hairy perennial to 25cm (usually much less) with 1 or more stems, usually purplish below, and basal rosette of *shiny dark green sinuate-lobed oblong leaves*. Distinguished from Hairy Rock-cress by having *only 1-4 stem leaves, part-clasping;* and *few (less than 5 per stem) creamy white flowers, 6-8mm* in diameter. Fruit to 50mm. Very rare on limestone rocks. **Fl** 3-6. **Br** As native, confined to Avon Gorge. Introduced in Somerset.

L Alpine Rock-cress *Arabis alpina* Hairy perennial to 40cm, creeping and mat-forming. Basal leaves oblong, coarsely toothed, in a rosette; stem leaves similar but *clasping stem with rounded lobes* (*see* Northern Rock-cress). Flowers white, *6-10mm* in diameter. Fruit to 35mm, spreading and curved upwards. On wet rock-ledges and screes in mountains. **Fl** 5-7. **Br** Very rare and confined to Skye.

M Honesty *Lunaria annua* Biennial to 1.5m, with densely hairy stem, branched above. Leaves coarsely and irregularly toothed, the *upper ones unstalked or almost so*. Flowers reddish purple (rarely white), 25-30mm in diameter. Fruit rounded or oval, flattened. Widespread as a garden escape. **Fl** 4-6. **Br** Frequent escape, especially near habitation.

N *Lunaria rediviva* Perennial to 1.5m, similar to Honesty but with *upper leaves stalked*. Flowers 20-25mm, and flattened fruit elliptical in outline. Widespread in damp, shady woodland, especially on calcareous soils; absent from the north and west. **Fl** 5-7. **Br** Introduced; rare garden escape.

O Small Alison *Alyssum alyssoides* Greyish-hairy annual or biennial to 25cm. Leaves to 30mm, lanceolate, stalked and untoothed. *Flowers pale yellow fading to whitish*, 3mm in diameter, in dense *compact* racemes. Fruit a rounded silicula, 3-4mm in diameter; sepals persistent in fruit. Local on open sandy or calcareous grassland or arable land. **Fl** 4-6. **Br** Rare and probably introduced in S and E England and E Scotland.

P *Alyssum montanum* Differs from Small Alison in having *bright yellow flowers*, 5mm in diameter. In rocky places in mountians. **Fl** 4-6. **Br** Absent.

Q Hoary Alison *Berteroa incana* Differs from Small Alison in having white flowers, 5-8mm in diameter, deeply notched petals (unusual for a crucifer); fruit elliptical, downy, 5-8mm in diameter. Local in arable and waste areas, usually on sandy soils. **Fl** 6-10. **Br** Naturalised in a few localities; casual elsewhere.

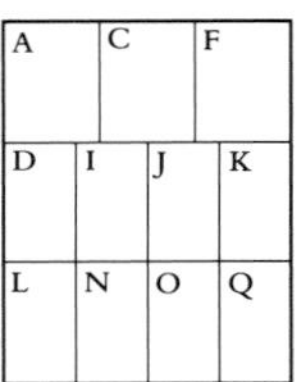

A Northern Rock-cress

C Tall Rock-cress

F Hairy Rock-cress

D Tower Mustard

I Tower Cress

J *Arabis recta*

K Bristol Rock-cress

L Alpine Rock-cress

N *Lunaria rediviva*

O Small Alison

Q Hoary Alison

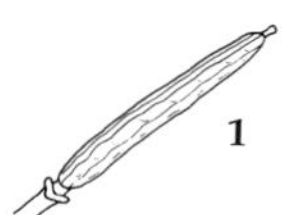

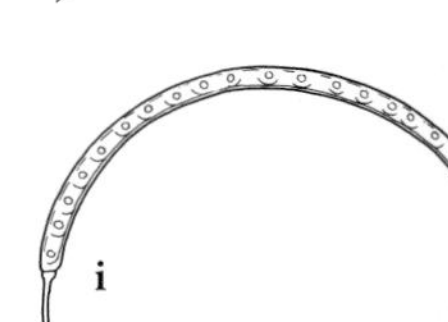

A

B

C

D

G

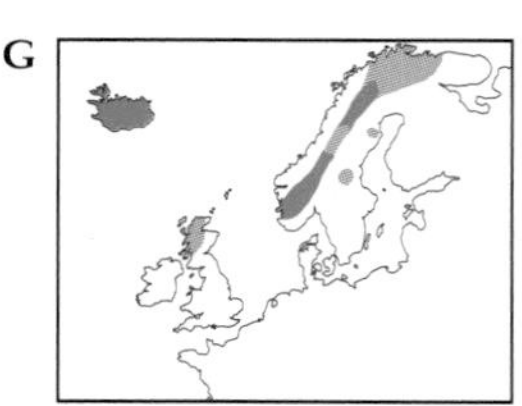

H

J

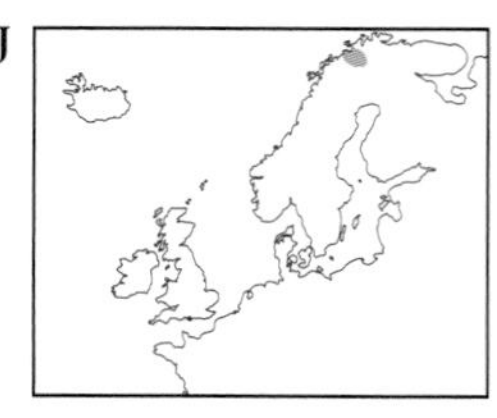

K

M

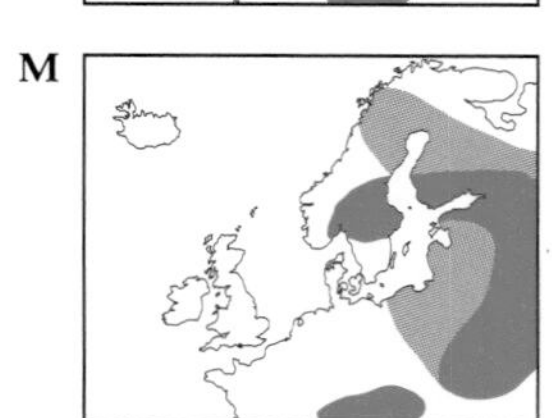

WHITLOWGRASSES *Draba* Leaves simple. Stem leaves few or none; occasionally numerous (Hoary and Wall Whitlowgrass; *D. nemorosa*). Fruit (**1**) a many-seeded silicula with valves flat, midrib in lower part only. Petals not deeply cleft (*see* Common Whitlowgrass).

(1) Flowers bright yellow.

A **Yellow Whitlowgrass** *Draba aizoides* Tufted perennial to only 15cm. Leaves only in basal rosettes, *linear-lanceolate* and stiff with marginal bristles; tip of leaf has long white bristle. Flowers bright yellow, *8-9mm* in diameter, in dense terminal clusters. Fruit 6-12mm long. Very local on cliffs, rocky places in mountains and on old walls; mainly a S and central European species. **Fl** 3-5. **Br** Very rare, and mainly confined to limestone rocks in S Wales where it is probably native; also introduced and naturalised on old walls.

B *Draba alpina* Variable, densely tufted, hairy perennial to 20cm. Leaves only in basal rosettes, *elliptical*. Flowers bright yellow, *4-8mm* in dense terminal clusters. Fruit 4-10mm. Very local in rocky and gravelly places; in Arctic and sub-Arctic. **Fl** 7-8. **Br** Absent.

(2) Flowers pale yellow, cream or white.

(a) Stem leaves few (to 4) or none.

C *Draba crassifolia* Tufted perennial to 7cm, with *hairless stems* and thick but soft *spoon-shaped basal leaves* and no stem leaves. Flowers few, pale yellow, 3-4mm in diameter. Fruit to 7mm. Very local in bare, stony places; in Arctic. **Fl** 6-7. **Br** Absent.

D *Draba nivalis* Densely tufted, hairy perennial to 5cm. Leaves bluish green, narrow-oblong, untoothed and usually only in a basal rosette; *densely covered with stellate hairs*. Flowers white, 5-6mm in diameter, in dense 2- to 5-flowered inflorescence. Fruit 4-9mm, hairless. Very local on screes and rocky mountain habitats; in Arctic and sub-Arctic. **Fl** 6-7. **Br** Absent.

E *Draba subcapitata* Differs from *D. nivalis* in having unbranched hairs on leaves, as well as stellate hairs. In rocky places and screes; Spitzbergen. **Fl** 6-7. **Br** Absent.

F *Draba cacuminum* Like *D. subcapitata*, but has hairy fruit. In rocky places; in mountains of Norway. **Fl** 6-7. **Br** Absent.

G **Rock Whitlowgrass** *Draba norvegica* Variable, tufted, hairy perennial to 5cm when in flower. *Stems hairy with stellate hairs*. Leaves in basal rosette, hairy with mainly simple hairs, usually untoothed; *stem leaves absent*, or occasionally 1-2. Flowers white, 4-5mm in diameter, with notched petals. Fruit to 6mm. Local on mountain screes and in rocky places; mainly in Arctic and sub-Arctic, but extending to Britain. **Fl** 7-8. **Br** Very rare in Scottish Highlands.

H *Draba fladnizensis* Tufted perennial to 10cm when in flower, *mainly hairless*. Leaves oblong, in basal rosette, with a few marginal hairs. Flowers white, 3-5mm with unnotched petals. Fruit to 8mm. Very local in mountain grassland and rocky places. **Fl** 6-8. **Br** Absent.

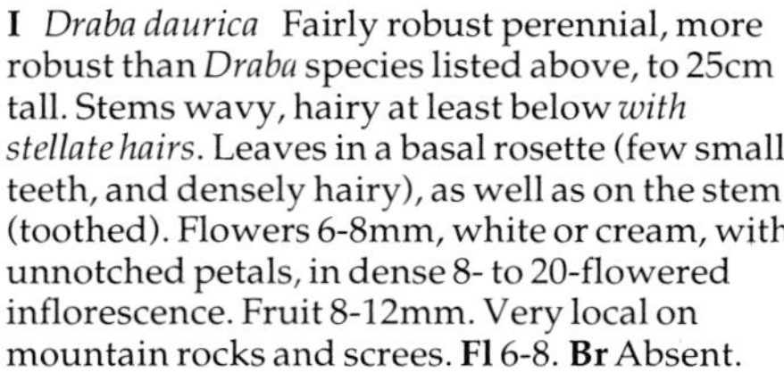

I *Draba daurica* Fairly robust perennial, more robust than *Draba* species listed above, to 25cm tall. Stems wavy, hairy at least below *with stellate hairs*. Leaves in a basal rosette (few small teeth, and densely hairy), as well as on the stem (toothed). Flowers 6-8mm, white or cream, with unnotched petals, in dense 8- to 20-flowered inflorescence. Fruit 8-12mm. Very local on mountain rocks and screes. **Fl** 6-8. **Br** Absent.

J *Draba cinerea* Very similar to *D. daurica*, but has stems densely hairy above as well as below. Very rare on rocks and in stony places. **Fl** 6-8. **Br** Absent.

(b) Stem leaves usually numerous (more than 4) except in dwarf plants.

K **Hoary Whitlowgrass** *Draba incana* Robust biennial or perennial, to 35cm, *usually with numerous stem leaves*. Basal leaves in a rosette, lanceolate, hairy, slightly toothed or untoothed; stem leaves lanceolate, usually coarsely toothed, *densely hairy*. Flowers white, 3-5mm in diameter, in 10- to 40-flowered terminal cluster; *petals slightly notched*. Fruit hairless to 9mm, twisted when ripe. Very local on rocks and cliffs, especially on limestone; usually in mountains, but occasionally on dunes. **Fl** 6-7. **Br** Very local from N Wales to N Scotland.

L **Wall Whitlowgrass** *Draba muralis* Very similar to Hoary Whitlowgrass, but slightly hairy annual, to 30cm, with *broadly oval, clasping stem leaves* and flowers 2-3mm with white *unnotched petals*. Fruit to 6mm, not twisted when ripe; fruit stalk as long as or slightly longer than fruit. Occasional on walls and rocks, mainly on limestone. **Fl** 4-5. **Br** Very local in SW and N England, often on south-facing slopes and occasionally in open rocky oakwoods; occasionally introduced in garden nurseries and on walls, or a casual on railways.

M *Draba nemorosa* Very like Wall Whitlowgrass, but *stems hairless above* and *flowers initially pale yellow*, fading to white. Fruit stalks much longer than fruit. Local in rocky places or waste ground. **Fl** 4-6. **Br** Absent.

N **Common Whitlowgrass** *Erophila verna* Annual to 20cm, slightly hairy below. Leaves only in a basal rosette, elliptical or lanceolate. Flowers white, 3-6mm in diameter, with petals deeply cleft (this distinguishes *Erophila* from the *Draba* species). Fruit to 9mm. Widespread and common in bare places, on walls and rocks, but absent from much of Scandinavia. **Fl** 3-6. **Br** Common throughout.

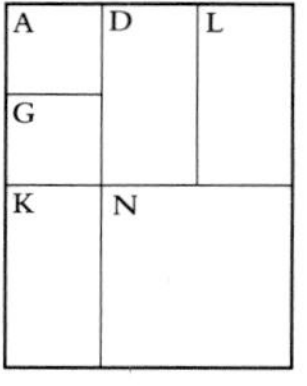

A **Yellow Whitlowgrass**

D *Draba nivalis*

L **Wall Whitlowgrass**

G **Rock Whitlowgrass**

K **Hoary Whitlowgrass**

N **Common Whitlowgrass**

B

E

G

H

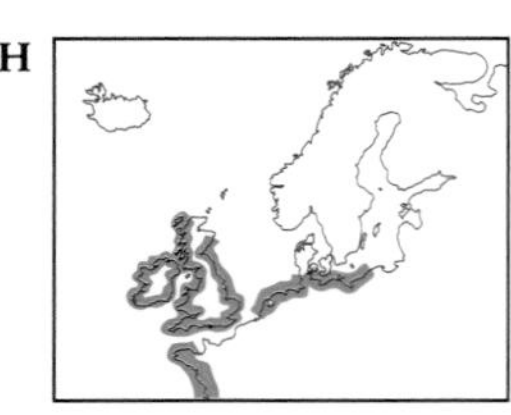

I

K

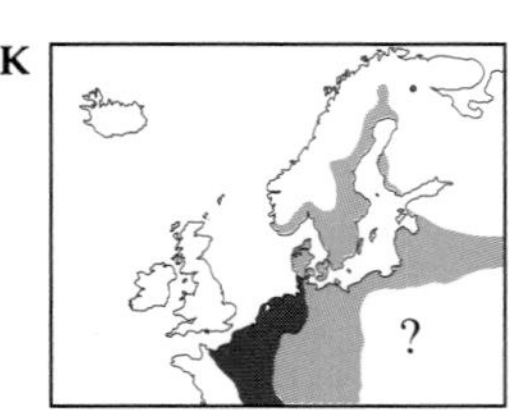

Q

R

SCURVYGRASSES *Cochlearia* Annuals or perennials with simple, often fleshy, leaves; flowers white or reddish with 6 stamens; fruit a swollen, rounded silicula. Often coastal.

(1) Plants with no stem leaves.

A *Cochlearia groenlandica* Biennial or perennial to 15cm, with numerous stout leafless stems and kidney-shaped basal leaves. Flowers white, 4-6mm in diameter. Fruit elliptical, 3-6mm. Local in gravelly, sandy and rocky places both on coast and inland; in Iceland and Spitzbergen. **Fl** 6-9. **Br** Absent.

(2) Plants with upper stem leaves stalked.

B **Danish Scurvygrass** *Cochlearia danica* Annual to 20cm. Basal leaves long-stalked, roundish with a heart-shaped base; upper stem leaves stalked, the lowest ivy-shaped with 3-7 lobes. Flowers white or pale mauve, 4-6mm in diameter. Fruit ovoid, to 6mm. Locally frequent on coastal cliffs, sandy ground or walls; occasionally on disturbed ground inland. **Fl** 1-8. **Br** Frequent all round the coasts.

(3) Plants with upper stem leaves unstalked; basal leaves with heart-shaped base.

C **Common Scurvygrass** *Cochlearia officinalis* Very variable biennial or perennial to 50cm, with kidney-shaped *basal leaves more than 20mm long*, and oblong stem leaves, often coarsely toothed with the upper ones clasping the stem. *Flowers white, 8-10mm.* Fruit ovoid 4-7mm, longer than its stalk. Widespread and locally common on coastal salt-marshes, cliffs, walls and mountains inland (especially on basic rocks). **Fl** 4-9. **Br** Locally common.

D **Alpine Scurvygrass** *Cochlearia pyrenaica* Differs from Common Scurvygrass in having *smaller basal leaves (under 20mm), smaller flowers (5-8mm)* and fruit elliptical, narrowed above and below, shorter than its stalk. Local inland species of mountains, rocky places, stream-margins, spoil heaps or meadows. **Fl** 6-9. **Br** Widely scattered but often local. Sometimes separated into ssp *pyrenaica* found on lead- or zinc-rich spoil heaps; and ssp *alpina* found in rocky places in W and N Britain.

E *Cochlearia aestuaria* Differs from Alpine Scurvygrass in that *fruit* (**e**) *is truncated or notched at apex*. Local on coastal mud. **Fl** 5-9. **Br** Absent.

F *Cochlearia fenestrata* Differs from *C. aestuaria* in having *fruit 3-4 times longer than wide* (**f1**). Leaves (**f2**). Local in rocky or gravelly places; in Arctic and sub-Arctic areas. **Fl** 6-8. **Br** Absent.

G **Scottish Scurvygrass** *Cochlearia scotica* Dwarf, to only 5cm, with squarish petals and *flowers only 5-6mm* in diameter, pale mauve or sometimes whitish. Leaves (**g**). On coastal sand or rocks. **Fl** 6-8. **Br** Endemic, NW Scotland, NW Ireland, Isle of Man.

(4) Plants with upper stem leaves unstalked; basal leaves narrowed into stalk.

H **English Scurvygrass** *Cochlearia anglica* Biennial or perennial to 35cm, with rather stiff stems, and oblong basal leaves narrowed at the base, often with a few teeth; upper leaves clasping the stem. Flowers white, 10-14mm in diameter. Fruit elliptical and compressed, 8-15mm. Locally common; coastal muds and estuaries. **Fl** 4-7. **Br** Locally common. on most coasts.

I *Kernera saxatilis* Branched perennial to 30cm, with both stem leaves and leaves in a basal rosette. Stem leaves lanceolate, clasping; basal leaves spoon-shaped or lanceolate, often toothed. Flowers white in loose racemes; petals rounded. Local in rocky places in mountains, usually on limestone. **Fl** 6-8. **Br** Absent.

Camelina Annuals or perennials, the species here all have arrow-shaped leaves and yellow flowers. Fruit oval or distinctively pear-shaped with many seeds (compare with Ball Mustard below, which is 1-seeded).

J **Gold-of-Pleasure** *Camelina sativa* Hairless annual to 70cm. Flowers yellow, 3-4mm. Fruit yellowish, elliptical, 6-9mm. **Fl** 5-7. Local casual on arable land; possibly cultivated as a crop in prehistoric era. **Br** Introduced and local.

K *Camelina microcarpa* Differs from Gold-of-Pleasure in having hairy stems and grey-green fruit. Rare casual on arable land. **Fl** 5-7. **Br** Rare.

L *Camelina alyssum* Differs from *C. mircrocarpa* in having fruit notched or truncated at the top, with valves soft and easily compressible between fingers. Rare casual on arable land. **Fl** 5-7. **Br** Rare.

M *Camelina macrocarpa* Has large fruit, 10-12mm. Rare on arable land. **Fl** 5-7. **Br** Rare.

N **Ball Mustard** *Neslia paniculata* Hairy annual to 60cm, with lanceolate arrow-shaped leaves, the stem leaves clasping. Flowers bright yellow, 3-4mm, in branched racemes. Fruit a rounded, wrinkled silicula, 3-4mm. In arable and disturbed areas. **Fl** 6-9. **Br** Rare casual.

O **Shepherd's-purse** *Capsella bursa-pastoris* Annual or biennial to 40cm, dull green. Basal leaves oblong-lanceolate, varying from deeply lobed to unlobed; upper leaves usually toothed, clasping the stem. Flowers white, 2-3mm in loose racemes; petals up to twice the length of sepals. Fruit distinctively triangular, flattened and notched. Widespread and often abundant in disturbed places or tracksides. **Fl** 1-12. **Br** Common throughout.

P *Capsella rubella* Differs from Shepherd's-purse in having pink or red flower buds, *petals pink- or red-flushed and only just exceeding sepals;* fruit hardly notched. More local in similar habitats. **Fl** 1-12. **Br** Very local in S England.

Q **Hutchinsia** *Hornungia petraea* Delicate annual to 15cm, with stems often branched at the base. Basal leaves stalked in a rosette, pinnate with elliptical segments; stem leaves similar but unstalked. Flowers minute (about 1mm), greenish white. Fruit a flattened silicula, 2-4mm on spreading stalk. Locally frequent on calcareous rocks or sandy places. **Fl** 3-5. **Br** Rare in W and N, from Mendips to NW Yorkshire.

R *Hymenolobus procumbens* Very similar to Hutchinsia, but *stems usually spreading, stem leaves undivided,* and flowers 2-3mm in diameter. Sandy places, often coastal. **Fl** 4-6. **Br** Absent.

S **Shepherd's Cress** *Teesdalia nudicaulis* Annual or biennial to 25cm, with few or no stem leaves and basal rosette of pinnately lobed leaves. Flowers distinctive, 2mm, with white petals, *2 much shorter than the other pair.* Fruit heart-shaped, notched above, 3-4mm. Local to locally common in dry sandy places or shingle. **Fl** 4-6. **Br** Local in the south, rare in the north and Ireland.

B	C	D
H	I	K
O	N	P
Q	R	S

B **Danish Scurvygrass**

C **Common Scurvygrass**

D **Alpine Scurvygrass**

H **English Scurvygrass**

I *Kernera saxatilis*

K *Camelina microcarpa*

O **Shepherd's-purse**

N **Ball Mustard**

P *Capsella rubella*

Q **Hutchinsia**

R *Hymenolobus procumbens*

S **Shepherd's Cress**

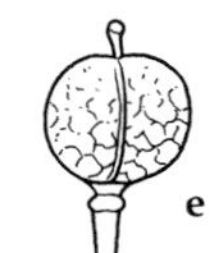

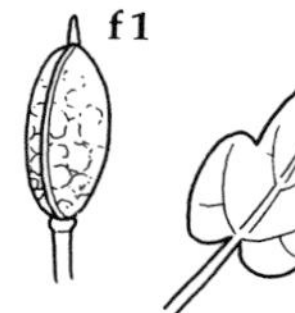

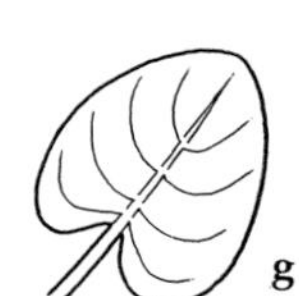

B

C

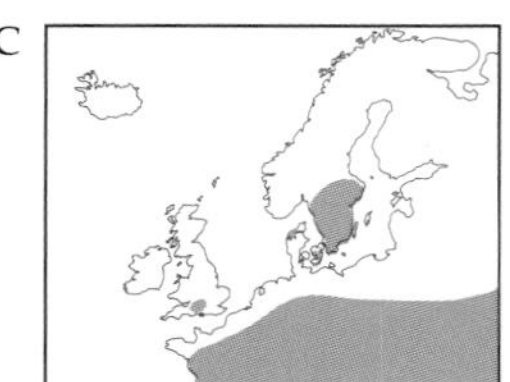

D

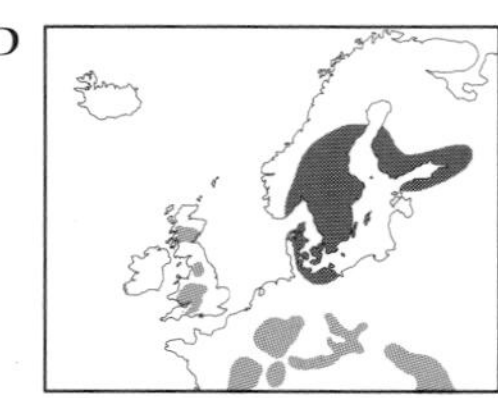

E

F

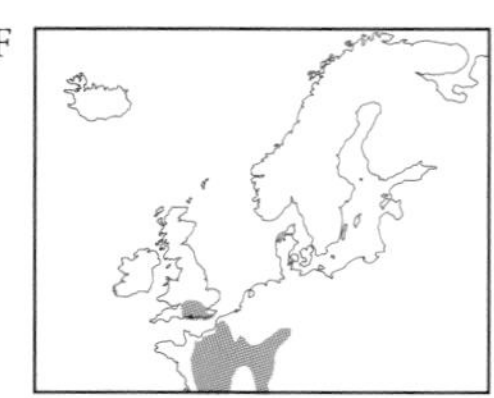

G

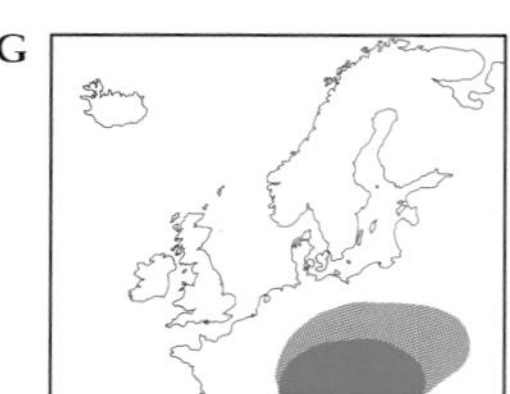

I

PENNY-CRESSES *Thlaspi* Stem leaves unstalked and often clasping. Flowers white or occasionally lilac. Fruit a flattened silicula with an apical notch and the valves winged and keeled. Seeds 2 or more per cell (compare with pepperworts, *see* below).

A Field Penny-cress *Thlaspi arvense* *Hairless annual* to 50cm, emitting a fetid smell when crushed. No basal rosette of leaves; stem leaves lanceolate, toothed and *clasping with arrow-shaped base*. Flowers white, 4-6mm, with *yellow anthers*. Fruit a circular silicula, 10-15mm indiameter with a deep notch. Widespread and common as weed of arable and waste areas. **Fl** 5-7. **Br** Common throughout.

B Garlic Penny-cress *Thlaspi alliaceum* Very similar to Field Penny-cress, but *stem is hairy below*, and fruit is heart-shaped with a shallow apical notch and narrow wings. Similar habitats. **Fl** 4-6. **Br** Rare casual.

C Perfoliate Penny-cress *Thlaspi perfoliatum* Overwintering annual to 25cm. Basal leaves in a rosette, grey-green, oblong and often toothed; *stem leaves clasping with rounded bases*. Flowers 3-4mm with yellow anthers. Fruit heart-shaped, 4-6mm long, with broad wings; style shorter than notch. Local in bare or stony areas, usually on limestone. **Fl** 4-5. **Br** Rare in and around Cotswolds.

D Alpine Penny-cress *Thlaspi alpestre* Very similar to Perfoliate Penny-cress, but perennial with *leaves untoothed*; flowers white or lilac, 3-4mm, with *violet anthers*; fruit with style equalling or longer than apical notch. Very local on limestone rocks, screes or spoil from old lead mines. **Fl** 4-8. **Br** Very local from SW England to Scotland.

E *Thlaspi montanum* Differs from Alpine Penny-cress in having large white flowers, 9-12mm, with *yellow anthers*. Fruit with style much longer than notch. Very local on limestone rocks. **Fl** 4-6.

F Wild Candytuft *Iberis amara* Annual to 30cm, distinctive for being branched above, having spoon-shaped basal leaves (often toothed), and flowers in flattened heads, white or mauve with outer 2 petals much longer than inner 2. Fruit a rounded, winged silicula with deep notch. Local in calcareous grassland, especially where disturbed. **Fl** 7-8. **Br** Local in Chilterns, Surrey and Cambridgeshire; rare elsewhere.

G Buckler Mustard *Biscutella laevigata* Hairy perennial to 30cm with lanceolate basal leaves, deeply lobed, and only 1 or 2 stem leaves. Flowers yellow, 6-10mm, in branched racemes. Fruit distinctive: wide with 2, almost circular, lobes. Local in bare places on limestone, or casual on calcareous soils. **Fl** 5-7. **Br** Absent.

PEPPERWORTS *Lepidium* These resemble penny-cresses, but fruits have only 1 seed per cell as opposed to 2 or more.

(1) Fruit same length or longer than its stalk.

H Field Pepperwort *Lepidium campestre* Greyish, hairy annual or biennial to 60cm. Basal leaves ovate-lanceolate, untoothed and soon withering; stem leaves arrow-shaped, *clasping stem*. Flowers white, 2mm, with *yellow anthers*. Fruit shaped like a coal-shovel when viewed from the side, 5-6mm, notched and *covered with small white vesicles*; style equals notch; fruit stalk spreading, but fruit erect. Widespread, and locally common, on dry grassland, arable or disturbed ground. **Fl** 5-8. **Br** Fairly common, less so in the north.

I Smith's Cress *Lepidium heterophyllum* Differs from previous species in being perennial, having *violet anthers* and *smooth fruit*, with style longer than notch (**i**). Similar habitats. **Fl** 5-8. **Br** frequent, especially in the south and west.

J *Lepidium hirtum* Differs from Field Pepperwort in being perennial, with *fruit hairy, without vesicles*, and with style longer than notch (**j1**). Leaves (**j2**). Similar habitats. **Fl** 5-8. **Br** Casual.

K Garden Cress *Lepidium sativum* Differs from Field Pepperwort in having *stem leaves lobed and not clasping*, the uppermost being linear. Similar habitats. **Fl** 5-8. **Br** Garden escape.

(2) Fruit shorter than its stalk; upper part of fruit not broadly winged but often narrowly so.

L *Lepidium densiflorum* Greyish annual or biennial to 60cm with *deeply toothed, long-stalked elliptical basal leaves*. Flowers greenish white, 2mm. Fruit with shallow notch. Rare in disturbed or waste areas. **Fl** 5-7. **Br** Rare casual.

M Narrow-leaved Pepperwort *Lepidium ruderale* Annual or biennial to 30cm, *with fetid smell* when crushed. *Basal leaves deeply pinnately lobed*, the segments long and narrow; upper stem leaves oblong and untoothed. Flowers tiny, greenish, 1mm, with petals usually absent. Fruit small and elliptical, deeply notched. In waste areas, often by the coast. **Fl** 5-7. **Br** Throughout England, occasional in the south, but rare in Scotland and apparently absent from Ireland.

N *Lepidium perfoliatum* Annual or biennial to 40cm, distinctive for its ovate, pointed upper *stem leaves which are clasping with overlapping basal lobes* (**n1**), *thus appearing to be completely surrounding the stem*; lower leaves pinnately lobed. Flowers pale yellow, 1-2mm. Fruit rounded, hardly notched (**n2**). Very local or rare in arable and waste areas. **Fl** 5-6. **Br** Formerly frequent casual; now rare.

O Dittander *Lepidium latifolium* Stout perennial to 1.2m with *large (to 30cm) oval, toothed leaves*(**o1**), the lower ones stalked, and a dense pyramidal panicle of white flowers, 2-3mm in diameter. Fruit rounded, 2mm, unnotched or hardly so (**o2**). In salt-marshes and wet sandy areas. **Fl** 5-7. **Br** Very local as both native and introduction.

P *Lepidium graminifolium* Perennial to 60cm, dark green. Rosette leaves toothed or pinnately lobed, withering early. Lower stem leaves to 50mm, simple, untoothed and acute at apex. *Upper stem leaves linear*, narrow and untoothed. Fruit oval and pointed, unnotched. **Fl** 5-7. **Br** Rare casual in England and S Wales.

Q Hoary Cress *Cardaria draba* Variable perennial to 90cm, green or greyish with or without hairs. Basal and stem leaves ovate or lanceolate, variably toothed, the latter *clasping the stem* with rounded or acute basal lobes. *Fruit heart-shaped*, inflated and not splitting. Widespread and often common in a variety of habitats, including arable land, waste areas and salt-marshes. **Fl** 4-10. **Br** Common in England; uncommon elsewhere. Originally introduced via a number of ports in 1802.

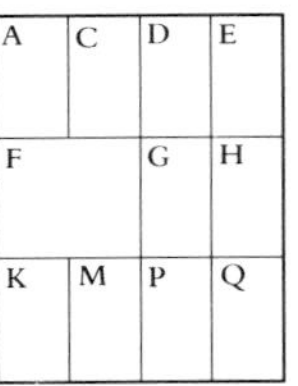

A Field Penny-cress
C Perfoliate Penny-cress
D Alpine Penny-cress
E *Thalspi montanum*
F Wild Candytuft
G Buckler Mustard
H Field Pepperwort
K Garden Cress
M Narrow-leaved Pepperwort
P *Lepidium graminifolium*
Q Hoary Cress

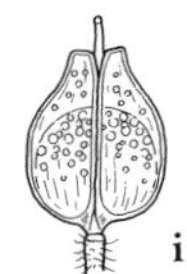

i

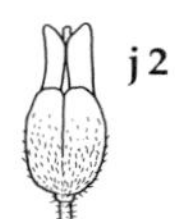

j 2

j 1

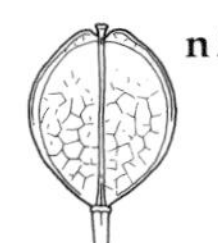

n 2

n 1

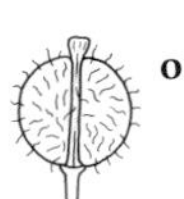

o 2

o 1

C
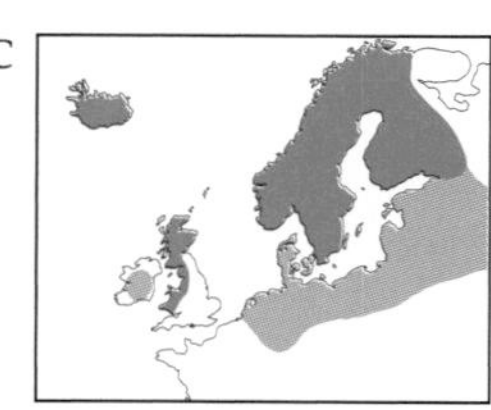

D
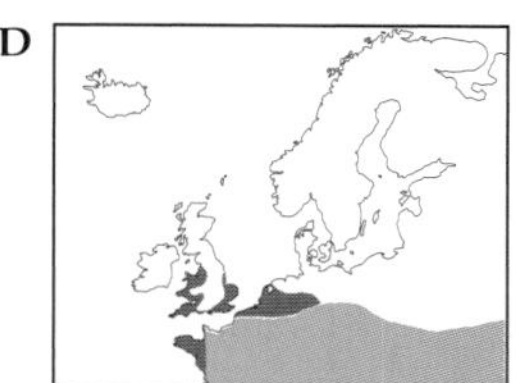

E
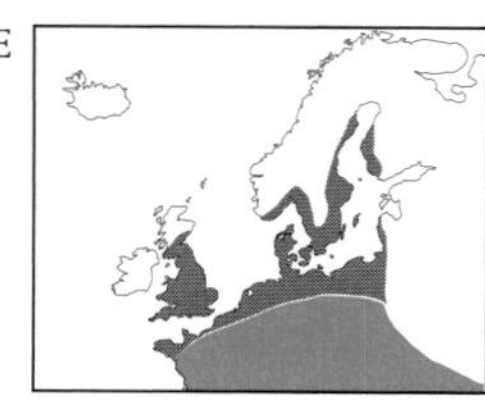

F
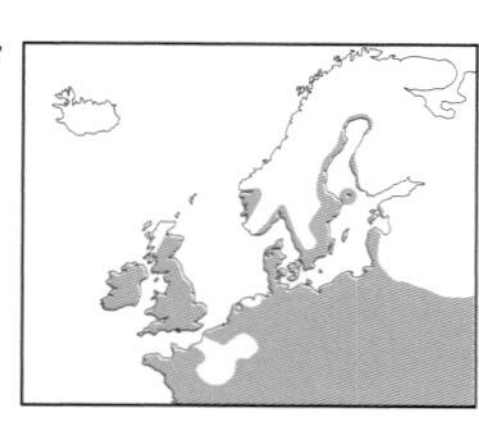

H

A Swine-cress *Coronopus squamatus* Prostrate annual or biennial to 30cm, with ascending stems bearing pinnate light green leaves, the leaflets coarsely toothed. Flowers white, 2.5mm in diameter, in dense racemes opposite leaves or in axils of branches. Fruit kidney-shaped, pointed above and with network of raised ridges (**a**). Locally common in waste and disturbed areas and paths. **Fl** 5-10. **Br** Common throughout S and E England, locally frequent elsewhere; usually near coast.

B Lesser Swine-cress *Coronopus didymus* Very similar to Swine-cress, but flowers usually have no petals (or, if present, they are shorter than sepals), and fruit is notched above and below, shaped like a dumb-bell (**b**). Locally common in waste and disturbed areas; absent from many inland areas. **Fl** 6-10. **Br** Naturalised throughout, but rarely abundant.

C Awlwort *Subularia aquatica* Distinctive aquatic annual to 12cm, bright green. Leaves distinctively awl-shaped, to 60mm, in basal rosette, rather flattened or triangular in cross-section and tapering to a fine point. Flowers tiny, white and in loose terminal clusters. Fruit ovoid, 2mm. Local to rare in the shallow water and gravelly bottoms of base-poor lakes. **Fl** 6-9. **Br** Local in Scotland; uncommon in N and W Ireland; rare in Wales and Cumbria.

D Hare's-ear Mustard *Conringia orientalis* Hairless annual to 40cm, distinctive for its oval greyish-green untoothed stem leaves, strongly clasping at base with blunt auricles. Flowers yellowish or greenish white, 9-12mm. Fruit a long 4-angled siliqua, to 14cm. Local and decreasing in arable and waste areas, docks and cliffs. **Fl** 5-9. **Br** Formerly frequent casual, now rare in England and Wales.

WALL-ROCKETS *Diplotaxis* Flowers yellow or lilac and fruit (siliqua) with single vein on each valve and 2 rows of seeds per cell.

E Perennial Wall-rocket *Diplotaxis tenuifolia* Perennial to 80cm, with erect leafy stems, branched above, fetid when bruised. Leaves pinnatifid, untoothed with oblong blunt lobes. Flowers large, 15-30mm, yellow, occasionally flushed red. Fruit to 60mm. Locally common in waste areas, on old walls and roadsides. **Fl** 5-9. **Br** Naturalised and most frequent in SE uncommon or rare elsewhere.

F Annual Wall-rocket, Stinkweed *Diplotaxis muralis* Annual to 60cm, with erect or ascending stems branched mainly below. Leaves mainly in basal rosette, pinnatifid with oblong lobes, very fetid when bruised. Flowers yellow, 10-15mm in diameter. Fruit to 40mm. Locally common in waste areas and arable land, on sandy soils and walls. **Fl** 5-9. **Br** Naturalised or casual, widespread in England and Wales but rare in Scotland and Ireland.

G White Wall-rocket *Diplotaxis erucoides* Differs from Annual Wall-rocket in having coarsely toothed leaves (**g**) and flowers white, soon becoming lilac. Mainly S European, now rare and declining in the north-west. **Fl** 5-9. **Br** Former casual, now apparently extinct.

BRASSICAS *Brassica* Leaves entire or pinnately lobed; petals yellow or white; fruit a beaked siliqua with 1 row of seeds, and valves rounded on back with only 1 strong vein (**1**).

H Wild Cabbage *Brassica oleracea* Biennial or perennial to 1.5m, greyish green with a thick woody stem below bearing obvious leaf scars. . Basal leaves fleshy and large, to 30cm, undulate, lobed and with winged stalks; upper stem leaves to 7cm, unstalked, unlobed and clasping. Flowers pale yellow, 3-4cm in elongated racemes. Fruit to 9cm, ascending. Coastal, usually on calcareous cliffs and often near sea-bird colonies which disperse the seeds. **Fl** 4-9. **Br** Local and possibly introduced in S and SW England and Wales.

I Rape *Brassica napus* ssp *oleifera* Annual or biennial to 1.3m, greyish green. Rosette leaves to 40cm, pinnately lobed, soon withering; lower stem leaves similar but clasping; upper stem leaves unlobed and also clasping with rounded bases. Flowers pale yellow with petals 13-18mm. Buds overtopping or same level as open flowers. Fruit to 10cm. Common in arable and waste areas, and roadsides. **Fl** 4-9. **Br** Common casual wherever Rape is grown.

J Wild Turnip *Brassica rapa* ssp *sylvestris* Similar to previous species, but petals 6-13mm, and open flowers usually overtop buds. Common in arable and waste areas. **Fl** 5-9. **Br** Common throughout.

K Black Mustard *Brassica nigra* Tall annual to 2m, often greyish and hairy below. Leaves all stalked, the lower ones pinnately lobed. Flowers yellow, 12-15mm in diameter. Fruits to only 30mm, flattened and distinctively pressed close to stem (unlike any other *Brassica* species). Frequent on riverbanks and sea-cliffs; casual in arable and waste areas. **Fl** 5-9. **Br** Native and locally frequent in England and Wales; rare in S Scotland; also a frequent casual.

L Brown Mustard *Brassica juncea* Like Black Mustard, has stalked upper stem leaves, but fruits not pressed to stem. Similar to *Sinapis* species, but hairless, sepals usually ascending and fruit valves with only 1 strong vein. In waste areas and docks. **Fl** 5-10. **Br** Rare casual.

SINAPSIS *Sinapis* Differ from *Brassica* in that the fruit valves (**2**) have 3-7 strong veins, not 1, and from *Coincya* (*see* page 84) in having spreading (not erect) sepals.

M Charlock *Sinapis arvensis* Tall annual to 2m, dark green or purplish, hairy below. Lower leaves large, stalked, coarsely toothed, often lyre-shaped; upper leaves stalked or not, and unlobed. Flowers yellow, 15-20mm, in crowded terminal clusters; sepals usually spreading or down-turned. Fruit beak rounded (compare with White Mustard). Common in arable and waste areas. **Fl** 4-10. **Br** Common throughout.

N White Mustard *Sinapis alba* Differs from Charlock in having upper leaves pinnately lobed and fruit beak flattened. Locally common casual of arable and waste areas; absent from much of the extreme north. **Fl** 5-9. **Br** Frequent in SE; scattered elsewhere.

O Hoary Mustard *Hirschfeldia incana* Tall erect annual to 1.3m. Lower leaves stalked and pinnate with oblong terminal lobe and up to 9 pairs of smaller lateral lobes; uppermost leaves unlobed. Flowers pale yellow, in crowded terminal racemes; sepals ascending. Fruit to 16mm, pressed close to stem; peg-shaped with slightly swollen, shorter upper segment (1-seeded) and flattened lower segment (2-6 seeds per cell). Locally common in waste areas and docks. **Fl** 5-10. **Br** Common in S Wales, London and Channel Islands; scattered elsewhere.

A	C	G
E F	H	
I	M	
J	K	O

A Swine-cress
C Awlwort
G White Wall-rocket
E Perennial Wall-rocket
F Annual Wall-rocket
H Wild Cabbage
I Rape
M Charlock
J Wild Turnip
K Black Mustard
O Hoary Mustard

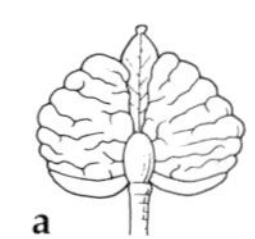
a

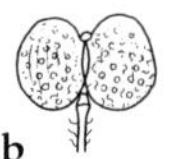
b

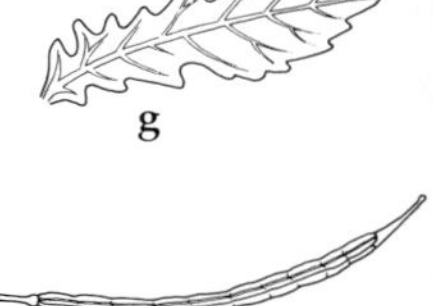
g

1

2

B

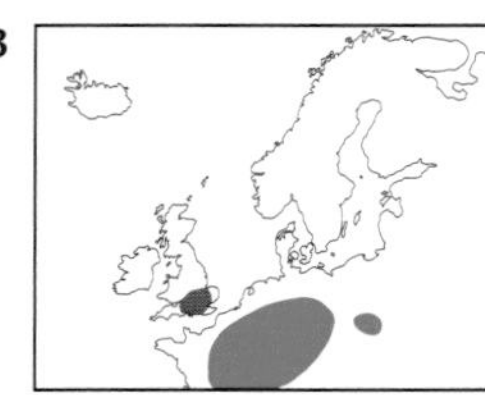

D

G

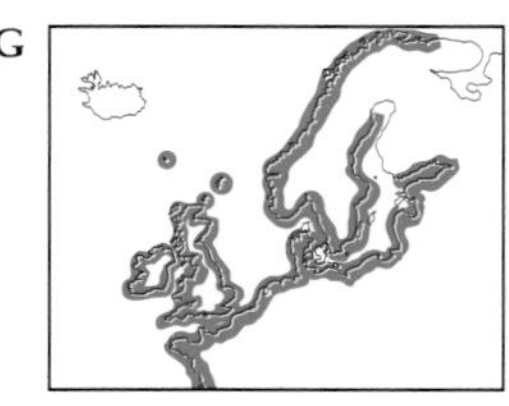

I

J

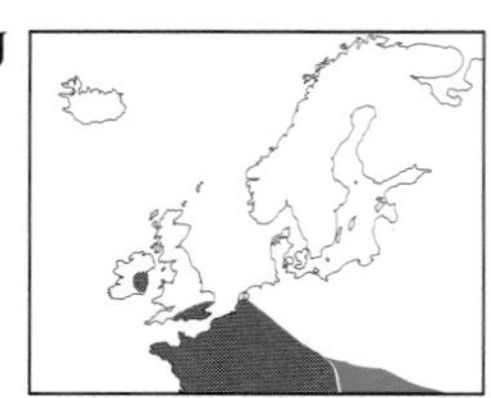

P

A Garden Rocket *Eruca sativa* Annual to 80cm, strong-smelling. Leaves mainly stalked and lobed (**a**). Flowers distinctive, pale yellow with dark veins. Fruit to 4cm with terminal segment half the length of valves which have 1 strong vein like *Brassica* species (*see* page 82), but the seeds are in 2 rows per cell. Uncommon casual in waste areas. **Fl** 5-11. **Br** Rare casual, formerly frequent and once cultivated.

B Hairy Rocket *Erucastrum gallicum* Hairy annual to 60cm, with *bipinnatifid leaves* (**b**). Flowers pale yellow, 10-15mm in diameter, in crowded terminal heads; lower part of flower stalk has *pinnately lobed bracts*. Fruit to 45mm, with seeds in 1 row and valves with 1 strong vein. Uncommon in dry waste areas and docks. **Fl** 5-11. **Br** Rare to occasional casual.

C *Erucastrum nasturtiifolium* Differs from Hairy Rocket in having clasping upper stem leaves and no bracts. Local in disturbed areas. **Fl** 5-11. **Br** Rare casual.

Coincya Flowers yellow, often with darker veins on petals, and with erect sepals. Fruit a siliqua with seeds in 1 row and the valves having 3 strong veins and a terminal sword-shaped beak with 1-6 seeds (**1**).

D Wallflower Cabbage *Coincya monensis* ssp *recurvata* Annual or biennial to 50cm, hairless above and with erect stems, branched below. Leaves stalked, pinnately lobed, hairy beneath. Flowers yellow, the petals often with darker veins. Fruit to 80mm. Local in dry areas, sand-dunes and roadsides. **Fl** 5-10. **Br** Local in S Wales and Channel Islands; rare in England.

E Isle of Man Cabbage *Coincya monensis* ssp *monensis* Differs from Wallflower Cabbage in that it is prostrate or ascending in habit, and leaf surfaces (**e1**) are hairless. Fruit to 70mm (**e2**). Sandy shores and coastal dunes. **Fl** 5-9. **Br** Endemic. Locally abundant on Isle of Man; very local and declining on W coast of Britain.

F Lundy Cabbage *Coincya wrightii* Perennial to 90cm, with erect stems branched below and greyish leaves, densely hairy above and below. Fruit to 65mm. On sea-cliffs. **Fl** 5-8. **Br** Endemic and rare on Lundy Island.

G Sea Rocket *Cakile maritima* Annual to 30cm with sprawling stems and shiny green hairless and succulent leaves, pinnatifid or shallowly lobed. Flowers white, pink or lilac, 6-12mm in diameter, in crowded racemes. Fruit erect, to 20mm, with 2 segments, 1 above the other, the lower with 2 shoulder-like projections. Frequent on sandy beaches, open dunes (early coloniser), and shingle. **Fl** 6-9. **Br** Frequent around the coasts.

H *Cakile edentula* Differs from Sea Rocket in having no projections on lower segment of fruit. Iceland; local on coast sand, shingle. **Fl** 6-9.

I Sea-kale *Crambe maritima* Distinctive hairless bushy perennial to 50cm, greyish green or flushed purple. Leaves broad, succulent, wavy and variable in shape from oval to elliptical, often coarsely toothed and lobed. Flowers white in dense flattish terminal heads. Fruit globular with 1-2 seeds. On sand, shingle coasts above drift-line. **Fl** 5-8. **Br** Occasional to very locally abundant; possibly declining.

J Bastard Cabbage *Rapistrum rugosum* Annual to 1m, with erect stems branched below. Leaves stiffly hairy, the lower ones pinnately lobed with a large terminal lobe. Flowers pale yellow, in crowded racemes. Fruit with 2 segments, the lower 1 narrow and elliptical, the upper 1 larger and ovoid; fruits pressed close to stem. Casual in waste areas and arable land. **Fl** 5-10. **Br** Locally abundant in England and Wales; rare elsewhere.

K White Ball Mustard *Calepina irregularis* Hairless annual or biennial to 70cm. Basal leaves strongly toothed or pinnately lobed, stem leaves clasping. Flowers white, 2-4mm, with unequal petals. *Fruit ovoid with a short conical beak.* **Fl** 5-6. **Br** Rare casual.

L Wild Radish *Raphanus raphanistrum* Annual to 1m, hairy below. Basal and lower stem leaves pinnate with up to 7 pairs of toothed lateral lobes; upper leaves lanceolate. Flowers white to yellow (sometimes purplish) with darker veins on petals; sepals erect. Fruit beaded with up to 10 segments, 2-5mm wide, often with narrow constrictions in between; terminal part conical and pointed. Common in arable and waste areas. **Fl** 6-10. **Br** Common throughout.

M Sea Radish *Raphanus raphanistrum* ssp *maritimus* Flowers almost always yellow and fruit with up to 5 strongly beaded segments, 5-10mm wide. On sand-dunes, sea-cliffs and coastal grassland. **Fl** 5-7. **Br** Scattered around the coasts; locally abundant in S and W.

N Garden Radish *Raphanus sativus* Flowers white to pink, leaves with very large oval terminal lobe and only 1-3 small lateral lobes; fruits usually not beaded. Escape from cultivation. **Fl** 5-11. **Br** Widespread, but infrequent.

Mignonette Family
Resedaceae

Annuals or perennials with spirally arranged leaves and flowers in spikes or racemes. Petals 4-8, often deeply divided. Sepals 4-8.

O Weld *Reseda luteola* Tall hairless biennial to 1.5m, with stiffly erect, ribbed, hollow stems. Basal rosette of narrow oblong leaves withering after 1st season; stem leaves unlobed with wavy margins. Flowers 4-petalled, yellowish green in long slender racemes. Common in disturbed or stony ground, on calcareous soils. **Fl** 6-9. **Br** Mostly common, local in N and W Britain.

P Wild Mignonette *Reseda lutea* Similar to previous species but stems solid, to 75cm. Stem leaves pinnately lobed with 1-2 pairs of lobes, the margins slightly wavy. Flowers 6-petalled, greenish yellow in more compact conical racemes. Common in disturbed areas on calcareous soils. **Fl** 6-8. **Br** Locally common; absent N Scotland; probably not native Ireland.

Q White Mignonette *Reseda alba* Leaves with at least 5 pairs of lobes. Flowers white. In disturbed areas, stony places, on old walls and docks. **Fl** 6-8. **Br** Casual, mainly in SW England.

R *Reseda phyteuma* Leaves paddle-shaped usually with no lobes (occasionally 1-2). White flowers. Similar habitats to White Mignonette. **Fl** 6-8. **Br** Rare casual in S England.

S *Sesamoides canescens* Perennial to only 15cm, with lanceolate unlobed leaves in both a basal rosette and along the stem. Flowers white, 6-petalled in long dense spikes. Fruit star-shaped. Very local in rocky and grassy places. **Fl** 7-8. **Br** Absent.

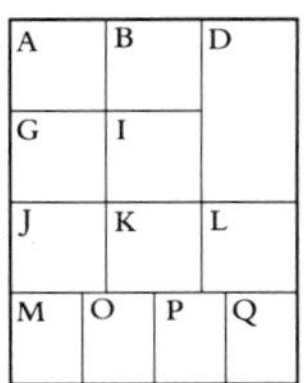

A **Garden Rocket**
B **Hairy Rocket**
D **Wallflower Cabbage**
G **Sea Rocket**
I **Sea-kale**
J **Bastard Cabbage**
K **White Ball Mustard**
L **Wild Radish**
M **Sea Radish**
O **Weld**
P **Wild Mignonette**
Q **White Mignonette**

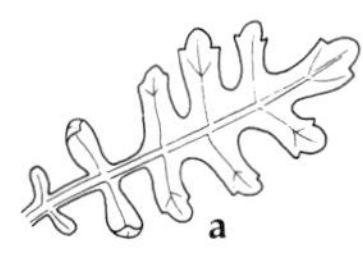
a

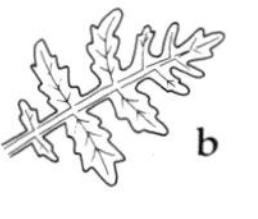
b

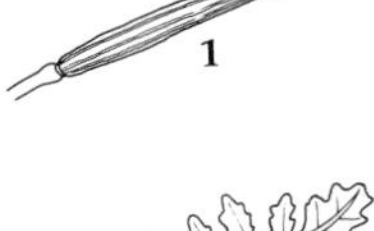
1

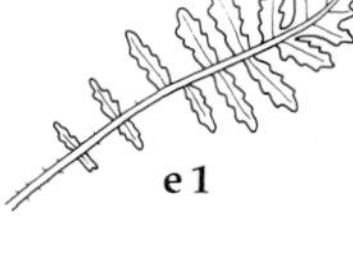
e1

e2

B 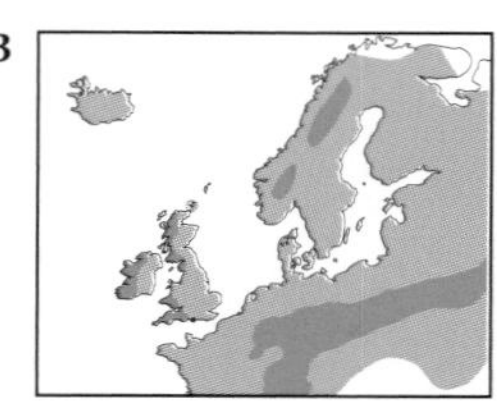

C 

D 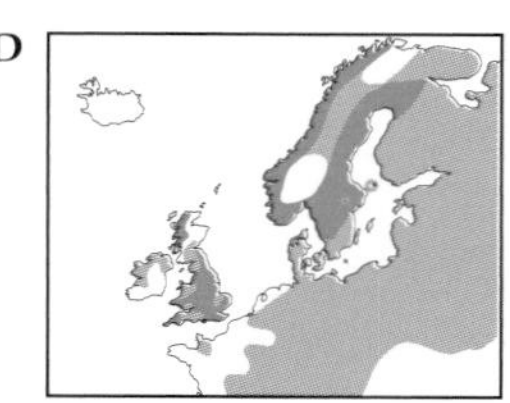

E 

F 

G 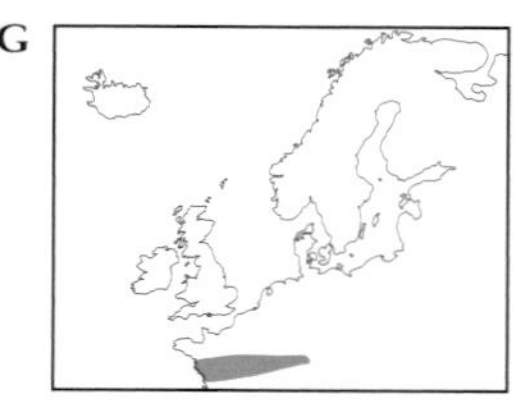

I 

Pitcherplant Family
Sarraceniaceae

Perennial insectiverous herbs with both sepals and petals free at the base (compare with sundew family, below). Insects are attracted to the pitchers by nectar secreted near the entrance, and due to the arrangement of downward-pointing hairs on the lining they are unable to climb out again. Eventually they slip down into an enzyme-rich liquid at the bottom of the pitcher and are slowly broken down and absorbed by the plant.

A **Pitcherplant** *Sarracenia purpurea* Very distinctive perennial to 40cm, with stem leaves converted into the 10-15cm 'pitchers', dark green flushed with purple, hooded at the top. Flowers purplish red, about 5cm in diameter with 5 sepals and petals. Introduced from N America and naturalised in bogs. **Fl** 6-7. **Br** Scattered localities in Ireland and S England.

Sundew Family Droseraceae

Perennial insectiverous herbs with leaves that have long glandular hairs adapted to trapping insects, and sepals united at the base. The leaves secrete enzymes which help to digest the insects.

B **Round-leaved Sundew** *Drosera rotundifolia* Reddish plant to 25cm when in flower, with leaves in a basal rosette, rounded to 1cm in diameter, long-stalked and spreading. Flowers white (only opening in full sun) on long erect stalks, 2-4 times the length of leaves, arising from the centre of the rosette. Fruit a capsule. Locally frequent in wet peaty areas on moors and heaths. **Fl** 6-8. **Br** Much decreased through habitat destruction, most frequent in N Britain and Ireland; increasingly local in S England.

C **Oblong-leaved Sundew** *Drosera intermedia* Differs from Round-leaved Sundew in having narrow oblong leaves to 1cm, *tapering abruptly into the stalk*. Flower stalk arises below the rosette, and is usually not much longer than the leaves. Wet peaty places on heaths or moors, sometimes on sphagnum. More local than Round-leaved Sundew. **Fl** 6-8. **Br** Decreasing, as previous species, but least local in W Britain, Ireland and parts of S England.

D **Great Sundew** *Drosera anglica* Long narrow leaves to 3cm, *gradually tapering into stalk*. Flower stalk arises from centre of rosette, up to twice the length of leaves. Wettest parts of peatbogs, decreasing in Europe through habitat destruction. **Fl** 6-8. **Br** Locally frequent in N and W Scotland and W Ireland; rare in England and Wales.

Stonecrop Family
Crassulaceae

Succulent plants with fleshy undivided leaves and 5-petalled flowers; 3-20 sepals and petals, the stamens equalling or twice this number.

Crassula Small low-growing plants with opposite, fused leaves, 3-4 free petals and equal number of stamens; mostly annuals.

E **Mossy Stonecrop** *Crassula tillaea* Tiny, often reddish, annual with creeping and ascending stems to 5cm. Leaves very crowded, blunt, 1-2mm long. Flowers whitish, minute (1-2mm) and numerous in leaf axils, with 3 petals and 3 longer sepals. Very local in bare, damp, sandy or gravelly ground. **Fl** 6-9. **Br** Very local in S and E England.

F **Pigmyweed** *Crassula aquatica* Differs from Mossy Stonecrop in having pointed linear leaves widely spaced, 3-6mm long, and flowers (also unstalked) with 4 petals and sepals. Local or rare on muddy pond-margins. **Fl** 6-9. **Br** In 1 site near Inverness, probably not native.

G *Crassula vaillantii* Like Pigmyweed but has slender-stalked flowers. Very local in France on muddy ground. **Fl** 6-9.

H **New Zealand Pigmyweed** *Crassula helmsii* Differs from previous 2 species in being perennial, patch-forming, with stems up to 30cm in water, leaves 4-12mm and stalked flowers pink or white. Introduced from New Zealand and well established on shallow pond-margins and damp ground. **Fl** 6-9. **Br** Scattered localities and increasing; becoming a serious problem in many localities such as the New Forest where it out-competes native plants.

I **Navelwort, Wall Pennywort** *Umbilicus rupestris* Distinctive hairless perennial to 40cm, with stalked, rounded fleshy leaves, mostly basal, with a central navel-like depression and very broad blunt teeth. Flowers tubular, greenish-white and drooping in many-flowered spikes. Locally common on old walls, rocks, cliffs and hedgebanks. **Fl** 6-9. **Br** Common in the west; scarce elsewhere.

J **House-leek** *Sempervivum tectorum* Perennial to 60cm, with dense basal rosettes of spiny-pointed leaves, bluish green but dull red above. Flowers dull red with up to 18 petals, 2-3cm in diameter, in dense rounded terminal clusters. Native in rocky mountain habitats in France and Germany; widely cultivated, and occasionally escapes. **Fl** 6-7. **Br** Introduced on old walls; scattered.

K *Jovibarba sobolifera* Similar to previous species, but with yellow flowers and closed leaf rosettes. Sandy and stony ground; in central and S Germany and Poland. **Fl** 6-7. **Br** Absent.

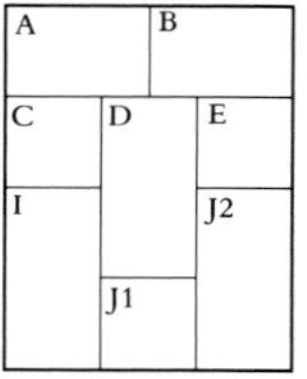

A **Pitcherplant**

B **Round-leaved Sundew**

C **Oblong-leaved Sundew**

D **Great Sundew**

E **Mossy Stonecrop**

I **Navelwort**

J **1 House-leek** showing basal leave rosettes

J **2 House-leek**

B
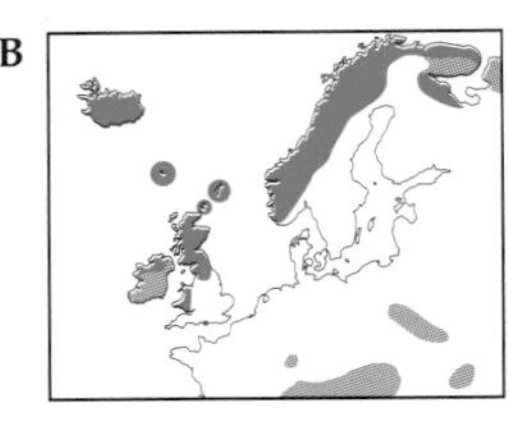

C

D
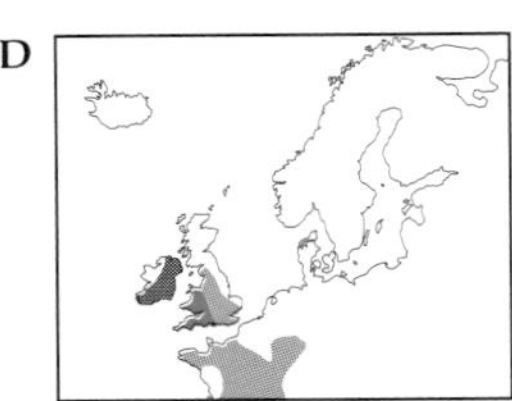

F
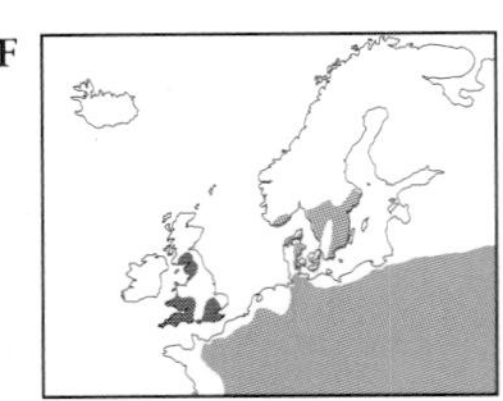

H
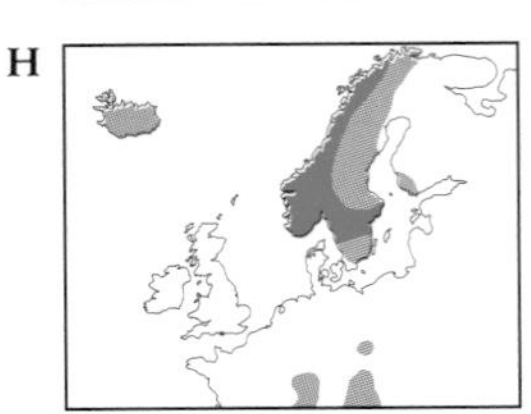

I
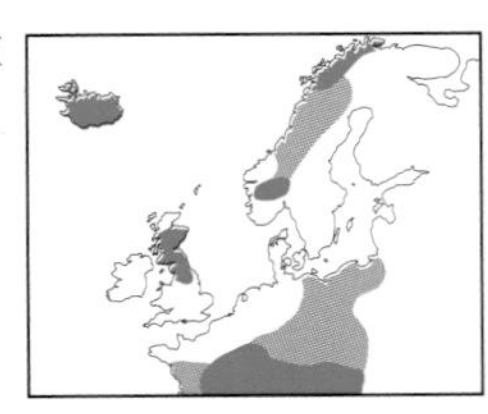

K
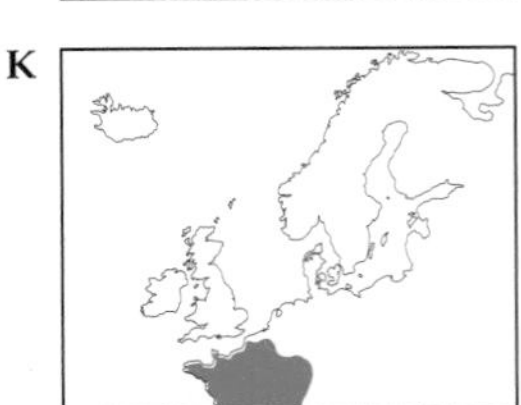

N
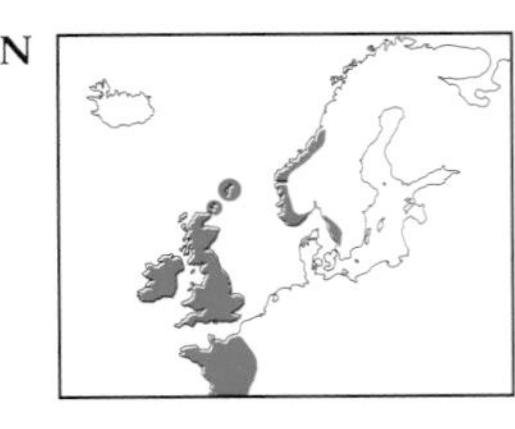

O
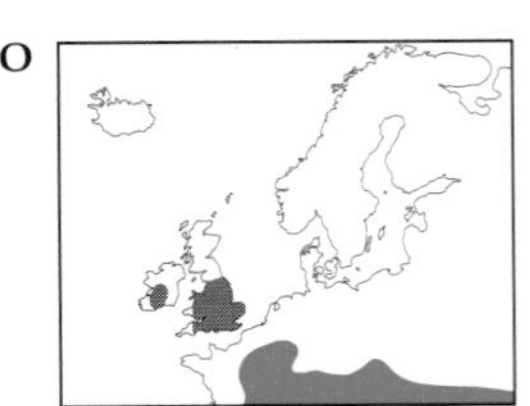

STONECROPS *Sedum* Leaves fleshy, alternate or whorled (occasionally opposite), flowers in cymes with petals free, usually 5 in number (can be 3-10) and stamens twice the number of petals. The shape and colour of the leaves plus the flower's colour help to separate species.

(1) Plants with broad, flat leaves.

A **Orpine** *Sedum telephium* Perennial to 60cm, with red-tinged erect stems in clusters. Leaves oval, alternate and irregularly toothed. Flowers purplish red or lilac, in dense terminal cymes; good nectar source for insects. Locally common in shady places in woodlands or hedgerows and scrub. **Fl** 7-9. **Br** Local but widespread; very rare in N Scotland, and not native in Ireland.

B **Rose-root** *Rhodiola rosea* Greyish perennial to 30cm, with clustered erect stems bearing alternate, thick, overlapping, variably toothed leaves and terminal clusters of greenish-yellow, or dull yellow, 4-petalled flowers. Fruit orange. Locally frequent in mountain rocks, screes and sea-cliffs. **Fl** 5-8. **Br** Locally common from Wales northwards and in N and W Ireland.

(2) Plants with narrow leaves, either rounded in cross-section or flat above and rounded beneath.

(a) Yellow flowers.

C **Reflexed Stonecrop** *Sedum reflexum* Greyish mat-forming perennial to 30cm. Leaves rounded in cross-section, linear and evenly spread up stem. Flowers, many, in terminal cyme, drooping in bud, bright or pale yellow; petals usually 7. Locally common in stony or rocky places or on walls. **Fl** 6-8. **Br** Introduced and naturalised on old walls.

D **Rock Stonecrop** *Sedum forsteranum* Perennial with flowers very similar to previous species, but leaves flat on top and in distinctive terminal clusters on non-flowering shoots; dead leaves persist below. Local in rocky places and screes. **Fl** 6-8. **Br** Very local in SW England and Wales; naturalised elsewhere.

E **Biting Stonecrop** *Sedum acre* Hairless mat-forming evergreen to only 10cm. Leaves beak-shaped, broadest towards base, densely crowded and pressed to stem on non-flowering shoots; peppery taste. Flowers bright yellow, 10-12mm in diameter, in few-flowered terminal clusters. Frequent in dry places, sand-dunes and on old walls. **Fl** 5-7. **Br** Frequent almost throughout.

F **Tasteless Stonecrop** *Sedum sexangulare* Very similar to Biting Stonecrop, but has bright green leaves spreading and parallel-sided or broadest towards tip. No peppery taste. Flowers 9mm in diameter. Locally frequent in rocky places and on old walls. **Fl** 7-8. **Br** Introduced and naturalised in a few places.

G *Sedum alpestre* Very similar to previous 2 species, but has leaves spreading, rather flattened, and streaked with red. Flowers only 6-8mm in diameter. In rocky places in mountains. **Fl** 6-7.

H *Sedum annuum* Annual or biennial tinged with red and branched from near the base. Leaves alternate, flattened on both sides. Flowering shoots ascending with a few yellow flowers, 3-5mm in diameter, on short stalks. In rocky places in mountains, moraines and sandy ground. **Fl** 5-7. **Br** Absent.

(b) Pink or white flowers.

I **Hairy Stonecrop** *Sedum villosum* Perennial to 15cm, usually reddish. Leaves distinctive, spirally arranged, flat above and with many stickily hairy glands. Flowers pink, 6-8mm, on long stalks; flower buds erect (compare with *S. hirsutum*). Rather local in wet places, sandy or stony ground, and streamsides. **Fl** 6-8. **Br** Local from Yorkshire northwards.

J *Sedum hirsutum* Glandular hairy, like the previous species, but leaves rounded above and flower buds drooping. Very local in dry rocky or stony places; N central France. **Fl** 6-8. **Br** Absent.

K *Sedum rubens* Greyish annual to 10cm, stems glandular hairy above (compare with following species). Leaves linear, alternate, slightly flattened and greyish streaked with red; 10-20mm long. Flowers pink or white, 9-11mm in diameter, and unstalked. Local in rocky and stony places. **Fl** 5-7. **Br** Absent.

L *Sedum andegavense* Very like previous species, but without glandular hairs on upper stem; flowers with short stalks.Local in damp, sandy or grassy places. **Fl** 5-7. **Br** Absent.

M **White Stonecrop** *Sedum album* Hairless, evergreen, mat-forming perennial to 15cm. Leaves oblong, 6-12mm, rather shiny, green or reddish. Flowers white (often pink beneath), 6-9mm in diameter, in many-flowered, flat-topped cymes. Local to locally common in rocky places and on old walls. **Fl** 6-8. **Br** Widespread, but local, and possibly only native in SW England.

N **English Stonecrop** *Sedum anglicum* Hairless, evergreen, mat-forming perennial to only 5cm. Leaves oblong, 3-6mm, alternate (compare with following species), greyish green or red-tinged. Flowers almost unstalked, white (pink beneath), 12mm in diameter, in terminal clusters of 3-6. Locally common in a wide variety of dry, sandy or rocky places and shingle. **Fl** 6-9. **Br** Most common in the west and Ireland; scattered localities near S and E coasts.

O **Thick-leaved Stonecrop** *Sedum dasyphyllum* Very similar to previous species, but leaves mainly opposite, always greyish with glandular hairs, and often falling and rooting to form new plants. Flowers 6mm in diameter, in small cymes. Local in rocky places, on old walls and banks. **Fl** 6-9. **Br** Introduced in S and central England; possibly native near Cork in Ireland.

A	B	C
E	I	F
G		H
K	M	N

A **Orpine**
B **Rose-root**
C **Reflexed Stonecrop**
E **Biting Stonecrop**
I **Hairy Stonecrop**
F **Tasteless Stonecrop**
G *Sedum alpestre*
H *Sedum anuum*
K *Sedum rubens*
M **White Stonecrop**
N **English Stonecrop**

A

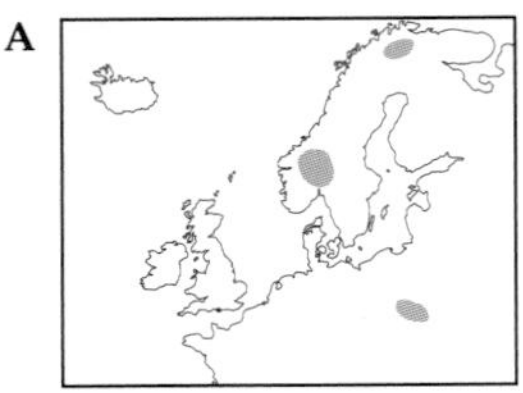

B

D

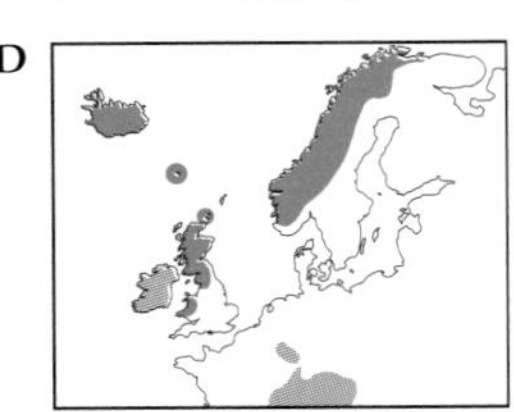

J

M

O

Saxifrage Family
Saxifragaceae

Mainly perennial herbs with leaves simple; usually alternate or spiral, or entirely in basal rosette. Flowers with 5 petals and sepals (*Saxifraga*) or 4 sepals but no petals (*Chrysosplenium*), and twice the number of stamens. Carpels 2, united at the base but free above. Fruit a capsule with numerous seeds.

(1) Leaves broad, rounded or spoon-shaped in basal rosettes; stems leafless.

A *Saxifraga hieracifolia* Hairy perennial to 40cm, with oval, slightly toothed, leaves, all in a basal rosette. Flowers greenish, often with a purple hue, *in a distinctive spike of separate clusters, each subtended by a large leafy bract*. Very local in damp, often rocky places in mountains; in Norway and Poland. **Fl** 7-8. **Br** Absent.

B **Alpine Saxifrage** *Saxifraga nivalis* Perennial to 20cm, with glandular hairs on purplish stem and leaf margins. Leaves thick and spoon-shaped, *purplish beneath*, all in basal rosette. Flowers white or pink (without spots), *short-stalked* in dense terminal cluster. Sepals erect or spreading. In wet, often shady, rocks, screes and moraines; most frequent in Scandinavia. **Fl** 7-8. **Br** Rare in N Wales, NW England, Scotland and W Ireland.

C *Saxifraga tenuis* Differs from Alpine Saxifrage in having long-stalked flowers. Similar habitats. **Fl** 7-8. **Br** Absent.

D **Starry Saxifrage** *Saxifraga stellaris* Perennial to 30cm, slightly hairy and often tufted. Leaves thick and oblong, toothed, *hardly stalked*, and all in basal rosettes. Inflorescence an open, loose panicle of up to 14 white flowers, the *petals having 2 yellow spots near the base but no red spots above*; sepals down-turned. Locally frequent in streamsides, mountain flushes and damp places. **Fl** 6-8. **Br** Frequent in mountains.

E *Saxifraga foliosa* Differs in not being tufted, and in usually having only 1 terminal flower, the rest being replaced by vegetative reproductive bulbils. Local in damp rocky places in Arctic and sub-Arctic areas. **Fl** 7-8. **Br** Absent.

F **St Patrick's-cabbage** *Saxifraga spathularis* Tufted perennial to 30cm, with reddish stem. Leaves thick, long-stalked, spoon-shaped, *sharply toothed* and *ascending*, in a basal rosette; often red-tinged beneath and with a narrow cartilaginous border; *hairless*. Inflorescence an open, loose panicle; flowers white, the *petals having 1-3 yellow spots at the base and numerous crimson dots above*; sepals down-turned. In damp, rocky places, in the shade or open; Ireland only. **Fl** 6-8. **Br** Very locally abundant in W Ireland and Wicklow.

G **Pyrenean Saxifrage** *Saxifraga umbrosa* Very similar to St Patrick's-cabbage, the most obvious difference being in the basal leaves which are *spreading* and have *blunt teeth*. Rarely naturalised in damp, shady places; native in Pyrenees. **Fl** 6-7. **Br** Naturalised in Yorkshire.

H **London-pride** *Saxifraga × urbium* Hybrid between the previous 2 species. Intermediate in character and with some hairs on upper surface. Naturalised from gardens in Britain, Ireland and France; uncommon naturally in the wild. **Fl** 5-8. **Br** Scattered localities, mainly in Ireland and the north and west.

I **Kidney Saxifrage** *Saxifraga hirsuta* Perennial to 30cm, similar to previous 2 species but having *rounded or kidney-shaped leaves, hairy on both sides*. Flowers often without red dots on petals. In damp, shady rocks and streamsides; in Ireland. **Fl** 5-7. **Br** SW Ireland only.

(2) Leaves oblong, mostly in basal rosettes, with some much smaller stem leaves.

J *Saxifraga cotyledon* Perennial to 30cm. Leaves mostly in dense basal rosettes, oblong-lanceolate, to 60mm long and 15mm wide, finely toothed and bristle-tipped; stem leaves similar, but smaller. Flowers white, 10-18mm, numerous in loose branched panicles. Mountain rocks and moraines; in Scandinavia and Iceland. **Fl** 7-8. **Br** Absent.

K *Saxifraga paniculata* Perennial to 30cm. Leaves almost entirely in hemispherical basal rosettes, but *leaf much smaller than previous species*, to 40mm long, 8mm wide, broadest above middle; stem leaves much smaller. Flowers white or cream, 6-12mm in diameter, numerous in loose branched panicle. Local in rocky places, cliffs, moraines and screes; in central and E Europe. **Fl** 6-8. **Br** Absent.

(3) Leaves broadly rounded, stems leafy.

L **Meadow Saxifrage** *Saxifraga granulata* Hairy perennial to 50cm. Leaves mostly basal, rounded or kidney-shaped, with numerous shallow, *blunt teeth* all around the margin; at the base of the leaf stalks, below ground, are a number of bulbils by which the plant overwinters. Flowers white, 15-30mm in diameter, 2-12 in terminal loose clusters; petals twice the length of sepals. Widespread and locally frequent in grassland, usually on well-drained neutral or basic soils, but occasionally in damp or wet meadows. **Fl** 4-6. **Br** Rather local, most common in the east; very local in E Ireland.

M *Saxifraga rotundifolia* Perennial to 40cm, with rosettes of leaves similar to previous species, but also with numerous stem leaves, the lower ones long-stalked, *with pointed teeth. Flowers white with yellow spots at the base and red dots above*. Very local in damp, shady places in or near mountains; in central and E Europe. **Fl** 6-10. **Br** Rarely naturalised in Scotland.

(4) Leaves lobed.

N **Rue-leaved Saxifrage** *Saxifraga tridactylites* Annual to 15cm, glandular hairy and usually reddish. *Lower leaves stalked* with 1-3 finger-like lobes; upper leaves simple. Flowers white, only 4-6mm in diameter, in loose clusters or solitary. Locally frequent on old walls and rocks, dry, sandy or calcareous ground. **Fl** 6-9. **Br** Widespread but ranging from very local to locally frequent, rare in Scotland.

O *Saxifraga adscendens* Biennial to 20cm. Leaves wedge-shaped, *unstalked*, in a basal rosette as well as along the stem; 2-5 broadly triangular lobes towards the apex of each leaf. Flowers white, 6-10mm, in loose clusters. Local on damp rocks, screes and grassy places in mountains. **Fl** 6-8. **Br** Absent.

P *Saxifraga osloensis* Hybrid between the previous 2 species, with stalked wedge-shaped leaves; flowers 6-10mm in diameter. Rare in similar habitats; in Sweden and SE Norway only. **Br** Absent.

B	D	F
	H	I
J	K	
L	M	N	O

B Alpine Saxifrage

D Starry Saxifrage

F St Patrick's-cabbage

H London-pride

I Kidney Saxifrage

J *Saxifraga cotyledon*

K *Saxifraga paniculata*

L Meadow Saxifrage

M *Saxifraga rotundifolia*

N Rue-leaved Saxifrage

O *Saxifraga adscendens*

A

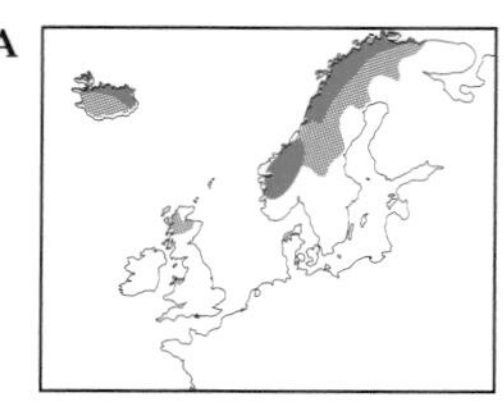

C

F

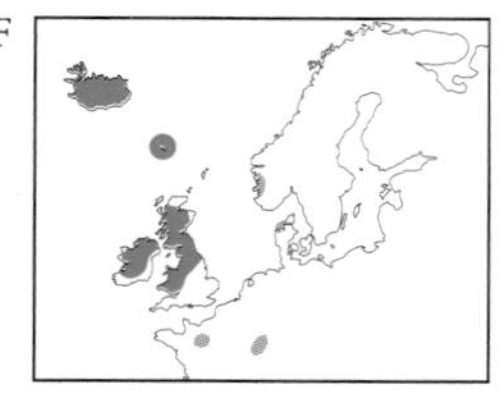

G

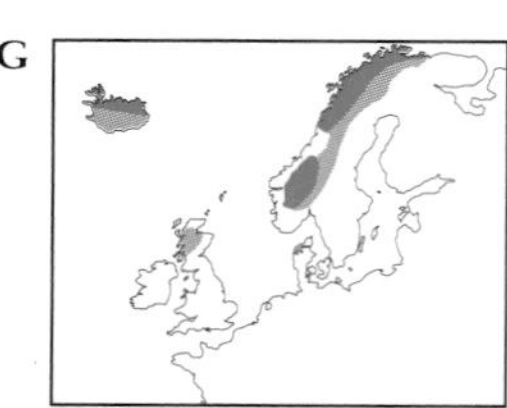

H

I

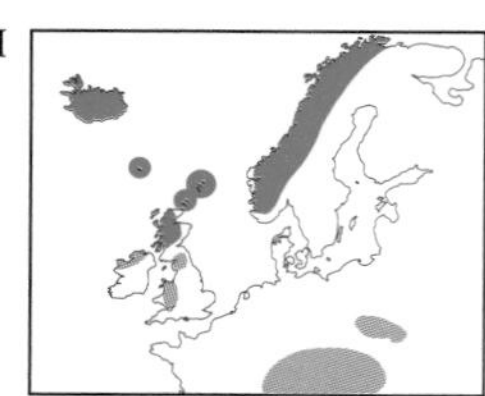

K

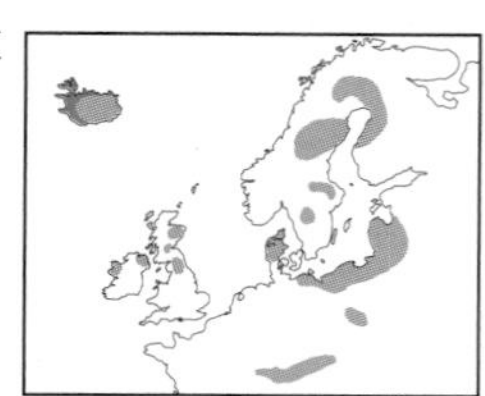

L

N

A Tufted Saxifrage *Saxifraga caespitosa* Densely tufted, low, compact cushion-forming perennial to only 10cm. Leaves 3- to 5-lobed with *blunt, finger-like lobes*. Flowers 1-5, *dull white*, 7-10mm. On mountain rocks; locally frequent in the north. **Fl** 6-7. **Br** Very rare in N Wales and Scottish Highlands.

B *Saxifraga hartii* Differs in having leaves with 5-7 *pointed lobes* and *flowers pure white*. On sea-cliffs. **Fl** 6-7. **Br** Endemic to NW Ireland and very rare.

C Irish Saxifrage *Saxifraga rosacea* Rather compact, cushion-forming perennial to 20cm. Leaves wedge-shaped with 3-7 lobes, *each pointed* (compare with Tufted Saxifrage). Flowers white, *12-18mm in diameter*, 1-8 in loose terminal cluster. Local in damp rocky places or streamsides in mountains, or sea-cliffs. **Fl** 6-8. **Br** Very local in S and W Ireland; extinct in N Wales.

D *Saxifraga moschata* Rather distinctive, densely cushion-forming hairy perennial to only 10cm, with many barren leafy shoots. Leaves mainly basal, glandular hairy, and usually deeply divided into 3-5 narrow finger-like lobes. *Flowers pale yellow or creamy*, 5-8mm in diameter, solitary or in loose clusters of 2-7; *petals narrow and not touching*. In rocky places in mountains of central Europe. **Fl** 7-8. **Br** Absent.

E *Saxifraga exarata* Differs from *S. moschata* in having white or pink flowers with petals touching. Similar habitats. **Fl** 7-8. **Br** Absent.

F Mossy Saxifrage *Saxifraga hypnoides* Mat-forming perennial to 20cm, characterised by having, in addition to the erect flowering shoots, *numerous procumbent non-flowering shoots bearing leafy bulbils in the axils of the leaves*. Leaves 3- to 5-lobed with narrow, pointed, linear lobes. Flowers white, 10-15mm in diameter, 1-5 in terminal cluster; buds nodding. Very local on rocks, screes and in grassy places; with a distinct north-west distribution. **Fl** 5-7. **Br** Locally frequent from N England to N Scotland; rare in Mendips; very local in N and W Ireland.

G Highland Saxifrage *Saxifraga rivularis* Short perennial to only 8cm. Leaves mainly basal, palmate with *3-7 shallow, blunt lobes*; no bulbils in axils of stem leaves. *Several flower stems, usually not much longer than basal leaves*, and each bearing 1-3 white flowers, 6-8mm in diameter. On wet rocks and ledges; mostly Arctic and sub-Arctic. **Fl** 7-8. **Br** Very rare in the Scottish Highlands.

H Drooping Saxifrage *Saxifraga cernua* Slender perennial to 15cm. Basal leaves in a rosette, shallowly palmately lobed, like Highland Saxifrage, with 3-5 lobes. Flowers white, 12-18mm in diameter, *solitary or often absent*, all or remaining flowers being replaced by *reproductive red bulbils in axils of bracts*. Local to very rare, in rocky, often shady places in mountains. **Fl** 6-7. **Br** Very rare in Scottish Highlands.

(5) Flowers pink to purple; leaves opposite, densely set all along stems.

I Purple Saxifrage *Saxifraga oppositifolia* Low, mat-forming perennial with creeping stems. Distinctive in having *opposite leaves* and *purple flowers*. Leaves dark green, oblong and thick, 2-6mm long with a thickened tip bearing 1-5 lime-secreting pores, and bristly margins. Flowers solitary on a short stalk, rosy purple and 10-20mm in diameter. Local to locally frequent, on damp basic rocks in mountains, sea-cliffs and stony ground down to sea level. **Fl** 3-5 (occasionally also 7-8). **Br** Local to rare in Wales and N England; locally frequent in Scottish Highlands, more local elsewhere in Scotland; very rare in NW Ireland.

J *Saxifraga biflora* Low, cushion-forming perennial with closely set, broad, oval leaves to 10mm, each bearing only 1 line-pore, and striking reddish-purple flowers, 16-20mm in diameter with a yellowish centre. Unlike previous species, petals are distinctly separate from each other. Damp screes and river-gravels in the Alps. **Fl** 6-8. **Br** Absent.

(6) Bright yellow flowers; narrow-oblong leaves.

K Marsh Saxifrage *Saxifraga hirculus* Perennial to 20cm, with leafy flowering stem bearing reddish hairs above. Leaves lanceolate, untoothed, and *stalked*. Flowers bright yellow, 20-30mm in diameter, *often solitary or 2-3 in a cluster*; petals often bearing orange dots near the base. Very local to locally frequent, in wet grassy places on moors or mountains. **Fl** 7-8. **Br** Very local and rare in N England, Scotland and Ireland. Shy flowering, and so easily overlooked.

L Yellow Saxifrage *Saxifraga aizoides* Perennial to 20cm, with leafy, slightly hairy, flowering stem. Leaves rather thick, lanceolate, *unstalked* and often toothed. Flowers bright yellow or orange-yellow, 7-15mm in diameter, *in a loose cluster of 1-10 flowers*; petals often bearing red dots near the base. Locally common, on wet stony ground and streamsides, usually in mountains but descending to sea level. **Fl** 6-9. **Br** Locally common in N England, Scotland and N Ireland.

GOLDEN-SAXIFRAGES *Chrysosplenium* Perennials with stalked leaves and small apetalous 4-sepalled flowers in flat leafy clusters.

M Opposite-leaved Golden-saxifrage *Chrysosplenium oppositifolium* Patch-forming perennial to 15cm, with creeping, rooting stems. Leaves in opposite pairs, slightly hairy, stalked and rounded with numerous blunt teeth, *the stalk usually no longer than the blade*. Flowers yellow, without petals and only 3-5mm in diameter, in dense flat clusters subtended by greenish-yellow bracts. Widespread and locally common in shady streamsides, damp woodland flushes and mountain rocks; absent from most of Scandinavia and the far east of the region. **Fl** 4-7. **Br** Locally common to common in most areas, but more local in E England.

N Alternate-leaved Golden-saxifrage *Chrysosplenium alternifolium* Patch-forming and slightly hairy, as previous species, but has *creeping leafless stolons* instead of leafy stems, and *long-stalked, kidney-shaped leaves* with blunt teeth. Flowers very similar, but 5-6mm in diameter, with bracts deeply toothed. Local to very local, in damp, shady woodlands, usually on base-rich soils; also on mountain rocks. More frequent than previous species in Scandinavia and the east. **Fl** 3-6. **Br** More local than previous species, absent from the extreme north, extreme west and Ireland.

O *Chrysosplenium tetrandrum* Differs in being hairless and having 4 stamens instead of 8. In wet Arctic places. **Fl** 6-8. **Br** Absent.

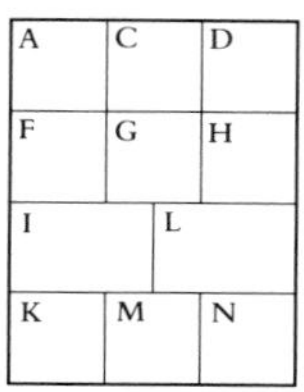

A Tufted Saxifrage

C Irish Saxifrage

D *Saxifraga moschata*

F Mossy Saxifrage

G Highland Saxifrage

H Drooping Saxifrage

I Purple Saxifrage

L Yellow Saxifrage

K Marsh Saxifrage

M Opposite-leaved Golden-saxifrage

N Alternate-leaved Golden-saxifrage

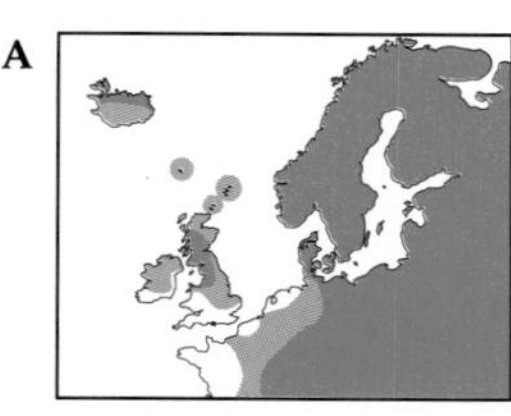

A

D

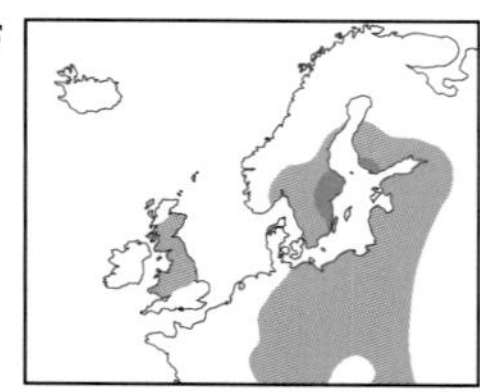

F

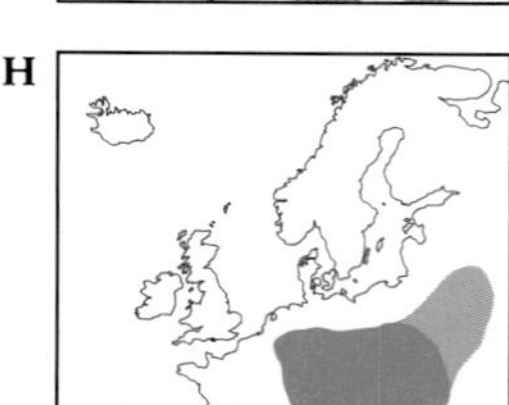

H

Grass-of-Parnassus Family
Parnassaceae

Perennials with simple alternate leaves, mainly basal, and solitary regular flowers with 5 petals, 5 sepals and 5 stamens plus a characteristic ring of 5 staminodes inside and opposite the petals.

A **Grass of Parnassus** *Parnassia palustris* Hairless tufted perennial to 30cm. Basal leaves stalked and heart-shaped, often red-spotted beneath; stem leaf solitary and clasping. Flower solitary, white, 15-30mm in diameter; petals have conspicuous greenish veins. Locally frequent in marshes, moors and fens. **Fl** 6-10. **Br** Widespread but varying from rare to locally frequent; most frequent in the north; rare in central S England; absent from extreme south.

Currant Family
Grossulariaceae

Small deciduous shrubs to about 3m, with palmately lobed leaves and 4- to 5-parted flowers, the petals usually shorter than sepals.

B **Red Currant** *Ribes rubrum* Shrub to 2m, with erect stems and 5-lobed leaves, not strongly smelling when bruised. Flowers 5-8mm, pale green and purple-edged, in drooping racemes of *up to 20 flowers*; flower structure distinctive, the receptacle being saucer-shaped with a 5-angled raised rim. Bract much shorter than flower stalk. *Fruit a shiny red berry.* Widespread and locally frequent; native in the west but often naturalised elsewhere, in wet woodlands, fens and streamsides. Absent from most of Scandinavia and the east. **Fl** 4-5. **Br** Locally common, but introduced in Scotland and Ireland.

C **Black Currant** *Ribes nigrum* Very similar in overall appearance to previous species, differing in having *leaves with aromatic glands beneath giving a strong smell when bruised*; racemes *up to 10-flowered*; flowers drooping and rather bell-shaped; *fruit a black berry.* Locally frequent in damp woodland, hedgerows and fens; more widespread than Red Currant, but often naturalised and exact native distribution difficult to evaluate. **Fl** 4-5. **Br** Widespread and locally common, especially in the south.

D *Ribes petraeum* Shrub to 3m, rather similar in appearance to Black Currant with 5-lobed leaves and bell-shaped flowers, but spreading or drooping racemes are *20-35 flowered* and flowers are pinkish; fruit dark purplish red. In woodlands and rocky places in mountains. **Fl** 4-6. **Br** Absent.

E **Downy Currant** *Ribes spicatum* Very similar to Red Currant with red berries, but has *racemes of flowers spreading or ascending rather than drooping* (except when in fruit), and flowers with rounded (non-angled) receptacle, not saucer-shaped; *bracts much shorter than flower stalks* (compare with Mountain Currant). Local in woods on basic soils; mainly in Scandinavia. **Fl** 4-5. **Br** Very local in N England and Scotland.

F **Mountain Currant** *Ribes alpinum* Shrub to 2m, with 3-lobed leaves. Flowers yellowish green, male and female on separate plants and borne on *upright racemes; each bract longer than flower stalk.* Local in rocky woods and cliffs, usually on limestone; widely escaped and naturalised outside its native area. **Fl** 4-6. **Br** Very local or rare in N Wales and N England; naturalised elsewhere.

G **Gooseberry** *Ribes uva-crispa* Shrub to 1.5m, with spreading, *spiny stems.* Flowers 10mm in diameter, drooping, 1-3 in clusters; petals greenish with red tinge. Fruit an oval pale green berry, usually bristly. In damp woodlands and hedgerows; often native but widely naturalised. **Fl** 3-5. **Br** Widespread and frequent, but often an escape; introduced in Ireland.

Rose Family Rosaceae

A very large and diverse family of trees, shrubs and herbs always possessing alternate, non-fleshy leaves (often lobed) and usually with stipules. A common feature is that the stamens and petals are attached to the sepals by their bases, so that when the sepals are removed the stamens and petals come with them. Flowers regular with parts usually in 5s, but sometimes 4s (lady's-mantles, burnets and cinquefoils), or rarely 6s. An epicalyx (outer ring of sepals below true sepals) is often present. Fruit very variable, ranging from capsule or collection of achenes to drupes (cherries and plums), drupelets (blackberries) or pomes (apples and pears).

H **Goat's-beard Spiraea** *Aruncus dioicus* Stout perennial to 2m, with erect stems. Leaves up to 1m long, bipinnate with numerous pairs of oval, sharply toothed leaflets. Flowers white, 5mm, virtually unstalked and in multiple dense spreading or ascending spikes. In damp shady places, mountain woods; in Belgium, France and Germany. **Fl** 5-8. **Br** Absent.

I **Meadowsweet** *Filipendula ulmaria* Perennial to 1.2m, with compound leaves bearing 2 types of leaflets: 2-5 pairs of larger sharply toothed leaflets, each 20-80mm, and between these a number of tiny leaflets, each 1-4mm; terminal leaflet 3- to 5-lobed. Inflorescence consisting of dense showy panicles of many creamy, fragrant flowers, each 4-8mm in diameter. Fruit a distinctive spirally twisted achene. Widespread and common in a variety of damp or wet habitats such as marshes, fens, streamsides, ditches and wet open woodland. **Fl** 6-9. **Br** Common throughout.

J **Dropwort** *Filipendula vulgaris* Perennial to 50cm, with similar features to previous species, the leaves bearing 2 types of leaflets, but differing in having 8-20 pairs of larger leaflets, each 5-15mm and *deeply pinnately cut into narrow lobes.* Inflorescence differs in being *flat-topped,* an inverted triangular shape and consisting of numerous, larger, creamy white flowers, reddish beneath and 10-20mm across. Rather local from S Sweden southwards; in dry calcareous grassland. **Fl** 5-8. **Br** Local or sometimes locally abundant, north to Yorkshire and in Wales; very rare in E Scotland; very local in W Ireland.

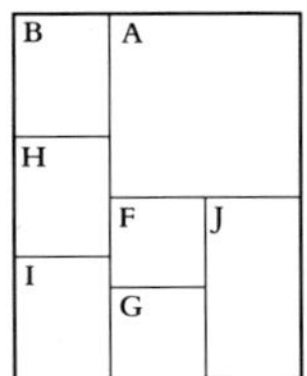

B **Red Currant**

A **Grass-of-Parnassus**

H **Goat's-beard Spiraea**

F **Mountain Currant**

I **Meadowsweet**

G **Gooseberry**

J **Dropwort**

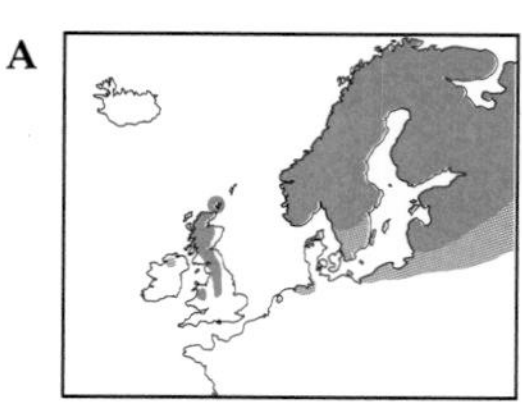

A

B

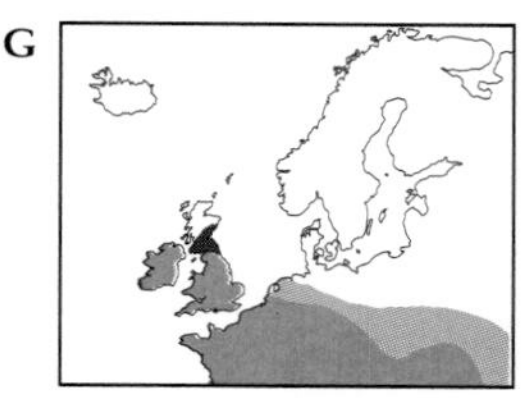

G

H

BRAMBLES *Rubus* Perennials, often prickly and scrambling, and usually with compound leaves (except Cloudberry), the leaflets having stipules. Flowers with 5 sepals joined below, 5(-8) separate petals but no epicalyx; carpels on a conical receptacle (contrast with *Rosa* species). Fruit an aggregate of 1-seeded fleshy drupelets.

A **Cloudberry** *Rubus chamaemorus* Low, downy creeping perennial to 20cm, without prickles and often forming patches. Leaves few, 1-3 per plant, rounded to 80mm in diameter, somewhat wrinkled and palmately lobed with 5-7 lobes. Flowers white (often absent), 15-25mm in diameter, solitary on a terminal stalk; usually dioecious. Fruit becoming red, then orange, a collection of about 20 drupelets. Locally abundant in mountain moors and bogs. **Fl** 6-8. **Br** Locally abundant from N England to N Scotland; rare in N Wales; very rare in Ireland.

B **Arctic Bramble** *Rubus arcticus* Creeping perennial to 40cm, without prickles. Leaves trifoliate with toothed leaflets. *Flowers solitary*, 15-20mm in diameter, *bright pink*. Fruit dark red, a collection of many drupelets. Locally frequent in moors and grassy places in mountains; Scandinavia only. **Fl** 6-7. **Br** Apparently extinct, but formerly in Scottish Highlands.

C **Stone Bramble** *Rubus saxatilis* Creeping perennial to 40cm, with either weak prickles or none. Leaves trifoliate, toothed, paler and slightly hairy beneath. Inflorescence consisting of *2-10 dull white flowers*, 5-10mm in diameter, and with 5 erect narrow petals equalling down-turned sepals. Fruit shiny red with 2-6 large drupelets. Mainly local to locally frequent on shaded rocks and in wooded areas, especially on limestone; most frequent in Scandinavia, and absent from the far west of mainland Europe. **Fl** 6-8. **Br** Local from Wales to Scotland, local also in Ireland; very rare in S England.

D **Raspberry** *Rubus idaeus* Tall erect perennial with arching biennial stems to 1.6m, bearing weak prickles. *Leaves pinnate with 3-7 toothed leaflets, markedly downy beneath.* Flowers white, about 10mm in diameter, in loose clusters of up to 10 flowers; petals narrow, erect and equalling sepals. Fruit red, not shiny, but downy with many drupelets. Widespread and common in woods, heaths and rocky places. **Fl** 6-8. **Br** Common throughout.

E **Bramble, Blackberry** *Rubus fruticosus* agg Very complex aggregate of hundreds of microspecies, too complex and difficult for this work, and separated by minute variations in structure. Generally, the aggregate comprises scrambling shrubs to 3m tall with biennial arching woody stems, variably prickled and angled. *Leaves with 3-5 (rarely 7), toothed leaflets, often prickly.* Flowers white or pink, 20-30mm in diameter, in loose panicles. Fruit changing from green to red, then shiny black or purplish red when ripe. Common in a variety of habitats ranging from damp woodland and scrub to dry open heaths and waste ground; most frequent in the west, and absent from much of the far north. **Fl** 5-9. **Br** Very common throughout.

F **Dewberry** *Rubus caesius* Rather prostrate, sprawling perennial, with *very weak prickles* and weak biennial stems. *Leaves trifoliate*, toothed and rather wrinkled. Flowers always white, 20-25mm. Fruit bluish black, *covered with a characteristic plum-like waxy bloom*; lateral fruits with 2-5 drupelets, terminal fruit with 14-20. Widespread and common in a variety of habitats ranging from dry grassland or scrub (often on calcareous soils) to fen carr; absent from the far north. **Fl** 6-9. **Br** Generally common, but rare in N Scotland, and locally frequent in Ireland.

ROSES *Rosa* Shrubs with prickly stems, pinnate leaves, well-developed stipules, and flowers with 5 showy petals and 5 sepals, but no epicalyx. The genus differs from brambles in having a deep or concave receptacle, which ripens to the fleshy fruit, or hip, containing numerous achenes. Styles protrude through the orifice of a central disc, the character of which can help to separate species.

(1) Prickles strongly hooked.

(a) Styles united into a column.

G **Field Rose** *Rosa arvensis* Shrub to 1m, with *weak trailing or scrambling stems*, often purple- tinted. Prickles sparse and hooked, all about equal. Leaflets 5-7, to 35mm. Inflorescence of 1-6 white flowers, 30-50mm in diameter, with styles distinctively united into a *long column equalling the shortest stamens*. Outer 2 sepals have a few narrow, lateral, pinnate lobes. Fruit red, oblong or ovoid, the sepals not persisting. Widespread in woods, scrub and hedges. **Fl** 6-8. **Br** Very common in S England, Wales and Ireland; becoming rare towards N England, and absent from Scotland.

H *Rosa stylosa* Shrub to 4m, with *arching stems* and hooked prickles (**h1**), often with stout bases. Leaflets 5-7, singly toothed and hairy beneath. Flowers 1-many, 30-60mm in diameter, white or pale pink (**h2**); styles united into a column, *shorter than inner stamens* (compare with Field Rose). Outer sepals with narrow side-lobes, not persisting in fruit. Widespread but local in the west of the region; in hedgerows, rough grassy areas and scrub. **Fl** 6-7. **Br** Local north to Lancaster, N Wales in the west and Suffolk in the east.

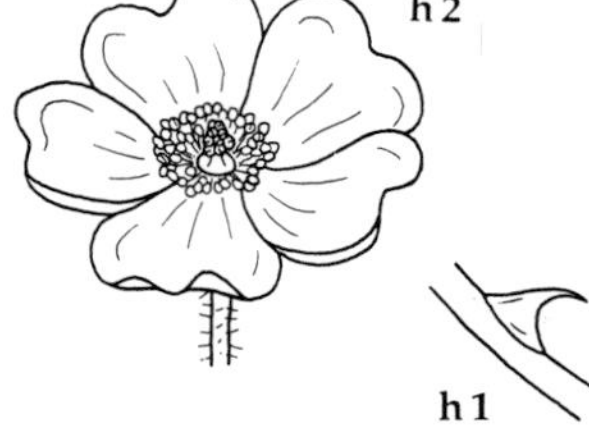

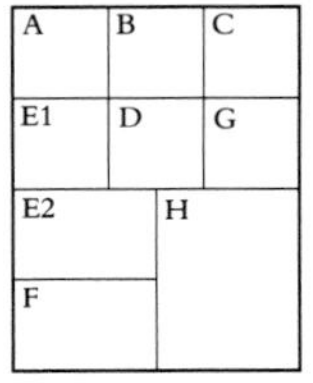

A **Cloudberry**

B **Arctic Bramble**

C **Stone Bramble** showing leaves

E **1 Bramble** showing flowers

D **Raspberry** showing leaves and fruit

G **Field Rose**

E **2 Bramble** showing fruit

F **Dewberry**

H *Rosa stylosa*

A

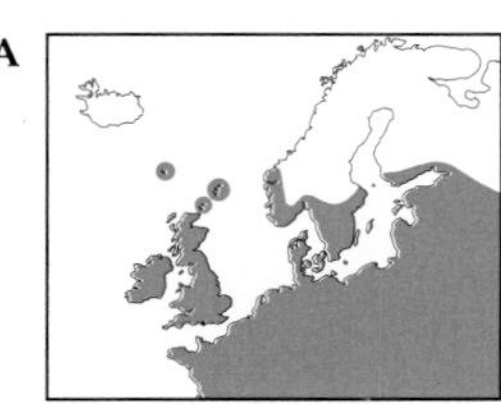

B

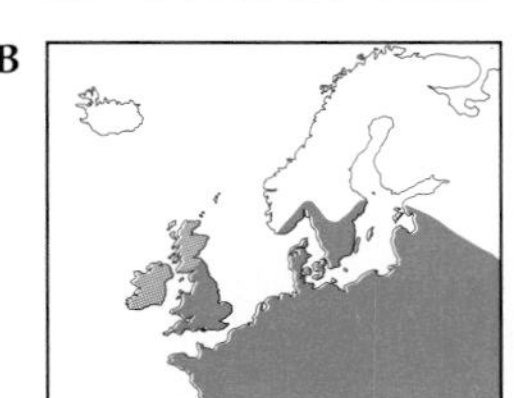

B1

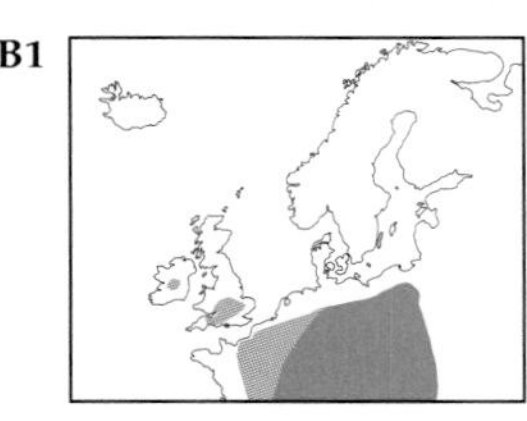

B2

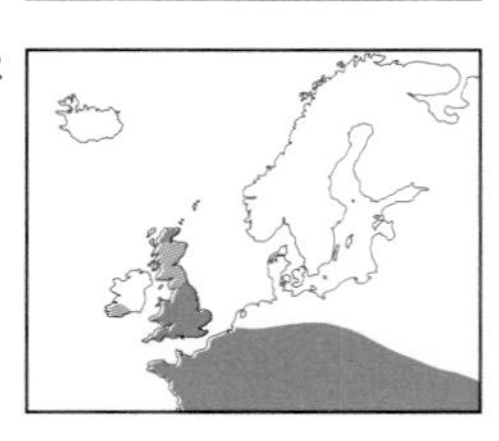

C

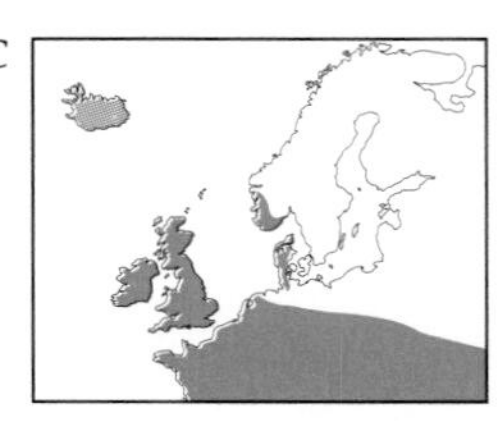

D

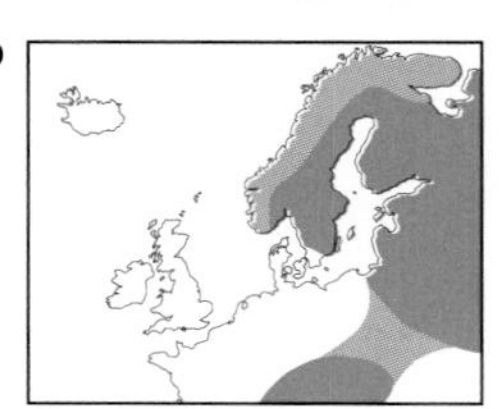

F

G

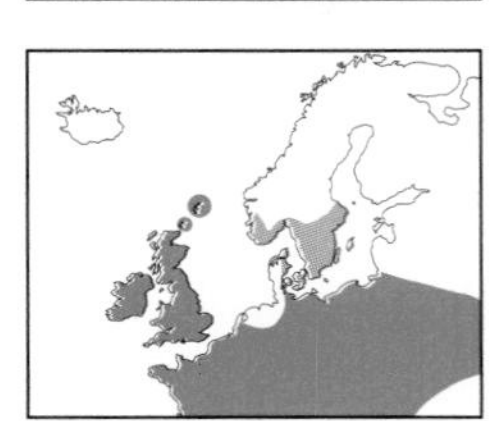

(b) Styles not united into a column.

***Rosa canina* group** Distinguished by having stout curved or hooked prickles (**a**) and leaflets usually either without glands or with glands only on main veins; not scented when bruised (compare with *R. rubiginosa* group). Outer sepals with narrow, projecting side-lobes.

A **Dog-rose** *Rosa canina* Shrub to 4m with arching stems. Leaflets 5-7, to 40mm long, hairless. Flowers 1-4, pink or white, 30-50mm in diameter. Disc wide with narrow orifice, up to 1mm wide. Flower stalk 10-20mm, hairless and without glands. Fruit red, hairless, oval or rounded and without sepals when ripe. Widespread and common in hedges, scrub and woodland margins. **Fl** 6-7. **Br** Throughout, but commonest in the south and becoming rare in N Scotland.

The following 5 species in the group are very close to Dog-rose, with similar habitats and flowering times, but have critical differences:

(i) Species with hairless leaflets.

Rosa squarrosa Leaf stalk and veins glandular; leaves doubly toothed. Probably widespread, but more frequent to the east. **Br** Distribution imperfectly known.

Rosa vosagiaca Stems reddish; leaflets bluish green; sepals persistent on fruit. Widespread almost throughout. **Br** Absent.

(ii) Species with hairy leaflets.

Round-leaved Dog-rose *Rosa obtusifolia* Veins glandular; flower stalk without glands. Mainly western and as far north as S Sweden. **Br** As far north as Northumberland, and in Ireland.

Rosa corymbifera Veins without glands; flower stalk without glands. Most frequent towards the south and east. **Br** Distribution imperfectly known.

Rosa caesia Leaflets densely hairy beneath; sepals persistent on fruit. Widespread throughout. **Br** Commonest in central and N Scotland where it replaces Dog-rose.

***Rosa rubiginosa* group** Prickles hooked or curved and leaves stickily brown glandular beneath, smelling of apples when bruised (compare with *R. canina* group); leaves sometimes hairy but never tomentose (compare with *R. tomentosa* group). Outer sepals with narrow side-lobes.

B **Sweet-briar** *Rosa rubiginosa* Shrub to 3m, with erect stems, the prickles (**b**) usually interspersed with bristles and glands. Leaflets 5-7, compound-toothed. Flowers 1-3, deep pink, 20-30mm in diameter. Sepals persistent in fruit. Widespread and often common in woods, hedges, scrub and rough grassy areas. **Fl** 6-7. **Br** Locally common in England and Wales, but more scarce in Scotland and Ireland.

The following 3 species in the group, which have similar habitats and flowering times, are described by their differences from Sweet-briar.

Rosa elliptica Stems without bristles or glands. W and central Europe (**B1**). **Br** Very rare in England and Ireland.

Small-leaved Sweet-briar *Rosa agrestis* Flowers white; sepals not glandular and not persistent in fruit. Widespread but rare in the north and east. **Br** Very rare in England and Ireland.

Small-flowered Sweet-briar *Rosa micrantha* Stems arching. Flowers white like Small-leaved Sweet-briar but sepals glandular. Widespread but absent from the north (**B2**). **Br** Widespread in England and Wales but rare in Scotland and only in SW of Ireland.

(2) Prickles straight or slightly curved.

C **Burnet Rose** *Rosa pimpinellifolia* Small patch-forming shrub to only 50cm, suckering freely. Prickles abundant and straight (**c**), long on main stems but shorter and less numerous on flowering stems. Leaflets 7-11, each oval, and up to 15mm long. Flowers solitary, creamy white (rarely pink), 20-30mm in diameter. Fruit spherical, small (about 6mm in diameter) and purplish-black when ripe. Widespread, but only locally frequent, on heaths, dunes, calcareous grassland, limestone pavement and mountain-ledges. **Fl** 5-7. **Br** Local throughout.

D **Cinnamon Rose** *Rosa majalis* Patch-forming with stems up to 2m, distinctive for its reddish-brown bark and the slender straight or slightly curved prickles in pairs at the nodes (**d1**). Leaflets 5-7, to 45mm, bluish green, downy and paler beneath. Flowers solitary, purplish pink and 30-50mm in diameter (**d2**). Fruit spherical, red and bearing the persistent sepals. In woods, hedges and scrub; Eastern and northern Europe. **Fl** 6-7. **Br** Absent.

The following 2 species resemble Cinnamon Rose, but have critical differences:

Rosa acicularis Stems have many slender bristles as well as long straight prickles, which do not occur in pairs. Similar habitats. **Fl** 6-7. **Br** Absent.

Rosa glauca Prickles not in pairs; leaves hairless, bluish green; flowers in clusters of 1-5; outer sepals usually with a few narrow side-lobes. On woodland edges and stony places in mountains; central and S Europe. **Fl** 6-8. **Br** Absent.

E **Japanese Rose** *Rosa rugosa* Stems erect to 1.5m. Leaflets 5-9, shiny above and thick; flower stalks downy; flowers white to red, 60-90mm. Fruit spherical, large to 20-50mm in diameter. Widely naturalised or planted in hedgerows, roadsides and motorway-verges. **Fl** 6-8. **Br** Introduced and naturalised, often on dunes.

F *Rosa gallica* Erect stems to 1m, suckering. Leaves leathery, with 3-5 leaflets, glandular beneath. Flowers solitary, pink to red, 70-90mm. Outer sepals with a few narrow projecting side-lobes and fruit bristly. Very local in hedges and wood-margins; in S and central Europe, extending to Belgium. **Fl** 5-8. **Br** Absent.

***Rosa tomentosa* group** Prickles straight or slightly curved (**g**). Leaflets densely hairy or tomentose, usually on both surfaces, and glands give a resinous smell when bruised. Sepals usually with narrow side-lobes.

G **Downy-rose** *Rosa tomentosa* Rather compact shrub to 2m, with arching stems. Leaflets soft, densely tomentose, 20-40mm. Flowers 1-5, pink or white, 30-40mm in diameter. Sepals not persistent in fruit. Flower stalk about 20mm. Fruit rounded or pear-shaped, covered with glands. Locally common in woods, hedges, scrub and rough grassy margins. **Fl** 6-7. **Br** Fairly common almost throughout, but rare in Scotland.

The following species differ from Downy-rose as follows:

Rosa scabriuscula Leaflets rough to touch. Sepals persistent in fruit. Probably widespread in Europe except in the north. **Fl** 6-7. **Br** Distribution imperfectly known.

Sherard's Downy-rose *Rosa sherardii* Stems have a whitish bloom and flowers always pink. Sepals soon falling in fruit. Locally frequent but absent from the south-east. **Fl** 6-7. **Br** Locally frequent in N England and Scotland; rare elsewhere.

Rosa villosa Leaflets noticeably bluish green, 30-50mm. Flower stalk only 5-10mm. Sepals persistent in fruit. Local in central and S Europe, extending north to Netherlands. **Fl** 6-7. **Br** Absent.

Soft Downy-rose *Rosa mollis* Leaflets grey green, 10-35mm. Young stems with whitish bloom and flowers deep pink. Sepals persistent in fruit. Mainly in N and W Europe. **Fl** 6-7. **Br** Locally common in S Wales and N Britain.

A1	B	
A2	G2	
G1		
C	G3	E

A **1 Dog-rose**
B **Sweet-briar**
A **2 Dog-rose** hips
G **1 Downy-rose**
G **2 Sherard's Downy-rose**
C **Burnet Rose**
G **3** *Rosa villosa*
E **Japanese Rose**

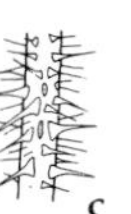

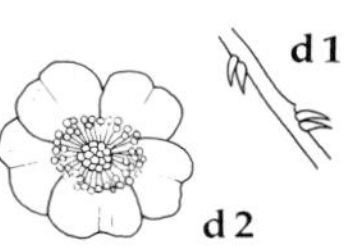

H

I

J

A **Agrimony** *Agrimonia eupatoria* Softly hairy perennial to 60cm, often with reddish stems and slight sweet smell when bruised. . Lower leaves pinnate with 3-6 pairs of larger, toothed leaflets, between which are 2-3 pairs of smaller ones; *undersurface of leaf covered with white or greyish tomentum*. Flowers yellow, 5-8mm in diameter, and numerous in dense narrow spikes. Fruit a bur-like achene with spreading (not backward-pointing) spines. Widespread and generally common in hedgebanks, road-verges and rough grassy areas, but absent from the far north. **Fl** 6-8. **Br** Common almost throughout, but rare in N Scotland and absent from Orkney and Shetland.

B *Agrimonia pilosa* Differs in having *leaves green below* and *flowers 3-5mm*. Similar habitats and flowering time. **Fl** 6-8. **Br** Absent.

C **Fragrant Agrimony** *Agrimonia procera* Similar to Agrimony but taller, to 1m, and markedly fragrant when bruised. *Leaves green on both sides*, with yellow glands on under-surface. *Flowers larger, 6-10mm in diameter*. Fruit with lower spines backward-pointing. Similar habitats and distribution, but more local on lighter acid soils. **Fl** 6-8. **Br** More local; absent from N Scotland.

D **Bastard Agrimony** *Aremonia agrimonoides* Perennial to 40cm, with stems often reddish below. Leaves pinnate with 2-4 pairs of larger toothed leaflets (*progressively longer towards the tip*), between which are 1-3 pairs of smaller ones. Flowers yellow, 7-10mm in diameter, *in loose, short terminal clusters*, and often not opening. Fruit spineless. Very local in mountain woods and scrub; in the south-east of the region. **Fl** 5-6. **Br** Introduced and naturalised in central Scotland.

E **Salad Burnet** *Sanguisorba minor* Short perennial to 40cm, hairy below. Basal leaves in a rosette, pinnate with 4-12 pairs of toothed leaflets progressively larger to 20mm, towards apex. Flowers tiny, green and in compact rounded heads, dioecious with petalless male flowers below, and red-styled female flowers above. Fruit 4-angled and ridged. Widespread, and often common, in grassland, especially on calcareous soils, but absent from much of the far north. **Fl** 5-8. **Br** Generally locally abundant but very local in Scotland, and absent from the north.

F **Great Burnet** *Sanguisorba officinalis* Rather tall perennial to 1m. Leaves distinctive, pinnate with long-stalked toothed leaflets (to 40mm), progressively larger towards the apex and often with reddish stalks. Flowers tiny, dull crimson or purplish red and in compact oblong heads on long stalks. Ranging from very local to locally frequent; in damp grassy places. **Fl** 6-9. **Br** Local and decreasing due to agricultural improvement; absent from N Scotland and very local or rare in S England.

G **Pirri-pirri-bur** *Acaena anserinifolia* Perennial undershrub to 15cm, rather similar to Salad Burnet, but creeping and much-branched with pinnate leaves having 3-4 pairs of toothed leaflets. Flowers white, in rounded compact heads, solitary on erect stalks. Fruit with soft reddish spines. Introduced from New Zealand, possibly with imported wool, and naturalised in Britain and Ireland. **Fl** 6-7. **Br** Spreading in a number of places, usually dry and sandy, especially coastal.

H **Mountain Avens** *Dryas octopetala* Creeping undershrub to only 8cm tall, with distinctive bluntly toothed, oblong evergreen leaves to 20mm, dark green above with deep veins and grey tomentose beneath. Flowers white with yellow stamens, to 40mm across and with 8 or more petals. Fruit a head of achenes made noticeable from a distance by the long feathery styles. Local to locally abundant on basic rocks, from sea level to 2,000m. **Br** Local to locally frequent in Scotland and W Ireland; rare in N Wales and N England. Descends to sea level in W Ireland and N Scotland.

Geum Perennials distinctive for their combination of flowers with parts in 5s or 7s, an epicalyx and an erect terminal style persistent in fruit and often hooked for dispersal by animals.

I *Geum reptans* Hairy, patch-forming perennial with reddish runners. Leaves mostly in basal rosettes, pinnate with toothed leaflets, the *terminal leaflet less than 4 times longer than leaflet immediately below* (compare with *G. montanum*). Flowers solitary, bright yellow, 25-40mm in diameter with 6 petals. Fruit distinctive with red feathery styles. In rocky or gravelly places in mountains. **Fl** 7-8. **Br** Absent.

J *Geum montanum* Very similar to previous species but without runners and *with terminal leaflet more than 4 times longer than side-leaflet immediately below*. Similar habitats and flowering time. **Fl** 7-8. **Br** Absent.

K **Water Avens** *Geum rivale* Tufted downy perennial to 60cm. Basal leaves pinnate with 3-6 pairs of side-leaflets and large, rounded, toothed terminal leaflet; stem leaves trifoliate. Flowers nodding, cup-shaped with orange-pink petals, and purple sepals and epicalyx. Fruit a collection of feathery achenes. Widespread and locally common in wet meadows, marshes, moist woods and on mountain-ledges, usually in base-rich conditions. **Fl** 4-9. **Br** Locally common but rare in SW England and absent from the south-east.

L **Wood Avens** *Geum urbanum* Hairy perennial to 60cm. Basal leaves pinnate with unequal toothed leaflets and large terminal leaflet usually 3-lobed; stipules large (often greater than 10mm) and leafy; stem leaves usually 3-lobed. Flowers yellow, 8-15mm with 5 rounded petals and sepals, erect at first but soon drooping. Fruit a rounded cluster of feathery achenes. Common in woods, hedgebanks and shady places. **Fl** 5-9. **Br** Common throughout.
Hybridises with Water Avens to produce *G.* × *intermedium*, which can have a range of characteristics from either parent.

M *Geum hispidum* Differs from Wood Avens in being more hairy and in having stipules less than 10mm. Rare in damp semi-shaded places in SE Sweden. **Fl** 6-7. **Br** Absent.

A	E	F
G	J	
D	H	I
K	L1	L2

A **Agrimony**

E **Salad Burnet**

F **Great Burnet**

G **Pirri-pirri-bur**

J *Geum montanum*

D **Bastard Agrimony**

H **Mountain Avens**

I *Geum reptans*

K **Water Avens**

L **1** Showing flowers (left to right) of **Water Avens,** *Geum* × *intermedium* and **Wood Avens**

L **2 Wood Avens**

B

E

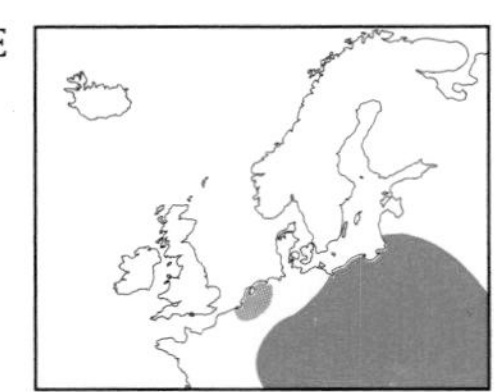

H

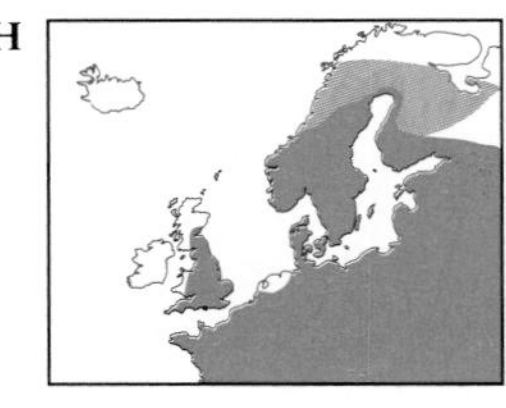

J

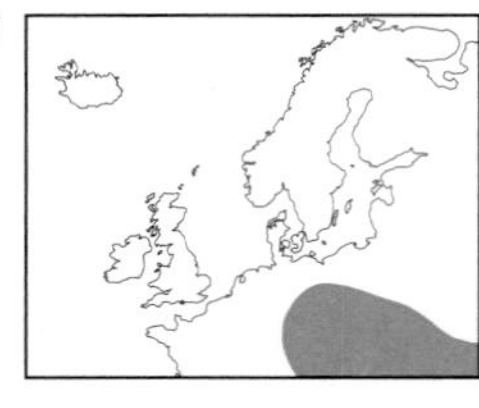

K

L

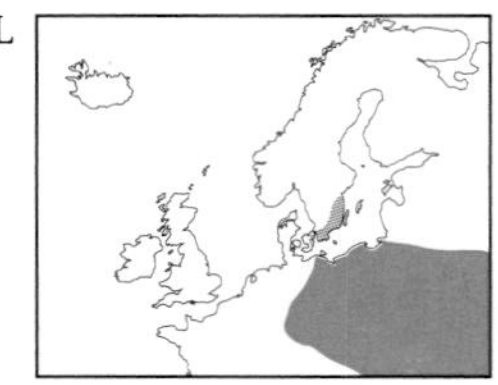

M

N

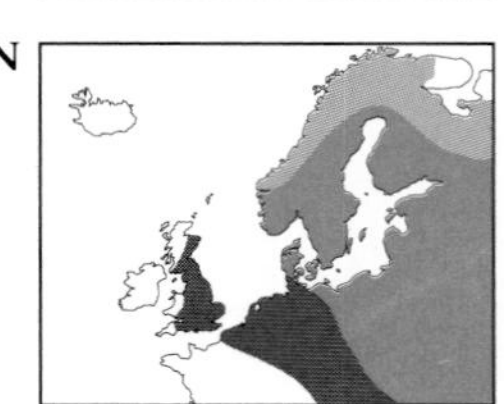

R

CINQUEFOILS *Potentilla* Herbs or small shrubs, usually perennial. Leaves lobed, pinnate or digitate. Flowers with 4-6 petals, usually 5; epicalyx present; styles not persistent and feathery in fruit (collection of achenes).

A Marsh Cinquefoil *Potentilla palustris* Hairless perennial to 45cm. Leaves greyish green, the lower ones pinnate with 5-7 leaflets and the upper ones trifoliate or palmate. Flowers distinctive, dull dark purple or red-wine coloured with 5 sharply pointed petals shorter than the (darker) purplish sepals. Widespread and locally frequent, in fens, marshes and pool-margins. **Fl** 5-7. **Br** Locally frequent in N Britain and Ireland; much more local in the south.

(1) Species with yellow flowers and leaflets not joined at the same point.

B Shrubby Cinquefoil *Potentilla fruticosa* Deciduous downy *shrub* to 1m, distinctive *untoothed greyish-green leaves* with 3-7 lanceolate leaflets. Flowers yellow, 20mm in diameter, solitary or in loose clusters, dioecious. Rare in damp rocky places (usually basic) and riverbanks. **Fl** 5-7. **Br** Rare in Teesdale and Lake District; very local in W Ireland.

C Silverweed *Potentilla anserina* Creeping perennial with long stolons to 80cm. Basal leaves pinnate, *toothed and silvery*, either on both sides or underside only; *tiny leaflets alternate with larger ones*. Flowers yellow, 15-20mm, solitary with unnotched petals. Widespread and common, in a variety of damp places such as roadsides, dunes and grassland. **Fl** 5-8. **Br** Common throughout.

D *Potentilla multifida* Hairy perennial to 40cm, distinctive for its pinnate leaves with *very narrow linear, untoothed segments with rolled edges*; greyish silky underneath. Flowers yellow, 10-14mm, in loose clusters. Rare, in rocky places in mountains of N Sweden. **Fl** 7-8. **Br** Absent.

E *Potentilla supina* Annual or short-lived perennial with stems prostrate or ascending to 40cm. Leaves green, pinnate with 5-11 sharply toothed leaflets. Stipules spreading, almost as broad as long. Flowers yellow, 6-8mm, *petals shorter than sepals*. Local, in meadows and grassy places. **Fl** 6-8. **Br** Absent.

(2) Species with yellow flowers and leaflets joined at the same point.

(a) Leaves grey or silvery below.

F *Potentilla nivea* Tufted perennial to 20cm, with trifoliate toothed leaves densely white tomentose beneath; *leaf stalk with only curled hairs*. Flowers yellow, 12-15mm, in loose clusters. Very local, in rocky places, cliffs and screes; in mountains of Scandinavia and central Europe. **Fl** 6-8. **Br** Absent.

G *Potentilla chamissonis* Differs in having only *straight hairs* on leaf stalk. Local, in rocky or gravelly Arctic habitats. **Br** Absent.

H Hoary Cinquefoil *Potentilla argentea* Downy perennial to 50cm, with spreading and ascending stems *covered with dense silvery hairs*. Leaves digitate, the 5 narrow leaflets with coarse forward-pointing teeth (basal leaves have 2-7 bluntish teeth (compare with *P. neglecta* below); *undersurface silvery white with dense hairs all curled over*. Flowers yellow, 8-12mm, in loose branched clusters; *style conical* (compare with *P. collina*). In dry places, often sandy, gravelly or rocky. **Fl** 6-9. **Br** North to mid-Scotland; local in the east and south-east but rare to the west; absent from Ireland.

I *Potentilla neglecta* Differs from Hoary Cinquefoil in having basal leaf lobes with 9-11 acute teeth and flowers slightly larger, 9-14mm. Similar habitats and flowering time. Precise distribution unknown as a result of confusion with previous species. **Fl** 6-9. **Br** Absent.

J *Potentilla inclinata* Hairy perennial to 50cm, similar to Hoary Cinquefoil but with *hairs spreading, long and straight*, and leaflets 5-7, sometimes pinnately lobed, *grey beneath rather than silvery white*. Local in rocky and short grassy places. **Fl** 6-7. **Br** Absent.

K *Potentilla collina* Almost identical to Hoary Cinquefoil, but shorter, to 30cm, and *with club-shaped style*. Sometimes hairless. Locally frequent in rocky and grassy places. **Fl** 6-8. **Br** Absent.

L *Potentilla cinerea* Densely hairy, mat-forming perennial to 20cm, with woody, procumbent, rooting stems. Leaves usually trifoliate, but sometimes with 5 leaflets, *grey cottony on both sides* due to dense mat of hairs, both simple and branched. Flowers yellow, 10-15mm, solitary or 2-6. In dry grassy and rocky places; in the east of the region. **Fl** 4-7. **Br** Absent.

M *Potentilla aurea* Low, mat-forming perennial, *leaflets having distinctive silky margins* and *terminal tooth much smaller than adjacent lateral ones* (*see* Alpine Cinquefoil, page 104). Flowers golden yellow, often orange in centre, 15-25mm in diameter. In rocky and grassy places in mountains. **Fl** 6-9. **Br** Absent.

(b) Leaves green below.

(i) Leaves apparently with 3 leaflets.

N *Potentilla norvegica* Annual or short-lived hairy perennial to 70cm. Leaves trifoliate, green on both sides. Flowers bright yellow, 8-15mm in branched clusters; petals no longer than sepals. Locally frequent in rocky and waste places or roadsides; widely naturalised outside its native range **Fl** 6-9. **Br** Introduced and naturalised, mainly in SE England.

O *Potentilla brauniana* *Dwarf* perennial to only 5cm, *sparsely hairy*. Leaves trifoliate, to 10mm. Flowers yellow, 7-12mm, solitary or in clusters of 2-5. In rocky and grassy places in the Alps and Jura, often near snow. **Fl** 6-8. **Br** Absent.

P *Potentilla frigida* Differs from *P. brauniana* in being taller, to 10cm, and having *leaflets densely hairy*. Similar habitats. **Fl** 6-8.

(ii) Leaves appearing to have 5 or more leaflets.

Q *Potentilla intermedia* Similar to *P. norvegica*, but differs in being perennial and *usually having 5 leaflets*, sometimes grey beneath. Introduced from USSR and naturalised on waste ground in many countries. **Fl** 6-9. **Br** Introduced and occasionally naturalised.

R Sulphur Cinquefoil *Potentilla recta* *Stiffly erect*, hairy perennial to 70cm. Leaves digitate with 5-7 toothed hairy leaflets. *Flowering stems terminal*; flowers pale yellow, 20-25mm, the notched petals longer than sepals. Local in dry grassy and waste places. Widely naturalised outside its native ranges. **Fl** 6-9. **Br** Introduced and naturalised in E and S England.

B	C	
D	A	F
	H	M
L	R	O

B Shrubby Cinquefoil
C Silverweed
D *Potentilla multifida*
A Marsh Cinquefoil
F *Potentilla nivea*
L *Potentilla cinerea*
H Hoary Cinquefoil
M *Potentilla aurea*
R Sulphur Cinquefoil
O *Potentilla brauniana*

A

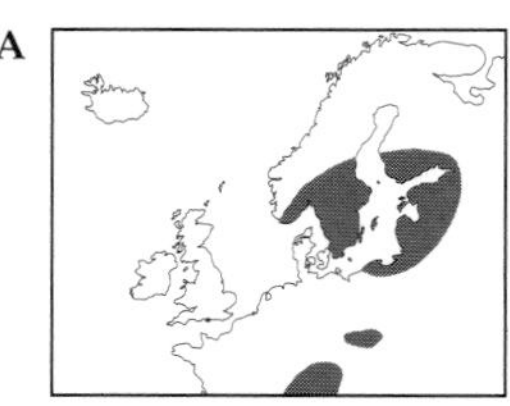

B

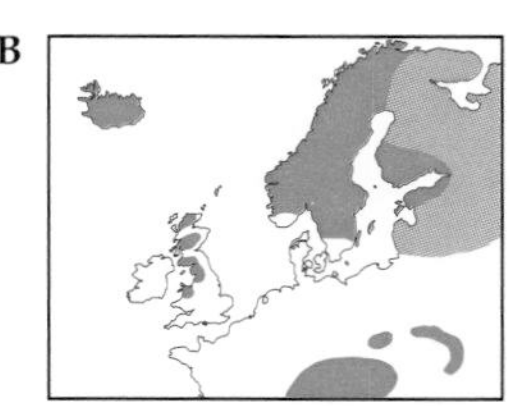

C

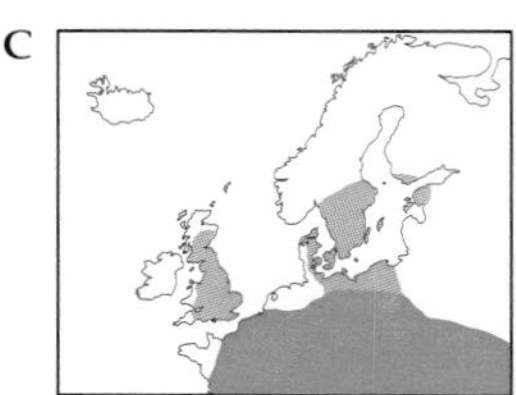

D

I

J

N

O

A *Potentilla thuringiaca* Very hairy perennial to 50cm. Leaves with 5-9 oblong-lanceolate coarsely toothed lobes. *Flowering stems lateral*; flowers yellow, 15-22mm, in loose clusters; flower stems lateral. Very local in meadows and stony places; in mountains; France and Gemany; introduced in Scandinavia. **Fl** 6-8. **Br** Absent.

B Alpine Cinquefoil *Potentilla crantzii* Hairy perennial to 25cm, not mat-forming. Leaves digitate with 5 wedge-shaped toothed leaflets, *the terminal tooth about equal to the adjacent lateral ones* (compare with *P. thuringiaca* and *P. aurea* *see* page 102). Stipules of basal leaves broadly ovate (ccompare with Spring Cinquefoil). Flowers yellow, 15-25mm in diameter, often with orange spot at base of each petal. Local to locally frequent in rocky and gravelly places, usually in mountains except in the extreme north. **Fl** 6-7. **Br** Very local in N Wales, N England and the Scottish Highlands.

C Spring Cinquefoil *Potentilla tabernaemontani* Mat-forming perennial to 20cm, with *prostrate rooting branches* and *stems woody at base*. Basal leaves digitate with 5-7 toothed leaflets; upper leaves stalkless with 3 leaflets; hairiness of leaves variable, but *with simple, unbranched hairs* only (compare with *P. pusilla*). Stipules of basal leaves very narrow (compare with Alpine Cinquefoil and *P. heptaphylla*). Flowers yellow, 10-20mm, in loose clusters on lateral flowering stems. Locally frequent in dry, calcareous grassland and rocky places on limestone; from S Sweden southwards. **Fl** 4-6. **Br** Widely scattered but very local or rare from Hampshire and Somerset north to mid-Scotland.

D *Potentilla heptaphylla* Resembles Spring Cinquefoil, but more erect, *not mat-forming* and *with reddish glandular hairs on stem*. Stipules of basal leaves ovate. Fruit stalk nodding. Flowers 10-15mm. Local in dry grassland and roadsides, usually on calcareous soils; eastern Europe. **Fl** 4-7. **Br** Absent.

E *Potentilla pusilla* Possibly a distant hybrid between Spring Cinquefoil and *P. cinerea*. Very similar to Spring Cinquefoil, but *sparingly hairy leaves have both simple and branched hairs*. Grassy places in mountains of France and S Germany. **Fl** 6-7. **Br** Absent.

F Tormentil *Potentilla erecta* Perennial with creeping and ascending stems to 30cm, but no rooting stolons. *Leaves unstalked*, almost entirely trifoliate, but often appearing digitate with 5 leaflets due to large stipules at leaf base; leaflets silky hairy on margins and veins beneath. Flowers yellow, 7-11mm, *with usually 4 petals*, on 20-40mm stalks. Common in a wide range of habitats from grassy places and woodland rides to heaths and moors. **Fl** 5-9. **Br** Common throughout.

G Creeping Cinquefoil *Potentilla reptans* Similar to Tormentil but has creeping flowering stems rooting at nodes, and *long-stalked hairless leaves* with 5-7 leaflets. Also, flowers are 17-25mm in diameter *with 5 petals*. Common in grassy places, waste areas and waysides. **Fl** 6-9. **Br** Common throughout.

H Trailing Tormentil *Potentilla anglica* Features intermediate between previous 2 species, but unlike the true hybrid it is not sterile. Creeping stems root at intervals like Creeping Cinquefoil, but leaves are mostly trifoliate and *hairy* like Tormentil, the *lower ones on short 10-20mm stalks and the upper ones on 5mm stalks. Flowers mostly with 4 petals, sometimes 5*, 14-18mm in diameter. Local to locally frequent in grassy places, heaths and waysides. **Fl** 6-9. **Br** Widespread and frequent in the south, but increasingly local northwards.

(3) Species with white flowers.

I Rock Cinquefoil *Potentilla rupestris* Hairy perennial to 50cm. *Basal leaves pinnate* with 5-9 oval, toothed leaflets, increasing in size from base to apex; stem leaves few, trifoliate. Flowers white, 15-25mm in diameter, in loose cymes. Local to rare on semi-shaded calcareous rocks. **Fl** 5-6. **Br** Very rare in mid-Wales and NE Scotland.

J *Potentilla alba* Hairy perennial to 25cm. *Leaves digitate* with 5 toothed leaflets, *green above but silvery hairy beneath*. Flowers white, 15-20mm in diameter, in loose clusters of 2-6; petals notched. In rocky and grassy places in mountains. **Fl** 4-6.

K *Potentilla caulescens* Very similar to previous species, but *leaves green on both sides* and petals pointed. Limestone rocks; in E France and S Germany. **Fl** 5-7. **Br** Absent.

L *Potentilla montana* Creeping perennial with long stolons. Leaves trifoliate, *green above and silky grey beneath*, toothed only towards tip. Flowers white, 15-25mm. In rocky places and woodlands, either lowland or to 1,500m. **Fl** 5-6.

M Barren Strawberry *Potentilla sterilis* Hairy perennial to 15cm *with long rooting stolons*. Leaves dull bluish green, trifoliate and with terminal tooth of leaflet shorter than adjacent ones. Flowers white, 10-15mm in diameter, the petals widely separated. *Epicalyx segments shorter than sepals*. Fruit not fleshy. NB Wild Strawberry (*see* page 106) has shiny leaves with long terminal tooth and fleshy fruits. In open woodland, grassy places and waysides. Widespread and common in the west; very local or absent from the east and far north. **Fl** 2-5. **Br** Common almost throughout; absent from N Scotland.

N *Potentilla micrantha* Very similar to previous species, but *without runners* and with *epicalyx segments equal to sepals*. Flowers usually pink, sometimes white. In rocky places and open woodlands to 1,600m; very local in central and E Europe. **Fl** 5-7. **Br** Absent.

O Sibbaldia *Sibbaldia procumbens* Dwarf, stiffly hairy, tufted perennial to 3cm. Leaves bluish green and distinctive: trifoliate, ovate and rather wedge-shaped, broadening towards the tip which has 3 teeth, the central one often being narrower than the 2 lateral ones. Flowers small, about 5mm in diameter, pale yellow or greenish in dense clusters; petals often diminutive or absent. Local to locally frequent in short turf and rocky places in mountains. **Fl** 7-8. **Br** Local in Scottish Highlands; very rare in N England.

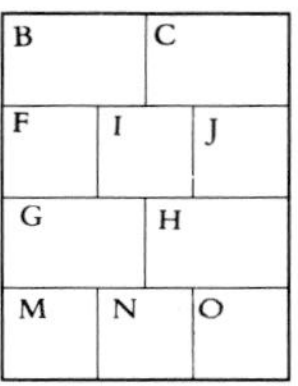

B Alpine Cinquefoil

C Spring Cinquefoil

F Tormentil

I Rock Cinquefoil

J *Potentilla alba*

G Creeping Cinquefoil

H Trailing Tormentil

M Barren Strawberry

N *Potentilla micrantha*

O Sibbaldia

B

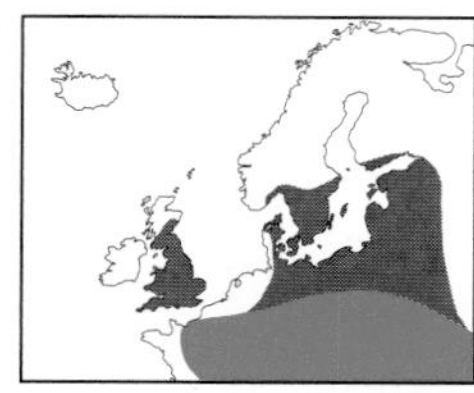

E1

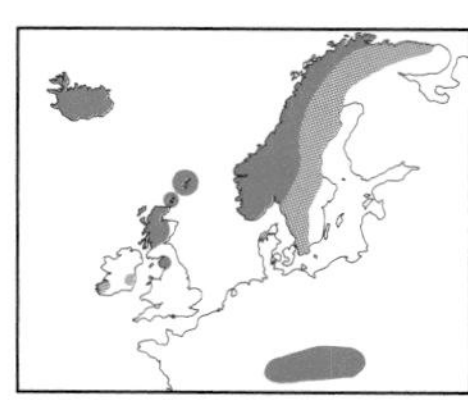

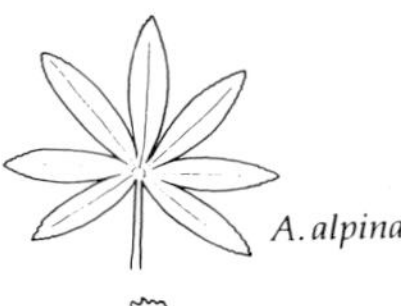
A. alpina

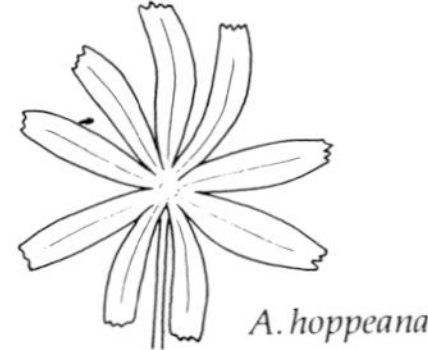
A. hoppeana

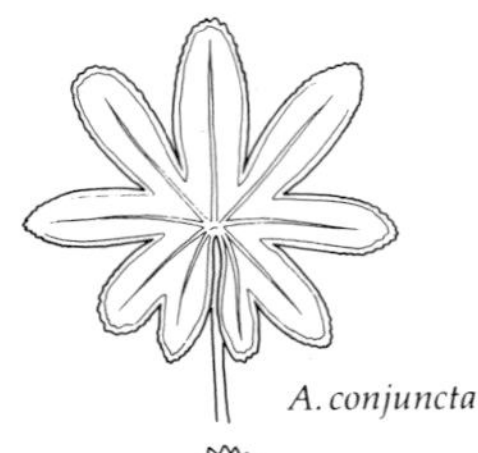
A. conjuncta

A. faeroensis

A. incisa

A. monticola

A. glaucescens

A. subcrenata

STRAWBERRIES *Fragaria* Like *Potentilla* species but leaves always trifoliate in basal rosette and fruit fleshy and brightly coloured.

A **Wild Strawberry** *Fragaria vesca* Perennial to 30cm, with long rooting stolons. Leaflets hairy, bright green above, toothed, the terminal tooth usually longer than the 2 immediately adjacent (compare with Barren Strawberry, *see* page 104). Flowers white, 12-18mm, in loose stalked clusters hardly longer than leaves. Fruit (strawberry) 10-20mm long with projecting achenes. In dry grassy (often calcareous) places, woods and banks. **Fl** 4-7. **Br** Common.

B **Hautbois Strawberry** *Fragaria moschata* Differs from previous species in having few or no runners, stalked leaflets and flowering stems noticeably overtopping leaves. Fruit has no achenes near base. Similar habitats. **Fl** 4-7. **Br** Introduced and naturalised.

C *Fragaria viridis* Resembles Wild Strawberry with flowering stems hardly longer than leaves, but has 10mm fruit with achenes usually not projecting and absent from base. Similar habitats. **Fl** 4-7.

D **Garden Strawberry** *Fragaria x ananassa* Distinctive large stalked leaflets to 80mm long, large white flowers 20-35mm in diameter with stalks hardly exceeding leaves; fruit large, about 30mm. Widely cultivated; often escaping to become naturalised. **Br** Widely naturalised.

E **LADY'S-MANTLES** *Alchemilla* Tufted perennials with palmate or palmately lobed toothed leaves. Flowers tiny, greenish yellow in characteristic rounded or flat-topped cymes.

(1) Plants with leaves divided almost to base into narrow lobes.

Alpine Lady's-mantle *Alchemilla alpina* To 25cm. Leaf lobes 5-7, pointed, with terminal teeth, middle lobe free at base; leaflets hairless above, silky hairy beneath. Flower clusters dense, hardly overtopping leaves. In grassy and rocky places in mountains; upland areas throughout Europe (**E1**). **Fl** 6-8. **Br** Locally abundant on acid rocks in NW England and Scotland; very rare in Ireland.

Alchemilla pallens As *A. alpina*, but leaf lobes 7-9, bluish green below. Similar habitats. **Fl** 6-8. **Br** Absent.

Alchemilla hoppeana To 25cm. Leaf lobes 7-9, linear, blunt and all joined at base; hairless above, sparsely hairy and greenish beneath; terminal teeth only. In grassy and rocky places in mountains, usually on limestone. **Fl** 6-8. **Br** Absent.

(2) Plants with leaves divided to at least one-third into narrow lobes, but not to base.

Alchemilla conjuncta To 40cm. Leaves divided up to four-fifths, with 7-9 leaf lobes hairless above and silky hairy beneath; teeth very indistinct and hidden by marginal hairs. In damp rocky places in mountains; Alps and Jura. **Fl** 6-7. **Br** Glen Clova, Scotland and Isle of Arran (probably naturalised in both places).

Alchemilla faeroensis To 20cm. Leaves lobed to a half to two-thirds with 7 lobes silky hairy beneath, the acute teeth extending more than half-way down side of lobe. In rocky places and streamsides. **Fl** 6-7. **Br** Absent.

Alchemilla incisa To 15cm. Leaves lobed to half-way (occasionally to one-third) with 7-9 lobes, almost hairless above and beneath. In rocky and grassy places in mountains. **Fl** 6-9. **Br** Absent.

(3) Plants with leaves palmately lobed to half-way or less into rounded or triangular lobes.

(a) Basal sinus closed.

(i) Leaf stalks hairless.

Alchemilla propinqua To 35cm. Leaves hairy with 7-9 lobes, the middle with 13-15 bluntish teeth. Basal lobes overlapping. In grassy places and streamsides. **Fl** 6-9. **Br** Absent.

(ii) Leaf stalks hairy.

Alchemilla monticola To 50cm. Leaves densely hairy, the hairs spreading; 9-11 lobes, the middle with 7-9 acute teeth. Leaf stalks with spreading hairs. In meadows and grassy places; mainly in E Europe and Scandinavia. **Fl** 6-9. **Br** Very locally abundant in Weardale and Teesdale; naturalised in S England.

Alchemilla glaucescens To 20cm. Leaves densely hairy with 7-9 lobes, the middle with 9-13 teeth. Leaf stalk reddish at base, densely hairy. In grassy or rocky places, usually on limestone; mainly in E Europe and Scandinavia. **Fl** 6-9. **Br** Scattered localities in Yorkshire and Scotland; very rare in Ireland.

Alchemilla subglobosa To 50cm. Leaves roughly hairy with 8-10 lobes, the middle with 13-17 equal teeth. Basal lobes overlapping. Leaf stalks hairy. In grassy places; mainly in Scandinavia. **Fl** 6-8. **Br** Absent.

Alchemilla subcrenata To 50cm. Leaves undulate, sparsely hairy above but densely hairy beneath; 7-9 lobes with unequal teeth. Leaf stalks with spreading hairs. Basal sinus occasionally open. In grassland; mainly in E Europe and Scandinavia. **Fl** 6-9. **Br** Very local in Teesdale and Weardale.

Alchemilla wichurae To 30cm. Leaves hairless except on veins beneath, with 7-9 rounded lobes, the middle having 17-19 equal teeth. Between each lobe is a narrow indentation called an 'incision'. Leaf stalks with appressed hairs. In mountain grassland and basic rock-ledges; mainly in Scandinavia. **Fl** 6-8. **Br** Very local from Yorkshire to N Scotland.

(b) Basal sinus open.

(i) Leaf stalks with appressed hairs.

Alchemilla glomerulans To 40cm. Leaves variably hairy with 9 rounded semicircular lobes, each with 13-15 wide unequal teeth. Sinus widely open. Leaf stalks and stem with dense closely pressed hairs. In damp grassy places and streamsides. **Fl** 5-8. **Br** Very local from Teesdale northwards.

Alchemilla gracilis To 50cm. Leaves softly hairy, the hairs somewhat pressed to the surface; 9-11 rounded lobes each with more or less equal teeth. In grassy places. **Fl** 6-9. **Br** Northumberland only.

(ii) Leaf stalks with spreading hairs or hairless.

Smooth Lady's-mantle *Alchemilla glabra* To 60cm, with flowering stems overtopping hairless leaves. Lobes 9-11, not overlapping and with 11-17 unequal teeth on middle lobes; apical tooth noticeably narrower than neighbours. In grassland and open woods; locally frequent. **Fl** 6-9. **Br** Local in the north and west; commonest species on mountains; rare in S England and absent from SE Ireland.

Alchemilla acutiloba Large, to 65cm. Leaves variably hairy, the hairs erect; 9-11 triangular, straight-sided lobes, the middle having 15-19 unequal teeth; apical tooth markedly smaller than others. In grassland. **Fl** 6-9. **Br** Very local in Teesdale and Weardale.

Alchemilla xanthochlora Robust, to 50cm, often yellowish green. Stems and leaf stalks with dense spreading hairs. Leaves hairless above with 7-9 rounded lobes, the middle with 13-15 equal teeth. Sinus widely open. In grassy places. **Fl** 5-7. **Br** Common, except in SE England and S Ireland.

Hairy Lady's-mantle *Alchemilla filicaulis* To 40cm. Leaves hairy (often only on folds above and veins beneath) with 7-9 lobes, the middle ones with 11-17 unequal teeth. Sinus widely open. Base of leaf stalk reddish. There are 2 subspecies: ssp *filicaulis* has upper part of stem, flower stalks and leaf stalks hairless. In dry or grassy places. **Fl** 6-9. **Br** Local in mountains from N Wales and Derbyshire northwards; ssp *vestita* is hairy throughout. In grassland; locally frequent. **Fl** 6-9. **Br** Almost throughout, and the most frequent species in S England.

Alchemilla minima Very dwarf, to only 5cm. Leaves with 5 wide lobes. In limestone grassland. **Fl** 7-9. **Br** Rare endemic in N England.

A	E1	E2
E3	E4	E5
E6	E7	
E8	E9	E10

A **Wild Strawberry**

E 1 **Alpine Lady's-mantle**

E 2 *Alchemilla hoppeana*

E 3 *Alchemilla conjuncta*

E 4 *Alchemilla wichurae*

E 5 *Alchemilla glomerulans*

E 6 *Alchemilla glabra*

E 7 *Alchemilla acutiloba*

E 8 *Alchemilla xanthochlora*

E 9 *Alchemilla filicaulis*

E 10 *Alchemilla minima*

A. wichurae

A. glomerulans

A. glabra

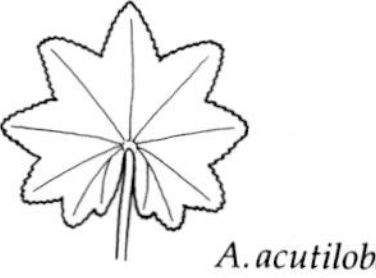
A. acutiloba

A. xanthochl

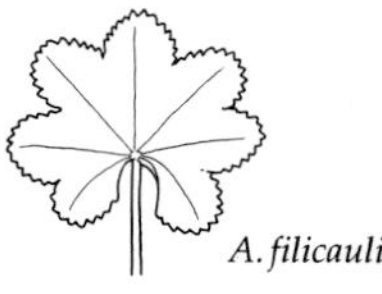
A. filicaulis

A. minima

B

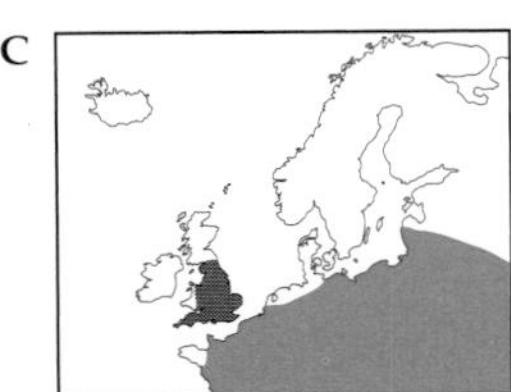

C

D

A Parsley-piert *Aphanes arvensis* Rather inconspicuous *greyish* downy annual to 20cm (usually much smaller). Leaves 2-10mm, short-stalked and fan-shaped, divided into 3 segments, each of which has a number of finger-shaped lobes. Flowers minute, green, petalless and in unstalked dense clusters along stem, each cluster surrounded by a cup of leafy stipules with *triangular lobes*. Widespread and common in arable and dry bare soils. **Fl** 4-10. **Br** Common throughout.

B Slender Parsley-piert *Aphanes microcarpa* Very like previous species, but differs in being *green* not greyish green, and in having *oblong stipule lobes*, not triangular. Local to locally common in open habitats, usually on sandy soils. **Fl** 4-10. **Br** Throughout, but less common than Parsley-piert.

C Wild Pear *Pyrus pyraster* Deciduous tree to 20m, with roughly fissured bark. Branches spreading or ascending, usually spiny. Leaves oval, toothed, usually hairless (at least above). Flowers white in umbel-like clusters, the *main stalk of the inflorescence no longer than 10mm*, and the *petals 10-15mm*. *Anthers red or purple* (compare with Crab Apple below). Fruit rounded or pear-shaped, 20-40mm. In woods and hedges. **Fl** 4. **Br** Widespread in England and Wales; rare in Ireland.

D Plymouth Pear *Pyrus cordaster* Deciduous shrub or small tree to 6m. Branches spiny, young twigs purplish. Leaves oval, slightly toothed and hairless. Flowers white or pinkish in clusters, the *main stalk of the inflorescence 10-30mm long*, and the *petals 8-10mm*. Fruit 12-18mm, rounded or ovoid. Very local in woods, hedges and scrub. **Fl** 4-5. **Br** Rare, restricted to Plymouth area.

E *Pyrus salvifolia* Deciduous tree to 15m. Differs from Wild Pear in having *leaves untoothed* and grey tòmentose beneath. **Fl** 5-6. **Br** Absent.

F Crab Apple *Malus sylvestris* Deciduous shrub or tree to 10m. Bark greyish brown, scaly and fissured. Branches usually thorny. Leaves oval, toothed and pointed. Flowers white with pink flush beneath petals; *anthers yellow*. Fruit apple-shaped, 20mm, yellow or flushed with red. Generally common except in the far north; in woods, scrub and hedgerows. **Fl** 5. **Br** Throughout; mostly common, but rare in central and N Scotland.

Sorbus A complex genus of deciduous shrubs or trees with simple, lobed or pinnate leaves, differing from *Pyrus* and *Malus* species in being thornless and in having compound heads of flowers instead of simple ones. Flowers usually white, occasionally pink, with 5 petals. Fruit a pome, often berry-like. This account describes the most widespread species, with many of the closely related species left out because they often differ only by subtle differences in leaf structure.

(1) Leaves pinnate with end-leaflet same size as side-leaflets.

G Rowan, Mountain Ash *Sorbus aucuparia* Slender tree to 20m, with *smooth, greyish bark*. Leaves with 4-9 pairs of oblong toothed leaflets, hairless when mature but downy below when young. Flower heads dense and flattish with flowers 8-12mm. *Fruit a red berry*. Generally common in woods, hedges, upland moors and mountains. **Fl** 5-6. **Br** Throughout, most frequent in the north.

H Service Tree *Sorbus domestica* Differs from previous species in having *bark finely fissured*, flowers 16-18mm in diameter and *fruit apple- or pear-shaped*, 20-30mm. Local in woods and hedges. **Fl** 5. **Br** Absent.

(2) Leaves pinnate with end-leaflet much larger than side-leaflets.

Sorbus hybrida Tree to 20m, with leaves pinnately lobed, but *only first 2 pairs of leaflets free* (**h1**), the others joined at the base; all greyish downy beneath. Fruit a red berry. In rocky places and woods; Scandinavia. **Fl** 5-6. **Br** Absent.

Sorbus meinichii Tree to 10m, with leaves pinnately lobed, but *only first 4-5 leaflets free* (**h2**), greyish downy beneath. Fruit a red berry. Local in rocky places; Scandinavia. **Fl** 6-7. **Br** Absent.

(3) Leaves simple but lobed (sometimes lobes very shallow).

I Wild Service-tree *Sorbus torminalis* Shrub or tree to 25m, with bark dark grey and fissured. Young twigs downy, purplish brown with greenish buds. Leaves toothed and distinctly shaped, *deeply lobed and rather maple-like*, but unlike maple the lobes are sharply pointed. Flowers white, 10-15mm, the stalks very hairy. Fruit brown with warty spots, 12-16mm, longer than broad. Local to locally frequent in woods, usually on clay; most frequent in southern central part of the region. **Fl** 5-6. **Br** Locally frequent in England and Wales.

J Swedish Whitebeam *Sorbus intermedia* Large shrub or tree to 15m, leaves yellowish grey and woolly beneath, lobes extending up to half-way to midrib. Widespread in the north of the area as a native, but also widely planted elsewhere. **Fl** 5-6. **Br** Planted.

The following are very closely related, with very shallow lobes. All are endemic to the British Isles.

Sorbus minima Shrub to 3m, with leaves under 80mm long, grey woolly beneath. **Fl** 5-6. **Br** Brecon, Wales on limestone crags.

Sorbus anglica Shrub to 2m, with leaves to 11cm, whitish grey woolly beneath. **Fl** 5. **Br** Very local on carboniferous limestone crags.

Sorbus subcuneata Tree to 5m, with leaves more than 1½ times longer than broad, grey woolly beneath. **Fl** 5-6. **Br** Oakwoods in Somerset and Devon.

Sorbus devoniensis Tree to 6m, with dense crown, leaves greenish grey woolly beneath. **Fl** 5-6. **Br** Devon (commonest *Sorbus* species), Cornwall and SW Ireland.

Sorbus bristoliensis Tree to 6m, leaves bright glossy yellowish green above and grey woolly beneath. **Fl** 5-6. **Br** Avon Gorge.

(4) Leaves simple, not lobed.

K Whitebeam *Sorbus aria* Large shrub or tree to 20m, with dense crown, rather variable. Bark greenish grey and smooth, although broken up into plates on older trees. Twigs reddish brown with many dark dots, downy when young. Leaves *dull yellow green above*, densely woolly hairy beneath, the teeth somewhat curved towards the apex of leaf. Fruit bright red berry, 8-15mm, and longer than wide. Local to locally frequent in woods, scrub and hedges, usually on calcareous soil; most frequent in southern-central part of region. **Fl** 5-6. **Br** Local in S England; rare in Ireland.

L Rock Whitebeam *Sorbus rupicola* Shrub to only 2m, with leaves *dark green above*, white woolly beneath and with teeth asymmetrical, being more curved on the outer side so that they point towards apex of leaf. Fruit broader than long, 12-15mm, when ripe dark red on 1 side and greenish on the other. Very local on limestone; in Scandinavia and Britain. **Fl** 5-6. **Br** Very local in the north and west.

Sorbus vexans Differs from Rock Whitebeam in having *fruit longer than broad* with few dots, and entirely scarlet. **Fl** 5. **Br** Endemic in Devon and Somerset.

Sorbus lancastriensis Differs from Rock Whitebeam in having teeth pointing outwards. **Fl** 5-6. **Br** Endemic on limestone near Morecambe Bay.

C A D
G F
H J
I K L

C **Wild Pear** showing fruit

A **Parsley-piert**

D **Plymouth Pear**

G **Rowan**

F **Crab Apple**

H **Service-tree**

J **Swedish Whitebeam** showing leaves and fruit

I **Wild Service-tree** showing autumn leaves and fruit

K **Whitebeam**

L **Rock Whitebeam** showing leaves

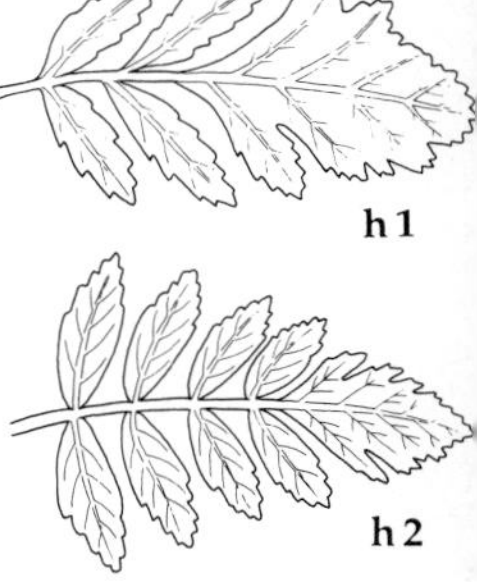

C
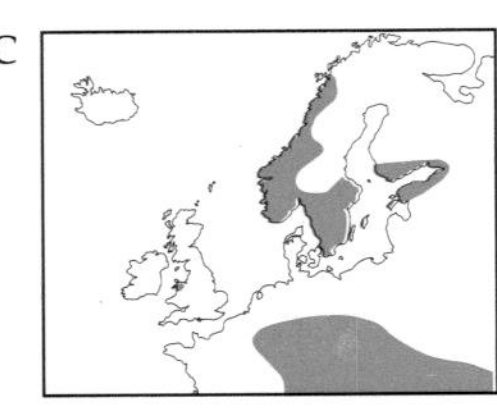

D
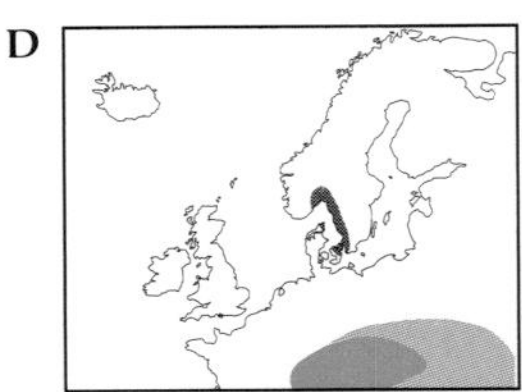

E
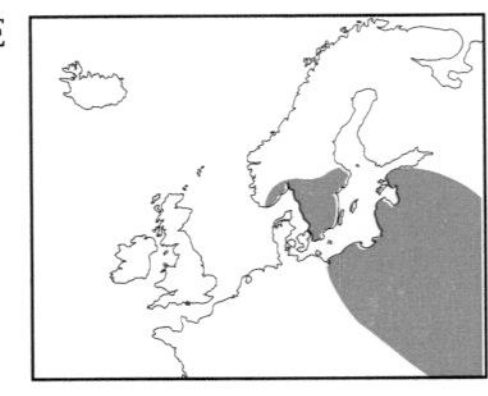

I
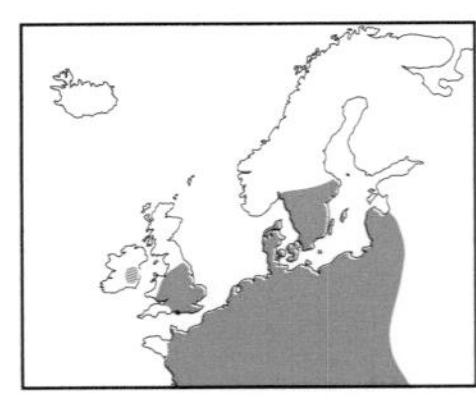

J
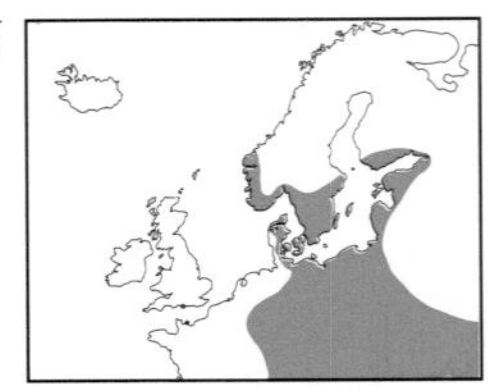

R
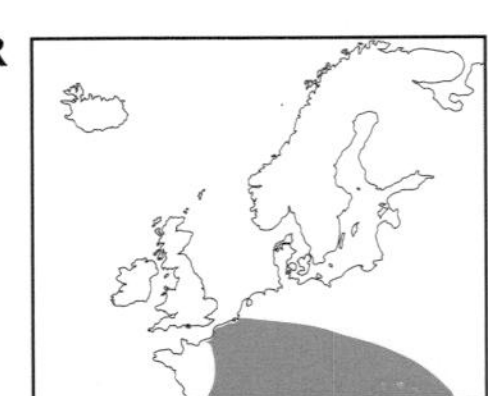

A Snowy Mespilus *Amelanchier ovalis* Deciduous shrub or small tree to 6m, spineless with oval, coarsely toothed leaves (3-5 per centimetre), hairless when mature. Flowers creamy white, petals 10-13mm. Fruit bluish-black berry. Local in open woods and scrub. **Fl** 4-5. **Br** Absent.

B June-berry *Amelanchier grandiflora* Leaves finely-toothed (6-12 per centimetre), purplish when young and petals 15-18mm. Widely naturalised. **Fl** 4-5. **Br** Locally common.

COTONEASTERS *Cotoneaster* Thornless shrubs, deciduous or evergreen, with untoothed leaves, small flowers (under 1cm) and fleshy fruits.

C Wild Cotoneaster *Cotoneaster integerrimus* Deciduous shrub to 1m, with leaves 15-40mm, grey downy beneath, and *clusters of 2-3 pink flowers* with erect petals. Fruit red. In rocky places, often limestone. **Fl** 4-6. **Br** Great Orme's Head, N Wales.

D *Cotoneaster nebrodensis* Differs from Wild Cotoneaster in having *3-12 flowers per cluster*, red on the outside. On calcareous rocks; in the south-east of the region. **Fl** 4-5. **Br** Absent.

E *Cotoneaster niger* Differs from Wild Cotoneaster in having 3-8 flowers per cluster, and *black berries*. In rocky places; in the east of the region. **Fl** 6-7. **Br** Absent.

F Wall Cotoneaster *Cotoneaster horizontalis* Spreading, under 50cm with *solitary pink flowers* and *small leaves 10mm or less*. Introduced, rarely naturalised. **Fl** 5-7. **Br** Rare on calcareous soils.

G Small-leaved Cotoneaster *Cotoneaster microphyllus* Prostrate stiffly branched evergreen, *leaves under 10mm* and *white flowers* with spreading petals. Introduced and naturalised on coastal limestone. **Fl** 5-6. **Br** Scattered localities, especially near the sea.

HAWTHORNS *Crataegus* Spiny deciduous trees or shrubs with leaves lobed and toothed.

H Hawthorn *Crataegus monogyna* Shrub or tree to 10m, with leaves of short shoots to 35mm, *rather sharply and deeply lobed at least half-way to midrib*. Flowers 8-15mm, usually white in flat-topped clusters. Fruit a red berry. Widespread and generally common in woods, scrub, hedges and open places; absent from the far north. **Fl** 5-6. **Br** Common throughout.

I Midland Hawthorn *Crataegus laevigata* Differs from Hawthorn in having *leaves of short shoots bluntly and shallowly lobed towards the tip, less than half-way to midrib*. Local in woods or hedges. **Fl** 5-6. **Br** Local, most frequent in the east; absent from Scotland and Ireland.

J *Crataegus calycina* Leaves similar to Hawthorn, being lobed over half-way to midrib, but larger (to 60mm). Flowers 15-20mm in diameter. Similar habitats. **Fl** 5-6. **Br** Absent.

CHERRIES AND PLUMS *Prunus* Mostly deciduous (occasionally evergreen) trees or shrubs with leaves unlobed and fruit a drupe.

(1) Flowers solitary, or 2-3.

K Blackthorn *Prunus spinosa* Shrub to 4m, with blackish bark and suckering to form hedges and thickets. *Twigs downy at first, with many lateral thorns*. Leaves 20-40mm, hairy on midrib beneath. *Flowers white, solitary (occasionally in pairs), but often several along flowering shoots*; flowers appear before leaves. Fruit (sloe) blue-black, 10-15mm, rounded and fleshy with a single stone. Widespread and common in woods, scrub and hedges, except in the far north. **Fl** 3-5. **Br** Common throughout.

L Wild Plum *Prunus domestica* Similar to previous species, but usually more tree-like to 8m, with smooth brown bark. *Twigs downy at first, with no, or few, thorns*. Leaves 4-10cm, often downy below. Flowers white, *1-3 together*, with several clusters on flowering shoots; flowers appear with leaves. Fruit rounded, 20-40mm, varies from blue-black to yellow. Widespread and locally frequent in hedges and scrub; absent from the far north. **Fl** 4-5. **Br** Introduced and naturalised, more frequent in the south.

M Bullace *Prunus domestica* ssp *insititia* Differs from Wild Plum in being usually *thorny* with *markedly downy young twigs. Leaves markedly downy below* and *flower stalks also downy*. Fruit 20-40mm, usually greenish purple. Widely naturalised in woods and hedgerows. **Br** Rather local, but widespread.

N Cherry Plum *Prunus cerasifera* Shrub to 3m, with *hairless glossy twigs and leaves*, the latter with rounded teeth. Flowers white, usually solitary. Widely planted and naturalised in hedges. **Fl** 2-4. **Br** Occasional.

(2) Flowers in umbel-like clusters.

O Wild Cherry *Prunus avium* Tree to 25m, usually suckering. Bark reddish brown, smooth with horizontal lines when young. Leaves light green, *dull and hairless above, downy beneath*; leaf stalk with 2 prominent rounded glands at top. Flowers white, *2-6 per umbel*, each flower on a stalk; petals 9-15mm; base of inflorescence with persistent large scales. Widespread in woods and hedges; absent from the far north. **Fl** 4-5. **Br** Common, except in N Scotland.

P Dwarf Cherry *Prunus cerasus* Differs from Wild Cherry in being a shrub to about 5m, with *shiny green leaves, hairless beneath*. Petals also 9-15mm. Introduced and widely naturalised in hedgerows and scrub. **Br** Local in S England, Wales and Ireland; rare elsewhere.

Q *Prunus fruticosa is* Shrub to only 1m, also with shiny leaves, but with *petals only 5-7mm*. Introduced and widely naturalised in hedges. **Fl** 4-5. **Br** Widespread, but local.

R *Prunus mahaleb* Usually a shrub, occasionally a small tree to 10m. Leaves hairless or slightly downy beneath, with conspicuous marginal glands. Flowers white, 3-10, *in corymbs*. Fruit black, 8-10mm. Very locally frequent in dry scrub and woods. **Fl** 4-5. **Br** Introduced and occasionally naturalised.

(3) Flowers in drooping racemes.

S Bird Cherry *Prunus padus* Tree to 15m, with malodorous peeling bark, smooth with horizontal lines. Leaves dull green, mostly hairless except for leaf axils beneath. Flowers white, 10-4, in elongated drooping racemes. Fruit shiny black, 6-8mm. In woods, scrub and moors; most frequent in the east of the region. **Fl** 5-6. **Br** Widespread; not native in S England.

(4) Flowers in erect racemes.

T Cherry Laurel *Prunus laurocerasus* *Evergreen* shrub to 8m, with elliptical leathery leaves, slightly toothed, and stiff, erect racemes of white flowers. Fruit black. Introduced and widely naturalised. **Fl** 4-5. **Br** Scattered in the south and west.

A	C	F
G	H	I
K	M	O
R	S	T

A Snowy Mespilus
C Wild Cotoneaster
F Wall Cotoneaster
G Small-leaved Cotoneaster
H Hawthorn
I Midland Hawthorn showing fruit and leaves
K Blackthorn showing flowers
M Bullace showing leaves and fruit
O Wild Cherry
R *Prunus mahaleb*
S Bird Cherry
T Cherry Laurel

A
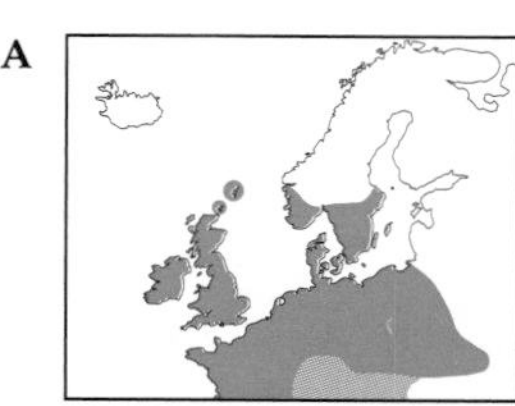
E
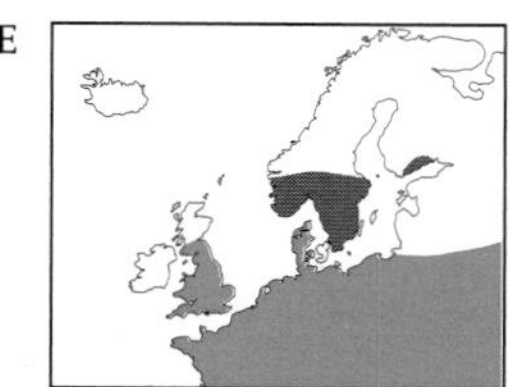
F
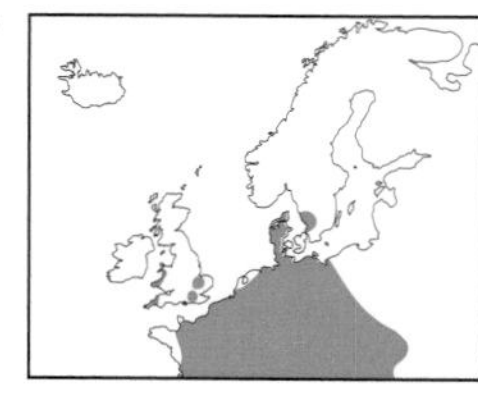
G
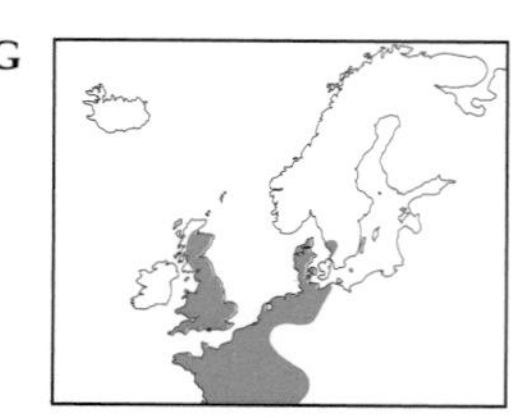
I
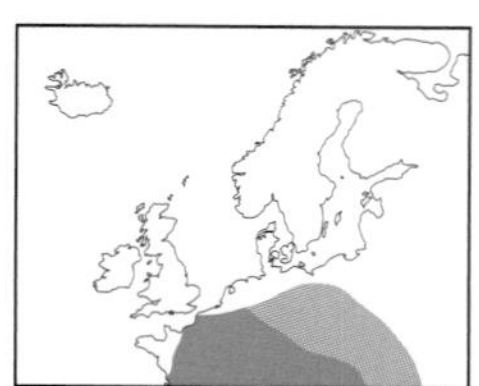
J
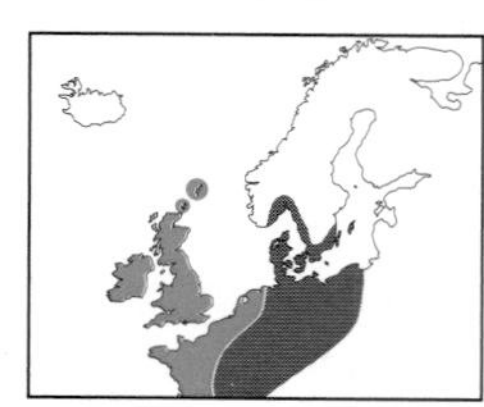
L

Pea Family Leguminosae

A very distinctive and well-known family, variable in form, but with easily recognised pea-like flowers. Trees, shrubs or herbs, with leaves usually opposite, simple to bipinnate. Flowers 5-petalled, with an erect standard at the top, 2 wing petals at the sides, and the lower 2 petals joined into a keel; 10 stamens and 1 style. Fruit usually an elongated pod.

A **Broom** *Cytisus scoparius* Much-branched, erect, spineless deciduous shrub to 2m, with long green straight hairless 5-angled stems. Leaves usually trifoliate, short-stalked, but may be simple and unstalked on young twigs. Flowers golden yellow, solitary or in pairs, up to 2cm long and short-stalked; pods oblong, becoming black. Common and widespread, mainly on acid soils, in scrub and grassy places; from S Sweden southwards. **Fl** 5-7. **Br** Common throughout.
Ssp *maritimus* is prostrate, with silky-hairy twigs. Occurs in coastal areas of W Britain and France.

B **Black Broom** *Lembotropis nigricans* Rather similar to Broom, though smaller, with smaller yellow flowers in long leafless racemes; corolla blackens on drying. In dry habitats; from central Germany eastwards. **Fl** 5-6. **Br** Absent.

C *Chamaecytisus ratisbonensis* Spreading or ascending shrub to 45cm. Leaves trifoliate, leaflets roughly ovate, hairless when mature. Flowers in short 1-sided inflorescences; corolla yellow with orange-red spots on standard. Dry habitats; Germany eastwards. **Fl** 5-6. **Br** Absent.

D *Chamaecytisus supinus* Similar to *C. ratisbonensis*, though generally more erect, to 60cm. Flowers in terminal inflorescences of 2-8. South-eastwards from central France and S Germany; in dry rocky places. **Fl** 5-7. **Br** Absent.

E **Dyer's Greenweed** *Genista tinctoria* Tufted erect or ascending small shrub to 1m or more. Leaves linear-lanceolate, simple, variable, to 30mm long, usually hairy on margins only and sometimes downy all over. Flowers in long usually terminal racemes, corolla yellow, about 15mm long, hairless; pods oblong, flat, hairless. Widespread and locally common throughout except N Scandinavia; in pastures and scrub on heavier soils. **Fl** 6-7. **Br** Locally common in England, Wales and S Scotland.

F **Hairy Greenweed** *Genista pilosa* Spreading or ascending low spineless shrub, up to 1.5m high but usually much less. Leaves small, to 1cm long, ovate to oblong, *very silvery downy below* but hairless above, unstalked or short-stalked. Flowers borne in short leafy racemes; corolla yellow, about 1cm long, with corolla, calyx and stalks all downy; *pods downy*, pointed, flat. On heaths and sea-cliffs; from S Sweden southwards, mainly western. **Fl** 4-6. **Br** Very local, in SW England and Wales.

G **Petty Whin** *Genista anglica* Erect or spreading small shrub, to about 1m, hairless or hairy, but *with strong spines*. Leaves hairless, lanceolate to elliptical, up to 10mm long and rather waxy. Flowers in short, leafy terminal racemes; corolla pale yellow, hairless, 6-8mm long; pods hairless, pointed, becoming swollen. Scattered on heaths and moors; from S Sweden southwards. **Fl** 4-6. **Br** Scattered throughout, but local; absent from Ireland.

H **German Greenweed** *Genista germanica* Erect branched shrub to 60cm, with branched spines (occasionally spineless). Leaves elliptical to lanceolate, with long hairs on undersurface. Flowers yellow, about 1cm, in loose racemes, with *hairy petals and sepals*; bracts very small; pod pointed, curved, slightly inflated. Local on heaths and grassland; from S Sweden southwards. **Fl** 5-6. **Br** Absent.

I **Winged Broom** *Chamaespartium sagittale* Spreading subshrub, mat-forming, with stems to 50cm. Distinctive by its *strongly winged stems*, constricted at the nodes. Leaves elliptical, to 20mm long, downy below. Flowers yellow, 10-15mm, in short terminal clusters. In dry and rocky places; from SE Belgium and S Germany southwards. **Fl** 5-6. **Br** Absent.

J **Common Gorse** *Ulex europaeus* Familiar spiny dense bushy evergreen shrub to 2m. Twigs hairy or downy. Has trifoliate leaves only when young; *terminal spines 15-25mm long, straight*, stout, *deeply furrowed*, hairless (**j**). Flowers pale yellow, 20mm across, coconut-scented; little bracts at base at least 2mm wide and 3-5mm long; calyx with spreading hairs. Common and widespread on rough grasslands and heathy areas, usually on acid soils, from Holland southwards; mainly western, introduced elsewhere. **Fl** 1-12, mainly in spring. **Br** Common almost throughout.

K **Dwarf Gorse** *Ulex minor* Smaller shrub than above, to 1m but usually less, often spreading. *Spines about 10mm long*, not rigid, *weakly furrowed* or striped (**k**). *Flowers deep yellow*, 10-12mm long, with bracts at base only 0.5mm long; calyx teeth divergent. On heaths and moors in Britain and W France only. **Fl** 7-9. **Br** Mainly southern and eastern, extending to S Scotland.

L **Western Gorse** *Ulex gallii* Very similar to Dwarf Gorse, but usually slightly taller and more robust. Spines more rigid, *longer to 25mm* and *faintly ridged* (**l**). Calyx teeth convergent. On heaths and moors; strongly western in distribution, from Scotland and W France southwards. **Fl** 7-9. **Br** Strongly western, barely overlapping with Dwarf Gorse, from S Scotland southwards.

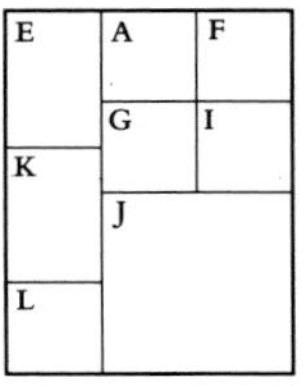

E **Dyer's Greenweed**
A **Broom**
F **Hairy Greenweed**
G **Petty Whin**
I **Winged Broom**
K **Dwarf Gorse**
J **Common Gorse**
L **Western Gorse**

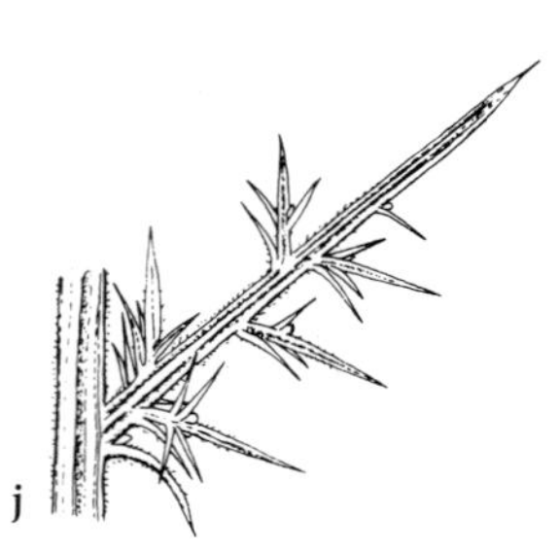
j

k

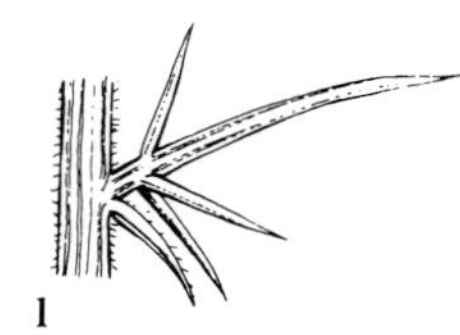
l

A
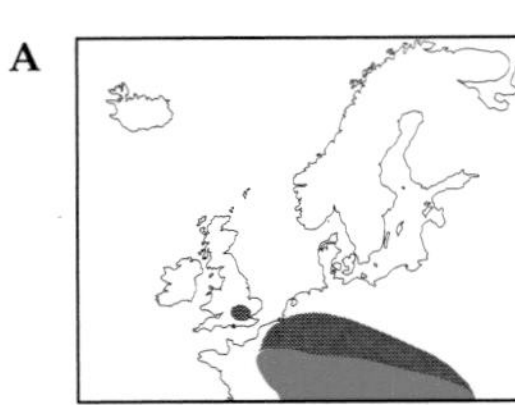

C
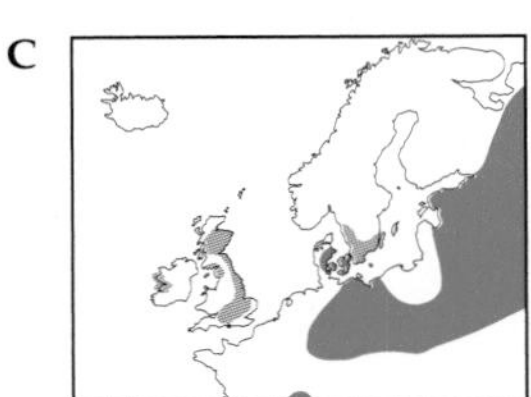

H
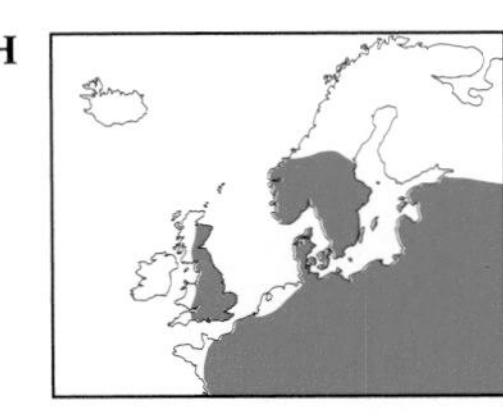

L

M
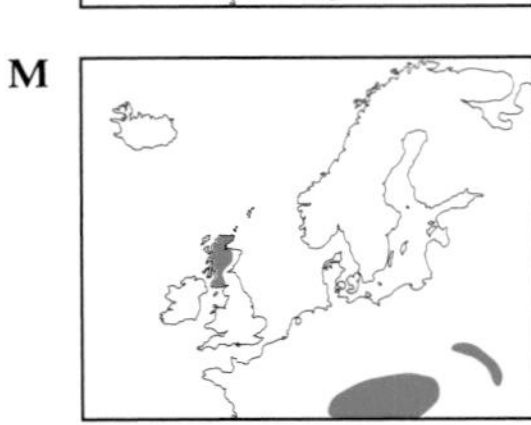

A Bladder Senna *Colutea arborescens* Branched shrub to 6m. Leaves pinnate with 4-5 pairs of oval leaflets, silky-hairy below. Inflorescence has 3-8 flowers, corolla 15-20mm, yellow marked with red; *pods to 70mm long, strongly inflated*, becoming brown and papery – very distinctive. On dry slopes, rocky places and scrub, mainly on lime-rich soils; native from N-central France and S Germany southwards, naturalised elsewhere. **Fl** 5-7. **Br** Locally naturalised, mainly SE England.

Astragalus Annual or perennial herbs, with pinnate leaves terminating in a single leaflet. Flowers in lateral clusters, often dense; keel blunt (**1**), without small tooth-like point (*see also* the very similar *Oxytropis*, in which the keel has a tooth at the tip).

B Wild Lentil *Astragalus cicer* Strong-growing ascending or almost erect perennial to 60cm, rarely more. Leaves to 13cm long with 10-15 pairs of ovate shortly hairy leaflets. Flowers pale yellow, in dense long-stalked inflorescences; standard 14-16mm long. The pods are distinctive: *inflated*, ovoid-globose, *papery, covered with short black and white hairs*. Grassy places and woodland margins; southwards from Belgium and N France; occasionally naturalised elsewhere. **Fl** 6-7. **Br** Absent.

C Purple Milk-vetch *Astragalus danicus* Slender spreading or ascending perennial herb to 35cm. Leaves hairy, 4-10cm long, with 6-13 pairs of leaflets; *stipules joined at base*. Flowers purplish-blue in clusters on stalks 1½- to 2-times as long as leaves; each flower 15-18mm long; fruit dark brown, *swollen*, with white hairs. From S Sweden southwards; on dry or calcareous grasslands, but very scattered and absent from large areas. **Fl** 5-7. **Br** Scattered almost throughout but very local; very rare in Ireland.

D *Astragalus frigidus* Stout erect perennial to 40cm, hairless, usually unbranched. Leaves with 3-8 pairs of leaflets. Flowers in narrow racemes, on stalks 1- to 1½-times as long as leaves; corolla pale yellowish-white, with standard 12-14mm long; calyx has densely black-hairy teeth. In mountain habitats; in Norway and Sweden (and the Alps). **Fl** 7-8. **Br** Absent.

E *Astragalus penduliflorus* Very similar to *A. frigidus*, but hairy below; leaves have *7-15 pairs of leaflets*; flowers *deeper* yellow. Mountain habitat;, central Sweden only (and the Alps and Pyrenees). **Fl** 7-8. **Br** Absent.

F Alpine Milk-vetch *Astragalus alpinus* Slender spreading or ascending perennial, similar to Purple Milk-vetch. Leaflets 7-15 pairs, with *stipules usually not joined at base*. Flowers in inflorescences with stalks 1- to 2-times as long as leaves; corolla blue; calyx teeth lanceolate and pointed; *fruit not swollen*, black-hairy when young then smooth. Mountain habitats, mainly on calcareous soils; in Scandinavia, N Scotland, and mountains of central and southern Europe. **Fl** 7-8. **Br** Very rare in mountains of central Scotland only.

G *Astragalus norvegicus* Rather similar to Alpine Milk-vetch, but differing in that there are usually only *6-7 pairs* of leaflets. *Corolla pale violet, calyx teeth triangular and blunt*. Open habitats, including roadsides; N Scandinavia only. **Fl** 7-8. **Br** Absent.

H Wild Liquorice *Astragalus glycyphyllos* Sprawling robust herb, with zigzagging stems to 1m long. Leaves to 20cm long, with 4-6 pairs of broadly ovate leaflets, sparsely hairy below; stipules large, to 2cm long. Flowers 10-15cm long, in racemes on stalks shorter than leaves; corolla dull greenish cream; pods to 4cm long, slightly curved. In grassy places and scrub; throughout except the far north. **Fl** 6-8. **Br** Scattered through England to S Scotland, rare in the north.

I *Astragalus arenarius* Slender spreading plant to 30cm. Leaves with 2-9 pairs of narrow leaflets, hairy on both sides; stipules joined at base. Inflorescence loose, with 3-8 purplish or lilac flowers, on stalks shorter than leaves; standard 13-17mm long; pods oblong, hairy. In grassy places; very local, Germany and Sweden only, occasionally naturalised elsewhere. **Fl** 6-7. **Br** Absent.

J *Astragalus baionensis* Very similar to above, but leaflets are a broader oblong; *inflorescence stalk as long as leaves; flowers pale blue*. On coastal sands; from W France southwards, very local. **Fl** 5-7. **Br** Absent.

Oxytropis Very similar to *Astragalus*, differing mainly in the tooth-like point on the keel (**2**).

K *Oxytropis lapponica* Low tufted spreading plant to rarely more than 10cm. Leaves with 8-14 pairs of leaflets, hairy on both surfaces; stipules joined together for about half their length. Flowers in *almost spherical heads*, violet-blue; standard 8-12mm long; pod narrowly oblong, hairy and *pendent*. In mountain habitats; Scandinavia only (and central Europe). **Fl** 7-8. **Br** Absent.

L Yellow Milk-vetch *Oxytropis campestris* Silky-hairy tufted perennial, with stems to 20cm and leaves up to 15cm long. Leaflets 10-15 pairs, lanceolate; stipules joined for about half their length. Inflorescence roughly *oval*, with 5-15 flowers; *corolla pale yellow* (occasionally pale violet); standard 15-20mm long; *fruit erect*, hairy. In calcareous mountain habitats; in N Scandinavia, Scotland and high mountains further south. **Fl** 6-7. **Br** Very rare in mountains of central Scotland only.

M Purple Oxytropis *Oxytropis halleri* Similar in form and hairiness to Yellow Milk-vetch, but with inflorescence of purple flowers on stout erect leafless stalks, which is *much longer* than leaves; corolla about 20mm long, keels tipped with dark purple. Fruit about 25mm long and downy. Mountains, mainly calcareous; in Scotland and central and S Europe. **Fl** 6-7. **Br** Local in central and N Scotland only.

N *Oxytropis pilosa* Similar to above species, though less silky. *Inflorescence stalks leafy* (leafless in above 2 species); corolla light yellow (darker than Yellow Milk-vetch). Rare in mountain habitats in S Sweden and Alps. **Fl** 6-8. **Br** Absent.

f

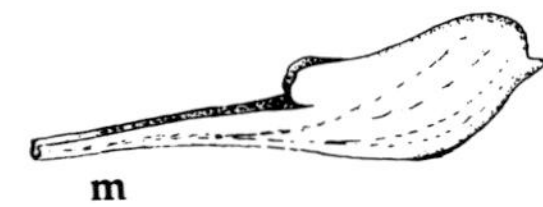
m

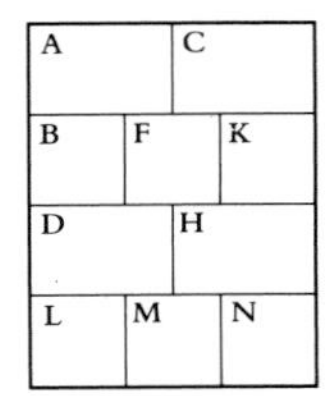

A Bladder Senna fruits and flower centre right

C Purple Milk-vetch

B Wild Lentil

F Alpine Milk-vetch

K *Oxytropis lapponica*

D *Astragalus frigidus*

H Wild Liquorice

L Yellow Milk-vetch

M Purple Oxytropis

N *Oxytropis pilosa*

A

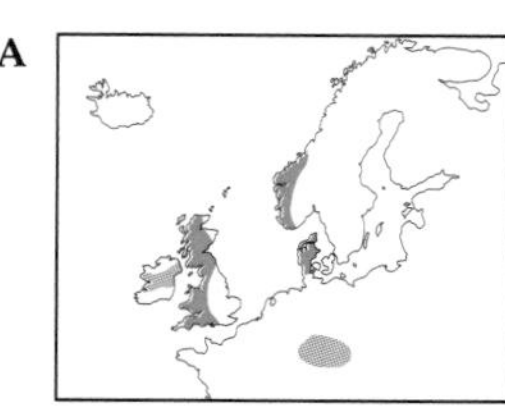

C

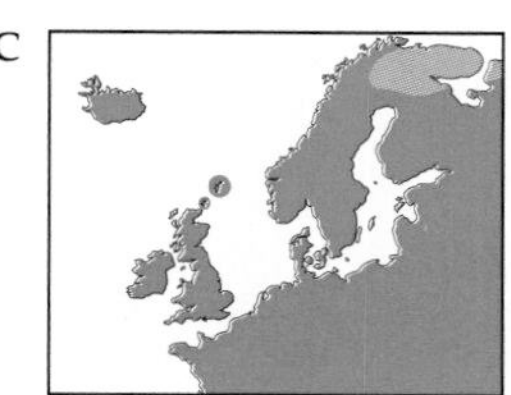

F

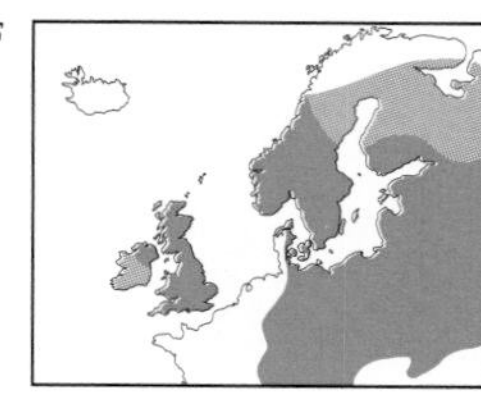

H

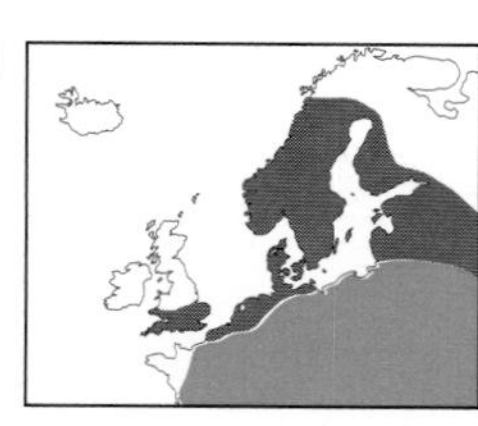

I

J

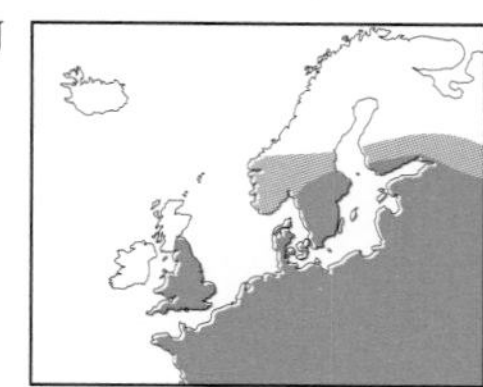

VETCHES *Vicia* Climbing or scrambling annual or perennial herbs; stems rounded or ridged, not winged. Leaves pinnate, with 2 to many pairs of leaflets, ending in a tendril or a point, but not a leaflet. Flowers solitary or in axillary racemes.

(1) Plants without tendrils.

A **Wood Bitter-vetch** *Vicia orobus* Spreading or erect downy perennial to 60cm, with round stems. Leaves pinnate, ending at a point not a tendril; stipules toothed. Inflorescences short, rounded and long-stalked; flowers very pale lilac with purple veins, 12-15mm long; pod oblong, pointed and hairless, to 30mm long. In grassland and scrub in hilly districts; mainly western from Norway southwards, though local. **Fl** 5-7. **Br** Scattered almost throughout, mainly western, but local and declining; rare in Ireland.

(2) Plants with tendrils.

B *Vicia pisiformis* Hairless scrambling perennial to 2m long. Leaflets oval, in 3-5 pairs, rather pea-like. Racemes cylindrical, slightly 1-sided, with 8-30 flowers; corolla pale yellow, 15-20mm long; pod to 40mm, pale brown and hairless. In semi-shaded places; S Norway and Sweden, Germany and E France. **Fl** 6-8. **Br** Absent.

C **Tufted Vetch** *Vicia cracca* Downy or hairless perennial scrambling herb to 2m long. Leaves pinnate, with 6-12 (rarely 15) pairs of narrow-oblong leaflets, very short-stalked; stipules half-arrow shaped, untoothed; tendrils branched. Flowers in *long narrow raceme* to 10cm; *corolla bluish violet*, 8-12mm long, with limb of standard roughly equal to its claw. Generally common in grassy and bushy places; throughout the area. **Fl** 6-8. **Br** Common and widespread throughout.

D *Vicia tenuifolia* Very similar to Tufted Vetch, except that leaflets are slightly narrower and flowers larger, to 18mm, with *limb of standard longer than its claw*. From S Sweden southwards, mainly southern, but distribution not fully known. Similar habitats. **Fl** 6-8. **Br** Not native; rarely established.

E *Vicia cassubica* Similar to Tufted Vetch, but *inflorescences shorter than or equal to leaves*; corolla 10-13mm long, blue or red-purple with *whitish wings and keel*. In grassy and rocky places; from S Scandinavia southwards, but very local. **Fl** 6-8. **Br** An occasional casual of waste places.

F **Wood Vetch** *Vicia sylvatica* Straggling or climbing perennial, with hairless *rounded stems* to 2m long. Leaves with 5-12 pairs of oblong leaflets, tipped with points; tendrils much branched; stipules roughly semi-circular with numerous fine teeth. Inflorescence loose, somewhat 1-sided, long-stalked, with 5-20 flowers; corolla 12-20mm long, whitish with purple veins; pods black and hairless. In woods, wood-margins and coastal cliffs; throughout, except Holland and Belgium, though local. **Fl** 6-8. **Br** Scattered throughout, but local; rare in Ireland.

G *Vicia dumetorum* Rather similar to Wood Vetch, but has *angled stems*, only *3-5 pairs of broad leaflets*, and blue-purple flowers; *pods brown*, not black. From S Sweden southwards, but mainly eastern; in rocky and grassy places, and woods. **Fl** 6-8. **Br** Absent.

H *Vicia villosa* Variable hairy scrambling annual, with stems to 2m. Leaves with 4-12 pairs of linear to elliptical leaflets; stipules narrowly triangular and untoothed. Inflorescence longer than its leaf; corolla violet to blue, often *with yellowish wings*, up to 20mm long; calyx strongly inflated at base; pod brown, 20-40mm long. In disturbed and cultivated ground; from France and Germany southwards; naturalised further north. **Fl** 6-8. **Br** An occasional casual of waste places.

I **Hairy Tare** *Vicia hirsuta* Very slender trailing or scrambling downy annual to 70cm. Leaves with *4-10 pairs of leaflets*, often borne alternately, linear to ovate but usually truncated or notched. Inflorescences on slender stalks with *1-9 flowers*; corolla whitish-mauve, 2-4mm long, *calyx teeth roughly equal*, longer than tube (**i**); *pod oblong and downy*, usually 2-seeded. Throughout the area, widespread and common in grassy and rough places, especially on neutral or calcareous soils. **Fl** 5-8. **Br** Throughout except the extreme north, rarer in Ireland.

J **Smooth Tare** *Vicia tetrasperma* Slender, virtually hairless, scrambling annual to 60cm. Leaves with *2-5 pairs of leaflets*, usually narrow and pointed, but variable. Inflorescence *1-2 flowered*, about equal in length to leaves; corolla purple, 4-8mm long, with *calyx teeth unequal*, upper 2 shorter than tube (**j**); *pod usually hairless*, with 3-5 (usually 4) seeds. Throughout the area, except the far north; in grassy and bushy places on approximately neutral soils. **Fl** 5-8. **Br** Frequent in England and Wales, rare and mainly naturalised elsewhere.

K **Slender Tare** *Vicia tenuissima* Similar to Smooth Tare, but with longer narrower leaflets (up to 25mm; less than 20mm in Smooth Tare); flowers larger, to 8mm or more, with 2-5 flowers per inflorescence; fruit brown, hairy or hairless, with 4-6 seeds. In grassy places on heavier soils; from Holland and central England southwards. **Fl** 6-8. **Br** Central and S England only; rare.

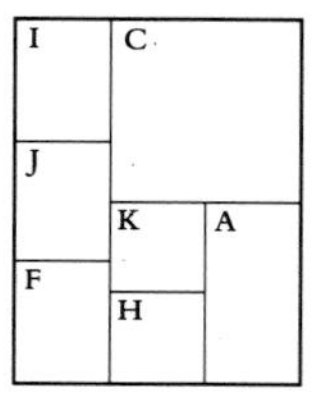

I **Hairy Tare**
C **Tufted Vetch**
J **Smooth Tare**
K **Slender Tare**
A **Wood Bitter-vetch**
F **Wood Vetch**
H *Vicia villosa*

i

j

A

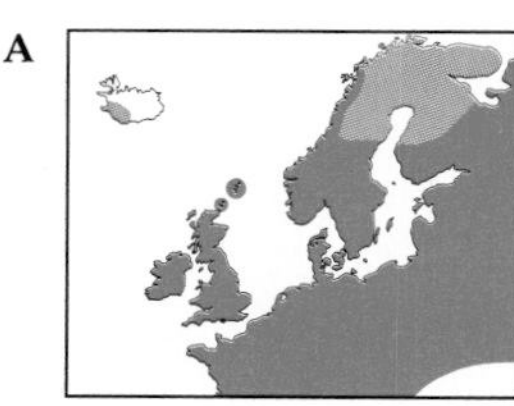

B

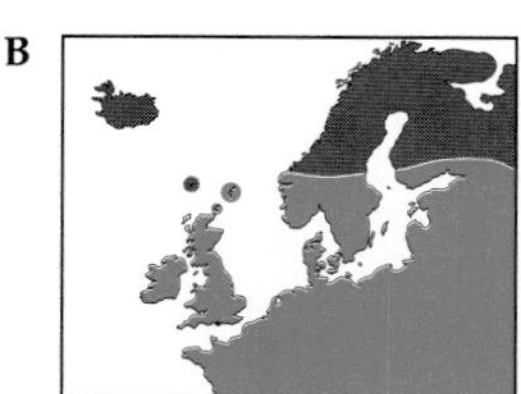

C

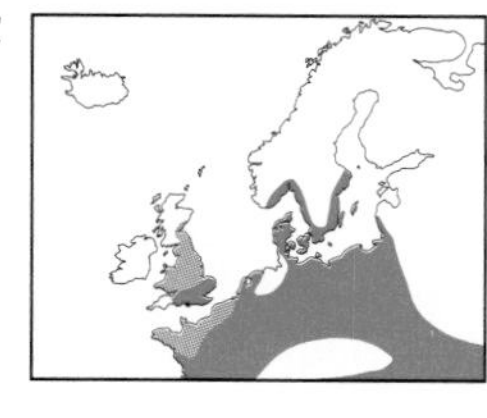

D

E

G

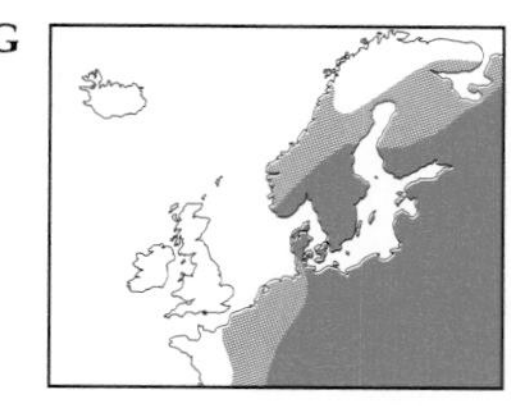

I

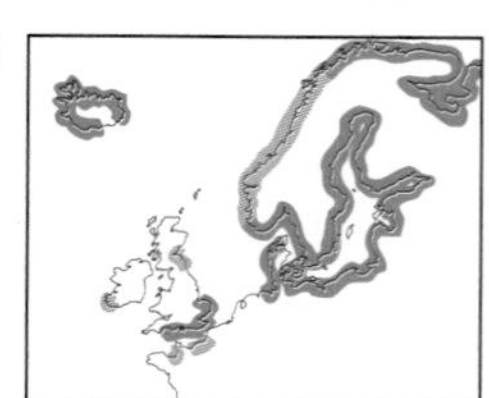

A Bush Vetch *Vicia sepium* Scrambling or spreading perennial to 1m, downy or almost hairless. Leaves with 3-9 pairs of ovate or almost round leaflets, with a bristle-point at the tip; tendrils branched, stipules half-arrow shaped, usually untoothed, spotted. *Inflorescence 2-6 flowered*, short-stalked; corolla distinctive *dull bluish-purple* with darker veins 12-15mm long; calyx teeth unequal, shorter than tube; pods black and hairless, to 25mm. Throughout the area except the extreme north; in bushy and grassy places. **Fl** 5-8. **Br** Common throughout.

B Common Vetch *Vicia sativa* Downy scrambling, trailing or ascending annual to 80cm. Leaves with 3-8 pairs of linear to ovate leaflets which may be pointed, blunt or bristle-tipped; tendrils branched or simple; stipules half-arrow shaped, usually toothed, often with a dark blotch. *Flowers in groups of 1-2* (rarely more), corolla to 30mm, purplish-red; calyx teeth equal; pods very variable. The main wild form is ssp *nigra* which has narrow leaflets, corolla all reddish-purple, 10-18mm long. Ssp *sativa* is the cultivated and naturalised form from S Europe, which has broader leaflets, flowers to 30mm, usually with wings darker than remainder. Ssp *nigra* is widespread and common in grassy places throughout except the extreme north; ssp *sativa* is mainly southern, but widely cultivated and naturalised further north. **Fl** 5-9. **Br** Ssp *nigra* is common throughout; ssp *sativa* is locally naturalised.

C Spring Vetch *Vicia lathyroides* Similar to Common Vetch, but small and spreading. Leaves with *2-4 pairs of leaflets*, bristle-tipped; tendrils unbranched; stipules unspotted. *Flowers small, 5-8mm long*, unstalked, solitary, red-purple; pods black, to 25mm. From S Finland southwards; in sandy grassland, mainly coastal. **Fl** 4-6. **Br** Widespread but local almost throughout.

D Yellow Vetch *Vicia lutea* Tufted prostrate hairless or hairy annual to 60cm. Leaves with 3-10 pairs of linear to oblong bristle-tipped leaflets; tendrils simple or branched; stipules small and triangular. Flowers in groups of 1-3, distinctively pale yellow, often tinged with purple, up to 35mm long; calyx teeth unequal, with lower ones longer than tube; pod yellowish-brown, hairy, to 40mm. On stabilised shingle and grassy coastal habitats; England and France southwards; naturalised in Germany. **Fl** 6-9. **Br** Very local, mainly southern.

E Bithynian Vetch *Vicia bithynica* Climbing or trailing hairless or downy annual (or perennial) herb to 60cm. Leaves with 2-3 pairs of elliptical to ovate leaflets, with branched tendrils; *stipules large and conspicuous, toothed* (**e**). Flowers 15-20mm, in groups of 1-3, with standard purplish, wings and keel creamy white; pods yellow-brown, hairy, to 50mm. In bushy and grassy places, hedgerows, often coastal; from Britain and France southwards. **Fl** 5-6. **Br** Rare and local, declining, in S England, S Wales, and very rare in SW Scotland.

F *Vicia narbonensis* Downy erect annual to 60cm. Leaves with 1-3 pairs of ovate leaflets, lower leaves without tendrils. Flowers 1-6 together, corolla dark purple, 2-3cm, calyx teeth unequal. Bushy and rocky habitats, often coastal; from W France southwards. **Fl** 5-7. **Br** Absent.

Lathyrus Similar to the vetches, differing mainly in the winged stems, and fewer leaflets, which are usually parallel-veined, though the differences between the 2 groups are small and inconsistent.

G Spring Pea *Lathyrus vernus* Erect or spreading tufted hairless or slightly hairy perennial to 40cm, with stems angled but not winged. Leaves with 2-4 pairs of ovate to lanceolate pointed leaflets, without tendrils; stipules similar, with arrow-shaped base. Flowers 3-10 together in a raceme, with reddish corolla ageing to blue, to 2cm long. Pods brown, hairless, to 6cm long. Almost throughout continental Europe, except the extreme north, and not native in Belgium and Holland; in woods and rough grassy places. **Fl** 4-6. **Br** Absent, except in cultivation.

H Black Pea *Lathyrus niger* Rather similar to Spring Pea, but with blunter leaflets, pinnately-veined (roughly parallel-veined in Spring Pea), and stipules much smaller than leaflets. Flowers smaller, to 15mm, 2-8 per raceme, *purple becoming blue; pods becoming black* when ripe, to 60mm long. In rocky and hilly woods; throughout continental Europe except N Scandinavia, and absent locally from many lowland areas. **Fl** 6-7. **Br** Formerly E Scotland, now extinct.

I Sea Pea *Lathyrus japonicus* Prostrate grey-green more or less hairless perennial herb, with angled (but not winged) stems to 1m long. Leaves with 2-5 pairs of *oval, blunt and slightly fleshy leaflets*; tendrils present or absent; stipules broadly triangular, with arrow-shaped base. Inflorescence with 2-15 purple flowers, ageing to blue, to 2cm long; pod to 5cm long, swollen, hairless. On coastal shingle and sand, rarely inland; on the coasts of NW Europe, northwards from England. **Fl** 6-8. **Br** Mainly on the coasts of S and E England, locally common, rare elsewhere.

J *Lathyrus pannonicus* Perennial herb, with unwinged or slightly winged stems to 50cm. Leaves with 1-4 pairs of narrow leaflets. Flowers pale creamy reddish, 1-2cm long, with 3-9 in inflorescence. Pods pale brown, 3-6cm. From NW France and S Germany southwards; in grassy and bushy habitats. **Fl** 5-7. **Br** Absent.

e

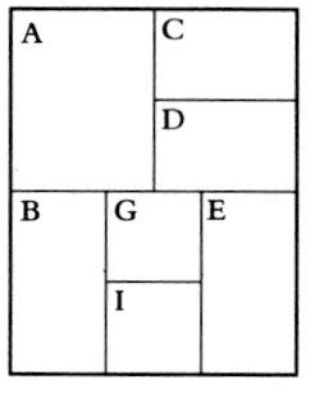

A Bush Vetch

C Spring Vetch

D Yellow Vetch

B Common Vetch ssp *sativa*

G Spring Pea

E Bithynian Vetch

I Sea Pea

A
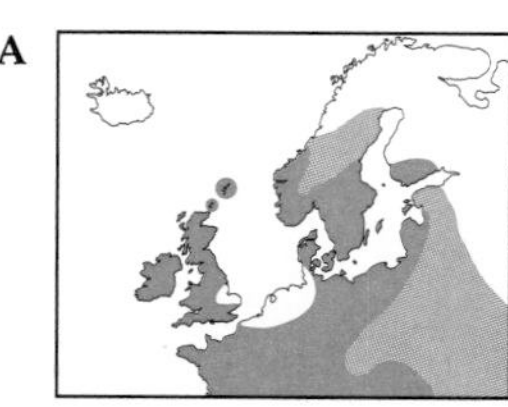

C
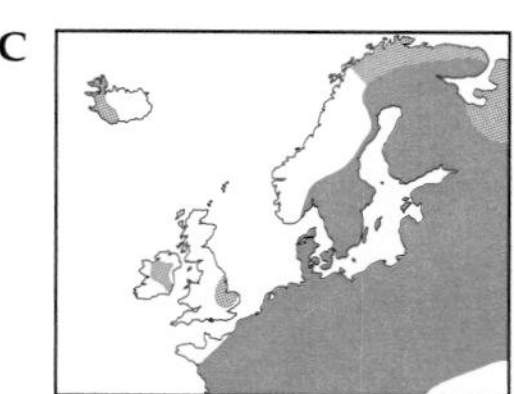

D
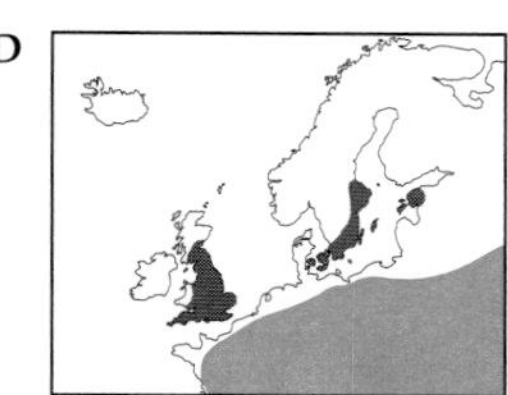

E
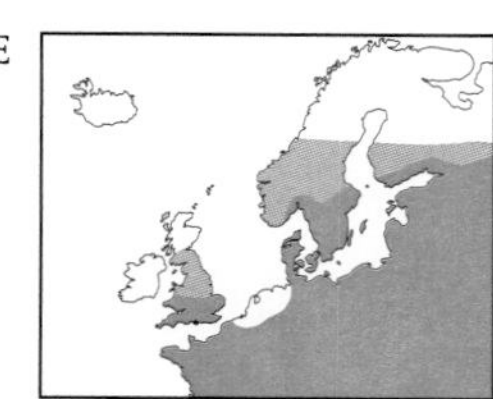

F
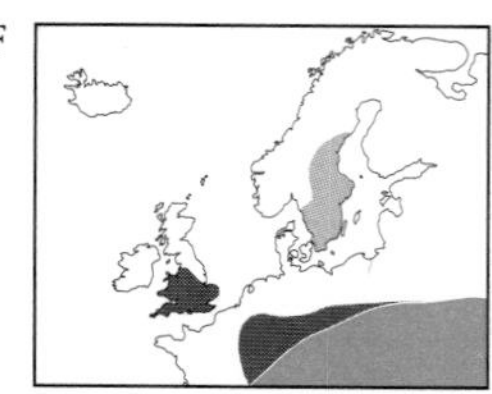

J
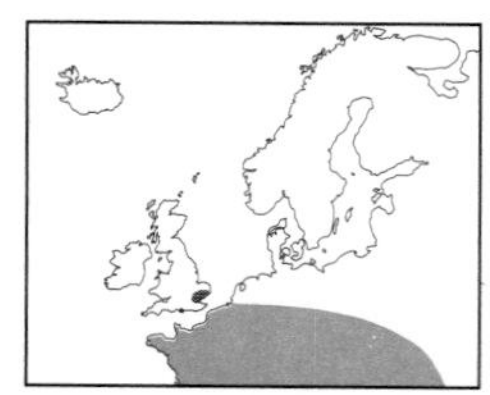

K
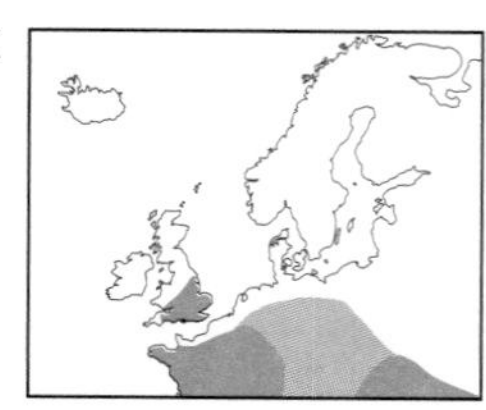

L
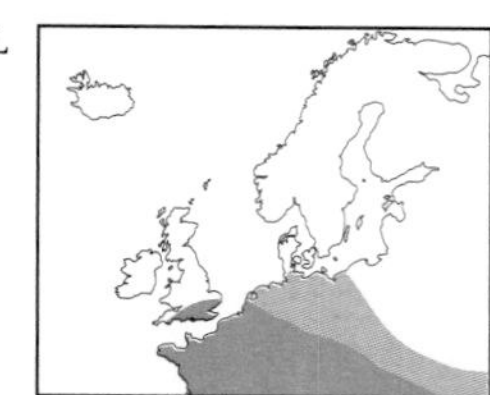

A Bitter-vetch *Lathyrus montanus* Erect, virtually hairless perennial with *winged stems* to 50cm. Leaves with 2-4 pairs of narrowly lanceolate to elliptical leaflets, usually pointed and without tendrils; stipules narrow with arrow-shaped base. Inflorescence with 2-6 flowers; corolla crimson-red, becoming bluish or greenish, to 16mm long; pod red-brown, hairless, to 40mm long. In woods, pastures and scrub, especially in hilly or acid regions; throughout except in the extreme north. **Fl** 4-7. **Br** Widespread and locally common, though absent from a few areas.

B Meadow Vetchling *Lathyrus pratensis* Scrambling hairless or downy perennial, with angled stems to 1.2m long. Leaves with 1 pair of grey-green narrowly lanceolate parallel-veined pointed leaflets, with a tendril; stipules with arrow-shaped base, about the same size as leaflets. Inflorescence long-stalked, with 5-12 yellow flowers, each about 15-18mm long; pod to 35mm long, black when ripe. In grassy and bushy places; throughout the area. **Fl** 5-8. **Br** Common throughout.

C Marsh Pea *Lathyrus palustris* Erect climbing or scrambling slightly downy perennial herb, with winged stems to 1.2m. Leaves with 2-5 pairs of narrowly lanceolate leaflets, branched tendrils, and half-arrow shaped stipules. Inflorescences long-stalked, with 2-8 flowers; corolla pale purplish-blue, to 2cm long; pod flattened, to 5cm long, hairless. In damp or wet grassy places, usually calcareous; throughout though very local. **Fl** 5-7. **Br** Scattered through England and Wales, local; rare in Ireland.

D Tuberous Pea or Fyfield Pea *Lathyrus tuberosus* Hairless scrambling perennial, with *angled, but unwinged, stems* to 1.2m. Leaves with 1 pair of roughly elliptical leaflets, and simple or branched tendrils; stipules narrowly half-arrow shaped. Inflorescence long-stalked, with 2-7 bright reddish-purple flowers, to 2cm long; pods brown, hairless, to 4cm long. In grassy places and waste ground; throughout, except Scandinavia and Britain, though naturalised locally there. **Fl** 6-7. **Br** Very locally naturalised, mainly in England.

E Narrow-leaved Everlasting-pea *Lathyrus sylvestris* Climbing hairless or downy perennial herb, with *broadly winged stems* to 3m. Leaves with 1 pair of narrowly lanceolate leaflets, to 15cm long, with branched tendrils; *stipules lanceolate, less than half width of stem*, to 2cm long. Inflorescence long-stalked, with 3-12 flowers; corolla pinkish-purple flushed yellow, to 2cm long (**e**); calyx teeth shorter than tube; pods brown, hairless, to 7cm. In scrub, grassland and wood-margins; throughout except the far north. **Fl** 6-8. **Br** Scattered throughout, local and mainly southern; also naturalised from gardens.

F Broad-leaved Everlasting-pea *Lathyrus latifolius* Similar to Narrow-leaved Everlasting-pea, but leaflets oval to rounded and blunt; *stipules more than half width of stem* (**f**); flowers larger, to 3cm, magenta-pink; calyx teeth longer than tube. In rough grassy and bushy places; native from N France southwards; naturalised further north along railway lines, hedgebanks etc. **Fl** 6-8. **Br** Locally naturalised in S Britain.

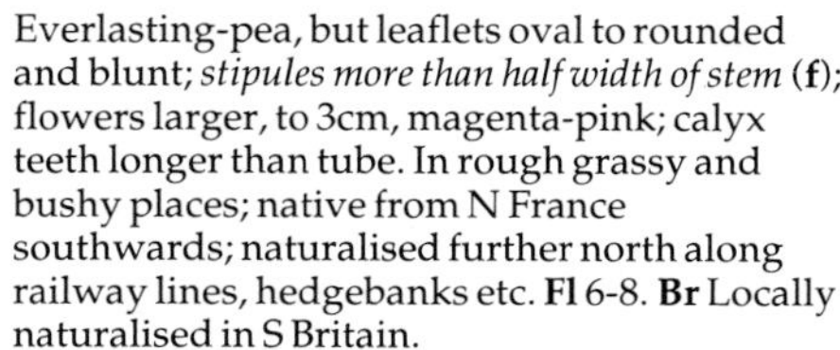

G *Lathyrus heterophyllus* Similar to Broad-leaved Everlasting-pea, but has 2-3 pairs of leaflets on upper leaves; flowers smaller, to 22mm only. Similar habitats; north to S Sweden in mainland Europe. **Fl** 6-8. **Br** Absent.

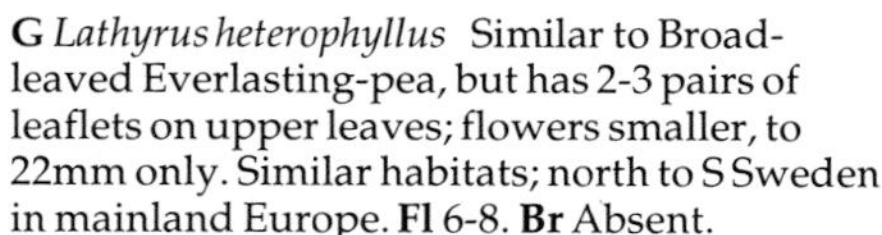

H *Lathyrus sphaericus* Hairless or downy annual, with angled, but not winged, stems to 50cm. Leaves with 1 pair of narrow linear to lanceolate pointed leaflets, with tendrils; stipules narrow, half-arrow shaped. *Flowers solitary* on slender stems, *orange-red*, to 13mm long; pod brown, hairless. Grassy and bushy places; in S Sweden and Denmark, and from N France southwards. **Fl** 6-8. **Br** Absent.

I *Lathyrus angulatus* Similar to *L. sphaericus*, but stipules broader, flower stalks longer (to 7cm, compared to 2cm), with flowers purple or pale blue, solitary or paired. In sandy places; from N France southwards. **Fl** 6-8. **Br** Absent.

J Hairy Vetchling *Lathyrus hirsutus* Hairless or downy scrambling annual, with winged stems to 1.2m. Leaves with 1 pair of linear to oblong leaflets, with a branched tendril; stipules narrow, half-arrow shaped. *Inflorescence with 1-3 flowers* on a long stalk; standard reddish-purple, wings pale blue, keel creamy white; pod densely hairy, ripening brown. In grassy and disturbed places, especially on clay soil; from N France, Belgium and S Germany southwards. **Fl** 6-8. **Br** Rarely naturalised, possibly native in Essex.

K Grass Vetchling *Lathyrus nissolia* Erect hairless or slightly downy annual, with unwinged stems to 90cm. Leaves reduced to grass-like midribs only, without leaflets or tendril – plant looks like grass when not in flower; stipules very small and narrow. Flowers solitary or paired, long-stalked, with crimson corolla to 18mm long; pods pale brown. A distinctive plant. In grassy places, especially on heavier soils; more common near the coast, from Holland and Britain southwards. **Fl** 5-7. **Br** Scattered and local through England, commoner in the south but declining.

L Yellow Vetchling *Lathyrus aphaca* Hairless waxy grey-green scrambling annual with angled stems to 1m. Leaves reduced to a tendril only, but stipules very large and leaf-like, broad-triangular, paired, to 30mm long. Flowers solitary and erect on long stalks, with corolla yellow, to 12mm long; pod to 35mm, curved, hairless, brown. In dry grassy and disturbed places; from Holland and Britain southwards, mainly western, and probably not native in north of range. **Fl** 6-8. **Br** In S England and Wales, on sandy and chalky soil.

D	A	F
	B	
E	J	
C	K	L

D Tuberous Pea

A Bitter-vetch

F Broad-leaved Everlasting-pea

B Meadow Vetchling

E Narrow-leaved Everlasting-pea

J Hairy Vetchling

C Marsh Pea

K Grass Vetchling

L Yellow Vetchling

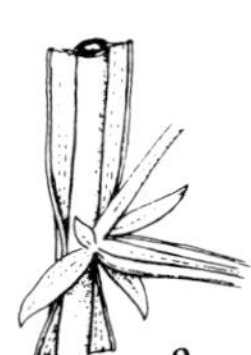

e

f

C

D

G
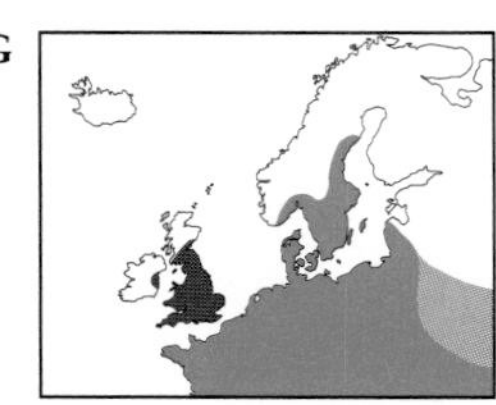

H
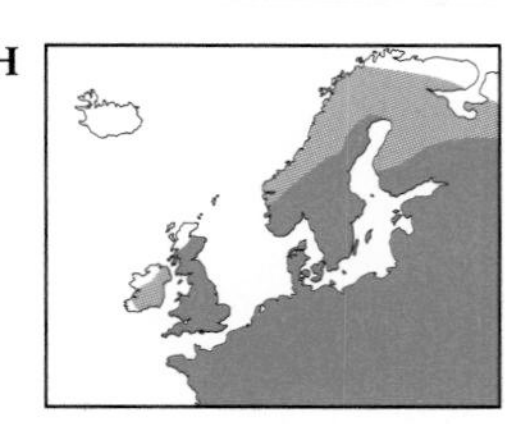

J
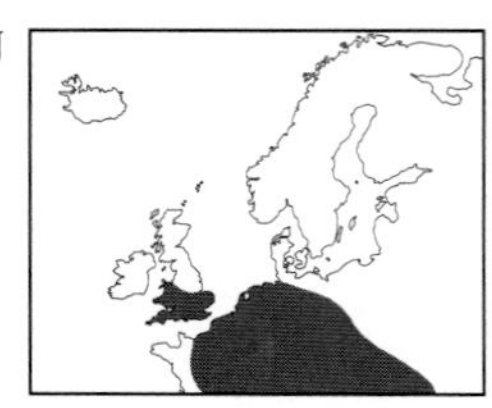

K

RESTHARROWS *Ononis* Annual or perennial herbs or dwarf shrubs, usually sticky-hairy. Leaves trifoliate, usually toothed. Standard petal broad.

(1) Flowers yellow.

A **Large Yellow Restharrow** *Ononis natrix* Small sticky-hairy subshrub to 60cm. Leaves trifoliate, with roughly ovate toothed leaflets. Flowers large, to 20mm, yellow with reddish veins, in loose leafy inflorescences: corolla twice as long as calyx. From N France and S Germany southwards; in dry grassy or rocky places, often calcareous. **Fl** 6-8. **Br** Absent.

B *Ononis pusilla* Similar to Large Yellow Restharrow in having yellow flowers, but differs in much smaller (to 12mm) clear yellow flowers, with corolla roughly equal to calyx. Similar habitats; from N France southwards. **Fl** 6-8. **Br** Absent.

(2) Flowers pink to red.

C **Common Restharrow** *Ononis repens* Creeping, ascending or spreading perennial subshrub to 70cm; stems variably *hairy all round, usually spineless*. Leaves trifoliate or with a single leaflet (**c**), sticky-hairy. Flowers in loose irregular leafy inflorescences; corolla pink, 10-18mm long, with wings equal to keel, calyx very hairy; pods erect, to 7mm long, shorter than calyx. In grassland and on dunes, especially neutral to calcareous; widespread and generally common throughout except the far north. **Fl** 6-9. **Br** Scattered throughout, locally common in calcareous areas, rare elsewhere.

D **Spiny Restharrow** *Ononis spinosa* Similar to Common Restharrow, but differing in that: *stems hairy mainly on 2 opposite sides*, and *long spines usually present*. Leaflets narrower and more pointed (**d**); flowers deeper pink, with wings shorter than keel; pods longer than calyx. In grassland on heavy, often calcareous soils, from S Scandinavia southwards; commonest near the coast. **Fl** 6-9. **Br** Local through England and Wales, though declining; rare in Scotland and absent from Ireland.

E **Small Restharrow** *Ononis reclinata* Small spreading annual to 15cm, with hairy stems, spineless. Flowers small, to 10mm, pink, with corolla equalling calyx; pods pendent when ripe, 10-14mm. In dry grassy and rocky places, usually by the sea; from SW Britain and W France southwards; local. **Fl** 6-7. **Br** Rare and local in SW England and S Wales only.

F *Ononis arvensis* Similar to Spiny Restharrow, but has no spines, and flowers are paired at each node not solitary. From S Scandinavia southwards in similar habitats. **Fl** 5-8. **Br** Absent.

MELILOTS *Melilotus* Annuals or short-lived perennials. Similar to clovers, with trifoliate toothed leaves, but flowers in elongated inflorescences; pods oval, short and straight.

G **Tall Melilot** *Melilotus altissima* Tall branched biennial or short-lived perennial to 1.5m. Leaflets oblong-ovate, with upper ones almost parallel-sided, toothed; stipules bristle-like. Flowers yellow, 50-70mm long, in long racemes to 50mm; corolla has wings, standard and keel all equal; pods are oval, 5-6mm long, pointed, downy, black when ripe, with net-veined surface, style persistent in fruit (**g**). In damp places, saline habitats, open woods and waste ground; from S Scandinavia southwards, though naturalised elsewhere. **Fl** 6-8. **Br** Local through England and Wales, absent from most of Scotland and very rare in Ireland.

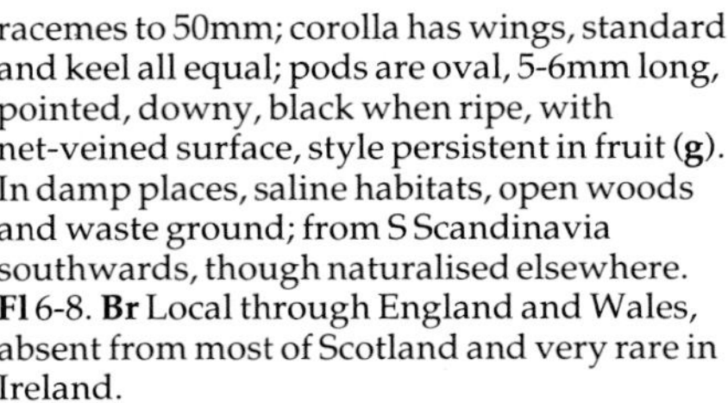

H **Ribbed, Common, Melilot** *Melilotus officinalis* Biennial to 2.5m, erect or spreading. Differs from Tall Melilot in that upper leaflets not parallel-sided; *wings and standard petals longer than keel*; pods hairless, 3-5mm long, wrinkled, blunt (with bristle-point), brown when ripe, *style not persisting* (**h**). In cultivated and disturbed ground, often on heavy or saline soils; throughout though not native in the north. **Fl** 6-9. **Br** Locally common as naturalised plant, mainly in south and east; rare in Ireland.

I **Small-flowered Melilot** *Melilotus dentata* Similar to Ribbed Melilot, but differs in having smaller flowers (corolla to 3mm, compared to 4-7mm), with wings shorter than standard but longer than keel; pod faintly net-veined, hairless, blackish-brown (**i**). Similar habitats; from S Sweden southwards to Germany, local. **Fl** 6-8. **Br** Absent.

J **Small Melilot** *Melilotus indica* Similar to Small-flowered Melilot, with very small flowers to 2mm, with wings and keel equal, shorter than standard; *pod only 2-3mm long, almost globose, strongly net-veined*, hairless and green (**j**). Naturalised on waste ground; from Holland and Britain southwards. **Fl** 6-8. **Br** Locally naturalised, mainly in S England and Wales.

K **White Melilot** *Melilotus alba* The only Melilot in N Europe with white flowers. Very similar otherwise to Ribbed Melilot, with hairless brown fruits, but these are strongly net-veined, as in Tall Melilot. Throughout except the far north in disturbed habitats, but not native over much of north of range. **Fl** 6-8. **Br** Naturalised locally in S and E Britain.

L **Trigonella** *Trigonella monspeliaca* Downy annual, to 35cm. Leaves trifoliate. Flowers 3-4mm long, yellow in short-stalked umbel-like clusters of 4-14; pod narrow and pendent, to 20mm long. Found in waste and cultivated ground; from Belgium and N France southwards. **Fl** 6-7. **Br** Absent.

M **Classical Fenugreek** *Trigonella foenum-graecum* Slightly downy annual to 50cm. Leaves trifoliate, with finely toothed ovate leaflets. Flowers solitary or paired, virtually unstalked; corolla creamy white, 10-15mm long, suffused with violet at base; pod erect, up to 10cm long. Cultivated and widely naturalised; from Belgium and Germany southwards. **Fl** 4-6. **Br** Absent.

N *Trigonella caerulea* Similar to Classical Fenugreek, with smaller blue or white flowers to 6mm, in dense globose clusters on stalks up to 50mm. Cultivated and widely naturalised, except in the north. **Fl** 6-8. **Br** Absent.

A	C	
D	H	K
G	J	M

A **Large Yellow Restharrow**

C **Common Restharrow**

D **Spiny Restharrow**

H **Ribbed Melilot**

K **White Melilot**

G **Tall Melilot**

J **Small Melilot**

M **Classical Fenugreek**

c

d

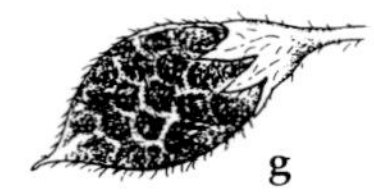
g

h

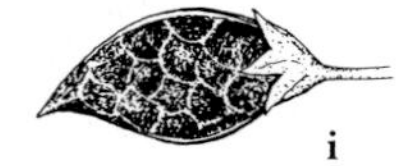
i

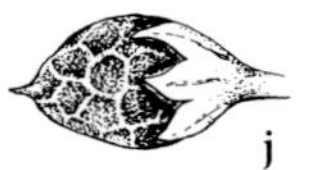
j

B

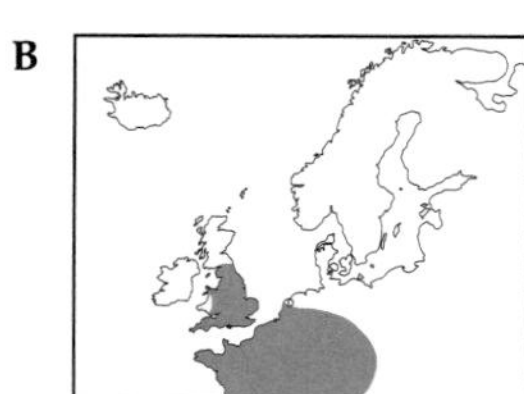

G

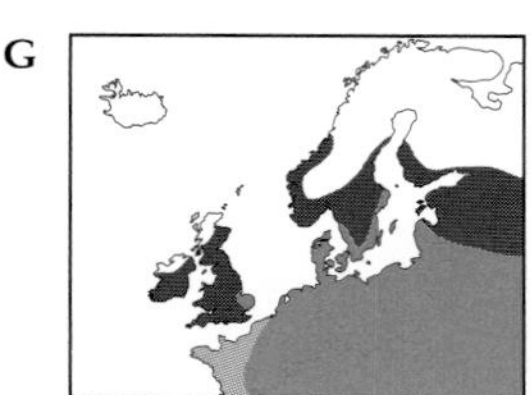

H

I

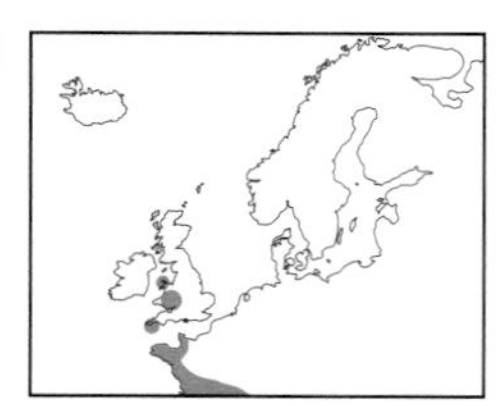

M

N

O

P

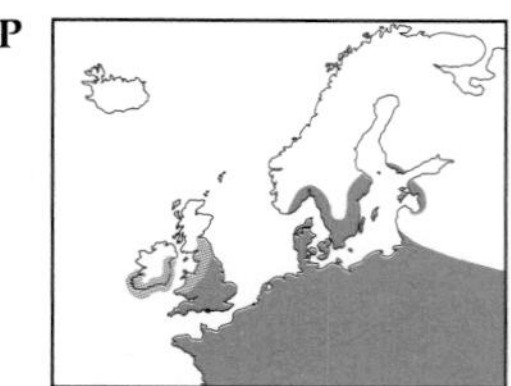

MEDICKS *Medicago* Similar to clovers (*see below*), with trifoliate leaves and compact heads of flowers, but differ in their sickle-shaped or spiral fruits, often spiny.

A **Black Medick** *Medicago lupulina* *Downy* annual or short-lived perennial to 60cm. Leaves trifoliate, leaflets usually having a triangular tooth in the terminal notch. Inflorescence globular, up to 9mm in diameter, with 10-50 very small yellow flowers; pods coiled in a full turn, black when ripe, *not spiny*, hairless. Very common in grasslands and waste places throughout except the extreme north. **Fl** 4-8. **Br** Common throughout.

B **Spotted Medick** *Medicago arabica* Prostrate, *virtually hairless* annual to 50cm. Leaves trifoliate, with toothed heart-shaped leaflets, *each dark-spotted, stiplues evenly toothed.* Flower heads with only 1-6 flowers, yellow, 5-7mm in diameter. Fruit tightly coiled (with 3-7 turns) becoming roughly globular, usually with hooked spines in a double row. In dry grasslands, especially coastal, from Holland and Britain southwards. **Fl** 4-9. **Br** Scattered, mainly S and E England, especially near coast.

C **Toothed Medick** *Medicago polymorpha* Similar to Spotted Medick, but usually hairier on stem; *leaflets unspotted*, with *jaggedly toothed stipules.* Fruit similar, but flatter, with fewer turns to spiral, *strongly net-veined*. Similar habitats; from Britain and France southwards, naturalised further north. **Fl** 4-9. **Br** Local around S and E coasts; occasional elsewhere.

D *Medicago marina* Similar to above species, but *densely white downy*, with flowers in dense globular heads. *Fruit downy*, spiralled with a central hole. Local on coastal sands, from S Brittany southwards. **Fl** 5-7. **Br** Absent.

E **Bur Medick** *Medicago minima* Short downy annual to 20cm (not as white downy as above). Inflorescences with 1-6 yellow flowers; pods 3-5mm in diameter, spiralled 3-5 times, *hairy*, usually spiny. From S Sweden southwards in dry, sandy and disturbed grasslands, mainly coastal. **Fl** 5-7. **Br** Local only around SE coasts and in Brecklands.

F **Lucerne** *Medicago sativa* ssp *sativa* Variable downy perennial to 80cm, quite different from above species superficially. Leaves trifoliate, with narrow leaflets, toothed towards tips. Flowers purple to lilac, in cylindrical heads of 5-40 flowers on stalks shorter than calyx tubes; *pod hairless, spiralled* 1½-3½ times, not spiny. Widely cultivated and often naturalised throughout, except the far north. **Fl** 6-9. **Br** Naturalised locally almost throughout, except the far north.

G **Sickle Medick** *Medicago sativa* ssp *falcata* Often distinguished as a separate species. Distinguished from Lucerne by the *yellow flowers*, with flower stalks longer than calyx tube; and *curved or sickle-shaped (not spiralled) pods*. Native in grassy places throughout except the far north, and locally naturalised. **Fl** 6-8. **Br** Native in Brecklands; introduced elsewhere.

CLOVERS *Trifolium* Herbs with trifoliate leaves, flowers in heads (corolla persistent in fruit) and stipules different from leaflets (compare with trefoils where stipules are very like leaflets).

H **Fenugreek** *Trifolium ornithopodioides* Rather inconspicuous, prostrate, hairless annual with stems 2-20cm. Leaflets oval and toothed. Stipules lanceolate and long-pointed. Flowers 5-8mm, white or pink, in small heads of 1-5. Very local in open, dry, sandy or gravelly places, often coastal and damp in winter. **Fl** 5-10. **Br** Very local, mainly south of a line from Anglesey to the Wash, and S and E Ireland.

I **Upright Clover** *Trifolium strictum* Erect or ascending stiff hairless annual to 20cm. Leaflets of upper leaves narrowly elliptical, sharply toothed. *Stipules distinctive, broad and toothed with a darker margin.* Flowers small, pinkish-purple in long-stalked rounded heads, 7-10mm in diameter. Very local to rare in open grassy places on dry acid soils. **Fl** 5-7. **Br** Very rare in SW England, Wales and Channel Islands.

J **Mountain Clover** *Trifolium montanum* Hairy perennial to 60cm with woody stem base. *Leaflets of upper leaves narrow-elliptical*, hairy below but not above. Flowers white or pale creamy yellow, becoming yellow-brown with age, in rounded (often paired) heads, 15-30mm in diameter. Dry grassy places or open woods, usually in uplands; most frequent towards the south-east of the region. **Fl** 5-7. **Br** Absent.

K **White Clover** *Trifolium repens* Creeping perennial to 50cm, *rooting at nodes. Leaflets oval often with whitish band and translucent lateral veins.* Stipules oblong and pointed. Flowers scented, white or pale pinkish in long-stalked rounded heads to 20mm in diameter, becoming light brown with age. Widespread throughout; often abundant in grassy places. **Fl** 5-10. **Br** Common throughout.

L **Alsike Clover** *Trifolium hybridum* Differs from White Clover in being erect, *not rooting at nodes* with *leaflets not having a whitish band* and flowers purple or white at first, then pink and brown. Widely cultivated and naturalised in meadows and roadsides. **Fl** 6-10. **Br** Frequent throughout, more so in the south.

M **Western Clover** *Trifolium occidentale* Similar to White Clover, but *leaflets without whitish marks* and with *lateral veins not translucent*; stipules reddish and flowers scentless in heads to 25mm in diameter. Very locally frequent on dry, exposed, coastal habitats. **Fl** 4-7. **Br** SW England, Scilly Isles and Channel Islands.

N **Clustered Clover** *Trifolium glomeratum* Prostrate *hairless* annual to 10-35cm. Leaflets oval, often with pale patch. Flowers pinkish purple in rounded *unstalked heads* 8-12mm in diameter. Dry bare or grassy places, often near the sea. **Fl** 5-8. **Br** Rare in S and E England.

O **Suffocated Clover** *Trifolium suffocatum* Very distinctive low, tufted, hairless annual to only 5cm. Leaves with oval leaflets overtopping the *unstalked* rounded 5mm heads of white flowers clustered at the base of the plant. Rare in dry sandy or gravelly ground, usually near coasts; W France and England only. **Fl** 4-5. **Br** Rare in S and E England.

P **Strawberry Clover** *Trifolium fragiferum* Creeping perennial with stems to 30cm, rooting at nodes. Leaflets oval, without whitish marks. Flowers pink or purplish in rounded heads 10-15mm in diameter. Calyx swells in fruit giving the flower head the appearance of a pinkish berry. Local to very locally common in short grassland on heavier soils. **Fl** 7-9. **Br** Local but widely scattered; locally common near sea in the south.

A	B	D
F	H	I
K	L	M
N	O	P

A **Black Medick**
B **Spotted Medick**
D *Medicago marina*
F **Lucerne** (left), G **Sickle Medick** (right)
H **Fenugreek**
I **Upright Clover**
K **White Clover**
L **Alsike Clover**
M **Western Clover**
N **Clustered Clover**
O **Suffocated Clover**
P **Strawberry Clover**

B

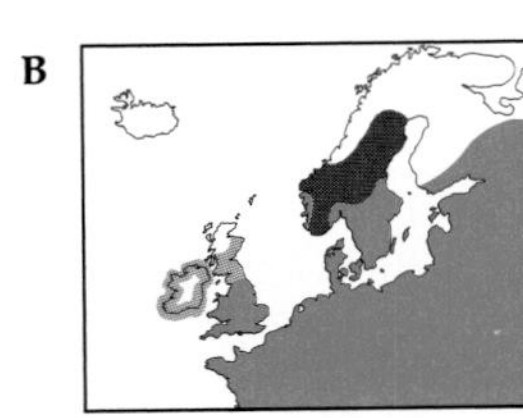

C

E

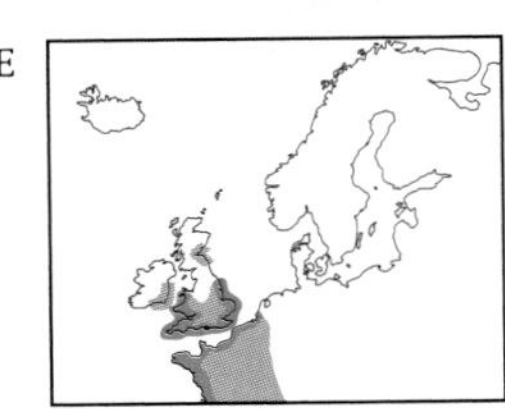

L

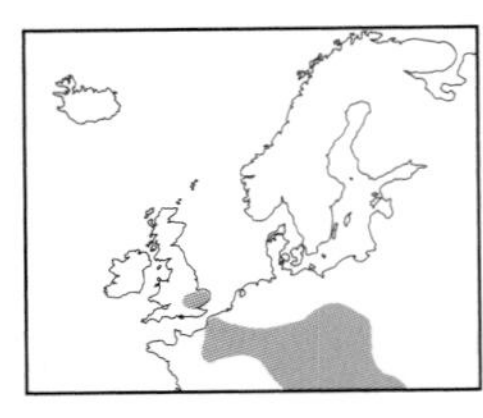

M

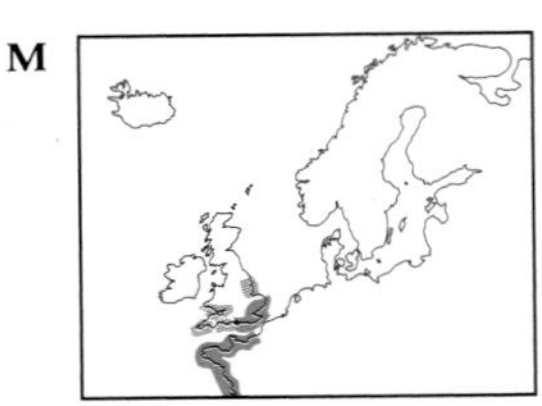

Q

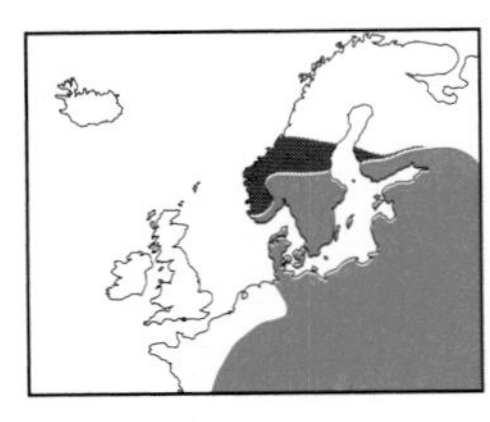

R

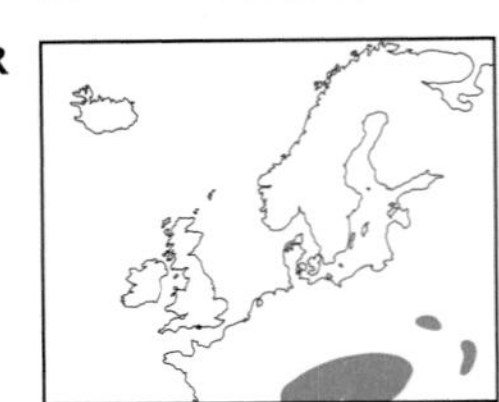

A **Reversed Clover** *Trifolium resupinatum* Differs from Strawberry Clover in that the flower heads droop. Introduced and widely naturalised. **Fl** 5-7. **Br** Casual, often near docks.

B **Hare's-foot Clover** *Trifolium arvense* Softly hairy annual to 30cm, with narrow leaflets, scarcely toothed. Flowers pale pink or white in *dense elongated oval or cylindrical stalked heads*, up to 25mm long, the flowers often shorter than the soft calyx teeth. Locally frequent in dry grassland, sandy or gravelly areas. **Fl** 5-9. **Br** Locally common, but absent from N Scotland.

C **Knotted Clover** *Trifolium striatum* Hairy, usually procumbent annual, 5-25cm. Leaflets spoon-shaped, hairy on both sides; *lateral veins not prominent* (compare with Rough Clover). Flowers 5mm, pink in *unstalked* ovoid heads to 15mm. Widespread but local to very local in dry grassy or heathy areas, sandy or gravelly places. **Fl** 5-7. **Br** Widely scattered but very local to local in England and Wales; rare in Scotland and E Ireland.

D **Twin-headed Clover** *Trifolium bocconei* Erect downy annual to 20cm, similar to previous species but leaflets hairless above, unstalked flower heads usually in pairs, and flowers white at first, then pale pink. Rare in dry grassy areas on coasts; N France and SW England only. **Fl** 5-6. **Br** Very rare on the Lizard and Jersey.

E **Rough Clover** *Trifolium scabrum* Erect or prostrate *rather downy* annual to 20cm, similar to Knotted Clover, but leaflets with *prominent lateral veins* which curve back towards the margins; flowers white in *unstalked heads* to 10mm. Local in dry grassland, dunes, sandy or gravelly soils. **Fl** 5-7. **Br** Local and mainly coastal except in the Brecks.

F **Starry Clover** *Trifolium stellatum* Erect downy annual to 20cm, with ovoid leaflets and flowers usually pink (rarely yellow or purple) in rounded heads to 25mm. *Calyx has long pointed sepals*, usually reddish, spreading and persistent in fruit giving a 'starry' appearance. Introduced from S Europe, and very rarely naturalised in dry bare places. **Fl** 6-7. **Br** Introduced and naturalised in Sussex.

G **Long-headed Clover** *Trifolium incarnatum* ssp *molinerii* Erect downy robust annual to 30cm, with oval leaflets. *Hairs pressed close to stems* (compare with ssp *incarnatum*). Flowers pink or cream with hairy calyces, in cylindrical heads to 4cm long. Very rare in short grassland on clifftops; W France and SW England. **Fl** 5-6. **Br** Very rare on the Lizard and in Jersey. Ssp *incarnatum* differs in having crimson flowers and *hairs on stems spreading*. Cultivated and widely naturalised **Fl** 5-9. **Br** Introduced and naturalised, especially in the south.

H **Red Clover** *Trifolium pratense* Downy perennial to 45cm. Leaflets oval, usually with a crescentic white mark. Stipules triangular towards tip and bristle-pointed. Flowers pinkish red, in rounded *unstalked heads* to 3cm in diameter. Common throughout in grassy places. **Fl** 5-9. **Br** Widespread and common.

I **Zig-zag Clover** *Trifolium medium* Downy perennial to 50cm, very similar to previous species but with stems rather wavy, leaflets narrowly elliptical, stipules lanceolate but not bristle-pointed and *shortly-stalked flower heads*, reddish-purple, to 30mm in diameter. Common in old grassland. **Fl** 5-7. **Br** Widespread, but local in the south, more common in the north.

J *Trifolium alpestre* Differs from Zig-zag Clover in having stipules with a downy tip and flowers usually purple. Grassy places, often in mountains. **Fl** 5-7. **Br** Absent.

K *Trifolium rubens* Hairless and has elongated flower heads to 8cm. Dry grassland, stony places; mainly in the south-east of the region. **Fl** 6-8. **Br** Absent.

L **Sulphur Clover** *Trifolium ochroleucon* Downy erect perennial to 50cm, similar to Red Clover but with lemon-yellow flowers and unmarked leaflets. Very local in grassy places on clay. **Fl** 6-7. **Br** Very local in E England.

M **Sea Clover** *Trifolium squamosum* Rather downy erect annual to 30cm, (usually much shorter) with unmarked narrow elliptical leaves and oblong stipules. Flowers pinkish red in small, rounded, short-stalked heads to 1cm, each head subtended by a pair of leaves; flowers only slightly longer than calyx, the teeth of which become prominent by spreading in fruit. Very local or rare in salt-marshes, short open coastal turf and dykesides. **Fl** 6-7. **Br** Increasingly rare northwards to Lancashire and Lincolnshire.

N **Subterranean Clover** *Trifolium subterraneum* Distinctive low-growing *prostrate* hairy annual with stems to 50cm. Leaflets broadly ovate and notched. Some flowers sterile, without corollas, but with enlarged calyx teeth; fertile flowers creamy, 8-12mm long, in clusters of only 2-6 in leaf axils. The distinctive pods are pushed down into the soil by elongating stalks. Local in dry, sandy coastal soils. **Fl** 5-6. **Br** local, mainly in the south.

O **Hop Trefoil** *Trifolium campestre* Erect or ascending *hairy* annual to 30cm. Leaves alternate; terminal leaflet longer-stalked than lateral leaflets. Flowers yellow, 4-5mm long, with 20-30 in rounded *heads up to 15mm in diameter*. Widespread and common, but almost absent from the north; in dry grassy places. **Fl** 5-10. **Br** Common; more local in Ireland.

P **Lesser Hop Trefoil** *Trifolium dubium* Very similar to Hop Trefoil, but smaller, *almost hairless* with flowers up to 3.5mm long, 3-20 in *heads 8-9mm in diameter*. Differs from Black Medick in not being downy and not having a tiny point in the terminal notch of each leaflet. Widespread and generally common, in dry grassy places, but absent from the far north. **Fl** 5-10. **Br** Common.

Q **Large Hop Trefoil** *Trifolium aureum* Similar to Hop Trefoil, but with *terminal leaflet almost stalkless*, flowers 6-7mm long, heads to 16mm. Local to locally frequent in rough grassland and waste areas; most frequent in S Scandinavia. **Fl** 6-9. **Br** Introduced and occasionally naturalised, especially in SE England.

R **Brown Clover** *Trifolium badium* Tufted hairy perennial, similar to the hop trefoils but upper leaves almost opposite, leaflets virtually stalkless and flowers 7-9mm long in heads to 25mm. In mountain grassland, usually calcareous; in central Europe. **Fl** 7-8. **Br** Absent.

S *Trifolium spadiceum* Differs from Brown Clover in being annual and having flowers to 6mm long. In grassy places in mountains, usually on acid soils; in central Europe and Scandinavia. **Fl** 6-8. **Br** Absent.

B	C	E
F	G	H
I	L	M
N	O	P

B **Hare's-foot Clover**
C **Knotted Clover**
E **Rough Clover**
F **Starry Clover**
G **Long-headed Clover**
H **Red Clover**
I **Zig-zag Clover**
L **Sulphur Clover**
M **Sea Clover**
N **Subterranean Clover**
O **Hop Trefoil**
P **Lesser Hop Trefoil**

A

C

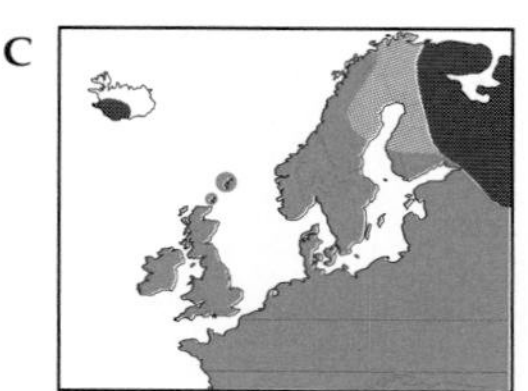

E

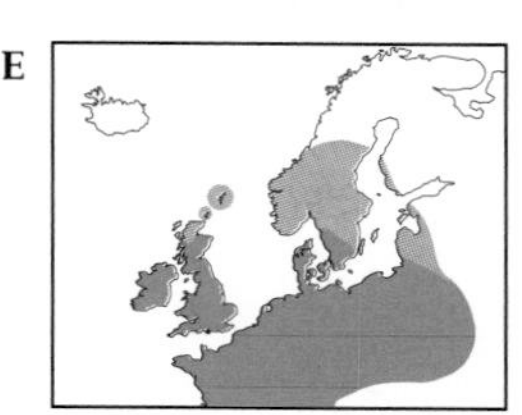

H

I

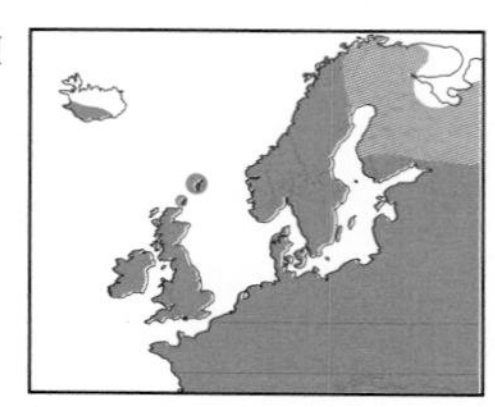

J

A Slender Trefoil *Trifolium micranthum* Erect or ascending annual to 10cm, with short-stalked leaflets. Flowers yellow and tiny, 2-3mm, in loose heads of 2-6 stalked flowers. Local in dry grassland, sandy or gravelly places. **Fl** 6-8. **Br** Widespread but generally local; rare in N England, Scotland and Ireland.

B *Dorycnium pentaphyllum* ssp *germanicum* Hairy perennial to 50cm, with pinnate leaves each having 5 elliptical untoothed leaflets. Flowers distinctive, *white with a reddish keel*, in compact stalked heads. Grassy places, often on sandy soils; in central Europe. **Fl** 6-7. **Br** Absent.

BIRD'S-FOOT-TREFOILS *Lotus* Low herbs with pinnate leaves that appear trifoliate because the lower pair is at the base of the stalk, looking like large stipules; actual stipules minute, brown. Flowers yellow, in small heads on long stalks from leaf axils. Pods, when ripe, spread out stiffly like a bird's foot.

C Common Bird's-foot-trefoil *Lotus corniculatus* Variable, often sprawling or creeping, perennial, usually almost hairless, occasionally hairy. Stems solid, to 40cm long. Leaflets ovate to lanceolate, occasionally nearly round. Heads 2-8 flowered, on stout stalks up to 80mm long; flowers yellow, about 15mm long, deep red in bud; calyx teeth (**c**) erect in bud, the 2 upper ones having an obtuse angle between them. Widespread and common in grasslands on all but the most acid soils; throughout the north, except the extreme north. **Fl** 6-9. **Br** Very common throughout.

D Narrow-leaved Bird's-foot-trefoil *Lotus tenuis* Similar to Common Bird's-foot-trefoil, but more slender, often more erect; leaflets narrow, tapering to a point, less than 4mm wide. Flowers in heads of 2-4, small; 2 upper calyx teeth convergent (**d**). In dry grasslands, widespread except in the north; more local than above. **Fl** 6-8. **Br** Local, but more frequent in the south, rare in the north. Commonest on clay soils.

E Greater Bird's-foot-trefoil *Lotus uliginosus* Similar to Common Bird's-foot-trefoil, but usually more erect, taller (to 60cm), and very hairy; stem hollow. Leaflets broadly oval, blunt, rather bluish green. Inflorescence stalks up to 15cm long; flowers usually without reddish tinge; upper calyx teeth separated by an acute angle (**e**). In damp grassy places and fens; throughout except most of Arctic Europe. **Fl** 6-8. **Br** Locally common throughout, except the far north.

F Hairy Bird's-foot-trefoil *Lotus subbiflorus* Annual or perennial, spreading, up to 30cm (rarely more). Leaflets all very hairy. Flowers small, to 1cm, in heads of 2-4, on stalks equalling or exceeding leaves; calyx teeth longer than tube. In dry places, mainly coastal; from S Britain and W France southwards; local. **Fl** 7-8. **Br** Local along southern coasts from Hampshire westwards.

G Slender Bird's-foot-trefoil *Lotus angustissimus* Similar to Hairy Bird's-foot-trefoil, but always annual, very slender, less hairy; heads 1- to 2-flowered, on stalks shorter than leaves; flowers sometimes purple-veined. In dry, usually coastal, grassland; from S England southwards. **Fl** 7-8. **Br** S coast of England only; very local.

H Dragon's-teeth *Tetragonolobus maritimus* Differs from bird's-foot-trefoils in having trifoliate leaves (with triangular stipules), and solitary flowers. Flowers on long stalks, with trifoliate bract below calyx; corolla pale yellow; fruit up to 5cm long, 4-angled, winged on angles. Widespread on mainland Europe southwards from S Sweden; in grassy, usually calcareous places. **Fl** 5-8. **Br** Probably introduced; very locally common in SE England.

I Kidney Vetch *Anthyllis vulneraria* Prostrate or ascending, silky-hairy perennial up to 40cm. Leaves pinnate, lower ones with fewer leaflets; leaflets linear to oblong, silky-white below, green above, terminal leaflet much larger. Flowers in close-set paired heads, up to 4cm across, with numerous yellow flowers (rarely pink, white or purple) and conspicuous woolly, inflated calyces between; pods very short. In dry grasslands, often coastal or calcareous, and in rocky places; throughout the area except the far north. **Fl** 5-9. **Br** Widespread and locally common in calcareous and coastal areas.

J Bird's-foot *Ornithopus perpusillus* Prostrate downy annual to 40cm, usually less. Leaves pinnate, with 4-13 pairs and a terminal leaflet. Flowers in heads of 3-8, with a pinnate bract just below head; corolla creamy and veined red (appearing orange at first sight), 3-5mm long; pods to 2cm long, curved, constricted between seeds, spreading out like a bird's foot. Found in dry sandy places; from S Sweden southwards, locally common. **Fl** 5-8. **Br** Locally common in England and Wales, rarer further north; very local in Ireland.

K Orange Bird's-foot *Ornithopus pinnatus* Similar to Bird's-foot, but less downy, *flowers wholly orange-yellow*, slightly larger (6-8mm), *without bract below flower head*; pods 20-30mm long, with less marked constrictions. Sandy turf, usually coastal, from Scilly Isles and W France southwards. **Fl** 4-8. **Br** Scilly Isles and Channel Islands only.

L Goat's Rue *Galega officinalis* An erect, perennial, hairless or slightly downy herb to 1.5m. Leaves pinnate, with 9-17 oblong to ovate leaflets. Flowers white to bluish-mauve, in erect, long-stalked, cylindrical inflorescences; calyx teeth bristle-like; pods cylindrical, not angled or inflated, 2-3cm long. Widely naturalised (from S Europe) on waste ground as far north as Britain and Belgium. **Fl** 5-8. **Br** Naturalised, mainly in S and central Britain.

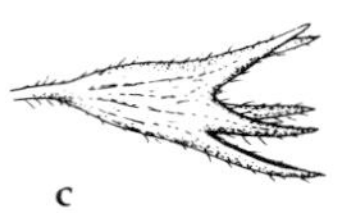

c

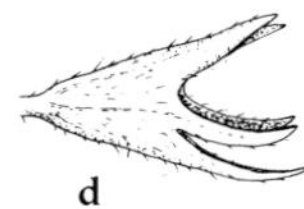

d

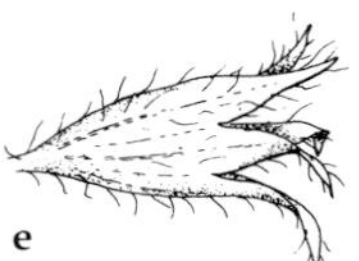

e

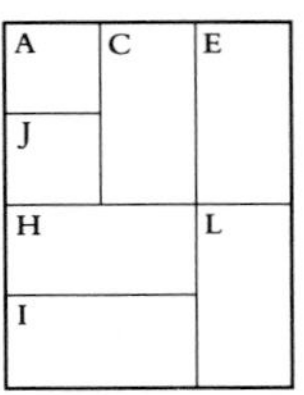

A **Slender Trefoil**

C **Common Bird's-foot-trefoil**

E **Greater Bird's-foot-trefoil**

J **Bird's-foot**

H **Dragon's-teeth**

I **Kidney Vetch**

L **Goat's Rue**

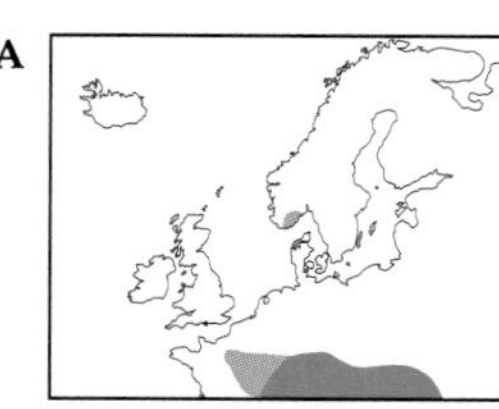

A

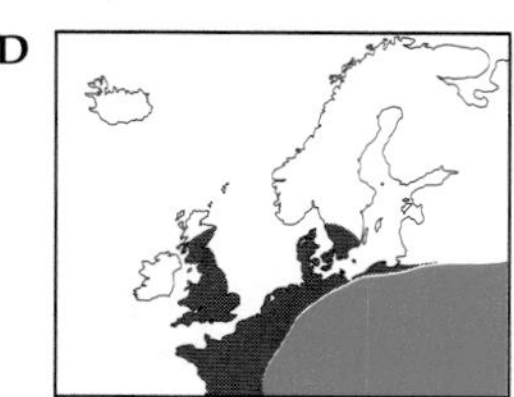

D

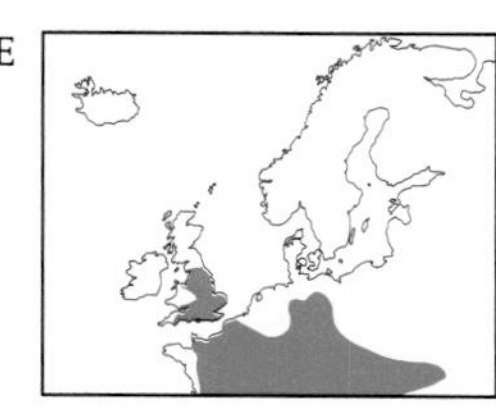

E

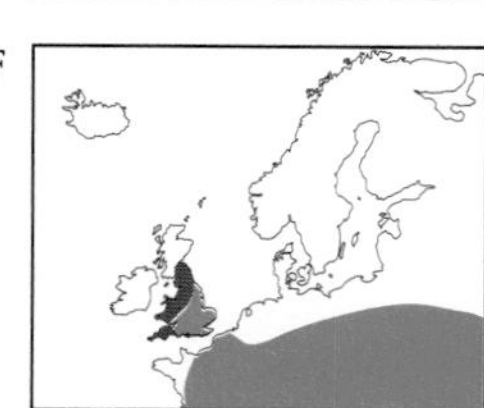

F

A False Senna *Coronilla emerus* Low loose shrub to 1m, rarely more. Leaves with 2-4 pairs of greyish-green leaflets, with tiny point in notch at tip; stipules not joined, papery, 1-2mm long. Flowers in clusters of 1-5, with corolla pale yellow, 14-20mm long; pods to 10cm long, narrow, with numerous divisions. (Bladder Senna [*see* page 114] has leaves with 4-5 pairs, usually, with flowers in clusters of 3-8; fruit inflated and quite different.) In rocky places, usually shady, especially on limestone; from S Scandinavia southwards, mainly eastern. **Fl** 4-5. **Br** Absent.

B Small Scorpion Vetch *Coronilla vaginalis* Small shrub to 50cm high. Leaves with 2-6 pairs of ovate to almost circular leaflets, with short stalks and rough margins; stipules 3-8mm long. Flowers in heads of 4-10, corolla yellow, 6-10mm long; pods up to 30mm long, segmented, 6-angled. Found in grassy places and scrub on calcareous soils and in mountain regions from France and Germany southwards. **Fl** 6-8. **Br** Absent.

C *Coronilla minima* Similar to Small Scorpion Vetch, with *unstalked leaflets, stipules only 1mm long;* corolla 5-8mm long, yellow. Dry open and grassy habitats, usually on calcareous soils; from NW France southwards. **Fl** 6-9. **Br** Absent.

D Crown Vetch *Coronilla varia* Straggling or ascending hairless perennial herb to 1m. Leaves pinnate, with 7-12 pairs of oblong-ovate leaflets; stipules papery, up to 6mm long. Flowers in heads of 10-20, corolla white or pink (rarely purplish), 10-15mm long; pods 4-angled, to 60mm long. In grassy and bushy places, often on calcareous soils; probably native from Holland and Germany southwards, but naturalised further north. **Fl** 6-8. **Br** Introduced; naturalised in scattered localities.

E Horseshoe Vetch *Hippocrepis comosa* Spreading, almost hairless perennial herb with woody rootstock, to 40cm. *Leaves pinnate,* with 3-8 pairs of ovate to linear leaflets; almost hairless or downy below; stipules small and narrowly triangular. Heads with 5-12 flowers on long stalks; corolla pale yellow, 5-10mm long; pods in form of bird's foot, to 30mm long, strongly wavy, breaking up into small horseshoe-shaped segments. Widespread and locally common in short, dry turf on calcareous soils from Holland and Britain southwards. **Fl** 5-7. **Br** Local, to locally common in England, rarer in Wales and absent elsewhere.

F Sainfoin *Onobrychis viciifolia* Erect or occasionally prostrate, downy to almost hairless perennial herb up to 80cm. Leaves pinnate, with 6-14 pairs of oblong to lanceolate leaflets; stipules triangular, papery and brown. Flowers in conical spikes, up to 90mm long, with numerous pink, red-veined flowers; calyx teeth much longer than downy tube; pods small, to 8mm, downy and oval, with toothed margins. In dry grassland, roadsides and disturbed ground, mainly on calcareous soils; throughout as far north as S Sweden, but probably not native through most of range. **Fl** 6-8. **Br** Mainly introduced, widespread on roadsides and grassy places; possibly native in dwarfer form in SE England.

Wood Sorrel Family
Oxalidaceae

Herbs with trifoliate untoothed leaves. Flowers solitary or in small clusters, 5-parted. Only Wood Sorrel is native to the area – all other species are introduced.

(1) Flowers white or very pale pink.

G Wood Sorrel *Oxalis acetosella* Creeping perennial herb, rarely more than 10cm. Leaves trifoliate and long-stalked, with drooping leaflets, yellowish-green above, purplish below. Flowers solitary on slender stalks to 10cm, bell-shaped, to 25mm in diameter, white or pale pink with lilac veins; fruit is a hairless capsule, 5-veined. In shady places, especially beech and oak woodland; throughout. **Fl** 4-6. **Br** Locally common throughout, especially in ancient woodland.

(2) Flowers yellow.

H *Oxalis corniculata* Creeping rooting downy perennial. *Leaves alternate,* with small eared stipules. Flowers yellow, petals 4-7mm long, in umbels of 1-7, with stalks reflexed in fruit. In dry open habitats, northwards to S Norway, possibly native in south of range. **Fl** 5-9. **Br** Introduced, locally naturalised.

I *Oxalis exilis* Similar to *O. corniculata*, but very small, with solitary flowers.

J *Oxalis europaea* Very similar to *O. corniculata*, but more erect, to 40cm, without rooting nodes. *Leaves opposite or in whorls,* stipules absent. Fruit stalks erect. A naturalised weed throughout except the far north. **Fl** 6-9. **Br** Local, southern.

K Bermuda Buttercup *Oxalis pes-caprae* Bulbous plant, with all leaves from base. Flowers in umbels, with large yellow flowers to 40mm in diameter. Fruit rare. Naturalised in SW England and France in cultivated land. **Fl** 3-6. **Br** Only in coastal areas of SW England.

(3) Flowers deep pink.

L Pink Oxalis *Oxalis articulata* Downy tufted perennial to 35cm. Leaves in rosettes, with downy leaflets, orange-spotted below. Flowers pink, in umbels, with petals 12-20mm long. Naturalised in waste ground from Britain southwards. **Fl** 4-9. **Br** Mainly in SW Britain.

M *Oxalis incarnata* Rather similar to Pink Oxalis, but has leaves up the stem, and bulbs rather than rhizomes. Flowers lilac with darker veins. Similar habitats; in SW England and W France. **Fl** 4-9. **Br** Local in SW England.

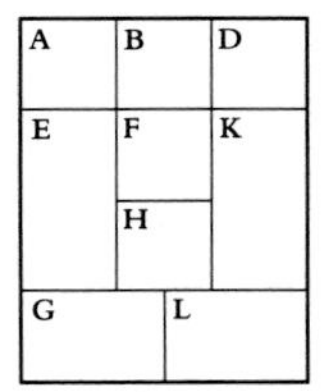

A **False Senna**

B **Small Scorpion Vetch**

D **Crown Vetch**

E **Horseshoe Vetch**

F **Sainfoin**

K **Bermuda Buttercup**

H *Oxalis corniculata*

G **Wood Sorrel**

L **Pink Oxalis**

A

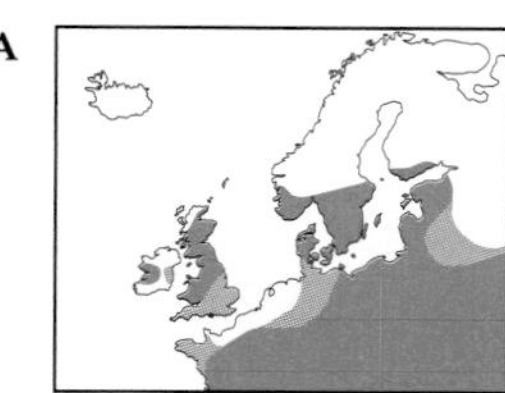

B

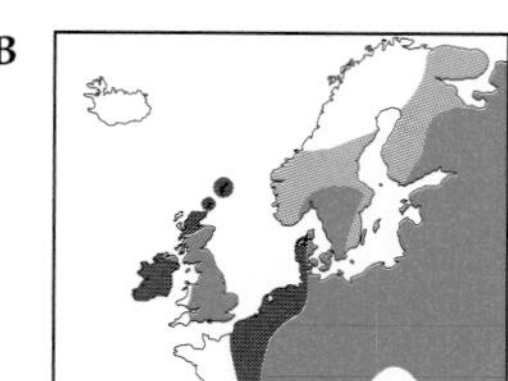

D

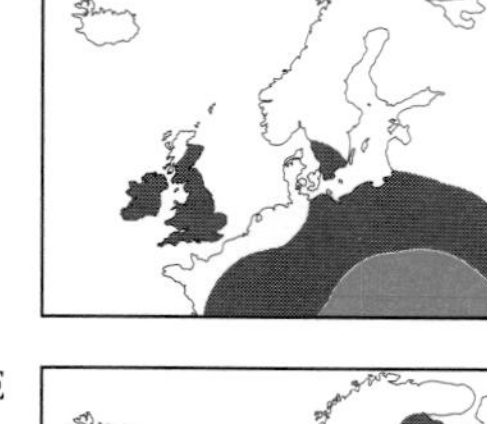

E

H

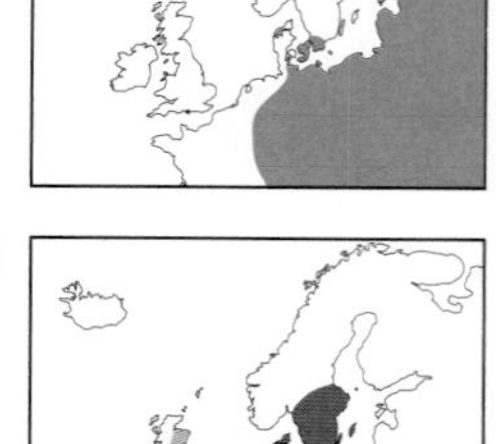

I

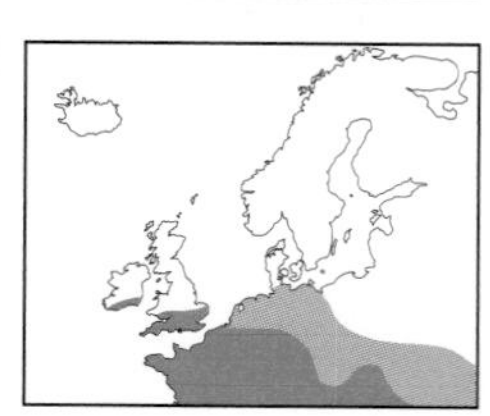

L

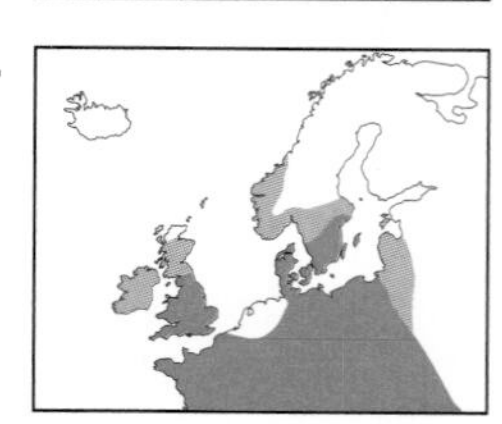

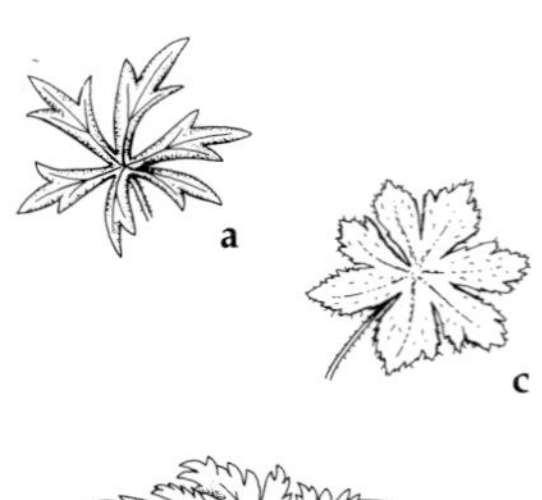

Crane's-bill Family
Geraniaceae

CRANE'S-BILLS *Geranium* Differ from the closely related Stork's-bills *(Erodium)* species in having palmately lobed leaves (not pinnate), and fruits whose beaks roll up to release the seeds (rather than twisting spirally and retaining the seeds).

A Bloody Crane's-bill *Geranium sanguineum* Low to medium perennial herb, much-branched and spreading. Leaves mainly basal, 30-50mm wide, deeply cut into 5-7 divided lobes (**a**). Flowers clear deep pink to reddish-purple, 20-30mm in diameter, usually solitary on long stalks, with a tiny pair of bracts half-way up. Widespread but local on light often base-rich soils, usually in open habitats such as grassland, limestone pavement and stable dunes; from S Scandinavia southwards. **Fl** 6-8. **Br** Local throughout; absent from SE England.

B Meadow Crane's-bill *Geranium pratense* Medium to tall hairy perennial herb, often in clumps, up to 80cm. Leaves about 10cm wide, deeply divided, almost to the base, into 5-7 divided lobes (**b**). Flowers large, 25-35mm in diameter, *clear blue* with very little red in, borne in pairs on stalks 20-40mm long; petals rounded. Widespread and locally common, on roadsides and in meadows, usually on base-rich soils, but absent from the far north of Europe. **Fl** 6-9. **Br** Locally common especially in the Midlands and the north.

C Wood Crane's-bill *Geranium sylvaticum* Medium tufted perennial to 60cm. Similar to Meadow Crane's-bill, but leaves have broader, blunter lobes (**c**); flowers are slightly smaller, 20-25mm, more cupped, and usually *reddish-purple to pinkish-violet*, not clear blue. Centre often white. Widespread and locally common throughout, in damper grasslands, open woods, mountain pastures and hedgebanks, usually on lime-rich soils. **Fl** 6-8. **Br** Rare in the south, frequent from N England northwards.

D Dusky Crane's-bill *Geranium phaeum* Medium, erect, tufted perennial to 70cm, usually hairy. Leaves divided just beyond half-way into 5-7 toothed lobes. Flowers distinctive – *deep blackish-purple* in colour, 15-20mm across, in pairs, petals somewhat reflexed, stamens in tight central cluster. Native from central France and S Germany southwards, but widely naturalised northwards to S Sweden. Occurs on woodland edges, roadsides, and damp semi-shaded places. **Fl** 5-7. **Br** Locally naturalised, absent from the north.

E Marsh Crane's-bill *Geranium palustre* Medium, tufted perennial to 60cm, erect or rather spreading, with short rhizomes. Leaves up to 10cm wide, divided just beyond the middle into 5 (or 7) lobes, each sharply toothed (**e**). Flowers purplish-red, 20-30mm in diameter, cup-shaped with rounded petals; produced in pairs in open inflorescences. Fruits hairy and erect, but with stalks reflexed. Local in mainland Europe in wet meadows and marshes, absent from Holland and N Scandinavia. **Fl** 6-8. **Br** Absent.

F *Geranium divaricatum* Annual, with similar leaves to Marsh Crane's-bill. Flowers are 8-12mm in diameter, in small clusters, petals pink, notched, same length as sepals. In shady places, from E France and S Germany southwards. **Fl** 5-8. **Br** Absent.

G *Geranium bohemicum* Rather similar to *G. divaricatum*, with violet-blue flowers, 15-18mm in diameter; sepals shorter than petals and bristle-tipped. Grassy places, locally from S Scandinavia southwards. **Fl** 5-9. **Br** Absent.

H Hedgerow Crane's-bill *Geranium pyrenaicum* Short to medium hairy perennial, ascending or erect to 70cm, though often much shorter. Leaves rounded in outline, divided about half-way into 5-7 lobes and toothed only at the ends (**h**). Basal leaves long-stalked. Flowers pinkish to purple, 12-18mm in diameter, borne *in pairs, petals deeply notched*. Sepals bristle-tipped. Fruit and stalks hairy, reflexed. Local, in meadows and roadsides, rough ground; native to S areas of Europe, naturalised through much of central Europe. **Fl** 6-8. **Br** Probably introduced. Frequent, but rare in W and N Britain.

I Round-leaved Crane's-bill *Geranium rotundifolium* Rather similar to Hedgerow Crane's-bill, but an annual plant to 40cm; leaves scarcely cut (**i**). Flowers numerous in open groups, with stalks less than 15mm long, pink, 10-12mm in diameter, with *petals barely notched*, and sepals not bristle-tipped. In dry sandy or calcareous places; from Germany and Belgium southwards. **Fl** 6-7. **Br** Mainly southern, absent from Scotland and very rare in Ireland.

J Dove's-foot Crane's-bill *Geranium molle* Low very hairy annual to 40cm, branched and spreading. Stems have very long hairs. Leaves grey-green, hairy and rounded but divided beyond half-way into 5-7 lobes (**j**). Upper stem leaves more divided. Flowers pink, 5-10mm in diameter, in pairs, with notched petals barely longer than sepals. Fruit is hairless. Widespread and common throughout, except in the extreme north, in dry open habitats, including meadows, dunes, roadsides and cultivated areas. **Fl** 4-9. **Br** Common and widespread, though rarer in the north.

K Small-flowered Crane's-bill *Geranium pusillum* Very like Dove's-foot Crane's-bill, but with shorter hairs, wider gaps between leaf lobes (**k**), smaller (4-6mm) pale flowers, and hairy fruits. Widespread throughout in dry open places, except in the far north. **Fl** 6-9. **Br** Widespread, mainly southern and eastern.

L Long-stalked Crane's-bill *Geranium columbinum* Short or medium, shortly hairy annual, erect or ascending to 60cm. Leaves divided almost to the base into narrow divided lobes (**l**); lower leaves long-stalked. Flowers pink-purple, 12-18mm in diameter, on *long slender stalks, standing clear of leaves*; petals not notched. Fruits hairless or almost so. Widespread in grassland, arable land and other open sites, usually on base-rich soil, except in the far north. **Fl** 6-8. **Br** Local in England and Wales; rare further north.

M Cut-leaved Crane's-bill *Geranium dissectum* Rather similar to Long-stalked Crane's-bill with leaves cut almost to base (**m**). Flowers on shorter stalks, less than 15mm; petals usually with small broad point at tip, not notched; fruit hairy. Widespread and common in cultivated and waste ground, grassy places, except in the extreme north. **Fl** 5-8. **Br** Mostly common, though very local in N Scotland.

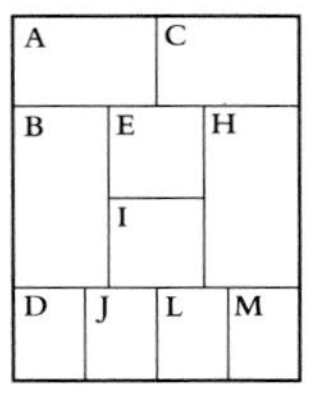

A Bloody Crane's-bill
C Wood Crane's-bill
B Meadow Crane's-bill
E Marsh Crane's-bill
H Hedgerow Crane's-bill
I Round-leaved Crane's-bill
D Dusky Crane's-bill
J Dove's-foot Crane's-bill
L Long-stalked Crane's-bill
M Cut-leaved Crane's-bill

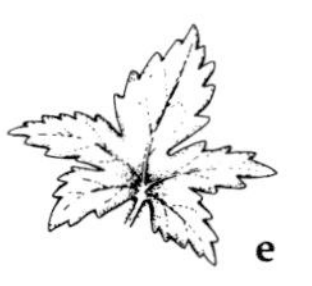

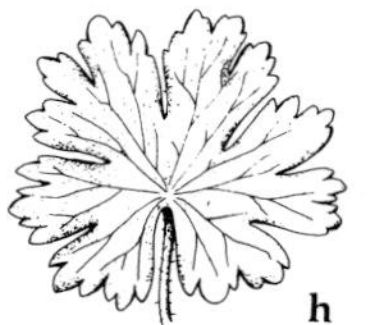

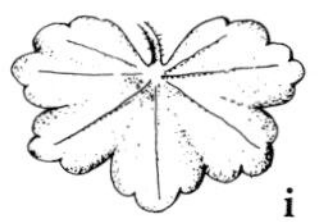

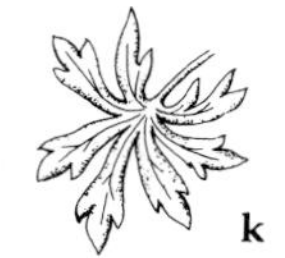

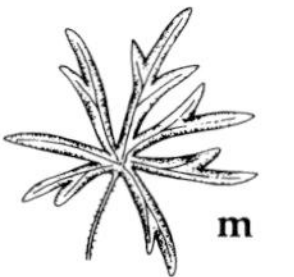

A

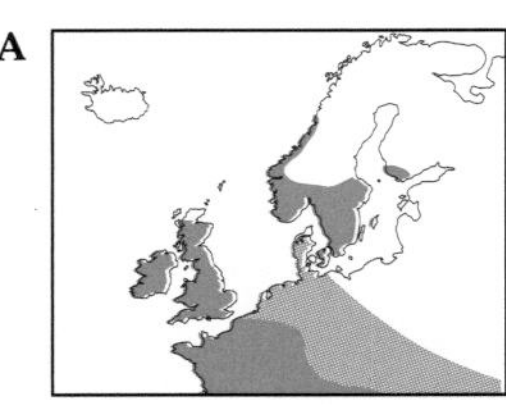

B

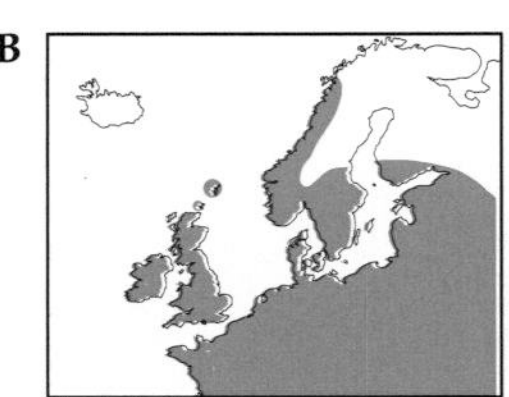

D

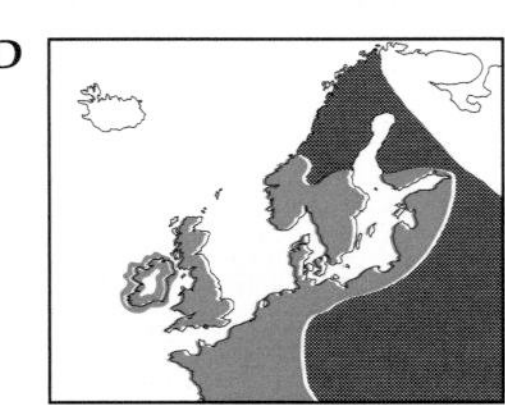

E

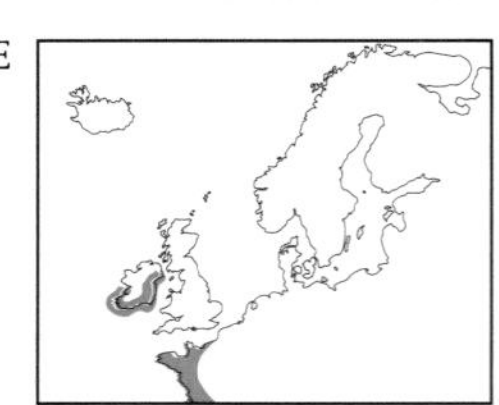

H

K

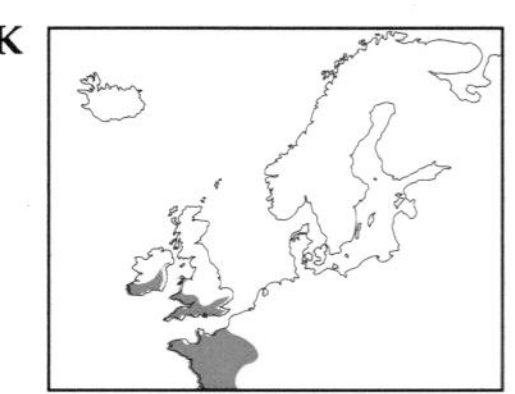

M

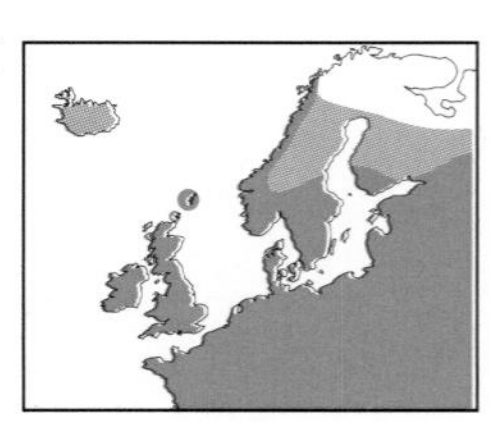

N

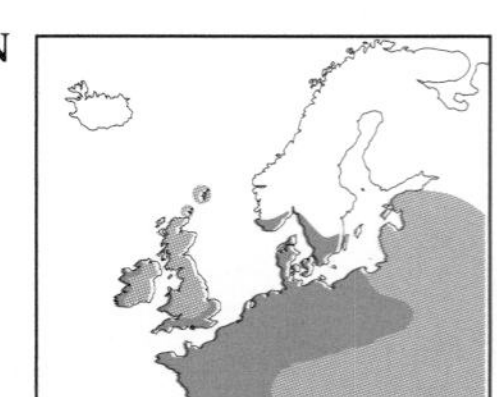

A Shining Crane's-bill *Geranium lucidum* Short, branched, ascending, almost hairless annual to 40cm. Leaves *shiny green*, often red-tinged, long-stalked; rounded in outline, divided about half-way into 5-7 lobes, each oval and bluntly toothed. Flowers pale pink, usually in pairs, 10-15mm in diameter, petals unnotched, and with a marked claw. Fruit hairless. Widespread in shady places, especially on rocks and walls, usually on limestone; not in the far north. **Fl** 4-8. **Br** Widespread, mainly western or upland, though rare in N Scotland.

B Herb Robert *Geranium robertianum* Short-medium hairy annual (though often overwintering), spreading or erect to 50cm, with strong unpleasant smell. Leaves divided to base into 5 pinnately divided lobes, hairy, and often red-tinged. Flowers bright pink, occasionally white, 12-16mm in diameter, petals unnotched, with a marked claw; pollen orange. Fruit hairy. Mainly shady places, woodland margins, hedges and walls, but also on shingle, where it is more prostrate. Throughout except in the far north. **Fl** 4-9. **Br** Common throughout.

C Little Robin *Geranium purpureum* Similar to Herb Robert, but smaller in all respects and less red; flowers 7-14mm in diameter, fruit more wrinkled; pollen yellow not orange. Uncommon on shingle or rocks close to the sea; in W France, Eire and England only. **Fl** 4-9. **Br** Very local in SW England, as far east as Sussex, and S Ireland.

STORK'S-BILLS *Erodium* Closely related to crane's-bills, differing mainly in details of fruit and leaves (*see* also Crane's-bills).

D Common Stork's-bill *Erodium cicutarium* Variable spreading annual up to 60cm (usually less), normally stickily hairy. Leaves pinnate, up to 15cm long, with lobes pinnately cut, with conspicuous whitish *pointed stipules* (**d**). Flowers in loose umbels of 1-12; petals 4-10mm long, rose-pink (occasionally white), usually unequal, and with dark spot at base of 2 upper larger petals. Widespread and common throughout, except in the extreme north; in dry sandy places and disturbed ground, especially near the coast. **Fl** 6-9. **Br** Widespread and locally common throughout; mainly coastal.

E Musk Stork's-bill *Erodium moschatum* Similar to Common Stork's-bill, but plant always sticky-hairy and smelling of musk. Leaves pinnate, with lobes toothed but not pinnately lobed; *stipules broad and blunt* (**e**). Flowers larger, with petals up to 15mm long. Found in cultivated and sandy ground, from Holland southwards, mainly coastal, local. **Fl** 5-7. **Br** Mainly coastal, on S and W coasts, and most of Ireland; introduced inland.

F *Erodium malacoides* Stalked oval leaves, toothed or sometimes 3-lobed, but not normally pinnate (**f**). Umbels with 3-7 flowers, bracts rounded ovate, petals pink, 5-9mm long. In dry sandy places; W France southwards. **Fl** 5-8. **Br** Absent.

G Sea Stork's-bill *Erodium maritimum* Prostrate annual, with similar leaves to *E. malacoides*. Flowers solitary or paired, petals very small, to 3mm, absent or falling early. Dry sandy coastal grasslands in Britain and France only (and further south). **Fl** 5-9. **Br** On S and W coasts, including Ireland, local.

Flax Family Linaceae

A small family of erect hairless herbs, with narrow untoothed unstalked leaves. Flowers with 4 or 5 parts, petals contorted in bud; fruit a globose dry capsule.

H Perennial Flax *Linum perenne* Erect or spreading hairless perennial, rather woody at base, to 60cm. Leaves linear, narrow to 2.5mm wide, 1-veined (or obscurely 3-veined), greyish-green. Flowers numerous in loose inflorescence, individually 20-25mm in diameter, pale to mid-blue; outer sepals narrow and pointed, inner sepals broader and blunt. Ssp *anglicum* is more procumbent than type, with stems curved at base. Local in dry, often calcareous grasslands. Ssp *perenne* occurs in E France and S Germany only; ssp *anglicum* is confined to Britain. **Fl** 6-7. **Br** In England only, mainly eastern, from Durham southwards.

I *Linum austriacum* Similar to Perennial Flax but flower stalks are usually reflexed. Similar habitats; E France, S Germany. **Fl** 6-7. **Br** Absent.

J *Linum leonii* Similar to above 2 species, but shorter (to 30cm only) and usually spreading; inflorescence few-flowered; flowers have anthers and stigmas at same height (different heights in above 2 species). Similar habitats, France and W Germany only. **Fl** 6-7. **Br** Absent.

K Pale Flax *Linum bienne* Annual to perennial with slender erect or spreading stems, often branched, to 60cm. Leaves narrow and pointed, normally 3-veined. Flowers pale blue or lilac, *12-18mm in diameter; sepals all ovate*, pointed; inner ones with a rough, hairy margin. In dry grassland, often calcareous and most frequently near the coast; in Britain and W France only. **Fl** 5-9. **Br** Local, almost entirely southern from Kent to SW Ireland; occasional further north.

L *Linum tenuifolium* Similar to Pale Flax, but shorter, with very narrow 1-veined leaves. Flowers pink, 10-15mm in diameter, with sepals all pointed. Found in calcareous grasslands, from Belgium and S Germany southwards. **Fl** 6-7. **Br** Absent.

M *Linum suffruticosum* Similar to Pale Flax, but with flowers much larger, to 30mm in diameter, pink to white, with a deep-pink claw. From N France southwards, in grassy and rocky places. **Fl** 5-7. **Br** Absent.

N Fairy Flax *Linum catharticum* Slender erect annual (rarely biennial) herb to 15cm. Leaves narrow, ovate-lanceolate, blunt and 1-veined. Flowers in very open forked inflorescence; white, only 4-6mm in diameter, nodding in bud; sepals lanceolate and glandular-hairy. In a wide range of dry or damp habitats, usually calcareous or neutral; common throughout except in the extreme north. **Fl** 6-9. **Br** Locally common throughout.

O Allseed *Radiola linoides* Very small bushy annual plant, rarely exceeding 8cm, often less, with branched stems. Leaves elliptical, in opposite pairs, 1-veined, to 3mm long (**o1**). Flowers numerous, in branched inflorescences; each is 1-2mm in diameter, with 4 tiny white petals, equal in length to the sepals (**o2**). Widespread but local on damp, sandy or peaty ground, usually acidic; throughout except in the north. **Fl** 6-8. **Br** Widespread but very local; frequent only in SW England.

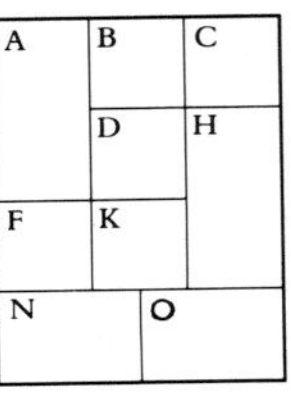

A **Shining Crane's-bill**
B **Herb Robert**
C **Little Robin**
D **Common Stork's-bill**
H **Perennial Flax**
F *Erodium malacoides*
K **Pale Flax**
N **Fairy Flax**
O **Allseed**

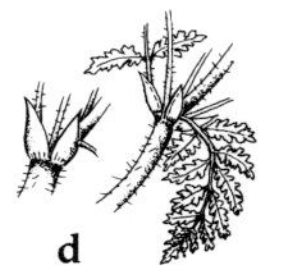

d

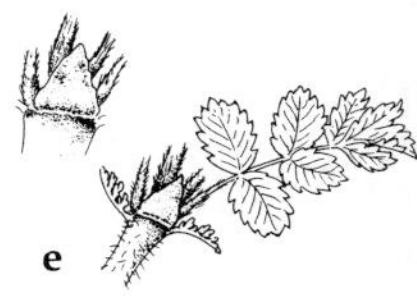

e

f

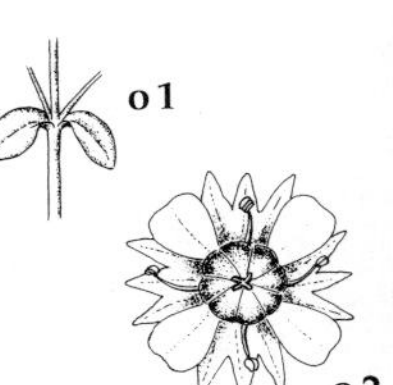

B 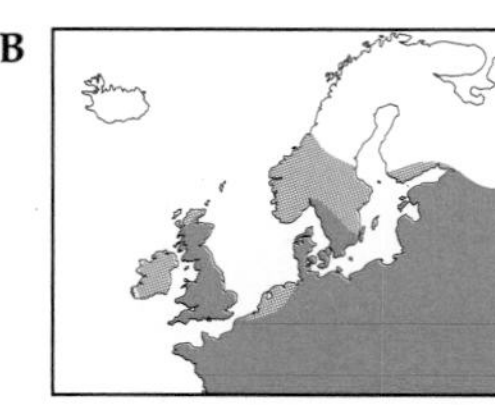

C 

E 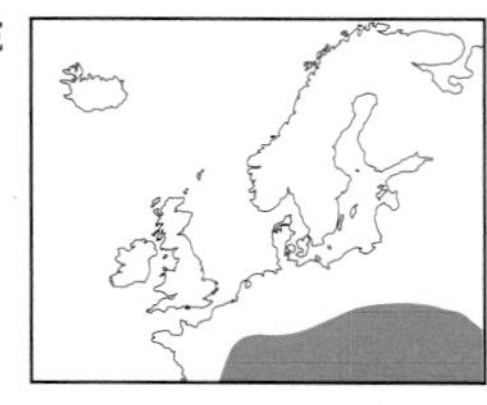

F 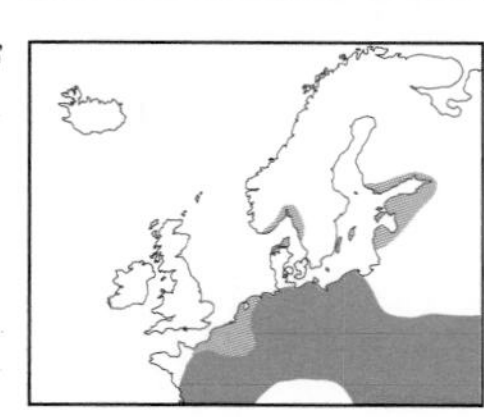

G 

Spurge Family Euphorbiaceae

All herbaceous plants (in N Europe), usually with latex, with alternate simple leaves. Flowers regular, single-sex, (on the same, or separate, plants), without petals, in umbel-like terminal heads (*Euphorbia*) or in spikes from leaf axils (*Mercurialis*).

A **Annual Mercury** *Mercurialis annua* Erect annual to 50cm, often branched and virtually hairless. Leaves ovate to elliptical, shiny green, to 50mm long, with regular rounded teeth. Male flowers (usually on separate plants) in long erect spikes; female flowers few, almost stalkless; all yellowish-green, 2-4mm. Fruit bristly. In waste places and cultivated ground, widespread, though rare and probably not native in most of Scandinavia. **Fl** 7-10. **Br** Locally common in S Britain, increasingly rare to the north.

B **Dog's Mercury** *Mercurialis perenne* Perennial, rather similar to Annual Mercury, but with erect unbranched stems to 40cm, from creeping rhizomes, and *downy all over*. Leaves lanceolate-ovate (generally broader on female plants), to 80mm long, short-stalked, with rounded teeth. Male flowers 3-5mm in long spikes, female flowers 1-3 on short stalk, producing hairy fruits. Widespread throughout except in the far north, in woods, less commonly on rock-ledges or limestone pavement. **Fl** 2-4. **Br** Generally common except in N Scotland, very rare in Ireland.

SPURGES *Euphorbia* Distinctive group of mainly erect plants with acrid milky latex, alternate (occasionally opposite) undivided leaves, and umbel-like flower heads. Flowers consist of cups with toothed rims, and 4-5 conspicuous rounded or crescent-shaped glands, with a single female flower and several 1-stamened male flowers in each.

(1) Leaves in opposite pairs.

C **Purple Spurge** *Euphorbia peplis Prostrate* annual plant with *forked red-purple stems*, up to 40cm long. Leaves oblong, with single lobe at base, to 11mm long, short-stalked, greyish green; stipules divided into narrow lobes. Flowers tiny with semicircular undivided glands. On sandy beaches, very local; from W France and possibly SW Britain southwards. **Fl** 7-9. **Br** Formerly in SW England and Channel Islands, probably extinct.

D **Caper Spurge** *Euphorbia lathyrus* Tall erect grey-green biennial up to 1.5m. Leaves linear to oblong, to 15cm long, untoothed and unstalked, in opposite pairs appearing in 4 rows. Inflorescence has 2-6 main rays; upper bracts heart-shaped at base; glands crescent-shaped, with blunt horns; fruit large, to 17mm across. In waste and cultivated ground, less frequent in open woods; probably native only in S and E Europe, but widely naturalised as far north as Holland. **Fl** 6-7. **Br** Frequently naturalised in gardens, possibly native in a few S England woodland sites.

(2) Leaves alternate, and with flower glands rounded on both edges, not horned or crescent-shaped.

E **Hairy Spurge** *Euphorbia villosa* Stout erect hairless or downy perennial to 1.2m, with clumps of flower and non-flower stems from rhizomes. Leaves oblong, to 10cm long, blunt or pointed, usually finely toothed towards apex, unstalked and wedge-shaped at base. Inflorescence with 4-6 or more main rays, often with lower axillary flower branches; bracts yellowish-green, oval, to 20mm long; glands oval, undivided (**e**), fruit almost globose, 4-8mm in diameter, smooth and often downy. In damp meadows, and open woods, from N France and S Germany southwards; uncommon. **Fl** 5-7. **Br** Formerly in woodland near Bath, now extinct.

F **Marsh Spurge** *Euphorbia palustris* Robust, hairless, tufted and much-branched perennial to 1.5m, with numerous non-flower branches. Leaves oblong to oblong-lanceolate, up to 60mm long. Rays 5 or more. Fruit capsule 4-6mm in diameter, covered with short warts. Widespread in marshy places, especially by rivers or coasts, from central Scandinavia southwards, but absent from many areas. **Fl** 5-7. **Br** Absent.

G **Irish Spurge** *Euphorbia hyberna* Hairless erect tufted perennial, with numerous unbranched stems to 60cm. Leaves roughly oblong, to 10cm, blunt, tapered to the base, virtually stalkless (**g1**), hairless above but often downy below. Rays 4-6, bracts elliptical, yellow; upper bracts yellow with heart-shaped bases; glands 5, yellowish, kidney-shaped and undivided (**g2**); fruit 5-6mm in diameter, with slender long warts. In woods and shady places; from SW Britain southwards; local. **Fl** 5-7. **Br** In SW England and SW Ireland only; local.

H **Sweet Spurge** *Euphorbia dulcis* Similar to Irish Spurge, but generally more slender, with smaller leaves (**h1**). Upper bracts truncated at base (not heart-shaped); glands almost round (**h2**), soon turning dark purple; fruits smaller, 3-4mm in diameter, with long warts. In damp and shady habitats, from Holland and Germany southwards; local. **Fl** 5-7. **Br** Rarely naturalised, mainly northern.

I *Euphorbia brittingeri* Similar to Sweet Spurge, but leaves less than 30mm long; upper bracts yellowish, turning purple later. Fruit 3-4mm in diameter, with numerous warts. In open woods and grassland, from Belgium and S Germany southwards. **Fl** 5-7. **Br** Absent.

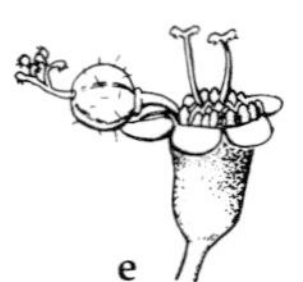

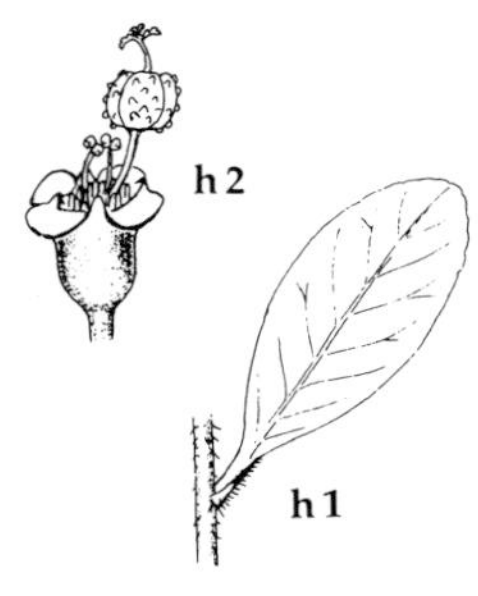

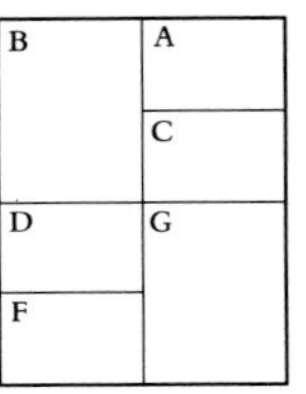

B **Dog's Mercury**
A **Annual Mercury**
C **Purple Spurge**
D **Caper Spurge**
G **Irish Spurge**
F **Marsh Spurge**

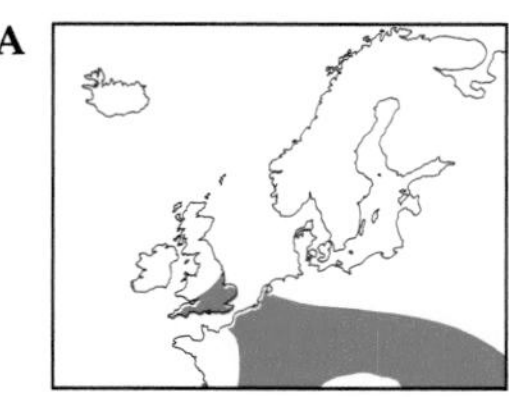
A
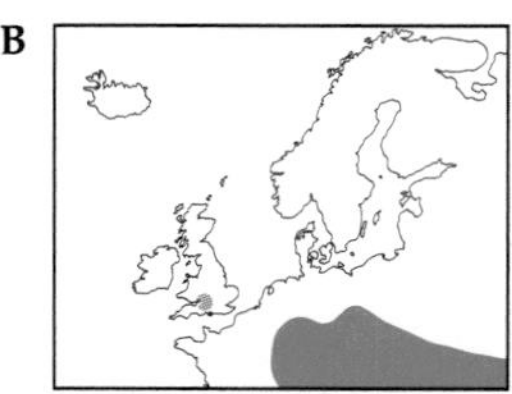
B
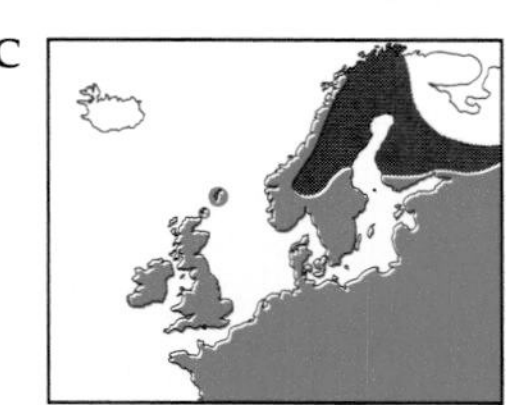
C
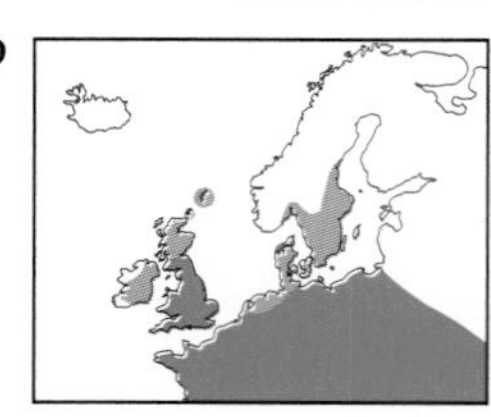
D

G
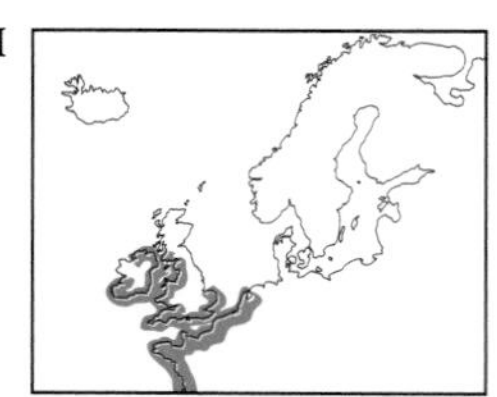
H
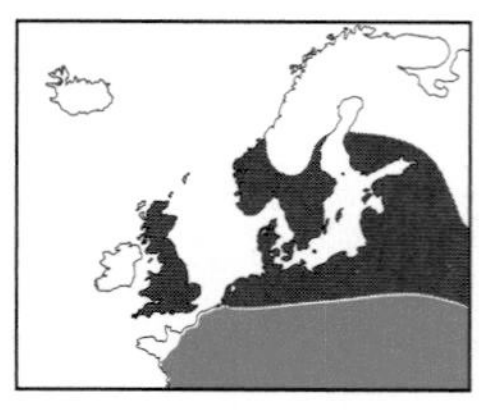
J
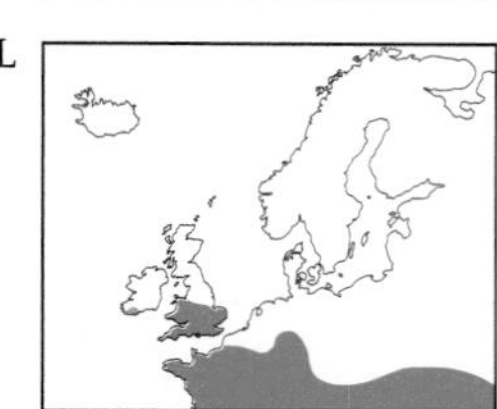
L

A Broad-leaved Spurge *Euphorbia platyphyllos* Hairless or downy erect annual to 80cm. Leaves roughly oblong, to 50mm, pointed, deeply heart-shaped at base and finely toothed except at base (**a**). Umbels usually with 5 main rays, each with 3 rays; glands almost round, unlobed; fruit 2-3mm in diameter, with *hemispherical* (not long and cylindrical) warts. In cultivated and waste ground; from Holland southwards. **Fl** 6-10. **Br** Uncommon, in S and E England.

B Upright Spurge *Euphorbia serrulata* Rather similar to Broad-leaved Spurge, but more slender and *always hairless*; bracts becoming gradually more heart-shaped upwards, without the abrupt change noticeable in Broad-leaved Spurge; fruit 2-3mm in diameter, 3-angled and covered with *cylindrical warts*. From Holland southwards, in open woodland on limestone, uncommon. **Fl** 6-9. **Br** Very local, in the Forest of Dean area only.

C Sun Spurge *Euphorbia helioscopia* Erect hairless annual, usually with a single stem, to 50cm. Leaves ovate, broadest towards tip, or almost spoon-shaped, up to 40mm long, toothed towards tip (**c**). Umbel usually *5-rayed, with 5 large distinctive yellow-green bracts at base*; glands oval, green and untoothed; fruit 2.5-3.5mm in diameter, smooth. Generally common on disturbed, open and waste ground, almost throughout the region but rare and irregular in far north. **Fl** 5-11. **Br** Common throughout.

(3) Leaves alternate, but with flower glands crescent-shaped, or with marked horns on outer side.

D Dwarf Spurge *Euphorbia exigua* Small *grey-green* annual to 35cm, usually much less, often branched from the base. Leaves differ from other species in being very narrow, lanceolate (to 25mm long × *2mm wide*), untoothed and unstalked. Rays 3-5, with narrowly triangular bracts; glands crescent-shaped. On cultivated ground; throughout except the far north. **Fl** 6-10. **Br** Locally common in the south, much rarer to the north, mainly on calcareous soils.

E *Euphorbia falcata* Rather similar to Dwarf Spurge, but usually less branched at the base. Leaves more oblong and broader, *to 5mm wide*, usually with 8 or more lateral inflorescences. Similar habitats, from N France and S Germany southwards. **Fl** 6-8. **Br** Absent.

F Petty Spurge *Euphorbia peplus* Erect hairless annual to 40cm, with 2 or more branches from base and up to 3 side flowering branches. Leaves oval, blunt, to 25mm long, untoothed but stalked. *Umbels 3-rayed, with 3 unstalked spoon-shaped bracts at base*; glands crescent-shaped, with long slender horns (**f**). Fruit 2mm in diameter, smooth. Very common on arable and disturbed land; throughout except for Arctic areas. **Fl** 4-11. **Br** Common throughout.

G Portland Spurge *Euphorbia portlandica* Hairless perennial up to 40cm, usually branched from the base, ascending or prostrate. Leaves ovate to spoon-shaped, *broadest towards tip*, tapering to base, usually untoothed, grey-green and with midrib prominent below. Umbels 3- to 6-rayed, with oval lower but triangular to diamond-shaped upper bracts; glands yellow and *crescent-shaped with prominent horns* (**g**); seeds pitted. On coastal sands, rocks and grassland; from Britain and W France southwards. **Fl** 5-9. **Br** S and W coasts from Sussex to S Scotland, common around Irish coasts.

H Sea Spurge *Euphorbia paralias* Rather similar to Portland Spurge, found in similar habitats, but differing in that it is usually stiffly erect, with several branches, to 70cm. Leaves oval, thick and fleshy, grey-green, untoothed, closely set on stem, *broadest towards base*, midrib obscure below. *Glands roughly kidney-shaped*, with horns (**h**); seeds smooth. On sand-dunes and beaches; from Holland southwards. **Fl** 6-10. **Br** Round most of the coasts except NE England and much of Scotland.

I *Euphorbia seguierana* Similar to Sea Spurge, but has narrower and less fleshy leaves; glands slightly crescent-shaped, with very short horns. Dry habitats from Holland southwards. **Fl** 5-8. **Br** Absent.

J Cypress Spurge *Euphorbia cyparissias* Distinctive patch-forming hairless perennial herb, with numerous erect and sterile flowering stems, to 50cm high. Leaves numerous, linear, up to 40mm long × *3mm wide*, untoothed and unstalked. Umbel with 9-15 rays, with lower axillary flower branches often present; upper bracts triangular, *yellow turning red*; glands crescent-shaped with 2 horns. In grassland, scrub, and open woodland, often on calcareous soils; widespread except in the far north, but not considered native in Scandinavia. **Fl** 5-7. **Br** Possibly native in a few S England localities, introduced elsewhere.

K Leafy Spurge *Euphorbia esula* Robust erect perennial to 1.2m. Leaves linear to ovate, *broadest towards apex*, about 10mm wide; glands with 2 short horns. Similar distribution to Cypress Spurge, often in damper habitats. **Fl**. 5-7. **Br** Very local, almost certainly not native.

L Wood Spurge *Euphorbia amygdaloides* Erect tufted downy perennial to 90cm. Rhizomes produce short overwintering stems with terminal rosettes, from which the following year's flower stems develop. Leaves of sterile shoots tapering into short stalk, strap-shaped, *dark green* and downy, up to 70mm long; leaves of flower shoots not tapering. Umbels with 5-10 rays, with *upper bracts joined in pairs, yellow*; glands crescent-shaped with 2 horns. Locally common in woodland and scrub, from Holland and Germany southwards. **Fl** 4-6. **Br** Absent from Scotland, rare in N England and Ireland, common in S England and Wales.

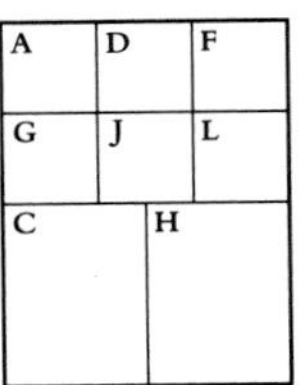

A Broad-leaved Spurge
D Dwarf Spurge
F Petty Spurge
G Portland Spurge
J Cypress Spurge
L Wood Spurge
C Sun Spurge
H Sea Spurge

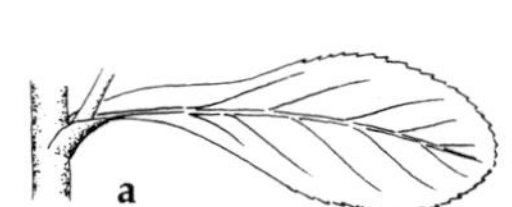

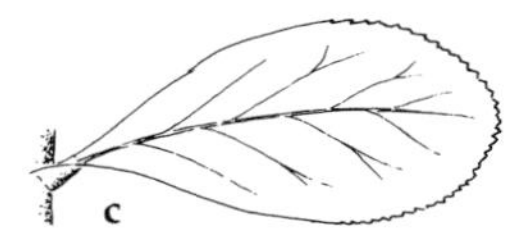

D

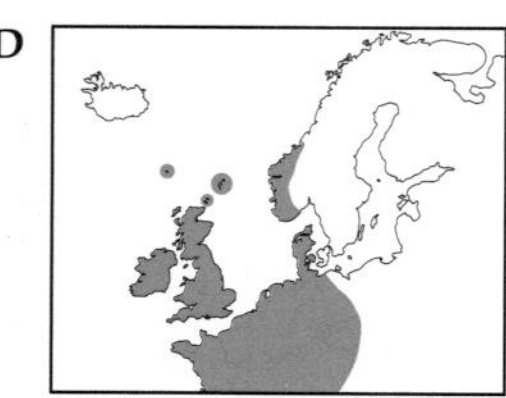

E

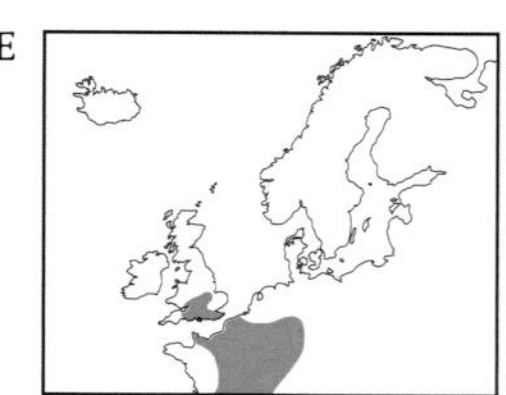

F

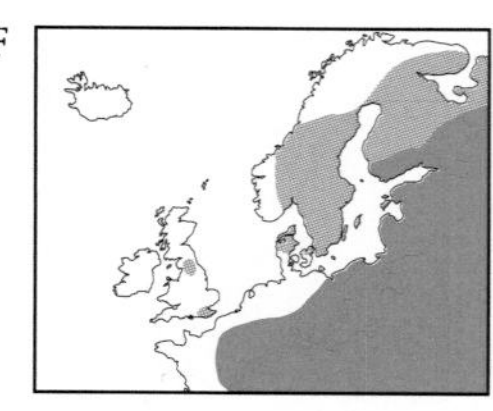

G

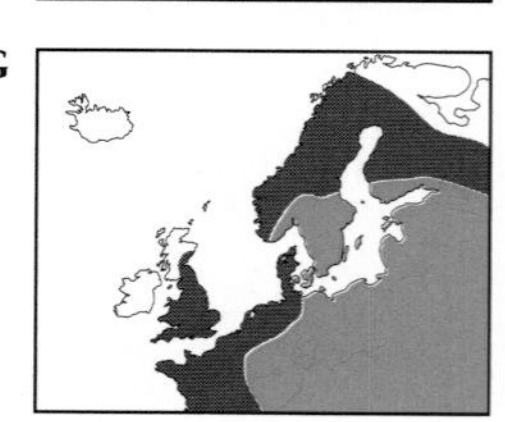

H

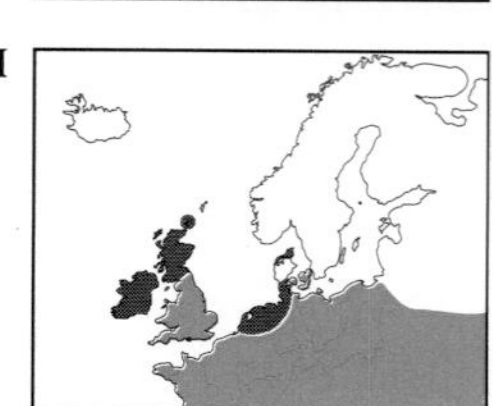

Milkwort Family
Polygalaceae

A small family of low herbaceous or shrubby perennials, with simple leaves. The flowers (of *Polygala*) are irregular and distinctive, with 3 tiny outer sepals, 2 large coloured petal-like inner ones, (the 'wings'), and 3 small petals joined into a whitish fringed tube with 8 stamens attached to it. The lower petal differs from the other 2, and is called the 'keel'.

A Shrubby Milkwort *Polygala chamaebuxus* Low mat-forming shrubby perennial to 15cm. Leaves alternate, ovate to linear-lanceolate, leathery, to 30mm long. Flowers solitary or paired from leaf axils; wings large, may be white, yellow or purple; corolla 10-14mm, with keel bright yellow, and remaining petals the same colour as the wings. In woods, mountain grassland and rocky slopes, mainly in hilly areas; from E France and S Germany southwards. **Fl** 5-9. **Br** Absent.

The remaining species of milkwort are all rather similar to each other, though 2 groups can easily be distinguished:

(1) Plants without a basal rosette, upper leaves larger than lower.

B Common Milkwort *Polygala vulgaris* Small ascending or erect plant, to 35cm (usually much less), hairless or slightly hairy, stems often branched. *Leaves all alternate*, pointed, widest at or below the middle, lowest ones shorter and broader, to 10mm long. Inflorescence with 10-40 flowers, which are blue, white or pink, and 6-8mm long; bracts very small; wings ovate but with a small point, and with much-branched veins. Common throughout in neutral and base-rich grassy places, except Iceland and Spitzbergen. **Fl** 5-9. **Br** Locally common throughout.

C *Polygala comosa* Similar to Common Milkwort, but flowers usually lilac-pink and smaller, with bracts distinctly longer, 3-5mm long. In calcareous grassland, from S Sweden southwards. **Fl** 5-7. **Br** Absent.

D Heath Milkwort *Polygala serpyllifolia* Very similar to Common Milkwort, differing in that the plants are usually smaller and more spreading. *Lower leaves to some extent in opposite pairs.* Inflorescence with fewer flowers (3-10), that are most commonly dull blue and 5-6mm long. Widespread and common on more acid soils, from SW Norway southwards, mainly western. **Fl** 5-9. **Br** Locally common throughout.

(2) Plants with a distinct basal rosette, lower leaves larger than upper.

E Chalk Milkwort *Polygala calcarea* Small perennial to 20cm, with a rosette of blunt leaves *slightly above ground level*; stem leaves alternate, widest above the middle. Inflorescences have 6-20 flowers, each 5-6mm long, most commonly bright blue, occasionally bluish-white; veins of wings much less branched than in group (1). In calcareous grassland, from Belgium and S Britain southwards. **Fl** 5-6 (not continuing through summer). **Br** S and E England only.

F Dwarf Milkwort *Polygala amarella* This is the current name for 2 formerly separate species, *P. amara* and *P. austriaca*. It differs from Chalk Milkwort in having *unstalked basal leaf rosettes.* Flowers are small, only 3-5mm long, dull blue, pink or white; wings much narrower than ripe fruit. In calcareous grassland, widespread but very local, from S Scandinavia southwards. **Fl** 5-8. **Br** In SE England and N England only, very local.

Maple Family Aceraceae

Deciduous trees, with opposite leaves. Flowers in racemes, small, greenish and 5-parted. Fruit a pair of winged samaras.

G Norway Maple *Acer platanoides* Large spreading deciduous tree, up to 30m. Bark pale grey and smooth, becoming shallowly furrowed. Leaves palmate, 5- to 7-lobed, up to 15cm long, with sharp teeth on lobes (**g1**). Flowers about 8mm in diameter, in erect hairless spreading inflorescences, appearing before the leaves; petals bright yellowish-green; fruit a double key, with widely spreading lobes, each 30-50mm long (**g2**). From S Scandinavia southwards, though absent from many western areas, and confined to mountains in the south. **Fl** 4-5. **Br** Not native; widely planted and occasionally naturalised.

H Field Maple *Acer campestre* Deciduous large shrub or small-medium tree to 20m. Bark light grey-brown, finely fissured and flaking; twigs downy. Leaves palmate, 3- to 5-lobed, with blunt, barely toothed lobes, leathery, 40-70mm long (**h1**). Flowers few, about 6mm in diameter, *in an erect rounded panicle*, appearing with the leaves; the yellow-green petals are less bright than in Norway Maple; fruit is usually downy, with *2 horizontally spreading lobes*, each 20-40mm long (**h2**). From S Sweden southwards, in woods and hedgerows, usually on heavy or base-rich soils. **Fl** 5-6. **Br** Common in S and central England, becoming rarer to the north and west, and absent as a native from Scotland and Ireland.

I Sycamore *Acer pseudoplatanus* Broad deciduous tree up to 30m. Bark smooth when young, becoming flaky later. Leaves palmate, 5-lobed, large (to 15cm long), with bluntly pointed teeth (**i1**). Flowers numerous, each about 6mm in diameter, in a cylindrical drooping inflorescence, up to 20cm long, usually appearing with the leaves; petals greenish; fruit with lobes spreading at an acute angle, or curved inwards at tips, each lobe 3-5cm long (**i2**). In woods and scrub, especially in mountain areas (as a native), from S Germany and Belgium southwards, though widely planted and naturalised elsewhere. **Fl** 4-6. **Br** Introduced 4-500 years ago, now widely naturalised and very common.

J Montpelier Maple *Acer monspessulanus* Small tree to 12m with dark, finely fissured bark. *Leaves 3-lobed*, with untoothed leathery lobes, shiny above (**j1**). Flowers greenish-yellow, in erect then drooping loose inflorescences. Fruit with 2 lobes almost parallel, each 2-4cm long (**j2**). Found in woods and scrub, from S Germany and NE France southwards. **Fl** 5-6. **Br** Absent.

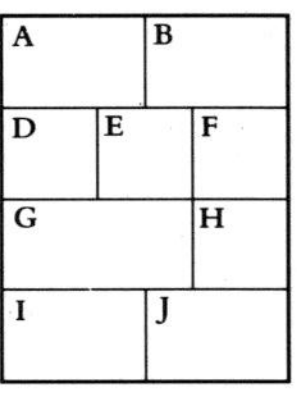

A Shrubby Milkwort
B Common Milkwort
D Heath Milkwort
E Chalk Milkwort
F Dwarf Milkwort
G Norway Maple
H Field Maple
I Sycamore
J Montpellier Maple

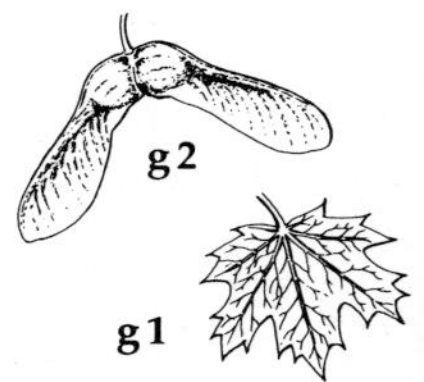

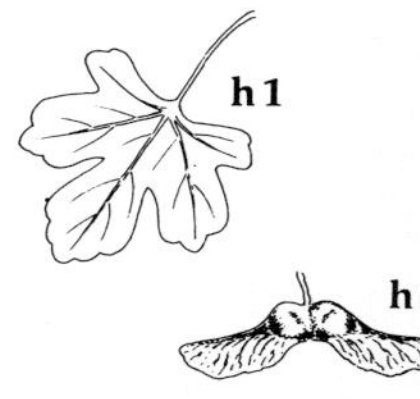

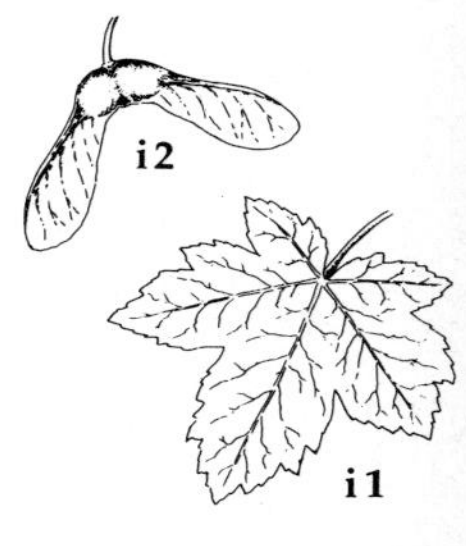

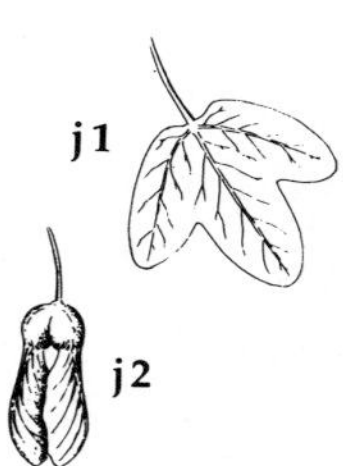

A

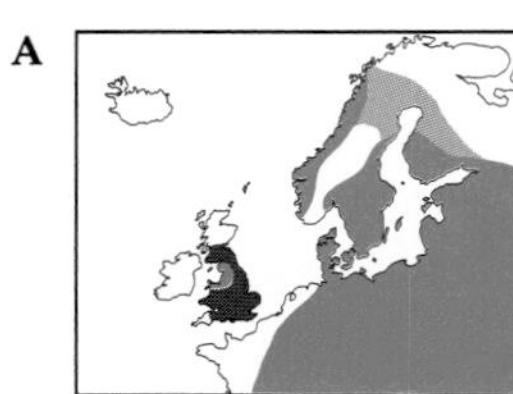

E

F

G

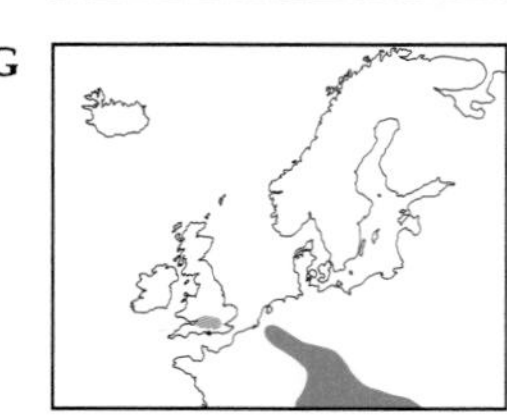

H

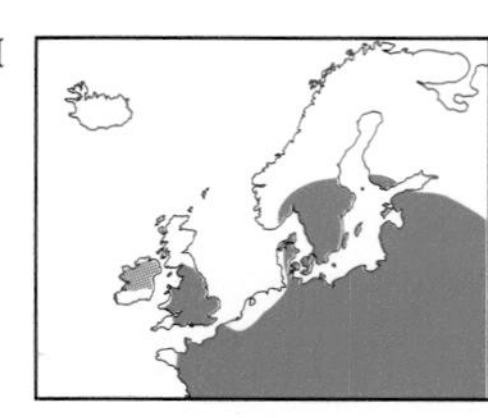

J

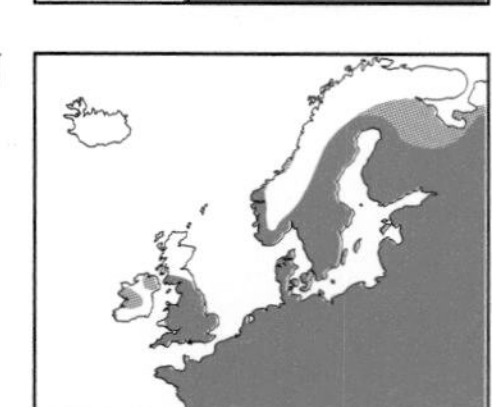

Balsam Family
Balsaminaceae

Herbs, with simple leaves. Flowers distinctive, with 5 parts, but only 3 sepals of which the lowest is prolonged into a spur. Fruit is an explosive capsule.

A **Touch-me-not Balsam** *Impatiens noli-tangere* Hairless erect annual plant to 1.8m, with branched or unbranched stems. Leaves alternate and roughly ovate, to 10cm long, with 7-16 usually pointed teeth on each side. Flowers in loose inflorescences of 3-6 from leaf axils; petals yellow with small brown spots, 20-35mm long including the curving, tapering spur; fruit linear in shape. In damp and shady places, widespread except in the far north. **Fl** 7-9. **Br** Native and locally common in N Wales and NW England; introduced elsewhere.

B **Orange Balsam** *Impatiens capensis* Similar to Touch-me-not, but differs in that its leaves are often wavy, with less than 10 teeth. Flowers orange, with reddish-brown blotches; spur contracts abruptly and is bent into a hook. A N American species, naturalised in Britain and France by rivers and canals. **Fl** 6-8. **Br** Local, in England and Wales only.

C **Small Balsam** *Impatiens parviflora* Rather similar to Orange Balsam, but leaves have 20-35 teeth on each side. *Flowers pale yellow, smaller,* up to 16mm, with short (1-7mm), *almost straight spur.* Widely naturalised from central Asia, in woods and shaded disturbed ground, but absent from N and W Scandinavia. **Fl** 6-10. **Br** Widespread, except in the far north, spreading.

D **Himalayan Balsam** *Impatiens glandulifera* Tall annual to 2m, branched or unbranched, with reddish stem. Leaves lanceolate to elliptical, to 18cm long, opposite or in whorls of 3. Flowers purplish-pink or white, up to 4cm long, with short curved spur. Fruit club-shaped. Naturalised from the Himalayas; on riverbanks and damp or shady waste ground; widespread northwards to central Scandinavia. **Fl** 7-10. **Br** Now widespread almost throughout.

Holly Family Aquifoliaceae

Trees or shrubs with alternate simple leaves. Flowers regular, with males and females on separate plants (in *Ilex*). Fruit is a berry.

E **Holly** *Ilex aquifolium* Familiar shrub or small tree to 10m (taller in cultivation). Bark pale grey and smooth; twigs green. Leaves oval, alternate, dark glossy green above, leathery, usually with large strong teeth on margins (leaves towards top of tree often spineless). Male and female plants separate; flowers 6-8mm in diameter, greenish-white, 4-petalled, in small crowded inflorescences. Fruit a globose scarlet berry, 7-12mm in diameter. Common in woods, hedges and scrub from Denmark southwards, commonest in the west. **Fl** 5-7. **Br** Generally common, though absent from NW Scotland; rare in some areas.

Spindle Family Celastraceae

Shrubs or trees, with simple leaves. Flowers 4- to 5-parted, hermaphrodite or unisexual, with fleshy disc. Fruit variable in form.

F **Spindle** *Euonymus europaeus* Bushy deciduous shrub or very small tree to 6m. Twigs green, 4-angled. Leaves ovate-lanceolate, to 10 cm long, opposite, pointed and finely toothed. Flowers in branched inflorescences in leaf axils, with up to 8 greenish-white, 4-parted flowers, each 8-10mm in diameter. Fruit 4-lobed, 10-15mm wide, coral pink, opening to expose the orange seeds. In woods and scrub, often on calcareous soils; throughout except N Scandinavia. **Fl** 5-6. **Br** Common in England, rarer northwards; absent from N Scotland.

Box Family Buxaceae

Evergreen shrubs or small trees. Flowers 4-parted, regular and usually single-sex.

G **Box** *Buxus sempervirens* Evergreen shrub or very small tree to 5m, rarely more; twigs green, 4-angled, with white down when young. Leaves roughly oval, to 3cm long, shiny, leathery, blunt, short-stalked and opposite, with incurled untoothed margins. Flowers in clusters in leaf axils: each cluster is made up of a terminal female flower, with 4 sepals, and several male flowers, all greenish-white; fruit is a 3-horned capsule. In woods, scrub and rocky ground, usually dry and/or calcareous; locally abundant from central Germany and S Britain southwards. **Fl** 4-5. **Br** Very local as a native, in SE England only; widely planted elsewhere.

Buckthorn Family
Rhamnaceae

Trees or shrubs. Flowers 4-5-parted, unisexual or hermaphrodite. Fruit is often fleshy.

H **Buckthorn** *Rhamnus catharcticus* Deciduous shrub or small tree to 6m, usually *with scattered thorns;* buds have dark scales. Leaves ovate to elliptical, to 70mm long, opposite, hairless and finely toothed, with 2-4 pairs of conspicuous side-veins, curving in towards tip of leaf. Flowers in small clusters on short shoots from previous year's wood; 4-petalled, greenish, about 4mm in diameter; male and female flowers are separate; fruit is a globular berry, 6-8mm in diameter, becoming black. Widespread and locally common, except in the far north, in scrub, woodland and fens, usually calcareous. **Fl** 5-6. **Br** Common in the south and east, but increasingly rare or absent to the north and west.

I *Rhamnus saxatilis* Similar to Buckthorn, but is a lower, and usually spreading, very spiny shrub to 2m; leaf stalk about a quarter the length of blade (*see* length in Buckthorn); blade less than 3cm long. In dry, rocky, lime-rich sites; from S Germany and NE France southwards. **Fl** 5-7. **Br** Absent.

J **Alder Buckthorn** *Frangula alnus* Deciduous shrub or very small tree to 5m, *without spines; buds without scales,* but densely brown hairy. Leaves are oval, alternate, untoothed, with about 7 pairs of lateral veins, not markedly curved in towards tip. Flowers in small clusters, greenish-white, with 5 petals, about 3mm in diameter; fruit a globular berry, 6-10mm in diameter, red for a long period, then black. Widespread and locally common throughout, except the far north; in damp woods and boggy places, on acid soils. **Fl** 5-6. **Br** Locally common in England and Wales, rare in Ireland, absent in Scotland as a native species.

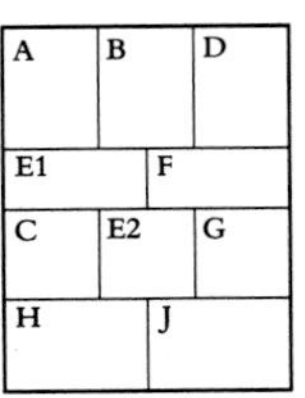

A **Touch-me-not Balsam**

B **Orange Balsam**

D **Himalayan Balsam**

E **1 Holly** berries

F **Spindle** in fruit

C **Small Balsam**

E **2 Holly** male flowers

G **Box**

H **Buckthorn**

J **Alder Buckthorn**

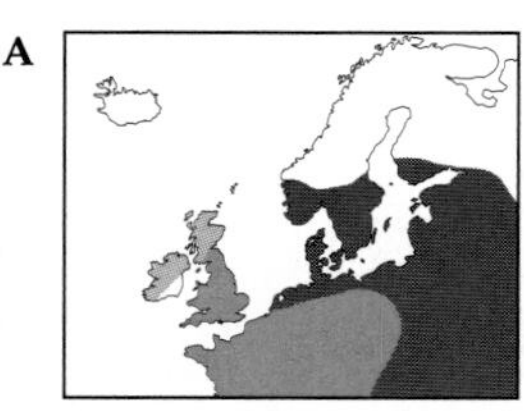
A

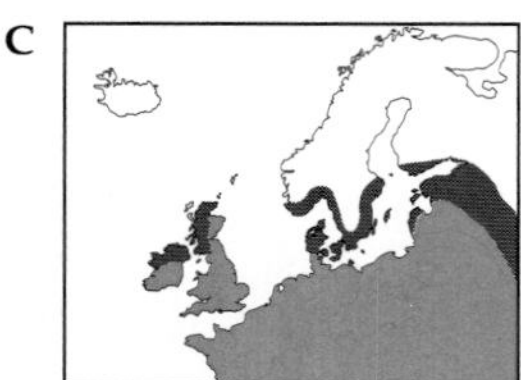
C

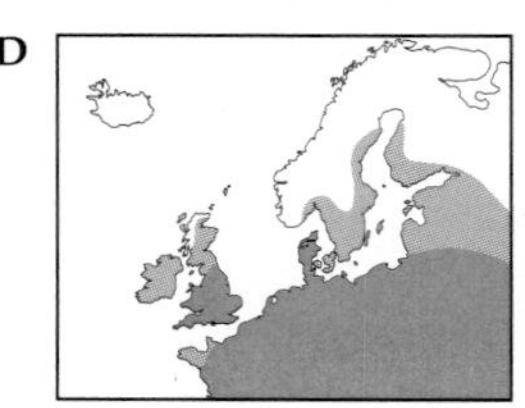
D

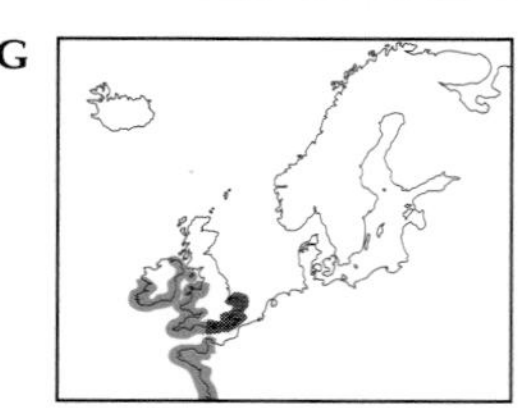
G

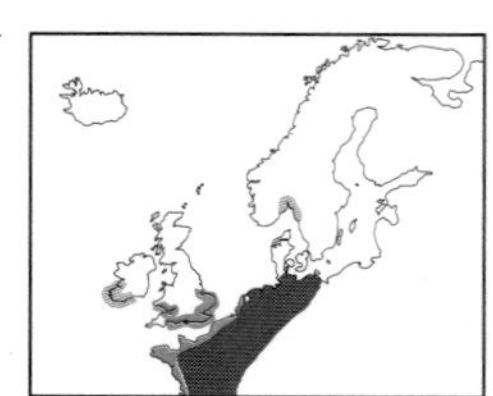
J

Mallow Family Malvaceae

Herbs or shrubs, usually softly hairy or downy with star-like hairs. Leaves alternate, with stipules present. Flowers 5-parted and often showy, with numerous stamens joined into a tube at the base; ovary superior, with numerous carpels joining into a flattened ring. An epicalyx is present below the true calyx, made up of 3 free segments in *Malva*, 3 joined segments in *Lavatera*, and 6-9 segments in *Althaea*.

A **Musk Mallow** *Malva moschata* Erect, often-branched, perennial herb to 80cm, with scattered *simple hairs*. Basal leaves roughly kidney-shaped, 3-lobed, to 8cm long, long-stalked; stem leaves deeply cut palmately into narrow further-divided segments. Flowers bright rose-pink, 3-6cm in diameter, 1-2 in leaf axils, and in loose terminal cluster; epicalyx segments linear-lanceolate and narrowed at both ends. In grassy and rocky places; from Holland and N Germany southwards. **Fl** 6-8. **Br** Throughout except the far north, local in Ireland.

B *Malva alcea* Rather similar to Musk Mallow, but differs in having *starry hairs* and leaves with less sharply pointed lobes. Epicalyx segments are triangular-oval. In grassy places, from S Sweden southwards. **Fl** 6-9. **Br** Absent.

C **Common Mallow** *Malva sylvestris* Erect or spreading perennial herb up to 1.5m, woolly at base. Leaves variable, roughly kidney-shaped, 5-10cm across, palmately divided into 3-7 toothed lobes and long-stalked. Flowers pinky purple with darker veins, 25-40mm in diameter, stalked, in small clusters from leaf axils; *petals about 4 times as long as downy sepals. Fruit sharply angled*, not winged, netted. Widespread and common throughout, except in the north, in grassy and waste places. **Fl** 6-9. **Br** Common in S Britain, rarer or absent further north.

D **Dwarf Mallow** *Malva neglecta* Prostrate downy annual. Leaves are similar to Common Mallow, though smaller (4-7cm across) and more shallowly lobed. Flowers in clusters of 3-6 along stem, 1-2cm in diameter, pale lilac with darker veins, with *petals 2- to 3-times length of sepals. Fruit smooth*, with blunt angles. Widespread almost throughout, except in the far north, on waste ground, roadsides and beaches. **Fl** 6-9. **Br** Widespread and locally common in the south, much rarer further north.

E *Malva pusilla* Very similar to Dwarf Mallow, but has *very small flowers, approximately 5mm in diameter*, in clusters of up to 10; petals are pale pink; fruit netted, with winged angles. Widespread though local on waste ground, and dry coastal habitats, as far south as Belgium. **Br** Local, in scattered sites throughout, but not native.

F *Malva parviflora* Very similar to *M pusilla*, but more erect (to 50cm). Flowers 7-10mm in diameter, in clusters of 2-4. Sepals membranous, *greatly enlarging and spreading in fruit* (barely enlarged in *M. pusilla*). In waste places, but rarely persisting except in south of area. **Fl** 6-9. **Br** Not native; rare in S Britain, usually casual.

G **Tree Mallow** *Lavatera arborea* Erect woody biennial to 3m tall, downy above with starry hairs. Leaves rounded, palmately 5- to 7-lobed, up to 20cm long and velvety. Flowers in clusters of 2-7 from leaf axils, forming a long terminal inflorescence; flowers are purplish-pink, veined darker, 3-5cm in diameter; epicalyx with 3 lobes joined into cup, *lobes longer than sepals*, greatly enlarged in fruit. In rocky places and waste ground, normally near the sea; from Britain and France southwards. **Fl** 6-9. **Br** Around the S and W coasts of Britain northwards to S Scotland, and in S and W Ireland.

H *Lavatera cretica* Annual or biennial, looking most similar to Common Mallow. It differs from it in having *broad epicalyx segments, fused at the base*; starry hairs, and rounded angles to the seeds. It differs from Tree Mallow in not being woody, *epicalyx segments not longer than sepals*, and smooth (not sharply angled) seeds. In waste places, mainly coastal; from SW England and W France southwards. **Fl** 6-7. **Br** W Cornwall and Jersey only.

I **Rough Mallow** *Althaea hirsuta* Ascending annual to 60cm, rough with simple and star-like hairs, with swollen bases. Lower leaves rounded and kidney-shaped, 30-60mm across, long-stalked, toothed or shallowly lobed, becoming more deeply palmately lobed upwards. Flowers solitary, long-stalked, small, *cup-shaped*, 25mm in diameter, with pink *petals barely exceeding sepals*; epicalyx segments 6-9, lanceolate, nearly as long as sepals. In scrub, downland and field-borders; from S Germany and S England southwards, casual elsewhere. **Fl** 6-7. **Br** In Kent and possibly Somerset, as a native; casual elsewhere.

J **Marsh Mallow** *Althaea officinalis* Downy, velvety erect perennial to 2m, with all hairs star-like. Leaves triangular-ovate, slightly 3- to 5-lobed, often folded like a fan, 50-90mm across. Flowers 25-40mm in diameter, solitary or clustered, axillary and terminal, pale lilac-pink. Damp coastal habitats, especially upper salt-marshes; from Denmark southwards, local. **Fl** 8-9. **Br** A plant of S coasts.

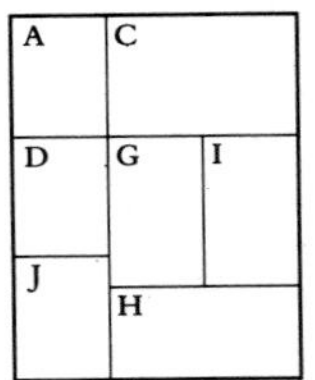

A **Musk Mallow**
C **Common Mallow**
D **Dwarf Mallow**
G **Tree Mallow**
I **Rough Mallow**
J **Marsh Mallow**
H *Lavatera cretica*

A

B

D

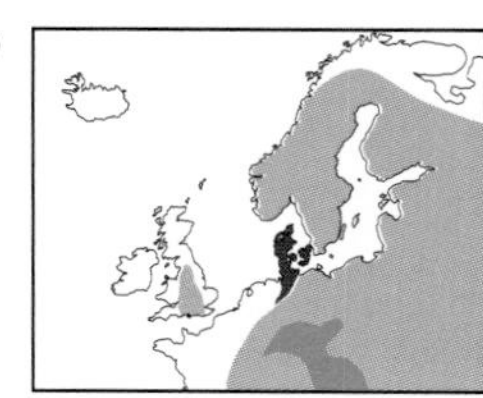

E

G

Lime Family Tiliaceae

Deciduous trees, with simple alternate leaves. Flowers are 5-parted and hermaphrodite, insect-pollinated in *Tilia*. Fruit is a globular nut.

A **Large-leaved Lime** *Tilia platyphyllos* Large tree up to 40m, with spreading branches; bark is smooth and dark brown, *without bosses on trunk*. Leaves alternate, long-stalked, heart-shaped, up to 12cm long, *grey downy below* and hairless or downy above; tertiary veins prominent. Inflorescence with 2-5 flowers (usually 3), *drooping*; flowers greenish-white, 5-parted, about 10mm in diameter with numerous stamens; inflorescence stalk partly fused to an oblong bract. Fruit roughly globose, strongly 5-ribbed and downy, 8-10mm in diameter (**a**). Native in woods and calcareous cliffs, from S Sweden southwards, local. **Fl** 6-7, but slightly earlier than next 2 species. **Br** Very local as native tree in limestone areas; also widely planted.

B **Small-leaved Lime** *Tilia cordata* Similar to above, but differing in that its bark is generally paler. Leaves more rounded, sometimes almost circular, usually smaller, to 70mm long; hairless below except for *tufts of reddish hairs in axils of veins*; tertiary veins not prominent. Inflorescence with 4-15 flowers, *obliquely erect or horizontal*; fruit smooth or faintly ribbed, pointed, 6mm in diameter (**b**). Widespread throughout except in the far north, in woods and on limestone cliffs, local. **Fl** 7. **Br** Scattered through England and Wales, local; also planted.

C **Common Lime** *Tilia* × *vulgaris* The hybrid between the above two species, occurring naturally but also planted. Key features include the presence of *large irregular bosses on the trunk*; leaves hairless below except for *tufts of whitish hairs in vein axils*. Inflorescence pendent, with 5-10 flowers; fruit ovoid, about 8mm in diameter, rounded at ends and slightly ribbed (**c**). Occurs locally throughout range of parents, but also very widely planted and occasionally naturalised. **Fl** 7. **Br** Very commonly planted, very rare as a naturally occurring hybrid.

Daphne Family Thymelaceae

Small shrubs or herbs with simple, untoothed, leaves. Flowers hermaphrodite in clusters, 4-parted; petals absent; fruit is a berry or nut.

D **Mezereon** *Daphne mezereum* Erect bushy deciduous shrub to 2m. Leaves oblong to lanceolate, up to 80mm long, thin, short-stalked, pale green, alternate and crowded towards tips of shoots. *Flowers rich rose-pink*, 8-12mm across, in long cylindrical inflorescence, usually appearing before or with leaves; individual flowers have 4 petal-like sepals on long tube (true petals absent); very fragrant. *Fruit is a red globular drupe*. Widespread, except in the far north, and parts of the west, in woods and scrub on calcareous soils. **Fl** 2-4. **Br** Scattered in England, but rare; absent elsewhere, except as introduction.

E **Spurge Laurel** *Daphne laureola* Erect evergreen hairless shrub to 1m tall, with greenish young shoots. Leaves leathery, lanceolate, alternate, dark shiny green, clustered towards tops of shoots. Flowers borne in short tight clusters on previous year's growth; *yellowish green*, 8-12mm across, slightly pendulous, with 4 petal-like sepal lobes, fragrant; *fruit is globose and black* when ripe. In woods, especially of beech, usually on calcareous soils; from Britain and S Germany southwards. **Fl** 2-4. **Br** Local in England, rare in Wales, absent from Ireland and most of Scotland.

F *Thymelaea passerina* Erect hairless (occasionally downy) annual up to 50cm. Leaves narrow linear, to 15mm long × 2mm wide. Flowers tiny and greenish, arising from a tuft of silky hairs, with 2 narrow bracts. In dry places, from Belgium and S Germany southwards, local. **Fl** 7-9. **Br** Absent.

Oleaster Family Eleagnaceae

Trees or shrubs, densely covered with scale-like hairs. Flowers may be solitary or in small clusters; petals absent; fruit like a drupe, with fleshy receptacle.

G **Sea Buckthorn** *Hippophae rhamnoides* Thorny, dense and much-branched deciduous shrub or small tree, normally to 3m, but occasionally to 10m; twigs covered with silvery scales. Leaves alternate, linear-lanceolate, untoothed, to 60mm long, covered with silvery or rusty scales. Flowers very small, about 3mm in diameter, with 2 sepals, in short spikes in leaf axils, before leaves open. Fruit globose, orange, 6-8mm in diameter. Widespread except in the far north, but confined as a native plant to coasts and mountain areas. **Fl** 3-4. **Br** Native on the E coast, introduced elsewhere; usually on sand-dunes; locally abundant.

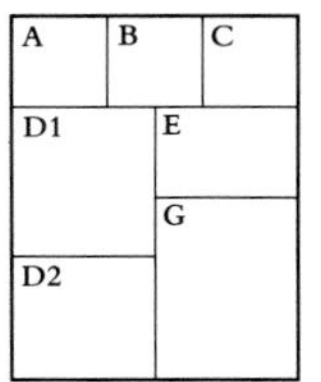

A **Large-leaved Lime** in fruit

B **Small-leaved Lime**

C **Common Lime** in fruit

D **1 Mezereon**

E **Spurge Laurel**

D **2 Mezereon** in fruit

G **Sea Buckthorn**

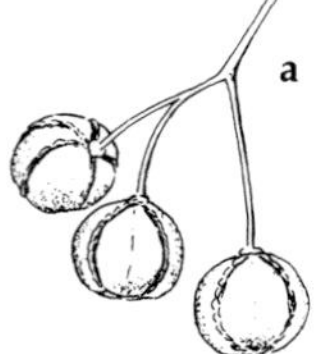

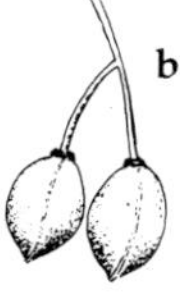

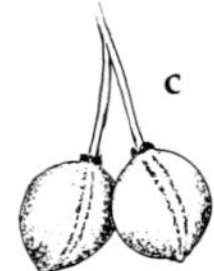

A

B

C

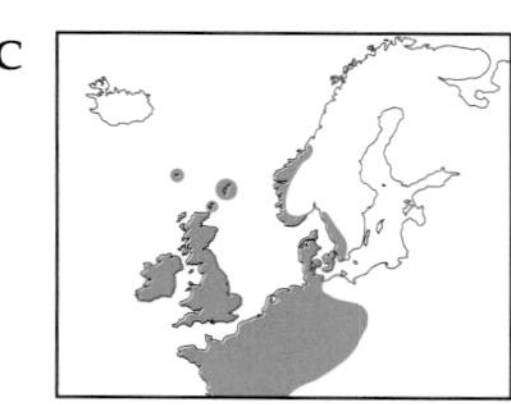

D

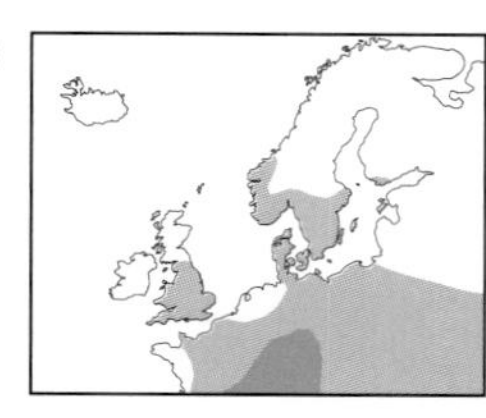

E

F

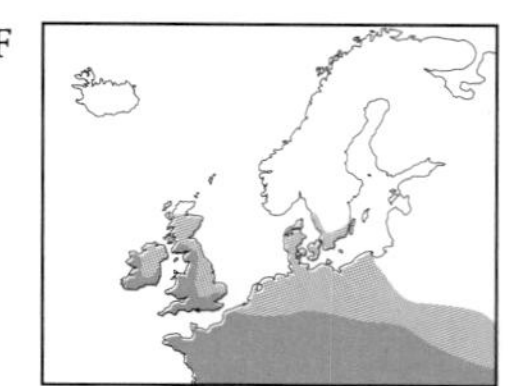

G

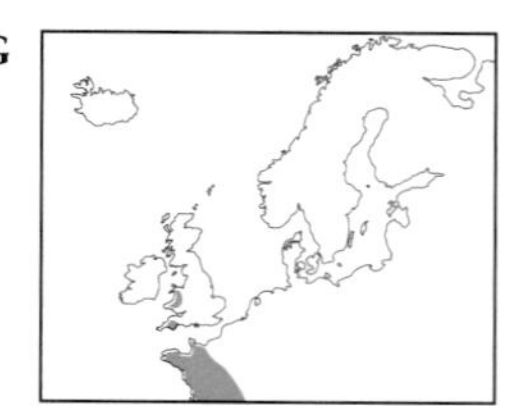

I

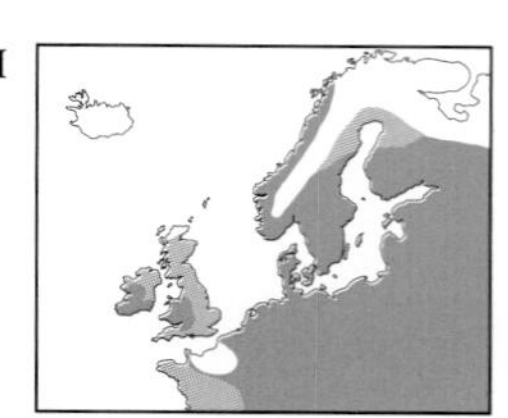

J

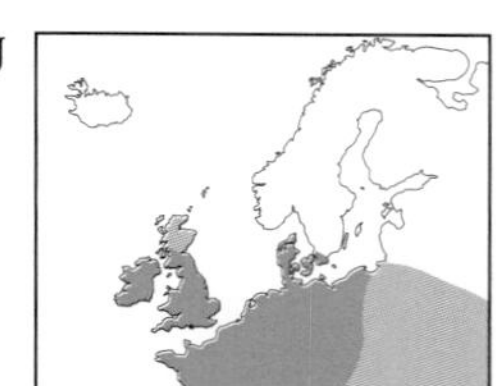

St John's-wort Family
Guttiferae (Hypericaceae)

Shrubs or herbs, commonly with numerous translucent glands in the leaves, and scattered black or red glands; leaves simple, opposite or whorled. Flowers regular and yellow, usually with 5 free petals and sepals, and numerous stamens; ovary superior, with 3-5 styles.

(1) Plant shrubby.

A Tutsan *Hypericum androsaemum* Spreading or ascending shrub to 70cm, with 2-edged stems. Leaves roughly oval, to 15cm, unstalked. Flowers relatively few, about 20mm in diameter, with yellow petals; sepals about as long as petals, broadly ovate, unequal, enlarging and turning back in fruit; fruit a fleshy ovoid berry (fruit is a dry capsule in all other native species), 6-8mm in diameter, red then black. In woods and shady places; from Belgium and Britain southwards, with a markedly western distribution. **Fl** 5-8. **Br** Scattered throughout, but generally commonest in the south and west.

(2) Plants herbaceous, with stem smooth, or with only 2 lines or angles.

B Hairy St John's-wort *Hypericum hirsutum* Erect *downy* perennial to 1m, with *round stems.* Leaves oblong to elliptical, to 50mm long, downy, with strongly marked veins, and translucent dots. Flowers numerous, in roughly cylindrical inflorescence; pale yellow, about 15mm in diameter, with pointed sepals that have stalked black glands on margins. Widespread and generally common, except in the extreme north; in grassy places, scrub, and open woods, usually on calcareous soils. **Fl** 7-8. **Br** Widespread, though local, and rare in the north and west.

C Slender St John's-wort *Hypericum pulchrum* *Hairless*, stiffly erect plant to 90cm, usually less, with *round reddish stems.* Leaves oval, to 20mm long, blunt, with heart-shaped base, and translucent dots. Inflorescence narrowly cylindrical or pyramidal; flowers about 15mm in diameter, orange-yellow, with red dots, and black dots on edges of petals and sepals. On heaths, dry grassland and open woods, avoiding lime-rich soils; from S Scandinavia southwards, local. **Fl** 6-8. **Br** Widespread and locally common, except in calcareous areas.

D Pale St John's-wort *Hypericum montanum* Rather similar in form to Hairy St John's-wort, except that the whole plant is hairless, and the leaves have no translucent dots. In scrub, woodland and rocky places, usually on calcareous soils; from S Finland southwards; local. **Fl** 6-8. **Br** Local in England and Wales; rare or absent elsewhere.

E Marsh St John's-wort *Hypericum elodes* Distinctive creeping grey-hairy herb, with rounded stems. Leaves oval to almost circular, up to 30mm long, *grey-hairy*, slightly clasping the stem. Flowers in loose terminal groups on erect stems, individually small, 10-15mm across, not opening widely, yellow, with *erect red-hairy sepals*. In wet acid and peaty places, from Holland and Germany southwards. **Fl** 6-8. **Br** Scattered throughout except in the far north, local, though more common in acid hilly districts.

F Trailing St John's-wort *Hypericum humifusum* *Creeping* hairless perennial, branching and rooting near the base; *stems with 2 ridges*. Leaves small, to 15mm, elliptical-oval, with translucent glands (**f**). Inflorescence few-flowered; flowers pale yellow, 8-10mm diameter, with petals equalling or up to 1½ times as long as sepals; sepals unequal, usually with scattered black glands. In open habitats, usually acidic, from S Sweden southwards. **Fl** 6-9. **Br** Throughout.

G Flax-leaved St John's-wort *Hypericum linarifolium* Very similar to Trailing St John's-wort, except that the flower stems are more erect; leaves are longer, to 35mm, usually without translucent dots (**g**); petals at least *twice as long as sepals*, and sepals strongly marked with black dots and streaks. In W France and SW Britain only (and further south to Spain), in dry open and rocky habitats, on acid soils. **Fl** 6-7. **Br** In SW England and N Wales only, very local.

H Perforate St John's-wort *Hypericum perforatum* Erect herb to 1m (usually less), with 2-lined stem (**h**) – an easy way to distinguish it from the otherwise similar Imperforate St John's-wort. Leaves ovate to linear, to 30mm, barely stalked, hairless and blunt, with numerous translucent dots. Flowers rich yellow, 20mm in diameter, often with black dots on petal edges; sepals pointed, usually with a few black dots. Throughout, except in the extreme north, in scrub, grasslands, open woods and roadsides. **Fl** 6-9. **Br** Common almost throughout, but rare in N Scotland.

(3) Plants herbaceous, stem 4-angled or 4-winged.

I Imperforate St John's-wort *Hypericum maculatum* Most similar to Perforate St John's-wort, differing in having *square but unwinged stems* (**i**); translucent leaf dots absent; petals usually have black dots and streaks all over; and sepals are blunt. Widespread and generally common throughout, in scrub, wood-margins and roadsides. **Fl** 6-8. **Br** Widespread, though local, and absent from the far north.

J Square-stalked St John's-wort *Hypericum tetrapterum* Rather similar to Imperforate St John's-wort, but with *winged corners on the square stem* (**j**). Leaves oval, with small translucent dots. Flowers pale yellow, sepals narrow and pointed, without black dots. In wet marshy places, from S Sweden southwards. **Fl** 6-9. **Br** Throughout, except N Scotland, though local in many areas.

K Wavy St John's-wort *Hypericum undulatum* Similar to Square-stalked St John's-wort in having 4-winged stems, but *leaves wavy-edged* and red-tinged; sepals lanceolate, pointed, with conspicuous black dots. From Wales and W France southwards, in marshy areas, rare. **Fl** 8-9. **Br** In SW England and SW Wales only, rare.

L Irish St John's-wort *Hypericum canadense* Slender annual or perennial to 25cm, with 4-winged stems. Leaves narrow linear, to 20mm long, 1-3 veined. Flowers 6-8mm in diameter; petals narrow and widely separated, looking more star-like than other species. Wet heaths; in Ireland and Holland only, very rare. Probably native. **Fl** 7-9. **Br** In W Ireland only.

A	B	C
D	E	G
	H	F
I	J	K

A Tutsan
B Hairy St John's-wort
C Slender St John's-wort
D Pale St John's-wort
E Marsh St John's-wort
G Flax-leaved St John's-wort
H Perforate St John's-wort
F Trailing St John's-wort
I Imperforate St John's-wort
J Square-stalked St John's-wort
K Wavy St John's-wort

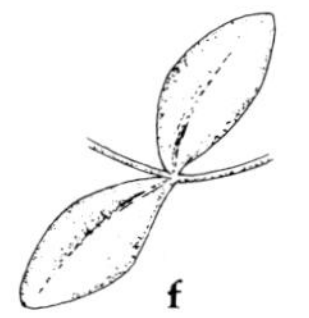

f

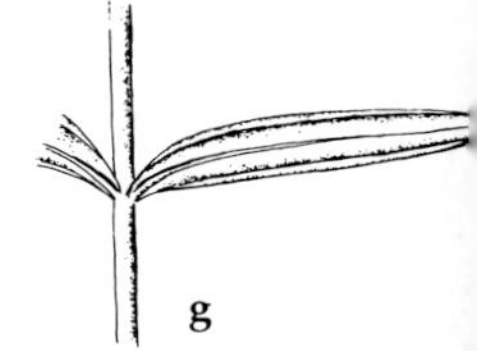

g

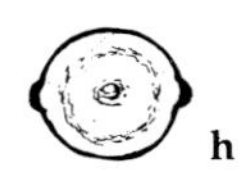

h

i

j

A

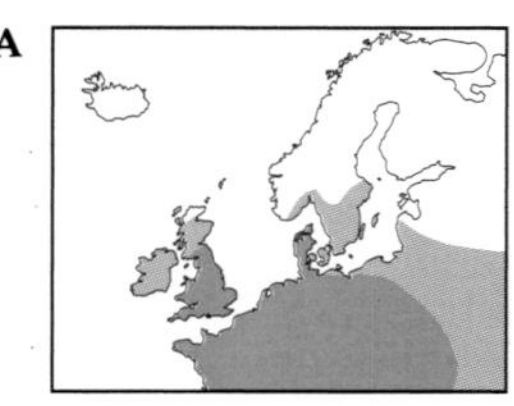

C

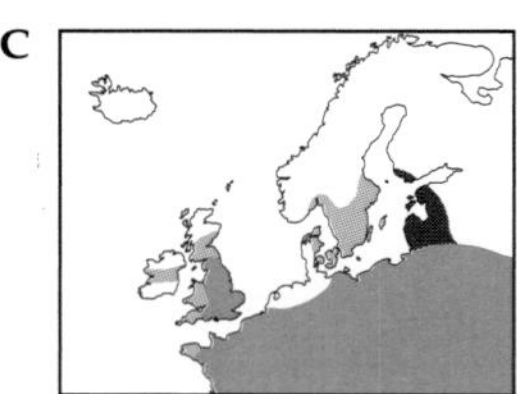

E

F

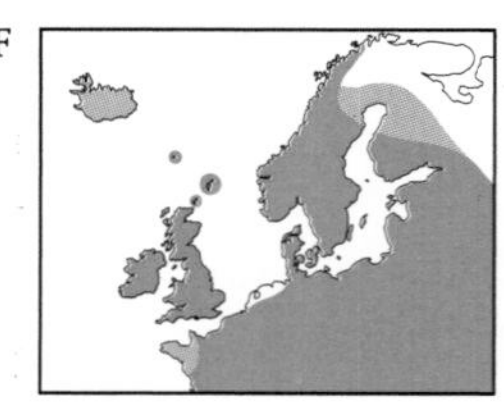

G

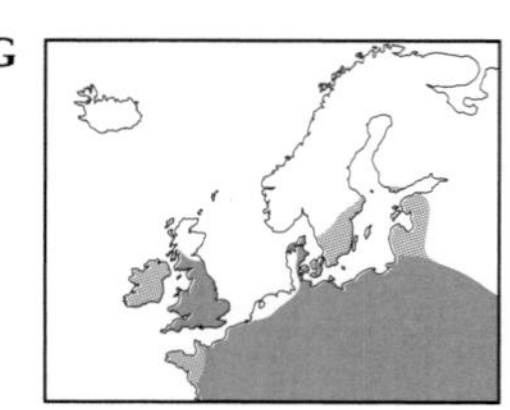

H

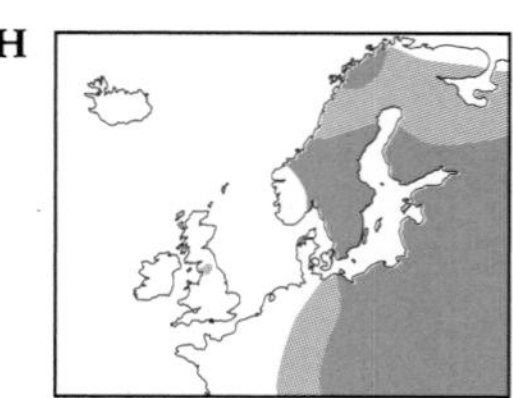

J

K

N

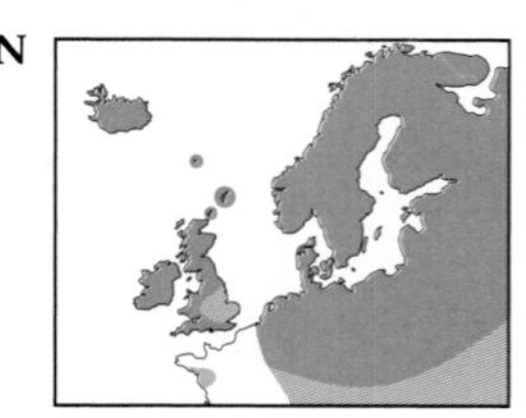

Violet Family Violaceae

Herbs, with alternate stalked leaves with paired stipules at the base. Flowers with 5 sepals, each extended backwards into an appendage; and 5 petals, of which the lower lip has a spur. All species in N Europe are within the genus *Viola*, though this divides into Violets and Pansies.

(1) Violets. Plants with leaf stipules undivided or fringed.

A **Sweet Violet** *Viola odorata* Small perennial herb to 15cm, with leaves and flowers arising directly from rootstock, closely downy, and long rooting runners. Leaves rounded and kidney-shaped, to 60mm long, heart-shaped at base, long-stalked, rather shiny, slightly hairy and becoming larger in summer; stipules usually fringed (**a**). Flowers fragrant, dark violet or white, 15mm long, sepals oblong with spreading appendages. In woods, scrub and hedgerows, usually on calcareous soils, throughout except the far north. **Fl** 3-5. **Br** Widespread as far north as S Scotland, locally common.

B *Viola alba* Rather similar to Sweet Violet, but always has white flowers; runners do not root; stipules have long (not short) fringes; side-petals bearded; spur yellow-green. In similar habitats, E France, Germany, and Oland, Sweden. **Fl** 3-6. **Br** Absent.

C **Hairy Violet** *Viola hirta* Similar to Sweet Violet, but hairier with spreading hairs on leaves and stalks; leaves narrower and runners completely absent. Flowers violet but not fragrant and paler than those of Sweet Violet. In grassland, scrub and rocky areas, usually calcareous, throughout except the far north. **Fl** 3-5. **Br** Frequent through England and Wales, becoming rare then absent further north.

D *Viola collina* Very similar to Hairy Violet, but has very narrow, long-fringed stipules (**d**); flowers pale blue and faintly fragrant; spur very pale, short (not dark violet). Similar habitats, local from S Scandinavia southwards. **Fl** 3-5. **Br** Absent.

E *Viola mirabilis* Similar to *V. collina*, but has a line of hairs up the stem; sepals and leaves pointed, sepals without a fringe; petals pale violet. Mainly northern and eastern, in woods. **Fl** 4-5. **Br** Absent.

F **Common Dog-violet** *Viola riviniana* Differs in form from the Hairy and Sweet Violet group, in having leafy flower-bearing shoots around a central non-flower rosette; plant is virtually hairless. Leaves heart-shaped, up to 40mm, long- stalked; stipules over 10mm long, narrow, with short wavy fringes. Flowers blue-violet, 15-25mm across, with dark purple lines on central area, especially on lower petal; *spur blunt, stout, paler than petals*, often whitish, *notched at tip*; sepals pointed, with large squared appendages (**f**). In grassland and open woods; throughout, generally common. **Fl** 3-6, and sometimes again in autumn. **Br** Common throughout.

G **Early Dog-violet** *Viola reichenbachiana* Very similar to Common Dog-violet in general form, though leaves and stipules are slightly narrower. Flowers slightly paler violet, with narrower petals, 15-20mm across; spur straight, *pointed, not notched, darker than petals*; sepals with shorter appendages (**g**). In dry, often calcareous, woods; from S Sweden southwards. **Fl** 3-5. **Br** Locally common in the south, rarer to the north, mainly in ancient woodland.

H **Teesdale Violet** *Viola rupestris* Similar in form to Common Dog-violet, but finely downy all over (rarely hairless). Flowers 10-15mm across, pale blue to violet but lacking darker throat markings of Common Dog-violet; spur thick, pale violet, furrowed. Open, generally dry habitats, on limestone; very local, but scattered throughout N Europe. **Fl** 4-6. **Br** Very rare, in Upper Teesdale and Cumbria only.

I **Heath Dog-violet** *Viola canina* Low perennial herb to 40cm, without basal rosette of leaves. *Leaves narrow* oval-lanceolate, *with rounded heart-shaped bases;* stipules third length of leaf stalk, barely toothed, or with broad teeth. Flowers slate-blue or white, 12-18mm across, with white or greenish straight spur. Widespread and locally common throughout, in heathy grasslands, heaths and fens. **Fl** 4-6. **Br** Local throughout.

J **Pale Dog-violet** *Viola lactea* Very similar in form to Heath Dog-violet, but *leaves even narrower, wedge-shaped to rounded at base* and not heart-shaped; stipules fringed with narrower teeth, upper stipules as long as leaf stalks. Flowers pale grey-violet, spur greenish. Very local on heaths, from Ireland and W France southwards. **Fl** 5-6. **Br** Scattered locally through England, Wales and Ireland, but only frequent in the south-west.

K **Fen Violet** *Viola persicifolia* Very similar to Pale Dog-violet, but leaves have truncated to slightly heart-shaped bases. *Petals rounded* and bluish-white; *spur greenish and very short*, barely longer than calyx appendages (much longer in Pale Dog-violet). Widespread though local throughout, except the far north, in fens and marshy areas. **Fl** 5-6. **Br** Local and rare, in E central England and W Ireland (locally common around seasonal lakes).

L *Viola pumila* Similar to Fen Violet, but the whole plant is hairless; spur no longer than calyx appendages; stipules large. In grassland; mainland Europe from S Sweden southwards, local. **Fl** 5-6. **Br** Absent.

M *Viola elatior* Very similar to *V. pumila*, but taller and larger, downy, with stipules up to 50mm long. In damp grassland and scrub; scattered localities from S Sweden southwards. **Fl** 5-6. **Br** Absent.

N **Marsh Violet** *Viola palustris* Distinctive low species, with few-leaved rosettes from creeping runners. Leaves long-stalked, *kidney-shaped*, 20-40mm long, rounded, hairless, wider than long; stipules ovate to lanceolate, untoothed or finely toothed. Flowers pale lilac with darker veins, with very rounded petals, 10-15mm across; spur blunt and pale lilac. Widespread throughout; in bogs and acid wet places, rather local. **Fl** 4-7. **Br** Local, throughout in suitable habitats.

O *Viola uliginosa* Very similar to Marsh Violet, but has stipules partly attached to leaf stalks (wholly free in Marsh Violet). Similar habitats and flowering time; from Germany and Denmark eastwards. **Fl** 4-7. **Br** Absent.

P *Viola epipsila* Very similar to Marsh Violet, but larger in all respects, with leaves always in pairs, slightly hairy below and slightly longer than wide. Similar habitats, N Germany and Scandinavia. **Fl** 5-7. **Br** Absent.

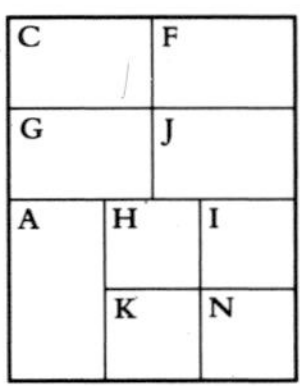

C **Hairy Violet**
F **Common Dog-violet**
G **Early Dog-violet**
J **Pale Dog-violet**
A **Sweet Violet**
H **Teesdale Violet**
I **Heath Dog-violet**
K **Fen Violet**
N **Marsh Violet**

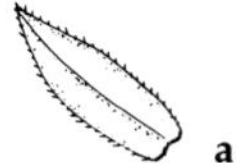

a

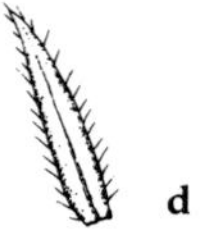

d

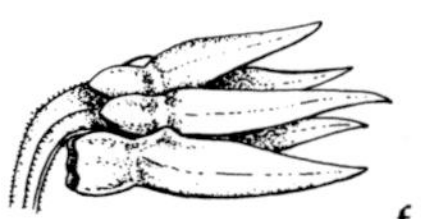

f

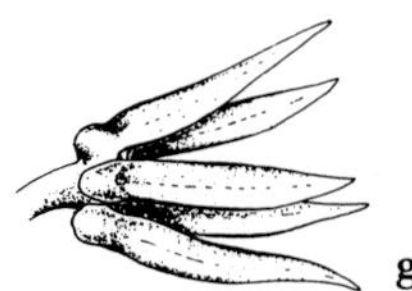

g

A

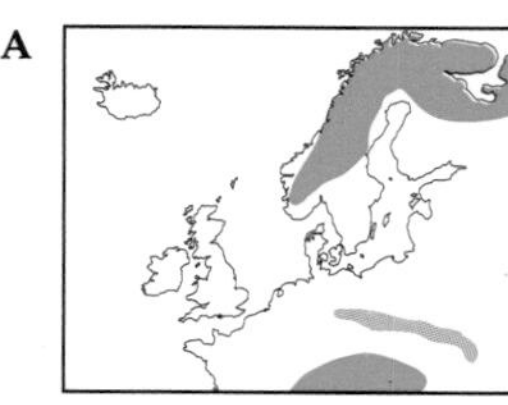

B

D

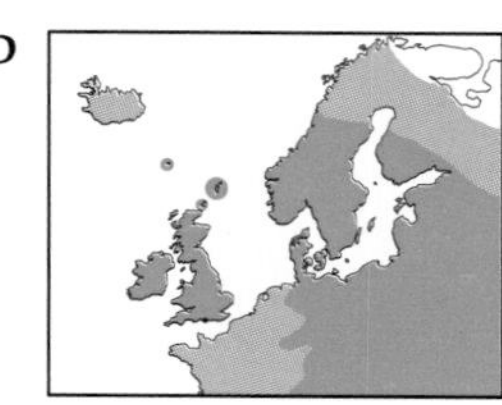

E

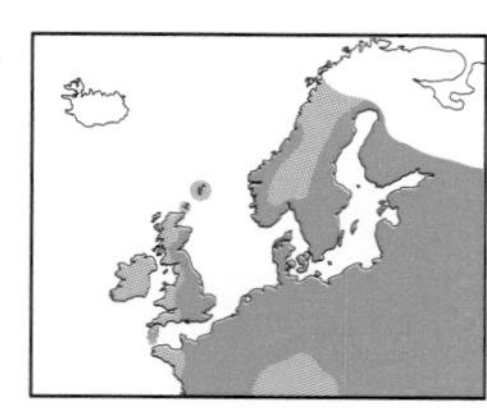

G

H

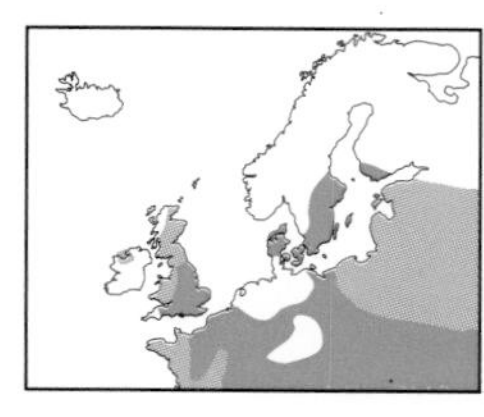

J

K

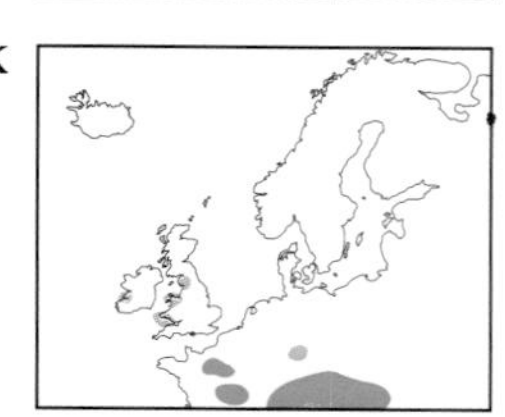

L

A Yellow Wood-violet *Viola biflora* Distinctive species. Low creeping perennial, with basal leaf rosettes and ascending leafy flower shoots. Leaves rounded kidney-shaped, toothed; stipules small, with hairy margins. Flowers yellow, 15mm across, solitary or paired, with 4 upper petals curved upwards; spur 2-3mm. In damp or shady places, mainly in mountains; in N Scandinavia, and from the Alps southwards. **Fl** 5-8. **Br** Absent.

(2)Pansies. Plants with stipules leafy, palmately or pinnately lobed; style expanded into a globe-like head.

B Mountain Pansy *Viola lutea* Almost hairless, creeping perennial to 40cm. Leaves ovate to lanceolate, hairless or slightly downy; stipules palmately or pinnately divided into 3-5 segments (**b**). *Flowers 15-30mm*, on long stalks, may be bright yellow, blue-violet, or mixed, with lower petal having darker markings. In neutral or calcareous upland grassland, very local from Germany and Scotland southwards. **Fl** 5-8. **Br** Locally common in mountains of N Wales, N England and Scotland.

C Rouen Pansy *Viola hispida* Perennial, *with spreading hairs*. Leaves rounded and heart-shaped at base; stipules palmately divided. Flowers violet or yellowish, 17-20mm across. On calcareous cliffs and grassland, only near Rouen (N France). **Fl** 5-7. **Br** Absent.

D Wild Pansy, Heartsease *Viola tricolor* Variable plant, occurring both as an annual plant in cultivated ground (ssp *tricolor*) or as a tufted perennial in dry grassland (ssp *curtisii*). Stipules deeply pinnately lobed, with end-lobe large, leaf-like and toothed. Flowers 15-25mm across, yellow, blue-violet, or mixed, with *petals distinctly exceeding sepals*. Widespread throughout in cultivated or waste ground; ssp *curtisii* in dry, mainly coastal, grasslands. **Fl** 4-9. **Br** Widespread and common. Ssp *curtisii* is mainly coastal in south and west, including Ireland.

E Field Pansy *Viola arvensis* Rather similar to annual forms of Wild Pansy. Flowers smaller, to 15mm, with *sepals at least as long as petals*; petals variable, creamy yellow to bluish-violet; lowest petal cream or yellow; whole flower more or less flat. Common in arable and disturbed ground throughout, except in the extreme north and Iceland. **Fl** 4-10. **Br** Common throughout.

F Dwarf Pansy *Viola kitaibeliana* Tiny annual to 10cm; flowers very small, to 5mm, concave and creamy white to yellow. In dry open turf or arable, mainly coastal; SW England and W France. **Fl** 4-7. **Br** Channel Islands and Scillies only, rare.

Rock-rose Family Cistaceae

Low, downy, usually perennial shrubby plants, with opposite undivided leaves (except Fumana). Flowers have 2 small outer, and 3 large inner sepals, often striped; 5 equal petals, and numerous stamens. Fruit is a small 3- or 5-valved capsule.

G Spotted Rock-rose *Tuberaria guttata Erect hairy annual* to 30cm. Leaves in a basal rosette and in opposite pairs on stems, elliptical and hairy, to 15mm long. Flowers in terminal inflorescences, yellow, 10-20mm in diameter, often with *red spot at each petal base*, petals usually falling by midday, rendering the plants inconspicuous. In dry, often acid places, especially near the coast, from Holland and N Wales southwards. **Fl** 4-8. **Br** Very rare in Channel Islands, and as var. *breweri* in N Wales and W Ireland.

H Common Rock-rose *Helianthemum nummularium* Spreading or ascending sub-shrub to 50cm, often much-branched from the base. Leaves oval-oblong, to 50mm long, *white woolly below*, usually with inrolled untoothed margins; short-stalked, with narrow stipules longer than stalk. Flowers in loose inflorescences, bright yellow, to 25mm in diameter, with petals crumpled in bud. In dry grassland and rocky places, often calcareous; throughout, except in the north. **Fl** 6-9. **Br** Widespread generally, though absent from parts of the north and west, and extremely rare in Ireland.

I *Helianthemum oelandicum* Resembles Common Rock-rose, but *leaves are green on both surfaces and have no stipules*. Similar habitats; Oland, Sweden and the Alps. **Fl** 5-7. **Br** Absent.

J White Rock-rose *Helianthemum apenninum* Similar in form to Common Rock-rose, differing in that the leaves are *grey downy above as well as below*, with strongly inrolled margins, and stipules no longer than leaf stalks. *Flowers white*. In dry limestone pastures and rocky areas, from S England and Belgium southwards, local. **Fl** 4-7. **Br** Very local, in Devon and Somerset only.

K Hoary Rock-rose *Helianthemum canum* Similar in form to Common Rock-rose, but with *leaves very narrow*, grey-white below, and lacking stipules. Flowers yellow, smaller, (10-15mm in diameter), with *style strongly bent in the middle* (**k**) – straight in all the above species. In dry grassy and rocky places, usually limestone; in S Sweden, and from Ireland and Germany southwards. **Fl** 5-7. **Br** Very rare, though locally common, in N England, Wales and Ireland.

L Fumana *Fumana procumbens* Prostrate or spreading shrub to 40cm. *Leaves linear, very narrow* and finely pointed, without stipules, alternate. Flowers solitary in leaf axils (not forming terminal inflorescence); petals yellow, with squared ends. In dry rocky and grassy places; Oland and Gotland, and from Belgium southwards. **Fl** 5-7. **Br** Absent.

A Yellow Wood-violet

B Mountain Pansy

D Wild Pansy

E Field Pansy

G Spotted Rock-rose

J White Rock-rose

H Common Rock-rose

K Hoary Rock-rose

L Fumana

b

k

A

B

C

D

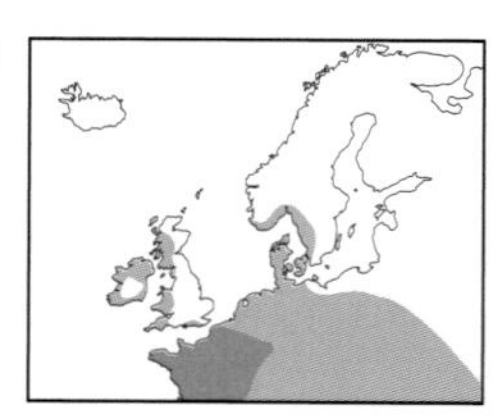

E

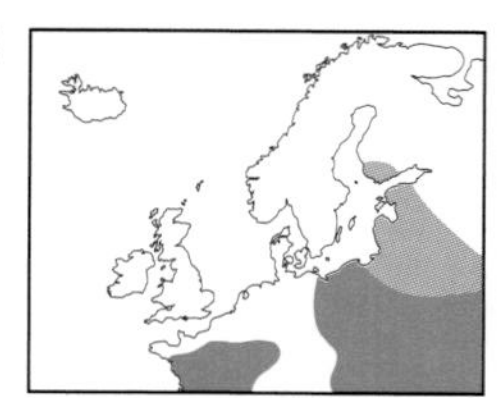

G

H

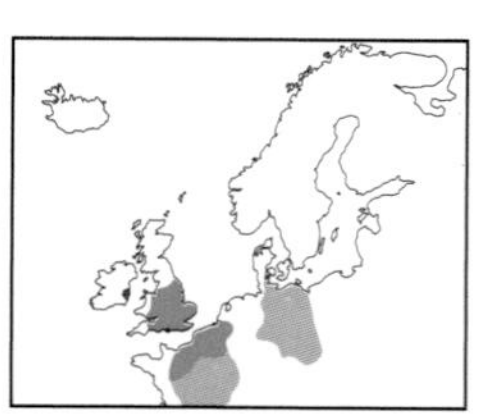

J

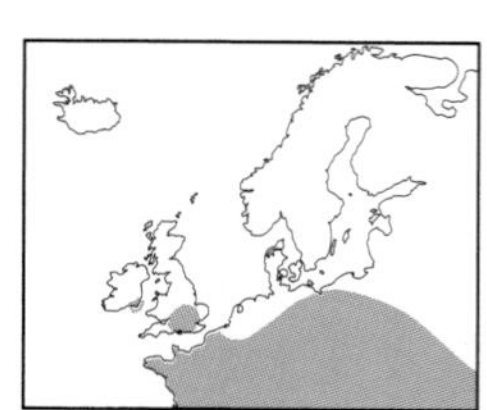

L

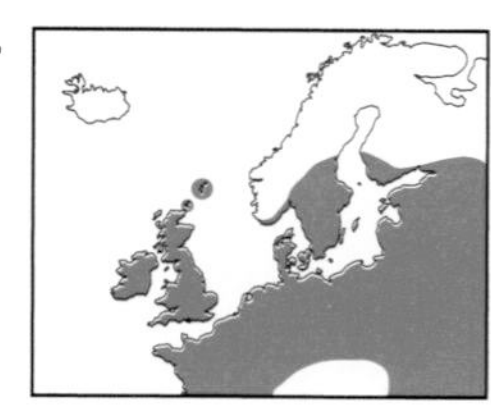

Tamarisk Family
Tamaricaceae

Shrubs or small trees. Flowers hermaphrodite, 4- or 5-parted, in long racemes; seeds fluffy.

A Tamarisk *Tamarix gallica* Hairless bushy shrub or small tree to 3m, with red-brown twigs and bark. Leaves very small, scale-like, 1-3mm long, grey-green and closely overlapping. Flowers pink, in dense spikes, with 5 tiny petals (about 1mm long), sepals, and stamens. Native in coastal habitats from NW France southwards, planted elsewhere. **Fl** 6-9. **Br** Introduced, occasionally naturalised.

B **Myricaria** *Myricaria germanica* Hairless shrub to 2.5m, with erect branches. Leaves small, grey-green and closely overlapping. Flowers pink, 5-6mm across, in terminal or axillary spikes. On river-gravels and bare stony places, in Scandinavia, and mountain areas further south. **Fl** 5-8. **Br** Absent.

Sea-heath Family
Frankeniaceae

Herbs with reduced heather-like leaves. Flowers hermaphrodite with 4-6 petals and usually 6 stamens.

C **Sea-heath** *Frankenia laevis* Prostrate, branched, mat-forming, finely hairy woody perennial up to 40cm. Leaves linear and very small, with inrolled edges, opposite but densely crowded on short lateral shoots. Flowers regular, pink, 5mm in diameter, with 5 crinkly petals, and 6 stamens. In drier parts of salt-marshes, or on shingle, from SE England and NW France southwards, local. **Fl** 6-8. **Br** Local around S and E coasts of England, from Norfolk to Hampshire.

Waterwort Family Elatinaceae

Herbaceous aquatic or marsh plants; leaves usually opposite.

D **Six-stamened Waterwort** *Elatine hexandra* Annual or short-lived perennial to 10cm. Leaves strap-shaped to spoon-shaped, about 10mm long, stalk shorter than blade, opposite or in 4s, untoothed. Flowers tiny, short-stalked, with *3 blunt sepals, 3 pinkish petals*, slightly longer than sepals, and *6 stamens*. In shallow still water, and muddy lake margins, generally acid; throughout as far north as S Sweden. **Fl** 6-9. **Br** Scattered almost throughout, but always very local.

E *Elatine alsinastrum* Larger plant than Six-stamened Waterwort, to 80cm, with leaves *in whorls of 3-18*. *Flowers 4-parted*. Wet places, SW Finland, and N France southwards. **Fl** 6-9. **Br** Absent.

F **Eight-stamened Waterwort** *Elatine hydropiper* Very similar to Six-stamened Waterwort, but *flowers unstalked*, and with *4 petals and sepals*, and *8 stamens*. Similar habitats; throughout but very local. **Fl** 7-9. **Br** Scattered localities, but very rare.

G *Elatine triandra* Similar to Eight-stamened Waterwort, but always annual; flowers white or red and unstalked, with 3 petals, sepals and stamens. Local throughout most of N Europe. **Fl** 6-9. **Br** Absent.

Gourd Family Cucurbitaceae

H **White Bryony** *Bryonia dioica* (*B. cretica* ssp *dioica*) Climbing perennial herb up to 4m, with bristly angled stems, and simple unbranched spirally-coiled tendrils. Leaves palmately lobed, 40-80mm across, with curved stalks. Plants dioecious. Flowers pale green in short axillary inflorescences; male flowers 12-18mm in diameter, 5-parted; female flowers smaller, with 3 forked stigmas. Fruit is a red berry, 6-10mm in diameter. In grassland, hedges and wood-margins; from Britain and Holland southwards, naturalised further north. **Fl** 5-9. **Br** Common in most of England, rarer to west and north, absent from Scotland and Ireland.

Purple-loosestrife Family
Lythraceae

Herbs, with simple untoothed leaves, opposite or whorled.

I **Purple-loosestrife** *Lythrum salicaria* Downy erect perennial herb, to 1.5m, with stems bearing 4 or more raised lines. Leaves oval-lanceolate, 40-70mm long, unstalked, pointed and untoothed, in opposite pairs, or whorls of 3 below and alternate above. Flowers 10-15mm in diameter, in long terminal spike with leafy bracts; 6 red-purple petals, with 12 stamens. In fens, damp grassland, and water-margins; throughout, except the extreme north. **Fl** 6-8. **Br** Locally common throughout, except for parts of N Scotland.

J **Grass-poly** *Lythrum hyssopifolia* Erect or spreading *hairless* annual to 25cm. Leaves narrow linear, alternate, usually less than 15mm long. Flowers pale pink, 6- (occasionally 5-) parted, 4-5mm in diameter, solitary in leaf axils. On seasonally flooded, bare or disturbed ground, often arable; widespread from N Germany southwards, but very local. **Fl** 6-8. **Br** Very rare and local in Cambridgeshire and Dorset only, casual elsewhere.

K *Lythrum borysthenicum* Similar to Grass-poly, but *rough hairy*, with broader leaves, and minute flowers with tiny purplish petals, falling early or wholly absent. Similar habitats, from NW France southwards. **Fl** 6-8. **Br** Absent.

L **Water-purslane** *Lythrum portula* *Hairless creeping* annual plant, with stems to 25cm, rooting at the nodes. Leaves opposite, to 15mm long, oval to spoon-shaped, broadest towards tip and rather fleshy. Flowers tiny, solitary in the leaf axils, 6-parted (usually), 1-2mm in diameter with pink petals falling early, or absent. On damp bare ground, or in shallow water, generally in acid conditions, throughout except the extreme north. **Fl** 6-10. **Br** Local throughout; rare or absent in parts of Scotland.

Water Chestnut Family
Trapaceae

M **Water Chestnut** *Trapa natans* Aquatic annual, rooted in mud. Floating leaves diamond-shaped, in spreading rosette, stalks often swollen. Flowers white, 15mm in diameter, with 4 petals and sepals. Fruit distinctively horned and edible. In nutrient-rich neutral to slightly acid waters; from S Germany and central France southwards. **Fl** 6-7. **Br** Absent.

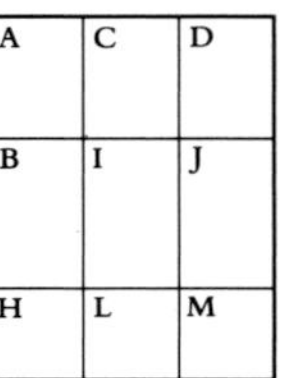

A **Tamarisk**
C **Sea-heath**
D **Six-stamened Waterwort**
B **Myricaria**
I **Purple-loosestrife**
J **Grass-poly**
H **White Bryony**
L **Water-purslane**
M **Water Chestnut**

A

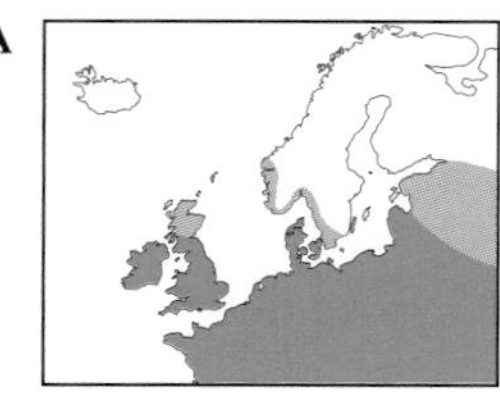

B

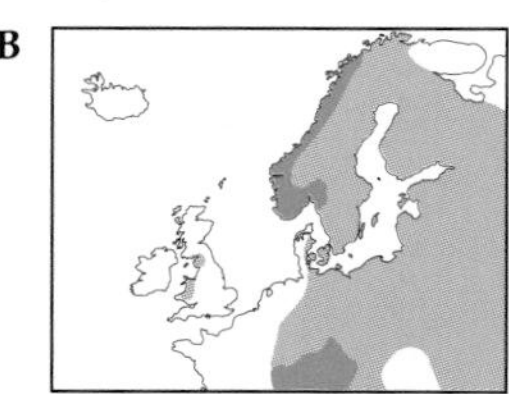

I

Willowherb Family
Onagraceae

Herbs or shrubs with opposite leaves (alternate in *Oenothera*). Flower parts in 4s, or 2s in *Circaea*; style solitary and ovary inferior.

ENCHANTER'S-NIGHTSHADES *Circaea* These plants have only 2 white petals, each deeply divided; 2 stamens; bristly fruit.

A **Enchanter's-nightshade** *Circaea lutetiana* Perennial herb to 70cm, with creeping stolons, and erect sparsely downy stems, swollen at the nodes. Leaves opposite, oval, to 10cm, rounded or slightly heart-shaped at base, *with round stalks* (**a**). Flowers in a spike-like inflorescence, held well above leaves, *continuing to elongate as flowers open;* petals white, 2 stamens, stigma 2-lobed; fruit densely covered with stiff white bristles. Widespread throughout, except in the north, in woods, hedgerows, and cultivated ground. **Fl** 6-8. **Br** Common throughout except in the far north.

B **Alpine Enchanter's-nightshade** *Circaea alpina* Smaller plant, to 20cm, almost hairless and sometimes spreading. Leaves to 6cm long, heart-shaped at base, more strongly toothed, with *winged stalks* (**b**). Inflorescences do not elongate until after petals have dropped, so *terminal flowers are always in a tighter cluster;* fruit has softer, less-hooked bristles. Throughout, in damp woods, but increasingly confined to mountain areas in the south; local. **Fl** 7-8. **Br** In hilly W districts, from S Wales northwards.

C **Upland Enchanter's-nightshade** *Circaea* × *intermedia* Sterile hybrid of the above 2 species, intermediate between them in characters, with elongate flower spikes and strongly toothed leaves. It can occur wherever both species are present. **Fl** 7-8. **Br** From Gloucester northwards, mainly western.

EVENING-PRIMROSES *Oenothera* These are all of American origin, becoming naturalised widely in Europe. All have 4 yellow, rarely pink, petals, a 4-lobed stigma, and alternate leaves. Only a few species are described here.

(1) Plants with tips of sepals pressed together in bud; inflorescence erect.

D **Common Evening-primrose** *Oenothera biennis* Tall erect biennial to 1.5m, with downy stems lacking red spots. Leaves lanceolate, with red veins when mature. Flowers yellow, 4-5cm in diameter, calyx green. On waste and open ground; throughout except the far north. **Fl** 6-9. **Br** Widespread and locally common.

E *Oenothera erythrosepala* Similar to Common Evening-primrose, but hairs on stem have red swollen bases; flowers 5-8cm in diameter, with sepals striped red or wholly red. Waste ground from Denmark southwards. **Fl** 6-9. **Br** Local in England and Wales.

F *Oenothera rubricaulis* Similar to *O. erythrosepala* in having red-based hairs, but the flowers are smaller, and the calyx is green. Waste ground; from S Britain, N France and S Germany southwards. **Fl** 6-9. **Br** Occasional, on waste ground.

(2) Plants with tips of sepals diverging in bud; inflorescence somewhat nodding at flower time.

G **Small-flowered Evening-primrose** *Oenanthe parviflora* Has stout leafy erect stems to 2m, with small red-based hairs on upper part of stem. Flowers small, to 18mm in diameter, in leafy inflorescence with a nodding tip; sepal-tips diverge in U-shaped pairs. Waste ground from Holland and Norway southwards. **Fl** 6-9. **Br** Local in the south-west only.

H *Oenanthe ammophila* Similar to Small-flowered Evening-primrose, but shorter (less than 1m), often spreading; leaves white hairy; sepal tips long and curved; capsule red-striped (all green in Small-flowered Evening-primrose) when young. In open sandy places, especially coastal; from France to Denmark. **Fl** 6-9. **Br** Absent.

I **Hampshire-purslane** *Ludwigia palustris* Creeping, hairless, reddish perennial, with stems to 50cm, rooting at the nodes. Leaves opposite, oval to elliptical, to 4cm long and short-stalked. Flowers inconspicuous, lacking petals, with 4 sepals and stamens, and 4-lobed stigma. In wet, muddy places, local, from Holland and England southwards. **Fl** 6-8. **Br** Very rare, almost confined to the New Forest.

WILLOWHERBS *Epilobium* A difficult group of perennial herbs, complicated by the occurrence of many hybrids. Flowers are pink or reddish, sepals and petals 4, stigma club-shaped (**1**) or 4-lobed (**2**), and fruit is a slender capsule splitting along its length to release plumed seeds.

(1) Leaves alternate, flowers large.

J **Rosebay Willowherb** *Epilobium angustifolium* Familiar showy tall erect perennial to 2m. Leaves lanceolate, alternate and spirally arranged up stem. Flowers in a long terminal raceme, rose-purple, 2-3cm in diameter, spreading horizontally from stem; style sharply bent at first, becoming erect as anthers mature and bend down. Generally common throughout on waste ground, roadsides, in mountain areas, cleared woodland and riversides, on a variety of soils. **Fl** 7-9. **Br** Common throughout.

K **River Beauty** *Epilobium latifolium* Rather similar to Rosebay Willowherb, but a spreading plant, with *very large rose-pink flowers* (to 5cm in diameter) in lax 1-sided few-flowered inflorescence. In rocky and gravelly places, only in Iceland within N Europe. **Fl** 7-9. **Br** Absent.

L *Epilobium fleischeri* Rather similar to Rosebay Willowherb, but is usually shorter and bushier, with very narow, lance-shaped leaves. Flowers similar, but with narrow, pointed petals, in the shape of a cross. Grassy, gravelly and rocky places in mountains, mainly on acid soils; from S Germany southwards. **Fl** 7-9. **Br** Absent.

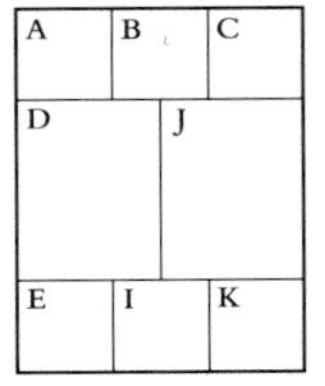

A **Enchanter's-nightshade**

B **Alpine Enchanter's-nightshade**

C **Upland Enchanter's-nightshade**

D **Common Evening-primrose**

J **Rosebay Willowherb**

E *Oenothera erythrosepala*

I **Hampshire-purslane**

K **River Beauty**

A

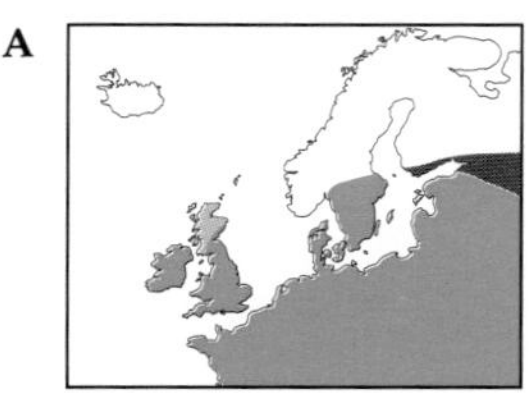

B

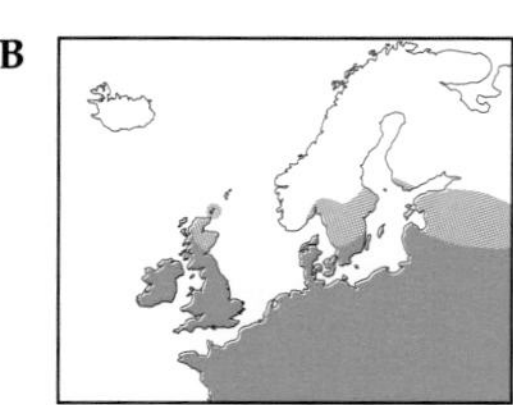

F

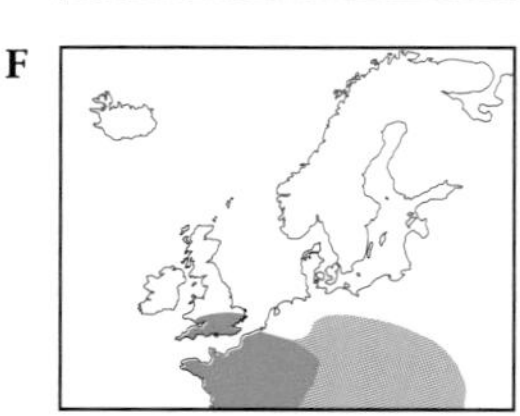

G

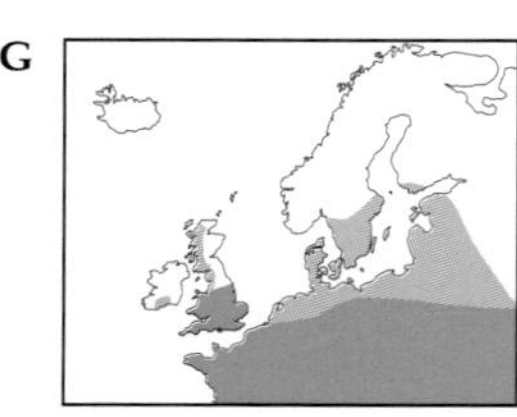

I

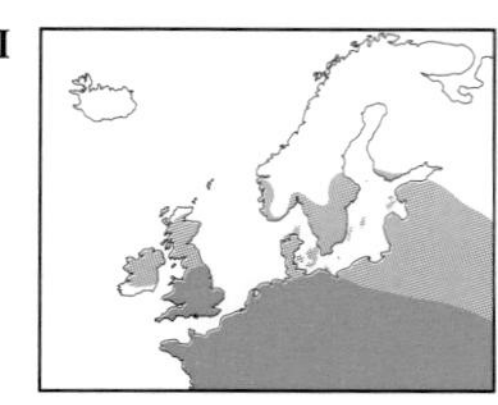

L

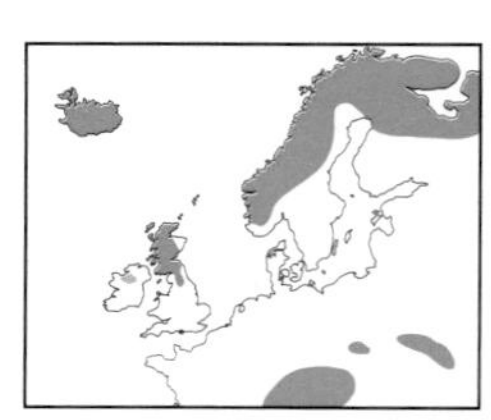

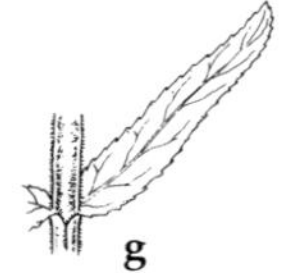

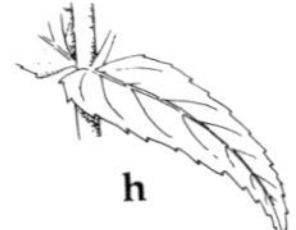

(2) Leaves opposite, at least on lower part of stem; stigma distinctly 4-lobed.

A **Great Willowherb** *Epilobium hirsutum* Tall perennial herb to 2m, with round stems, densely downy with spreading hairs. Leaves oblong-lanceolate, clasping, stalkless, with sharp teeth, to 12cm long. Flowers strong purplish-pink, to 25mm in diameter, in loose leafy terminal inflorescence; stigma with 4 arching lobes. In damp places, often among tall vegetation; widespread and common except in the far north. **Fl** 7-8. **Br** Common throughout except in far NW Scotland.

B **Hoary Willowherb** *Epilobium parviflorum* Similar to Great Willowherb, but smaller, to 75cm at most; leaves not clasping; flowers paler pink, much smaller (to 12mm in diameter). Similar habitats, distribution and flowering time. **Fl** 7-8. **Br** Common throughout the year except in NW Scotland.

C *Epilobium duriaei* Rather similar to Hoary Willowherb, but downy with appressed hairs; leaves short-stalked, with rounded bases; flowers pale pink. Mountain areas, from Vosges southwards. **Fl** 6-9. **Br** Absent.

D **Broad-leaved Willowherb** *Epilobium montanum* Similar in form to Hoary Willowherb, to 80cm tall, but *almost hairless;* leaves short-stalked with rounded bases, oval-lanceolate, up to 80mm long by 40mm wide (**d**); flowers 6-10mm in diameter, with pale pink petals; buds pointed. In woods, hedgerows, waste ground and rocky places, almost throughout. **Fl** 6-8. **Br** Common and widespread.

E *Epilobium collinum* Very similar to Broad-leaved Willowherb, but leaves smaller, up to 50 × 15mm, buds blunt and flowers smaller, 5-8mm in diameter. Widespread in similar places in mainland Europe. **Fl** 5-8. **Br** Absent.

F **Spear-leaved Willowherb** *Epilobium lanceolatum* Similar in form to Broad-leaved Willowherb, but *leaves alternate* above, leaf bases wedge-shaped, leaf stalks up to 10mm long (**f**); flowers white, turning pink later. In rocky and semi-shaded places; from S Britain and Holland southwards. **Fl** 7-9. **Br** Local, in S England and S Wales only.

(3) Leaves opposite, as for (2), but stigmas club-shaped, not lobed.

G **Square-stalked Willowherb** *Epilobium tetragonum* Medium to tall perennial herb up to 1m, overwintering by rosettes produced on short stolons; *stem has 4 conspicuously raised ridges, often winged,* downy above but not glandular. Leaves narrow, to 70mm long, almost parallel-sided, virtually unstalked, running down into stem, finely toothed (**g**). Flowers pink, 6-8mm in diameter, with erect pointed buds; *fruit 6-10cm long.* Widespread except in N and W Scandinavia, in damp woodland clearings, hedgerows and streamsides. **Fl** 7-8. **Br** Common in England and Wales; rare or absent elsewhere.

H **Short-fruited Willowherb** *Epilobium obscurum* Very similar to Square-stalked Willowherb, but leaves broader ovate (**h**), calyx with a few glandular hairs (none in Square-stalked Willowherb), and *fruits less than 60mm long.* In wet places; throughout except the far north. **Fl** 7-8. **Br** Common throughout.

I **Pale Willowherb** *Epilobium roseum* Similar to Short-fruited Willowherb, though 4 lines less distinct. Leaves lanceolate to elliptical, with wedge-shaped base and stalk up to 20mm long (**i**). Inflorescence and capsule have sticky glandular hairs; petals are whitish, streaked pink. In shady places, hedgebanks and waste ground, throughout except the far north. **Fl** 7-8. **Br** Frequent only in lowland England and Wales; rare elsewhere.

J **Marsh Willowherb** *Epilobium palustre* Erect slender plant to 60cm, with cylindrical unridged stems. Leaves strap-shaped, less than 10mm wide and narrowed at each end, unstalked and untoothed (**j**). Flowers pale pink or white, only 4-7mm in diameter, held horizontally. In bogs and other wet acid places, throughout. **Fl** 7-8. **Br** Locally common throughout.

K *Epilobium davuricum* Very similar to Marsh Willowherb, but it overwinters by rosettes not stolons, and the stem is more glandular-hairy. Similar habitats, N Scandinavia only. **Fl** 7-8. **Br** Absent.

L **Alpine Willowherb** *Epilobium anagallidifolium* Low creeping hairless perennial, with leafy stolons, stems up to 10cm, very slender (1-2mm in diameter). Leaves ovate to elliptical, to 25mm long, short-stalked and faintly toothed (**l**). Flowers small, 4-5mm in diameter, pale purplish, with the top of the inflorescence drooping in flower and young fruit. In wet areas, especially flushes, in mountains, and more widespread in N Scandinavia. **Fl** 7-8. **Br** Very local in mountain areas from N England northwards.

M **Chickweed Willowherb** *Epilobium alsinifolium* Perennial, with ascending stems (2-3mm in diameter) to 20cm, and long underground stolons; stems hairless except for 2 lines of hairs up faint ridges. Leaves ovate to ovate-lanceolate, distantly toothed, rounded at base, narrowed into short stalk (**m**). Flowers larger, 8-11mm in diameter, bright purplish-pink. Similar habitats to Alpine Willowherb, over a similar range. **Fl** 7-8. **Br** Very local in mountain areas from N England northwards; very rare in Ireland.

N **American Willowherb** *Epilobium adenocaulon* Perennial, with erect stems to 1m, with *4 raised lines,* and numerous *spreading glandular hairs,* especially above. Leaves oval-lanceolate, to 10cm, finely toothed, short-stalked and hairless (**n**). Flowers 8-10mm in diameter, purplish-pink or white, with deeply notched petals; fruit glandular-hairy. Widespread almost throughout in waste ground, shady and rocky places; naturalised from N America. **Fl** 6-8. **Br** Widespread in England and Wales, rarer in Scotland, but still spreading.

O **New Zealand Willowherb** *Epilobium nerterioides* Creeping perennial, rooting at the nodes. Leaves broadly ovate or almost circular, in opposite pairs, up to 10mm long, untoothed or slightly toothed (**o**). Flowers solitary from leaf axils on long erect stalks to 75mm; petals 3-4mm, pink or white; fruit hairless. **Fl** 7-8. **Br** A distinctive species, introduced from New Zealand, but widespread in mountain regions of N Britain and Ireland, appearing to be native, most commonly in mountain rills and flushes.

A	B	C
	D	H
M	J	L
	N	O

A **Great Willowherb**

B **Hoary Willowherb**

C *Epilobium duriaei*

D **Broad-leaved Willowherb**

H **Short-fruited Willowherb**

M **Chickweed Willowherb**

J **Marsh Willowherb**

L **Alpine Willowherb**

N **American Willowherb**

O **New Zealand Willowherb**

o

E

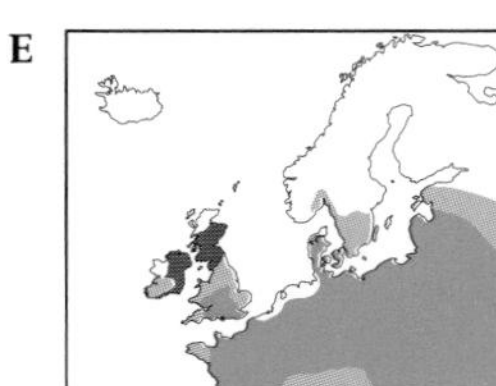

F

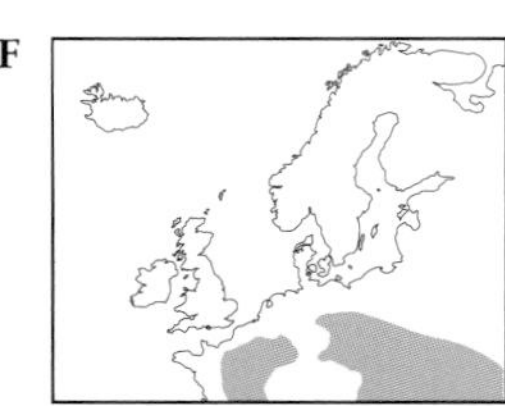

G

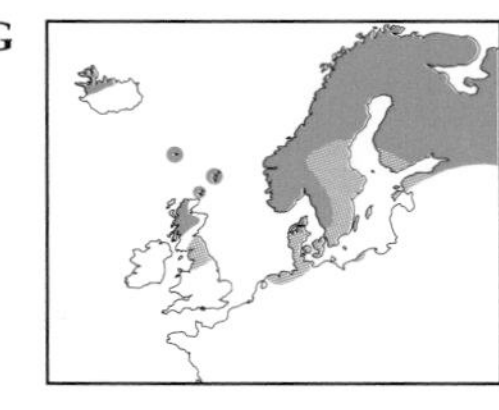

H

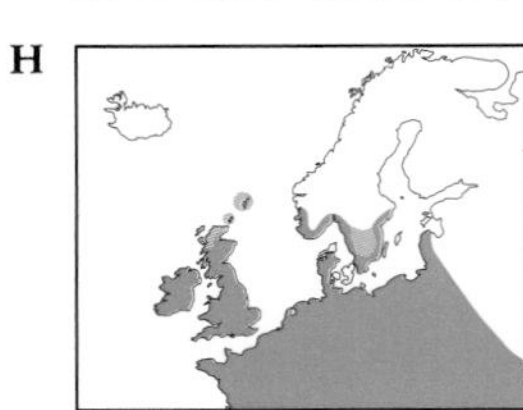

Water-milfoil Family
Haloragaceae

Aquatic perennial hairless herbs, with finely divided leaves and spikes of usually 4-parted flowers.

A **Whorled Water-milfoil** *Myriophyllum verticillatum* Aquatic, with stems up to 3m long. Leaves in whorls of 5, (4 or 6 occasionally), finely pinnate with narrow bristle-like segments, up to 45mm long. Flowers in emergent spikes, with long *pinnately divided bracts* (**a1**) below each whorl of tiny reddish 4-parted flowers (**a2**). Fruit is rounded and smooth. Widespread and locally common almost throughout, in still or slow-flowing base-rich waters. **Fl** 7-8. **Br** Local in lowland areas, absent from the north and west; declining.

B **Spiked Water-milfoil** *Myriophyllum spicatum* Similar to Whorled Water-milfoil, but leaves usually 4 in a whorl, rather shorter (to 30mm); tiny reddish flowers in whorls of 4 with *undivided bracts*, much shorter than the flowers. Fruit rounded, finely warty. In still and slow-flowing waters; common throughout. **Fl** 6-8. **Br** Locally common throughout.

C **Alternate-flowered Water-milfoil** *Myriophyllum alterniflorum* Slenderer and smaller than Spiked Water-milfoil, with 3-4 leaves per whorl, less than 25mm long. Flowers whorled below, alternate above, *with tiny bracts;* petals are yellow with red streaks. Fruit warty and elongated. Throughout the area, most commonly in acid waters. **Fl** 5-8. **Br** Widespread, though rather rare and declining, in lowland areas.

Mare's-tail Family
Hippuridaceae

Aquatic herbs, with whorled linear leaves, and solitary flowers in the axils; single stamens.

D **Mare's-tail** *Hippuris vulgaris* Aquatic perennial, with creeping rhizomes producing stout erect cylindrical spongy emergent stems. Leaves narrow strap-shaped, to 70mm long, in regular whorls of 6-12. Male and female flowers separate, produced at base of leaves on emergent stems; both sexes greenish, tiny and without petals; male has one reddish anther. Widespread and common throughout; in neutral to base-rich still and flowing waters. **Fl** 6-7. **Br** Locally common throughout.

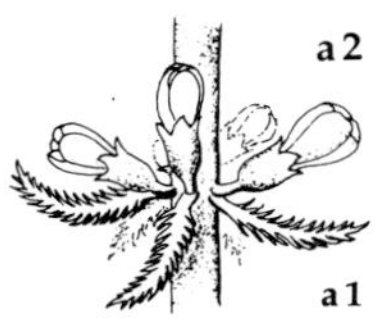

Dogwood Family Cornaceae

Shrubs with simple opposite leaves. Flowers 4-parted, in umbels.

E **Dogwood** *Cornus sanguinea* Deciduous shrub to 4m tall, with dark red twigs. Leaves broadly elliptical to ovate, up to 10cm long, pointed, rounded at base and untoothed, with 3-5 main veins on each side curving round to tip of leaf. Flowers dull white and small, in a flat-topped umbel up to 50mm in diameter; petals, sepals and stamens all 4; fruit is a purplish-black globose drupe, 5-8mm in diameter Widespread throughout except in the far north (and naturalised locally in Finland), in scrub, woodland and grassland, usually on calcareous soils. **Fl** 5-7. **Br** Common in England and Wales, rare in Ireland, absent from Scotland.

F **Cornelian Cherry** *Cornus mas* Shrub or small tree to 8m, with greenish-yellow twigs. Leaves similar to Dogwood. Flowers are produced in umbels in leaf axils (not terminal), with 4 bracts at base, before leaves open; individual flowers are yellow, 3-4mm across. Fruit is shiny, scarlet and oval, to 15mm long. In scrub and woodland, on calcareous soils; from N France and Belgium southwards, introduced elsewhere. **Fl** 2-4. **Br** Introduced only.

G **Dwarf Cornel** *Cornus suecica* Low creeping perennial herb, with flower stems to 25cm. Leaves similar to Dogwood. Flowers in a terminal umbel with 4 large conspicuous whitish bracts below it, resembling a single flower, 20mm across; individual flowers are tiny and blackish-purple, in a cluster of up to 25. Fruit is red, globular, to 5mm across. On moors, heaths and tundra, from Holland and N England northwards, becoming locally abundant towards the Arctic. **Fl** 7-9. **Br** From N England northwards, becoming locally common in central Scotland.

Ivy Family Araliaceae

Woody climbers (or trees or shrubs, outside Europe). Leaves alternate. Flowers small, often in umbel-like heads, usually 5-parted. Fruit is a drupe or berry.

H **Ivy** *Hedera helix* Familiar evergreen woody climber, reaching 30m, though also spreading widely at ground level in shade; stems covered with adhesive roots. Leaves glossy dark green above, paler below and hairless, 50-90mm long; palmately lobed on non-flowering stems, elliptical to ovate and unlobed, on flowering stems. Flowers in dense spherical umbels at tops of stems in sunny conditions; flowers are 4-parted and greenish-white; berry globular, black, 6-8mm in diameter. Widespread and generally common throughout, except in NE Europe, in woods, hedgerows and waste ground. **Fl** 9-11. **Br** Common throughout.

B D F1
E F2
G1 G2
H

B **Spiked Water-milfoil**
D **Mare's-tail**
F **1 Cornelian Cherry** in fruit
E **Dogwood**
F **2 Cornelian Cherry** in flower
G **1 Dwarf Cornel** in flower
G **2 Dwarf Cornel** in fruit
H **Ivy**

A
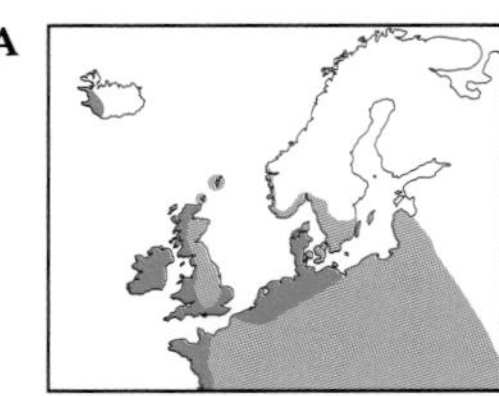
B
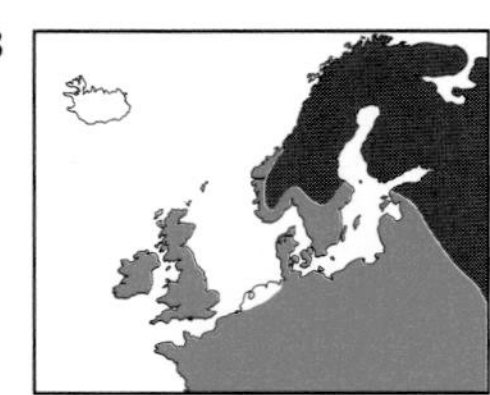
C
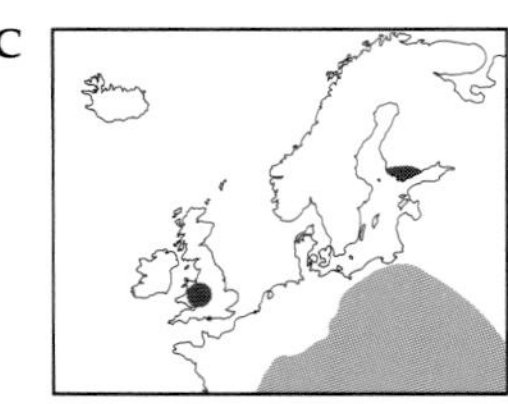
D
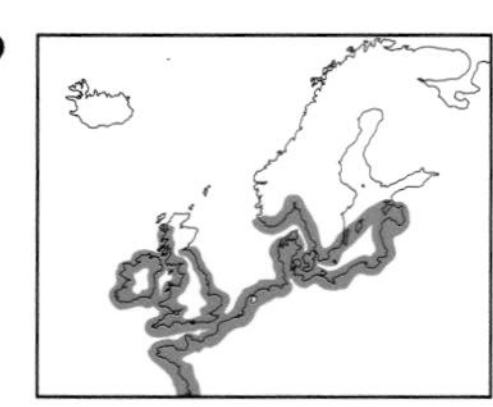
F
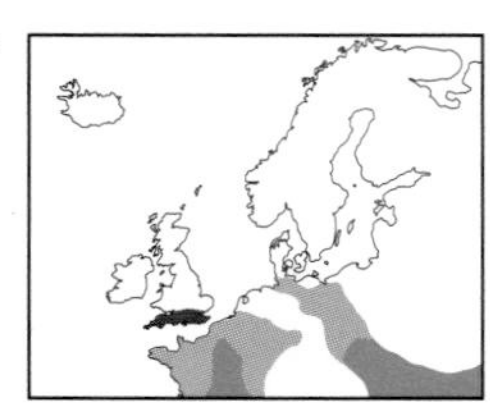
G
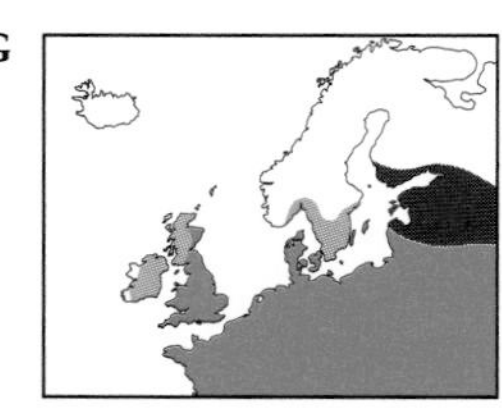
H

K
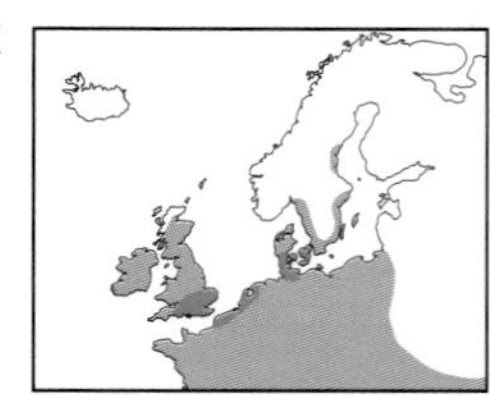

Carrot Family Umbelliferae

A large family of annual to perennial herbs. Leaves alternate, without stipules, usually much-divided and often with sheathing bases. Flowers usually in compound umbels, i.e. the umbels themselves are in umbels; individual flowers have 5 free petals, 5 sepals (often absent), 5 stamens and 2 stigmas; ovary is inferior, enlarging to form a dry 2-part fruit of various shapes. A difficult family; key characters include: leaf shape; bracts to the main umbel, and for the secondary umbels (called 'bracteoles'); and shape of ripe fruit.

(1) Plants with leaves undivided or palmately lobed; not spiny.

A **Marsh Pennywort** *Hydrocotyle vulgaris* Low perennial plant with creeping stems rooting at the nodes. Leaves roughly circular, 20-50mm in diameter, with broad blunt teeth, often very long-stalked. Inflorescence small, 2-3mm across, consisting of whorls of tiny pinkish-green flowers, often partially hidden amongst the leaves; fruit rounded, 2mm wide and ridged. In damp or wet places, usually acidic, throughout except N Scandinavia. **Fl** 6-8. **Br** Locally common throughout.

B **Sanicle** *Sanicula europaea* Hairless erect perennial to 60cm. Basal leaves long-stalked and palmately lobed, with 3-7 toothed lobes; upper leaves smaller with shorter stalks. Umbels small with few rays; bracts 3-5mm long, simple or pinnately toothed; bracteoles undivided; flowers pink or white. Fruit oval, with hooked bristles. Throughout except the far north, in deciduous woodland, mainly on neutral to calcareous soils. **Fl** 5-8. **Br** Locally common throughout in older woodland, though rarer in the north.

C **Great Masterwort** *Astrantia major* Distinctive almost scabious-like umbellifer, with erect hairless stems to 1m. Basal leaves long-stalked and palmately lobed, to 15cm in diameter, strongly veined. Umbels simple, with *a conspicuous ruff of long narrow whitish bracts*, tinged with green and red, 20-30mm in diameter; flowers white or pink and very small. Fruit cylindrical, 6-8mm long. In woods and meadows; from France and Germany southwards, but naturalised further north. **Fl** 5-7. **Br** Introduced, very locally naturalised.

(2) Leaves with spiny lobes.

D **Sea-holly** *Eryngium maritimum* Branched hairless perennial to 60cm. *Leaves waxy grey-green*, 3- to 5-lobed, with thickened margins bearing long spines; basal leaves long-stalked, stem leaves unstalked. Umbels simple, oval, to 40mm long, with numerous densely packed small blue flowers, surrounded by a ruff of spiny bracts. Fruit bristly, 5mm long. On coastal sand and shingle; from S Norway southwards. **Fl** 7-9. **Br** Widespread around the coast.

E *Eryngium viviparum* Similar to Sea-holly, but *much smaller and more prostrate, less than 10cm high*. Basal leaves linear-lanceolate, toothed; inflorescence consists of numerous few-flowered tiny *greenish heads*, with lanceolate bracts. Rare, in coastal sites or winter-flooded habitats, W France. **Fl** 6-8. **Br** Absent.

F **Field Eryngo** *Eryngium campestre* Similar in form to Sea-holly, but *greyish or yellowish green*, with pinnate lanceolate spiny leaves, stalked at base, stalkless on stem. Flowers in numerous oval umbels, to 20mm long, with long narrow spiny bracts; *petals greenish white*, with individual flower bracts longer than flowers. Fruit only 3mm long. In dry grasslands, from N Germany southwards, becoming common in the south. **Fl** 7-8. **Br** Very rare in a few S England sites, and occasionally naturalised.

(3) Other species not as above.

Chaerophyllum Biennials or perennials with 2- to 3-pinnate leaves, compound umbels with few or no bracts, but several bracteoles; sepals absent or insignificant; petals notched; fruit oblong-ovoid.

G **Rough Chervil** *Chaerophyllum temulentum* An erect biennial up to 1m, with ridged, *solid, purple-spotted* (or almost all purple), *bristly stems*. Leaves 2- to 3-pinnate, dull dark green and hairy, with rather blunt-pointed lobes. Flowers white, 2mm in diameter, in compound umbels up to 60mm in diameter, nodding in bud; bracts usually absent, bracteoles 5-8, hairy, reflexed in fruit. Fruit oblong-ovoid, narrowing upwards, 5-8mm. Rather similar to Cow Parsley (*see* differences below), but flowering slightly later. Widespread and rather common on roadsides and hedgebanks, through much of N Europe, but absent from N Scandinavia. **Fl** 6-7. **Br** Widespread and common, except in N Scotland and W Ireland.

H *Chaerophyllum bulbosum* Similar to Rough Chervil, but has tuberous roots (not a tap-root), stems hairless above, bracteoles hairless. Extending westwards into Finland, Sweden, E France and Germany. **Fl** 6-7. **Br** Absent.

Anthriscus These are similar to *Chaerophyllum*, except that the stems are hollow.

I **Cow Parsley** *Anthriscus sylvestris* Tall downy erect perennial herb to 1.2m. Very similar to Rough Chervil, but *stems hollow and unspotted*; leaves fresher green, with more pointed segments (**i**). Flower and fruit very similar. Abundant throughout on roadsides, in meadows, and wood-borders. **Fl** 4-6 (earlier than Rough Chervil). **Br** Common throughout, especially on roadsides.

J *Anthriscus nitida* Very similar, but leaves dark green and glossy, with the lowest main segment nearly as large as the rest of the leaf. Mainly in mountains, from central Germany southwards. **Fl** 5-7. **Br** Absent.

K **Bur Chervil** *Anthriscus caucalis* Wiry annual to 50cm (rarely more), with hairless stems, purplish towards the base. Leaflets very small and feathery. Umbels 20-40mm in diameter, with 2-6 hairless rays; bracts absent, bracteoles fringed and pointed; fruit distinctively bur-like, 3mm, ovoid, covered with thick spines (**k**). In sandy and waste ground, especially near the sea; from S Sweden southwards. **Fl** 5-6. **Br** Widespread almost throughout, but local; most frequent in the south-east.

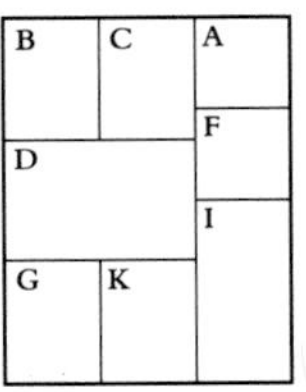

B **Sanicle**

C **Great Masterwort**

A **Marsh Pennywort** with flower cluster visible central right

D **Sea-holly**

F **Field Eryngo**

G **Rough Chervil**

K **Bur Chervil**

I **Cow Parsley**

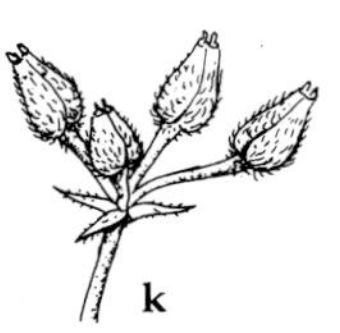

A

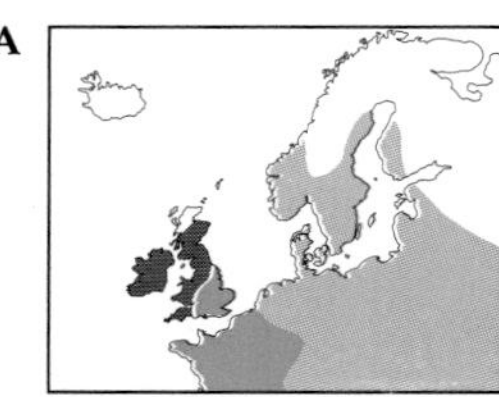

B

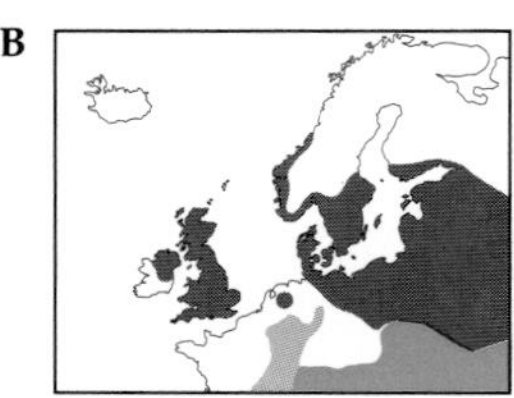

C

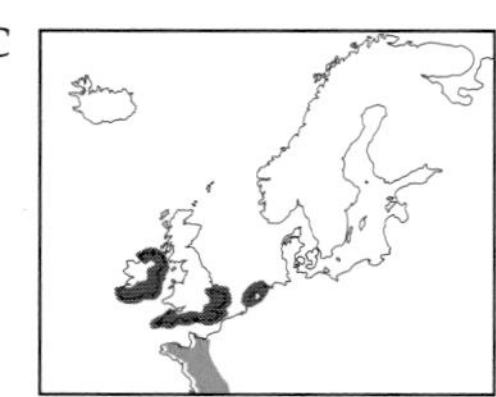

D

E

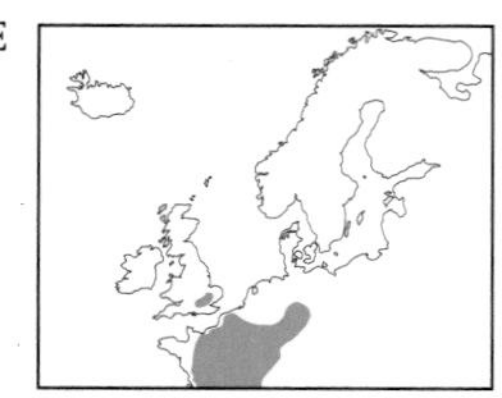

G

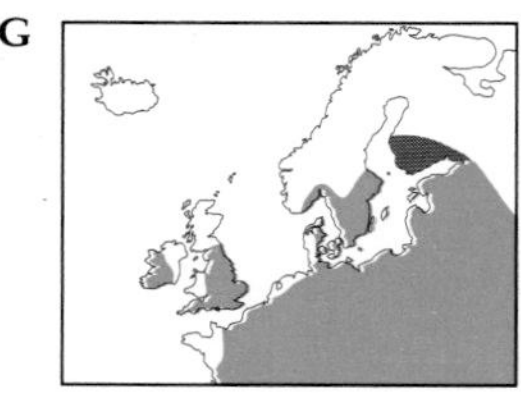

H

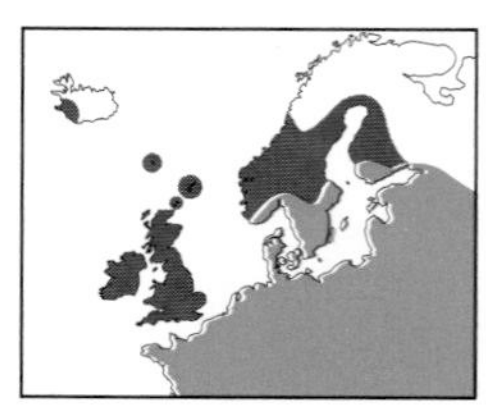

I

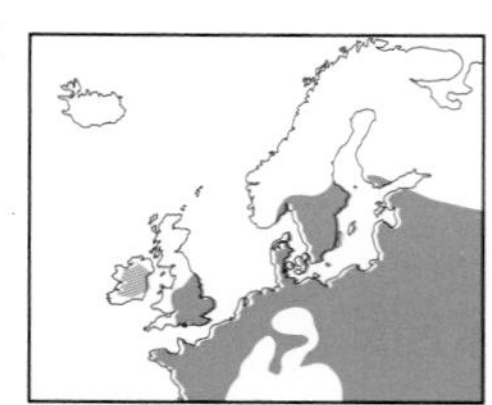

J

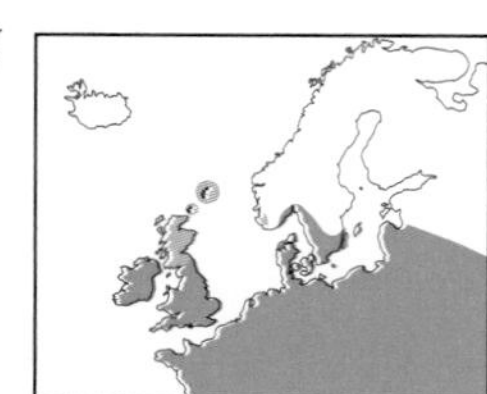

A Shepherd's-needle *Scandix pecten-veneris* Highly distinctive plant when in fruit. Annual, erect or spreading to 50cm. Leaves 2- to 3-pinnate, with segments widening towards tips. Umbels simple, or with 2-3 rays, and spiny-edged bracteoles; flowers small and white; *fruits elongating to 8cm long,* of which at least half is a distinctive slender flattened beak, the whole often forming a comb-like structure. In arable and disturbed land, northwards to S Sweden, but commoner in the south. **Fl** 5-7. **Br** Widespread, mainly in S and E England, but increasingly local and declining.

B Sweet Cicely *Myrrhis odorata* Bushy, downy, erect, strongly aromatic perennial to 2m, with hollow stems. Leaves 2- to 3-pinnate, fern-like, to 30cm long, with conspicuous basal sheaths. Umbels compound, with 4-20 rays; bracts usually absent, bracteoles narrow and pointed, usually 5; flowers white, heads up to 50mm in diameter; fruit linear to oblong, up to 25mm, beaked and strongly ridged, tasting of aniseed, becoming shiny dark brown when ripe (**b**). Native to mountains of central and S Europe, but widely naturalised northwards to S Sweden. **Fl** 5-6. **Br** Common in N England and S Scotland; local or absent elsewhere.

C Alexanders *Smyrnium olusatrum* Stout erect hairless biennial to 1.5m, with solid stems becoming hollow with age; whole plant rather celery-scented. Leaves shiny green, basal leaves 3-times trifoliate, triangular in outline, up to 30cm; upper leaves smaller, with short inflated stalks, becoming yellower upwards. Umbels terminal and axillary, with 7-15 rays; bracts and bracteoles few or absent; flowers yellow, about 3mm in diameter, without sepals; fruit broadly ovoid, 7-8mm, black when ripe. In waste places, especially near the sea; native from NW France southwards, but widely naturalised in Britain and Holland. **Fl** 4-6. **Br** Common around the coasts of England, Wales and Ireland, rare in Scotland.

D Pignut *Conopodium majus* Slender erect perennial, with smooth stems, emerging from deeply buried brown globose tuber. Basal leaves 2- to 3-pinnate, to 15cm long, withering early; basal part of stem without leaves; upper leaves 2-pinnate, with narrow segments. Flowers white in delicate umbels 30-70mm in diameter, with 6-12 rays; bracts usually absent, bracteoles 2 or more; fruit 3-4mm, oval, beaked, with short erect styles. In grassland and open woods, generally on dry, more acid soils; in Britain, France and Norway. **Fl** 4-6. **Br** Locally common throughout.

E Great Pignut *Bunium bulbocastanum* Similar to Pignut, but usually *larger,* to 1m; *stem remains solid after flowering* (becomes hollow in Pignut); umbels 3-8cm across, with 5-10 lanceolate bracts, and as many bracteoles; *styles bent* back on fruit, not straight. From S England and central Germany southwards, in rough calcareous grassland. **Fl** 6-7. **Br** Rare and local, only in E-central England.

F Burnet-saxifrage *Pimpinella saxifraga* Erect perennial to 60cm (occasionally 1m), with a round rough downy stem. Basal leaves usually singly pinnate, with 3-7 pairs of ovate toothed leaflets, 10-15cm long; stem leaves are very different, 2-pinnate, with very narrow segments. Umbels have 6-25 rays, usually without bracts, always without bracteoles; flowers 2mm in diameter, white or rarely pink, with short styles. Fruit oval, to 3mm, slightly ridged. Widespread and generally common, except in the far north, in dry, generally calcareous, grassy places. **Fl** 6-9. **Br** Common throughout, though rarer in the north, and absent in NW Scotland.

G Greater Burnet-saxifrage *Pimpinella major* Somewhat similar to Burnet-saxifrage, but generally larger, to 1.2m high. Stem hairless (very rarely downy), *deeply ridged* and hollow. Leaves usually 1-pinnate with deeply toothed pointed lobes, but very variable, to 20cm long. Umbels 30-60mm in diameter, with 10-25 rays, lacking bracts, bracteoles normally absent; petals white or pink; styles long. Fruit ovoid, ridged, 4mm long. In grassy places and scrub, often on heavy soils; throughout except the far north. **Fl** 6-9. **Br** Rather local, mainly in central England; rare or absent in most of the west and north.

H Ground-elder *Aegopodium podagraria* Erect hairless perennial to 1m, with robust hollow stems arising from slender far-creeping rhizomes. Basal leaves triangular in outline, 10-20cm long, twice trifoliate, fresh green, with toothed, roughly oval leaflets. Umbels terminal, 20-60mm in diameter, with 10-20 rays; bracts and bracteoles usually absent; flowers white, 1mm in diameter. Fruit ovoid, 4mm long, with slender bent-back styles. In cultivated ground (often as a persistent weed), riversides, and shady places; throughout except the far north, though natural limits uncertain. **Fl** 5-7. **Br** Throughout in lowland areas.

I Greater Water-parsnip *Sium latifolium* Robust, erect, hairless perennial to 2m, with hollow, strongly ridged stems. Stem leaves 1-pinnate, to 30cm long, long-stalked, with 4-9 pairs of toothed pointed leaflets. Umbels terminal, flat-topped, 6-10cm in diameter, with 20-30 rays; bracts 2-6, often large and leafy, bracteoles lanceolate, variable; flowers white, about 4mm in diameter, with calyx teeth present; fruit oval and ridged. Throughout, except the far north and west, in shallow water and fens. **Fl** 7-8. **Br** Scattered through to S Scotland, rare except in E Anglia.

J Lesser Water-parsnip *Berula erecta* Rather similar to Greater Water-parsnip, but smaller in all respects, and more spreading. Leaves 1-pinnate, to 25cm long, with 7-14 pairs of unstalked, deeply toothed, roughly oval and bluish-green leaflets. Umbels 30-60mm in diameter, short-stalked, with 10-20 rays; bracts and bracteoles numerous, often leaf-like, sometimes pinnately divided. Fruit 2mm, broader than long. In fens and shallow water; throughout except the north. **Fl** 7-9. **Br** Common through much of the lowlands, but rare in the north and in Ireland.

A	B	C
D	F	G
H	I	J

A Shepherd's Needle

B Sweet Cicely

C Alexanders

D Pignut

F Burnet Saxifrage

G Greater Burnet Saxifrage

H Ground Elder

I Greater Water-parsnip

J Lesser Water-parsnip

b

A
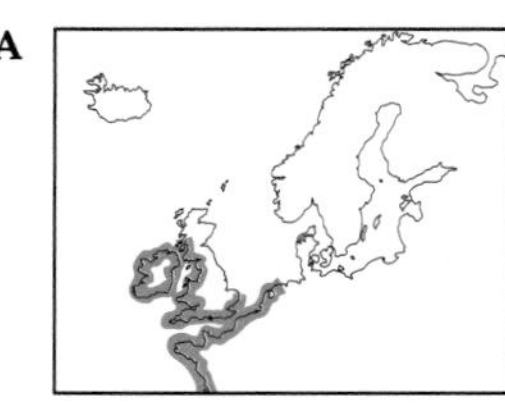

B
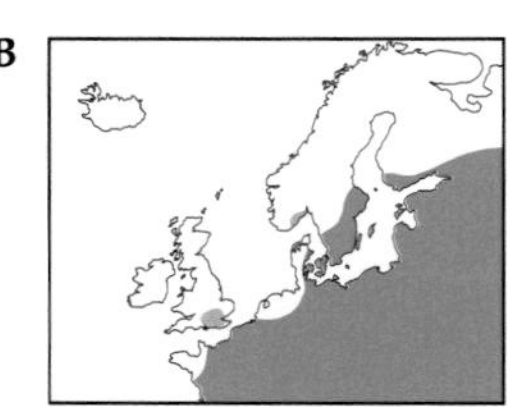

E
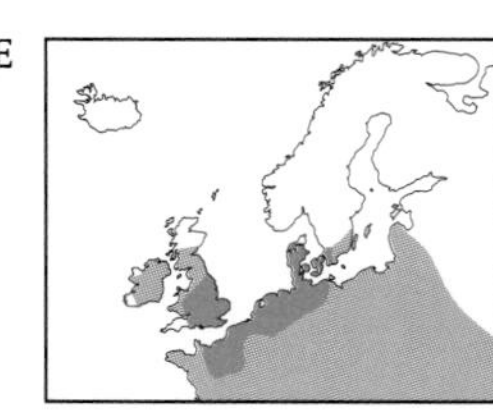

F

G

I
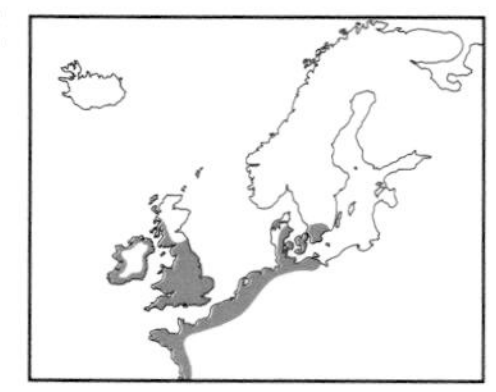

J
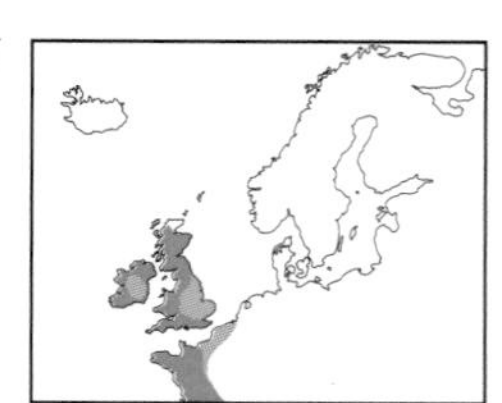

K
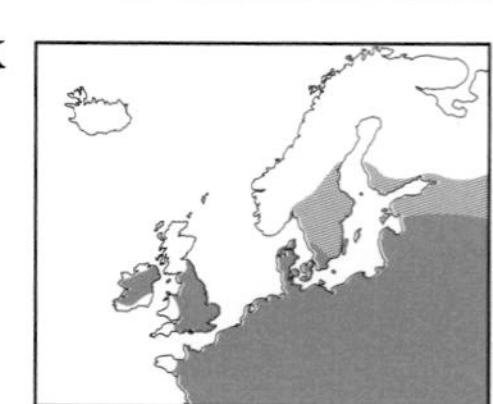

L
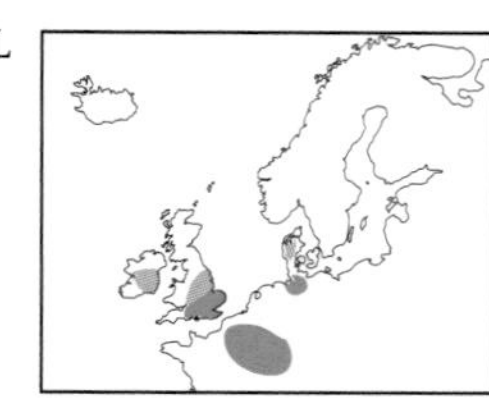

A Rock Samphire *Crithmum maritimum* Bushy spreading perennial, branched from the base, with hairless, solid, ridged stems. Leaves fleshy, triangular in outline, but divided 1-2 times trifoliately into narrow pointed segments. Umbels 30-60mm in diameter, with 8-30 rays; bracts and bracteoles numerous, narrowly triangular, turning back as flowers mature; petals yellowish-green, sepals absent. Fruit to 6mm, oval and corky, becoming purple. Coastal habitats, usually on rock; from Scotland and Holland southwards. **Fl** 6-8. **Br** Frequent around most of the coast except NE England and E Scotland.

B Moon Carrot *Seseli libanotis* Erect, stout, downy or almost hairless perennial to 1m, with solid ridged stems, and remains of old leaf bases persisting at base of stem as fibrous tuft. Lower leaves 1- to 3-pinnate (usually 2-pinnate), to 20cm long, with oblong pointed hairy lobes, spreading in different planes; some leaves opposite. Umbels terminal, 30-60mm in diameter, with 20-60 downy rays; bracts 8 or more, up to 15mm long, bracteoles 10-15, narrow; flowers white, or pink, 1-2mm in diameter, with long sepal lobes. Fruit oval, downy and ridged, with deflexed styles (**b**). Widespread, except in the north, on calcareous grassland, scrub and rocky areas. **Fl** 6-8. **Br** Very rare; in a few SE England localities only.

C *Seseli montanum* Similar to Moon Carrot, but smaller and slenderer, to 70cm, hairless. Basal leaves 2-pinnate, long-stalked, to 10cm long, oval in outline, leaflets narrow and linear, often forked; upper stem leaves 1-pinnate. Umbels smaller, without bracts but bracteoles present; calyx teeth short. Similar habitats; from N France southwards. **Fl** 6-8. **Br** Absent.

D *Seseli annuum* Similar to Moon Carrot, but smaller, with fewer-rayed umbels, downy on the inner faces; fruit hairless. From N France southwards. **Fl** 6-8. **Br** Absent.

WATER-DROPWORTS *Oenanthe* Perennial hairless herbs of wet places. Leaves 2- to 4-pinnate, usually with sharply pointed lobes; stalk often tubular, sheathing the stem at its base. Bracts and bracteoles are both numerous; petals white, notched and unequal.

E Tubular Water-dropwort *Oenanthe fistulosa* Erect perennial to 80cm (usually less), with slender hollow stems, inflated between leaf nodes. Leaves 1- (occasionally 2-) pinnate, with leaflets of lower leaves oval and stalked, and those of upper leaves narrowly linear and distant (**e1**); *leaf stalk inflated*, cylindrical and *longer* than blade. Umbels terminal, 2-4cm across, with 2-4 rays, bracts usually absent but bracteoles numerous; flowers white; secondary umbels form dense balls as the fruit ripens. Fruit 3mm, cylindrical, with styles as long as fruit (**e2**). In wet places and shallow water, from S Sweden southwards. **Fl** 7-9. **Br** Local in England, but rare elsewhere, absent from N Scotland.

F Corky-fruited Water-dropwort *Oenanthe pimpinelloides* The least water-demanding species of *Oenanthe*. Stems erect, solid and ridged, to 1m. Basal leaves 2-pinnate, with linear-ovate lobed leaflets; stem leaves usually 1-pinnate, with narrow unlobed leaflets (**f1**). Umbels terminal, 20-60mm in diameter, with 6-15 rays, flat-topped; bracts and bracteoles both bristle-like; flowers white; fruits cylindrical, about 3mm long, with *swollen corky bases* and erect styles as long as fruit (**f2**). In damp and clayey grasslands, often near the sea; in W areas from Holland southwards. **Fl** 5-8. **Br** Only in S, local and mainly near the coast.

G Narrow-leaved Water-dropwort *Oenanthe silaifolia* Similar to Corky-fruited Water-dropwort, but with *stems hollow*, and plant generally more robust. All leaves at least 2- pinnate, with narrow, pointed segments (**g1**). Umbels rather less dense, 3-5cm across, with rays becoming very stout in fruit; bracts are usually absent. Fruit is similar, but *strongly constricted* where it joins its stalk (**g2**). In wet places, especially in river valleys; from England and Germany southwards, local. **Fl** 6-7. **Br** Rare and decreasing; in S England only.

H *Oenanthe peucedanifolia* Very similar to Narrow-leaved Water-dropwort, but rays not thickened in fruit; fruit ovoid, with styles as long as fruit (almost as long as fruit in Narrow-leaved Water-dropwort). Wet places, Holland southwards. **Fl** 6-7. **Br** Absent.

I Parsley Water-dropwort *Oenanthe lachenalii* Rather similar to above species, especially Corky-fruited Water-dropwort. Stem solid. Basal leaves 2-pinnate, with elliptical to spoon-shaped blunt toothless leaflets (**i1**) – *stalk shorter than blade*. Bracts present; rays not thickened in fruit; fruit oval, without corky base (**i2**). In wet meadows and marshes, often coastal; from Denmark and S Sweden southwards. **Fl** 6-9. **Br** Scattered throughout, mainly near the coast; absent from N Scotland.

J Hemlock Water-dropwort *Oenanthe crocata* The most distinctive water-dropwort. A robust, branched plant to 1.5m, with hollow, grooved stems; all parts highly poisonous. Basal leaves triangular in outline, 3- to 4-times pinnate, with oval to rounded leaflets, toothed above, tapering to base; stem leaves 2- to 3-pinnate, with narrower lobes. Umbels terminal and stalked, 5-10cm in diameter, with 10-40 rays, not thickening in fruit; bracts and bracteoles numerous, linear-lanceolate, soon falling. Flowers white, with unequal petals; fruit cylindrical, with erect styles. In shady or sunny wet places; from Belgium and Britain southwards. **Fl** 6-7. **Br** Scattered throughout, but common only in the south and west.

K Fine-leaved Water-dropwort *Oenanthe aquatica* Erect bushy plant to 1.5m, from runners; stems hollow and grooved, with transverse joints, swollen near base. Submerged leaves are 3- to 4-pinnate with very fine segments (**k1**); aerial leaves 3-pinnate with ovate, lobed, pointed segments. Umbels terminal and axillary, 20-50mm diameter, bracts absent, bracteoles bristle-like. Flowers white, with equal petals; fruit oval, 3-4mm long, with styles as long (**k2**). Throughout, except the far north, in still or slow-flowing water. **Br** Scattered as far north as SE Scotland, but very local.

L River Water-dropwort *Oenanthe fluviatilis* Similar to Fine-leaved Water-dropwort, but stems mainly submerged. Leaves all 2-pinnate, submerged leaves with narrow, forked segments, aerial leaves with shallowly cut, blunt oval lobes. Umbels often absent, but similar to above. Fruit eliptical, 5-6mm. Generally in faster-flowing water, though also in ponds; in W Europe from Denmark southwards only. **Fl** 6-9. **Br** Rare in England and Wales, mainly southern; rare in Ireland.

A	B	E
F	G	I
J	K	L

A **Rock Samphire**
B **Moon Carrot**
E **Tubular Water-dropwort**
F **Corky-fruited Water-dropwort**
G **Narrow-leaved Water-dropwort**
I **Parsley Water-dropwort**
J **Hemlock Water-dropwort**
K **Fine-leaved Water-dropwort**
L **River Water-dropwort**

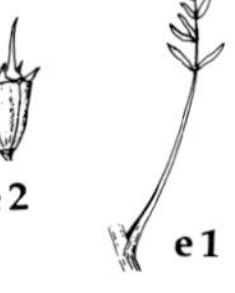

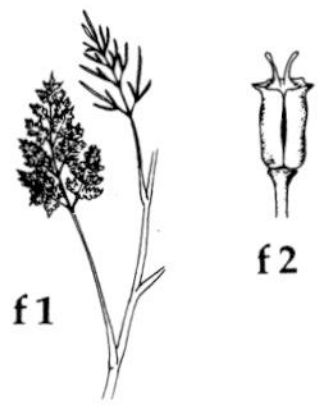

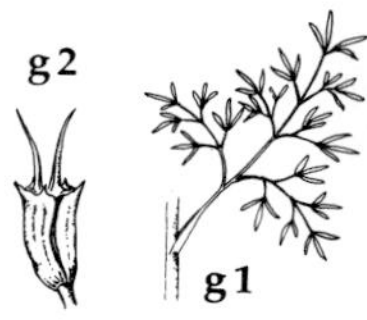

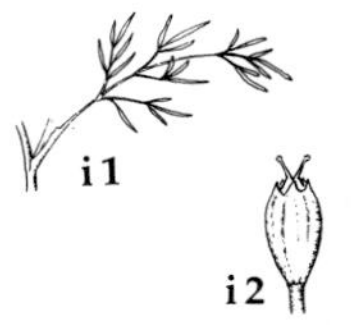

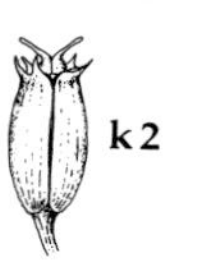

B

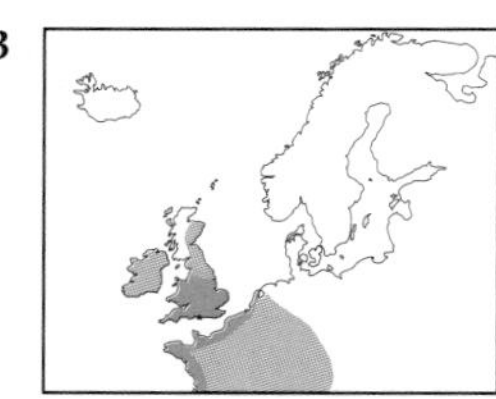

C

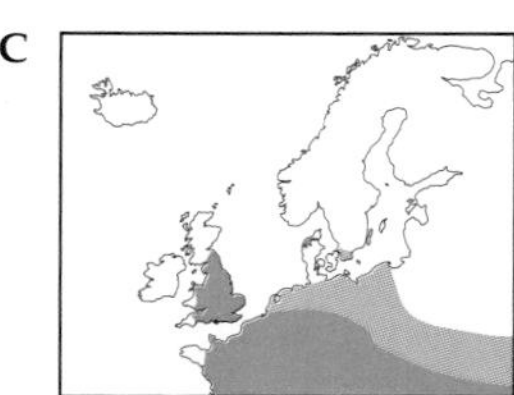

D

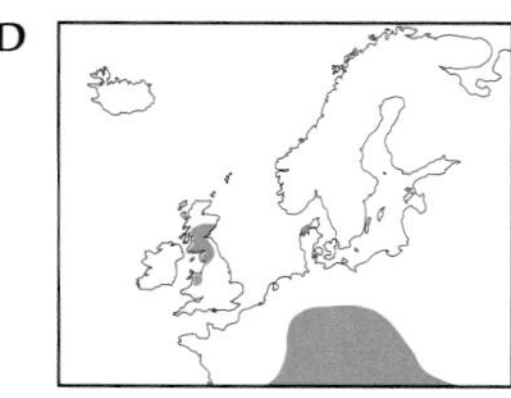

E

F

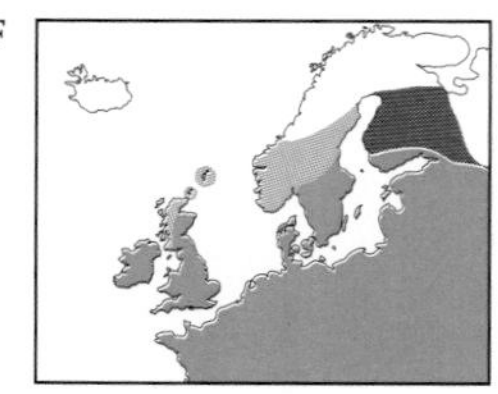

G

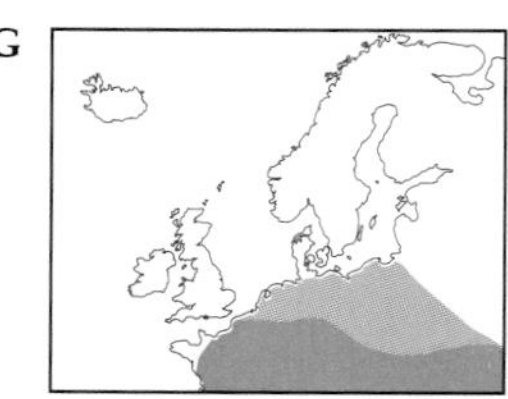

I

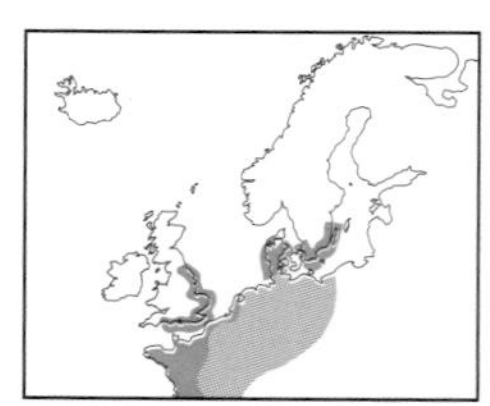

K

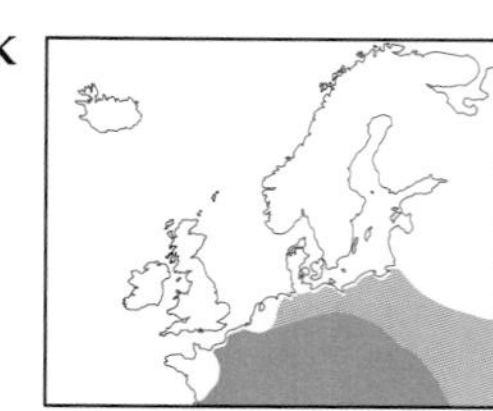

A Fool's Parsley *Aethusa cynapium* Annual hairless herb to 1.2m, usually much less. Leaves 2-pinnate. Bracts absent (occasionally 1); bracteoles are distinctive, long and narrow, hanging downwards conspicuously on outer side of secondary umbels; fruit oval and ridged, 3-4mm long. Widespread throughout as a weed of cultivated land; common.
Ssp cynapioides is taller, with less-ridged stems and long bracteoles, occurring in woods in S Sweden, Germany and France. **Fl** 6-8. **Br** Widespread and common in disturbed ground, except for N Scotland.

B Fennel *Foeniculum vulgare* Tall, stout, erect, hairless grey-green perennial to 2.5m, with a faintly ridged solid stem, developing a small hollow when old. Leaves very finely divided into waxy, grey-green, thread-like, spreading leaflets, with toughened points, 4-6mm long. Umbels terminal and axillary, 40-80mm in diameter, with numerous rays; bracts and bracteoles usually absent; flowers yellow; fruit ovoid and ridged. In coastal habitats; from Holland southwards, but probably native only in southern part of range. **Fl** 7-10. **Br** Coastal, in England, Wales and Ireland.

C Pepper-saxifrage *Silaum silaus* Hairless perennial to 1m, with solid ridged stems. Basal leaves triangular in outline, 2- to 4-pinnate, with linear, pointed leaflets, very finely toothed; stem leaves few and small. Umbels long-stalked, terminal and axillary, 20-60mm in diameter with 5-15 rays; bracts usually absent, or up to 3, bracteoles narrow; flowers bright yellow. Fruit ovoid to oblong, 5mm long. In grasslands, often on heavy soils; from S Sweden southwards, local. **Fl** 6-8. **Br** Locally common in England, rare elsewhere, absent from Ireland.

D Spignel, Baldmoney *Meum athamanticum* Hairless, strongly aromatic perennial to 60cm, with rootstock crowned by fibrous remains of previous year's leaf stalks; stem hollow and striped. Leaves mainly basal, 3- to 4-pinnate, with very fine bristle-like lobes, sometimes appearing to be in whorls (**e**). Umbels terminal or axillary, 30-60mm in diameter; bracts 0-2, bracteoles few, all bristle-like and small; fruit 6-10mm long, elliptical. In mountain areas in Belgium, France, Germany and Britain. **Fl** 6-7. **Br** From N Wales and N England northwards.

E Bladderseed *Physospermum cornubiense* Almost hairless perennial, with erect solid striped stems to 1m. Basal leaves long-stalked, twice-trifoliate, with long-stalked pinnately-lobed segments, wedge-shaped at bases. Umbels 20-50mm in diameter, with narrow, pointed bracts and bracteoles; fruits smooth and rounded, 3-4mm long, like little bladders (**f**). In shaded places; S Britain and France southwards. **Fl** 7-8. **Br** Rare, in Cornwall and Buckinghamshire.

F Hemlock *Conium maculatum* Erect branched biennial or winter annual, almost hairless, with purple-spotted stems to 2.5m; strong-smelling and poisonous. Lower leaves large, up to 40cm, triangular in outline, but 2- to 4-pinnate with fine leaflets, soft but hairless. Umbels terminal and axillary, 20-50mm in diameter, with a few small turned-back bracts, and similar but smaller bracteoles; flowers white. Fruit almost spherical, with wavy ridges. Throughout, except the far north, in a wide variety of habitats, especially riversides, scrub and waste ground. **Fl** 6-7. **Br** Throughout except the far north.

THOROW-WAX and **HARE'S-EARS**
Bupleurum Hairless annual or perennial plants with distinctive simple undivided leaves. Flowers yellow, not notched; sepals usually missing.

G Thorow-wax *Bupleurum rotundifolium* Erect grey-green annual to about 50cm, with hollow stems. Leaves elliptical to almost round, 2-5cm across, lower ones narrowing into a stalk, but *upper ones encircling stem completely*. Umbels 10-30mm across, few-rayed, bracts absent, but bracteoles conspicuous, ovate, joined together at base, yellowish-green, forming a ruff around the flowers; flowers yellow. In arable land and dry open habitats, rare and declining; from Belgium and Germany southwards. **Fl** 6-8. **Br** Now extinct as native plant.

H Small Hare's-ear *Bupleurum baldense* Slender erect annual, often less than 10cm high, frequently much-branched. Leaves linear to spoon-shaped and sharp-pointed. Umbels are few-flowered, 5-10mm in diameter, with *bracts longer than longest rays;* bracteoles are bristle-pointed and yellowish, almost hiding flowers. In dry open habitats, usually close to the sea, often calcareous; from England and N France southwards, rare. **Fl** 6-7. **Br** Very rare, in Devon, Sussex, and Channel Islands only.

I Slender Hare's-ear *Bupleurum tenuissimum* Slender spreading or erect annual, to 50cm, with wiry stems. Leaves linear-lanceolate to spoon-shaped, narrow, to 50mm long, pointed. *Umbels small, less than 5mm in diameter,* in leaf axils, very short-stalked. In grassy coastal habitats, upper salt-marshes; from Gotland (SE Sweden) southwards. **Fl** 7-9. **Br** Coasts of S and E England only.

J *Bupleurum gerardii* Similar to Slender Hare's-ear, but leaves are more sickle-shaped. In drier habitats; NW France southwards. **Fl** 7-9. **Br** Absent.

K Sickle-leaved Hare's-ear *Bupleurum falcatum* Erect hairless perennial, with hollow stems to 1.3m. *Leaves narrowly spoon-shaped,* 3-8cm long, *curved,* lower ones stalked, upper ones clasping the stem. Umbels stalked, to 40mm in diameter, with 3-15 rays; bracts 2-5, narrow and unequal; bracteoles 5, linear-lanceolate. Flowers are yellow, fruit is oblong and red-tipped. From Belgium and S England southwards, in grassy and waste places, often calcareous. **Fl** 7-9. **Br** Very rare, in Essex only.

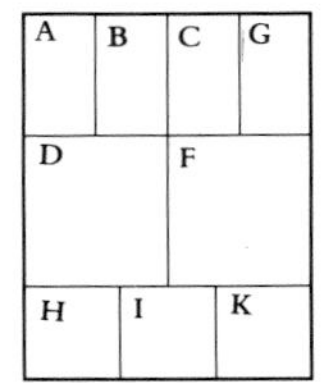

A Fool's Parsley
B Fennel
C Pepper-saxifrage
G Thorow-wax
D Spignel
F Hemlock
H Small Hare's-ear
I Slender Hare's-ear
K Sickle-leaved Hare's-ear

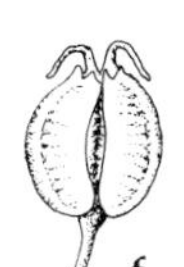

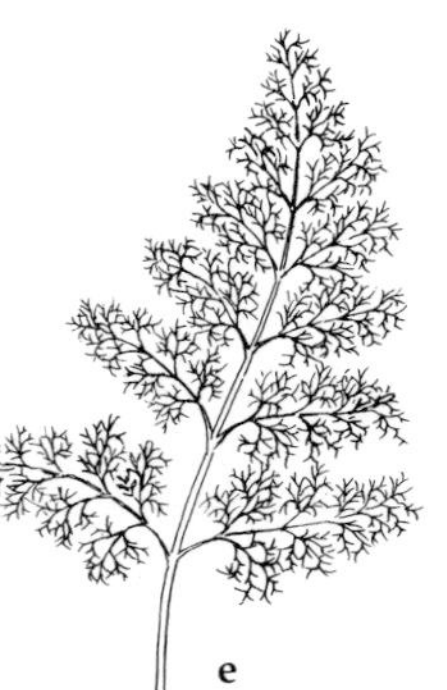

A

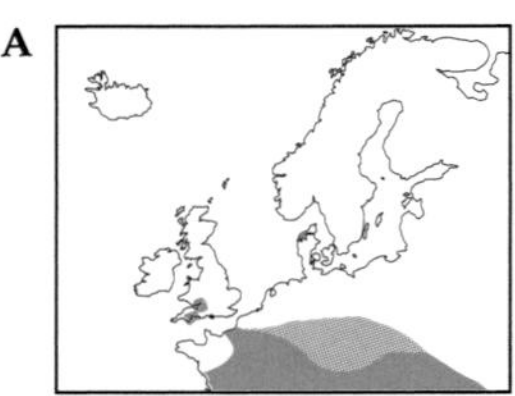

B

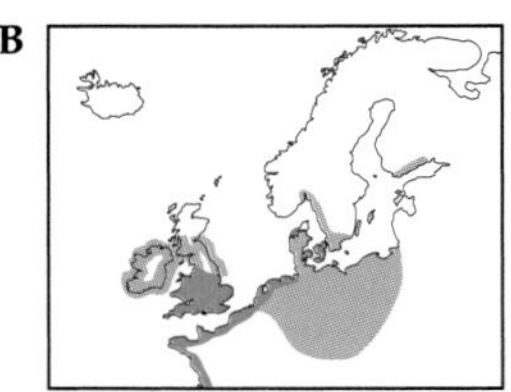

C

E

F

G

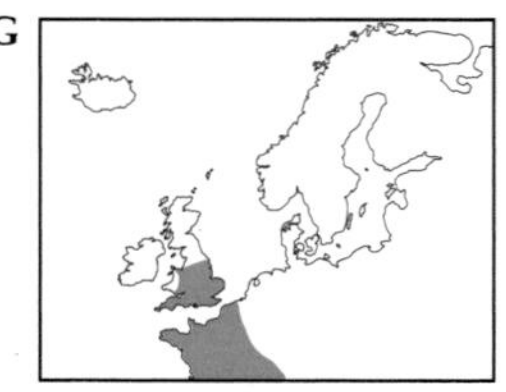

K

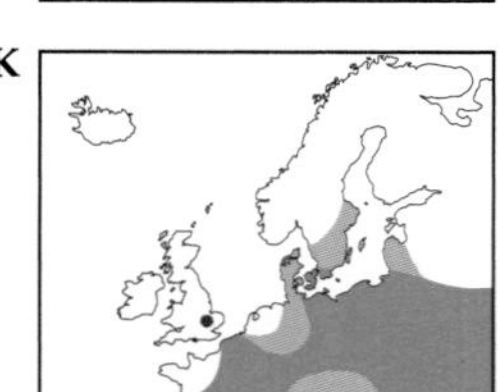

A Honewort *Trinia glauca* Hairless, erect, waxy grey-green perennial up to 50cm, though usually less and frequently branched from the base. Lower leaves 2- to 3-pinnate, with lobes to 30mm. Separate male and female plants; male plant umbels flat-topped, 10mm wide, with 4-7 equal rays; female plant umbels 30mm in diameter, with irregular rays; bracts absent or 1, 3-lobed; bracteoles 2-3, simple; fruit ovoid, ridged, about 2mm long. From S England and S Germany southwards, rare, in sunny limestone grassy and rocky areas. **Fl** 5-6. **Br** Very rare, S Devon and N Somerset.

Apium Hairless perennial herbs, with 1-pinnate or ternate leaves; bracts and bracteoles few or absent; sepals minute or absent; flowers more or less white.

B Wild Celery *Apium graveolens* Stout biennial up to 1m, with a strong characteristic celery smell; stems solid and grooved. Basal leaves 1-pinnate, with lobed and toothed diamond-shaped segments, occasionally almost 2-pinnate; upper stem leaves ternate, stalked. Umbels terminal and axillary, 40-60mm across, short-stalked or unstalked; bracts and bracteoles absent; flowers greenish-white. Fruit broadly ovoid, to 2mm. From Denmark southwards; in damp, usually saline, habitats, mainly coastal. **Fl** 6-8. **Br** Local around the coasts, occasionally inland, absent from N Scotland.

C Fool's Water-cress *Apium nodiflorum* Creeping perennial, with ascending hollow stems, rooting at lower nodes. Leaves 1-pinnate, with 4-6 pairs of bright green leaflets (compare with Lesser Water-parsnip, *see* page 164, which has more pairs of bluish leaflets). Umbels in leaf axils, with short stalks, 3-12 rays; bracts usually absent, 5 bracteoles, narrowly lanceolate; flowers white; fruit broadly oval. (Compare with Water-cress, which grows in similar places, but has very different flowers, and rather different leaves). In wet places, from Holland southwards, predominantly western. **Fl** 7-8. **Br** Generally common, rarer in Scotland, absent from the far north.

D *Apium repens* Very similar to Fool's Water-cress, but stem roots at all nodes; leaf segments broader and more rounded; 3-7 bracts are present, rays usually 3-6 only. Similar habitats, from Denmark southwards, but not fully recorded due to confusion with above. **Fl** 7-8. **Br** Very rare, central England only.

E Lesser Marshwort *Apium inundatum* Slender, straggling, often submerged perennial to 75cm, with almost smooth stems. Lower leaves 1-pinnate, with very narrow hair-like leaflets; upper leaves pinnate with broader often 3-lobed segments. Umbels axillary, stalked, to 35mm long, bracts absent, bracteoles 3-6, lanceolate; flowers white; fruit elliptical-oblong, 2mm. In wet or muddy places, local, from SE Sweden southwards. **Fl** 6-8. **Br** Scattered throughout except N Scotland, mainly in lowland areas.

F Corn Parsley *Petroselinum segetum* Slender, hairless, rather *dark grey-green* parsley-scented annual or biennial, with round solid stems up to 1m. Leaves 1-pinnate, with numerous ovate toothed or lobed segments, with hard forward-curving points. Umbels very irregular, up to 50mm in diameter, with only 2-5 rays of varying length; both bracts and bracteoles present and bristle-like; flowers white, few per umbel; fruit is ovoid, 2-4mm long (**f**). In hedgerows, fields and waste places, often near the coast, from Holland southwards. **Fl** 8-10. **Br** Local and decreasing in S and E England, rare in Wales, mainly coastal; absent elsewhere.

G Stone Parsley *Sison amomum* Erect, much-branched slender biennial, with solid stems to 1m, with an unpleasant smell when crushed (described as a mixture of nutmeg and petrol!). Lower leaves simply pinnate, long-stalked, with 7-9 pairs of ovate toothed lobes; upper leaves trifoliate, with narrower leaflets; all *leaves are bright green* (compare with Corn Parsley, *see* above). Umbels terminal and axillary, 10-40mm across, with only 3-6 slender unequal rays; bracts and bracteoles present and bristle-like; flowers white; fruit almost spherical, 3mm long. From England and N France southwards, in hedgerows and grasslands, usually on heavy soil. **Fl** 7-9. **Br** In England and Wales only, mainly in the south and east, local.

H Cowbane *Cicuta virosa* Stout, erect perennial to 1.2m, with ridged, hollow stems. Highly poisonous. Leaves triangular in outline, up to 30cm long, 2- to 3-pinnate, with narrow, sharply toothed, pointed leaflets; stalks long and hollow. Umbels terminal, long-stalked, large, to 13cm across, rounded on top; bracts absent, bracteoles numerous and strap-shaped, long; flowers numerous, white; fruit globular, 2mm long. In fens, water-sides and shallow water, throughout. **Fl** 7-8. **Br** Scattered almost throughout, but very local.

I Bullwort, False Bishop's Weed *Ammi majus* Erect, hairless annual or biennial up to 1m tall. Leaves pinnate, greyish-green, all segments with hard-tipped teeth. Flowers white, in umbels 3-6cm across, with up to 50 or more rays; bracts usually pinnately divided, about half the length of rays; fruit ovoid, pale, ridged, 2mm long. In waste places, or bare rocky areas; from N France southwards, casual further north. **Fl** 6-10. **Br** A rare casual only.

J *Ptychotis saxifraga* Hairless biennial to 60cm. Leaves pinnate, with lobes toothed or pinnately lobed; upper leaves finely divided, with sheathing bases. Flowers white, in small uneven umbels of 6-12 rays; bracts few, soon falling off. Fruit 3mm long, oblong, slightly ridged. In dry rocky and waste places, from N France southwards. **Fl** 6-8. **Br** Absent.

K Longleaf *Falcaria vulgaris* Distinctive greyish-green, branched annual or perennial, to 80cm, with solid smooth stems. Basal leaves long-stalked, 1- to 2-trifoliate, with long, narrow, sharply toothed, curved, pointed segments, up to 30cm long – a distinctive combination. Umbels terminal and axillary, 6-12cm across, with linear bracts and bracteoles; flowers white. Fruit oblong, ridged. From N France southwards in calcareous grassland, and further north where probably introduced. **Fl** 7-9. **Br** Introduced, rarely naturalised in S England.

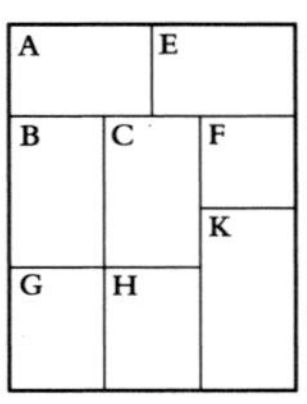

A Honewort

E Lesser Marshwort

B Wild Celery

C Fool's Water-cress

F Corn Parsley

K Longleaf

G Stone Parsley

H Cowbane

f

B
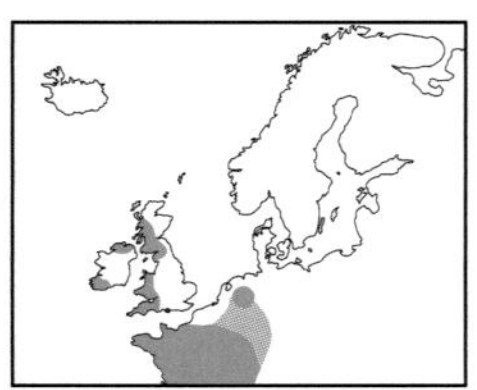
F
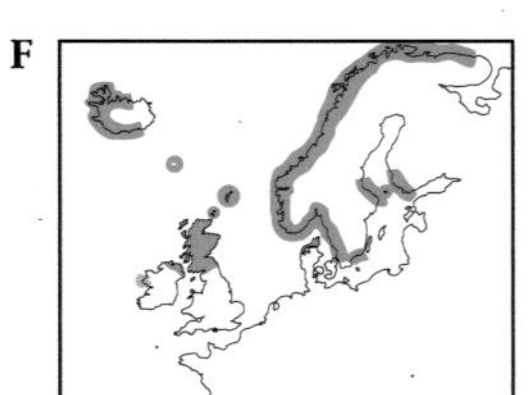
J
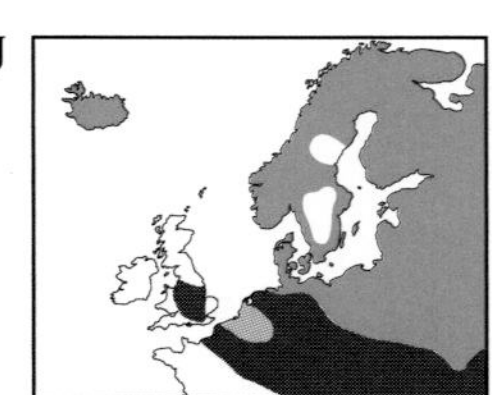

A Caraway *Carum carvi* Erect, branched, hairless perennial, with a striped, hollow stem to 1.5m, usually less. Leaves 2- to 3-pinnate, with linear lobes. Umbels long-stalked, 20-40mm in diameter and irregular; bracts and bracteoles usually absent, not bent back if present; flowers white or pink; fruit ovoid to 6mm long and aromatic if crushed – the caraway used in cooking. Native or naturalised in grassy areas and waste ground, throughout except the far north. **Fl** 6-7. **Br** Possibly native in the south-east, rare, locally naturalised elsewhere.

B Whorled Caraway *Carum verticillatum* Erect hairless perennial to 1m, usually less, with solid, little-branched stem with few leaves. Basal leaves up to 25cm, narrowly oblong in outline, with at least 20 pairs of deeply divided segments, appearing as if in a whorl (**b1**). Umbels 20-50mm in diameter, flat-topped, with numerous narrow, reflexed bracts and bracteoles; flowers white; fruit elliptical, about 2mm, with strong ridges (**b2**). In damp acidic grasslands and marshy areas, from Scotland and Holland southwards, predominantly western. **Fl** 6-8. **Br** Local in SW England, Wales, Ireland and W Scotland.

C *Cnidium dubium* Hairless perennial to 1m, with hollow stem, furrowed above. Leaves 2- to 3-pinnate, with narrow segments with a whitish tip; stem leaves have sheathing purplish stalks. Umbel rays winged on angles; bracteoles numerous, narrow; fruit globose, 2-3mm. Shady places and disturbed ground, usually coastal. S Scandinavia and Germany. **Fl** 7-9. **Br** Absent.

D Cambridge Milk-parsley *Selinum carvifolia* Tall, almost hairless perennial to 1m, with solid branched stems with winged angles. Leaves 2- to 4-pinnate, with linear-lanceolate minutely toothed lobes with short spine-tips (**d1**). Umbels terminal, long-stalked, 30-70mm in diameter, without bracts but with several linear bracteoles; flowers white; fruit oval, 3-4mm, flattened, with winged ridges (**d2**). Throughout, in fens and damp meadows. **Fl** 7-10. **Br** Rare, in E England only.

E *Selinum pyrenaeum* Similar to Cambridge Milk-parsley but smaller, stems ridged but unwinged, only 0-2 stem leaves. Mountain pastures, from the Vosges southwards. **Fl** 6-8. **Br** Absent.

F Scots Lovage *Ligusticum scoticum* Hairless, shiny bright green perennial to 90cm, often purplish at base. Leaves twice-trifoliate, bright green, with oval leaflets, toothed towards tips; leaf stalks inflated, sheathing stem. Umbels terminal, dense and long-stalked, 40-60mm in diameter, with narrow linear bracts and bracteoles; flowers greenish-white; fruit oblong-ovoid, 5-8mm long, with persistent calyx teeth. On rocky or shingle coasts, from Britain to Norway, and isolated localities on the Baltic in Sweden. **Fl** 6-8. **Br** Coasts of Scotland and N Ireland only, locally common.

G *Ligusticum mutellina* Has abundant coarse fibres around rootstock, 2- to 3-pinnate leaves, and red to purple flowers. Mountain habitats, from E France and S Germany southwards. **Fl** 7-8. **Br** Absent.

H Wild Angelica *Angelica sylvestris* Stout, almost hairless perennial with broad and hollow, purplish stems to 2m or more. Leaves large, to 60cm, triangular in outline, 2- to 3-pinnate, with oblong-oval, unequal-based, toothed leaflets (**h1**); stalk is very conspicuously broad, inflated, hollow and sheathing; uppermost leaves little more than sheaths. Umbels terminal and lateral, to 15cm in diameter, with numerous rays; bracts absent or very few, bracteoles few and very narrow; calyx teeth minute, petals white to pinkish; fruit oval, 5mm long, very flattened and winged (**h2**). Damp or shaded places, throughout, common. **Fl** 6-9. **Br** Widespread and generally common throughout.

I *Angelica palustris* Similar to Wild Angelica, usually rather smaller. Flowers have well-developed whitish sepals (absent in Wild Angelica). Similar habitats, central Germany eastwards. **Fl** 6-9. **Br** Absent.

J Garden Angelica *Angelica archangelica* Rather similar to Wild Angelica, but stems are usually green; leaf lobes more jaggedly cut and irregular, with terminal lobe deeply 3-lobed (**j1**); flowers are greenish-white to yellow; *fruit with thick corky* (not membranous) *wings* (**j2**). In pastures, riversides and damp places, northwards from Holland and Denmark. Used in the making of confectionery, and a liqueur. **Fl** 6-9. **Br** Locally naturalised.

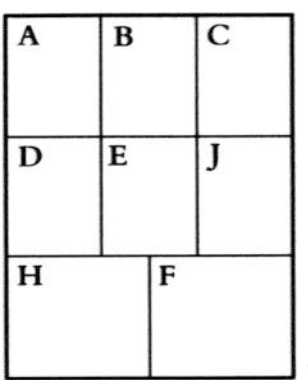

A Caraway
B Whorled Caraway
C *Cnidium dubium*
D Cambridge Milk-parsley
E *Selinum pyrenaeum*
J Garden Angelica
H Wild Angelica
F Scots Lovage

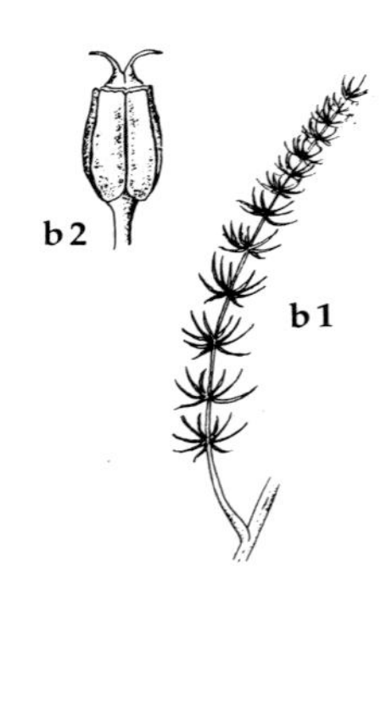

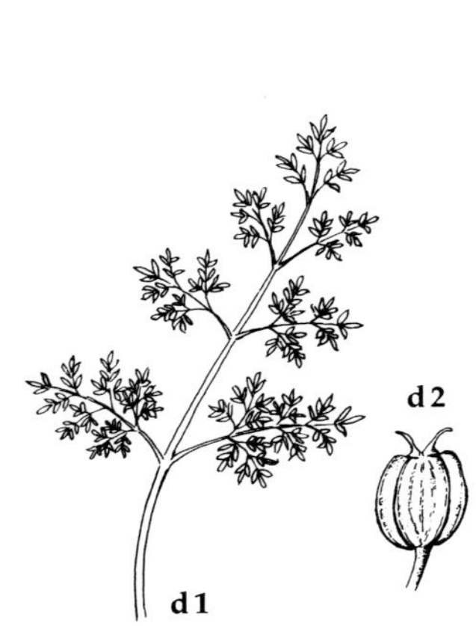

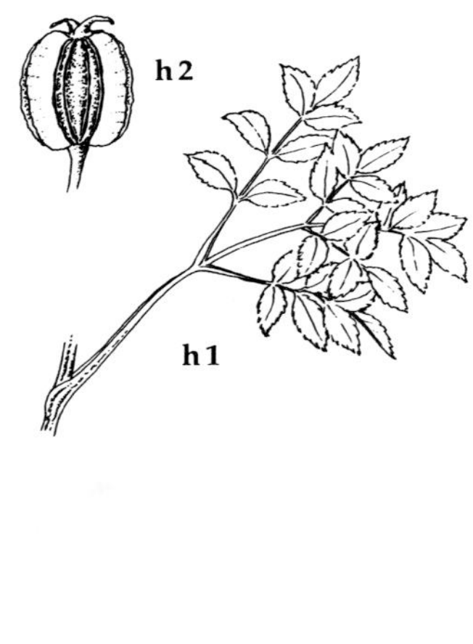

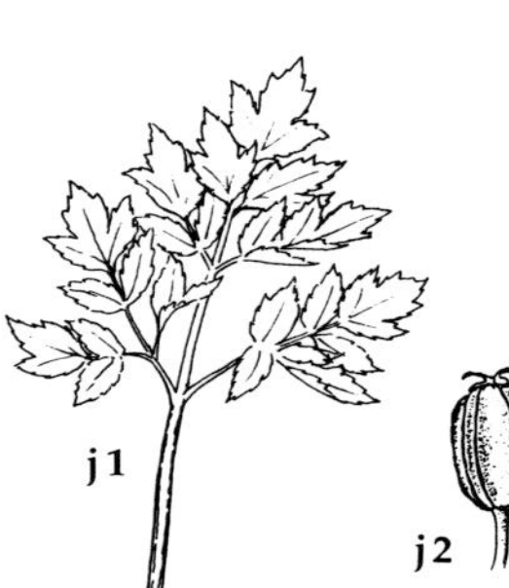

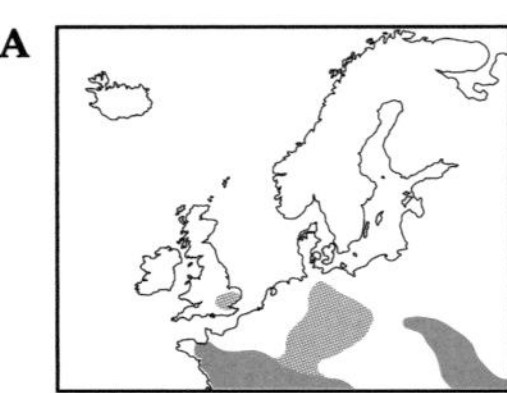

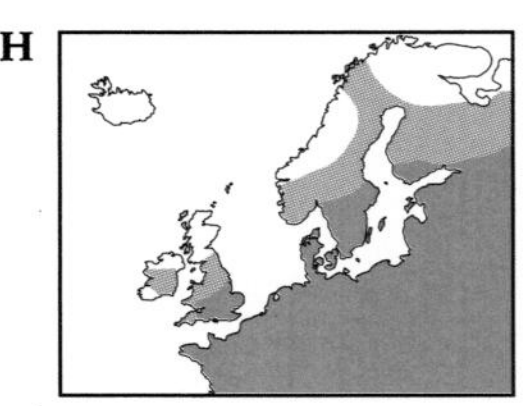

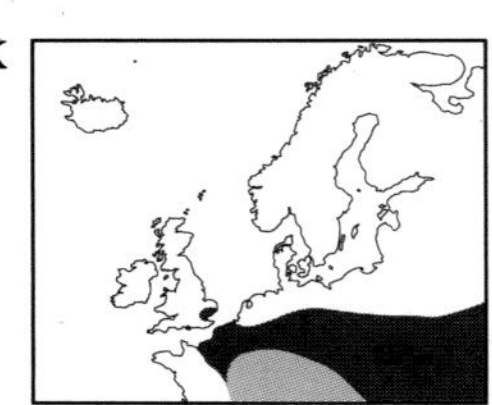

Peucedanum Perennials or biennials Leaves pinnate or ternate. Flowers white, yellow or pinkish, with broadly ovate petals; calyx teeth small or absent; fruit compressed, ridged and winged.

A **Hog's Fennel** *Peucedanum officinale* Robust, hairless perennial to 2m tall, with base of stem often very broad with abundant fibres; stem unridged or faintly ridged, solid. Leaves 4- to 6-times trifoliate, with flat linear untoothed leaflets, 4-10cm long and narrowed at both ends. Umbels terminal and axillary, up to 20cm in diameter, with numerous rays, nodding in bud but erect later; bracts absent or up to 3, bracteoles several, all very narrow; flowers sulphur-yellow; fruit oblong-ovate, to 1cm long, ridged. Rough grassland on clay, usually near the sea, from N France and S Germany southwards. **Fl** 7-9. **Br** Rare, though locally common, in SE England only, coastal.

B *Peucedanum carvifolia* Similar to Hog's Fennel, but with leaves 1-pinnate, with deeply pinnately lobed segments, shining on both sides; bracts absent, bracteoles few; fruit has transparent wings. In grassy and waste places, from Holland southwards. **Fl** 6-8. **Br** Absent.

C *Peucedanum oreoselinum* Tall perennial to 1m, with solid striped but unridged stems. Lower leaves triangular in outline, to 40cm, 2- to 3-pinnate, with stalks often wavy; lobes ovate and lobed. Umbels have numerous narrow turned-back bracts and bracteoles; sepals ovate, petals white or pinkish; fruit with thick wings. In grassy habitats, scrub and rocky places, from S Scandinavia southwards, local. **Fl** 6-8. **Br** Absent.

D *Peucedanum lancifolium* Similar to *P. oreoselinum*, but rootstock does not have fibres around it, and the leaf divisions are very narrow, untoothed; petals white or yellowish. In wet meadows and marshes, NW France only. **Fl** 7-10. **Br** Absent.

E **Milk Parsley** *Peucedanum palustre* Virtually hairless biennial up to 1.6m, with ridged, hollow, often purplish stems. Leaves triangular in outline, 2- to 4-pinnate (**e1**), with ultimate lobes linear-oblong and blunt; leaf stalks channelled and sometimes inflated. Umbels 3-8cm in diameter, with 20-40 rays; bracts and bracteoles 4 or more each, long and narrow, sometimes forked, bent back; petals white, sepals ovate; fruit oval, flattened and winged especially on edges (**e2**). In wet places, usually calcareous; throughout though local. **Fl** 7-9. **Br** Very local, mainly in E Anglia, with scattered sites in England only.

F *Peucedanum cervaria* Resembles Milk Parsley, but has a fibrous stem base, and less ridged stems. Leaf lobes are more pointed; bracts more numerous and often pinnately cut. In grassy habitats, central Europe, west to Belgium, France and Germany. **Fl** 7-9. **Br** Absent.

G **Masterwort** *Peucedanum ostruthium* Erect, downy biennial or perennial to 1m, with hollow, ridged stems. Leaves 1- to 2-ternate, with irregularly toothed lobes; stalks of upper stem leaves strongly inflated. Flowers white or pinkish, in umbels 6-12cm across, with up to 50 rays; bracts absent, bracteoles few, very narrow. Fruit almost spherical, winged, 4-5mm long. Native in grassy places in mountains, from France and Germany southwards, but naturalised occasionally. **Br** Mainly central and N Britain.

H **Wild Parsnip** *Pastinaca sativa* Erect, downy, branched biennial, with hollow, ridged and angled (occasionally solid and unridged) stems to 1m. Basal leaves 1-pinnate, with ovate, lobed and toothed segments. Umbels 3-10cm in diameter, with 5-20 rays; bracts and bracteoles absent or very few, falling early; flowers yellow; fruit oval and flattened, with narrowly winged edges. In grassland, scrub and waste ground, especially on dry or calcareous soils; widespread except in parts of the north. **Fl** 6-8. **Br** Widespread in S Britain, rare or absent from the north; not native in Ireland.

I **Hogweed** *Heracleum sphondylium* Robust, erect, roughly hairy perennial to 2.5m, with hollow, ridged stems. Leaves large, to 60cm, usually 1-pinnate, but variable, with toothed or lobed ovate leaflets, hairy on both surfaces. Umbels large, up to 20cm in diameter, with up to 45 rays; bracts usually absent, bracteoles bristle-like and turned back; flowers white, up to 1cm in diameter, with notched petals, very uneven in size on outer flowers; fruit elliptical, flattened and hairless. Widespread and common, except in the extreme north, in grassland, roadsides, waste places and open woods. **Fl** 5-8. **Br** Common throughout.

J **Giant Hogweed** *Heracleum mantegazzianum* Huge herbaceous biennial or perennial up *to 5m tall*, with stems hollow, ridged and purple-spotted, up to 10cm in diameter. Leaves similar to Hogweed, but larger, to 1m, with more sharply pointed leaflets. Umbels up to 50cm in diameter, with larger flowers. Can cause blistering of skin if touched in sunlight. Introduced from Caucasus, now naturalised almost throughout, especially along riversides. **Fl** 6-7. **Br** Widespread, though local.

K **Hartwort** *Tordylium maximum* Erect, branched annual or biennial to 1m or more, with adpressed bristles on ridged stem. Leaves pinnate; segments of lower leaves ovate or almost round, toothed; segments of upper leaves narrow lanceolate and strongly toothed (**k1**). Umbels terminal and axillary, long-stalked, with numerous narrow bracts and bracteoles, bristly; flowers white, with uneven petals, sepals as long as petals; fruit oblong and bristly, with thickened whitish ridges (**k2**). From Belgium and SE England southwards, in grassland, possibly not native in the north of range. **Fl** 6-7. **Br** Essex only, possibly native.

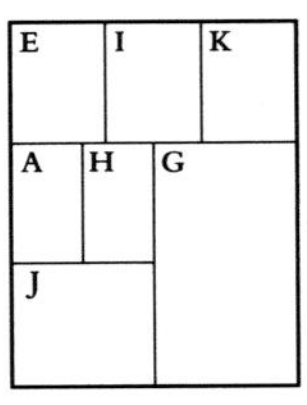

E **Milk Parsley**
I **Hogweed**
K **Hartwort**
A **Hog's Fennel**
H **Wild Parsnip**
G **Masterwort**
J **Giant Hogweed**

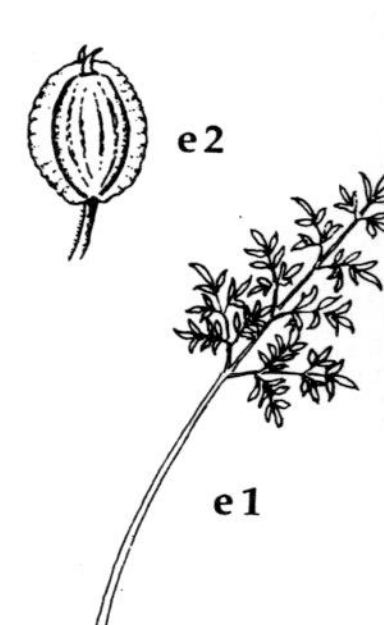

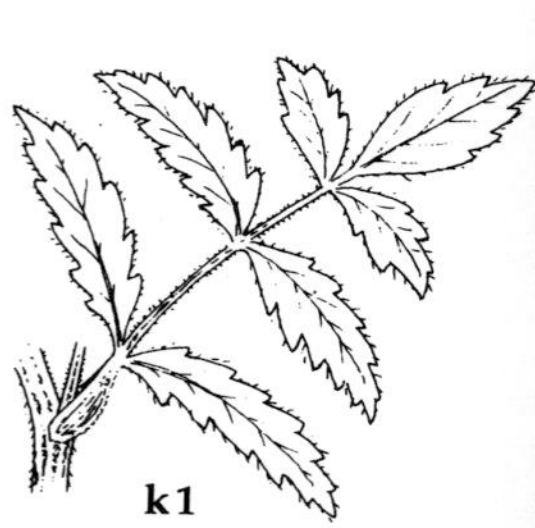

B

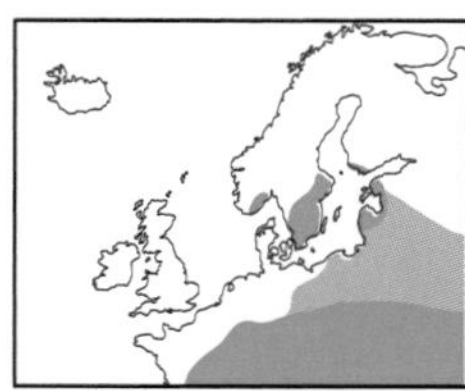

D

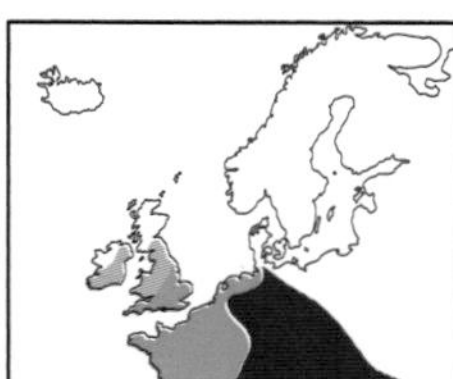

A *Laserpitium siler* Erect perennial to 1.2m, with ridged, almost hairless stems; fibrous leaf bases persist around base of stem. Leaves 3-pinnate, triangular in outline, with greyish-green untoothed segments. Flowers white, in large umbels to 14cm across, with up to 40 rays, and numerous reflexed bracts. Fruit ovoid, about 1cm, winged. In scrub and bare places on stony calcareous soils, from central France and Germany southwards. **Fl** 6-9. **Br** Absent.

B Sermountain *Laserpitium latifolium* Robust, almost hairless, grey-green perennial, with rounded, striped, solid stems to 2m. Leaves triangular in outline, 2-pinnate, with ovate toothed leaflets, unequally heart-shaped at bases; stalks of upper leaves strongly inflated (**b**). Umbels large, with 25-40 rays; bracts numerous, narrow and drooping, bracteoles few, very narrow; flowers white; fruit oval, 5-10mm long, winged but not flattened. From central Sweden southwards, widespread though local, in scrub, open woodland and rocky places, usually on limestone, and mainly in the mountains. **Fl** 6-8. **Br** Absent.

C *Laserpitium prutenicum* Biennial to 1m, with a more slender angled stem. Bracts and bracteoles both numerous and hairy (hairless in Sermountain); flowers white or yellowish. In mountain habitats, woods and grassland, from N Germany southwards. **Fl** 6-9. **Br** Absent.

D Knotted Hedge-parsley *Torilis nodosa* Prostrate or ascending slender annual to 50cm, with solid ridged stems with few deflexed hairs. Leaves less than 10cm, 1- to 2-pinnate, with deeply cut lobes. Umbels in leaf axils, small (less than 10mm in diameter) and virtually stalkless, with very short rays; bracts absent, bracteoles longer than flowers; petals pinkish-white, sepals very small; fruit 2-3mm long, covered with *warts and straight spines* (**d**). From Holland southwards, on dry banks and in arable fields, local, probably not native in the north of range. **Fl** 5-7. **Br** Scattered throughout, but mainly southern and eastern.

E Upright Hedge-parsley *Torilis japonica* Erect, slender annual, with solid, unspotted rough stems to 1.25m, with straight appressed hairs. Leaves 1- to 3-pinnate, dull green and hairy. Umbels terminal and axillary, stalked, to 40mm in diameter, with 5-12 rays; bracts and bracteoles present; flowers pinkish or purplish-white; fruit oval, to 4mm, with *hooked bristles* and bent-back styles (**e**). Roadsides, hedgerows, wood-margins and waste ground common throughout region except the far north. **Fl** 7-8 (later than Cow Parsley). **Br** Common throughout, except upland areas and N Scotland.

F Spreading Hedge-parsley *Torilis arvensis* Rather similar to Upright Hedge-parsley but smaller, to 50cm, usually spreading, branched or unbranched. Umbels long-stalked, with 3-5 rays, bracts absent, bracteoles rough hairy; fruit with spines *curved, but not hooked*, thickened at tip; styles spreading in fruit (**f**). In arable fields and disturbed ground, from Holland and S England southwards, local and declining. **Fl** 7-9. **Br** Now SE England only, declining.

G Small Bur-parsley *Caucalis platycarpos* Erect, slightly downy annual, with solid and somewhat angled stems to 40cm. Leaves 2- to 3-pinnate. Inflorescence similar to that of Hedge-parsley, but has conspicuous green sepals, and fruit to 10mm, with single rows of spines on ridges (**g**). In arable fields and waste places, especially on calcareous soils, from Holland and Germany southwards. **Fl** 6-7. **Br** A casual introduction only, not persisting.

H Greater Bur-parsley *Caucalis latifolia* Differs from Small Bur-parsley in being larger (to 60cm), more hispid, with simply pinnate leaves; umbels have 2-5 rays, with at least as many bracts and bracteoles; flowers 5mm wide (compared with 2mm in Small Bur-parsley); fruit 6-10mm, with 2-3 rows of spines on ridges. In cultivated and waste ground; from Germany and Belgium southwards. **Fl** 6-8. **Br** An uncommon casual.

I *Orlaya grandiflora* Erect annual to 40cm, simple or unbranched, hairy towards base. Leaves 2- to 3-pinnate. Umbels long-stalked with 5-12 rays; flowers white or pink, with outer petals up to 8 times as long as others. Fruit 7-8mm long, ovoid and flattened, with rows of hooked bristles. In dry grassy places; from Belgium and Germany southwards. **Fl** 6-8. **Br** Absent.

J Wild Carrot *Daucus carota* Variable erect or spreading annual or biennial to 1m, usually rough hairy; stems solid and ridged. Leaves 2- to 3-pinnate, with narrow linear segments. Umbels long-stalked, to 70mm in diameter, with numerous large pinnately divided leafy bracts forming a conspicuous ruff below each; bracteoles numerous; flowers white and dense, with central flower often reddish; fruit oval, 2-4mm long, with 4 spiny ridges; umbel rays become stiffly erect after flower, producing a concave fruit ball. Found in rough grassland, especially near the coast, throughout though rare in the far north. **Fl** 6-8. **Br** Throughout, except parts of the far north, and higher mountain areas.
Ssp *gummifer* has more fleshy, blunter leaves, umbels flat or convex in fruit, and fruit spines pointing upwards, more webbed together. Confined to coasts of S Britain and France.

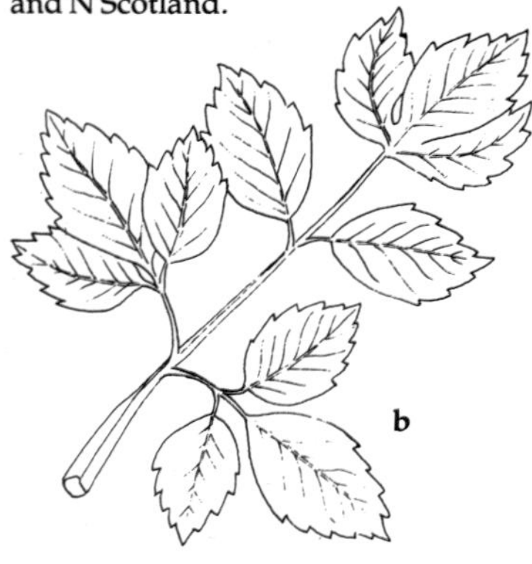

b

d

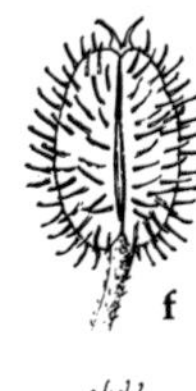

f

e

g

B Sermountain

D Knotted Hedge-parsley

F Spreading Hedge-parsley

J Wild Carrot

I *Orlaya grandiflora*

E Upright Hedge-parsley

G Small Bur-parsley

A
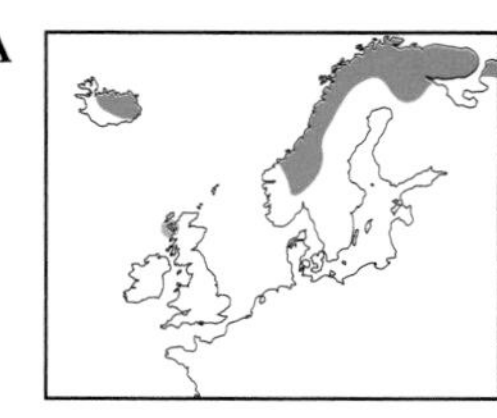

B
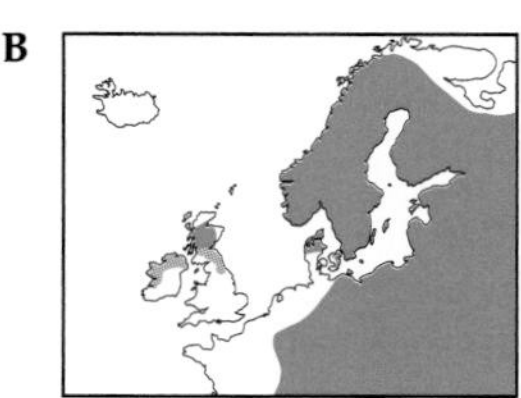

F

Diapensiaceae

Perennial herbs or low shrubs. Flowers regular, 5-parted, with superior ovary and 3-lobed stigma.

A **Diapensia** *Diapensia lapponica* Low-growing, dense, evergreen herb or subshrub, forming small cushions. Leaves small, to 1cm, leathery, deep green and shiny, roughly ovate and rounded at tip. Flowers with 5 parts, solitary but often numerous; petals creamy white, to 1cm long, rounded; stamens 5 alternating with petals, with wide filaments. Style single but 3-lobed; (compare with Saxifrage species, *see* page 90, which have 2 styles). Mountain habitats and tundra, especially exposed gravelly places, where it may be abundant. N Europe only. **Fl** 5-7. **Br** Very rare, in 2 W Scotland sites, discovered in 1951.

Wintergreen Family Pyrolaceae

Small perennial herbs with hermaphrodite 5- (occasionally 4-) parted flowers, petals separate, stamens usually 10.

B **Common Wintergreen** *Pyrola minor* Low evergreen herb, with erect flowering stems to 25cm. Leaves roughly elliptical, to 40mm wide, with rounded teeth, stalk shorter than leaf blade (**b1**). Inflorescence terminal, with individual flowers globose, 5-7mm in diameter; petals white to pale pink; style straight, 1-2mm long and *not protruding beyond petals* (**b2**). Widespread throughout in open woods, moorland and mountain habitats, rarely on dunes but frequently on calcareous soils. **Fl** 6-8. **Br** Uncommon and declining, and absent from many areas.

C **Intermediate Wintergreen** *Pyrola media* Similar to Common Wintergreen, though often slightly taller; leaves broader, to 6cm wide, more rounded, stalk shorter than or equal to blade (**c1**). Flowers larger, 7-10mm in diameter, globose, petals white to pink; style straight, but 4-6mm long, *protruding beyond petals* (**c2**), and expanded into a disc below the stigma. Widespread in N areas in woods (especially of Scots Pine), on moors and heaths. Absent from the far north and many lowland areas, such as Belgium and Holland. **Fl** 6-8.
Br Rare and declining, absent from most of the area, and frequent only in E Scotland.

D **Yellow Wintergreen** *Pyrola chlorantha* Low perennial, with yellow-green oblong to rounded leaves, darker below, stalk longer than blade. Flowers 8-12mm in diameter, bell-shaped and *yellowish-green*; style about 7mm long, curved, protruding, with expanded disc below stigma. Widespread in continental Europe, mostly in coniferous woods, less often in open grassland. **Fl** 6-7. **Br** Absent.

E **Round-leaved Wintergreen** *Pyrola rotundifolia* Low perennial, with ovate to rounded leaves, about 4 × 4cm, with round teeth; stalk distinctly longer than blade (**e1**). Flowers 8-12mm in diameter, bell-shaped but *opening widely*; petals clear white, *style S-shaped*, up to 10mm long, (though 4-6mm long in ssp *maritima*), *distinctly protruding* (**e2**), with expanded disc below stigma. Widespread throughout in fens, woodland and mountain pastures, often on base-rich soils. The commonest subspecies is ssp *rotundifolia*, but ssp *maritima*, which occurs in sand-dune slacks, is distinguished by shorter style, shorter flower stalks (less than 5mm), and 2-5 scales on the flowering stem, rather than 1-2. **Fl** 5-8. **Br** Rare and local, scattered throughout; ssp *maritima* is confined to N Wales and NW England.

F **Norwegian Wintergreen** *Pyrola norvegica* Rather similar to Round-leaved Wintergreen, but differs in that the leaf stalk is shorter than or equal to the blade (**f1**), which is rather leathery in texture; the flowers are usually larger, 10-25mm in diameter, and often pink, though they may be white; the curved style (**f2**) is *not expanded below the stigma*. Locally frequent on dry calcareous mountain slopes in N Scandinavia. **Fl** 6-8. **Br** Absent.

G **Serrated, or Nodding, Wintergreen** *Orthilia secunda* Generally similar in form to the *Pyrola* wintergreens. Leaves ovate to elliptical, 20-40mm long, distinctly toothed, light green, with stalk shorter than blade. Flower spikes differ in being strongly 1-sided, with individual flowers small, 5-6mm in diameter, greenish- white, with straight protruding style. Throughout as far as N Sweden; in coniferous and deciduous woodland, or open mountain habitats. **Fl** 6-8. **Br** Local from Wales and N England northwards, mainly in mountainous areas.

H **One-flowered Wintergreen** *Moneses uniflora* Similar in general appearance to *Pyrola*, but leaves are opposite (not alternate) and *flowers are solitary*. Leaves ovate to almost circular, toothed, stalk shorter than blade. Flowers large, 15-20mm in diameter, opening widely, nodding, solitary and white; style 5-7mm, straight. Widespread throughout, but very local; in old woods, usually coniferous, on acid soils. **Fl** 6-8. **Br** Rare, local and declining, confined to a few Scottish pinewoods, mainly eastern.

I **Umbellate Wintergreen** *Chimaphila umbellata* Low subshrub, with opposite or almost whorled leaves, which are ovate, dark green and leathery. Flowers distinctive, in *umbel-like clusters* on short stem; individual flowers pink, globose, 8-12mm in diameter; style short, not protruding. Local in coniferous woods and damp rocky places in N and E Europe only. Absent from much of W Europe. **Fl** 6-7. **Br** Absent.

J **Yellow Bird's-nest, Dutchman's Pipe** *Monotropa hypopitys* Short herb, totally lacking chlorophyll, living saprophytically on leaf mould. Leaves all scale-like and alternate; whole plant yellow to creamy white, becoming browner with age. Stems erect. Flowers in terminal drooping spike, individually narrowly bell-shaped, 9-14mm long, partially obscured by bracts. Unlikely to be mistaken for anything else, except possibly young Bird's-nest Orchid. Widespread throughout except the far north, though local; in damp coniferous and beechwoods. **Fl** 6-9. **Br** Scattered widely, but very local; usual habitat in beechwoods on chalk in S England, occasionally found in dune slacks.

A E
B C D G
H I J

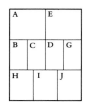

A **Diapensia**
E **Round-leaved Wintergreen**
B **Common Wintergreen**
C **Intermediate Wintergreen**
D **Yellow Wintergreen**
G **Serrated Wintergreen**
H **One-flowered Wintergreen**
I **Umbellate Wintergreen**
J **Yellow Bird's-nest**

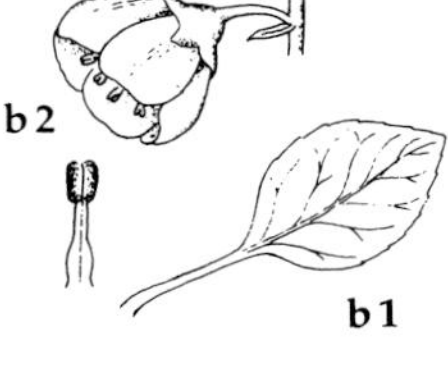

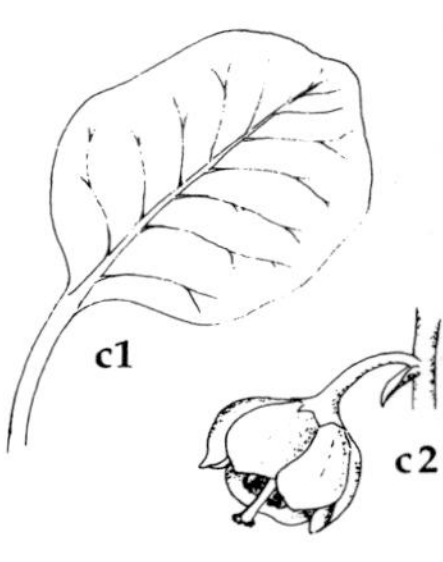

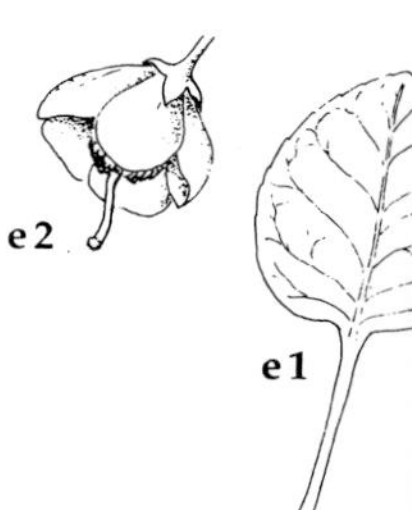

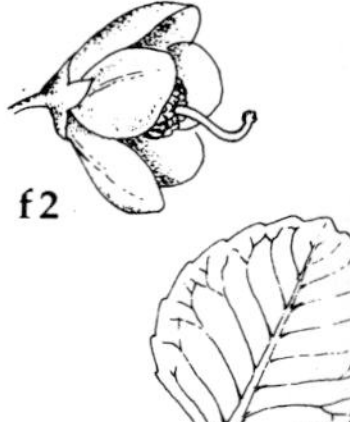

D

E

F

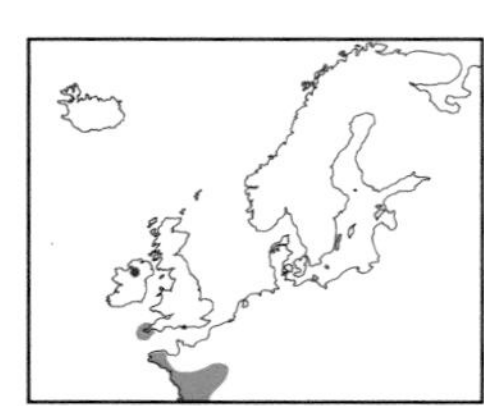

G

H

I

Heather Family Ericaeceae

Shrubby plants, usually low-growing, but including a few trees. Leaves simple, without stipules. Flower parts usually in 4s or 5s, with petals normally joined together, at least partially, often into a tube. Stamens usually twice as many as petals; ovary superior except in *Vaccinium*. Style simple, with an expanded head. A distinctive family, most often to be found in acid and frequently damp environments.

A **Heather, Ling** *Calluna vulgaris* Spreading evergreen undershrub up to 50-60cm. Downy or hairless, but distinctive for its very small (1-2mm) stalkless leaves in 4 tight rows, and its small, pale pink-purple flowers (about 4mm long). Widespread throughout, often dominant, on heaths, moors, dunes, bogs and open woodland, wet or dry but usually acid. **Fl** 7-9. **Br** Widespread and often abundant, especially in the north and west.

B **Cross-leaved Heath** *Erica tetralix* Low, greyish, downy undershrub, shorter (to 30cm), and more erect, than most heathers. Little-branched, and distinctive for its large, (about 7mm long), pale pink bell-flowers in tight 1-sided cluster, and its grey leaves in distinctive separate 4s (occasionally 5s) up the stem. Stamens hidden in corolla. *Fruits downy*. Widespread and locally frequent, always in wet or damp acid areas e.g. wet heaths, bogs. **Fl** 6-9. **Br** Almost throughout, though rare in central and E England.

C **Bell Heather** *Erica cinerea* Low hairless undershrub to 50cm, similar in habit to Cross-leaved Heath, but more spreading and with more flower spikes. Leaves in 3s, in less distinct whorls, dark green and hairless. Reddish-purple flowers, 5-6mm long, in scattered groups, not clustered at the top as in Cross-leaved Heath. Stamens hidden in corolla. Locally common on *drier* acid sites, often dominant. Widespread, but absent from the far north. **Fl** 6-9. **Br** Locally abundant or dominant, commoner in the west.

D **Dorset Heath** *Erica ciliaris* Usually taller than above species to 70cm, often in distinct clumps. Leaves in 3s, 2-3mm long, not downy but with glandular bristles on edges. Flowers large, 8-10mm long, in long, deep pink racemes, tapering towards top. *Fruit hairless*. Damp acidic areas, very local only in SW England, Ireland, and W France. **Fl** 6-9. **Br** Rare and local in England from Dorset westwards, and in W Eire. Hybridises with Cross-leaved Heath.

E **Mackay's Heath** *Erica mackaiana* Similar but with leaves darker green, in 4s, with smaller purplish flowers. **Br** W Eire only.

F **Cornish Heath** *Erica vagans* Bushy, medium-height shrub to 80-90cm. Leaves long, 8-10cm, linear, in 4s or 5s, edges recurved, whole plant hairless. Flowers small, 3-4mm long, on long stalks, pink, lilac or white, with brown anthers protruding, in long leafy racemes, usually with leafy tip. On drier heaths, rare but locally abundant only in SW England, NW Ireland and W France. **Fl** 7-9. **Br** Only in Cornwall and Fermanagh, though very locally abundant.

G **Irish Heath** *Erica erigena* Relatively tall hairless shrub to 2m high. Leaves in 4s, linear, 6-8mm long. Flowers 5-7mm, pale pink-purple, in long, leafy racemes, like Cornish Heath in form. Reddish anthers protruding half-way. Drier parts of bogs, very locally frequent in W Eire and W France only **Fl** Early (2)3-5. **Br** W Eire only, very local.

H *Erica scoparia* Taller than Irish Heath, to 2m with leaves in whorls of 3-4. Flowers in slender racemes, small, greenish-white, with anthers not protruding. Acid rocky places, especially open pinewoods, from N France southwards **Fl** 1-6. **Br** Absent.

I **Spring Heath** *Erica herbacea* Dwarf spreading shrub to 30cm only. Leaves densely set in whorls of 4. Flowers red or pink, in 1-sided racemes, with protruding purple anthers. Stony places and open woods; Germany only. **Fl** 3-6. **Br** Absent.

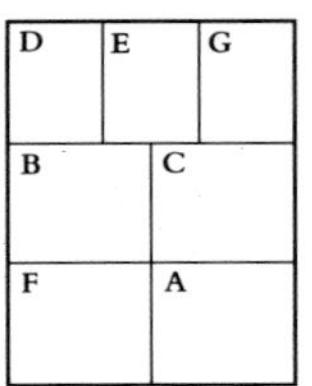

D **Dorset Heath**

E **Mackay's Heath**

G **Irish Heath**

B **Cross-leaved Heath**

C **Bell Heather**

F **Cornish Heath**

A **Heather**

A

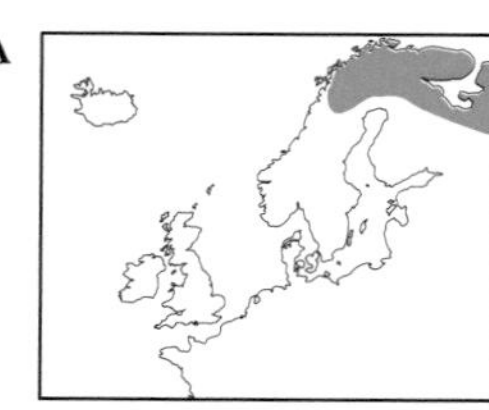

B

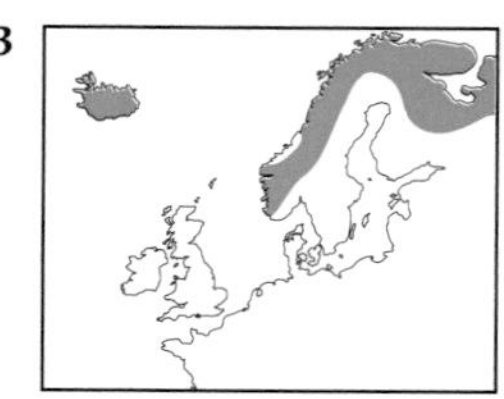

F

G

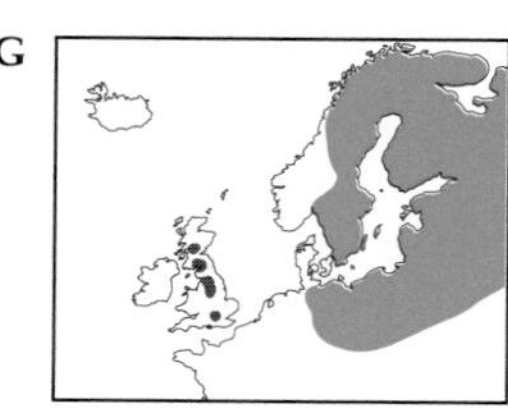

H

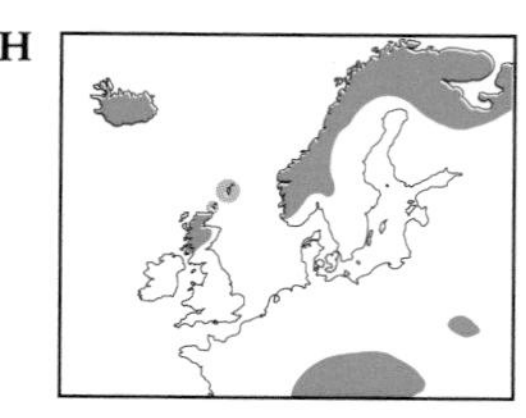

I

J

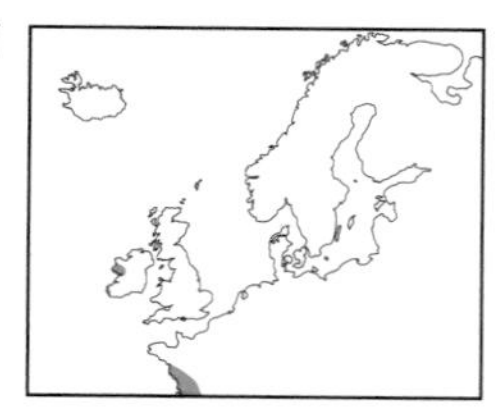

L

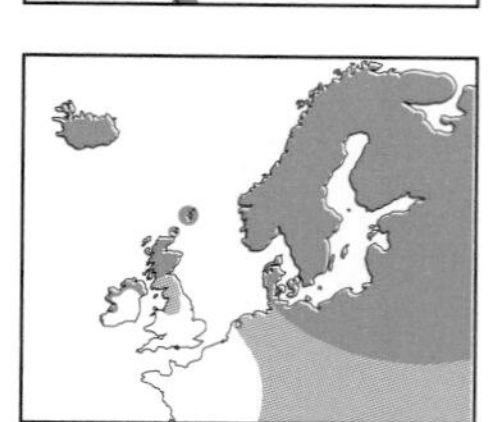

M

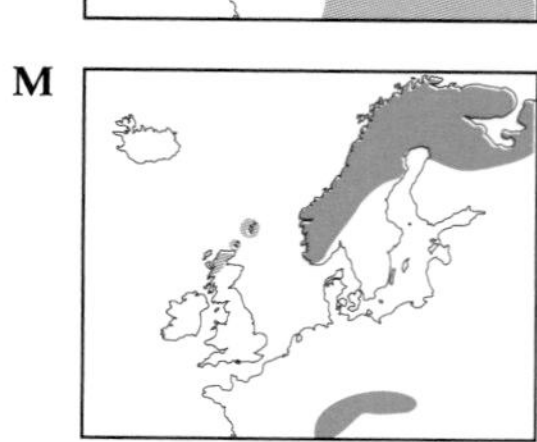

A Cassiope *Cassiope tetragona* Small evergreen dwarf shrub, creeping or ascending. Leaves dark green, scale-like, opposite and appressed to stem. *Flowers produced laterally*, solitary on red downy stalks, creamy white or pinkish, bell-shaped, pendulous and 5-8mm long. On dry, stony or sandy heaths and tundra, usually slightly calcareous, in Arctic Europe only. **Fl** 5-7. **Br** Absent.

B Matted Cassiope *Cassiope hypnoides* Prostrate, very dwarf subshrub forming mats. Leaves scale-like, alternate, not closely appressed to stem. *Flowers terminal on thin stalks*, white or tinged pink, bell-shaped and 4-5mm long, with crimson sepals. In mountains, by streams, in snow-hollows and other damp habitats, in Scandinavia and Iceland only. **Fl** 6-8. **Br** Absent.

C Rhododendron *Rhododendron ponticum* Erect, strong-growing, evergreen shrub, with spreading branches. Leaves elliptical, untoothed, leathery, dark shiny green above and paler below, 10-25cm long. Flowers in clusters, bell-shaped, 4-6cm long, violet-purple, pinkish or mauve. Introduced from E Europe/W Asia, but now widely naturalised on acid and damp soil, through much of W Europe. **Fl** 5-7. **Br** Widely naturalised, locally abundant, often becoming a problem through its invasive nature.

D Alpenrose *Rhododendron ferrugineum* Evergreen branching shrub to 1.2m high, with reddish scaly twigs. Leaves oblong to elliptical, dark shiny green above, reddish scaly below, with rolled-under margins. Flowers bell-shaped, pink to reddish, in clusters of 6-10. On open or lightly wooded mountain slopes, usually avoiding lime-rich soils, from S Germany and E France southwards. **Fl** 5-8. **Br** Absent.

E Hairy Alpenrose *Rhododendron hirsutum* Similar to Alpenrose, but lower (to 50cm), less scaly, with leaves hairy on edges, barely in-rolled. Flowers bright pink. Similar habitats, but usually on lime-rich soils in central and E Alps.

F Lapland Rhododendron *Rhododendron lapponicum* Creeping dwarf evergreen shrub, up to 60cm high, much-branched and forming mats. Leaves small, to 20mm, dark green above, rusty with scales below, with margins rolled under. Flowers in small clusters, violet-purple, bell-shaped, to 15mm long. In dry mountain habitats, on calcareous soils, in Scandinavia only. **Fl** 5-6. **Br** Absent. Occasionally cultivated.

G Labrador Tea *Ledum palustre* Evergreen, spreading or erect, small shrub, commonly to 1m, occasionally taller. Young twigs covered with rusty down. Leaves linear to oblong, 20-50mm long, rusty below with margins in-rolled. Flowers in umbels, creamy white, 10-15mm long, numerous, upright in flower, then reflexed in fruit. Widespread through N Europe from Germany northwards in bogs, damp woodland and heaths. **Fl** 5-7. **Br** Absent.

H Trailing, or Mountain, Azalea *Loiseleuria procumbens* Very small, prostrate, mat-forming, evergreen dwarf shrub. Leaves opposite, oblong, only 5-6mm long, not adpressed to stem, with margins rolled under. Flowers very small, about 5mm in diameter, pale to dark pink, bell-shaped, but deeply lobed – like a miniature rhododendron; petals soon falling, solitary or in small terminal clusters. Widespread and often common in mountain regions, on dry, stony or peaty acid situations. **Fl** 5-7. **Br** Local in the Scottish Highlands and northwards; most frequent in the Cairngorms.

I Blue, or Mountain, Heath *Phyllodoce caerulea* Dwarf, evergreen heather-like shrub, spreading, but producing erect flowering shots. Leaves small, to 12mm long, linear, rolled, alternate and leathery dark green. Flowers terminal on long reddish sticky stems, in clusters of most commonly 2; bell-shaped, 7-12mm long, pendulous and pink to purple. Stamens and style not protruding. Locally frequent on dry, usually acidic mountains and moorlands, in Iceland and Scandinavia north of S Norway, and in Scotland. **Fl** 6-8. **Br** Very rare, in a few Scottish Highland localities.

J St Dabeoc's Heath *Daboecia cantabrica* Dwarf evergreen heath-like straggling shrub, reaching 70cm if supported. Leaves variable in size, to 14mm, ovate to lanceolate, dark green and hairy above, white below, with rolled-under margins. Flowers in loose terminal spikes, urn-shaped, 10-14mm long, with 4 petal lobes, reddish-purple and hairy. Differs from *Erica* in the broader leaves, and the corolla that falls before the fruit ripens. Local on dry heaths and in open woods on acid soil, in W France and Ireland only. **Fl** 6-10. **Br** Locally common in central W Ireland.

K Strawberry Tree *Arbutus unedo* Evergreen shrub or small tree to 12m at most, usually less. Bark red-brown and peeling. Leaves roughly elliptical, tapering at both ends, 4-10cm long, usually toothed, leathery, shiny dark green above and paler below. Flowers white, often tinged pinkish or greenish, urn-shaped, 8-10mm long, in drooping clusters. Fruit a spherical berry to 20mm in diameter, covered with warts, ripening through yellow to deep red. Fruit and flower both present at the same time, because of long ripening process. Local in woods and rocky places in SW Ireland and W France. Also widely planted. **Fl** 9-12. **Br** Native only in SW Ireland, where it is locally abundant. Widely planted elsewhere, occasionally naturalised.

L Bearberry *Arctostaphylos uva-ursi* Prostrate mat-forming evergreen shrub producing long creeping shoots. Leaves oval, broadest towards tip, untoothed, leathery, dark shiny green above, paler below, with conspicuous net-veining and flat margins (I). Flowers in dense terminal clusters, individually urn-shaped, with 5 short spreading lobes, white to pink, 5-6mm long. Berry shiny red, 7-9mm in diameter. (Cowberry, *see* page 184, is similar, but distinguishable by less creeping habit, leaves not so net-veined, with in-rolled margins and more open flowers). Widespread and frequent in much of N Europe, especially in N and mountain areas; on heaths, moors and open woods. **Fl** 5-8. **Br** Rare in N England, commoner in Scotland.

M Alpine Bearberry *Arctostaphylos alpinus* Similar to Bearberry, but less far-creeping, *leaves toothed*, not leathery, withering by autumn (though persisting); berry often larger, to 10mm in diameter, *black* when ripe. Widespread in Scandinavia and mountains further south, on acid moors and tundra. **Fl** 5-7. **Br** Very local in N Scotland.

A	B	C
D	G	
H	I	J
K	L	M

A Cassiope

B Matted Cassiope

C Rhododendron

D Alpenrose

G Labrador Tea

H Trailing Azalea

I Blue Heath

J St Dabeoc's Heath

K Strawberry Tree

L Bearberry

M Alpine Bearberry

I

A
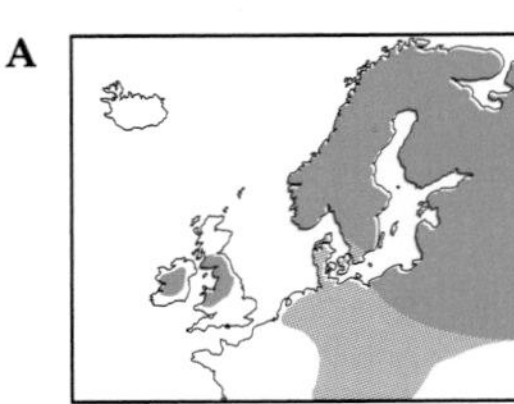

C
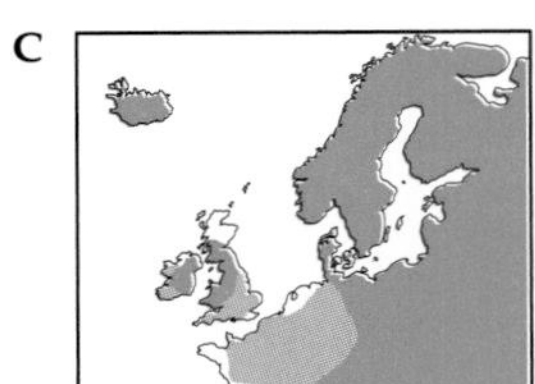

E
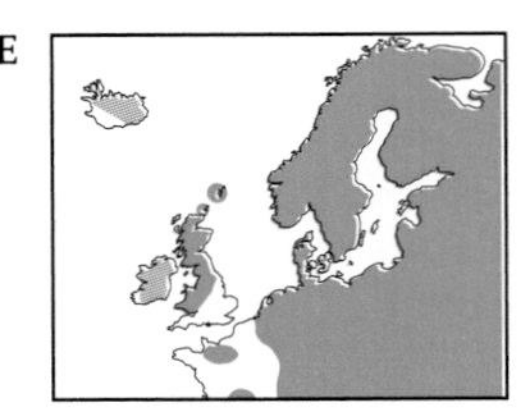

F
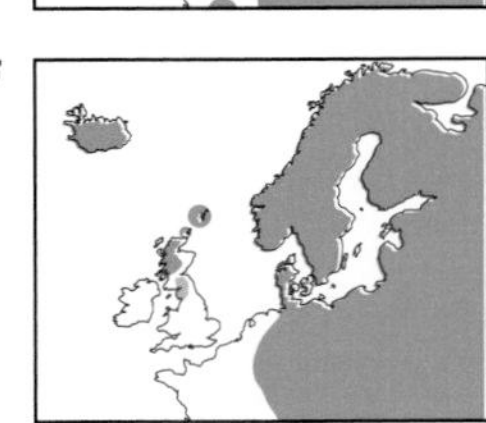

A Bog Rosemary *Andromeda polifolia* Low evergreen, hairless, little-branched shrub, reaching 30 (rarely 50) cm high. Leaves alternate, linear to oblong, pointed, untoothed, 10-30mm long, bluish green above, almost-white below, with rolled-under margins. Flowers in small terminal clusters, on thin stalks, rosy pink, fading paler, urn-shaped and 8-10mm long. Widespread in acidic bogs and similar habitats; absent from many lowland areas and confined to mountains in the south. **Fl** 5-9. **Br** Local, from mid-Wales and N England north to central Scotland; also central Ireland.

B *Chamaedaphne calyculata* Evergreen shrub, with alternate elliptical leaves which are scaly brown below. Flowers white, pendulous, in leafy racemes. In marshes and wet woods in NE Europe, south to Poland. **Fl** 6-7. **Br** Absent.

C Cranberry *Vaccinium oxycoccos* Distinctive tiny creeping evergreen shrub, with alternate widely spaced oblong leaves on long thread-like stems. Leaves dark green above, waxy greyish below, with in-rolled margins. Flowers (1-2) on long downy stalks; petals rosy pink, with 4 strongly reflexed lobes, exposing central cluster of stamens. Nothing else resembles it except Small Cranberry. Fruit globose, red or brownish. Throughout, except the extreme north, in wet peatbogs. **Fl** 5-7. **Br** Widespread but local, and absent from many lowland areas.

D Small Cranberry *Vaccinium microcarpum* Differs from Cranberry in its more triangular but narrower leaves (less than 2.5mm long), and in its hairless flower stalks. Rare in bogs in Scandinavia, Germany, Iceland and Scotland. **Br** Rare in NE Scotland only.

E Cowberry *Vaccinium vitis-idaea* Prostrate or scrambling evergreen dwarf shrub, with some erect stems. Leaves elliptical-oblong, leathery, untoothed, dark green above, paler dotted with glands below, with margins down-turned (**e**). Flowers in short dense clusters, bell-shaped, 5-8mm long, white or pink, with 4 or 5 lobes and with a protruding style. Berry globose, shiny red, to 10mm in diameter. Most easily confused with Bearberry (*see* page 182). Widespread on moors, heaths, montane pastures and in coniferous woods, on acid soils. **Fl** 6-8. **Br** In hilly or mountain areas, from N England northwards.

e

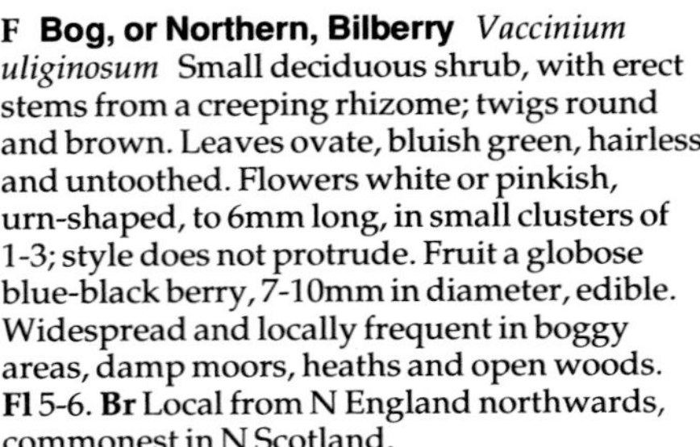

F Bog, or Northern, Bilberry *Vaccinium uliginosum* Small deciduous shrub, with erect stems from a creeping rhizome; twigs round and brown. Leaves ovate, bluish green, hairless and untoothed. Flowers white or pinkish, urn-shaped, to 6mm long, in small clusters of 1-3; style does not protrude. Fruit a globose blue-black berry, 7-10mm in diameter, edible. Widespread and locally frequent in boggy areas, damp moors, heaths and open woods. **Fl** 5-6. **Br** Local from N England northwards, commonest in N Scotland.

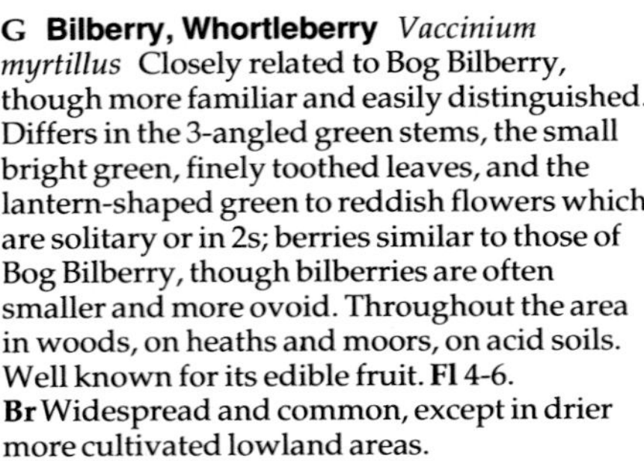

G Bilberry, Whortleberry *Vaccinium myrtillus* Closely related to Bog Bilberry, though more familiar and easily distinguished. Differs in the 3-angled green stems, the small bright green, finely toothed leaves, and the lantern-shaped green to reddish flowers which are solitary or in 2s; berries similar to those of Bog Bilberry, though bilberries are often smaller and more ovoid. Throughout the area in woods, on heaths and moors, on acid soils. Well known for its edible fruit. **Fl** 4-6. **Br** Widespread and common, except in drier more cultivated lowland areas.

Crowberry Family Empetraceae

A small family of evergreen heath-like shrubs. Leaves alternate, with flowers in leaf axils. 4-6 perianth segments in 2 similar whorls; 3 stamens.

H Crowberry *Empetrum nigrum* Prostrate heather-like, mat-forming shrub. Stems reddish when young. Leaves linear, crowded, to 7mm long, shiny green, with rolled margins. Flowers tiny at base of leaves, with 6 separate pinkish petals; male and female flowers separate. Fruit a black globose berry, 5-7mm in diameter, and much more visible than flowers. In acid, often damp, habitats including heaths, moors, tundra, and open woods. **Fl** 5-6. **Br** Frequent in N Britain, with outposts on southern uplands. Ssp *hermaphroditum* (sometimes treated as a separate species) has hermaphrodite flowers with stamens persisting on the fruit, and greenish stems, not rooting; slightly broader leaves, grooved beneath. Generally more northern, and the commonest subspecies in the Arctic. Very local in Scottish mountains

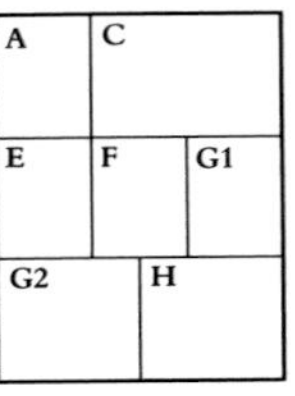

A Bog Rosemary
C Cranberry
E Cowberry
F Bog Bilberry in fruit
G 1 Bilberry
G 2 Bilberry in fruit
H Crowberry in fruit

A
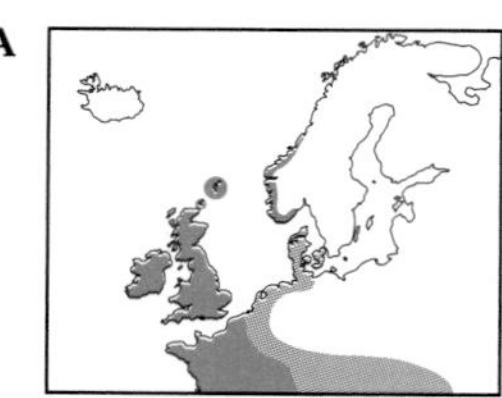
B
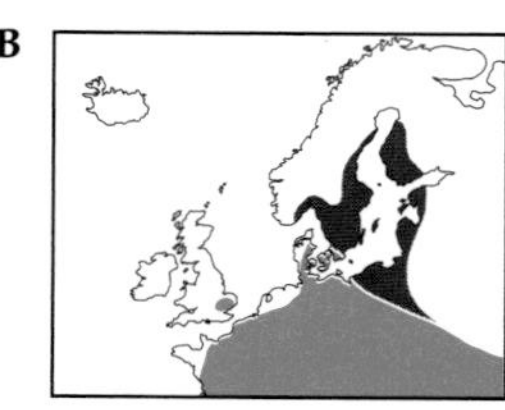
F
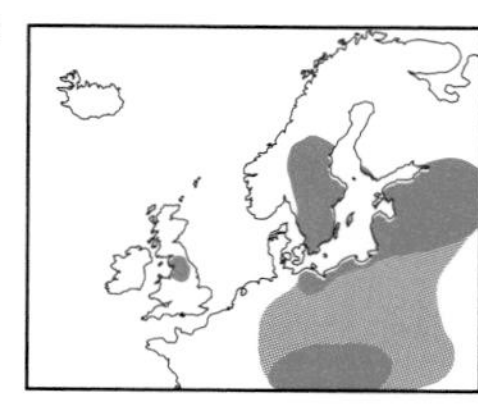
K
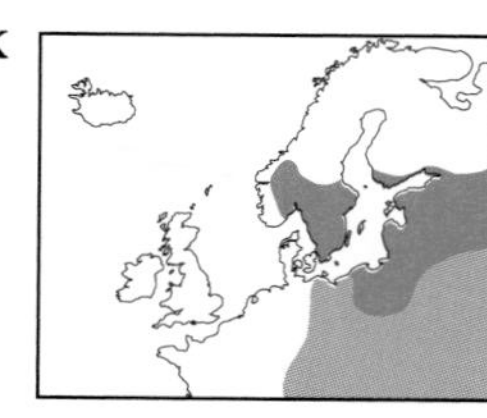
L
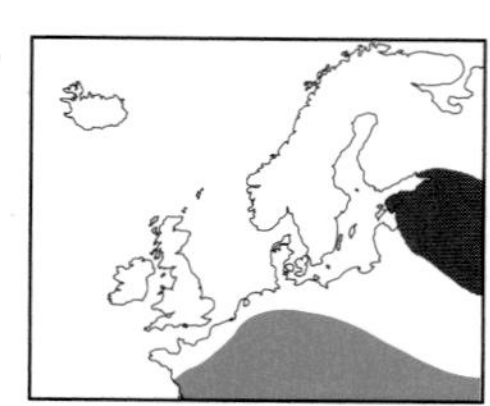
N
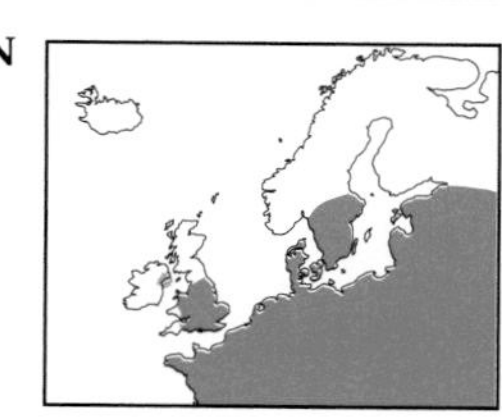
O
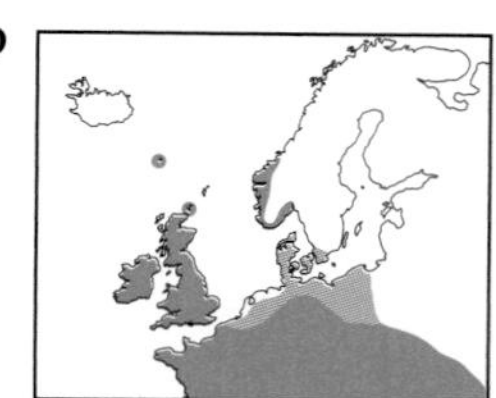

Primrose Family Primulaceae

Herbs with leaves without stipules, often in a basal rosette, usually simple. Flowers regular, usually with 5 parts, with the petals often joined at the base to form a tube.

A Primrose *Primula vulgaris* Familiar low herbaceous perennial, with a rosette of wrinkled, hairy, spoon-shaped leaves, to 15cm long, unstalked but tapering gradually to the base (**a**). *Flowers solitary* on long hairy stalks from rosette centre, often numerous; pale yellow, often with orange markings in centre, to 4cm in diameter, 5-lobed. Widespread, often abundant in damp shady places, or in pastures; absent over much of Scandinavia. **Fl** 2-5, normally. **Br** Widespread and common in many areas, least frequent in the south-east.

B Oxlip *Primula elatior* Similar plant to Primrose. *Leaves abruptly contracted* into long winged stalk, about as long as blade, less wrinkled than Primrose or Cowslip (**b**). Flowers in a 1-sided drooping umbel, with 10-20 pale yellow flowers, 15-25mm in diameter, very like smaller primroses; throat of corolla tube open, without folds. Widespread but local as far north as S Scandinavia, in woods, meadows and streamsides, usually on heavy soil. In mountain pastures further south. **Fl** 3-5. **Br** Locally common in a small area of E Anglia and adjacent counties, mainly in coppiced woodland.

C Cowslip *Primula veris* Rather similar to Oxlip, but leaves more wrinkled (**c**). Flowers 10-30 in an umbel, less strongly 1-sided than Oxlip; *flowers deeper yellow-orange*, with orange markings in centre, 8-15mm in diameter, with distinct folds at the mouth of the tube. Widespread and locally common throughout, except in the far north, in meadows, pastures and open woods, usually on drier sites than preceding 2 species. **Fl** 4-5. **Br** Widespread, sometimes frequent, as far north as central Scotland, usually on lime-rich soils. Decreasing through agricultural changes.

D False Oxlip *Primula veris × vulgaris* Common, naturally occurring hybrid, superficially similar to Oxlip, but differing in the less 1-sided umbels, and the folds in the throat of the corolla, though it is variable. Occurs where parents both grow. **Fl** 4-5. **Br** Widespread but local.

E Bear's-ear *Primula auricula* Small perennial, with a rosette of mealy leaves, and a leafless stem to 16cm. Leaves spoon-shaped, toothed. Flowers yellow, with a white centre, in terminal clusters of 2-20. In damp, rocky and grassy places, usually at high altitudes, from S Germany southwards. **Fl** 5-7. **Br** Absent.

F Bird's-eye Primrose *Primula farinosa* Small perennial herb, with rosette of spoon-shaped leaves, mealy white below and shallowly toothed. Flowers in umbels on long mealy stalks, pale pink to rosy violet, 10-16mm across, with yellow 'eye', and distinct gaps between petals. Calyx mealy, often tinged dark purple. In fens and damp meadows, usually in mountain areas, most often on base-rich soil, from S Sweden southwards. **Fl** 5-7. **Br** Local on calcareous soils in N England only.

G Scottish Primrose *Primula scotica* Similar to Bird's-eye Primrose, differing in untoothed leaves, widest at middle. Flowers smaller, 5-8mm across, purplish with large yellow eye, on shorter stalks, petals broader, without gaps. In damp pastures and dunes near the sea; N Scotland only. **Fl** Mainly 5-6, some 7-9. **Br** As above.

H *Primula scandinavica* Very similar to Scottish Primrose, but taller, with more flowers, and stigma globose, not 5-lobed, as in Scottish Primrose. Calcareous mountain areas in N Scandinavia only. **Fl** 6-8. **Br** Absent.

I *Primula stricta* Differs in having leaves that are not mealy, and violet to lilac flowers. Meadows and pastures, often coastal, in N Scandinavia and Iceland. **Fl** 6-8. **Br** Absent.

J *Primula nutans* Like *P. stricta*, but with larger flowers (10-20mm in diameter, compared to 4-9mm) and fleshy leaves. In coastal meadows and upper salt-marshes in far N Scandinavia. **Fl** 6-8. **Br** Absent.

K Northern Androsace, Rock-jasmine *Androsace septentrionalis* Small annual herb with a rosette of toothed, oblong-lanceolate leaves; flowers in umbels of 5-30 on long stalks, often several per rosette; petals white to pale pink, about 5mm long, much longer than sepals. Dry, often sandy, places from Scandinavia southwards, but mainly in mountains further south. **Fl** 5-7. **Br** Absent.

L Annual Androsace *Androsace maxima* Has tiny pink or white flowers, dwarfed by much larger sepals. In dry, open, mainly calcareous sites, from central Germany and France southwards. **Fl** 4-6. **Br** Absent.

M Elongate Androsace *Androsace elongata* Similar to Northern Androsace, but barely hairy, and calyx slightly longer than small white petals. Central Germany southwards. **Fl** 5-7. **Br** Absent.

N Water Violet *Hottonia palustris* Aquatic perennial herb, with pale green, submerged and floating leaves. Leaves finely divided, pinnate or bipinnate, with narrow flattened leaflets. Flowers emergent on erect robust hairless stems, with several whorls of flowers, individually pale lilac with central yellow eye, and 5 petals, 20-25mm across. Widespread and not uncommon as far north as S Sweden in shallow, still or slow-flowing fresh water. **Fl** 5-7. **Br** Local, mainly in S and E England; very rare in Wales; absent from Scotland.

O Yellow Pimpernel *Lysimachia nemorum* Evergreen prostrate perennial hairless herb, reaching 45cm long. Leaves oval, 20-30mm long, *pointed*, short-stalked, and in opposite pairs. Flowers solitary from leaf axils on *slender stalks, longer than leaves*, bright yellow, star-like, 10-15mm in diameter, with 5 petals; calyx very narrow, bristle-like. Widespread as far north as S Sweden; in damp and shady places. **Fl** 5-8. **Br** Widespread, often common almost throughout; rarest in dry and highly cultivated areas.

P Creeping Jenny *Lysimachia nummularia* Creeping hairless perennial, rooting at the nodes. Similar to Yellow Pimpernel, but leaves 10-20mm long, wider to almost round, *blunt* at tip; flowers larger, 15-25mm in diameter, on *stout stalks, shorter than leaves*, solitary or in pairs; calyx teeth ovate not bristle-like. Widespread and locally common in damp grassy habitats, throughout except the extreme north. **Fl** 6-8. **Br** Locally common through most of England, but rare to the north and south-west.

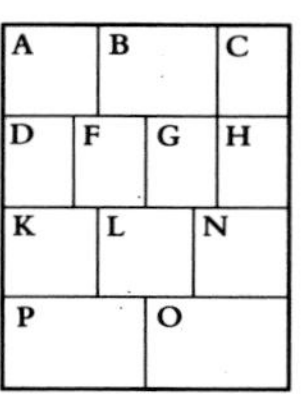

A Primrose
B Oxlip
C Cowslip
D False Oxlip
F Bird's-eye Primrose
G Scottish Primrose
H *Primula scandinavia*
K Northern Androsace
L Annual Androsace
N Water Violet
P Creeping Jenny – the circular, toothed leaves are Marsh Pennywort
O Yellow Pimpernel

a

b

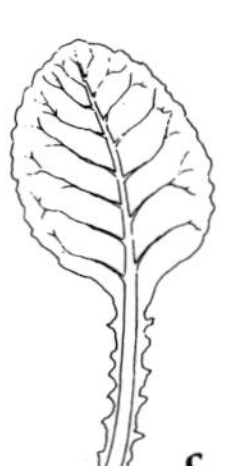
c

B

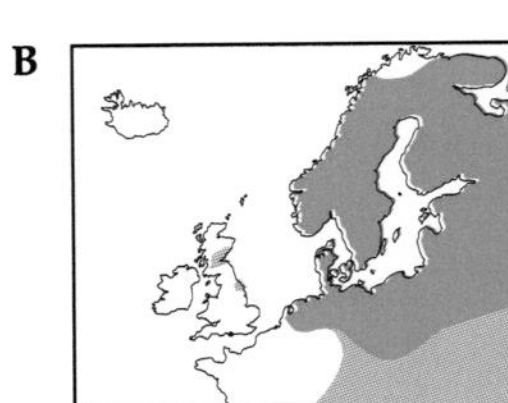

C

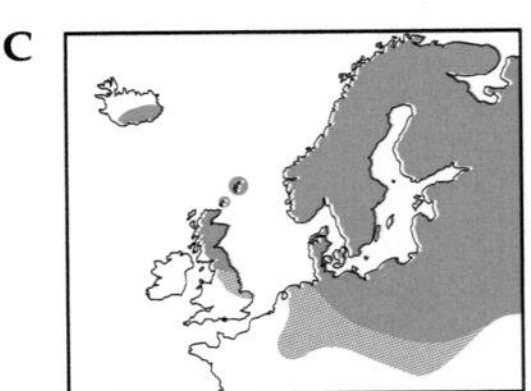

G

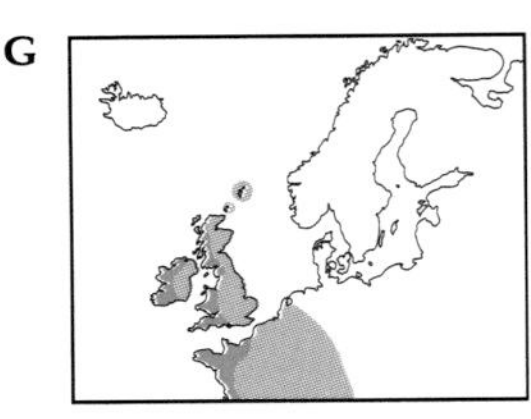

J

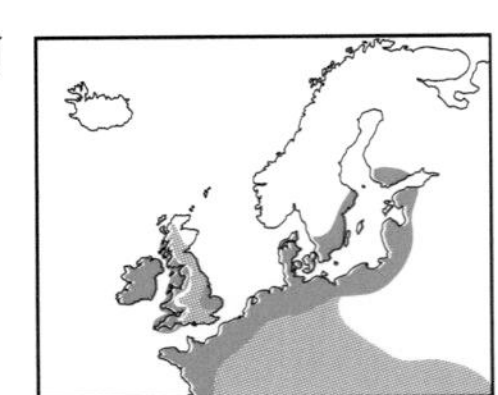

A Yellow Loosestrife *Lysimachia vulgaris* Medium or tall, softly hairy perennial, erect from creeping stems and reaching 1m or more. Leaves ovate, in pairs or whorls of 3-4, up to 10cm long, dotted with glands. Inflorescence forms a terminal panicle, made up of clusters of flowers from the upper nodes; flowers bright yellow, starry, 5-pointed, 15-20mm in diameter; sepals with red-orange margins. Widespread and frequent virtually throughout in wet habitats – fens, carr woodland, meadows and streamsides. **Fl** 6-8. **Br** Locally common through most of Britain except the far north.

B Tufted Loosestrife *Lysimachia thyrsiflora* Usually hairless perennial, with erect stems to 70cm from a creeping stem. Leaves in opposite pairs, unstalked, lanceolate, with numerous black glands. Flowers in dense, stalked clusters from nodes at centre of stem; individual flowers small, 5mm across, with 7 petals, dark yellow, stamens protruding. Wet habitats, often with standing water, from central France northwards, commonest in the north. **Fl** 6-7. **Br** Rare and local only in N England and central Scotland.

C Chickweed Wintergreen *Trientalis europaea* Low perennial, with slender stalks to 25cm arising from creeping rootstock. Leaves mostly in a whorl near top of stem, lanceolate to ovate, with a few small leaves below. Flowers arise from rosette, 1-2 together, on long stalks, starry, white, 12-18mm in diameter and with 5-9 (usually 7) petal lobes. A distinctive combination. Fruit a globular capsule. Widespread in N Europe in coniferous woods and mossy habitats; commoner in the north, confined to mountains in the south. **Fl** 6-7. **Br** Mainly in Scotland, where it is locally common, but extending into N England; rare in E Anglia.

D *Asterolinon linum-stellatum* Small, erect branched glabrous annual. Leaves lanceolate, to 7mm long. Flowers white, tiny (maximum 2mm), 5-parted, solitary in axils of upper leaves. Dry open places, NW France southwards. **Fl** 5-7. **Br** Absent.

E Sea Milkwort *Glaux maritima* Low, fleshy, partly procumbent herb, rooting at some nodes, with erect stems to 20cm. Leaves opposite below, alternate above, fleshy, elliptical, unstalked, up to 12mm long. Flowers on erect shoots, solitary at bases of leaves, pink or white, 5mm in diameter, without petals. Frequent in damp coastal habitats throughout N Europe and occasionally inland on saline soils. **Fl** 5-8. **Br** Common all around the coast; also inland in W Midlands (rare).

F Chaffweed *Anagallis minima* Tiny, more or less erect, hairless annual, 20-70mm tall. Leaves up to 5mm long, ovate, alternate. Flowers solitary in axils of upper leaves, tiny, white or pink, 5-parted. Fruit like tiny apples, 1-2mm in diameter. One of the smallest plants in N Europe. Easily overlooked. Throughout on damp sandy habitats, except in the extreme north. **Fl** 6-7. **Br** Local in coastal habitats, more widespread in S England.

G Bog Pimpernel *Anagallis tenella* Low, hairless, creeping, rooting perennial, with slender stems up to 15cm long. Leaves in pairs, elliptical to almost round, short-stalked, to 9mm long. Flowers pink (white, finely veined red), funnel-shaped, 5-lobed, to 10mm long, on long slender stalks. Petals 2-3 times longer than calyx. Numerous overlapping stems can often produce a dense mass of flowers. On damp open ground, especially near the coast, usually on acid soil. Frequent in W Europe, not in the north, and becoming rarer eastwards. **Fl** 6-8. **Br** Widespread, commonest in the west, rarest in the north and east; local or absent in many areas.

H Scarlet Pimpernel *Anagallis arvensis* Prostrate to ascending, low, hairless annual (occasionally biennial or longer-lived), with squarish stems. Leaves opposite in pairs, occasionally whorls, ovate, pointed, unstalked, up to 20mm long, both surfaces covered with minute glands (**h**). Flowers scarlet or orange-pink, occasionally blue or pink, borne singly on long stalks from leaf axils; calyx teeth narrow, almost as long as petals; corolla flat (opening most widely in sunshine), 10-15mm, petals fringed with hairs. Throughout, except Iceland, in bare sites, such as cultivated ground, sand-dunes, etc. **Fl** 5-10. **Br** Throughout, though rare and mainly coastal in Scotland.

I Blue Pimpernel *Anagallis foemina* Very similar to Scarlet Pimpernel (and formerly considered a subspecies of it), but differs in that leaves are narrower, lanceolate (**i**); flowers always blue, petals concealed by calyx in bud (visible in Scarlet Pimpernel), marginal hairs on petals sparse or absent. Throughout, except the far north, in similar habitats, most usually on chalky soils. **Fl** 6- 8. **Br** Widespread, but local, commoner in the south.

J Brookweed *Samolus valerandi* Perennial glabrous herb with a basal rosette and erect, flowering stems. Leaves spoon-shaped, rather shiny, short-stalked in rosette, becoming stalkless and alternate up stems. Flowers small, cup-shaped, 2-3mm across, white, 5-petalled, borne in long lax raceme; calyx fused into hemisphere with ovary, with 5 small free teeth. Damp, flushed habitats, most frequently saline or calcareous, usually open, occasionally shaded. Widespread as far north as S Finland. **Fl** 6-8. **Br** Local, but widespread; mainly coastal, except in E Anglia.

K Alpine Snowbell *Soldanella alpina* Distinctive creeping herb to 25cm. Leaves all basal, evergreen, leathery, long-stalked and kidney-shaped, to 4cm wide. Flowers bell-shaped with fringed edges, blue-violet, in terminal clusters of 2-4. Wet pastures and rocks in mountains, often flowering as the snow melts, from SW Germany southwards. **Fl** 4-8. **Br** Absent.

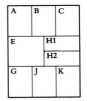

A	B	C
E	H1 / H2	
G	J	K

A Yellow Loosestrife

B Tufted Loosestrife

C Chickweed Wintergreen

E Sea Milkwort

H 1 Scarlet Pimpernel

H 2 Scarlet Pimpernel blue form

G Bog Pimpernel

J Brookweed

K Alpine Snowbell

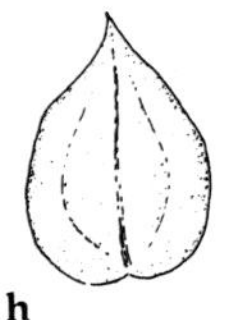

h

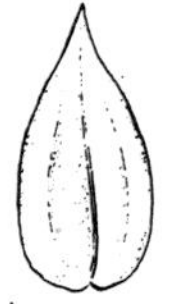

i

A

C

K

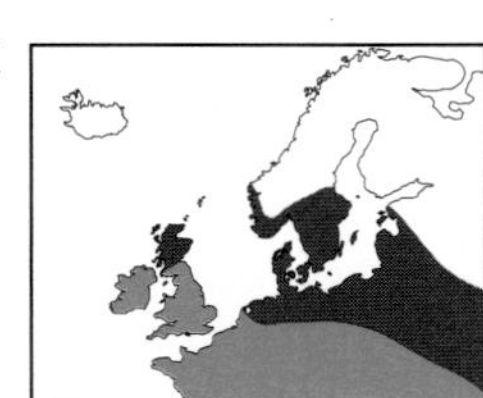

Sea-lavender Family
Plumbaginaceae

Perennial herbs, with basal rosettes of leaves. Flowers 5-parted, in tight heads or loose branched inflorescences.

A **Thrift** *Armeria maritima* Low, cushion-forming perennial, becoming woody at base. Leaves linear or thinly spoon-shaped, flattened, dark green, to 10cm long, 1-veined and in loose rosettes. Inflorescences borne on tall leafless slightly hairy stalks, 5-30cm long; beneath the globular head of flowers is a papery, brown bract, extending 20-30mm down stem; flowers pink or white, fragrant, 8-9mm in diameter. Throughout; mainly in coastal habitats, less frequent in mountains. **Fl** 4-10, mainly 5-6. **Br** Common around the coasts, uncommon on mountains in N England and Scotland.
A highly variable plant, for which a number of subspecies are recognised:
Ssp *elongata* is taller, with pale pink flowers, and leaves with shortly hairy edges. On dry grassland and sandy heaths; in Lincolnshire, and scattered localities in N Europe.
Ssp *halleri* has smaller flower heads (10-15mm in diameter), bright pink to red. In pastures and dry areas, especially on serpentine soils; in Holland, Denmark and Germany.

B **Jersey Thrift** *Armeria alliacea* Similar to Thrift, but leaves fewer, wider, 3- to 7-veined; calyx teeth spine-like; flowers often paler, on taller stems. Dry grassland, mainly in mountains, occasionally coastal. **Br** Dunes in Jersey.

SEA-LAVENDERS *Limonium* This is a difficult group, with many superficially similar species, distinguishable only on close examination. All are broadly similar to Common Sea-lavender, differing in the points described.

C **Common Sea-lavender** *Limonium vulgare* Short to medium, hairless perennial with a woody rootstock and rosette of ascending leaves. Leaves elliptical to spoon-shaped, 10-15cm long, with stalk from as long as to half the length of blade, veins pinnately branched, tip of leaf with tiny spine. Inflorescence branched only above the middle, up to 40cm tall (usually less), with dense, arching spikes of flowers in small clusters; each cluster has green bracts, with outer one rounded on back. Flowers small, 6-8mm, reddish to purple-blue; calyx papery, pale lilac, with 5 sharp teeth and 5 smaller teeth between. In coastal salt-marshes; from S Sweden southwards, locally frequent. **Fl** 7-8. **Br** Widespread, common in the south, rare in the north.

D **Lax-flowered Sea-lavender** *Limonium humile* Similar, but leaves narrower; inflorescence branches first below middle; flower clusters more spread out; outer green bracts ridged not rounded on back. Similar habitats and distribution. **Fl** 7-8. **Br** Local northwards to S Scotland.

E **Matted Sea-lavender** *Limonium bellidifolium* Short plant, with spoon-shaped 3-veined leaves that wither by flowering. Inflorescence spreading to prostrate, with numerous non-flowering branches below; outer bracts of flower clusters white and papery. Sandy, upper parts of salt-marshes. **Fl** 7-8. **Br** Local in Norfolk and Lincolnshire only.

F **Rock Sea-lavender** *Limonium binervosum* Low plant to 30cm, hairless. Leaves 3-veined (occasionally only 1 visible), spoon-shaped with winged stalk. Inflorescence branches low down, but spreads little, with no sterile shoots; flower clusters do not overlap. On sea-cliffs, shingle and drier salt-marshes; in Britain and W France, commoner towards the south. **Br** Local in the south, extending northwards to S Scotland.

G *Limonium recurvum* and *Limonium transwallianum* Highly local similar species. Similar to Rock Sea-Lavender but fewer clusters very densely set along branches. Leaves spoon-shaped and blunt in *L. recurvum*; leaves lanceolate and mucronate in *L. transwallianum*. **Br** The former is found at Portland, Dorset, and the latter in Pembrokeshire and W Ireland.

H *Limonium paradoxum* Has rounded heads with very short side-branches, and short 1-veined leaves. **Br** Found only in Pembrokeshire and NW Ireland.

I **Jersey, or Alderney, Sea-lavender** *Limonium auriculae-ursifolium* A robust plant, more like Common Sea-lavender in stature, but leaves broad, spoon-shaped, *3- to 7-veined, without pinnate veining*, grey-green; stalk broadly winged. Inflorescence without non-flowering shoots; inner flower cluster bracts have bright red, papery margins. Very local on coastal rocks in Channel Islands, and W France. **Br** Alderney and Jersey only.

Olive Family Oleaceae

Trees or shrubs, with leaves usually opposite. Flowers 4-parted, usually in branched inflorescences. Stamens usually 2, ovary superior.

J **Ash** *Fraxinus excelsior* Familiar deciduous tree up to 25m, occasionally more. Bark smooth and greyish at first, becoming fissured on older branches. Buds large and matt black. Leaves opposite, pinnate with 7-13 ovate toothed leaflets. Flowers male, female or mixed, appearing before leaves in clusters, with tufts of purplish stamens; petals and sepals absent. Fruit familiar as 'keys', green, turning brown, 3-5cm long. Widespread and common throughout, except in the extreme north; in woods, scrub and hedgerows, mainly on calcareous soil. **Fl** 4-5. **Br** Common throughout.

K **Privet** *Ligustrum vulgare* A deciduous or semi-evergreen shrub to 5m tall, densely branched. Leaves opposite, untoothed, lanceolate, 30-60mm long, thin. Flowers white or creamy, 4-5mm in diameter, in dense pyramidal clusters, fragrant. Fruit globose, 6-8mm, becoming shiny black when ripe, poisonous. Widespread and common in lowland areas as far north as SW Sweden; often on calcareous soils. Formerly used widely for hedging. **Fl** 6-7. **Br** Common northwards to Co. Durham, naturalised further north.

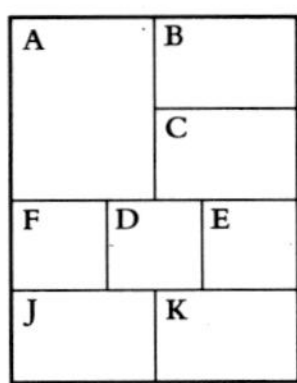

A **Thrift**
B **Jersey Thrift**
C **Common Sea-lavender**
F **Rock Sea-lavender**
D **Lax-flowered Sea-lavender**
E **Matted Sea-lavender**
J **Ash**
K **Privet**

A
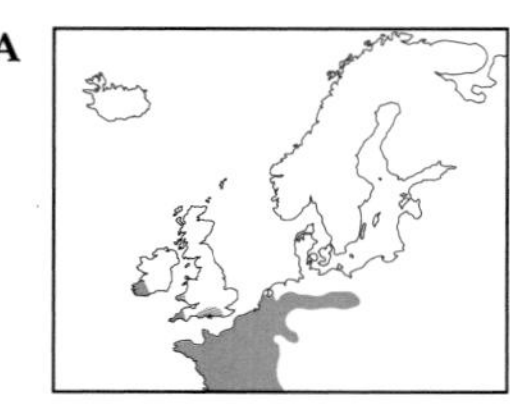
C
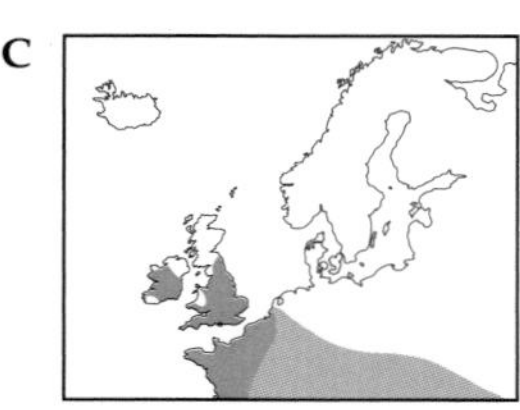
F
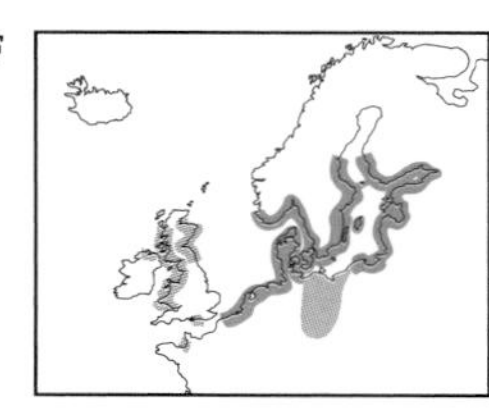
K
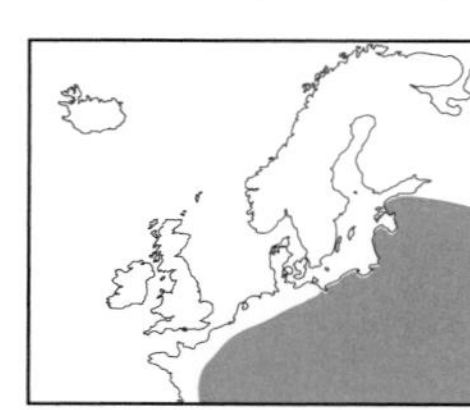
L
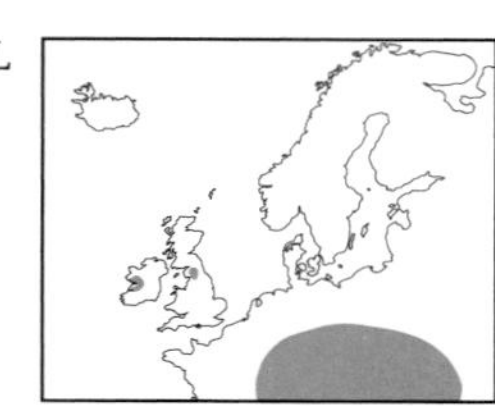
M
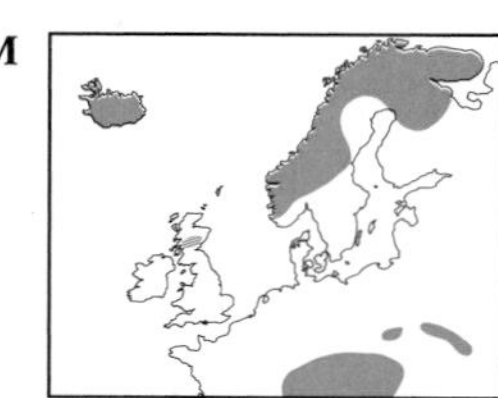

Gentian Family Gentianaceae

Usually hairless herbs, with opposite, untoothed and often stalkless leaves. Flowers regular, with 4-5 (occasionally more) lobes. Petals twisted together in bud. Ovary superior.

A **Yellow Centaury** *Cicendia filiformis* Slender annual herb 2-14cm tall, with erect simple or branched stems. Leaves linear, in widely spaced pairs, 2-6mm long. Flowers yellow, tiny, 3-6mm in diameter, corolla 4-lobed, opening only in sun, solitary on long stalks. Local, on damp sandy or peaty open ground, especially near the sea; from Holland and Germany southwards. **Fl** 6-10. **Br** Local, only in SW Briain.

B **Guernsey Centaury** *Exaculum pusillum* Similar to Yellow Centaury, but even smaller, with narrower leaves and pink or cream flowers. On damp sandy and grassy habitats near the coast; W France and Guernsey only. **Fl** 7-9. **Br** Guernsey only.

C **Yellow-wort** *Blackstonia perfoliata* Erect annual to 40cm high, waxy grey-green, with a basal rosette of leaves. Leaves ovate and spoon-shaped in rosette, stem leaves fused around the stem forming a distinctive feature. Flowers in loose, branching inflorescence, individually yellow, 10-15mm in diameter, with 6-8 petal lobes. Britain and continental Europe as far north as Holland and S Germany; in calcareous grassland and dunes, or lime-rich damp areas. **Fl** 6- 9. **Br** Locally common in England and Wales.

D **Common Centaury** *Centaurium erythraea* Variable, hairless, erect annual, with a basal rosette and 1 or more stems. Rosette leaves elliptical to oval, greyish-green, with 3-7 veins, blunt, 10-20mm wide; stem leaves narrower, 3-veined, *never parallel-sided*. Flowers pink, 10-15mm in diameter, in lax, branching inflorescence towards top of stem, often with scattered flowers lower down; petal lobes flat and spreading. Common throughout, though absent from NW Scandinavia; in drier grassy habitats, scrub and dunes. **Fl** 6-9. **Br** Common throughout, except NE Scotland.

E **Perennial Centaury** *Centaurium scilloides* Creeping, perennial herb, with erect, flowering and sterile stems to 30cm. Leaves on creeping stems rounded and stalked, about 10mm wide; upper leaves unstalked, oblong- lanceolate. Flowers large, 15-20mm in diameter, pink, in few-flowered heads. Very local on sea-cliffs and dunes; in NW France and SW Britain. **Fl** 7-8. **Br** Rare, only in Cornwall and Pembrokeshire.

F **Seaside Centaury** *Centaurium littorale* Similar to Common Centaury, but usually shorter; basal leaves narrow, to 5mm wide; *stem leaves parallel-sided*, strap-shaped, blunt with 1-3 veins. Flowers pink, 12-14mm in diameter, corolla more concave, in dense, umbel-like, flat-topped clusters. Locally common on dunes and other grassy habitats; mainly coastal from N France to S Scandinavia, more inland further north. **Fl** 6-8. **Br** Locally frequent on coasts of N and W Britain; very rare in the south.

G **Lesser Centaury** *Centaurium pulchellum* Small slender annual to 15cm at most, *without a basal rosette*, branching widely, often from below the middle. Leaves ovate-lanceolate, 3- to 7-veined. Inflorescence very open, with flowers in forks and at tips; flowers dark pink, 5-8mm in diameter, 5- (rarely 4-) lobed, short-stalked. In grazed or exposed sites, whole plant consists of single stem and 1 flower. Widespread in open, often damp, grassy places, frequently coastal; throughout except far N Scandinavia. **Fl** 6-9. **Br** England and Wales only, local, mainly coastal. Commonest in the south.

H **Slender Centaury** *Centaurium tenuiflorum* Similar to Lesser Centaury, but taller, branched only above middle with erect branches, rosette occasionally present. Inflorescence dense and flat-topped, pink, rarely white. Damp, grassy, mainly coastal habitats; in France and S Britain only. **Fl** 6-9. **Br** Very rare on S coast.

I **Yellow Centaury** *Centaurium maritimum* Small upright annual or biennial, with single stem to 20cm; rosette leaves wither by flowering time. Corolla yellow, or tinged pink, 8-10mm across. Coastal sandy and grassy places; NW France only. **Fl** 4-6. **Br** Absent.

J **Marsh Gentian** *Gentiana pneumonanthe* Procumbent or erect hairless perennial to 40cm, without basal rosette. Leaves on stem linear-oblong, blunt, 1-veined and rather fleshy. Flowers large, 25-45mm long, blue, in tight terminal cluster of 1-7 flowers; outside of corolla tube has 5 green stripes; calyx with 5 narrow, pointed teeth. Wet acidic sites, such as bogs and wet heaths; throughout except the far north. **Fl** 7-10. **Br** Scattered through England and Wales, very locally frequent in S England.

K **Cross Gentian** *Gentiana cruciata* Rather similar to Marsh Gentian, but leaves elliptical, much wider, longer than flowers; flowers smaller, 20-25mm long, with *4 petal lobes* in a cross, corolla green-speckled outside. In dry grassy habitats or open woods; Europe as far north as Holland. **Fl** 7- 10. **Br** Absent.

L **Spring Gentian** *Gentiana verna* Low, hairless, short-lived perennial, with basal leaf rosettes. Often forms loose clumps. Leaves lanceolate to ovate, 10-20mm long, bright green, mainly in rosette, with few opposite pairs on stem. Flowers bright blue, usually solitary terminal, but occasionally produced lower on stem on robust plants; corolla 5-lobed, spreading at 90° to corolla tube, 15-20mm in diameter. Calyx winged on angles. In limestone grassland, wet calcareous flushes, mountain habitats; in W Ireland, N England, and mountains in south of area only; oddly absent from Arctic Europe. **Fl** 4-6. **Br** Very locally frequent in Upper Teesdale and the Burren.

M **Alpine, or Snow, Gentian** *Gentiana nivalis* Very small slender annual, rather similar to Spring Gentian, but smaller in all respects. Leaves 6-10mm long. Flowers bright blue, but only 5-8mm in diameter, solitary or few together. Calyx angled but not winged. Throughout area, locally common in Arctic Europe, confined to mountains further south; in grassy, occasionally heathy habitats, and rock-ledges. **Fl** 6-9. **Br** Very rare, on a few Scottish mountains only.

N **Trumpet Gentian** *Gentiana clusii* Low tufted perennial, to about 10cm in flower (taller in fruit). Leaves mainly basal, elliptical to oblong, bright green, leathery. Flowers large, trumpet-shaped, mid to deep blue, 4-7cm long, opening widely in sun; calyx teeth triangular, at least half as long as tube. In grassy and stony places, often on limestone; from SW Germany and E France southwards. **Fl** 4-8. **Br** Absent.

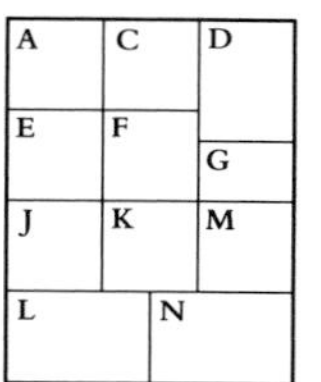

A **Yellow Centaury**
C **Yellow-wort**
D **Common Centaury**
E **Perennial Centaury**
F **Seaside Centaury**
G **Lesser Centaury**
J **Marsh Gentian**
K **Cross Gentian**
M **Alpine Gentian**
L **Spring Gentian**
N **Trumpet Gentian**

B

C
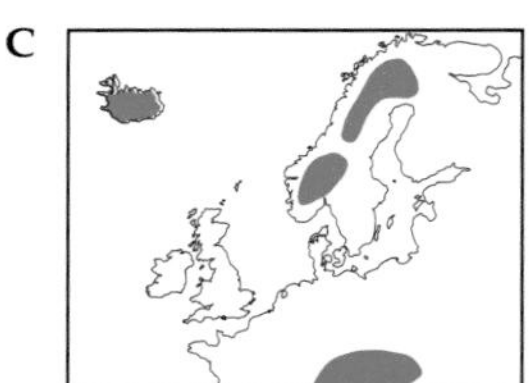
D

G
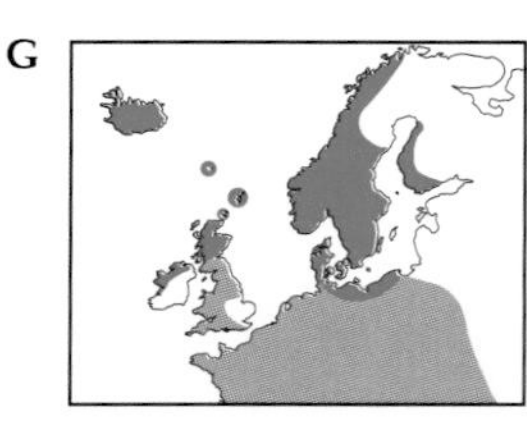
J
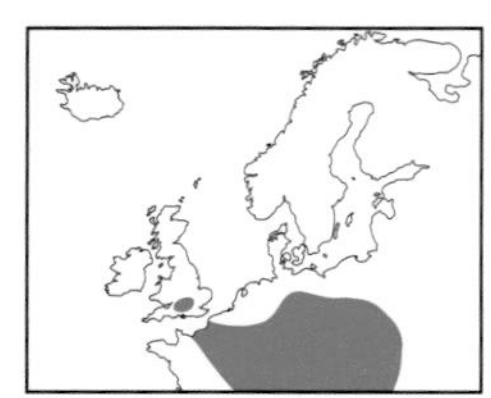
L
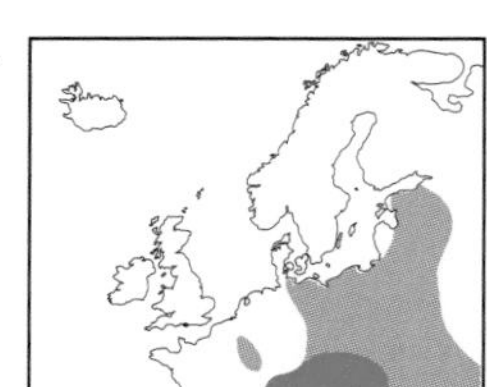

A Great Yellow Gentian *Gentiana lutea* Highly distinctive plant, in N Europe. Stout, erect plant to 1m or more, with broad strongly veined leaves, and whorls of yellow flowers with deeply separated petal lobes. Mainly southern, reaching into the region in the Vosges and S German mountains. **Fl** 6-8. **Br** Absent.

B Purple Gentian *Gentiana purpurea* Erect perennial to 60cm, with terminal cluster of trumpet-shaped, dull purple flowers, 20-25mm long, and a few in whorls below. Very local in mountains of central Europe, and S Norway; in grassy and rocky places. **Fl** 7-10. **Br** Absent.

Gentianella This genus differs from *Gentiana* in having no secondary lobes between the petals, and in having a fringe of hairs in the throat of the corolla (usually).

C Slender Gentian *Gentianella tenella* Tiny annual 2-10cm, with a basal rosette and several erect, flowering stems. Similar to Snow Gentian, differing in the genus differences described above, and in the 4-petalled flowers, usually blue, occasionally violet or yellowish. Local on acid often gravelly habitats in Arctic Europe, and mountains further south. **Fl** 7-9. **Br** Absent.

D Fringed Gentian *Gentianella ciliata* Low, unbranched biennial to 30cm. Very like a *Gentiana* species. There is no basal leaf rosette, lower leaves spoon-shaped, upper ones narrow. The flowers are large, 25-50mm, blue, with 4 triangular lobes, fringed with fine blue hairs. Very distinctive in flower. Dry grassy and rocky habitats throughout mainland Europe except the far north, but very local. **Fl** 8-10. **Br** Very rare; recently rediscovered in the Chilterns.

E *Gentianella detonsa* Similar to Fringed Gentian, except that flowers are smaller, darker blue and only slightly fringed on petals; calyx lobes not equal. Damp, often maritime habitats; in Arctic only. **Fl** 7-9. **Br** Absent.

F Autumn Gentian, Felwort *Gentianella amarella* Erect, simple or branched biennial to 30cm; 1st-year rosette dies before flowering. Stem leaves oval-lanceolate, pointed and 10-20mm long. Flowers in dense terminal and axillary clusters; individual flowers reddish-purple, bluish or creamy, 4- or 5-lobed, 10mm in diameter; corolla tube 14-22mm long, less than twice as long as calyx. Calyx has 4 or 5 equal lobes. Widespread and locally common throughout; in dry often calcareous grassland, dunes, mountain habitats. Ssp *septentrionalis* has corolla tube creamy white inside, reddish outside, and petal lobes erect; in Iceland and N Scotland only. **Fl** 7-10. **Br** Widespread and fairly common; replaced by ssp *septentrionalis* in NW Scotland.

G Field Gentian *Gentianella campestris* The commonest form, ssp *baltica*, is similar in form to Felwort, but differing mainly in that the flowers are usually more bluish, occasionally creamy, always with 4 petal lobes, and the calyx is distinctly separated into 2 large outer lobes overlapping the 2 smaller inner lobes. Grassland, dunes, heaths and montane habitats on acid-neutral soils; throughout the area except the extreme north, and rare towards the south. Ssp *baltica* is an annual, with corolla tube barely longer than calyx; found in a restricted area from S Sweden to N France. **Fl** 7-10. **Br** Rare in S England and Wales, commoner further north (ssp *campestris* only).

H Dune Gentian *Gentianella uliginosa* Differs from Felwort in that the upper leaves are ovate, terminal flowers very long-stalked, and the calyx teeth are spreading and unequal. In dune-slacks and damp meadows; local from N France northwards. **Fl** 7-10. **Br** S Wales only.

I Early Gentian *Gentianella anglica* Very similar generally to Felwort. The clearest distinction lies in the spring flowering time, but minor morphological differences include: plant short, 4-20cm; uppermost internode forms at least half the total height of plant; calyx lobes unequal, the longest roughly equal in length to corolla tube. **Fl** 4-6. **Br** Endemic and occuring in calcareous grassland and dune-slacks.

J Chiltern Gentian *Gentianella germanica* Broadly similar to Felwort in habit, differing in that the leaves taper from a broader base, 10mm wide or more; flowers are larger, lobes roughly 20mm in diameter, corolla tube 25-40mm long, at least twice the length of the calyx, which has 5 equal-length lobes. Annual (not biennial) plants sometimes occur, and are much smaller in all respects. Calcareous grassland and scrub; from Holland southwards, commonest in N France. **Fl** 8-10. **Br** Chilterns to N Hampshire, locally common.

K *Gentianella aurea* Broadly similar to Chiltern Gentian, but with pale yellow (rarely blue) flowers, which are smaller. Coasts and lake shores; Arctic Europe only. **Fl** 8-10. **Br** Absent.

L Marsh Felwort *Swertia perennis* Medium-height perennial to 60cm, with 4-angled stems. Differs from *Gentianella* in the deeply divided petals, and the fringed nectaries. Leaves roughly ovate, upper ones slightly clasping the stem. Flowers large, 15-30mm in diameter, star-shaped with 4-5 lobes, dull blue-violet, occasionally yellow-green or white, in branched clusters. Primarily a mountain species of S and central Europe, extending as far as S Germany and N central France; in marshy places and riversides. **Fl** 6-8. **Br** Absent.

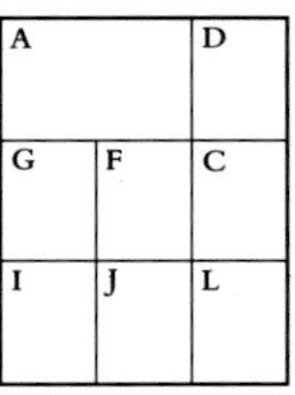

A **Great Yellow Gentian**
D **Fringed Gentian**
G **Field Gentian**
F **Autumn Gentian**
C **Slender Gentian**
I **Early Gentian**
J **Chiltern Gentian**
L **Marsh Felwort**

B

C
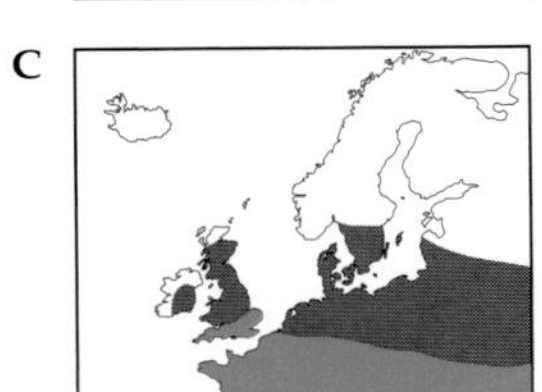

E
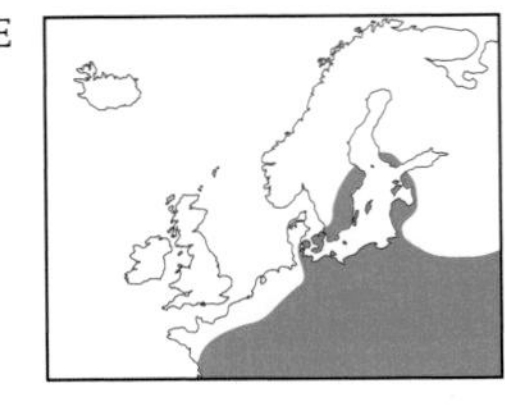

G
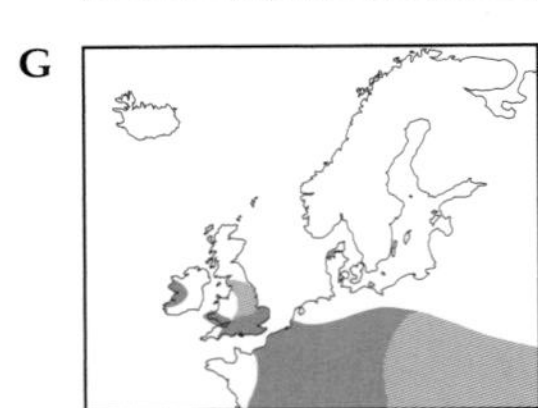

Bogbean Family
Menyanthaceae

Similar to Gentian family, but always aquatic or bog plants. Lower leaves alternate.

A **Bogbean** *Menyanthes trifoliata* Glabrous perennial with stout creeping rhizome, bearing erect leaves and flower stems. Mainly aquatic. Leaves all trifoliate, held above water level, reminiscent of broad-bean leaves in texture. Flowers in dense, erect spikes to 30cm, individual flowers with 5 petal lobes, star-shaped, 15mm across, pink-white and with conspicuous fringing of thick white hairs. No other N European plant is similar. In shallower water, or wet peaty areas; throughout, often common, though rare in Arctic. **Fl** 4-6. **Br** Widespread and common almost throughout, but local in central England.

B **Fringed Water-lily** *Nymphoides peltata* Floating aquatic, with creeping stems, resembling water-lilies in habit, but flowers very different. Leaves round to kidney-shaped, floating, 3-10cm in diameter. Flowers solitary or in small groups, orange-yellow, 3-4cm in diameter, with 5 strongly fringed petal lobes. Widespread and common as far north as S Sweden; in still and slow-flowing water; sometimes dominant. Also cultivated in garden ponds. **Fl** 6-9. **Br** Mainly S England, though becoming naturalised elsewhere.

Periwinkle Family
Apocynaceae

Woody plants, often climbing, with milky poisonous latex. Leaves opposite. Flowers 5-parted, usually solitary.

C **Lesser Periwinkle** *Vinca minor* Prostrate, trailing, evergreen perennial, forming mounded mats. Leaves shiny dark green, leathery, in opposite pairs, elliptical-ovate, 20-40mm long, short-stalked. Flowers solitary from leaf axils and long-stalked; corolla blue-violet, flat, 25-30mm in diameter, with 5 lobes obliquely truncated. *Calyx lobes narrowly triangular* and hairless (**c**). Widespread through Europe as far north as Denmark, but probably naturalised only in the N part of range; occurs in hedgerows, woods, and shady places. **Fl** 2-5. **Br** Possibly native in S England, certainly introduced elsewhere.

D **Greater Periwinkle** *Vinca major* Similar, but has larger, wider, longer-stalked leaves; flowers larger (40-50cm in diameter), *calyx lobes very narrow with densely hairy margins* (**d**). Similar habitats, but only as naturalised plant from S Europe. **Fl** 3-5. **Br** Naturalised as far north as central Scotland, commonest in the south.

Swallow-wort Family
Asclepiadaceae

Perennial shrubs or herbs, with opposite leaves. Flowers 5-parted, with lobes contorted in bud. Anthers joined in a ring, usually with the stigma.

E **Swallow-wort, Vincetoxicum** *Vincetoxicum hirundinaria* Perennial almost hairless herb, with erect stems to 1m tall. Leaves heart-shaped or narrower, 6-10cm long, opposite, pointed and stalked. Flowers greenish-yellow to almost white, starry, 5-lobed, 4-10mm in diameter, in lax clusters from the bases of the upper leaves. Fruits are long pods to 50mm containing silky seeds. Highly poisonous. Widespread and locally frequent in mainland Europe as far north as S Scandinavia; in grasslands, scrub and roadsides, often on calcareous soils. **Fl** 5-9. **Br** Absent.

Bedstraw Family Rubiaceae

Herbs (in N Europe) with opposite, or often apparently whorled, leaves (in fact, the intermediate leaves of the whorl are technically stipules not leaves), which are usually simple and untoothed. Flowers funnel-shaped, usually in open branching inflorescences, sometimes tight heads. Corolla 4- or 5-lobed; calyx very small. Ovary inferior. A mainly tropical, woody family.

F **Field Madder** *Sherardia arvensis* Procumbent, annual plant up to 40cm long, with leaves in whorls of 4-6. Lower leaves withering early, upper leaves 5-20mm long, pointed, elliptical, with backward-pointing prickles on edges. Inflorescence with 4-8 flowers in terminal heads, with a conspicuous ruff of leafy bracts below them; flowers pink to purple, 4-6mm in diameter; calyx 6-toothed, enlarging in fruit. Throughout, except the far north; in open disturbed habitats, such as margins of arable fields. **Fl** 5-10. **Br** Widespread and common, becoming rarer towards the north.

G **Squinancywort** *Asperula cynanchica* Perennial prostrate herb, with 4-angled ascending stems, reaching 20cm. Leaves whorled in 4s, narrowly linear, often uneven in length. Inflorescence consists of long-stalked branched clusters of pink flowers (whiter inside tube), 3-4mm in diameter and 4-lobed; calyx tiny. Fruit finely warty. Dry calcareous pastures and dunes; in continental Europe and UK as far north as N England and Holland. **Fl** 6-9. **Br** England and Wales only, locally common in S England, rare in the north.

H **Western Woodruff** *Asperula occidentalis* Differs from Squinancywort in its underground orange stolons; it is frequently not treated as a separate species. Very local on coastal sands; in W France, SW Britain and Ireland. **Fl** 5-7. **Br** Very local in coastal areas only.

I **Dyer's Woodruff** *Asperula tinctoria* Stoloniferous perennial producing erect robust stems to 80cm. Whole plant blackens when dried. Leaves in whorls of 4-6, up to 40mm long, narrowly lanceolate, rough-edged, 3-veined. Inflorescence freely branched, with numerous small 3-petalled white flowers. Fruit hairless, granular, 15-20mm in diameter. In grassy and scrub habitats; continental Europe from S Sweden southwards; local. **Fl** 6-9. **Br** Absent.

J **Blue, or Field, Woodruff** *Asperula arvensis* Annual to 50cm, with leaves in whorls of 6-8. Flowers 3-5mm across, bluish violet in groups, surrounded by ruff of leafy bracts. Corolla 4-lobed. In fields and waste ground; possibly native in S parts of region. **Fl** 4-7. **Br** A rare casual; England only.

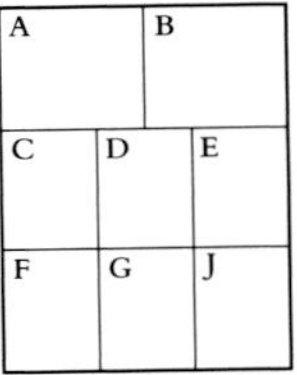

A **Bogbean**
B **Fringed Water-lily**
C **Lesser Periwinkle**
D **Greater Periwinkle**
E **Swallow-wort**
F **Field Madder**
G **Squinancywort**
J **Blue Woodruff**

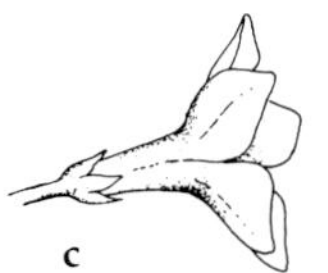
c

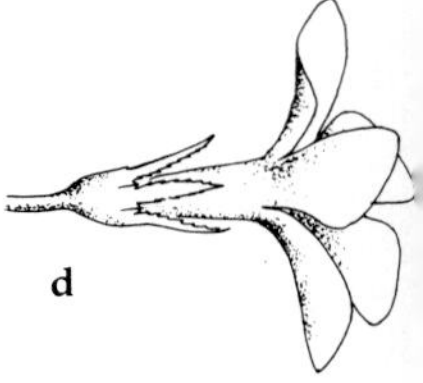
d

A

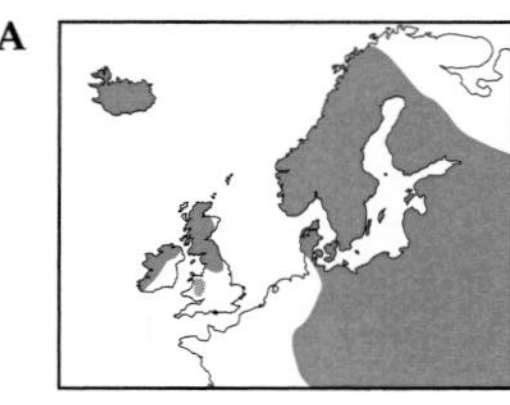

C

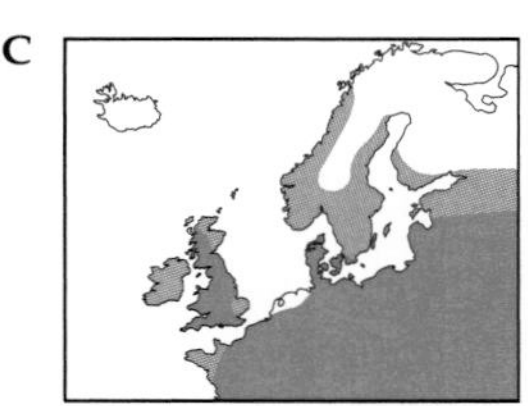

D

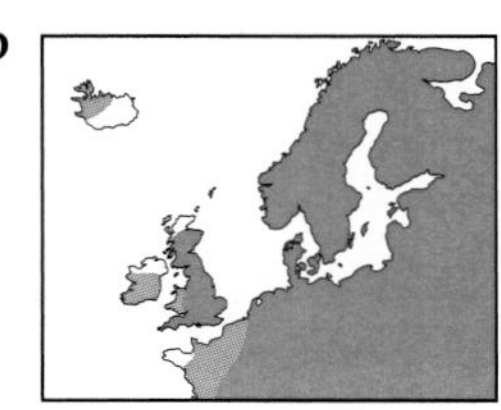

H

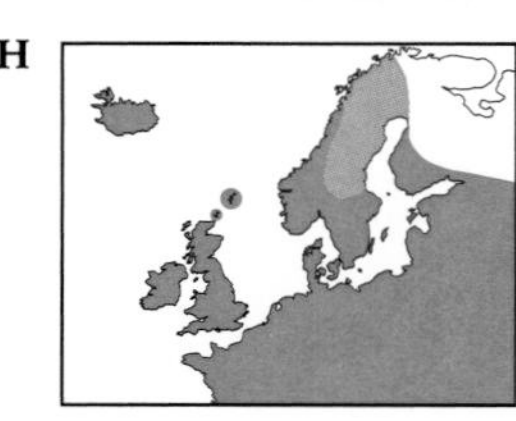

J

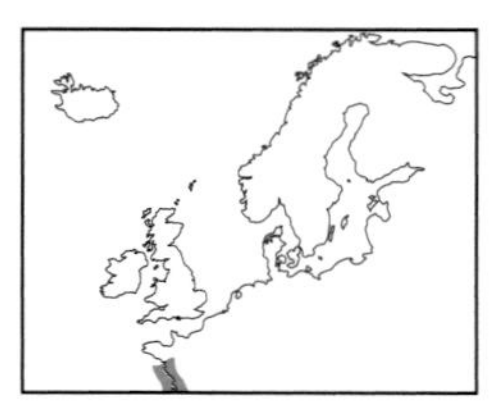

K

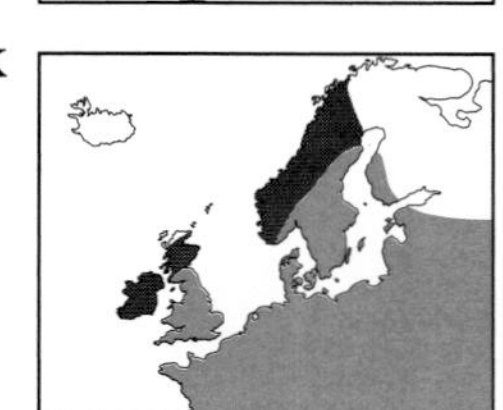

BEDSTRAWS *Galium* This is a difficult group, comprising almost 30 often similar species in this area. Detailed examination is required for many species to be identified accurately.

A **Northern Bedstraw** *Galium boreale* Stoloniferous perennial with ascending or erect, 4-angled stems to 60cm. Leaves dark green, 20-40mm long, in 4s, slightly leathery, widest at the middle, 3-veined and blunt. Flowers white, 4mm in diameter, in branched terminal inflorescences with numerous leafy bracts. Fruit brownish, 2-3mm across, with hooked bristles. Throughout, but local; in grassy and rocky places, and mountain habitats. One of the most easily recognised bedstraws. **Fl** 6-8. **Br** From N Wales and N England northwards.

B *Galium rotundifolium* Similar to Northern Bedstraw, but much shorter with leaves more rounded and less leathery; inflorescence few-flowered. Local in woods; as far north as S Sweden. **Fl** 6-9. **Br** Absent.

C **Sweet Woodruff** *Galium odoratum* Erect, virtually hairless perennial, with 4-angled stems to 30cm. Whole plant hay-scented. Leaves lanceolate-elliptical, to 40mm, in distant whorls of 6-8; leaf margins with forward-pointing prickles. Flowers white, in dense umbel-like terminal inflorescences, funnel-shaped, 4-lobed to roughly half-way, 6mm in diameter. Fruit 2-3mm across, with hooked black-tipped bristles. Frequent and widespread in base-rich, often damp, woods; throughout except the far north. **Fl** 5-6. **Br** Throughout, though rare in N Scotland.

D **Fen Bedstraw** *Galium uliginosum* Slender, straggling-ascending herb, with thin stems reaching 80-90cm, rough on the 4 angles, with backward-pointing prickles. Leaves 10-20mm long, narrowly lanceolate, with *spine at tip*, 1-veined, *in whorls of 6-8*, with backward-pointing prickles on margins (**d**). Flowers white, 2.5-3mm across in a narrow inflorescence; anthers yellow. Fruit 1mm across, wrinkled, brown, on deflexed stalks. Widespread and locally common throughout except the extreme north; in mainly calcareous marshes and fens. **Fl** 6-8. **Br** Throughout except N Scotland; frequent.

E **Common Marsh-bedstraw** *Galium palustre* Rather similar in habit and habitat to Fen Bedstraw. Usually rather more robust; leaves 5-20mm long, *4-6 in a whorl*, broadest towards the tip, *blunt or slightly pointed*, but *never with spine at tip* (**e**). Flowers white, 35-45mm in diameter, in wide-spreading branching inflorescence; anthers red. Widespread and common; in wet places throughout. **Fl** 6-8. **Br** Common throughout. Robust forms of Marsh-bedstraw, with leaves at least 20mm long, are sometimes distinguished as Great Marsh-bedstraw *G. elongatum*, or a subspecies of Marsh-bedstraw, though intermediate forms also occur.

F **Slender Marsh-bedstraw** *Galium debile* Very similar to Common Marsh-bedstraw, but plant smaller and more slender (up to only 60cm); *stems smooth* or barely rough; leaves 10mm long (maximum), not spine-tipped, with forward-pointing prickles on margins. Flowers 2-3mm across, in V-shaped inflorescences. Local or rare in England, Ireland and W France only. **Fl** 5-8. **Br** New Forest, Devon, Yorkshire and W Ireland only.

G *Galium trifidum* Resembles Marsh-bedstraw, but is a delicate low plant, with leaves in 4s, and 3-part flowers. Bogs and wet places in Scandinavia, NE Poland. **Fl** 6-8. **Br** Absent.

H **Lady's Bedstraw** *Galium verum* Distinctive as the only bedstraw with bright yellow flowers (but *see* succeeding 2 species). Stem creeping with erect flower stems to 80cm, faintly 4-angled, with 4 lines. Leaves linear, spine-tipped, 15-30mm long, dark green above, downy below, with rolled margins; 8-12 in a whorl. Flowers golden yellow, 2-3mm in diameter, in a dense oval terminal inflorescence and fragrant. Fruit 1.5mm across, smooth and black when ripe. Widespread and common throughout, except in the extreme north; in grasslands, hedgebanks and dunes. **Fl** 6-9. **Br** Common throughout.

I *Galium × pomeranicum* Natural hybrid between Lady's and Hedge Bedstraw. The result is more straggly than Lady's Bedstraw, with distinctly 4-angled stems, and pale yellow flowers. Throughout in grassy habitats, usually with both parents, but local. **Fl** 6-8. **Br** Local, scattered.

J **Sand Bedstraw** *Galium arenarium* Resembles a prostrate, dense Lady's Bedstraw. Stem 4-angled, to 50cm long. Leaves fleshy and shining, broadly lanceolate, margins not rolled under. Flowers dull yellow, 3-4mm in diameter, in a narrow terminal inflorescence, often almost horizontal. Fruit 3mm in diameter, globose and slightly fleshy. Very local on coastal sands; in W France, north into Brittany. **Fl** 5-7. **Br** Absent.

K **Hedge-bedstraw** *Galium mollugo* Variable scrambling perennial, sometimes climbing to 1-2m in hedges, etc. Stems 4-angled, smooth and solid. Leaves 10-25mm long, oblong to elliptical, 1-veined, pale green, bristle-tipped, with forward-pointing prickles on margins. Flowers white, 3mm in diameter, with 4 pointed lobes, in large loose branched inflorescences. Fruit hairless, wrinkled, 1-2mm across. In hedges, rough grassy places and scrub; throughout except the far north, generally common. **Fl** 6-9. **Br** Common in the south, rarer further north.

L **Upright Hedge-bedstraw** *Galium album* Very similar to Hedge Bedstraw, sometimes treated as a subspecies. Differs in having *erect stems* to 1.5m, thicker, rather leathery, narrower leaves, larger flowers, 3-5mm across, and more erect inflorescences, even in fruit. Grassy habitats; as far north as S Scandinavia. **Fl** 6-9. **Br** Local through the lowlands, usually on dry calcareous pastures.

M **Glaucous Bedstraw** *Galium glaucum* Bluish-green stoloniferous plant with rounded stems; leaves narrow in whorls of 8-10; flowers 4-6mm in diameter, white. Local on wood-margins, in dry grassland; from Belgium and Germany southwards. **Fl** 5-7. **Br** Absent.

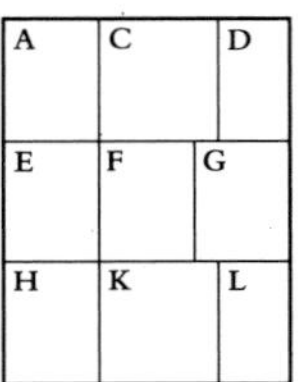

A **Northern Bedstraw**

C **Sweet Woodruff**

D **Fen Bedstraw**

E **Common Marsh Bedstraw**

F **Slender Bedstraw**

G *Galium trifidum*

H **Lady's Bedstraw**

K **Hedge-bedstraw**

L **Upright Hedge-bedstraw**

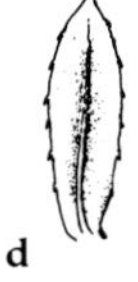

d

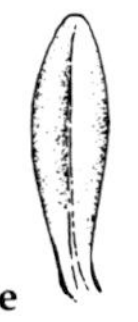

e

B

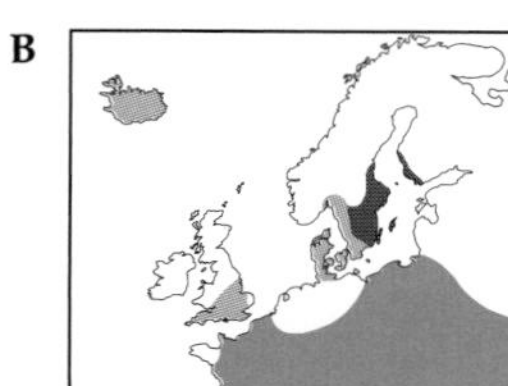

C

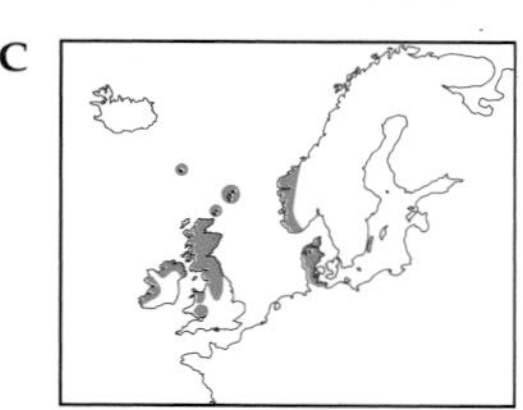

E

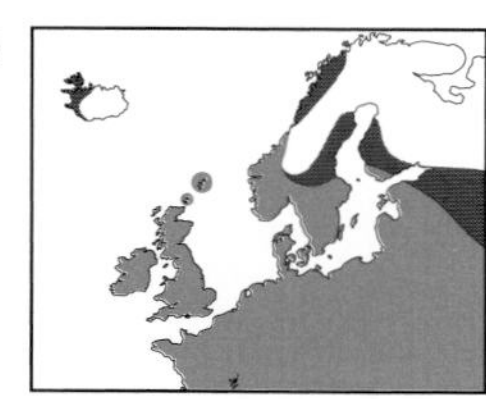

G

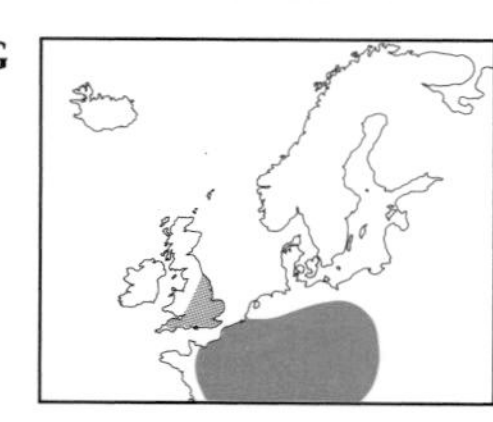

H

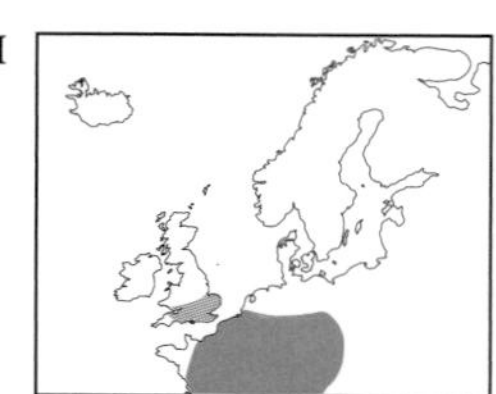

I

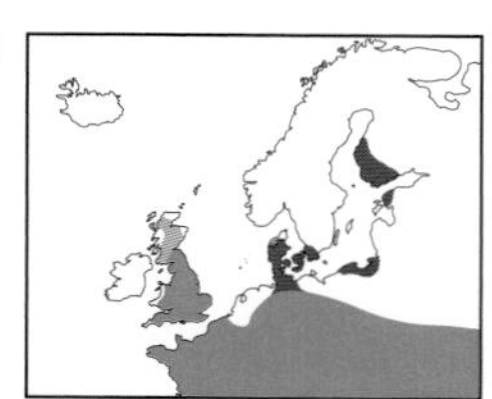

K

A Wood Bedstraw *Galium sylvaticum* Robust, bushy plant, with rounded hollow stems. Leaves elliptical to spoon-shaped, greyish green, up to 40mm long, 10mm wide, blunt, without strong edge prickles, in whorls of 6-8. Flowers on very fine stalks, *drooping in bud*, in branched terminal inflorescence; white, cup-shaped, 2-3mm in diameter. Fruit smooth, bluish green, 1-2mm. Local in woods, especially in hilly areas; in Belgium, France, Germany and Holland only. **Fl** 6-8. **Br** Absent.

B. Slender Bedstraw *Galium pumilum* Slender ascending plant to 30cm high, with smooth 4-angled stems. Leaves linear-lanceolate, often distinctly *sickle-shaped*, bristle-pointed, with few *backward-pointing prickles* on edges, in whorls of 6-9. Flowers white-cream, 2-3mm in diameter, in long loose inflorescences. Fruit about 1.5mm across, hairless, sometimes with blunt warts (*see G. sterneri*). Uncommon in grassland, scrub and open woodlands, usually on calcareous soil; in lowland areas, as far north as Denmark. **Fl** 6-7. **Br** S England only, local.

Four species are very similar to Slender Bedstraw, but are very local and difficult to distinguish. *Galium fleurotii* occurs on limestone cliffs and screes in NW France and Somerset; *Galium valdepilosum* occurs in dry grassland in Denmark and Germany; and *Galium suecicum* is local in dry grassland in N Germany and S Sweden. *Galium oelandicum* occurs on limestone in Oland, Sweden only.

C Limestone Bedstraw *Galium sterneri* Compact, mat-forming perennial with many non-flowering stems; whole plant turns dark greenish black on drying. Leaves narrowly oblong, 7-11mm long, with bristle-tip, and numerous *backward-pointing prickles on margins* (**c**), in crowded whorls of 7-8. Flowers creamy white or greenish, 3mm in diameter, in pyramidal inflorescence. Fruit 1-1.4mm and hairless with *pointed warts*. In dry grassy and rocky habitats, especially on limestone, frequently in hilly areas; from Ireland to Germany northwards to Finland. **Fl** 5-7. **Br** Mainly northern and western.

D Heath Bedstraw *Galium saxatile* Rather similar to Limestone Bedstraw, but always on acidic soils. Heath Bedstraw has *forward-pointing bristles on the leaf margins* (**d**), and the whole plant blackens on drying. Widespread and common throughout; on heaths, acid grassland and scrub. **Fl** 6-8. **Br** Common throughout where suitable habitats exist.

E Goosegrass, Cleavers *Galium aparine* Familiar sprawling, scrambling plant, reaching 1.8m long; stems very rough and square, with large backward-pointing prickles, hairy around the nodes. Whole plant very sticky, like velcro. Leaves robust, elliptical, abruptly contracted towards the tip with backward-pointing prickles on the margins, 6-8 in a whorl. Flowers greenish white, 2mm in diameter, in few-flowered axillary clusters *longer than the subtending leaves*. Fruit 3-6mm across, green becoming purplish, covered with dense hooked bristles with swollen bases. Widespread and common throughout, except in the far north of Europe; in cultivated land, hedgerows, woods, scrub and waste ground. **Fl** 5-9. **Br** Widespread and common.

F False Cleavers *Galium spurium* Very similar to Goosegrass, but a more prostrate plant; nodes less hairy, leaves narrower and shorter. *Only 2-3 bracts below flowers* (4-8 in Goosegrass). Fruit smaller, 1.5-3mm across, turning blackish when ripe, the hooked hairs without swollen bases. In cultivated land, hedgerows and waste ground; widespread in Europe except in the far north. **Br** Very rare in S England only

G Corn Cleavers *Galium tricornutum* Very similar to Goosegrass in general habit but differs in that the flowers are creamy white, 3-flowered *clusters equal to or shorter than the leaves*; flower stalks becoming strongly downcurved after flowering. Fruits hairless, warty but not prickly. An uncommon and decreasing plant of arable land and open habitats, usually on calcareous soils; mainly southern in distribution, as far north as Holland. **Fl** 6-9. **Br** Probably introduced, now very rare in S and E England only.

H Wall Bedstraw *Galium parisiense* Slender scrambling annual up to 40cm long, with 4-angled stem, rough on the corners with small downward-pointing prickles. Leaves narrow, to 3mm wide, and short, to 10mm, in whorls of 5-7, somewhat reflexed; margins with forward-pointing prickles. Flowers small, 2mm in diameter, greenish white inside, reddish outside, in small clusters forming long narrow inflorescence. Fruit small, 1mm across, warty but usually hairless. On old walls, and in sandy open habitats, including arable land; from E England and Germany southwards; local. **Fl** 6-7. **Br** Rare and local in S and E England only.

I Crosswort *Cruciata laevipes* Creeping perennial, with erect, *hairy*, 4-angled stems up to 60cm tall. Leaves in distinctive whorls of 4 (the 'cross' of the name), oval-elliptical, 3-veined, to 20mm long, yellow-green and hairy. Flowers yellow, 2-3mm in diameter, in dense axillary clusters which do not exceed the leaves. Fruit 2-3mm across, almost globose, blackening when ripe, smooth. Common in pastures, roadsides, woodland edges and scrub, often on calcareous soils; as far north as Holland and Germany (introduced in Denmark). **Fl** 4- 6. **Br** Common and widespread, becoming rarer to the north and west.

J *Cruciata glabra* Rather similar to Crosswort, but a smaller and more slender plant to 20cm high, *virtually hairless*, without the tiny (8mm) bracteoles at the base of the flowers that are present in Crosswort. Similar habitats, local, Holland southwards. **Fl** 4-6. **Br** Absent.

K Wild Madder *Rubia peregrina* Scrambling, trailing perennial, with long hairless 4-angled stems, prickly on the angles, reaching 1.5m. Leaves dark green, leathery, rigid, ovate-elliptical, to 60mm long, 1-veined, with curved prickles on the margins and midrib below. Flowers yellow-green, 4-6mm in diameter, in spreading axillary and terminal inflorescences, exceeding the leaves. Fruit a globular black berry, 4-6mm in diameter. Local in S Britain, Ireland and W France; in hedges, woods, coastal habitats, much rarer inland. **Fl** 6-8. **Br** S and W parts of England, Wales and Ireland, rarer inland.

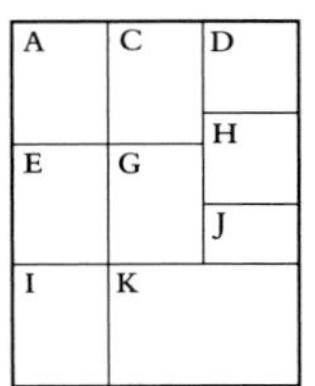

A **Wood Bedstraw**

C **Limestone Bedstraw**

D **Heath Bedstraw**

E **Goosegrass**

G **Corn Cleavers**

H **Wall Bedstraw**

J *Cruciata glabra*

I **Crosswort**

K **Wild Madder**

c

d

A

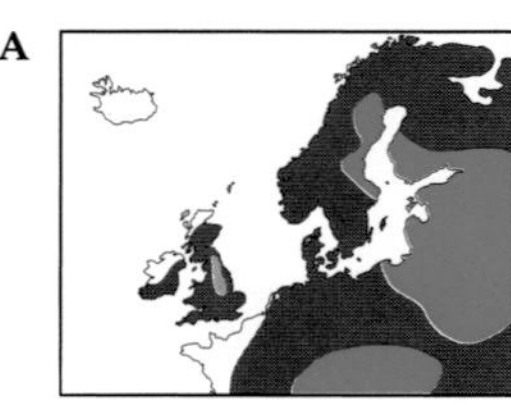

B

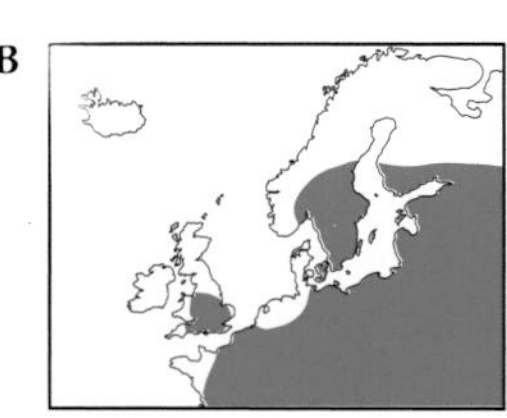

F

Jacob's-ladder Family
Polemoniaceae

Herbs or shrubs. Leaves without stipules. Flowers 5-parted, with lower parts of petals fused into a tube. Ovary superior.

A **Jacob's-ladder** *Polemonium caeruleum* Erect perennial herb up to 90cm high. Stems hollow, angled and downy above. Leaves pinnate, with 6-12 pairs of leaflets, 10-40cm long, alternate, hairless. Flowers in terminal heads, dense at first, petals blue (occasionally white), with a short tube and 5 spreading lobes, 2-3cm in diameter; stamens golden, style 3-lobed, both protruding. Local throughout except the far north and many lowland areas; commonest in hilly limestone areas, in grassland, scrub, rock-ledges and screes. **Fl** 6-7. **Br** N England only as a native, naturalised elsewhere.

Two similar species occur in Arctic Europe. *Polemonium acutifolium* has less than 8 pairs of leaflets per leaf; flowers smaller, more bell-shaped, with tiny hairs on petals. *Polemonium boreale* has only 1 stem leaf at most, flowers bell-shaped, without tiny hairs.

Bindweed Family
Convolvulaceae

A family of mainly climbing plants, with alternate leaves and twining stems. *Convolvulus* flowers are regular, with 5 sepals and 5 petals, 5-lobed or joined and 5-angled. The dodders *Cuscuta* species are wholly parasitic plants, lacking green colouring and with scale-like leaves.

B **Greater Dodder** *Cuscuta europaea* Reddish parasitic climbing plant, twining anticlockwise around its host plant; stems up to 1mm in diameter, frequently branching. Leaves scale-like. Flowers pinkish, 4-5mm in diameter, in dense pinkish heads 10-15mm in diameter, with bracts, stamens not protruding, corolla lobes blunt. Parasitic, mainly on nettles and hops, occasionally other plants. Widespread in continental Europe except in the far north; usually on roadsides and in hedges. **Fl** 7-10. **Br** Rare and local; only in S England.

C **Flax Dodder** *Cuscuta epilinum* Very similar to Greater Dodder, but parasitic on various flax *Linum* spp. Differs in that the stem is simple or slightly branched, and the *flowers are yellowish*, with spreading more pointed petal lobes. Usually in flax fields; throughout much of Europe, though rare in the north and west, decreasing. **Fl** 7-9. **Br** Extinct.

D **Common Dodder** *Cuscuta epithymum* Similar generally to Greater Dodder, with a mass of trailing, branched, very slender, red stems. Flowers pinkish, 3-4mm across, in dense clusters 6-10mm across; petals pointed, stamens protruding. Parasitic on gorse, heather, clover and other shrubs and herbs. Widespread and locally common throughout area except the extreme north; especially on heaths, moors and rough grasslands. **Fl** 7-9. **Br** Locally common in England, decreasing northwards; absent from N Scotland.

E *Cuscuta lupuliformis* Differs from Common Dodder in having a single style (not 2), stamens not protruding, parasitic on willows and other trees. Holland and Germany only. **Fl** 6-9. **Br** Absent.

F **Sea Bindweed** *Calystegia soldanella* Procumbent hairless perennial, with stems not, or barely, twisting. Leaves fleshy, kidney-shaped, 1-4cm long, broader than long and long-stalked. Flowers trumpet-shaped, 3-5cm, pink with white stripes, epicalyx shorter than sepals. Mainly on coastal dunes, occasionally shingle; on coast of W Europe from Denmark southwards. **Fl** 5-8. **Br** All around the coasts, though rare in N Scotland, mainly on acid sands.

G **Hedge Bindweed** *Calystegia sepium* Strong-growing climbing plant, often reaching 2-3m high on other plants or supports, with strongly twisting stems. Leaves arrow-shaped, to 15cm long. Flowers white (or very rarely pink), 3-4cm in diameter, 3-5cm in length; 2 epicalyx bracts, longer than sepals, surrounding them but not overlapping each other (**g**). Widespread and common throughout, except in the far north; in waste places, hedge- rows, riversides and woodland edges. **Fl** 6-9. **Br** Very common throughout, less so in the far north.
Ssp *roseata* is pubescent, more procumbent, with bright pink flowers. In salt-marshes and coastal areas from Denmark southwards. **Br** Local, coastal.

H **Large, or Great, Bindweed** *Calystegia sylvatica* Similar to Hedge Bindweed, and formerly treated as a subspecies of it. Differs in that the flowers are larger (60-75mm in diameter), white rarely striped pink; 2 epicalyx bracts strongly inflated and overlapping each other, concealing the sepals (**h**). Similar habitats. Locally naturalised, especially in France and Britain. **Fl** 6-9. **Br** Widespread and frequent, especially in England, but only in cultivated and waste habitats.

I **Field Bindweed** *Convolvulus arvensis* Creeping or climbing perennial, with stems up to 2m arising from fleshy rhizomes. Leaves arrow-shaped, 2-5cm long, stalk shorter than blade, often rather greyish. Flowers trumpet-shaped, white, or pink with white stripes, smaller than *Calystegia* species (about 2cm in diameter); sepals 5-lobed, without epicalyx bracts. Very common throughout, except the extreme north; in disturbed habitats and coastal grasslands. A persistent weed. **Fl** 6-9. **Br** Very common throughout, except N Scotland where it is rarer.

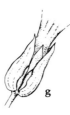

g

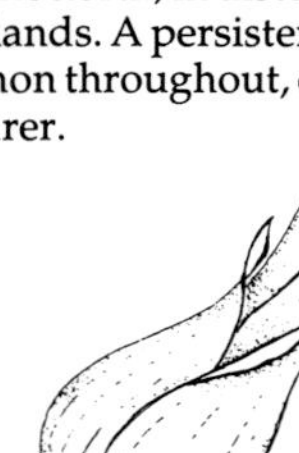

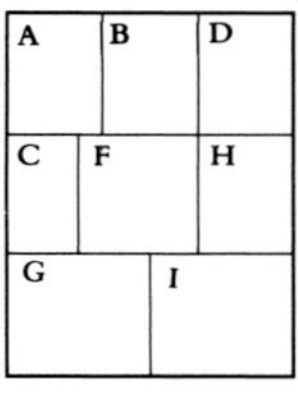

A **Jacob's-ladder**
B **Greater Dodder**
D **Common Dodder**
C **Flax Dodder**
F **Sea Bindweed**
H **Large Bindweed**
G **Hedge Bindweed**
I **Field Bindweed**

B
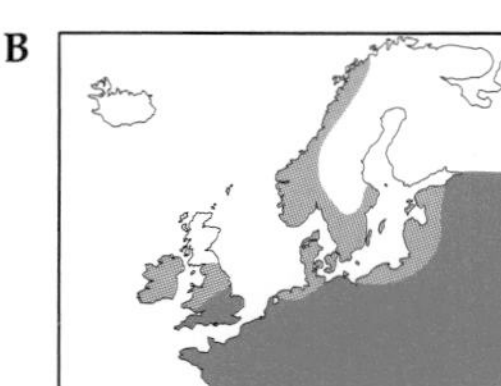
C

D
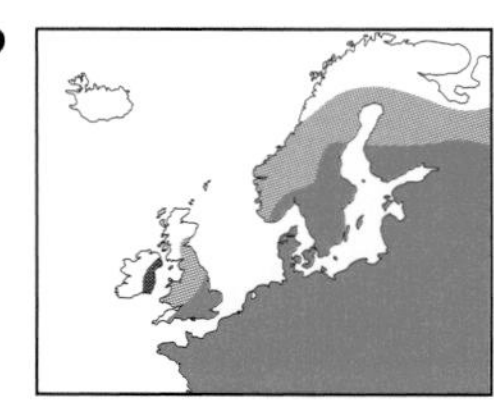
H
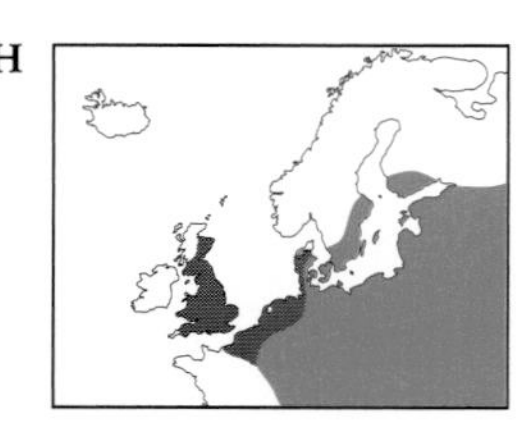
K
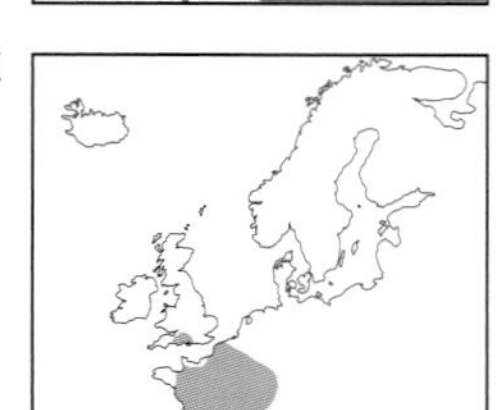

Borage Family Boraginaceae

Herbs or dwarf shrubs, frequently bristly-hairy. Leaves alternate, undivided and without stipules. Flowers usually in curved clusters (scorpioid cymes). Petals and sepals 5. Fruit 4 (occasionally 2) separate 1-seeded nutlets.

A **Heliotrope** *Heliotropium europaeum* Erect or ascending, hairy annual plants to 40cm. Leaves ovate-elliptical, stalked, greyish green and downy. Flowers white with yellow eye, 3-5mm in diameter, in markedly curled 1-sided spikes. In waste and disturbed ground; from France and S Germany southwards. **Fl** 5-7. **Br** Absent.

B **Common Gromwell** *Lithospermum officinale* Erect, downy perennial to 60cm, often in clusters. Leaves lanceolate, pointed, stalkless, to 10cm long, with strongly marked veins. Flowers greenish white, funnel-shaped, 3-4mm in diameter, in short dense clusters, elongating in fruit. Fruit consists of 4 shiny white porcelain-like nutlets, 3-4mm long, that persist well into winter. Widespread and common throughout, becoming rarer to the north and west; in scrub, grassland and wood-margins, often on calcareous soils. **Fl** 6-7. **Br** Local in England and Wales; much rarer further north.

C **Purple, or Blue, Gromwell** *Buglossoides purpurocaerulea* Creeping, downy, woody perennial, from which arise erect or arching stems. Leaves lanceolate, narrow, long-pointed, dark green and stalkless. Flowers reddish at first, becoming bright deep blue; corolla funnel-shaped, 12-15mm in diameter, tube twice as long as sepals; in terminal forked leafy inflorescences. Fruit white, smooth, shiny, 4-5mm long. Local from Belgium and Germany southwards; in woods, roadsides and scrub, on calcareous soils. **Fl** 4-6. **Br** Uncommon and local in S England and Wales only, in limestone areas.

D **Corn, or Field, Gromwell** *Buglossoides arvensis* Erect, downy annual, with barely branched stem to 50cm. Leaves oblong to strap-shaped, not sharp-pointed, upper ones unstalked, lower short-stalked, without marked side-veins. Flowers 3-4mm in diameter, white or bluish, with a violet corolla tube, in short clusters at tip of stem. Nutlets grey-brown and warty, 2.5-4mm long. Cultivated ground and dry open habitats; throughout most of Europe, except the far north. **Fl** 5-8. **Br** Local, most frequent in S and E England.

E *Lithodora diffusa* Dwarf low-growing shrub to 60cm, with linear-lanceolate rather blunt hispid leaves. Flowers 20-25mm in diameter, bright blue. Fruit smooth and pale brown. A SW European species, extending into NW France; in woods and hedges, usually on acid soils. **Fl** 4-6. **Br** Absent.

F **Viper's-bugloss** *Echium vulgare* Erect, roughly hispid biennial, with scattered red-based bristles, to 90cm tall, very variable in form. Root leaves stalked and 1-veined; stem leaves unstalked with rounded bases. Flowers usually bright blue or blue-violet, funnel-shaped, with 5 somewhat unequal petal lobes, 15-20mm long, in short curved axillary clusters. Stamens, 5, of which 4 protrude. Fruit rough nutlets. In open grassy places, often near the coast, frequently on light or calcareous soils; throughout area except the far north. **Fl** 6-9. **Br** Common through most of England, Wales and E Ireland; rarer elsewhere, or absent.

G **Purple Viper's-bugloss** *Echium plantagineum* Similar to Viper's-bugloss, but shorter and more softly hairy. Leaves with prominent lateral veins, stem leaves with heart-shaped bases; flowers reddish becoming blue, with only 2 stamens protruding. Dry sandy places near the sea in SW Britain and W France only. **Fl** 6-8. **Br** Cornwall and Jersey only.

H **Common Lungwort** *Pulmonaria officinalis* Low perennial herb, tufted and very rough-hairy. Basal leaves roughly ovate, sometimes heart-shaped at base, abruptly narrowed into long, winged stalk (**h**), normally white-spotted. Stem leaves ovate, unstalked, partly clasping the stem. Flowers pink in bud, becoming red-violet to blue, 10mm in diameter; calyx teeth between a third and a quarter the length of the cylindrical calyx tube. Fruit rounded oval nutlets. In shady or partially shaded places on chalk and clay soils; from Holland and S Sweden southwards. **Fl** 3-5. **Br** Introduced, locally naturalised.

I *Pulmonaria obscura* Very similar, but differs in having unspotted root leaves, with blade shorter than petiole. Similar habitats and distribution. **Fl** 3-5. **Br** Absent.

J **Mountain Lungwort** *Pulmonaria montana* Similar in form to Common Lungwort. Basal leaves lanceolate, narrowing gradually to the base (**j**), softly hairy, slightly sticky and normally without paler blotches; upper leaves with heart-shaped base, slightly clasping the stem. Local, in France, Germany and Belgium; in meadows and woods, usually in hilly areas. **Fl** 4-5. **Br** Absent.

K **Narrow-leaved Lungwort** *Pulmonaria longifolia* Similar in form to other lungworts. Basal leaves narrowly lanceolate, 10-20cm long, pointed, *very gradually narrowing to stalk* (**k**) and usually white-spotted (more frequently unspotted in E France); stem leaves similar but smaller, unstalked and clasping the stem. Flowers in short clusters, remaining dense throughout flowering period; corolla red, turning blue, with tufts of hairs in throat of corolla alternating with stamens; calyx teeth half the length of tube. In woods and scrub, often on heavy soils; north as far as France and S England. **Fl** 4- 5. **Br** Locally common in New Forest, Isle of Wight and E Dorset.

L *Pulmonaria angustifolia* Very similar to Narrow-leaved Lungwort, differing mainly in that the rosette leaves are covered with stiff, even bristles, without glandular hairs (compared to uneven bristles and scattered glandular hairs in Narrow-leaved Lungwort). S Sweden, Denmark and Germany; local, and rare in France. **Fl** 4-6. **Br** Absent.

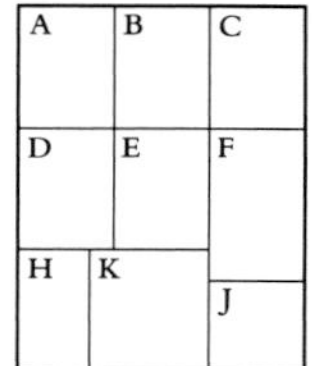

A **Heliotrope**

B **Common Gromwell**

C **Purple Gromwell**

D **Corn Gromwell**

E *Lithodora diffusa*

F **Viper's-bugloss**

H **Common Lungwort**

K **Narrow-leaved Lungwort**

J **Mountain Lungwort**

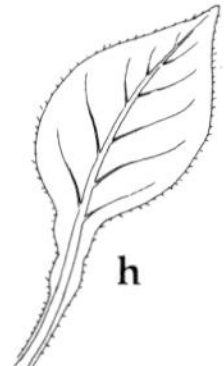

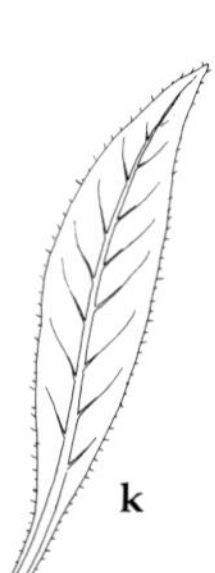

A
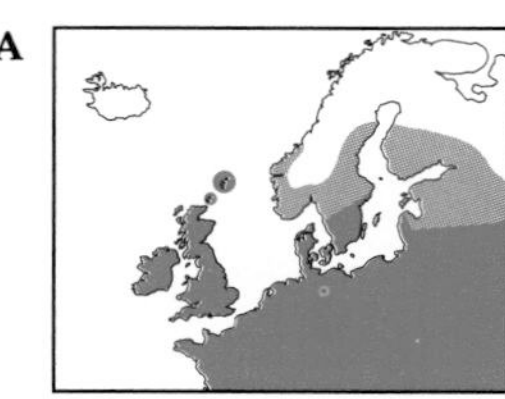

D
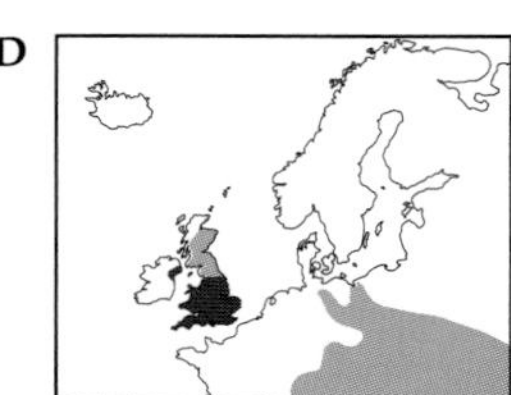

E
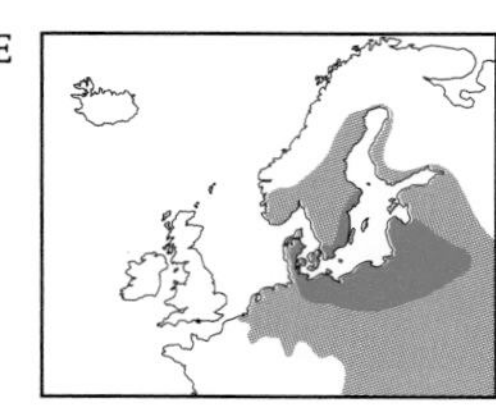

H
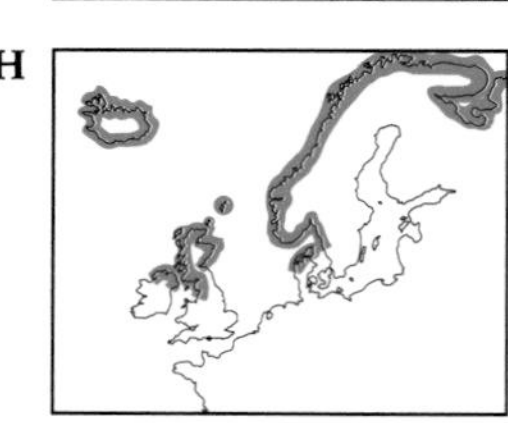

I
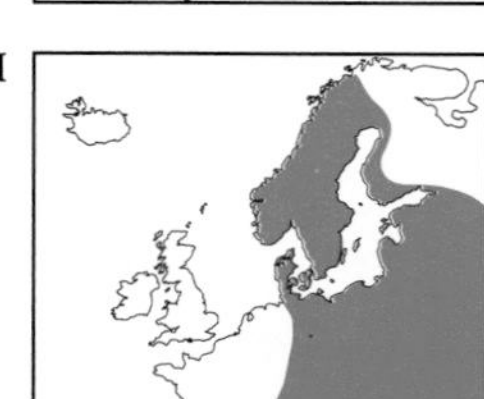

A Common Comfrey *Symphytum officinale* Erect bristly perennial, to 1.2m; stem strongly winged. Root leaves large, 15-25cm long, stalked, oval-lanceolate, softly hairy and untoothed; stem leaves smaller, unstalked, clasping stem, with bases running down stem. Flowers in branched coiled inflorescences; corolla tubular to bell-shaped, 12-18mm long, with short reflexed petal lobes, white, pink or purple-violet. On riverbanks and in damp grassland; through much of N Europe, but rarer and mainly naturalised further north. **Fl** 6-7. **Br** Common throughout southern half of Britain, rare in N Scotland and Ireland.

B Rough Comfrey *Symphytum asperum* Similar to Common Comfrey, but stems not winged, stem bristles hooked, calyx with blunt teeth, flowers pink turning blue. Introduced as fodder plant, now widely naturalised, including Britain. **Fl** 6-7. **Br** Locally naturalised throughout.

C Russian Comfrey *Symphytum × uplandicum* Stable hybrid, arising from Common Comfrey and Rough Comfrey. Intermediate between the parents, with very rough narrowly winged stems, upper leaves only forming short wings down stem. Petals purplish blue and variable. Now common in grassy places, especially roadsides, less so in damp places; throughout most of N Europe. **Fl** 5-8. **Br** Naturalised throughout most of Britain.

D Tuberous Comfrey *Symphytum tuberosum* Similar in habit to other comfreys, but has tuberous roots; stems simple or slightly branched, unwinged or slightly winged; middle leaves of stem longest, basal leaves disappearing by flowering time. Flowers yellow, 13-19mm long, corolla lobes turned back at the tip. Woods and damp shady places; from England and Germany southwards. **Fl** 6-7. **Br** Widespread, most frequent in Scotland, but rarely common.

E Alkanet *Anchusa officinalis* Hispid, erect perennial to 80cm, rarely more. Leaves long-lanceolate to oval-lanceolate, only lower ones stalked. Flowers bluish red or violet, rarely white or yellow, 10mm in diameter, with straight corolla tube, in long curling inflorescences. Bracts not wavy-edged. From S Scandinavia southwards; in scattered localities in grassy, rocky and disturbed places, often over limestone. **Fl** 6-9. **Br** Naturalised or casual in scattered localities, mainly S England.

F Bugloss *Anchusa arvensis* Erect or ascending very bristly annual to 60cm. Bristles mostly have swollen bases. Leaves linear-lanceolate or broader, wavy-edged and somewhat toothed, lower ones stalked, upper ones clasping stem. Flowers bright blue or rarely pale, with a curved corolla tube 4-7mm long, in branched leafy inflorescences; throat of corolla closed by 5 hairy scales. Fruit 3-4mm wide, irregularly ovoid, with net pattern on surface. Common and widespread on sandy and light soils, in grassland, dunes and waste ground. **Fl** 6-9. **Br** Locally common throughout much of Britain, rarer in the north, tending to be coastal.

G Green Alkanet *Pentaglottis sempervirens* Erect bristly perennial up to 80cm. Basal leaves ovate, narrowed into long petiole, stem leaves unstalked and untoothed. Flowers bright blue with whitish centre, 8-10mm in diameter, in stalked bristly clusters from the axils of the upper leaves; corolla throat closed by 5 hairy scales. Nutlets rough, netted on surface. Widely naturalised, originally from SW Europe; in hedges, roadsides and shaded areas, often close to habitation. **Fl** 4-6. **Br** Scattered, commonest in the south-west.

H Oyster Plant *Mertensia maritima* Distinctive, prostrate, hairless, fleshy, blue-grey plant, with stems to 60cm, sometimes forming mats. Leaves oval to spoon-shaped, lower ones stalked, upper unstalked. Flowers long-stalked, about 6mm across, bell-shaped, pink in bud becoming pink and blue, in branched leafy inflorescences; flower stalks become recurved as fruit ripens. On sandy or shingly shores, often amongst high-tide debris; from N England, N Ireland and Denmark northwards, frequent in the far north. **Fl** 6-8. **Br** From NW England northwards, locally frequent further north.

I Madwort *Asperugo procumbens* Hispid procumbent or climbing annual herb. Leaves lanceolate. Flowers purplish becoming blue, with white tube, about 3mm in diameter, solitary or paired in leaf axils, becoming surrounded by greatly enlarged leaf-like toothed sepals (**i**). In cultivated places and disturbed ground, usually rich in nitrogen; throughout much of N Europe, but often not native. **Fl** 5-9. **Br** Casual, occasionally naturalised, in scattered sites, mainly near ports.

J Hound's-tongue *Cynoglossum officinale* Erect, softly *grey-downy* biennial to 80cm. Basal leaves lanceolate-ovate, stalked and pointed, to 30cm; stem leaves smaller, unstalked and narrower. Flowers dull purplish red, funnel-shaped, 5-7mm in diameter, with 5 equal lobes; calyx lobes spreading in fruit; inflorescence long and often branched. Fruit consists of 4 flattened oval nutlets covered with hooked bristles, and with a raised border. Widespread and locally common throughout, except the far north; in dry open habitats especially near the coast. **Fl** 5-8. **Br** Commonest in the east, rarer in the west.

K Green Hound's-tongue *Cynoglossum germanicum* Similar to Hound's-tongue in form, but differs in that the *leaves are green*, bristly and barely hairy; flowers smaller, 5-6mm in diameter, and the nutlets have no thickened border. Central Europe extending north-west to England and Belgium; in woods and hedgerows, usually on basic soil. **Fl** 5-7. **Br** Very rare in S England.

L Blue Hound's-tongue *Cynoglossum creticum* Rather similar to Green Hound's-tongue, but hairier, with larger blue flowers, 7-10mm across, veined with purple. A S European plant, reaching N France. **Fl** 5-7. **Br** Absent.

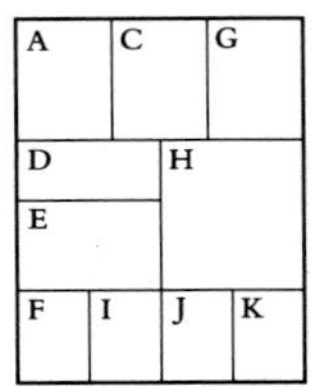

A Common Comfrey
C Russian Comfrey
G Green Alkanet
D Tuberous Comfrey
H Oyster Plant
E Alkanet
F Bugloss
I Madwort
J Hound's-tongue
K Green Hound's-tongue

D
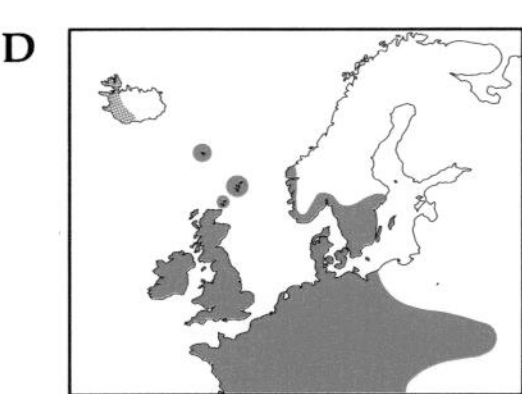

E
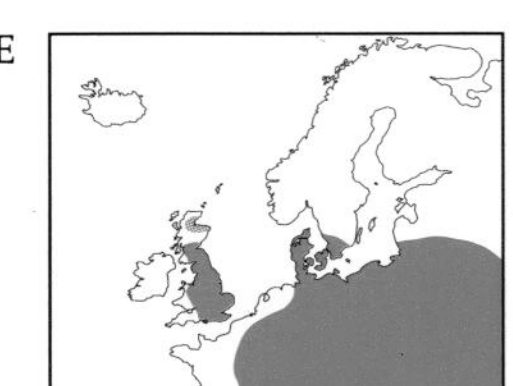

G
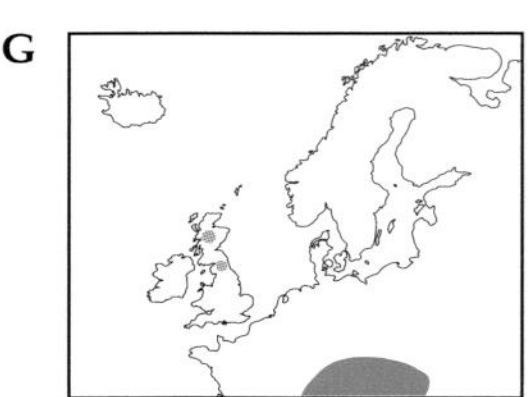

H
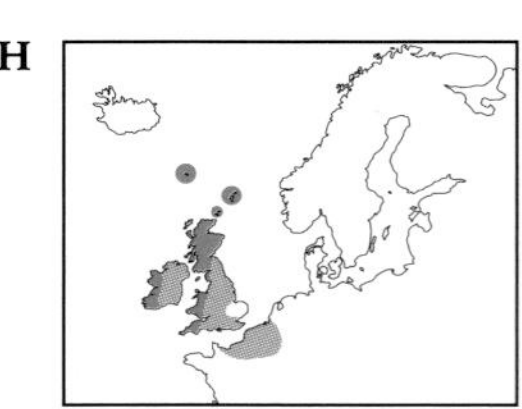

L
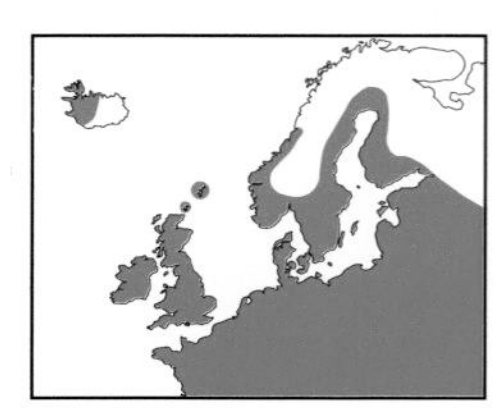

O
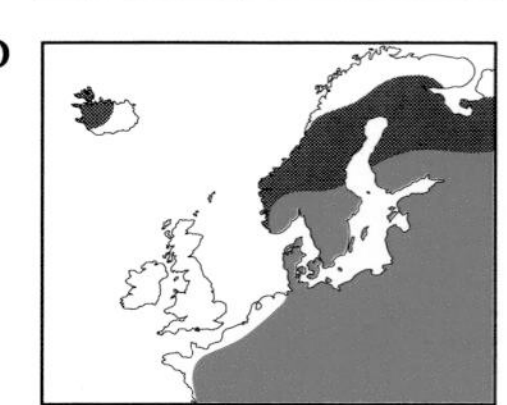

FORGET-ME-NOTS *Myosotis* Readily recognised group of small annual or perennial herbs, usually with pale blue flowers. Many species need close examination for certain identification; important features include the degree of hairiness and type of hairs on the sepals, length of the flower stalks, and presence or absence of leafy bracts in the inflorescence.

A **Field Forget-me-not** *Myosotis arvensis* Variable, erect, pubescent annual, occasionally perennial, stem branching, with spreading hairs. Lower leaves forming a loose rosette, roughly elliptical, broadest above the middle and barely stalked; stem leaves lanceolate and unstalked, with spreading hairs on both surfaces. Flowers pale to bright blue, with 5 concave lobes, up to 5mm in diameter, corolla tube shorter than calyx. Calyx bell-shaped, with hooked hairs on tube (**a**), lobes spreading when in fruit. Inflorescence without bracts. Flower stalks remain erect in fruit, and are roughly twice as long as calyx. Very common throughout; in dry grasslands, scrub, open woods and arable land. **Fl** 4-10. **Br** Common throughout except the far north.

B **Early Forget-me-not** *Myosotis ramossissima* Low hispid annual, only to 15cm. Similar characteristics to Field Forget-me-not, but stem with spreading hairs below, appressed hairs above; calyx teeth spreading in fruit, flowers only 2-3mm in diameter, inflorescence longer than leafy part of stem when in fruit. Flower stalks roughly equal to calyx when in fruit. Common in dry open habitats, especially on sand; throughout except the far north. **Fl** 4-6. **Br** Widespread and common, rarer in west and north.

C *Myosotis stricta* Very similar to Early Forget-me-not, but hairs on lower leaf surface and lower part of stem are hooked. Widespread in similar habitats. **Fl** 5-7. **Br** Absent.

D **Changing Forget-me-not** *Myosotis discolor* Similar to above 2 species, except that it is 8-20cm tall, *flowers open yellow* then change to blue, calyx with hooked hairs is longer than stalk (**d**), calyx teeth are erect in fruit. In dry open, often sandy, grasslands; almost throughout, except N Scandinavia. **Fl** 5-9. **Br** Locally common throughout.

E **Wood Forget-me-not** *Myosotis sylvatica* More robust, hairy perennial to 50cm, often much-branched and leafy, with spreading hairs on stem. Leaves with spreading hairs. Corolla pale blue, flat and *6-10mm in diameter*; calyx with stiffly hooked hairs (**e**); fruit stalks 1-2 times the length of calyx, spreading when ripe. Inflorescence not leafy, not longer than leafy part of stem when in fruit. Nutlets brown when ripe. In woods and shady or damp grassland; widespread and locally common, except in the north. **Fl** 4-8. **Br** Locally common, but rare in W and N Britain.

F *Myosotis decumbens* Very similar to Wood Forget-me-not, but has creeping rhizomes and corolla tube is distinctly longer than calyx (rather than roughly equal to it). Grassy and rocky places, mainly in mountains; in Germany and Scandinavia. **Br** Absent.

G **Alpine Forget-me-not** *Myosotis alpestris* Rather similar to Wood Forget-me-not, but usually shorter and tufted. Basal leaves commonly (though not always) long-stalked. Flowers bright blue. *Fruit stalks about the same length as calyx, which is densely silvery hairy* (**g**). Nutlets black when ripe. Mountain grasslands and rocky habitats from Scotland southwards, usually on calcareous rock. **Fl** 7-9. **Br** In Upper Teesdale and Scottish Highlands only; rare.

H **Creeping Forget-me-not** *Myosotis secunda* Creeping, rhizomatous perennial producing erect hairy branches. Flowers blue, 6-8mm in diameter, with slightly notched lobes; calyx divided half-way into pointed teeth, half the length of calyx (**h**), with straight hairs; *fruit stalks 3-5 times the length of calyx, reflexed when mature.* Lower part of inflorescence has leafy bracts. Nutlets dark brown and shiny. In acid marshes, bogs and wet places in Britain, France (local) and mountains further south. **Fl** 6-8. **Br** Common in W and N Britain, increasingly rare to the east.

I **Pale Forget-me-not** *Myosotis stolonifera* Similar to Creeping Forget-me-not, but smaller, with numerous stolons from lower part of plant; leaves oval, twice as long as wide; flowers smaller, 5mm in diameter. In wet places on mountains; Britain only. **Fl** 6-7. **Br** N England and Scotland only.

J **Tufted Forget-me-not** *Myosotis laxa* ssp *caespitosa* Rather similar to above 2 species, but without runners. *Hairs on stems, leaves, and calyx appressed*; petals blue, 2-4mm with rounded lobes; calyx with pointed teeth (**j**). Fruit stalks 2-3 times as long as calyx, spreading when in fruit. In wet and damp places; widespread, though rare in N Scandinavia. **Fl** 5-8. **Br** Throughout Britain; frequent.

K **Jersey Forget-me-not** *Myosotis sicula* Similar to Tufted Forget-me-not, with *almost hairless calyx with blunt teeth*; corolla saucer-shaped; inflorescence with flowers in 2 distinct rows. Dune-hollows in Jersey and NW France only. **Fl** 5-7. **Br** Rare in Jersey only.

L **Water Forget-me-not** *Myosotis scorpioides* Rather similar to Creeping Forget-me-not, but hairless or with appressed hairs on stem; fruit stalks only *1-2 times the length of calyx; calyx teeth short and triangular* (**l**), not more than a third of the length of calyx; corolla larger, 8-10mm in diameter; no leafy bracts on inflorescence. Wet habitats, often on neutral-basic soils; throughout, often common. **Fl** 5-9. **Br** Common and widespread.

M *Myosotis nemorosa* Very similar to above, but usually without stolons; leaves usually with deflexed hairs below; flowers less than 6mm in diameter. Wet meadows and woods; widespread, mainly eastern. **Fl** 5-7. **Br** Absent.

N **Deflexed Bur Forget-me-not** *Lappula deflexa* Rather similar in form and colouring to *Myosotis* forget-me-nots. Differs in that the corolla is more bell-shaped, 3-6mm across, with a shorter tube, and the nutlets have *distinctive hooked spines* – hence the name. In this species, the *fruits are strongly deflexed* as they ripen (**n**), and the corolla is 5-7mm in diameter. In rocky and mountain habitats; mainly central and S Scandinavia, on mountains in France and Germany. **Fl** 6-8. **Br** Absent.

O **Bur Forget-me-not** *Lappula squarrosa* Very similar to above, differing mainly in the smaller flowers (4mm in diameter) and the *erect fruits.* In dry habitats, disturbed, and waste ground; widespread in mainland Europe except in the far north, but often only casual or naturalised. **Br** Casual only.

A	B	D
E	G	H
J	L	O

A **Field Forget-me-not**

B **Early Forget-me-not**

D **Changing Forget-me-not**

E **Wood Forget-me-not**

G **Alpine Forget-me-not**

H **Creeping Forget-me-not**

J **Tufted Forget-me-not**

L **Water Forget-me-not**

O **Bur Forget-me-not**

a

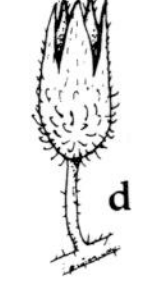
d

e

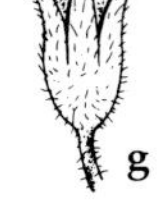
g

h

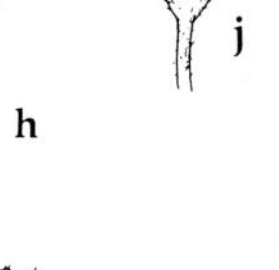
j

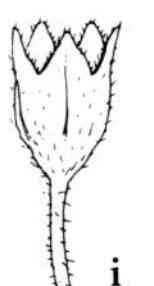
i

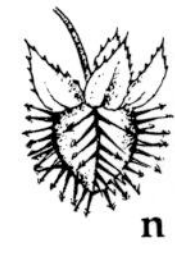
n

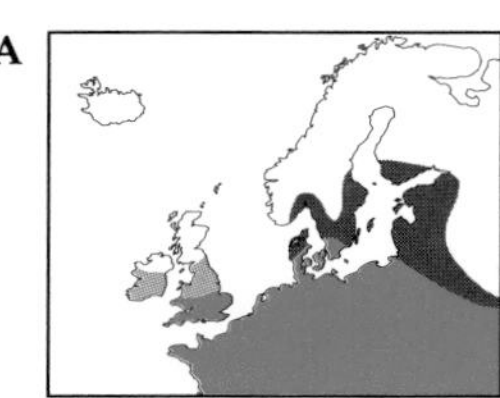

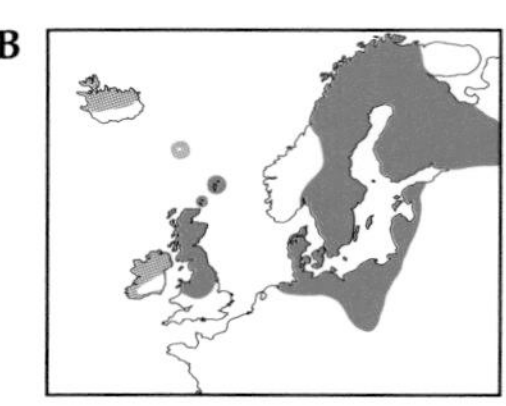

Vervain Family Verbenaceae

Herbs or shrubs with opposite leaves. Flowers 5- (or 4-) parted; corolla with flat petal lobes and short tube.

A Vervain *Verbena officinalis* Medium-tall erect perennial, with 4-angled stems, rough on corners. Lower leaves roughly rhomboid, but deeply cut, almost to the midrib, with the lobes often divided again. Upper leaves smaller, unstalked, barely divided. Flowers bluish pink, 4-5mm across, 5-lobed divided roughly into 2 lips, corolla tube twice the length of calyx; in long narrow, often branched, leafless spikes, 8-12cm long. Fruit separates into 4 ribbed nutlets. Widespread northwards to N Germany (and naturalised beyond that); in dry grasslands, woodland edges, roadsides, and scrub. **Fl** 6-9. **Br** Common and widespread through most of England and Wales, becoming increasingly rare northwards.

Water-starwort Family Callitrichaceae

The water-starworts are a difficult group of small aquatic or mud-dwelling plants. Most species can vary considerably in form according to conditions, and all except 2 produce different water and land forms. For reliable identification, close examination of ripe fruit is required. To simplify the process of identification, the species have been broken down into groups with certain similar characteristics.

(1) Species with leaves all linear, and normally submerged.

B Autumnal Water-starwort *Callitriche hermaphroditica* Submerged herb. Leaves yellow-green, mostly over 10mm long, *tapering slightly towards apex* which has distinctly notched tip (**b1**). Flowers solitary, bracts absent. Fruit roughly circular, 2mm, broadly winged (**b2**), produced in reasonable quantity. Throughout in lakes, canals and slow-flowing rivers. **Fl** 5-9. **Br** N Britain from Midlands northwards, and throughout Ireland.

C Short-leaved Water-starwort *Callitriche truncata* ssp *occidentalis* Rather similar to above, but stems reddish, leaves bluish-green, normally less than 10mm long, tips square cut and *barely notched* (**c**). Fruit rare, distinctly wider than long, to 1.5mm across, lobes unwinged. Only Britain, France and Belgium. **Br** Very rare, S and central England only.

D Intermediate Water-starwort *Callitriche hamulata* Similar to Autumnal Water-starwort, but with at least lower leaves up to 25mm long, spanner-shaped, parallel-sided but then *expanding to notched tip* (**d**). Floating leaves, where present, more elliptical. Flowers solitary, from submerged or floating leaf axils. Styles deflexed, bracts sickle-shaped, soon falling; fruit 1.5-2.5mm wide, with narrow wings on lobes and remnants of styles bent back. Widespread in often acid slow-moving or still waters; throughout except the far north. **Fl** 4-9. **Br** Common and widespread.

E Pedunculate Water-starwort *Callitriche brutia* Very similar to Intermediate Water-starwort, but more slender; tips of submerged leaves not enlarged though often irregularly notched (**e**); fruit broadly winged, 1-1.4mm, stalked in terrestrial forms. Scattered throughout but very local and incompletely recorded. **Fl** 5-9. **Br** Probably widespread.

(2) Leaves not all linear, with upper ones normally forming a floating rosette.

F Common Water-starwort *Callitriche stagnalis* Has no parallel-sided leaves, all leaves elliptical to oval, not (or barely) notched (**f1**); upper leaves, often 6, forming a rosette (**f2**); leaves commonly 5-veined. Flowers from rosette leaves only, solitary or paired; stigmas 2-3mm, becoming recurved; *fruit has all 4 lobes broadly winged*. Very common and widespread throughout; in still and slow-moving water, or on mud. **Fl** 5-9. **Br** Common throughout.

G Blunt-fruited Water-starwort *Callitriche obtusangula* Similar in form to Common Water-starwort, but differs in having submerged leaves linear, often deeply notched; *rosette leaves up to 12 together, roughly diamond-shaped*, strongly veined (**g**). Fruit slightly keeled but *not winged*, 1.5mm across. In fresh or brackish, still to slow-moving water; northwards to Holland and Germany. **Fl** 5-9. **Br** England and Wales only, scattered through Ireland.

H *Callitriche cophocarpa* Similar to Blunt-fruited Water-starwort, but leaves more rounded (**h1, h2**), fruit smaller (about 1mm). Widespread but local; in base-rich water. **Fl** 5-9. **Br** Very rare in highly base-rich waters.

I Various-leaved, or Long-styled, Water-starwort *Callitriche platycarpa* Broadly similar to above 3 species. Submerged leaves linear, not expanded at tip, but distinctly notched (**i1**); *rosette leaves few, elliptical*, narrowing to a stalk, dark green, 3-veined, forming a convex rosette (**i2**). Stigmas erect, 3-5mm, fruit brownish, with *lobes narrowly winged all round*, to 2mm across. Widespread almost throughout; in still or slow-moving, fresh, occasionally brackish, waters. **Fl** 4-10. **Br** Local, mainly in lowland areas.

J *Callitriche palustris* Very like Various-leaved Water-starwort, but flowers usually 2 together; fruit blackish with *lobes narrow-winged at tip only*. Throughout but local. **Fl** 6-9. **Br** Possibly present.

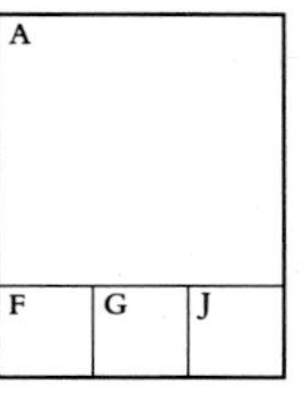

A Vervain with White Melolot visible in the centre

F Common Water-starwort

G Blunt-fruited Water-starwort

J *Callitriche palustris*

b1 b2 c

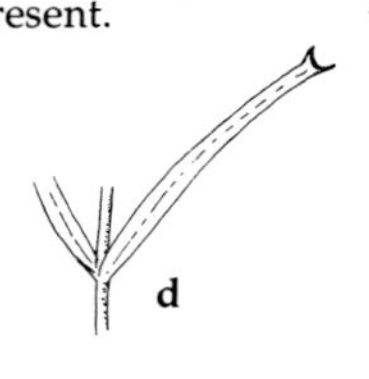

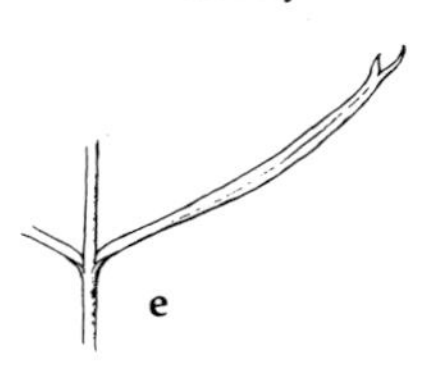

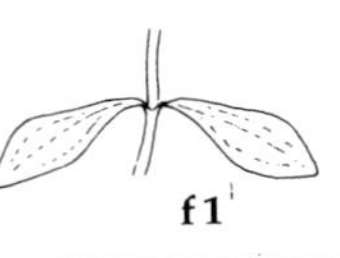

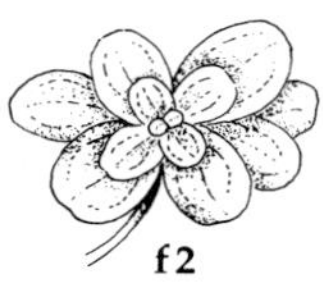

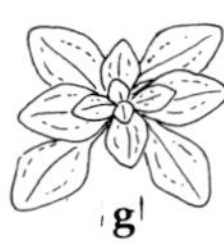

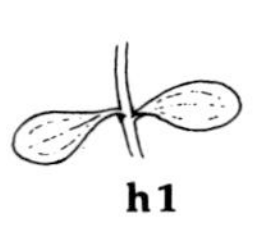

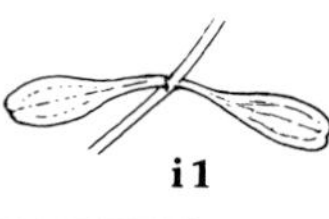

B

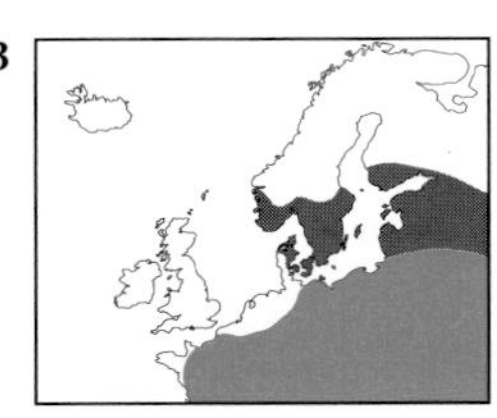

C

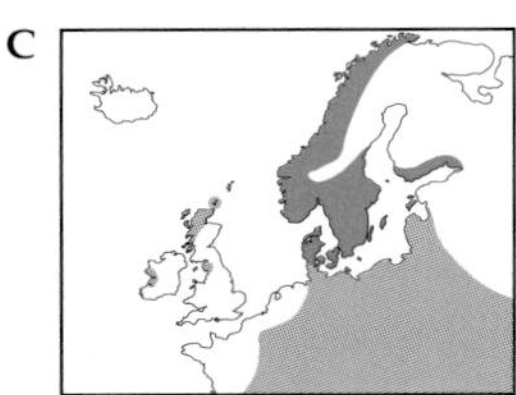

D

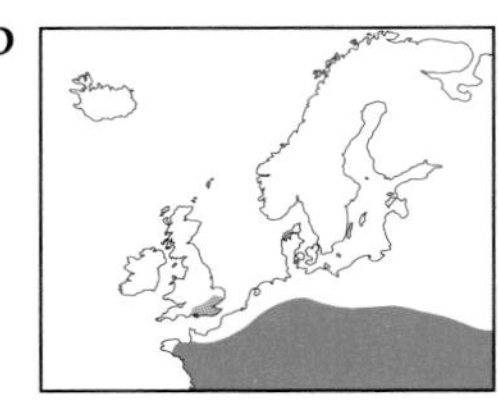

E

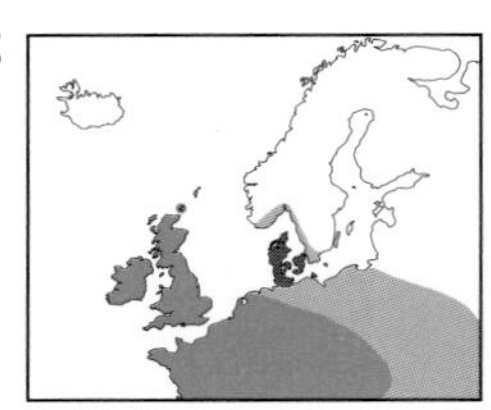

F

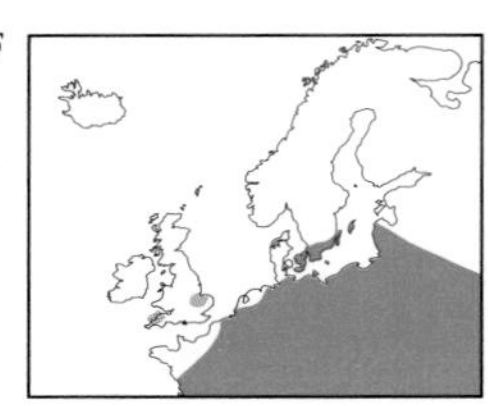

G

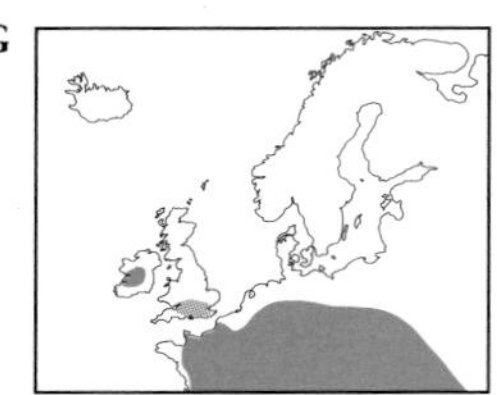

H

J

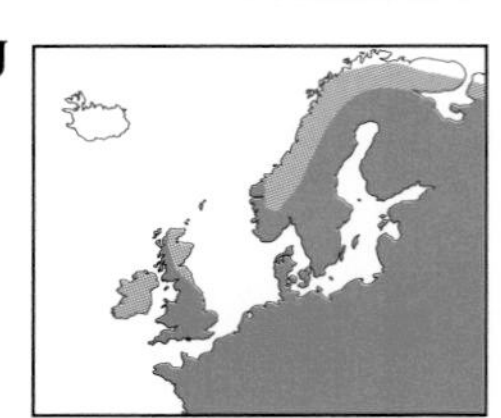

K

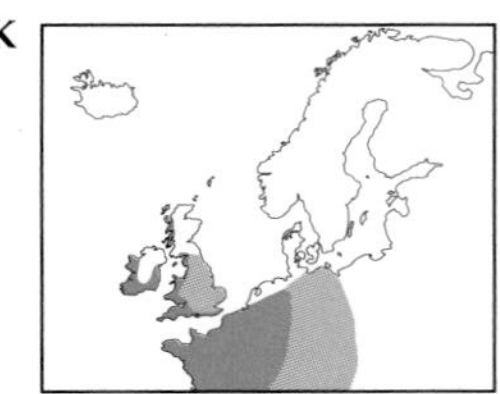

Mint Family Labiatae

Herbs or subshrubs, with square stems, and opposite leaves without stipules. Frequently aromatic, the source of many volatile oils. Flowers irregular, usually clearly 2-lipped, in apparent whorls in the axils of opposite leaf-like bracts. Calyx with 5 teeth.

A Bugle *Ajuga reptans* Small perennial herb, with long leafy rooting runners. Erect flower stems, up to 40cm, shortly hairy on 2 opposite faces only. Basal leaves between ovate and spoon-shaped, 40-70mm long, stalked, sometimes shallowly toothed; stem leaves in pairs, unstalked. Inflorescence made up of whorls of flowers from bracts, uppermost bracts shorter than flowers; corolla blue to blue-violet, 14-17mm long, lower lip often with white lines. Widespread and frequently common in woods and grasslands, often on heavy soils; as far north as S Norway. **Fl** 4-6. **Br** Very common, less so in the north.

B Blue Bugle *Ajuga genevensis* Similar in form to Bugle, differing in that there are no above-ground runners and the stem is normally *hairy on all 4 faces*; the leaves are toothed, with the lower ones withering by flowering time. Flowers similar, but *brighter*, richer blue. Stamens markedly protruding from tube. Locally common on mainland Europe northwards to Belgium and Germany; in woods, roadsides and dry rocky places, often on lime-rich soils. **Fl** 4-7. **Br** Absent as native, occasionally naturalised.

C Pyramidal Bugle *Ajuga pyramidalis* Similar to the above 2 species in form. *Stem hairy all round*. Basal leaves stalked, oval, remaining green at flowering time. Leafy bracts all much longer than the flowers, often purplish-tinged, hairy. Flowers blue, *stamens slightly protruding*. Grassy and rocky habitats, often in upland areas, usually on calcareous soils; from Belgium northwards (and in mountains further south). **Fl** 5-7. **Br** Local or rare in N England, Scotland and Ireland only.

D Ground-pine *Ajuga chamaepitys* Hairy, ascending, low annual to 20cm, quite different to other *Ajuga* species. Basal leaves withering early, stem leaves divided into 3 narrow linear lobes, smelling of pine when crushed. Flowers 7-15mm long, yellow with red-purple markings (rarely all purple), 2 (-4) at each node, much shorter than bracts. Widespread from Holland and Germany southwards, very local except to the south; in open calcareous habitats including arable fields. **Fl** 5-9. **Br** Rare and local, decreasing, in S England only.

E Wood Sage *Teucrium scorodonia* Medium, erect, downy, perennial herb to 60cm, usually less. Leaves oval, heart-shaped at base, to 70mm, stalked, wrinkled, with rounded teeth, aromatic. Flowers in pairs in bract axils, pale greenish yellow, with typical *Teucrium* shape (a single, 5-lobed, lower lip, 5-6mm long); stamens red, distinctly protruding. Inflorescence terminal, without true leaves. Widespread and common outside Scandinavia, local or naturalised in S Scandinavia; in dry grassy and wooded areas, heaths, usually on acid soils. **Fl** 7-9. **Br** Common throughout.

F Water Germander *Teucrium scordium* Softly hairy perennial, with creeping rhizomes or leafy runners, and erect flower stems to 40cm. Leaves oblong, coarsely toothed, rounded at base, more or less unstalked, grey-green and with garlic smell when crushed. Flowers typical *Teucrium* shape, pink-purple, lip to 10mm long, in whorls of 2-6 forming a loose terminal inflorescence. Wet, often calcareous damp places, including dune-slacks; local or rare, as far north as S Scandinavia. **Fl** 6-10. **Br** Very rare in a few sites in SW and E England and W Ireland only.

G Cut-leaved Germander *Teucrium botrys* Short, erect, downy annual or biennial, often with branched stems up to 30cm. Leaves stalked, *deeply pinnately lobed*, with lobes often cut further; bracts similar but smaller, longer than flowers. Flowers bright pink, lip about 8mm long, in whorls of 2-6 up stem. Dry grassland, disturbed sites, and rocky areas on calcareous soils; local or rare from Belgium and Holland southwards. **Fl** 6-9. **Br** Rare and local in S England only, from Cotswolds eastwards.

H Wall Germander *Teucrium chamaedrys* Tufted, hairy perennial, woody at the base, without creeping rhizomes. Stems erect or ascending, to 40cm. Leaves oval-oblong, about twice as long as wide, blunt, short-stalked, shiny dark green above and varying from untoothed to deeply toothed. Flowers pink-purple, corolla lip 8-10mm long, in whorls, upper bracts shorter than flowers. From Belgium and Holland southwards; on calcareous rocks, in grassland and on walls; often naturalised. **Fl** 6-9. **Br** In chalk grassland in Sussex, possibly native; rarely naturalised on walls elsewhere.

I Mountain Germander *Teucrium montanum* Dwarf spreading shrub, 10-25cm, with spreading hairs. Leaves linear-lanceolate, untoothed, grey-green above and *white hairy below* with edges rolled under. Flowers in dense rounded heads of *creamy yellow flowers*, 12-15mm long, with leaf-like bracts. On dry or rocky calcareous soils, including chalk downland; from Holland and Germany southwards. **Fl** 5-8. **Br** Absent.

J Skullcap *Scutellaria galericulata* Medium, creeping, downy or hairless perennial, with erect flower stems to 50cm. Leaves oval-lanceolate, 20-50mm long, slightly toothed, variably heart-shaped at base, stalked. Flowers blue-violet, much longer than calyx, 10-20mm long, tube curved slightly; in loose erratic inflorescence towards top of stem. Common and widespread throughout N Europe except in the far north; in marshes, riversides and wet woods. **Fl** 6-9. **Br** Common and widespread, though scarce in Ireland and NE Scotland.

K Lesser Skullcap *Scutellaria minor* Similar to Skullcap in form, but smaller, to 15cm tall and almost hairless. Leaves 10-30mm long, ovate to lanceolate, untoothed, though sometimes lobed near base. Flowers in pairs in axils of leaf-like bracts, pink and 2-lipped with lower lip purple-spotted; corolla tube 6-10mm long, 2-4 times length of calyx, straight. In damp, often acid, habitats; from Holland and Germany southwards (and very rare in Sweden). **Fl** 7-10. **Br** Widespread and local as far north as central Scotland, rarer further north.

L Spear-leaved Skullcap *Scutellaria hastifolia* Similar to Lesser Skullcap, but leaves arrow-shaped (I), purplish below; flowers blue-purple, tube strongly bent. Local in damp grassland, woods, throughout Europe except in far north. **Fl** 7-9. **Br** Very rare introduction only.

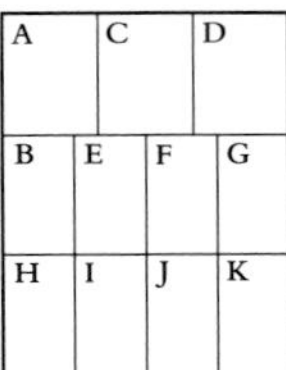

A Bugle
C Pyramidal Bugle
D Ground-pine
B Blue Bugle
E Wood Sage
F Water Germander
G Cut-leaved Germander
H Wall Germander
I Mountain Germander
J Skullcap
K Lesser Skullcap

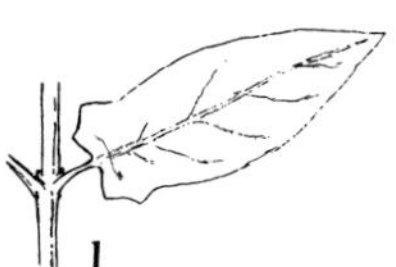

A

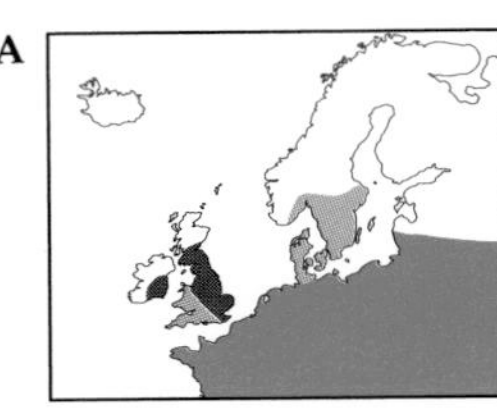

B

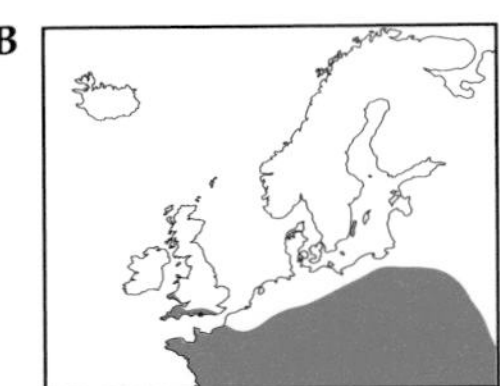

E

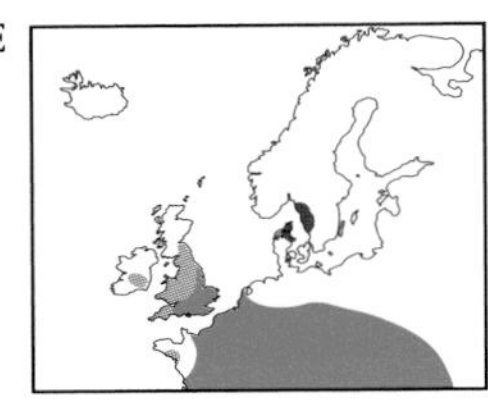

I

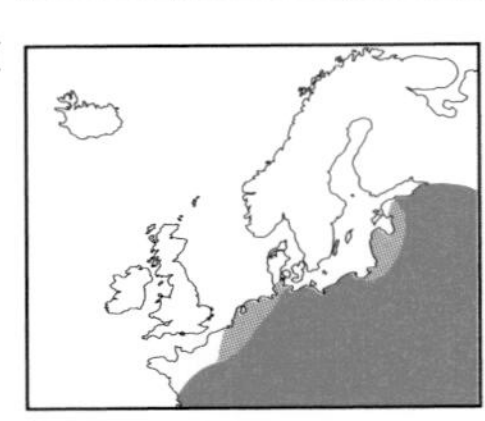

N

A White Horehound *Marrubium vulgare* Erect, white-downy perennial to 45cm, often with numerous non-flowering branches. Leaves rounded-oval, to 40mm long, wrinkled and greyish downy above, felted white below. Flowers white, 12-15mm long, in many-flowered separated whorls. Scattered localities northwards to S Sweden; on dry grasslands and waste places, especially near the coast. **Fl** 6-10. **Br** Occasional on the S coast in calcareous grassy sites; very rare elsewhere.

B Bastard Balm *Melittis melissophyllum* Perennial herb, with erect often clustered stems to 70cm, hairy and strong-smelling. Leaves ovate, to 80mm long, pointed, with rounded teeth and stalked. Flowers very large, 25-40mm long, white, pink, purple or a mixture of these, greatly exceeding the sepals, fragrant, in clusters of 2-6 from the upper leaf-like bract axils. Woodland edges and rides, hedgebanks, shady areas; as far north as Belgium and S Britain. Common in the south of area. **Fl** 5-7. **Br** Rare in S Britain, W Sussex; decreasing.

C Common Hemp-nettle *Galeopsis tetrahit* Erect branched annual, with bristly-hairy, slightly sticky, stems up to 60cm, *swollen at the nodes*. Leaves ovate to lanceolate, pointed, toothed, 3-10cm long, and stalked. Flowers pink-purple, rarely white, with darker markings, 15-20mm long, *corolla tube roughly equal to calyx*, middle lobe of lower corolla lip not notched; calyx bristly, with long pointed teeth. Inflorescence consists of leafy dense whorls in upper part of stem. Throughout; in disturbed habitats, tracksides and heaths. **Fl** 7-9. **Br** Common throughout.

D Lesser Hemp-nettle *Galeopsis bifida* Very similar to Common Hemp-nettle, but smaller in all parts, middle lobe of lip narrower, with deflexed sides, and notch in centre; darker colouring reaching edge of lower lip. Throughout, including Britain. **Fl** 7-9. **Br** Widespread almost throughout.

E Red, or Narrow-leaved, Hemp-nettle *Galeopsis angustifolia* Similar in form to Common Hemp-nettle. *Stem not swollen at nodes*. Leaves narrower, less than 10mm wide, with few small teeth, silkily hairy. Flowers deep reddish pink, to purplish, with yellow markings, 15-25mm long, *tube much longer than calyx teeth*. In arable land, on shingle, and other open habitats; local from Germany southwards, naturalised further north. **Fl** 7-10. **Br** Local and erratic in appearance, mainly in SE England, rare elsewhere.

F Broad-leaved Hemp-nettle *Galeopsis ladanum* Very similar to Red Hemp-nettle, but has broader, oval, strongly toothed leaves, not silky. *Corolla tube barely exceeds calyx*. Widespread in Europe except in the far north; on more acid soils. **Fl** 7-10. **Br** Very rare or extinct.

G Downy Hemp-nettle *Galeopsis segetum* Broadly similar to Red Hemp-nettle, except the flowers are pale yellow, to 30mm, much longer than calyx; and leaves (especially below) and calyx silkily hairy. Local in Europe northwards to Denmark; in arable land on acid soil. **Fl** 7-8. **Br** Very rare, possibly extinct.

H Large-flowered Hemp-nettle *Galeopsis speciosa* Resembles other hemp-nettles in form, but very distinctive. Stem stout, uniformly bristly-hairy, with additional yellow-tipped glandular hairs. Corolla 27-34mm long, yellow and violet, corolla tube twice the length of calyx. In arable land on acid and peaty soils, frequently with potatoes; throughout except the far north. **Fl** 7-9. **Br** Rather common in the north, much less frequent in the south.

I Spotted Dead-nettle *Lamium maculatum* Very variable, hairy, aromatic perennial, often forming patches with rhizomes, with erect flower stems to 60cm. Leaves triangular to ovate, pointed, toothed and stalked, often (but not always) with a large white to pale green blotch in the centre. Flowers pinkish purple, 20-35mm, with curved corolla tube, lateral lobes of corolla with a single tooth. Woodlands, hedgebanks and shady habitats; from Holland southwards on mainland Europe, naturalised elsewhere. **Fl** 4-10. **Br** Introduced, locally naturalised, most commonly as form with silver-blotched leaves.

J White Dead-nettle *Lamium album* Similar in form to Spotted Dead-nettle. Leaves ovate, heart-shaped at the base, coarsely toothed, roughly Stinging-nettle shape, but not stinging (hence the name). Flowers white, 20-25mm, with corolla tube curved near base, upper lip hairy, lower lip with 2-3 teeth on each side-lobe. A familiar, common and widespread species, in grassy, disturbed and semi-shaded habitats almost throughout, except the far north. **Fl** 4-12. **Br** Common almost throughout, except N Scotland.

K Red Dead-nettle *Lamium purpureum* More or less erect, downy annual to 40cm, usually much less, often branched near base, and purplish. Leaves oval to heart-shaped, 10-50mm long, all stalked, coarsely round-toothed. Inflorescence dense and leafy; flowers pink-purple, corolla 10-18mm, tube longer than calyx, straight; calyx downy, with teeth equal to tube length, becoming spreading as fruit ripens. In cultivated ground and waste places; throughout N Europe. **Fl** 3-10. **Br** Common throughout.

L Cut-leaved Dead-nettle *Lamium hybridum* Very similar to Red Dead-nettle, but slenderer and less downy; leaves and bracts irregularly deeply toothed and truncated at base, with blade running down stalk. Similar habitats; throughout. **Fl** 3-10. **Br** Local, throughout but rare in the west and north.

M Henbit Dead-nettle *Lamium amplexicaule* Rather similar to Red Dead-nettle. Lower leaves rounded to ovate, blunt-toothed and long-stalked; bracts quite different in appearance (stalkless, *rounded, clasping the stem in pairs*, sometimes appearing like a ruff below the flowers). Flowers pink-purple, mostly 15-20mm long, but some remaining small and closed; calyx tube with dense, white, spreading hairs, teeth shorter than tube (**m**), not spreading in fruit. Widespread throughout except the extreme north; in cultivated and disturbed ground. **Fl** 3-11. **Br** Throughout, but much rarer in the north, mainly on dry soils.

N Northern Dead-nettle *Lamium molucellifolium* Similar to Henbit Dead-nettle, but stronger-growing, bracts not clasping, lower ones stalked; calyx with appressed hairs, teeth longer than tube (**n**), spreading in fruit. Similar habitats from Scotland and central Germany northwards. **Fl** 5-10. **Br** Scotland, frequent; Ireland rare.

A	B	C	E
F	H	I	M
K	J		L

A **White Horehound**

B **Bastard Balm**

C **Common Hemp-nettle**

E **Red Hemp-nettle**

F **Broad-leaved Hemp-nettle**

H **Large-flowered Hemp-nettle**

I **Spotted Dead-nettle** in the unspotted form, common in continental Europe

M **Henbit Dead-nettle**

K **Red Dead-nettle**

J **White Dead-nettle**

L **Cut-leaved Dead-nettle**

m

n

A

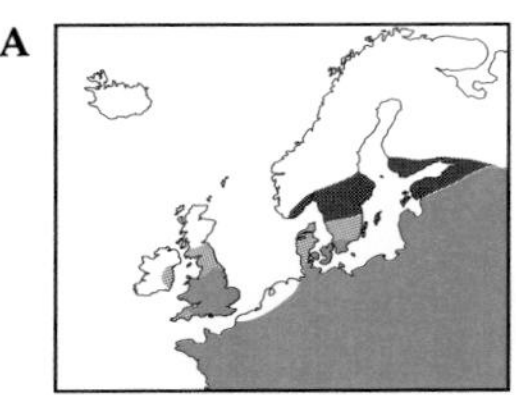

B

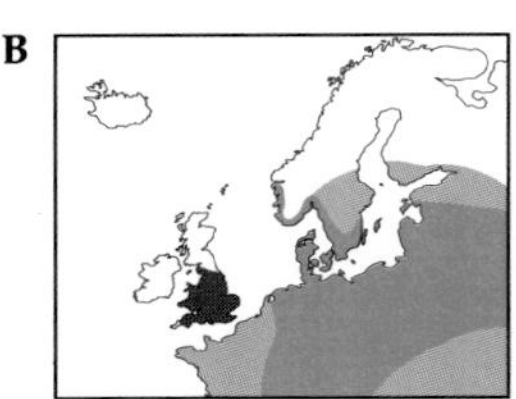

C

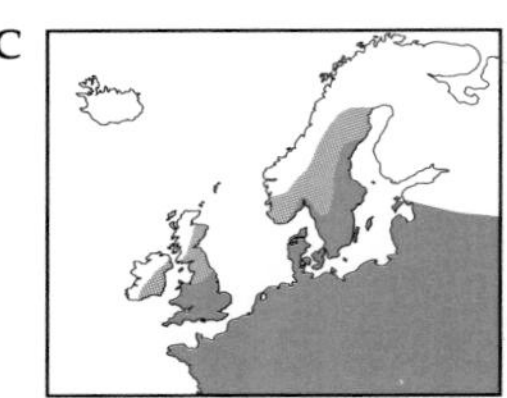

D

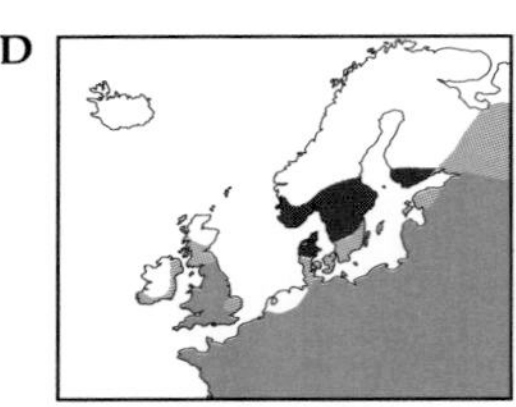

E

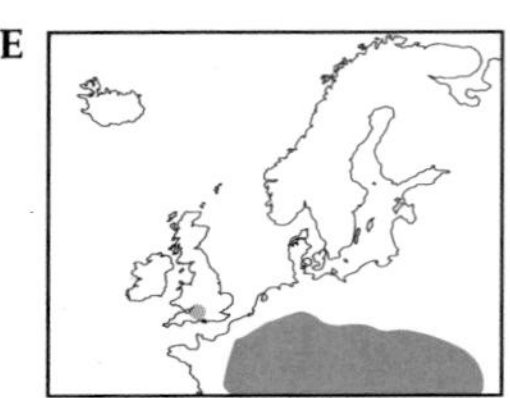

F

I

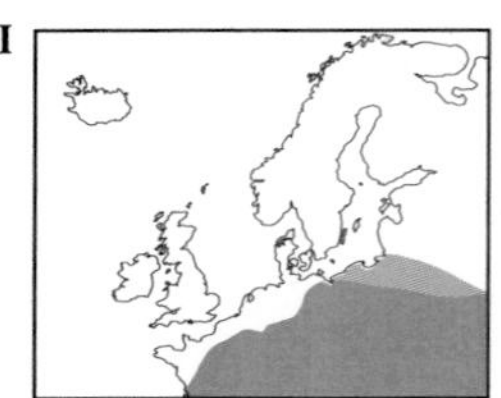

L

A Yellow Archangel *Lamiastrum galeobdolon* Hairy perennial, with long leafy runners, especially after flowering time; flower stems more or less erect, to 45cm. Very similar to dead-nettles, but with yellow flowers, 17-20mm long, streaked reddish, and lip of corolla divided into 3 equal lobes, with the middle lobe triangular and untoothed. In woods and hedgerows; as far north as S Scandinavia, most commonly on heavier base-rich soils. **Fl** 4-6. **Br** Frequent throughout most of England and Wales, much rarer further north and in Ireland.

B Motherwort *Leonurus cardiaca* Tall, variably hairy perennial, usually about 1m, occasionally more. Lower leaves palmately 3- to 7-lobed, with the lobes further toothed or lobed; upper leaves 3-lobed. Flowers pink or white, in whorls with conspicuous 3-lobed bracts; corolla 8-12mm, distinctly exceeding calyx, upper lip very hairy on back; calyx prominently 5-veined, with teeth almost as long as tube. In hedgebanks, woodland edges and shady waste places; widespread in mainland Europe except in the far north. **Fl** 7-9. **Br** Rarely naturalised.

C Black Horehound *Ballota nigra* Straggling to erect, roughly hairy perennial, to 80cm, with an unpleasant smell. Leaves ovate to heart-shaped, stalked, coarsely toothed, 30-80mm long. Flowers dull purple to pink, 12-18mm long, hairy, with concave upper lip; calyx funnel-shaped with 5 triangular long-pointed lobes; in dense leafy whorls. Widespread on roadsides and hedgebanks; from S Sweden southwards, probably not native in north of range. **Fl** 6-10. **Br** Common throughout England and Wales, rarer further north and in Ireland.

D Betony *Stachys officinalis* Erect, hairy or hairless perennial to 60cm. Basal leaves roughly oblong, heart-shaped at base, on long petioles; stem leaves narrower, with decreasing length stalks up the stem; all leaves with even rounded teeth. Inflorescence a short cylindrical dense terminal spike, sometimes with looser whorls below; *corolla red-purple*, 12-18mm, tube exceeding calyx; calyx has 5 bristle-pointed teeth. In open woods, pastures, hedgebanks, heaths, usually on lighter soils; from S Sweden and Scotland southwards; common. **Fl** 6-9. **Br** Common in England and Wales, rarer further north and in Ireland.

E Limestone, or Alpine, Woundwort *Stachys alpina* Softly hairy, erect or ascending perennial to 1m, with glandular hairs in the upper part. No creeping stems. Leaves ovate, heart-shaped at base, up to 18cm long, long-stalked, with rounded teeth. *Flowers dull purplish or pink*, sometimes with yellow centre, 15-22mm long, and hairy; individual flower bracteoles linear, roughly length of calyx; in dense leafy close-set whorls. Open woodland, wood-margins and rocky places, usually on limestone; commonest in hilly areas. **Fl** 6-8. **Br** Very rare on limestone in Gloucestershire and N Wales only.

F Downy Woundwort *Stachys germanica* Patch-forming biennial or perennial, with erect or ascending stems, wholly *densely felted with white hairs*. Leaves similar to Alpine Woundwort. Flowers rosy pink, hairy, in dense spikes. Rare in calcareous grassland and disturbed areas; from S England, Belgium and Germany southwards. **Fl** 7-8. **Br** Very rare, declining, in Oxfordshire only.

G Hedge Woundwort *Stachys sylvatica* Unpleasant-smelling bristly perennial, with erect stems to 90cm from a creeping rhizome. Leaves ovate, coarsely toothed, pointed, heart-shaped at base, blade 40-90mm long, with stalks to 70mm. Flowers 12-18mm long, *claret-red* with white markings, in whorls forming a long terminal spike; flower bracteoles minute; calyx with 5 rigid triangular teeth, more than the length of the tube. In shaded places and disturbed ground, almost throughout the area. **Fl** 7-9. **Br** Common almost throughout.

H Marsh Woundwort *Stachys palustris* Unscented bristly perennial, with erect stems to 1m or more from creeping rhizomes. Leaves narrow oblong to lanceolate, rounded or heart-shaped at base, lower ones short-stalked, upper stalkless, all coarsely toothed. *Flowers dull pink-purple*, with white markings, hairy outside, 12-15mm; calyx with narrowly triangular teeth, more than half as long as tube and hairy. In damp habitats such as ditchsides, lake-margins, marshes, occasionally in arable land; throughout. **Fl** 6-9. **Br** Throughout, frequent.

Marsh and Hedge Woundworts readily hybridise to produce *Stachys × ambigua*, intermediate between the parents, often in large clumps.

I Yellow Woundwort *Stachys recta* Variable, usually erect, aromatic perennial to 1m, slightly hairy but not glandular. Lower leaves oblong to ovate, rounded at base, wrinkled, dark green, usually downy; upper leaves narrower, unstalked. *Flowers in whorls of 6-16*, crowded towards the top; corolla pale yellow with red-purple streaks on lower lip, 15-20mm long. Calyx teeth broad, triangular, hairless, shorter than tube. In dry grassland and scrub; northwards to Belgium and Germany. **Fl** 6-8. **Br** Absent as native, rarely naturalised.

J Annual Woundwort *Stachys annua* Very similar to Yellow Woundwort but annual, hairless, to 30cm; flowers with corolla 10-16mm, *in whorls of 2-6 only*. In cultivated fields and open habitats, usually on calcareous soil, from Belgium and central Germany southwards. **Fl** 6-8. **Br** Occasional as casual.

K Field Woundwort *Stachys arvensis* Rather similar to Annual Woundwort, but with more rounded leaves and with *pink, purple-streaked flowers*. Almost throughout on sandy and disturbed acid ground. **Fl** 4-11. **Br** Locally common in the south and west, rarer in the north.

L Cat-mint *Nepeta cataria* Perennial mint-scented herb with grey-downy erect stems up to 80cm. Leaves ovate to heart-shaped, stalked, coarsely toothed, grey woolly below and downy but green above. Inflorescence cylindrical and spike-like, sometimes with separate lower whorls; flowers white with purple spots, 7-12mm, corolla tube curved, upper lip flat and rounded; calyx downy, with straight teeth. On dry banks, grassland and rocky areas, normally calcareous; native as far north as Holland, naturalised northwards into S Scandinavia. **Fl** 7-9. **Br** Only frequent in S and E England and Wales; very rare elsewhere.

A	B	D	
C	E	F	G
H	I	J	L

A Yellow Archangel
B Motherwort
D Betony
C Black Horehound
E Limestone Woundwort
F Downy Woundwort
G Hedge Woundwort
H Marsh Woundwort
I Yellow Woundwort
J Annual Woundwort
L Catmint

D
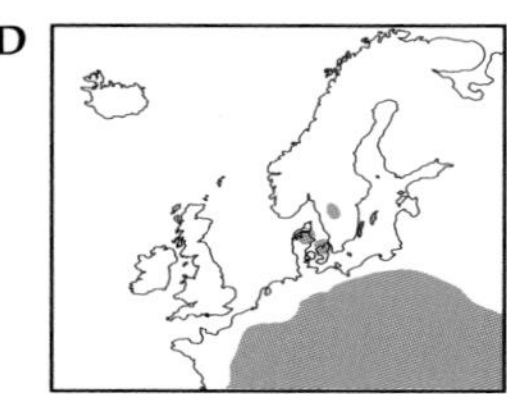
E
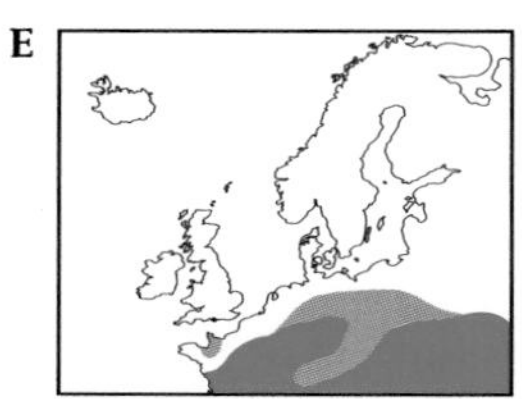
G
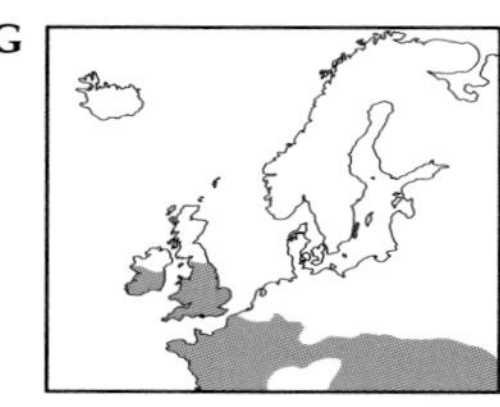
L
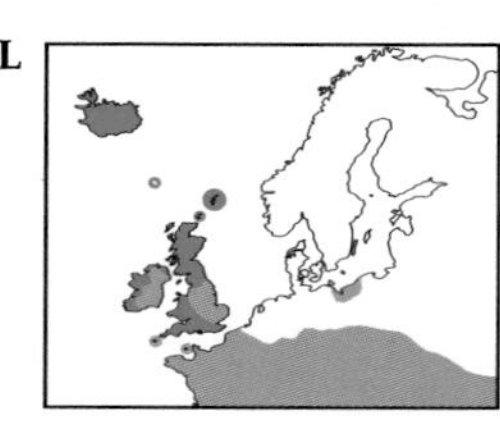
M
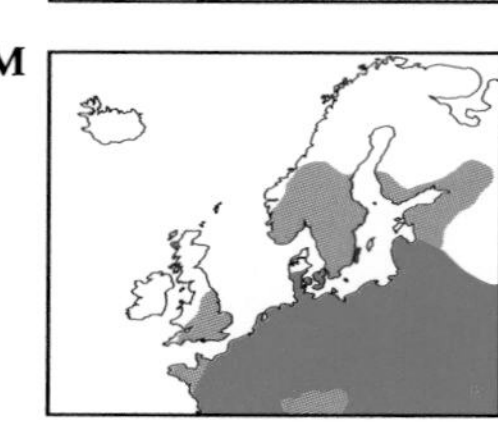

A Ground-ivy *Glechoma hederacea* Softly hairy, creeping perennial, rooting at the nodes, flowering stems erect, to 20cm. Leaves rounded, kidney-shaped, toothed, blunt at the tip, long-stalked, to 40mm long. Flowers in whorls of 2-4 with leaf-like bracts; corolla violet-blue, 15-20mm long, with purplish spots on lower lip, tube straight; calyx 2-lipped. Common throughout; in woods, grassland and waste ground. **Fl** 3-6. **Br** Common throughout.

B Northern Dragonhead *Dracocephalum ruyschiana* Hairless or slightly hairy perennial, with erect stems to 60cm. Leaves linear-lanceolate, untoothed. Flowers large (20-28mm) blue-violet, held erect in whorls forming a terminal spike. In mountain grassland and open woods; Scandinavia and Germany, local. **Fl** 7-9. **Br** Absent.

C Selfheal *Prunella vulgaris* More or less downy creeping herb, with erect flower stems to 20cm. Leaves oval to diamond-shaped, 10-30mm long, untoothed or slightly toothed, pointed and wedge-shaped at base. Flowers violet-blue, 10-15mm, with concave upper lip, in dense, cylindrical, terminal head; bracts purplish and hairy; calyx with 3 short bristle-pointed teeth and 2 long narrow teeth. Widespread and common throughout; in grassy places and open woods, on neutral-calcareous soils. **Fl** 6-10. **Br** Common throughout.

D Large Selfheal *Prunella grandiflora* Similar to Selfheal, but larger in all respects. Corolla 20-25mm, calyx large and purple; inflorescence with no leaves immediately below and touching it. Mainland Europe north to S Sweden; in woods and shady grasslands; commonest to the south. **Fl** 6-9. **Br** Absent.

E Cut-leaved Selfheal *Prunella laciniata* Similar to Selfheal, but leaves and bracts normally *pinnately lobed*, very downy, and *flowers white*. In grasslands on calcareous soils; north to Belgium and central Germany. **Fl** 6-10. **Br** Rare in S England only.

F Basil Thyme *Acinos arvensis* Pubescent annual, occasionally perennial, with ascending to erect hairy stems up to 20cm. Leaves small, to 15mm long, roughly ovate, stalked, slightly toothed, and wedge-shaped at base. Flowers blue-violet with white patches on lower lip, 7-10mm, in separate whorls of 3-8 flowers; calyx hairy, curved, constricted in middle of tube. Widespread throughout most of the area except the extreme north; in open and grassy calcareous habitats. **Fl** 5-9. **Br** Locally common in S and E England, much rarer elsewhere.

G Common Calamint *Calamintha sylvatica* ssp *ascendens* Erect, hairy perennial, producing tufts of stems from short rhizome, up to 60cm. Leaves ovate to almost circular, with 5-8 shallow teeth on each side, 20-40mm long, blunt, base truncated, hairy. Flowers pink-lilac, with darker spots on lower lip, 10-15mm long, usually short-stalked in whorls of 3-9 in upper leaf axils; calyx tubular, hairy on veins, calyx teeth with long hairs, 2 teeth longer than the other 3. Local on dry banks, wood-borders and hedgerows; from England and Germany southwards and eastwards. **Fl** 6-9. **Br** Locally common in the south; rare or absent elsewhere.

H Wood Calamint *Calamintha sylvatica* ssp *sylvatica* Very similar to Common Calamint, but with larger leaves (to 60mm long), larger rose-pink flowers, 15-22mm long, with often longer stalks. Uncommon in similar habitats, usually on calcareous soil; in Germany, France and England. **Fl** 7-10. **Br** In scrub on chalk in the Isle of Wight only.

I Lesser Calamint *Calamintha nepeta* Similar to Common Calamint, but more grey downy, strongly aromatic. *Leaves small*, only 10-20mm, *barely toothed*; flower stems often branched and bushy; flowers pale mauve, *barely spotted*, 10-15mm; calyx with 5 equal teeth, shortly hairy; *hairs protrude from calyx throat in fruit* (not protruding in other species). From S England and France southwards; on dry usually calcareous or sandy banks, roadsides and hedgebanks. **Fl** 7-9. **Br** Uncommon in S and E England only; declining.

J Wild Basil *Clinopodium vulgare* Erect, hairy, aromatic herb to 40cm, rarely to 80cm, simple or branched. Leaves ovate, 20-50mm, stalked, rounded or wedge-shaped at base, blunt at tip and shallowly toothed: Flowers bright pink-purple, corolla 12-22mm, in dense whorls; calyx tubular, somewhat 2-lipped, curved, hairy and 13-veined; flower bracts linear, about as long as calyx. Widespread and common throughout N Europe except the far north; in dry, often calcareous, habitats. **Fl** 6-9. **Br** Common in the south and east, rarer to the north, absent in the far north.

K Marjoram *Origanum vulgare* Erect, sparsely hairy, perennial herb to 70cm. Leaves oval, to 40mm long, stalked, untoothed or slightly toothed, aromatic. Flowers in dense terminal heads, with lower whorls; corolla pinky purple, 2-lipped, 6-8mm, with tube longer than calyx; stamens protruding; calyx 2-lipped but with 5 equal teeth. Widespread throughout, except the extreme north; in dry grassy usually calcareous habitats. **Fl** 7-9. **Br** Widespread and generally common, but increasingly rare to the north.

L Wild Thyme *Thymus praecox* ssp *arcticus* Familiar, mat-forming, creeping, slightly aromatic perennial with a woody base. Flower stems ascending, rarely more than 70mm, bluntly 4-angled and *very hairy on opposite faces*, virtually hairless on the other 2 (**l**). Leaves 4-8mm long, rounded to elliptical, short-stalked, flat. Flowers in dense terminal heads, petals rose-purple or pink, 3-4mm; calyx 2-lipped. In a wide range of habitats, usually dry, including short grassland, rocky areas, banks and cliffs; western, locally from Norway southwards. **Fl** 5-8. **Br** Common throughout.

M Large Thyme *Thymus pulegioides* Generally similar in appearance to Wild Thyme, though larger in most respects, and more strongly thyme-scented. Flower stems with *long hairs on the angles, 2 faces hairless, and 2 shortly hairy* (**m**). Flowers in more or less interrupted spikes of whorls, or in tighter heads in short-grazed grass, up to 20cm tall. Widespread and common in N Europe except in the far north; in dry acid or calcareous banks, grasslands and roadsides. **Fl** 6-8. **Br** Common only in the south, much rarer northwards.

N Breckland Thyme *Thymus serpyllum* Very similar to Wild Thyme, differing in that the *flower stems are almost round, with short white hairs all round* (**n**); and the leaves are held more erect. On dry, often acid or sandy sites such as dunes, heaths and grasslands; northwards from N France to N Scandinavia. **Fl** 5-9. **Br** In E Anglia only, in Breckland area.

A	B	C	D
E	F		G
H	J	K	
L		M	

A Ground-ivy
B Northern Dragonhead
C Selfheal
D Large Selfheal
E Cut-leaved Selfheal
F Basil Thyme
G Common Calamint
H Wood Calamint
J Wild Basil
K Marjoram
L Wild Thyme
M Large Thyme

l

m

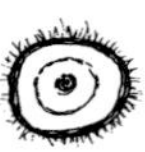
n

B

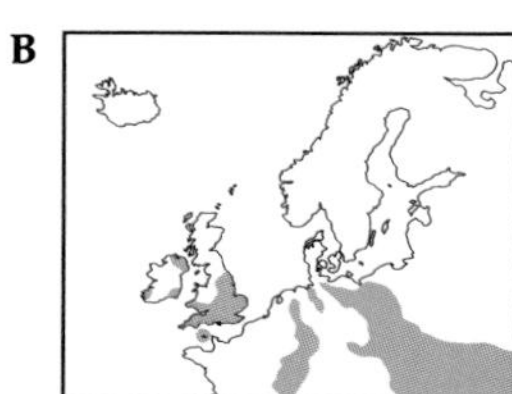

D

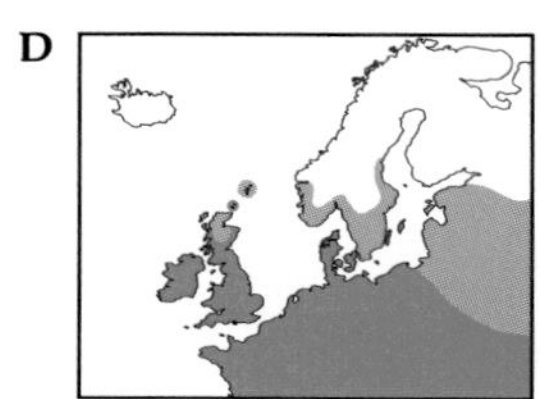

I

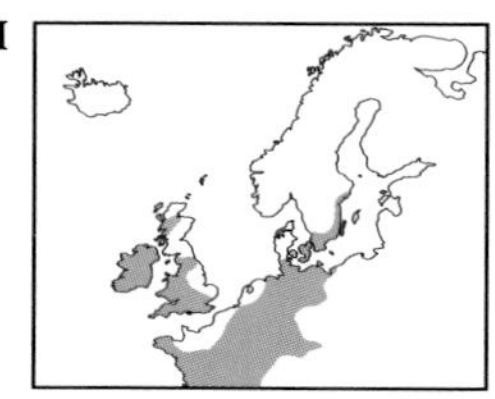

L

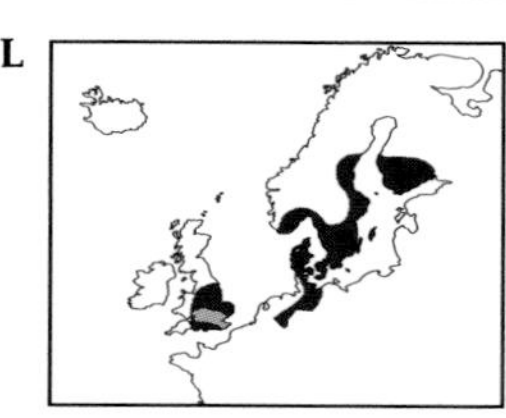

M

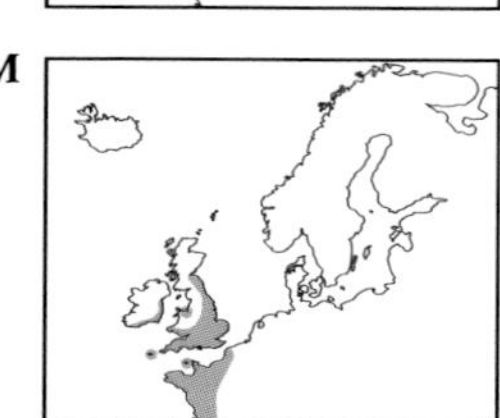

A Gipsywort *Lycopus europaeus* Variable, erect, rather hairy perennial, sometimes single-stemmed, less often a large, branched plant to 1m. Leaves ovate, but deeply pinnately lobed with narrow lobes, except at tip. Flowers small, 3mm in diameter, with 4 roughly equal corolla lobes, white and in dense whorls well spaced out up stem, each with a pair of lobed bracts. Common in wet habitats such as carr woodlands, pond-margins and ditchsides; throughout except the far north. **Fl** 6-9. **Br** Common almost throughout, rarer to the north-east.

MINTS *Mentha* Herbs with flowers divided into 4 nearly equal lobes, with 4 stamens. There are many hybrids involving both native and introduced species.

B Pennyroyal *Mentha pulegium* Prostrate, creeping perennial herb, usually hairy, with erect flower stems to 40cm, pungently aromatic. Leaves roughly oval, to 20mm long, finely downy, blunt, blunt-toothed with 1-6 teeth each side. Flowers mauve, 5-6mm long, corolla only hairy outside, calyx and flower stalks downy; in well-separated whorls, without a clear terminal head. Local or rare, scattered throughout N Europe except Scandinavia; in wet, grazed grassland, pondsides and muddy hollows. **Fl** 8-10. **Br** Rare and declining, mainly on commons in S England.

C Corn Mint *Mentha arvensis* Variable perennial, more or less hairy, erect to ascending, to 40cm, pleasantly mint-scented. Leaves oval to elliptical, to 60mm long, short-stalked, blunt, toothed, hairy on both sides. Flowers lilac, 3-4mm long, corolla hairy outside, stamens protruding; calyx bell-shaped, very hairy, with short triangular teeth; in dense well-separated whorls, with bracts much longer than flowers, and *no terminal head*. Common throughout; on paths, arable land, waste ground and damp habitats. **Fl** 5-10. **Br** Common throughout, though less so in the north.

D Water Mint *Mentha aquatica* Similar in form to Corn Mint, usually taller, to 60cm. Strongly mint-scented. *Flowers in terminal rounded heads*, about 20mm long, with separate whorls below; flowers mauve, stamens projecting, calyx hairy. Very common in wet places or standing water; throughout, except the far north. **Fl** 7-10. **Br** Common throughout.

E Whorled Mint *Mentha × verticillata* Natural hybrid between Corn and Water Mints. Very variable, intermediate between the parents. Flowers in whorls, *not forming a dense terminal head*; calyx tubular, hairy, with teeth about twice as long as broad; *stamens normally not projecting*. Common throughout; in damp habitats, not necessarily with parent species present. **Fl** 7-9. **Br** Common.

F Bushy Mint *Mentha × gentilis* Hybrid between Corn Mint and Spearmint. Variable. The key features include a pungent smell; flowers in distinctly separated whorls, with leaf-like bracts; flower stalks and *calyx hairless* (except for teeth, sometimes) but glandular; calyx bell-shaped, teeth narrow, about twice as long as broad; *stamens not protruding*. Widespread, often naturalised, except in the north. **Fl** 7-9. **Br** Local, rarer to the north.

G Tall Mint *Mentha × smithiana* Probably a secondary hybrid between Whorled Mint and Spearmint. Main features are pleasant, strong mint scent; leaves often reddish purple; flowers in separate whorls; calyx tube-shaped, *hairless* except for short hairs on the teeth; *stamens protruding*. Locally native or naturalised, not in Scandinavia. **Fl** 7-9. **Br** Local, throughout, but rare in Scotland and Ireland.

H Peppermint *Mentha × piperita* Hybrid between Water Mint and Spearmint. Familiar Peppermint smell. Leaves relatively long and narrow. *Flowers in a terminal spike*, usually with some separate whorls below. Calyx tubular, hairless except for the narrow teeth; stamens not protruding from corolla. Naturalised or spontaneous locally except Scandinavia. **Fl** 7-9. **Br** Locally naturalised throughout.

I Apple Mint *Mentha suaveolens* Creeping, strongly aromatic perennial, with erect very downy stems to 90cm. *Leaves oval to almost round*, white downy below, unstalked. Flowers in dense, terminal and axillary spikes, curving when young; flower stalks and calyx hairy; stamens usually protruding. In damp, grassy places, or waste ground; north to Holland as a native, naturalised from gardens further north. **Fl** 7-9. **Br** Throughout, but rare in the north, and probably only native in the south-west.

J Horse Mint *Mentha longifolia* Tall, erect perennial to 90cm. Leaves elliptical to lanceolate, up to 9cm long, pointed, often greyish, white downy below, *with unbranched hairs*, upper leaf surface not conspicuously wrinkled. Flowers in long terminal spikes, up to 10cm long, with whorls separating as it matures. Flower stalks and *calyx hairy*, stamens protruding. In damp grassy and waste places; from S Sweden southwards, but often naturalised. **Fl** 7-10. **Br** Probably not native; occasionally naturalised.

K Spearmint *Mentha spicata* Rather similar to Horse Mint in form and flower spikes, but leaves usually green, barely hairy with *a few branched hairs below*; scent of mint sauce. Flower stalks and *calyx tube hairless* (calyx teeth sometimes shortly hairy). Naturalised widely in damp places from its use as a pot herb; almost throughout. **Fl** 8-9. **Br** Naturalised locally.

L Meadow Clary *Salvia pratensis* Erect, perennial herb, with stems to 1m, downy at the base, glandular higher up. Basal leaves in a rosette, oval to oblong, heart-shaped at base, long-stalked, wrinkled and toothed. Stem leaves becoming stalkless higher up. Flowers with violet-blue corolla, *20-30mm*, with upper lip strongly curved, in a series of whorls of 4-6 forming a long spike; *calyx downy, without long white hairs*; style long-projecting. North to Holland and central Germany only; in dry grasslands, roadsides and rocky areas; commonest in the south of the area. **Fl** 5-7. **Br** A rare native in a few S England areas only.

M Wild Clary *Salvia verbenaca* Erect, downy perennial to 80cm, little-branched. Rosette leaves with deep irregular jagged teeth or lobes; upper stem leaves, bracts and calyces purplish blue. Flowers in whorled spikes, smaller than Meadow Clary, blue to violet, *8-15mm long, or much smaller* and unopened; *calyx sticky and downy, with long white hairs*. In dry grassy habitats, especially on lime-rich soils, frequent near the coast; in Britain and France only. **Fl** 5-8. **Br** Locally frequent in S and E England; rare elsewhere.

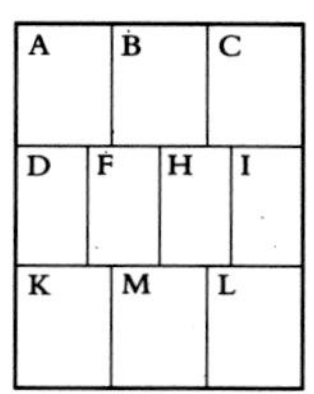

A **Gipsywort**
B **Pennyroyal**
C **Corn Mint**
D **Water Mint**
F **Bushy Mint**
H **Peppermint**
I **Apple Mint**
K **Spearmint**
M **Wild Clary**
L **Meadow Clary**

B

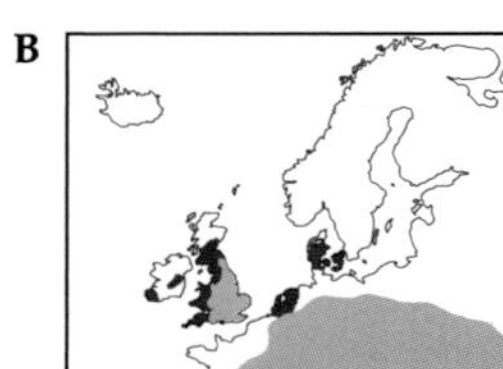

C

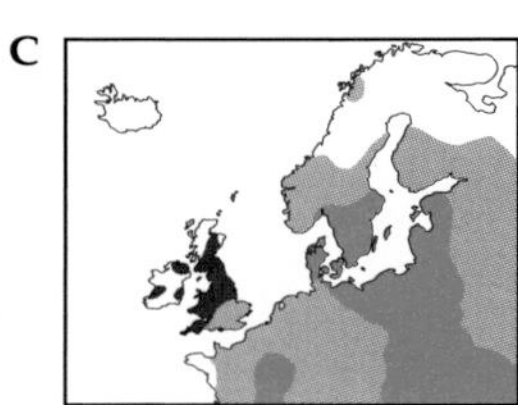

E

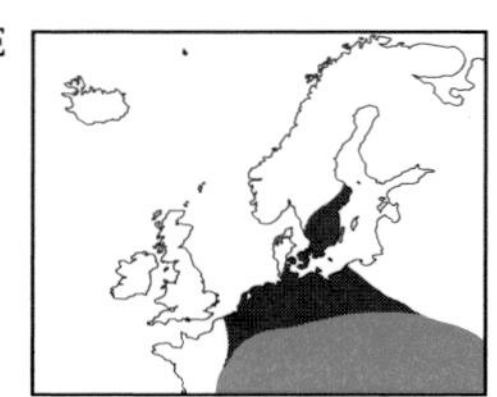

Nightshade or Potato Family
Solanaceae

A family of herbs or shrubs, with alternate leaves lacking stipules. Flowers normally regular, with 5 parts and 5 stamens, projecting in a tube in some genera. Ovary superior, forming a capsule or berry. Many members of the family are poisonous, whilst many are food plants.

A **Duke of Argyll's Teaplant** *Lycium barbarum* Deciduous shrub with arching grey-white barely spiny stems. Leaves narrowly elliptical, to 10cm, grey-green. Flowers red-purple or brownish, 8-10mm long, in groups of 1-3 on short shoots, with long projecting stamens. Fruit a red oval berry. Naturalised from W China; in rough habitats, especially coastal and near habitation, or sometimes in hedgerows. **Fl** 6-9. **Br** Local, mainly in England and Wales.

B **Deadly Nightshade** *Atropa belladonna* Stout, much-branched perennial up to 1.5m, hairless or downy glandular. Leaves oval, pointed, to 20cm long, alternate or opposite. Flowers 1-2, in leaf or branch axils, bell-shaped, hanging, dull purplish brown or green, 25-30mm long, stalked. Fruit a black fleshy glossy globose berry, 15-20mm in diameter, surrounded by the persistent calyx; highly poisonous, as is the rest of the plant. In scrub, semi-shaded areas, and damp places, most commonly on calcareous soils or in mountain areas; widespread as far north as N England and Holland, naturalised elsewhere. **Fl** 6-9. **Br** Locally common, mainly on chalky soils, in S and E England, rarer to the north and west.

C **Henbane** *Hyoscamus niger* Erect, branched or simple, stickily hairy annual or biennial to 80cm. Leaves oval to oblong, roughly toothed or lobed, 10-20cm long and strong-smelling, lower ones stalked, upper ones clasping the stem. Flowers unequally funnel-shaped, 20-30mm across, dull yellowish with purple veins and centre, stalkless in 2 rows in a forked curving inflorescence. Fruit a capsule, 12-20mm in diameter, opening at top. Whole plant poisonous. Widespread and locally common throughout most of N Europe except the far north, on bare, sandy and disturbed ground, most frequently near the sea. **Fl** 6-8. **Br** Local in S and E England, rare elsewhere.

D **Black Nightshade** *Solanum nigrum* Hairless or downy annual, erect or straggling, to 70cm. Leaves ovate, 30-60mm long, pointed, untoothed or wavy-toothed, not lobed at base and short-stalked. Flowers white with a cone of yellow anthers, 7-10mm in diameter, in stalked clusters of 5-10. Fruit globose, 7-9mm in diameter, becoming black. Common in cultivated and disturbed ground, including gardens; throughout most of N Europe, though probably not native to the north. **Fl** 7-10. **Br** Common in England and Wales; rare in Scotland and Ireland.

E **Hairy Nightshade** *Solanum luteum* Rather similar to Black Nightshade, but a much hairier and more glandular plant; flowers in clusters of 3-5, with peduncles only 7-13mm long (compared with 15-30mm long in Black Nightshade); *berries red* and oval in shape. In similar habitats, northwards to S Germany and N France. **Fl** 7-10. **Br** Absent, except as a casual.

F **Bittersweet, Woody Nightshade** *Solanum dulcamara* Woody, rather downy, scrambling perennial, reaching 2m. Leaves ovate, up to 80mm long, usually with distinct spreading lobes or teeth at base. Flowers have purple corolla, 10-15mm across, with 5 reflexed lobes and a cone of yellow stamens, in loose clusters of 10-25; fruit an ovoid berry, about 10mm long, green becoming red. Common in various grassy, wooded and semi-shaded habitats, often near water, and occasionally on shingle beaches; throughout except the far north. **Fl** 6-9. **Br** Common throughout except for N Scotland and Ireland where it is rare.

G **Thorn-apple** *Datura stramonium* Stout, erect, branched annual herb up to 1m, usually less. Leaves variable, ovate, up to 20cm long, toothed or lobed and long-stalked. Flowers large and trumpet-shaped, up to 10cm in diameter, usually white but occasionally purple, with long tube and 5 petal lobes. Fruit distinctive: large, ovoid, green, robustly spiny capsules, up to 5cm long. All parts highly poisonous. Naturalised on waste and cultivated ground; through much of N Europe except the far north, originally from central and S America. **Fl** 6-10. **Br** An occasional weed, varying in abundance with the weather.

Buddleja Family
Buddlejaceae

Shrubs, with simple opposite leaves. Flowers 4-parted, with corolla partly fused into a tube.

H **Butterfly Bush** *Buddleja davidii* Familiar shrub up to 5m tall, with long arching branches, bearing opposite grey-green downy lanceolate short-stalked leaves. Flowers mauve to lilac, with an orange centre, 3-4mm in diameter, tubular with 4 lobes; borne in long, dense tapering terminal inflorescences. A native of China, but commonly naturalised on waste ground from Holland southwards. **Fl** 6-9. **Br** Widely naturalised, and spreading.

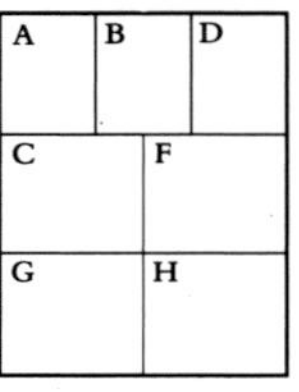

A **Duke of Argyll's Teaplant**

B **Deadly Nightshade**

D **Black Nightshade**

C **Henbane**

F **Bittersweet**

G **Thorn-apple**

H **Butterfly Bush** with Small Tortoiseshell

A
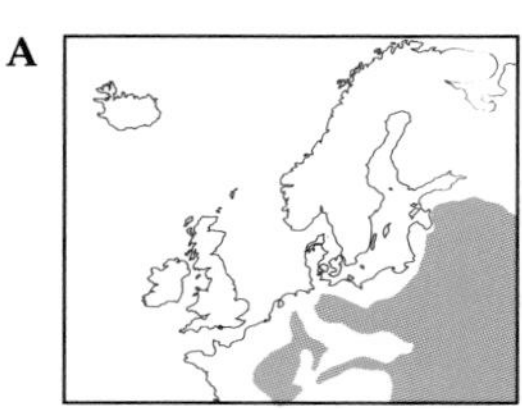

J

K

L
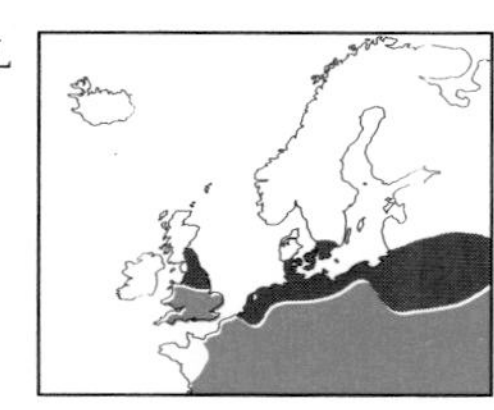

N
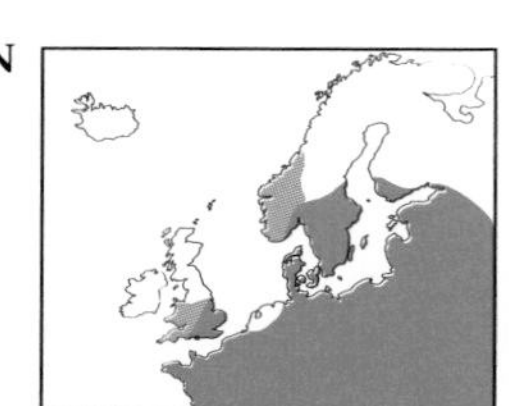

Figwort Family
Scrophulariaceae

Herbaceous plants, with leaves without stipules. Corolla irregular, usually 5-lobed.

A **Gratiole** *Gratiola officinalis* Perennial hairless herb, with erect 4-angled stems, to 50cm from a creeping base. Leaves linear-lanceolate, finely toothed or untoothed, 20-50mm long, unstalked. Flowers trumpet-shaped, white tinged with purplish red, 10-18mm long, in pairs from leaf axils. In wet grassy places; northwards to Holland and Germany. **Fl** 5-9. **Br** Absent.

B **Mudwort** *Limosella aquatica* Hairless annual, creeping by runners that produce rosettes of leaves. Upper leaves with stalks much longer than blade (**b**), lower ones spoon-shaped or linear, up to 12cm long. Flowers small, long-stalked from leaf axils, white or pink with bell-shaped corolla and 5 pointed lobes, 2-5mm in diameter; calyx longer than corolla tube. On muddy pond- margins, or areas where water has stood; rare or local but widespread throughout. **Fl** 6-10. **Br** Now very rare, and declining; mainly southern.

C **Welsh Mudwort** *Limosella australis* Very similar to Mudwort, but differing in that the leaves are all linear, narrow, to 40mm long (**c**); flowers are white with orange tube. Similar habitats; Wales only, though widespread outside Europe. **Fl** 7-10. **Br** Wales, very rare.

D **Monkeyflower** *Mimulus guttatus* Erect perennial to 50cm, hairless on lower parts, usually glandular downy above. Leaves opposite, ovate to oblong, to 70mm long, irregularly toothed, lower ones stalked and upper ones clasping. Flowers in loose leafy inflorescences, large (25-45mm), yellow *corolla dotted with small red spots in the throat*, almost closed by 2 hairy ridges; calyx and flower stalks downy. Introduced from N America, now naturalised, especially along streams, over most of N Europe. **Fl** 6-9. **Br** Widespread and locally common almost throughout.

E **Blood-drop-emlets** *Mimulus luteus* Very similar to Monkeyflower, but the corolla is more evenly 5-lobed, yellow with *large red blotches*, and the throat not closed; calyx and flower stalks hairless. Naturalised very locally, especially in Scotland; introduced from Chile. **Fl** 6-9. **Br** N England, Wales and Scotland.

F **Musk** *Mimulus moschatus* Rather similar to other *Mimulus* species, but smaller, prostrate, stickily hairy all over; corolla smaller (10-20mm), yellow, usually unspotted, calyx teeth roughly all equal (markedly unequal in other species). In wet and shady places; locally naturalised from France north to Holland; native to N America. **Fl** 6-9. **Br** Very locally naturalised.

MULLEINS *Verbascum* Tall, stout, white- or yellow-flowered herbs.

(1) Species with white or yellow hairs on stalks of stamens.

G **Great Mullein, Aaron's Rod** *Verbascum thapsus* Erect, stout, white-woolly biennial up to 2m, with a round, usually unbranched stem. Basal leaves broadly ovate to spoon-shaped, with winged leaf stalks; *stem leaves unstalked, running down stem to next leaf*. Flowers in long thin terminal spikes, occasionally with side-branches; petals bright yellow, with 5 roughly equal lobes, 15-35mm in diameter; stamens 5, with the upper 3 having stalks covered with yellow-white hairs, *lower 2 almost hairless*. Common throughout except the extreme north; in dry grassy areas, waste ground and roadsides. **Fl** 6-8. **Br** Common throughout, except N and W Scotland.

H **Orange Mullein** *Verbascum phlomoides* Similar to Great Mullein. The *upper leaves do not run down the stem far*; the flowers are larger (20-55mm in diameter) and flatter (rather concave in Great Mullein). Dry grassland in France and Germany, naturalised further north. **Fl** 7-9. **Br** Casual only.

I *Verbascum densiflorum* Very like Orange Mullein, with large flat flowers, but *leaf bases do run down the stems*, and the *flower bracts are much longer* (15-40mm long, compared to 10-15mm). Dry grassland, north to Holland and S Sweden. **Fl** 7-9. **Br** Casual only.

J **Hoary Mullein** *Verbascum pulverulentum* Similar to Great Mullein, but leaves thickly clothed with white wool that rubs off easily; upper stem leaves have heart-shaped bases; inflorescence with spreading branches, forming a pyramidal panicle; *all stamen stalks equally white hairy*. Dry grassland, mainly on calcareous soil; from Belgium and England southwards. **Fl** 7-9. **Br** Local, in E Anglia only.

K **White Mullein** *Verbascum lychnitis* Similar in general form to above species and up to 1.5m. Stem angled, downy-sticky above; leaves dark shiny green above, powdery white below. Inflorescence branched, *with the branches remaining erect, parallel to main stem*; flowers commonly white, but yellow in some areas, 15-20mm in diameter; stamen stalks equally clothed with white hairs. Dry grassland, usually on calcareous soils; from Holland and England southwards. **Fl** 7-8. **Br** Local in England; yellow form occurring in W Somerset.

(2) Species with purple hairs on stalks of stamens.

L **Moth Mullein** *Verbascum blattaria* Slender, with angled stems, stickily hairy above. Leaves dark shiny green, hairless, wrinkled. *Flowers solitary*, on stalks longer than calyx, forming a long loose spike; petals usually yellow, rarely whitish, 20-30mm in diameter; stamen stalks all with purple hairs. In waste places and grassy areas, often damp; from Holland southwards. **Fl** 6-9. **Br** Occasional in S and central England.

M **Twiggy Mullein** *Verbascum virgatum* Similar to Moth Mullein, but plant more glandular hairy; flowers 1-5 in axils of bracts, with *stalks shorter* than calyx. From England and France southwards. **Fl** 6-10. **Br** Rare, SW England only, as native.

N **Dark Mullein** *Verbascum nigrum* Tall, thin plant, not mealy, stems angled. Leaves dark green above, paler below, slightly hairy; lower leaves long-stalked, with heart-shaped bases, upper ones wedge-shaped at base, short-stalked to stalkless. Flowers yellow, 12-20mm in diameter, with dense purple hairs on stalks of all stamens, in long simple or branched spikes. In grassy places, waste ground and roadsides, often on calcareous or sandy soil; north to S Scandinavia. **Fl** 6-9. **Br** Locally common in S and E England, much rarer to the north and west.

A	B	D
E	F	I
K	J	G
L		N

A **Gratiole**
B **Mudwort**
D **Monkeyflower**
E **Blood-drop-emlets**
F **Musk**
I *Verbascum densiflorum*
K **White Mullein**
J **Hoary Mullein**
G **Great Mullein**
L **Moth Mullein**
N **Dark Mullein**

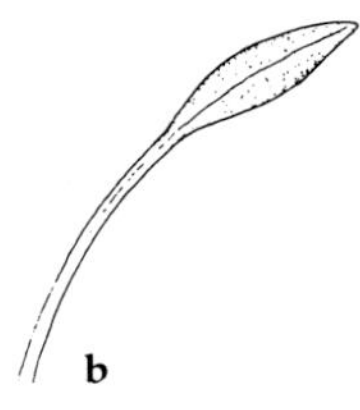
b

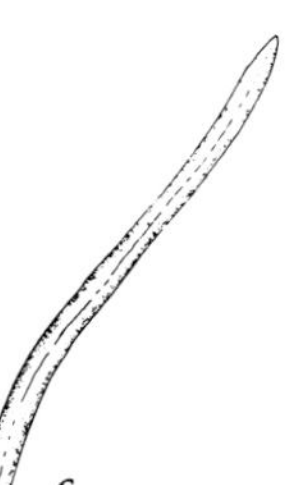
c

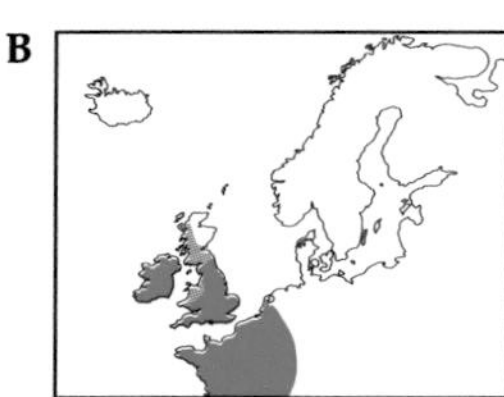

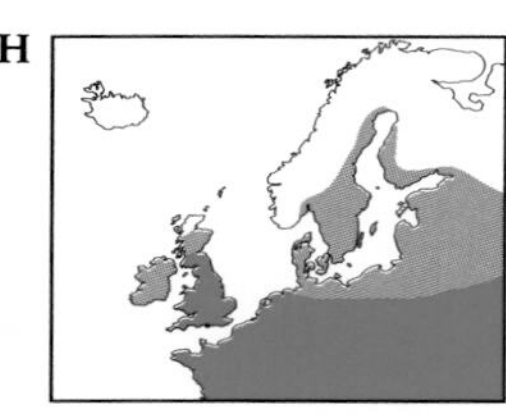

A Common Figwort *Scrophularia nodosa* Erect perennial to 80cm, from short rhizomes, with *square unwinged stems* which are hairless below the flowers. Leaves oval, pointed, coarsely toothed, truncated at base and short-stalked. Flowers 10mm long, with greenish tube, and purplish-red upper lip; stamens 4, plus 1 without an anther; calyx 5-lobed, with very *narrow white borders.* Common in damp woods, grassland, riverbanks and waste places; throughout, except the far north. **Fl** 6-9. **Br** Common throughout except N Scotland where it is rare.

B Water Figwort *Scrophularia auriculata* Similar in character to Common Figwort, but differing mainly in the *markedly 4-winged stems,* the blunt-tipped, round-toothed leaves, and the *broad white borders* to the sepal lobes. In wetter habitats, north to Holland, Scotland and Germany. **Fl** 6-9. **Br** Common in England, Wales and Ireland, rarer in Scotland.

C Balm-leaved Figwort *Scrophularia scorodonia* Similar to Common Figwort, but whole plant greyish downy. Leaves downy on both surfaces, *wrinkled,* double-toothed, with hair-points. Flowers purple, 8-12mm long, sterile, stamen rounded, calyx lobes with broad membranous margins. Very local in open woods, wet places and cliffs; in SW Britain and W France, occasionally abundant. **Fl** 5-8. **Br** Locally common in SW England and the Channel Islands.

D Green Figwort *Scrophularia umbrosa* Most similar in general appearance to Common Figwort, but with *stems very broadly winged; leaves pointed,* sharp-toothed, wrinkled and not heart-shaped at base. Flowers purplish brown, 6-9mm long; *sterile stamen with 2 lobes;* inflorescence very lax. Local, in damp and shaded places; from Denmark and Scotland southwards. **Fl** 7-9. **Br** Rare and local, patchily distributed as far north as the Moray Firth.

E Anarrhinum *Anarrhinum bellidifolium* Hairless, erect, biennial or perennial herb to 70cm. Basal leaves variable, spoon-shaped to elliptical, up to 80mm, stalked and blunt; stem leaves numerous, crowded, divided into 3-5 narrow lobes. Flowers blue to pale lilac, 4-5mm, in long slender terminal spikes. On dry banks, walls, and open woodland; very local in N France, commoner in S Europe. **Fl** 5-7. **Br** Absent.

F Snapdragon *Antirrhinum majus* The familiar garden plant. Erect or ascending and bushy, with linear to ovate leaves to 70mm. Flowers large, 30-45mm, unspurred, usually pink or purple, sometimes yellow. Widespread on old walls, and in waste places; only as a naturalised garden escape. **Fl** 6-9. **Br** Local, scattered.

G Lesser Snapdragon, Weasel's Snout *Misopates orontium* Erect, annual plant to 50cm, simple or branched, stickily hairy in upper parts. Leaves linear, narrowing to base, untoothed, to 50mm long. Flowers borne singly in upper leaf axils, forming a loose inflorescence; corolla 10-15mm, pinkish purple, without spur; calyx lobes long and narrow, equalling or exceeding the corolla. In cultivated and disturbed ground often on sandy soil; throughout much of area as far north as S Scandinavia, but doubtfully native in northern part. **Fl** 7-10. **Br** Uncommon and declining; mainly in S and E Britain.

H Small Toadflax *Chaenorhinum minus* Erect sticky-downy annual, reaching 25cm, occasionally more. Leaves linear-lanceolate to oblong, to 30mm, alternate, blunt, untoothed, narrowed to short stalk. Flowers 6-8mm, with pale purple corolla, with yellow patch, short-spurred, solitary on long stalks from upper leaf axils. Arable, disturbed and waste ground including roadsides and railways; throughout except the far north. **Fl** 5-10. **Br** Common throughout except N Scotland.

I Pale Toadflax *Linaria repens* Erect, grey-green, hairless perennial to 1m, with creeping rhizome and, often, numerous stems. Leaves linear, to 50mm, whorled on lower part of stem. Flowers with corolla pale lilac or white, 7-14mm, with violet stripes, and an orange spot on the lower lip; *spur straight, about a quarter of the length of corolla.* In dry places, rocky banks, grassland and cultivated soil, often on calcareous soils; from S Sweden southwards, though uncertainly native in northern parts. **Fl** 6-9. **Br** Throughout England and Wales, locally, possibly native.

J Jersey Toadflax *Linaria pelisseriana* Similar to Pale Toadflax, but smaller, to 30cm, annual, few-flowered; *flowers violet,* with white in throat, 10-15mm long, *spur slender, straight and almost as long as rest of corolla.* Heaths, cultivated ground and waste places; infrequent, only in W France and Jersey. **Fl** 5-7. **Br** Jersey only, local.

K Common Toadflax *Linaria vulgaris* Erect, almost hairless, grey-green perennial, with erect tufted stems to 80cm from a creeping rhizome. Leaves linear-lanceolate, 30-80mm, mostly alternate, but whorled lower down. Flowers in dense cylindrical terminal inflorescences; corolla yellow with orange central palate, 20-30mm long, with straight, stout long spur; sepals oval and pointed. Common throughout except the extreme north, in grassy places, waste ground, and cultivated land. **Fl** 7-10. **Br** Common almost throughout, though rare in N Scotland, local in Ireland.

L Sand Toadflax *Linaria arenaria* Stickily downy branched annual, rarely reaching 15cm. Leaves narrow, lanceolate, 10-20mm long, short-stalked. Flowers yellow, only 4-6mm long, with spur shorter than corolla, sometimes purple-tinged. In sandy coastal habitats; native only in W France, and further south. **Fl** 5- 9. **Br** Naturalised at Braunton Burrows, Devon.

M *Linaria arvensis* Low annual to 20cm, hairless below, and stickily hairy in the inflorescence. Leaves linear, hairless. Flowers pale lilac, 4-7mm, with short, strongly curved spur. In cultivated and bare ground; from N France and S Germany southwards. **Fl** 5-8. **Br** Absent.

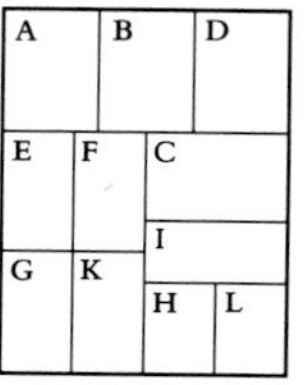

A **Common Figwort**
B **Water Figwort**
D **Green Figwort**
E **Anarrhinum**
F **Snapdragon**
C **Balm-leaved Figwort**
I **Pale Toadflax**
G **Lesser Snapdragon**
K **Common Toadflax**
H **Small Toadflax**
L **Sand Toadflax**

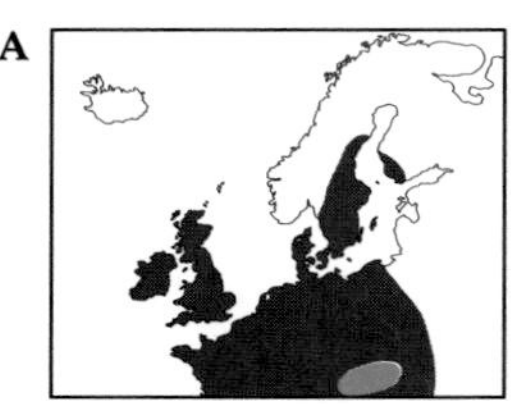
A

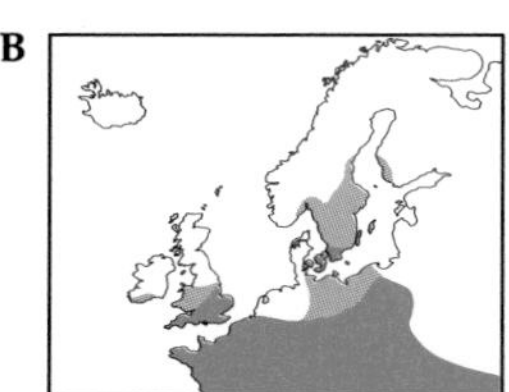
B

C

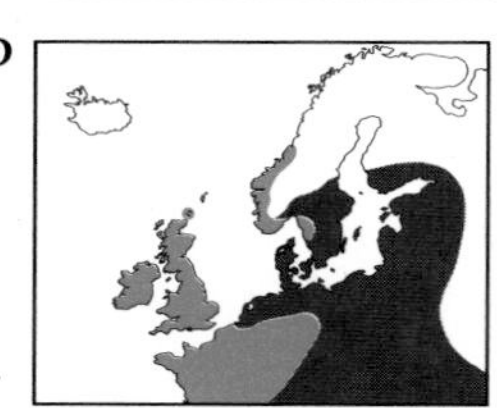
D

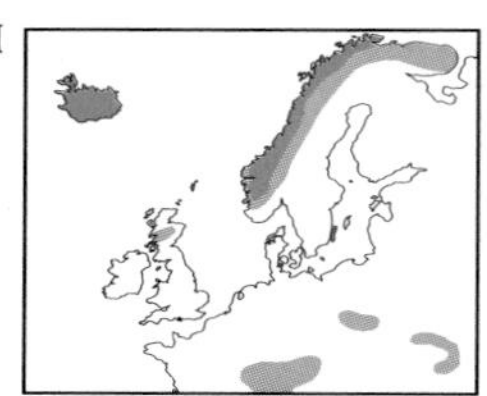
I

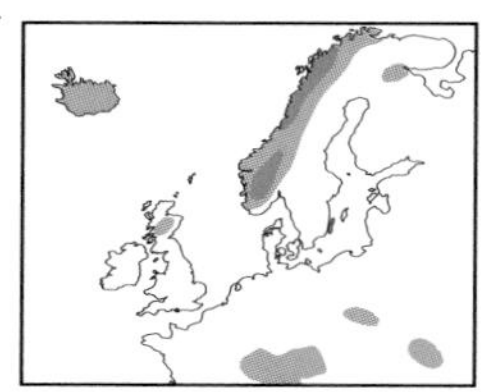
J

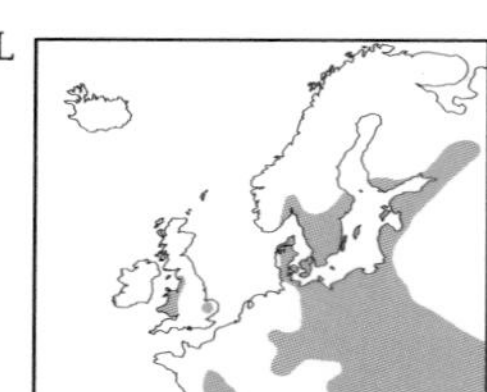
L

A Ivy-leaved Toadflax *Cymbalaria muralis* Trailing, hairless, or slightly downy, perennial with purplish stems to 80cm. Leaves roughly ivy-shaped to rounded, fleshy, 20-40mm long, long-stalked, alternate. Flowers solitary from leaf axils, long-stalked, corolla 10-15mm, violet to lilac (occasionally white), with white and yellow palate, spur curved and less than length of corolla. Flower stalks becoming recurved in fruit. Very widely naturalised on rocks and walls; as far north as S Scandinavia; native of S Europe. **Fl** 5-9. **Br** Commonly naturalised throughout, rare in N Scotland.

B Sharp-leaved Fluellen *Kickxia elatine* Prostrate, hairy, slightly glandular annual, with stems branching from base. Leaves usually *triangular, arrow-shaped*, pointed and stalked (**b**). Flowers solitary, long-stalked from leaf axils, with hairless stalks; corolla yellow with purple upper lip, *spur straight*. In cultivated and waste ground; as far north as S Scandinavia, though only native in the south of area; locally common. **Fl** 7-10. **Br** Local or common in S England; rare or absent elsewhere. Declining.

C Round-leaved Fluellen *Kickxia spuria* Very similar to Sharp-leaved Fluellen, but hairier and stickier; *leaves oval* (**c**); flowers with deeper purple upper lip, *spur curved*, flower stalks woolly. Similar habitats and distribution. **Fl** 7-10. **Br** Frequent in S and E England, becoming rare then absent to west and north.

D Foxglove *Digitalis purpurea* Erect, unbranched greyish-downy biennial or perennial reaching 1.8m. Leaves ovate- lanceolate, to 30cm long, downy above, with rounded teeth and winged stalk. Flowers familiar, in long terminal erect racemes; flowers tubular, 40-50mm long, pale purple, reddish pink or white, usually spotted inside; calyx much shorter. Widespread as far north as S Scandinavia; rarer or naturalised to north of range; in open woods, clearings and rocky areas, usually on acid soils. **Fl** 5- 8. **Br** Very common throughout in suitable habitats.

E Large Yellow Foxglove *Digitalis grandiflora* Similar in form to Foxglove, but generally shorter, to 1m. Leaves hairless, to 20cm, and shiny green above. Flowers tubular, 40-50mm long, pale yellow with faint red-brown markings inside, in long terminal racemes. In woods, rocky areas, and scrub; from Belgium southwards. **Fl** 6-8. **Br** Absent.

F Small Yellow Foxglove *Digitalis lutea* Similar to Large Yellow Foxglove, but with smaller flowers, with slender cylindrical tube, 15-20mm long, pale yellow. Similar habitats, usually calcareous; from Belgium southwards, naturalised further north. **Fl** 6-8. **Br** Absent.

G Fairy Foxglove *Erinus alpinus* Tufted perennial, with many erect shoots up to 30cm. Leaves oblong-lanceolate, toothed, in basal rosette. Flowers pinkish-purple, 10-15mm across, with 5 roughly equal lobes, in terminal clusters elongating into spikes. Stony places and mountains; S Germany and central France southwards, naturalised to north. **Fl** 5-9. **Br** Naturalised in N England and Scotland.

SPEEDWELLS *Veronica* Large genus, with some 25 species in N Europe, many of which look superficially similar. Herbaceous annuals or perennials, with opposite leaves. Corolla 4-lobed, flat or cup-shaped; calyx 4-lobed. Fruit flattened and heart-shaped. To assist in identification, the genus is divided into 3 groups, based on the structure of the inflorescence.

(1) Flowers in heads that terminate the main stems, not originating from lower leaf axils.

H Thyme-leaved Speedwell *Veronica serpyllifolia* Perennial herb, with creeping rooting stems to 30cm, more or less hairless; flower stems erect or ascending. Leaves oval, rounded at both ends, 10-20mm long, untoothed or faintly toothed and hairless. Flowers in loose, more or less erect terminal spikes, with oblong bracts longer than flower stalks. Corolla pale blue to white, with darker lines, 6-8mm in diameter; flower stalks longer than calyx; capsule broader than long and roughly equal to calyx (**g**). Common throughout; on bare, cultivated and sparsely grassy habitats, heaths and open woods. **Fl** 3-10. **Br** Common throughout. A mountain form, ssp *humifusa*, has larger flowers (7-10mm), brighter blue, in fewer-flowered inflorescences.

I Alpine Speedwell *Veronica alpina* Rather similar, to Thyme-leaved Speedwell, but leaves often more rounded-toothed and wedge-shaped at base. Inflorescence few-flowered, short, distinctly separate from leaves. Corolla deep dull blue, 7-8mm in diameter; style much shorter than fruit (**h**) (equal in Thyme-leaved Speedwell). Local in rocky or grassy mountain habitats; throughout. **Fl** 7-8. **Br** Very local, Scottish Highlands only.

J Rock Speedwell *Veronica fruticans* Perennial, with stem woody at base, and numerous ascending, often branching, shoots. Leaves oblong, to 10mm, untoothed or slightly toothed, wedge-shaped at base and almost stalkless. Flowers deep blue, with red-purple centre, 10-15mm in diameter, in rather loose few-flowered terminal clusters. Fruit oval, with a slight notch at tip (**i**). Rocky and grassy habitats, usually in mountains; local from the Alps northwards in suitable habitats. **Fl** 7-9. **Br** Very local in the Scottish Highlands.

K French Speedwell *Veronica acinifolia* Glandular annual, with ascending stems. Leaves oval, 10mm, barely toothed. Corolla blue, 2-3mm in diameter, longer than calyx. Fruit longer than broad and notched. In cultivated ground and damp grass; from N France southwards. **Fl** 4-6. **Br** Casual only.

L Spiked Speedwell *Veronica spicata* Distinctive, erect, downy perennial to 60cm, with several stems arising from a mat. Leaves oval at base of stem, stalked, shallowly toothed, becoming narrower and unstalked further up. Flowers in conspicuous, dense, long, leafless, many-flowered terminal inflorescences; corolla bright blue, 4-8mm in diameter, with a longish tube and narrow lobes. Fruit rounded (**k**). In dry grassland and rocky outcrops, frequently calcareous; from Scandinavia southwards, though often very local. **Fl** 7-9. **Br** Rare, in grassland in E Anglia, and limestone rocks in W England and Wales.

M Long-leaved Speedwell *Veronica longifolia* Rather similar to Spiked Speedwell, but leaves sometimes in 4s, sharply toothed and pointed; flowers in a terminal spike, but often with 1 or 2 lower spikes. Fruit hairless, heart-shaped, with persistent style much longer than capsule (**l**). Uncommon in damp woods and riverbanks; throughout mainland N Europe, but local. **Fl** 6- 8. **Br** Absent.

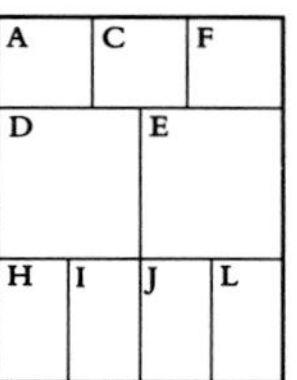

A **Ivy-leaved Toadflax**

C **Round-leaved Fluellen**

F **Small Yellow Foxglove**

D **Foxglove**

E **Large Yellow Foxglove**

H **Thyme-leaved Speedwell**

I **Alpine Speedwell**

J **Rock Speedwell**

L **Spiked Speedwell**

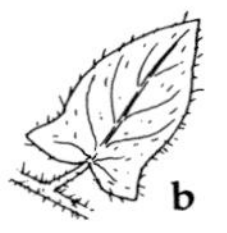
b

c

g

h

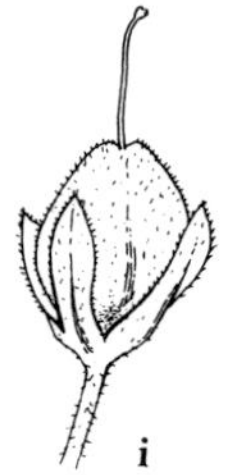
i

k

l

E

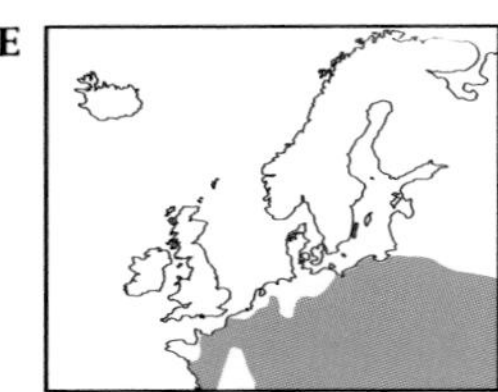

H

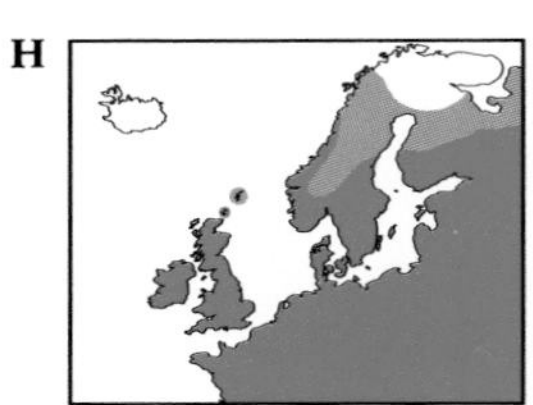

I

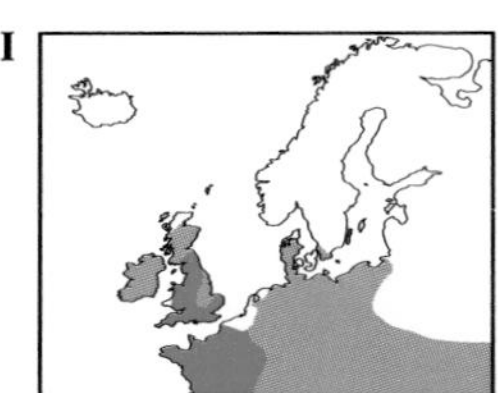

A Wall Speedwell *Veronica arvensis* Erect, downy, annual plant, to 25cm but very variable, often much smaller. Leaves triangular to ovate, coarsely round-toothed, to 15mm, lower ones stalked, upper ones unstalked. Flowers in terminal racemes, with upper bracts longer than flowers, flower stalks very short; corolla blue, 2-4mm in diameter. Fruit hairy, *heart-shaped, as long as broad* (**a**). Common in dry open habitats, on old walls, rocky banks and heaths; throughout the area. **Fl** 3-10. **Br** Common throughout.

B Spring Speedwell *Veronica verna* Similar to Wall Speedwell, differing in that it has deeply pinnate 3- to 7-lobed upper leaves, denser more glandular inflorescence, and *capsule broader than long* (**b**). In dry bare areas; local, throughout except the far north. **Fl** 4-6. **Br** Rare, in Breckland, E Anglia only.

C Fingered Speedwell *Veronica triphyllos* Similar to above, but with leaves palmately lobed into 3-7 lobes, like fingers. Flower stalks 5-8mm and longer than calyx. *Fruit as long as broad, shorter than calyx* (**c**). In dry grassland and cultivated areas; local S Sweden southwards. **Fl** 4-7. **Br** Very local, in E Anglia only.

D Breckland Speedwell *Veronica praecox* Similar to above in form. Leaves strongly toothed, but less lobed than previous 2 species. Flowers in long racemes. Upper bracts and calyx both shorter than flower stalks; corolla longer than calyx. *Fruit longer than broad and notched* (**d**). In cultivated land and dry bare places, local, from S Sweden southwards. **Fl** 3-6. **Br** Very rare, in fields in Breckland only.

(2) Species with flowers in inflorescences originating mainly from lower leaf axils, usually with a leafy non-flowering shoot at tip of plant.

E Large Speedwell *Veronica austriaca* ssp *teucrium* Variable, downy perennial, sprawling or erect, to 20cm. Leaves oval to oblong, unstalked, up to 60mm, deeply blunt-toothed. Flowers in *long, paired leafless inflorescences* from axils of opposite leaves; corolla bright blue, 9-14mm in diameter, with broad lobes. Fruit rounded to heart-shaped, usually longer than wide. In grassy and rocky places, usually on calcareous soil; northwards to Holland and Germany. **Fl** 5- 8. **Br** Absent.

F *Veronica prostrata* Similar to Large Speedwell, but shorter and more procumbent; leaves toothed, but not deeply, or untoothed; calyx and fruit hairless (sometimes hairy in Large Speedwell). From Holland southwards; in grassy habitats. **Fl** 6-8. **Br** Absent.

G Heath, or Common, Speedwell *Veronica officinalis* Mat-forming, perennial herb, with creeping rooting stems and erect flower spikes from leaf axils; stems hairy all round. Leaves oblong to ovate, 20-30mm, shallowly toothed, hairy on both sides, unstalked. Flowers in long-stalked cylindrical to pyramidal inflorescences from leaf axils; *corolla lilac-blue*, with darker veins, 6-8mm in diameter; flower stalks short, 2mm. Capsule heart-shaped, longer than calyx. Throughout N Europe, except Spitzbergen; common in grassy and heathy places. **Fl** 5-8. **Br** Common throughout in suitable habitats.

H Germander Speedwell, Bird's Eye *Veronica chamaedrys* Perennial herb with prostrate stems rooting at the nodes, and ascending flower stems; *stems with 2 opposite lines of long white hairs*, otherwise hairless. Leaves oval-triangular, to 30mm, very short-stalked, toothed, hairy. Flowers in loose long-stalked inflorescences from leaf axils, usually only 1 spike per leaf pair. *Corolla bright blue* with white eye, about 10mm across. Fruit heart-shaped, hairy on margin, shorter than calyx. Common throughout, except the far north; in grassland, scrub and open woods, often on damper ground. **Fl** 3-7. **Br** Common throughout.

I Wood Speedwell *Veronica montana* Similar to Germander Speedwell, but differing in that the *stem is hairy all round;* leaves are distinctly stalked (5-15mm long), light green in colour; *flowers lilac*, smaller (7-9mm); fruit heart-shaped to almost round, and longer than calyx lobes. Common northwards to Denmark and S Sweden; in woods, often on damp or less acid soils. **Fl** 4-7. **Br** Widespread and locally common, normally in ancient woodland; rare in N Scotland.

J Marsh Speedwell *Veronica scutellata* Hairless or slightly downy perennial, with creeping and ascending stems. *Leaves linear-lanceolate*, 20-40mm long, unstalked, *often reddish brown*, few-toothed, pointed. Flowers borne in long-stalked, lax, alternate inflorescences; flower stalks 7-10mm, much longer than bracts; *corolla pale pink-lilac*, or white, often with purplish lines, 6-7mm in diameter. Fruit flat, broader than long, much longer than calyx. Locally common throughout, except the extreme north; in bogs, marshy areas and pondsides. **Fl** 6-8. **Br** Locally common throughout.

K Brooklime *Veronica beccabunga* Hairless perennial, with creeping rooting stems, then ascending, rather fleshy. *Leaves oval-oblong*, rounded at base, blunt, 30-60mm long, thick, shallowly toothed and short-stalked. Flowers in paired racemes from leaf axils; flower bracts narrow, roughly equal to flower stalks; *corolla blue*, sometimes with red centre, 7-8mm in diameter; fruit rounded and shorter than calyx. In wet places and standing water; common throughout, except in Arctic region. **Fl** 5-9. **Br** Common throughout.

L Blue Water-speedwell *Veronica anagallis-aquatica* Hairless perennial (sometimes glandular hairy amongst flowers), with short-creeping rhizome and ascending stems to 30cm. *Leaves lanceolate-slightly oval and pointed, to 12cm long*, slightly toothed and unstalked. Flowers in paired, long racemes from leaf axils; flower stalk at least as long as bract, becoming erect after flowering; *corolla pale blue*, 5-6mm in diameter. Fruit almost round, slightly notched, slightly longer than broad. In wet places, water and damp woods; throughout except the far north, common. **Fl** 6-8. **Br** Locally common throughout in suitable habitats.

M Pink Water-speedwell *Veronica catenata* Similar to Blue Water-speedwell, but with *pink flowers*, inflorescence looser and more spreading; *flower stalks shorter than bracts*. Fruit more deeply notched, fruit stalks spreading not erect. In similar habitats; northwards to S Sweden. **Fl** 6-8. **Br** Locally common, except in Scotland.The hybrid between Pink and Blue Water-speedwells is widespread. It is always sterile.

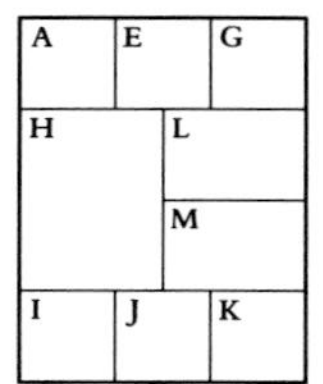

A **Wall Speedwell**
E **Large Speedwell**
G **Heath Speedwell**
H **Germander Speedwell**
L **Blue Water-speedwell**
M **Pink Water-speedwell**
I **Wood Speedwell**
J **Marsh Speedwell**
K **Brooklime**

a

b

c

d

G

H
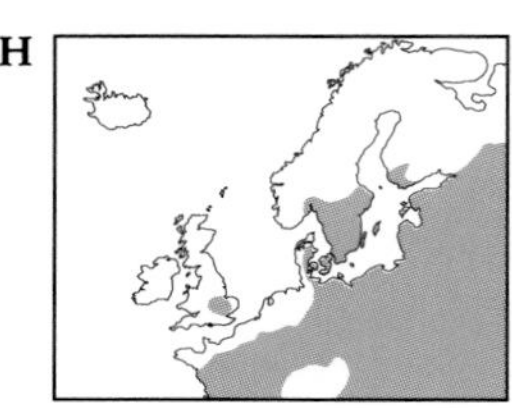
I
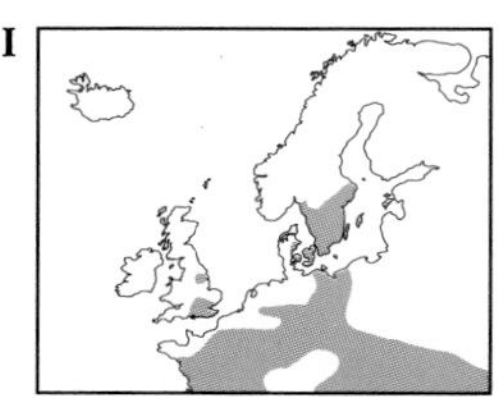
J

L
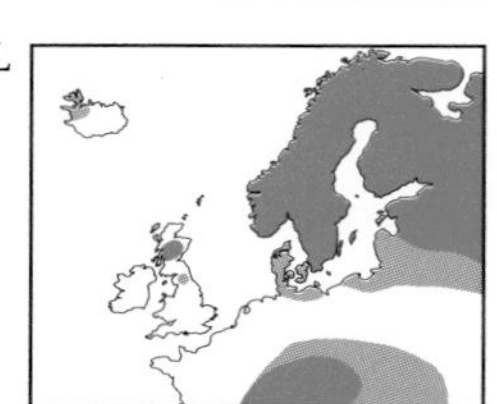

(3) Plants with solitary flowers in axils of ordinary leaves.

A **Common Field-speedwell** *Veronica persica* Procumbent, hairy, branched annual to 60cm long. Leaves triangular to ovate, 10-30mm long, short-stalked, light green, coarsely toothed and hairy below. Flowers solitary in leaf axils, stalks longer than leaves; corolla blue, *with white lower lip*, 8-12mm in diameter; calyx lobes oval, pointed and hairy, spreading when in fruit. Fruit hairy and twice as wide as long, with 2 divergent sharp-edged lobes (**a**). Common throughout, except in the extreme north, though almost certainly not native anywhere in area; in cultivated and bare ground. **Fl** All year. **Br** Common throughout.

B **Grey Field-speedwell** *Veronica polita* Similar to Common Field-speedwell, but smaller, with *grey-green leaves; flowers wholly blue*. Fruit with erect unkeeled lobes, covered with curled hairs, *calyx lobes overlapping in fruit* (**b**). In similar habitats; throughout, except the far north. **Fl** All year. **Br** Common in the south, rare to the north.

C **Green Field-speedwell** *Veronica agrestis* Similar to Grey Field-speedwell, but leaves all longer than broad (lower ones broader than long in Grey Field-speedwell); flowers have lower petal white; *calyx lobes oblong and blunt* (not oval and pointed); fruit with straight hairs only (**c**). Similar habitats, often acid; throughout N Europe except the far north. **Fl** All year. **Br** Widespread, but commoner in the north.

D *Veronica opaca* Similar to above, with flowers all blue, sepals narrowly spoon-shaped and blunt, not overlapping at base. Fruit with some curled hairs. Similar habitats and flowering time; mainland Europe only, north as far as S Scandinavia. **Fl** 4-10. **Br** Absent.

E **Slender Speedwell** *Veronica filiformis* Downy perennial plant, with numerous creeping stems, often forming mats. Leaves small, 5-10mm, short-stalked, rounded to kidney-shaped, with rounded teeth, opposite on non-flower stems, alternate on flower stems. Flowers blue with white lip, 8-10mm in diameter, stalks 2-3 times length of leaves. Fruit rarely produced. Native of Caucasus area, but now widespread in N Europe as far north as S Sweden; in lawns, pastures and waste places. **Fl** 4-7. **Br** Widespread, locally common in S Britain.

F **Ivy-leaved Speedwell** *Veronica hederifolia* Hairy, spreading annual, branched from the base. Leaves kidney-shaped, palmately lobed like ivy leaf, to 15mm long. Flowers in leaf axils on stalks shorter than leaves; corolla pale blue or lilac, shorter than calyx and 4-5mm in diameter; calyx lobes oval and heart-shaped at base. Fruit broader than long, barely flattened and hairless. Widespread and common throughout N Europe, except Arctic regions; in cultivated land, waste ground and woodlands. **Fl** 3-8. **Br** Common and widespread, though much rarer in the north.

G **Cornish Moneywort** *Sibthorpia europaea* Slender creeping perennial, with stems rooting at the nodes, hairy. Leaves alternate, kidney-shaped, to 20mm diameter, 5- to 7-lobed and long-stalked. Flowers solitary and short-stalked, 2 corolla lobes yellow and 3 pink, 1-2mm in diameter; 4 stamens. Very local, though occasionally common, in damp shady habitats in W France and S Britain only. **Fl** 7-10. **Br** Very local in S and SW Britain only.

H **Crested Cow-wheat** *Melampyrum cristatum* Erect, finely hairy annual to 50cm, usually unbranched. Leaves lanceolate, to 10cm, unstalked, toothed or not, in opposite pairs. *Flowers in dense 4-angled spikes*, with conspicuous narrowly heart-shaped bracts, curved back. Bracts have short, 2mm-long teeth on the lower half and are often pinky purple, but untoothed and green on the other half; corolla yellow suffused with purple, 12-16mm long. Widespread in N Europe except in the far north; on roadsides, rough grass and wood-borders. **Fl** 6-9. **Br** Rare, in central E England only.

I **Field Cow-wheat** *Melampyrum arvense* Similar to Crested Cow-wheat, but *spikes cylindrical* not 4-sided, and slightly looser; bracts more or less erect, with long teeth (to 8mm), *not heart-shaped at base*, bright rosy red. Corolla yellow and pink, 20-25mm long. In arable fields, grassland and roadsides; local, from S Finland southwards. **Fl** 5-10. **Br** Rare and local in scattered S England localities.

J *Melampyrum nemorosum* Beautiful and distinctive species, rather similar to Field Cow-wheat, but with wider leaves, *violet bracts*, and *yellow and violet flowers*. In woods, grassland and scrub; mainly Scandinavian extending south into Germany. **Fl** 6-9. **Br** Absent.

K **Common Cow-wheat** *Melampyrum pratense* Very variable, hairless or slightly bristly annual, single or branched, erect or ascending, to 40cm high. Leaves oval-lanceolate, to 80mm, short-stalked or unstalked and untoothed; bracts leaf-like, but usually toothed at base. Flowers paired in axils, turned to the same side; corolla pale yellow-white, 10-18mm, much longer than calyx, with *corolla mouth virtually closed*; calyx teeth erect. Common and widespread throughout, except in the extreme north; in woods, scrub and heaths. **Fl** 5-9. **Br** Locally common throughout, usually on acid soils.

L **Small Cow-wheat** *Melampyrum sylvaticum* Similar to Common Cow-wheat, but smaller; *corolla golden yellow*, only 8-10mm long, *mouth of tube open*, with the lower lip bent back, tube roughly equal to calyx; calyx teeth spreading. In birchwoods and pinewoods, moorlands and grassy areas; common in Scandinavia, but rarer and mainly in mountains further south. **Fl** 6-9. **Br** Rare and local, in N England and Scotland only; very rare in Ireland.

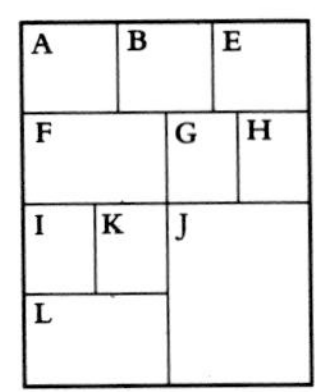

A **Common Field-speedwell**

B **Grey Field-speedwell**

E **Slender Speedwell**

F **Ivy-leaved Speedwell**

G **Cornish Moneywort**

H **Crested Cow-wheat**

I **Field Cow-wheat**

K **Common Cow-wheat**

J *Melampyrum nemorosum*

L **Small Cow-wheat**

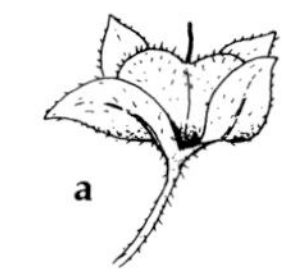
a

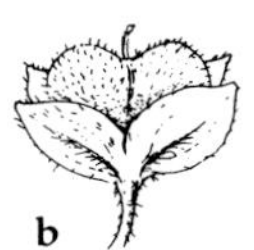
b

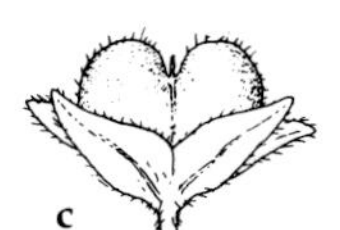
c

C
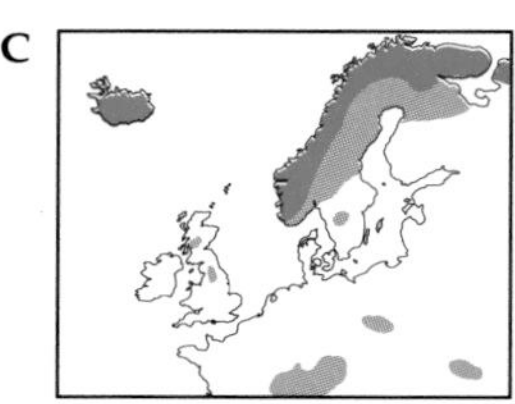

D
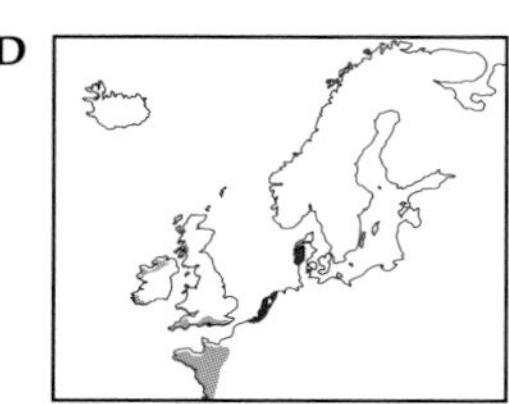

F
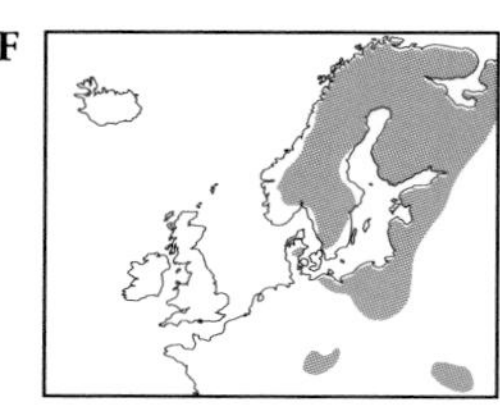

K
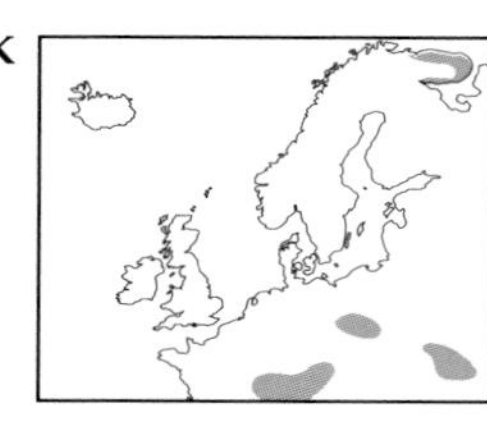

M
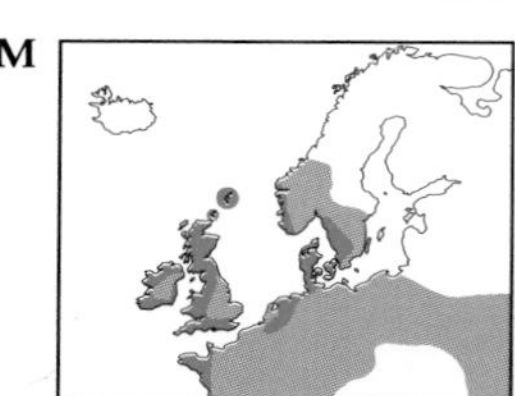

A Red Bartsia *Odontites verna* Erect, branching, downy annual to 50cm, often purple-tinged. Leaves oblong-lanceolate, 10-30mm long, usually few-toothed and unstalked. Flowers in long branched terminal leafy inflorescences; corolla reddish pink, 8-10mm, 2-lipped, tube about equalling calyx; anthers slightly protruding. Capsule downy and more or less equalling calyx. In meadows, pastures, tracks, roadsides and disturbed ground; throughout except the extreme north, generally common. **Fl** 6-9. **Br** Common throughout.

B Yellow Odontites *Odontites lutea* Generally similar to Red Bartsia, with untoothed or slightly toothed linear leaves; flowers bright yellow, anthers markedly protruding. Dry grassland and scrub; extending into N France from S Europe. **Fl** 7-9. **Br** Absent.

C Alpine Bartsia *Bartsia alpina* Erect, downy, unbranched perennial to 30cm, from a short rhizome. Leaves opposite, unstalked, oval, 10-20mm long and blunt, with rounded teeth; bracts similar, purplish and decreasing in size up stem, but longer than calyx. Flowers in short few-flowered terminal inflorescence; corolla dull dark purple, 15-20mm long, upper lip longer than lower. In damp base-rich habitats, frequently in mountains; in Scandinavia, then confined to mountains further south. **Fl** 6-8. **Br** Rare, in N England and parts of Scotland only.

D Yellow Bartsia *Parentucellia viscosa* Erect, very *sticky-hairy*, unbranched annual to 50cm, usually less. Leaves lanceolate, to 40mm, toothed, pointed and unstalked. Flowers in long loose terminal inflorescence with leaf-like bracts; corolla yellow, 16-24mm long, with lower 3-lobed lip much longer than upper; calyx tubular with 4 triangular teeth. Local in W Europe from France and Scotland southwards; often near the coast, in grassy and sandy habitats. **Fl** 6-10. **Br** Local, mainly in SW Britain, extending to SW Scotland.

E *Parentucellia latifolia* Similar to Yellow Bartsia, but smaller, with more triangular, more deeply toothed leaves. Flowers smaller, 8-10mm, red-purple or rarely white. In sandy or stony places; from S Europe to NW France. **Fl** 6-8. **Br** Absent.

LOUSEWORTS *Pedicularis* Perennial or occasionally annual herbs, semi-parasitic on other herbs. Leaves alternate or whorled, usually deeply divided pinnately. Flowers in dense terminal, often leafy, spikes. Corolla 2-lipped, upper lip compressed and hooded, lower lip 3-lobed and flatter. 4 stamens.

F Moor-king *Pedicularis sceptrum-carolinae* Large and distinctive species, with erect stems to 80cm, often reddish. Basal leaves in a rosette, lanceolate in shape but pinnately lobed with oval segments; stem leaves few. Flowers most often in whorls of 3 in a long lax spike; corolla large, to 32mm, erect, pale dirty yellow with orange-red margins to lower lip; corolla mouth usually closed with lower lip wrapped around upper. In boggy areas, marshes, and wet woodlands; in the lowlands of Scandinavia, extending south into Germany. **Fl** 6-8. **Br** Absent.

G Leafy Lousewort *Pedicularis foliosa* Distinctive species with long finely divided leaves, and leafy conical spikes of large (to 25mm) pale yellow flowers. In meadows and damp areas in mountains only; from the Vosges southwards. **Fl** 6-8. **Br** Absent.

H Hairy Lousewort *Pedicularis hirsuta* Perennial herb to 12cm, woolly-hairy above. Leaves pinnately lobed, bracts similar. Corolla bright pink, 10-13mm, upper lip nearly straight and not toothed. Calcareous Arctic habitats only. **Fl** 6-8. **Br** Absent.

I Crimson-tipped Lousewort *Pedicularis oederi* Erect perennial to 15cm, hairy above, with few stem leaves. Leaves lanceolate, pinnately divided, hairless. Flowers in dense terminal spike, becoming laxer when in fruit; corolla yellow with crimson tip to upper lip, 12-20mm long; calyx hairy. In damp grassland in mountains, or tundra; in N Scandinavia, and from central Germany southwards. **Fl** 7-8. **Br** Absent.

J *Pedicularis flammea* Similar to Crimson-tipped Lousewort, but smaller (to 10cm), upper lip of flower suffused with red, calyx hairless. Damp habitats; in Scandinavian mountains. **Br** Absent.

K Whorled, or Verticillate, Lousewort *Pedicularis verticillata* Similar to other species in general habit, but distinctive because of the whorls of 3-4 short-stalked, pinnately divided leaves, and similar unstalked bracts amongst the dense inflorescence. Corolla 12-18mm, purplish red (occasionally pale). A mountain species; in central and S Europe, reaching France and Germany, and reappearing in Arctic Russia. **Fl** 6-8. **Br** Absent.

L Marsh Lousewort, Red Rattle *Pedicularis palustris* Virtually hairless erect *annual*, reaching *60cm*, with a single branching stem. Leaves oblong in outline, to 60mm long, but deeply lobed pinnately, with toothed lobes. Flowers in loose leafy spikes; corolla pinky purple, 20-25mm, 2-lipped, *upper lip with 4 teeth* (**l**); calyx tubular, inflated at base, with 2 leafy lobes. Common and widespread in marshes, bogs and wet heaths and fens, though usually on slightly acid soils; throughout except the far north. **Fl** 5-9. **Br** Locally common and widespread, though decreasing through drainage. Much more scarce in central and southern England.

M Lousewort *Pedicularis sylvatica* Rather similar to Marsh Lousewort, but perennial, *shorter, to 20cm*, with many branches spreading from the base. Inflorescence fewer flowered; corolla paler pink, with *upper lip 2-toothed* (**m**); calyx 5-angled with 4 small leafy lobes. In bogs, heaths, moors, damp grassland and open woods, usually acid; frequent in N to central Sweden. **Fl** 4-7. **Br** Locally common almost throughout, especially in the west and north; scarce in central England..

N Lapland Lousewort *Pedicularis lapponica* Similar in form to others; perennial, erect, single-stemmed, to 25cm. Leaves linear, pinnately lobed. Corolla pale yellow in few-flowered spikes. Locally common on moors, open woods and tundra; in N Scandinavia only. **Fl** 6-7. **Br** Absent.

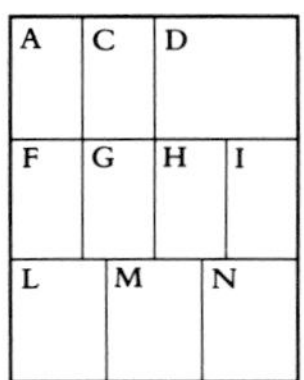

A Red Bartsia
C Alpine Bartsia
D Yellow Bartsia
F Moor-king
G Leafy Lousewort
H Hairy Lousewort
I Crimson-tipped Lousewort
L Marsh Lousewort
M Lousewort
N Lapland Lousewort

l

m

E

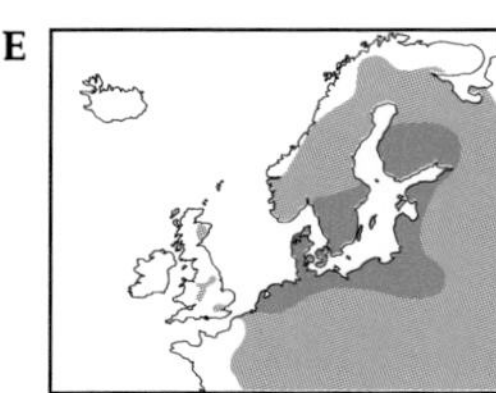

F

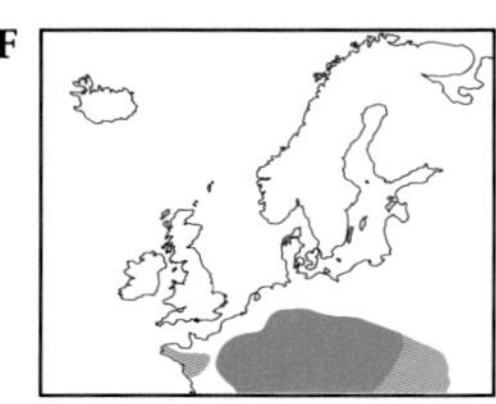

G

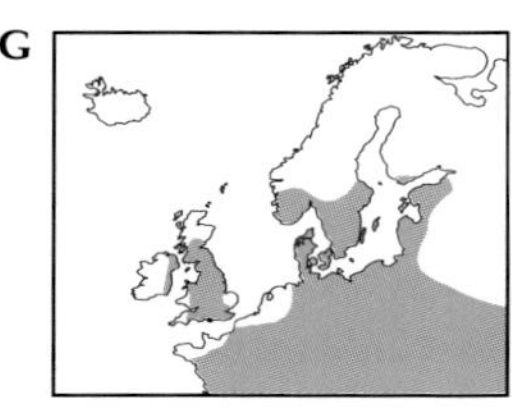

J

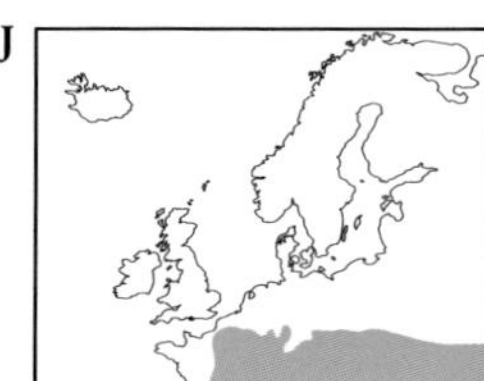

EYEBRIGHTS *Euphrasia* Annual, short, branched or simple, semi-parasitic herbs. Leaves opposite or alternate in upper part of stem. Flowers in leafy terminal inflorescences; corolla white, often with yellow and purple, 4-11mm, 2-lipped, with upper lip 2-lobed and lower lip 3-lobed. The eyebrights are a distinctive but exceptionally difficult group. Some 30 species occur in this area, but they are not readily identifiable by normal means, in that a number of samples from a population are often required, combined with extremely close examination. Many natural hybrids also occur. Only 2 of the commoner, more distinctive species are described.

A **Eyebright** *Euphrasia nemorosa* Erect plant to 35cm, with 1 to 9 pairs of ascending branches, often purplish. Leaves oval-triangular, 2-12mm, hairy below, sharply toothed; bracts (with flowers) oval, pointed, sharp-toothed and rounded at base. Flowers white to lilac, 5-7. 5mm long, lower lip longer than upper. Fruit more than twice as long as wide and hairy. In grassy places and open woods; throughout N Europe. **Fl** 7-9. **Br** Common in England and Wales, uncommon in Scotland and Ireland.

B *Euphrasia micrantha* Similar in general form, but plant usually strongly tinged with purple. Leaves hairless, not darker below, small (2-8mm). Corolla 4-6. 5mm and lilac-purple. Widespread on heaths, frequently associated with Ling, and probably semi-parasitic on it; throughout N Europe. **Fl** 7-9. **Br** Widespread, but only common in N and W Britain.

YELLOW-RATTLES *Rhinanthus* Small, but difficult group of annual semi-parasitic herbs, with opposite leaves, and leafy spikes of flowers. Corolla usually yellow, 2-lipped, with a long tube. Stamens 4 included in the upper lip.

C **Yellow-rattle** *Rhinanthus minor* Erect, almost hairless annual to 50cm, often with black-spotted stem. Leaves oblong to linear-lanceolate, 5-15mm wide, with rounded or pointed teeth, directed towards the leaf tip; bracts similar but more triangular, strongly toothed at base and pointed. Flowers in long terminal leafy inflorescences; corolla yellow, 2-lipped, 13-15mm long, upper lip with 2 short violet teeth (about 1mm); calyx flattened, becoming inflated when in fruit, hairless except for the margins. Common almost throughout; in grasslands, especially meadows and dunes. **Fl** 5-9. **Br** Common and widespread.

D *Rhinanthus groenlandicus* Similar to Yellow-rattle, but with stem hairy on 2 opposite sides, leaves more deeply toothed, with spreading teeth. Only Scandinavia from S Norway northwards. **Fl** 6-9. **Br** Absent.

E **Greater Yellow-rattle** *Rhinanthus angustifolius* Very similar to Yellow-rattle, differing in that the plant is often larger, *more branched*; bracts more yellowish green; corolla tube curved upwards (straight in Yellow-rattle), with the *teeth on the upper corolla lip at least 2mm long*, and about twice as long as broad. In meadows, cornfields and dunes; widespread in mainland Europe. **Fl** 5-9. **Br** Now very rare, in a few localities from central Scotland southwards.

F *Rhinanthus alectorolophus* Similar to other species, but *stem not black spotted*; basal teeth of bracts little different from others; corolla tube slightly curved; *calyx covered with long white hairs when in flower*. From Holland and N France southwards; local in meadows. **Fl** 5-9. **Br** Absent.

G **Toothwort** *Lathraea squamaria* Distinctive plant, wholly parasitic on the roots of Hazel, Maple and other woody plants. Stout and erect, with white or pink stems to 30cm. Leaves scale-like, alternate, clasping and untoothed. Flowers 15-17mm long, in a 1-sided spike with scale-like bracts; corolla pinky white, tubular and exceeding calyx; calyx with 4 equal lobes (compare with broomrapes, *see* pages 238-40, which have 2-lipped calyx). Widespread and locally common, though absent from the far north; mainly in woods on base-rich soils. **Fl** 3-5. **Br** Widespread but local, northwards to mid-Scotland. Often included in the Broomrape family, but now thought to be closer to the Figwort family.

H **Purple Toothwort** *Lathraea clandestina* Highly distinctive plant, with wholly subterranean stems, giving rise to large violet flowers, corolla 40-50mm. Often found in large clusters at the base of poplars, willows and alders on which it is parasitic. Local from Belgium southwards; in woods and parkland. **Fl** 3-5. **Br** Not native, but commonly introduced, occasionally naturalised.

Globularia Family
Globulariaceae

A small family of low herbs, with alternate untoothed leaves. Flowers with 5 parts, in dense heads; stamens 4; ovary superior (compare with inferior in similar Scabious family or Sheep's-bit.)

I **Common Globularia** *Globularia vulgaris* Hairless perennial evergreen herb, with a rosette of stalked, oval to spoon-shaped leaves, notched or 3-toothed at tip, lateral veins barely visible on top surface; stems erect and unbranched, to 20cm. Stem leaves alternate, stalkless, lanceolate. Flowers in dense terminal, rounded heads, 20-25mm in diameter; corolla blue, tubular, 2-lipped. In S Sweden only. **Fl** 4-7. **Br** Absent.

J *Globularia punctata* Similar to above, but basal leaves are notched or untoothed, *not 3-toothed; leaf veins are clearly visible above.* Flower heads smaller, to 15mm in diameter. From Belgium and N France southwards; in grassy and rocky habitats, often calcareous. **Fl** 5-6. **Br** Absent.

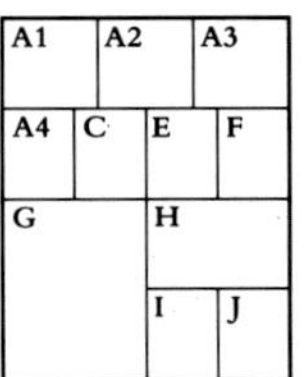

A **1** *Euphrasia rostkoviana*

A **2** *Euphrasia actica*

A **3 Eyebright** *Euphrasia nemorosa*

A **4** *Euphrasia stricta*

C **Yellow-rattle**

E **Greater Yellow-rattle**

F *Rhinanthus alectorolophus*

G **Toothwort**

H **Purple Toothwort**

I **Common Globularia**

J *Globularia punctata*

B

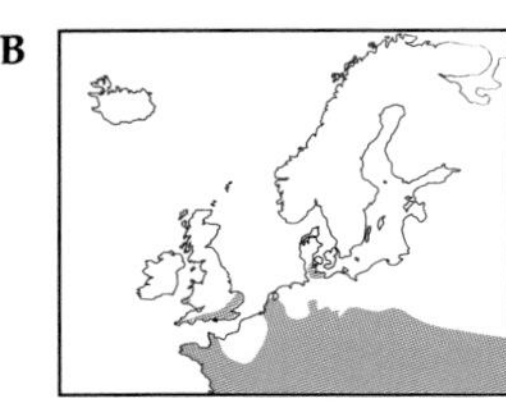

C

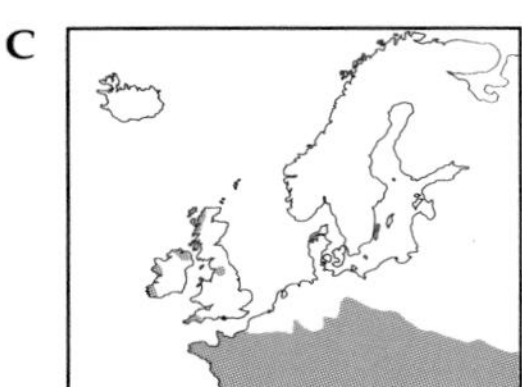

E

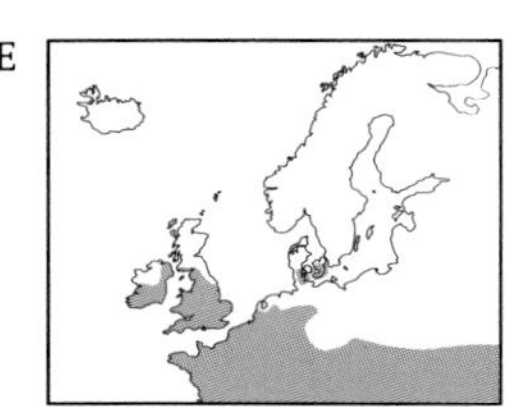

G

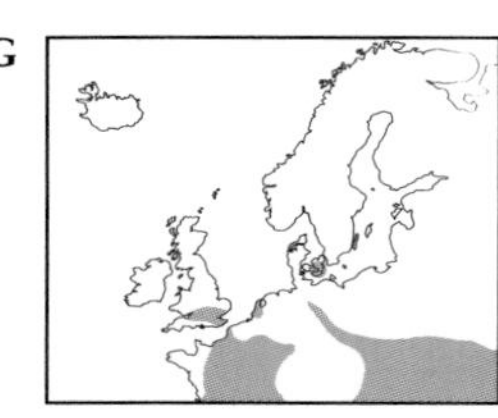

H

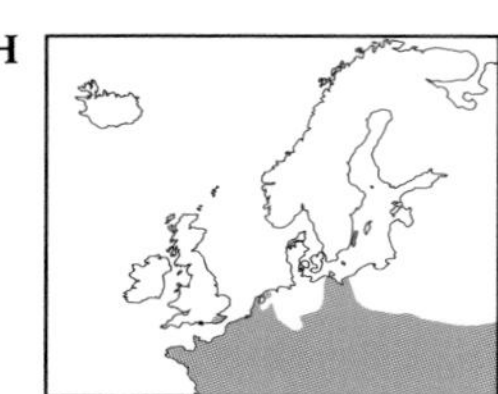

Broomrape Family
Orobanchaceae

Annual or perennial herbs, parasitic on a variety of other plants by means of root tubers. Plants totally lacking chlorophyll. Flower stems erect, with spikes of tubular 2-lipped flowers; stamens 4. The host plant, where known, can be a useful but not diagnostic aid to identification.

(1) Plants with 3 bracts below each flower (actually 1 bract plus 2 bracteoles) in addition to calyx lobes.

A **Hemp, Branched Broomrape** *Orobanche ramosa* Erect glandular stems to 30cm, usually branched (the only species in area that is). Scale-leaves oval and pointed. Bracts and bracteoles present, equalling calyx. Flowers violet or blue, 10-22mm long and glandular; filaments hairless, or hairy at base; stigma white or pale blue. A S European species, occasionally naturalised in the south of N Europe, parasitic on Hemp, Tobacco, and other herbaceous plants. **Fl** 6-9. **Br** Formerly in E England, possibly extinct, or casual only.

B **Yarrow Broomrape** *Orobanche purpurea* Erect unbranched stems to 60cm, minutely hairy and bluish. Flowers bluish-violet, with deeper violet veins, 18-25mm; stigma white or pale blue. Parasitic on Yarrow, occasionally other composites. Local N to SE Sweden; in rough grassy areas. **Fl** 6-7. **Br** Rare and local in scattered localities south of a line from Lincolnshire to SW Wales, only on Yarrow.

(2) Plants with single bracts below flowers, stigmas purple, orange or dark red at flowering time.

C **Thyme Broomrape** *Orobanche alba* Erect reddish stout plant, to 25cm high, glandular downy, with numerous reddish scale-leaves at base. Flowers few, *fragrant*, in loose spikes, bracts shorter than flowers; corolla dull red-purple, 15-20mm long; filaments somewhat hairy below (**c1**); stigma-lobes touching (**c2**); reddish. Parasitic on thyme, and other Labiates. From Oland, southwards, rare in north of area; in grasslands and rocky areas, often calcareous. **Fl** 5-8. **Br** Very local in maritime grasslands in Cornwall, W Scotland, and Ireland.

D **Thistle Broomrape** *Orobanche reticulata* Similar in form to Thyme Broomrape, though generally larger, to 70cm. Flowers barely fragrant; corolla 15-25mm, yellow with purple margins, lower lip with 3 equal lobes (central 1 larger in Thyme Broomrape); filaments slightly hairy or hairless; stigma-lobes touching, *dark purple*. On thistles, *Scabious* and relatives, in grasslands; as far north as S Scandinavia. **Fl** 6-8. **Br** Very rare, only in Yorkshire.

E **Common Broomrape** *Orobanche minor* Spikes to 50cm, usually yellowish flushed purple. Corolla usually pale yellow-tinged or veined with purple, 10-18mm long, with *back of tube arched in a smooth curve*; upper lip notched to 2-lobed, lower lip with 3 roughly equal lobes. Filaments hairy below (**e1**); stigmas purple (occasionally yellow, in pale yellow corolla), with separated lobes (**e2**). Most commonly parasitic on a variety of legumes, especially clovers, but also on many other herbaceous species. From Holland and Germany southwards. **Fl** 6-9. **Br** Common to the south and east, but rare or absent further west and north.

F *Orobanche amethystea* Similar to Common Broomrape, but corolla white or cream, tinged with violet; *bracts longer* (12-22mm rather than 7-15mm), stamens inserted 3-5mm above base of corolla (not 2-3mm). On Sea Holly, Wild Carrot, and various other herbs; from N France and S Britain southwards, local. **Fl** 6-8. **Br** Isle of Wight and Channel Islands only.

G **Oxtongue Broomrape** *Orobanche loricata* Very similar to above, but *back of corolla curved at base, then almost straight*; upper lip notched or not, but not distinctly 2-lobed; *corolla with pale glands*; filaments densely hairy below (**g1**), almost hairless above; *stigma-lobes just touching* (**g2**). On Hawkweed Oxtongue, Artemisia and other composites; locally from Denmark southwards. **Fl** 6-7. **Br** Very rare, S England only.

H **Bedstraw Broomrape** *Orobanche caryophyllacea* *Stem glandular hairy*, yellow or purplish. *Flowers large, 20-32mm*, pink or creamy yellow, strongly clove-scented; *corolla tube roughly bell-shaped* with curved back; filaments hairy below (**h1**); stigma-lobes purple, well separated (**h2**). On bedstraws, in grassy places; widespread north to S Norway. **Fl** 6-7. **Br** Only in E Kent, very rare on downs and dunes.

I **Germander Broomrape** *Orobanche teucrii* Similar to Bedstraw Broomrape, parasitic on germander species (*Teucrium*). Differs in shorter spikes, shorter calyx (less than 12mm, not 10-17mm), and back of corolla irregularly, not smoothly, curved. From Belgium and N France southwards, local; in dry grassy and rocky places. **Fl** 5-7. **Br** Absent.

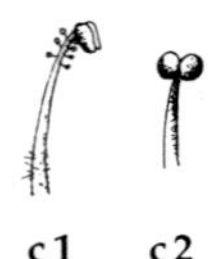

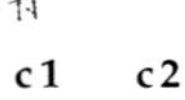

c1 c2

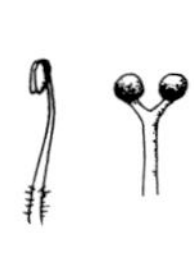

e1 e2

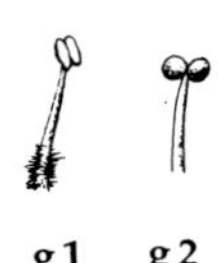

g1 g2

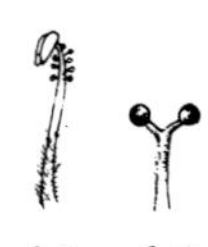

h1 h2

A	C	
B	D	E
F	G	H

A **Hemp Broomrape**
C **Thyme Broomrape**
B **Yarrow Broomrape**
D **Thistle Broomrape**
E **Common Broomrape**
F *Orobanche amethystea*
G **Oxtongue Broomrape**
H **Bedstraw Broomrape**

B

D

E

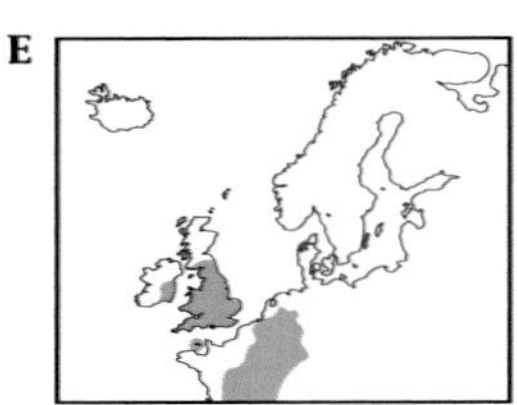

G

I

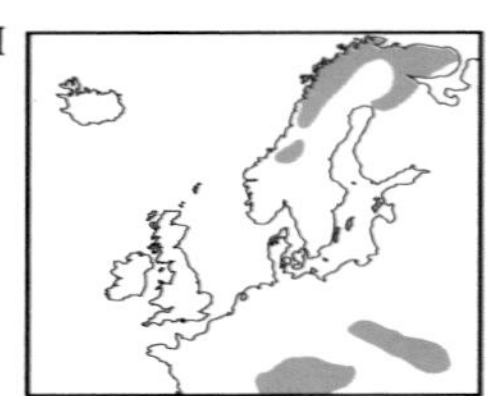

J

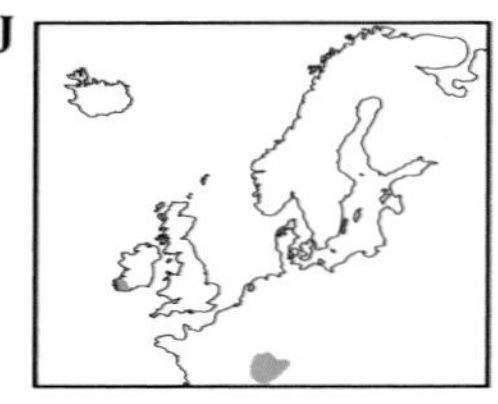

K

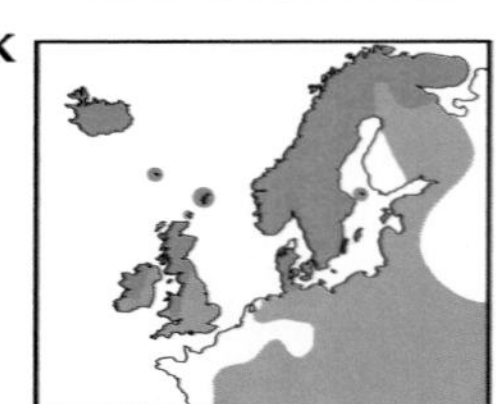

(3) Plants with a single bract below flowers, but stigmas white or yellow at flowering time.

A *Orobanche arenaria* To 60cm; corolla 25-35mm, bluish violet, filaments hairless, anthers hairy, stigma white. On Artemisia species, from N France and Germany southwards. **Fl** 6-7. **Br** Absent.

B Ivy Broomrape *Orobanche hederae* Stems to 60cm, usually less, glandular downy, yellow or red-purple, swollen at base. Corolla 10-22mm, cream, veined with purple; tube inflated near base, then straight; upper lip notched or entire, lower lip 3-lobed, central lobe square, margins not hairy; filaments slightly hairy (**b1**), stigma-lobes yellow and partly joined (**b2**). Parasitic on ivy, north to Ireland and Holland; locally frequent on limestone soils especially near the coast, rare elsewhere. **Fl** 5-7. **Br** Local in S Britain, commoner towards the west.

C *Orobanche lutea* Similar to Bedstraw Broomrape in most respects, but stems more swollen at base; corolla yellowish brown or reddish brown, not hairy on lower lip; stigma yellow or white. Parasitic on species of Medick and other legumes in grassy places; from Holland southwards. **Fl** 6-8. **Br** Absent.

D Knapweed Broomrape *Orobanche elatior* Relatively tall plant to 70cm, slightly glandular hairy, stem slightly swollen at base, yellowish or reddish. Bracts as long as flowers. Flowers numerous in dense long spike; corolla yellow, usually purple-tinged, 18-25mm, evenly curved on the back; corolla-lobes finely toothed, not hairy; filaments hairy below (**d1**), attached half-way up corolla tube; stigma-lobes (**d2**) yellow. Scattered in grassy areas; from Denmark and S Sweden southwards, parasitic on *Centaurea* species and other composites. **Fl** 6-7. **Br** Locally common in parts of S and E England, usually on shallow calcareous soils; rarer to the north and west, absent from Scotland.

E Greater Broomrape *Orobanche rapum-genistae* Large, often clumped plant to 80cm tall, with stout yellowish stems, *strongly swollen at bases*; flower spike long and dense. Bracts longer than flowers. Corolla 20-25mm, yellowish, tinged purple, with back curved evenly; upper lip barely lobed and untoothed; *filaments hairless at base*, with a few glands at top (**e1**), stamens attached at base of corolla tube; stigma-lobes separated (**e2**), yellow. Parasitic on Broom, Gorse and related shrubs, in dry grassy areas. Generally rare and declining, from Holland and central Germany southwards. **Fl** 5-7. **Br** Widespread to S Scotland, but local and rare, decreasing.

F Slender Broomrape *Orobanche gracilis* Stems slender, glandular, reddish or yellowish, to 60cm. Bracts triangular, shorter than flowers. Corolla yellow with red veins, deep shiny red inside tube. Filaments hairy, at least below; stigmas yellow, lobes separated. On various legumes, in grassy places; from central Germany southwards. **Fl** 6-7. **Br** Absent.

Butterwort Family
Lentibulariaceae

A distinctive family of small carnivorous herbs. Corolla 2-lipped, 5-lobed; calyx 5-lobed; stamens 2, attached to corolla. Fruit a many-seeded capsule. All species grow in wet places, often nutrient-poor, and have the ability to digest insects.

G Pale Butterwort *Pinguicula lusitanica* Small plant, with an overwintering rosette of 5-12 *pale grey-green*, oblong, blunt leaves, 10-20mm long, with rolled-up margins. Flowers on stalks up to 12cm long, downy, slender, 1-8 together; *corolla pale lilac-pink*, 7-9mm, yellow in throat; lobes of upper lip rounded, spur short (2-4mm), blunt and cylindrical. Locally frequent in bogs and wet heaths; in W Britain and W France only. **Fl** 6-10. **Br** Strongly western in distribution, from Hampshire to NW Scotland, and throughout Ireland.

H *Pinguicula villosa* Similar to Pale Butterwort, but overwintering as bud; leaves more rounded; *flower stalks very glandular hairy*; corolla pale violet. Only in bogs; from central Sweden northwards. **Fl** 6-8. **Br** Absent.

I Alpine Butterwort *Pinguicula alpina* Easily recognised species. Leaves yellowish green, overwintering as bud. *Flowers white with yellow spot* at mouth, 8-16mm. In bogs and other wet places; throughout Arctic Europe, and in mountains further south. **Fl** 6-8. **Br** Extinct, formerly in N Scotland.

J Large-flowered Butterwort *Pinguicula grandiflora* Overwinters as bud. Leaves in rosettes of 5-8, ovate to oblong, to 60mm long, bright yellow-green. Flower stalks to 18cm; *corolla violet* or paler, *25-30mm wide*, with long white purple-streaked patch at throat; *lobes of lower lip partially overlapping*, rounded and wavy. Spur 10-12mm, straight and backwardly directed, occasionally notched at tip. In bogs, wet rocks, flushed areas; in SW Ireland and mountains from Jura southwards. **Fl** 5-7. **Br** SW Eire, locally common; introduced in Cornwall.

K Common Butterwort *Pinguicula vulgaris* Rather similar to Large-flowered Butterwort, but smaller; flower stalks to 15cm; *corolla violet, 11-13mm wide*, with broad clear white patch at throat; *lobes of lower lip well separated* and flat. Spur 4-7mm, tapering to a point, slender. In bogs, fens and flushes, often calcareous; throughout the area, though absent from many southern lowland areas. **Fl** 5-7. **Br** Common in the north and west, but rare or absent in much of SE England.

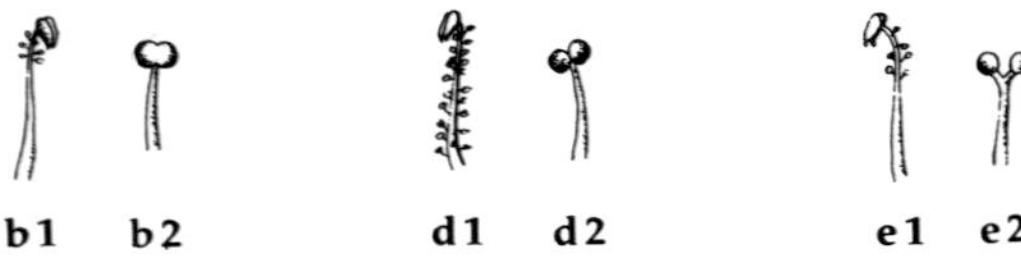

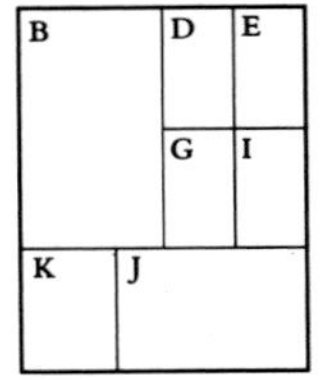

B **Ivy Broorape**

D **Knapweed Broorape**

E **Greater Broomrape**

G **Pale Butterwort**

I **Alpine Butterwort**

K **Common Butterwort**

J **Large-flowered Butterwort**

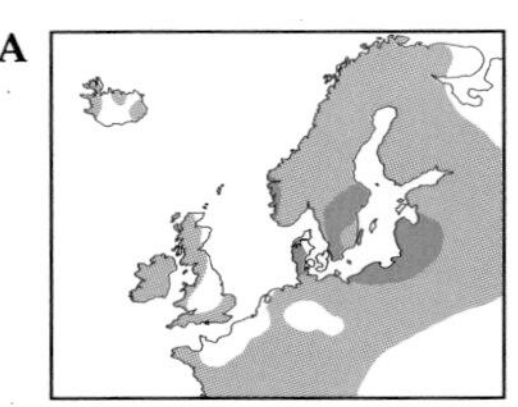

A

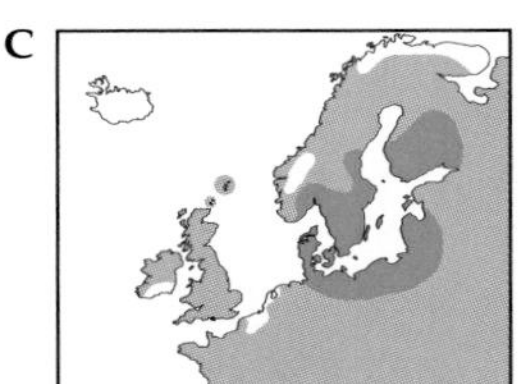

C

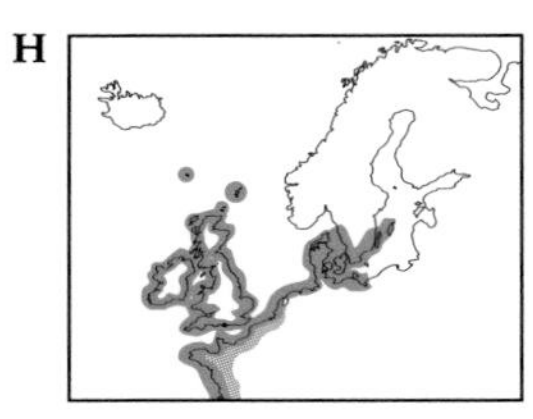

H

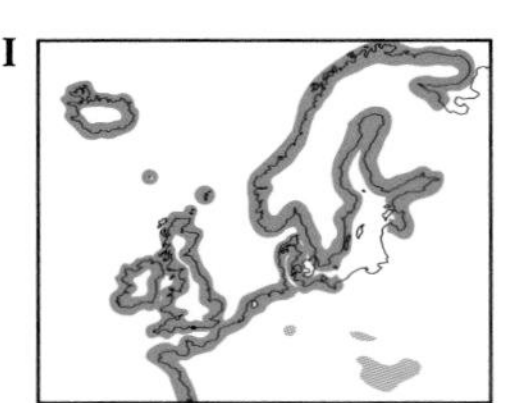

I

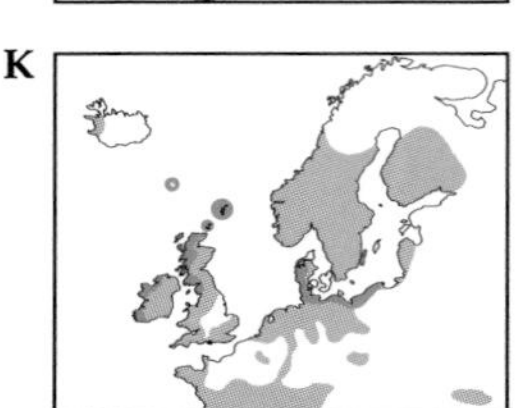

K

BLADDERWORTS *Utricularia* Loosely rooted aquatic plants, with erect emergent flower spikes and horizontal submerged stems with finely divided leaves; small, flask-shaped bladders which trap minute invertebrates.

(1) Plants with 2 kinds of stem: some with green leaves and a few bladders; others often buried, colourless, with few leaves and many bladders.

A **Lesser Bladderwort** *Utricularia minor* Main leaves finely divided into thread-like untoothed segments, only 3-10mm long, *without bristles*. Inflorescences 4-15cm tall, with 2-6 flowers; *corolla pale yellow, small* (6-8mm), with short blunt spur. In pools in bogs and other acid waters; throughout though local. **Fl** 6-9. **Br** Throughout, but local; mainly in NW Britain, though frequent in bogs in central and S England.

B **Intermediate Bladderwort** *Utricularia intermedia* Small plant, up to 25cm long. Flowers rare, with bright yellow corolla with reddish lines, 8-12mm long, in 2- to 4-flowered inflorescence to 20cm; spur conical. In shallow peaty water and bogs; throughout but local. **Fl** 7-9. **Br** Local in Scotland and Ireland, very local and rare elsewhere.

(2) Stems of one kind, all with green floating leaves with numerous bladders.

C **Greater Bladderwort** *Utricularia vulgaris* Stems up to 1m long bearing pinnately divided leaves, to 30mm long, toothed with *1 or more bristles on teeth*. Inflorescence to 30cm tall, 4-10 flowers; *corolla deep yellow*, 12-18mm long, *upper lip same length as central palate*, lower lip with vertically turned-back margin; spur conical and pointed. In still waters, up to about 1m deep; almost throughout, but local. **Fl** 7-8. **Br** Widespread but mainly eastern, most frequently in calcareous waters.

D *Utricularia australis* (also known as Greater Bladderwort) Very similar, and virtually indistinguishable from Greater Bladderwort except when it is in flower. Differs in that it is a more slender plant, with leaf-segments only having *solitary bristles*. Flowers pale lemon yellow; *lower lip of corolla almost flat with wavy margin, upper lip longer than palate*. Widespread in similar places, often acid, but distribution uncertain as flowers rarely produced in the north of range. **Br** Mainly western.

Plantain Family
Plantaginaceae

Herbs, usually with leaves in basal rosettes. Flowers usually in terminal inflorescences; very small, with reduced 4-lobed calyx and corolla, and 4 long conspicuous stamens. Normally hermaphrodite, but unisexual in *Littorella*.

E **Greater Plantain** *Plantago major* Perennial herb with basal rosette. Leaves broadly ovate to elliptical, up to 25cm long, 3- to 9-veined, usually hairless, narrowing abruptly into a petiole about as long as blade (**e**). Flower heads on unfurrowed hairy stalks, 10-15cm long, carrying long thin dense spike of flowers; corolla yellowish white, 3mm in diameter, anthers lilac then yellowish. Widespread throughout, and very common, in open cultivated and disturbed habitats. **Fl** 6-10. **Br** Common throughout.

Ssp *winteri* has leaves 3- to 5-veined, gradually narrowing into stalk; blade thin, yellowish green. Widespread in saline habitats. **Br** Absent.

F **Hoary Plantain** *Plantago media* Similar to Greater Plantain, but differs in that the leaves are elliptical (**f**), greyish downy, *gradually narrowing into a short stalk*, forming a flat rosette. Inflorescence cylindrical on long unfurrowed stalk (up to 30cm long), much longer than leaves. Flowers whitish, 2mm in diameter, scented; *filaments purple, anthers lilac*. In dry, grassy places, often on calcareous soils; widespread and frequent almost throughout. **Fl** 5-8. **Br** Common in England, but rare elsewhere.

G **Ribwort Plantain** *Plantago lanceolata* Basal leaves in a spreading rosette; *leaves lanceolate*, up to 20cm long (occasionally 30cm), with 3-5 strongly marked almost parallel veins, usually short-stalked. Inflorescence on long deeply furrowed stalks, up to 45cm, much longer than leaves; inflorescence short, usually less than 20mm; *corolla brownish*, 4mm in diameter; *stamens long and white*. In cultivated and waste land, grassy places and roadsides; almost throughout, very common. **Fl** 4-10. *Br* Common and widespread.

H **Buck's-horn Plantain** *Plantago coronopus* Distinctive plantain, with flat rosette of deeply pinnately divided leaves, to 20cm, 1-veined, with linear segments (though occasionally just toothed). Flower spikes numerous, with arching stems exceeding the leaves; spikes 20-40mm long; corolla brownish, lobes without a midrib, stamens yellow; bracts of flower spike with long spreading points. Common and widespread; in coastal habitats, less common on disturbed ground and grassland inland, mainly on sand or gravel soils. **Fl** 5-7. **Br** Common around the coasts, and inland in the south and east.

I **Sea Plantain** *Plantago maritima* Plant with woody rootstock and erect, loose rosette of linear, fleshy, faintly 3- to 5-veined, *untoothed leaves*. Flower stalks numerous, stout, unfurrowed, bearing cylindrical inflorescence 20-60mm long. Flowers about 3mm in diameter, corolla brownish with darker midrib, stamens pale yellow; flower bracts oval and appressed. Widespread and locally common throughout; mainly coastal but also on saline soils inland, and some mountains. **Fl** 6-8. **Br** Widespread around coasts, most frequently in salt-marshes, and local in mountains.

J **Branched Plantain** *Plantago arenaria* Differs from other plantains in its branched inflorescence, with many egg-shaped flower clusters; leaves linear, not fleshy. Annual. An uncommon casual, occasionally naturalised, in dry sandy places; north to Holland. Native to S Europe. **Fl** 5-8. **Br** Occasional.

K **Shoreweed** *Littorella uniflora* Dwarf, hairless perennial; aquatic, with slender rooting stolons. Leaves in erect basal rosettes, narrowly linear to 10cm, semicircular in section, spongy, with sheathing bases. Flowers unisexual: male flowers solitary on slender stalks 50-80mm long, with 4 tiny whitish petals, and 4 long-stalked white stamens; female flowers short-stalked, several at base of male stalk, with 1cm long style. Margins of lakes and ponds, usually acidic, to a depth of 4m. Local, but widespread almost throughout, except the far north. **Fl** 6-8. **Br** Locally common in Ireland and N Britain, rarer in the south and east.

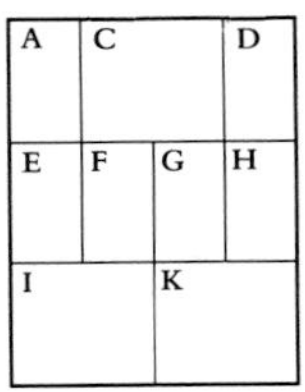

A **Lesser Bladderwort**

C **Greater Bladderwort** *Utricularia vulgaris*

D *Utricularia australis*

E **Greater Plantain**

F **Hoary Plantain**

G **Ribwort Plantain**

H **Buck's-horn Plantain**

I **Sea Plantain**

K **Shoreweed** with the leaves of Marsh Pennywort

e

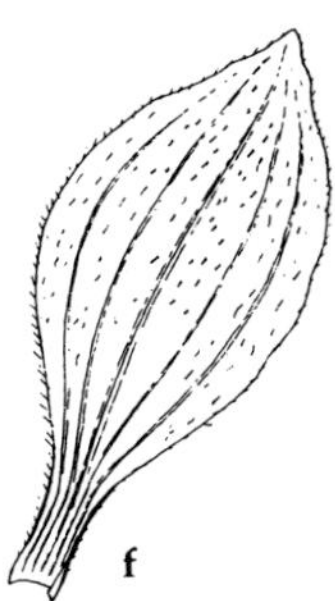

f

B

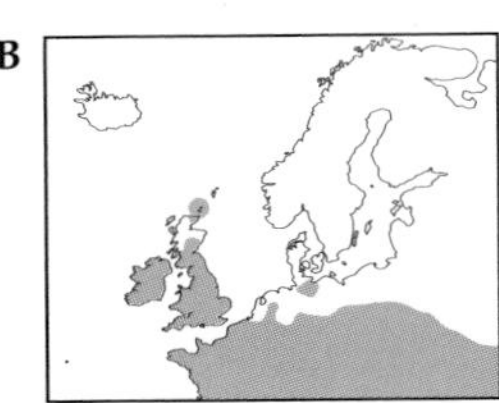

C

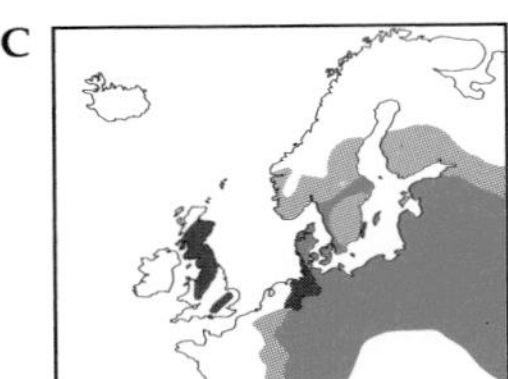

E

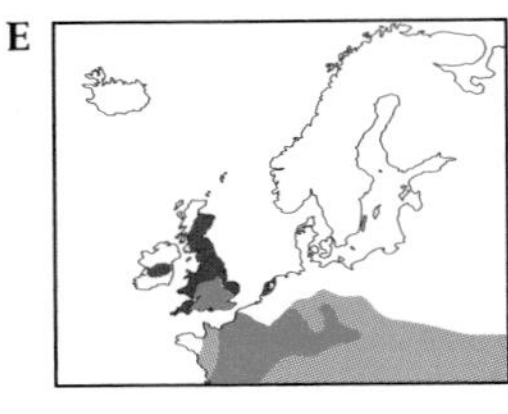

F

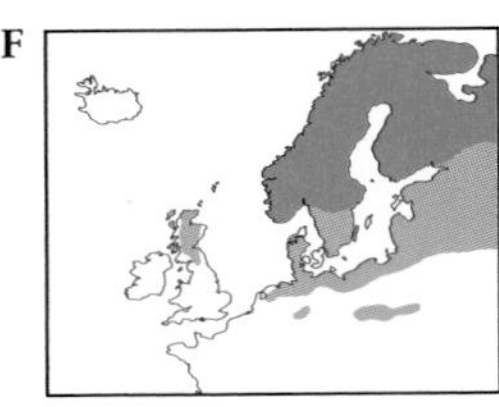

I

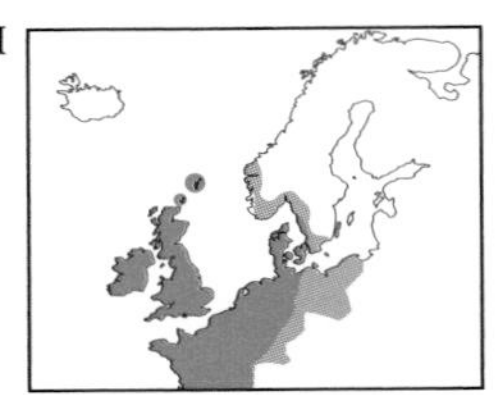

J

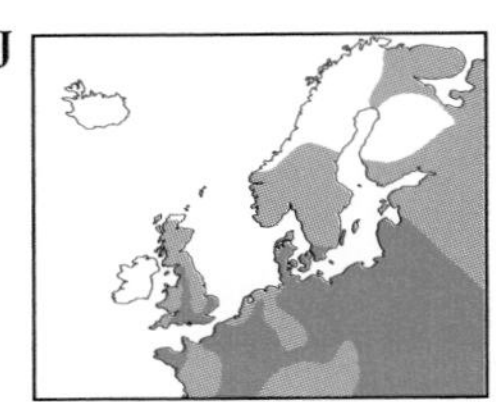

Honeysuckle Family
Caprifoliaceae

Woody perennial shrubs, occasionally herbs, with opposite paired leaves. Flowers usually 5-parted, often tubular; calyx small. Ovary inferior, fruit usually fleshy.

A **Elder** *Sambucus nigra* Common and familiar deciduous shrub to 10m, with ascending branches from base; bark brown-grey, furrowed and corky, interior of white pith. Leaves opposite, to 12cm long, pinnately divided with 5-7 toothed ovate leaflets. Inflorescence a terminal plate-like cluster, much-branched and almost flat-topped, 10-20cm in diameter; flowers creamy white, 5-lobed, about 5mm in diameter, strong-smelling. Fruit (the elderberry) a small globose shiny black berry, 6-8mm in diameter. Widespread and common throughout except the extreme north; in grasslands, rough land, etc., generally on lime-rich or nitrogen-rich soils. **Fl** 6-7. **Br** Common throughout except N Scotland.

B **Dwarf Elder, Danewort** *Sambucus ebulus* Strong-growing *herbaceous plant, to 2m*, with erect, grooved stems. All parts strong-smelling, unpleasant. Leaves pinnate with 7-13 narrower leaflets and conspicuous oval stipules at the base. Inflorescence flat-topped, with 3 main rays, smaller (7-14cm in diameter) and pinker than Common Elder; stamens purple. Fruit globose, 5-7mm in diameter, black, poisonous. In hedges, on roadsides, waste places; from Holland southwards, locally common. **Fl** 6-8. **Br** Not native, scattered through England, rare in Scotland.

C **Red-berried, or Alpine, Elder** *Sambucus racemosa* Deciduous shrub to 4m, with arching stems, grey bark and reddish pith. Leaves pinnate with 3-7 long-pointed leaflets, stipules barely visible, flowers in dense oval to pyramidal heads, 3-6cm in diameter; corolla yellowish or greenish white. Fruit globose, red, 5mm in diameter. From Belgium southwards; in woods, mainly in mountain areas; introduced elsewhere. **Fl** 4-6. **Br** Naturalised, mainly in E Scotland.

D **Guelder Rose** *Viburnum opulus* Deciduous much-branched shrub to 4m; twigs greyish, hairless, angled, buds scaly. Leaves opposite, palmately lobed, 50-80mm long, with 3-5 sharply toothed lobes, downy below, with short petiole. Flowers in flat umbel-like heads, 5-10cm in diameter; outer flowers large (15-20mm in diameter) and sterile, inner flowers smaller (4-7mm in diameter), all white. Fruit almost globose, 8mm in diameter, becoming red. Widespread and common throughout except the far north; in woods, scrub and hedges, usually on heavy soils. **Fl** 5-7. **Br** Common, except in N Scotland.

E **Wayfaring Tree** *Viburnum lantana* Deciduous shrub to 6m, with pale brown, downy, rounded twigs, buds without scales. Leaves ovate, to 10cm, pointed, wrinkled, finely toothed and densely downy below. Flowers in flat-topped umbel-like heads, 6-10cm in diameter, all flowers alike; corolla creamy white, 5-7mm in diameter. Fruit flattened ovoid, red then black, about 8mm long. From Belgium and England southwards; in scrub, hedgerows and open woods, usually on calcareous soils. **Fl** 5-6. **Br** Common in S and E England, especially on chalk, but rare or absent further north and west.

F **Twinflower** *Linnaea borealis* Low, creeping, evergreen subshrub, with long trailing stems. Leaves oval to almost round, 10-15mm long, bluntly toothed, in rather distant opposite pairs. Flowers usually paired, on erect glandular-downy stalks to 80mm, with flowers often hanging 1 to each side; corolla bell-shaped, 5-lobed, pink, 5-9mm long, and fragrant. A very distinctive plant when in flower. Widespread and common in Arctic Europe, becoming much rarer and increasingly confined to mountains southwards; mainly in coniferous woods and moorlands. **Fl** 6-8. **Br** Rare and declining in native pinewoods, NE Scotland only.

G **Fly Honeysuckle** *Lonicera xylosteum* Deciduous bushy shrub to 3m, with downy grey young twigs. Leaves variable, ovate or nearly round, to 7cm long, grey-green and stalked. Flowers in pairs on a shared downy stalk, 1-2cm long, from axils of leafy bracts; corolla about 1cm, creamy yellow, 2-lipped, downy on outside (**g**). Fruit bright red globose berry, paired but not fused. Widespread in mainland Europe throughout, except the extreme north; in woods, hedges and scrub. **Fl** 5-6. **Br** Very rare, only in Sussex as a native plant.

H **Blue-berried Honeysuckle** *Lonicera caerulea* Similar to Fly Honeysuckle, but with *bell-shaped flowers, with 5 equal lobes* (**h**); *berries blue-black* when ripe. Local in mountain woods; mainly NE Europe, from Finland southwards to NE France. **Fl** 5-7, **Br** Absent.

I **Honeysuckle, Woodbine** *Lonicera periclymenum* Vigorous, twining climbing shrub, reaching 6m on a support, though also low and spreading in shady places. Leaves grey-green, opposite pairs, oval-elliptical, to 9cm long, untoothed and pointed, lower ones short-stalked. Flowers familiar, in whorled terminal heads of creamy white or yellow, tinged red, trumpet-shaped flowers, 3-5cm long, 2-lipped; very fragrant, especially at night. Fruit red, globose and fleshy. From S Sweden southwards; in scrub, hedgerows and woods, widespread and common, mainly on acid soils. **Fl** 6-9. **Br** Common throughout.

Moschatel Family Adoxaceae

A family with only the one species. Family characteristics as for species.

J **Moschatel, Townhall Clock** *Adoxa moschatellina* Perennial herb, with creeping rhizomes, and short erect stems to 10cm. Basal leaves long-stalked, twice 3-lobed, with spine-tipped lobes; stem leaves only 1 opposite pair of stalked 3-lobed leaves, smaller than basal ones; all leaves fleshy, pale green. Flowers in long-stalked terminal head, 6-8mm in diameter, made up of 5 flowers, 4 in square facing outwards, 5th facing upwards; corolla green, 5-lobed (4-lobed in top flower), with 10 stamens (8 in top flower). Easily recognised when in flower. In woods, shady places and rock-ledges; through most of Europe, mainly on damp or heavy soils. **Fl** 4-5. **Br** Locally common, becoming rarer northwards.

A	B1	B2
C1	C2	D1
D2	E	F
G	I	J

A **Elder**

B **1 Dwarf Elder** in flower

B **2 Dwarf Elder** in fruit

C **1 Red-berried Elder** in flower

C **2 Red-berried Elder** in fruit

D **1 Guelder Rose** in flower

D **2 Guelder Rose** in fruit

E **Wayfaring Tree** in fruit

F **Twinflower**

G **Fly Honeysuckle**

I **Honeysuckle**

J **Moschatel**

g

h

A

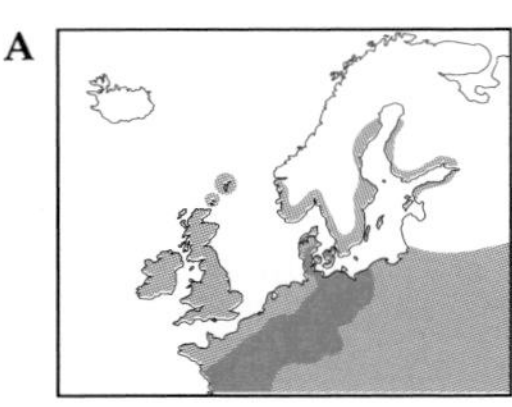

F

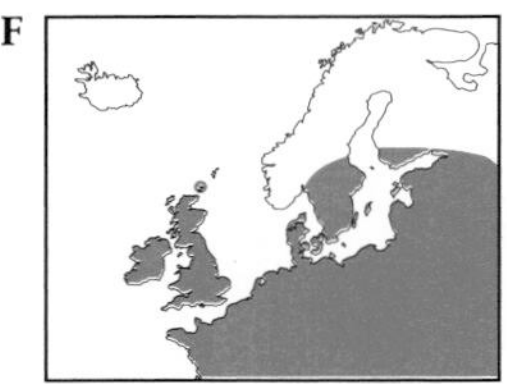

G

Valerian Family
Valerianaceae

Herbaceous plants with opposite leaves, without stipules. Flowers in dense umbel-like heads, or cylindrical. Calyx very small, toothed or not; corolla funnel-shaped, sometimes spurred, 5-lobed; ovary inferior.

CORNSALADS *Valerianella* Small annual plants with symmetrical branching; flowers small in clusters in axils of branches, and in terminal heads. The species are difficult to distinguish, and ripe fruit is required for certain identification.

(1) Species with minute, barely visible calyx.

A **Common Cornsalad, Lamb's Lettuce** *Valerianella locusta* Variable hairless annual, to 40cm, very forked in favourable conditions. Lower leaves spoon-shaped, to 70mm, blunt, sometimes toothed, upper ones oblong. Flowers in dense terminal heads, 10-20mm in diameter; corolla pale lilac-mauve, 1-2mm in diameter, 5-lobed; calyx very small, 1-toothed. Fruit 2.5 × 2mm, compressed laterally, with a corky bulge on the fertile seed-bearing cell (**a**). In dry grasslands, waste places, walls and dunes; throughout, though much rarer in the north. The commonest species in most areas. **Fl** 4-6. **Br** Widespread though local.

B **Keeled-fruited Cornsalad** *Valerianella carinata* Very similar to above, but the fruit is almost square in cross-section, 2 × 0.75mm, fertile cell thin-walled, not corky and swollen (**b**). Similar habitats; north to Holland. **Fl** 4-6. **Br** Local in south, very rare further north; absent from Scotland..

(2) Species with larger calyx, clearly visible.

C **Narrow-fruited Cornsalad** *Valerianella dentata* Similar to above species, up to 30cm, but with looser inflorescences. Fruit narrow egg-shaped (**c**), 2 × 1mm, with calyx about width of fruit, with 1 tooth bigger than others. In arable fields, usually on calcareous soil; northwards to S Sweden. **Fl** 6-7. **Br** Locally common in the south and east, rare or absent elsewhere; declining generally.

D **Broad-fruited Cornsalad** *Valerianella rimosa* Similar to Narrow-fruited Cornsalad, but has more angled stems, rougher on angles. Fruit broadly egg-shaped, (**d**) not flattened, 2 × 1.5mm; calyx above fruit small but visible, about a third of the width of fruit, minutely toothed. In arable fields; north to Denmark. **Fl** 7-8 (later than other species). **Br** Scattered sites in S England and Ireland; uncommon and decreasing.

E **Hairy-fruited Cornsalad** *Valerianella eriocarpa* Differs from above in *hairy fruits* (**e**), with *calyx as wide as fruit, deeply 5- to 6-toothed*. In arable land, and on walls; introduced from S Europe, occurring as far north as Scotland and Germany. **Fl** 6-7. **Br** Scattered and rare, as far north as central Scotland.

F **Common Valerian** *Valeriana officinalis* Tall erect perennial herb to 1.5m, singly or clustered. Leaves pinnate, to 20cm long, in opposite pairs, lower ones stalked, upper ones short-stalked; leaflets lanceolate and toothed. Flowers in terminal head, often with a few separate lower clusters; hermaphrodite; corolla funnel-shaped, pink, tube swollen at base, 2.5-5mm long and 5-lobed, with 3 protruding stamens. Fruit oblong, with a white, feathery pappus. Widespread and common almost throughout; in fens, riversides, wet woods and occasionally in dwarfer form in dry grasslands. **Fl** 6-8. **Br** Common throughout.

G **Marsh Valerian** *Valeriana dioica* Perennial, with creeping runners and erect stems to 30cm. *Root leaves long-stalked, roughly ovate,* blade 20-30mm long, untoothed and blunt; upper leaves virtually unstalked and pinnately divided. Male and female flowers produced on separate plants; flowers in terminal heads, pink: male heads larger, 40mm in diameter, with 5mm-diameter flowers; females 10-20mm in diameter, with 2mm-diameter flowers. Fruit similar to Common Valerian, but smaller. In fens and wet meadows; from SE Norway southwards, local. **Fl** 5-6. **Br** Local throughout England, Wales and S Scotland; absent from N Scotland and Ireland.

H **Three-leaved Valerian** *Valeriana tripteris* Stems to 40cm, hairy at nodes; numerous non-flowering shoots. *Middle stem leaves trifoliate;* flowers in heads, pink. In woods and scrub from the Vosges southwards. **Fl** 5-8. **Br** Absent.

I *Valeriana montana* Very similar, with simple or pinnately lobed middle stem leaves. Similar habitats and distribution. **Fl** 4-7. **Br** Absent.

J **Red Valerian** *Centranthus ruber* Branched ascending perennial to 80cm. *Leaves grey-green,* opposite, *ovate,* 5-10cm long and usually *untoothed;* lower ones narrowed into stalk, upper ones stalkless. Flowers in terminal inflorescence; *corolla red, pink or white,* tubular, 8-10mm long, with a pointed 3-4mm spur; 1 stamen, protruding. Fruit with hairy pappus. Native to S Europe, but widely naturalised on walls and rocky places, especially coastal; from Holland southwards. **Fl** 6-8. **Br** Widespread, commonest in the west, absent from the far north.

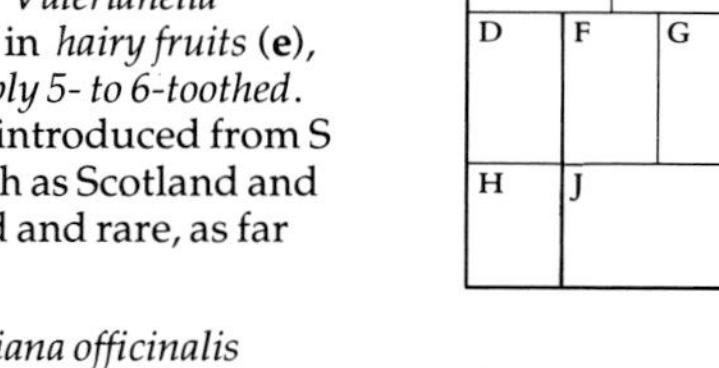

A **Common Cornsalad**
B **Keeled-fruited Cornsalad**
D **Broad-fruited Cornsalad**
F **Common Valerian**
G **Marsh Valerian**
H **Three-leaved Valerian**
J **Red Valerian**

a

b

c

d

e

A

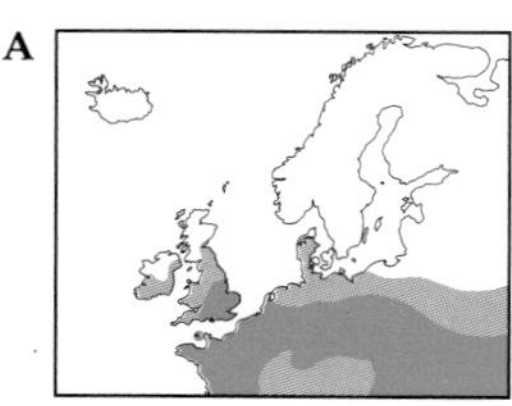

C

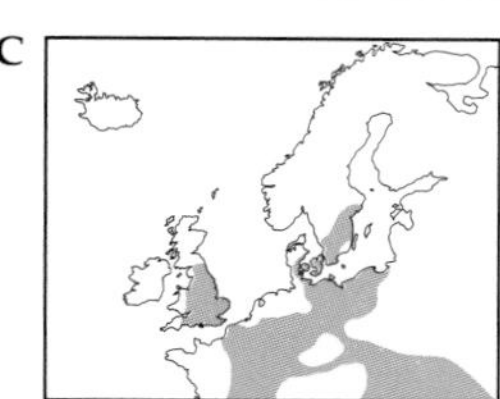

F

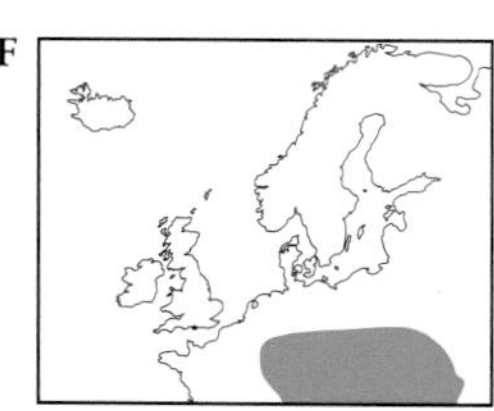

G

Teasel Family Dipsacaceae

Comprises the teasels and scabiouses. Annual or perennial herbs, with opposite leaves, erect stems, and dense clearly defined heads of flowers surrounded by a whorl of bracts. Corolla tubular, 4- to 5-lobed, or 2-lipped; stamens 2 or 4, long-protruding, not joined together, style long, ovary inferior. The rather similar rampions and Sheep's-bit (*see* page 252) differ in their lack of protruding stamens, and short calyx teeth. (*See also* Compositae page 254).

A **Wild Teasel** *Dipsacus fullonum* Stout erect biennial herb to 2m, with angled stems, prickly on angles; in 1st year, produces a rosette of short-stalked, roughly oblong, untoothed leaves with swollen-based prickles; in 2nd year, these die, and tall flower stem is produced bearing opposite leaves joined at base to form a cup. Flowers in dense egg-shaped heads, to 8cm, surrounded by a whorl of long thin spiny bracts, to 9cm long; corolla pink-purple, not all opening at once. Widespread and common, but absent from Scandinavia; in grassy places, woods and damp places, especially on heavy soils. **Fl** 7-8.
Br Locally common in S Britain, absent from N Scotland, rare in Ireland.

B *Dipsacus laciniatus* Similar to Wild Teasel, but with slender stem prickles, *pinnately lobed leaves*, shorter flower heads, and pale pink corolla. Similar habitats; mainland Europe from N Germany southwards. **Fl** 7-8. **Br** Absent.

C **Small Teasel** *Dipsacus pilosus* Erect, slender, branched plant to 1.2m, sparsely prickly. Basal rosette leaves ovate, long-stalked, hairy and prickly on midrib below; stem leaves roughly oval, sometimes with 2 basal lobes, not joined around stem. Flowers in globose heads, 15-20mm, surrounded by narrowly triangular bracts, shorter than head; corolla white or pinkish. Local in damp or shady places; from Denmark southwards. **Fl** 7-9. **Br** Local through England and Wales, absent elsewhere.

D **Devil's-bit Scabious** *Succisa pratensis* Erect perennial to 1m (usually less), with hairy or hairless stems. Basal leaves oval to spoon-shaped, to 30cm, usually untoothed, short-stalked and firm in texture; stems leaves narrower. Flower heads long-stalked and hemispherical, 15-25mm in diameter, with all florets the same size; corolla mauve to dark violet-blue, with 4 roughly equal lobes, calyx with 5 bristle teeth; heads either hermaphrodite (with conspicuously protruding anthers) or female only, with shorter anthers. Widespread and common, except for the extreme north; in meadows, fens, damp woods and downlands. **Fl** 6-10. **Br** Common throughout.

E **Field Scabious** *Knautia arvensis* Stout biennial or perennial plant, with roughly hairy stems to 75cm. Basal leaves roughly spoon-shaped, roughly hairy, undivided, toothed, or lobed; *stem leaves pinnately divided* with ovate-lanceolate terminal leaflet, all roughly hairy. Flowers in hemispherical heads, 3-4cm in diameter, on long hairy stalks; corolla blue-violet to lilac, marginal flowers larger than central ones; bracts below head ovate, calyx with 8 bristle teeth. In meadows, pastures and open woods; throughout except the far north, common. **Fl** 7-9. **Br** Common and widespread except in N and W Scotland.

F **Wood Scabious** *Knautia dipsacifolia* Similar to Field Scabious, but less hairy; upper stem leaves toothed, heart-shaped to clasping at base, but not divided or deeply lobed. In shady habitats; Belgium and central Germany southwards. **Fl** 7-9. **Br** Absent.

G **Small Scabious** *Scabiosa columbaria* Slender erect perennial, with branching stems to 70cm. Rosette leaves long-stalked, spoon-shaped but toothed or roughly pinnately lobed, with large end-leaflet; stem leaves pinnate, with narrow lobes. Flower heads 2-3cm in diameter on long, rather slender downy stalks. Involucral bracts narrow, about 10 in 1 row, shorter than flowers; outer flowers larger than inner; corolla bluish violet with 5 lobes, calyx with 5 long blackish bristle teeth. In calcareous grassy areas; from Denmark and S Sweden southwards; locally common. **Fl** 6-9. **Br** Locally common in much of England and Wales, rarer to the north, absent from much of Scotland and all of Ireland.

H *Scabiosa canescens* Similar to Small Scabious, with untoothed narrower grey-downy basal leaves, pale lilac flowers in slightly smaller heads (15-25mm in diameter). Uncommon in dry grasslands; northwards to S Sweden. **Fl** 7-9. **Br** Absent.

I *Scabiosa ochroleuca* Has yellowish flowers, with less deeply cut lower leaves than Small Scabious. An eastern species, extending into Germany. **Fl** 7-9. **Br** Absent.

A	B	C
D	E	F
G	H	I

A **Wild Teasel**
B *Dipsacus laciniatus*
C **Small Teasel**
D **Devil's-bit Scabious**
E **Field Scabious**
F **Wood Scabious**
G **Small Scabious**
H *Scabiosa canescens*
I *Scabiosa ochroleuca*

B

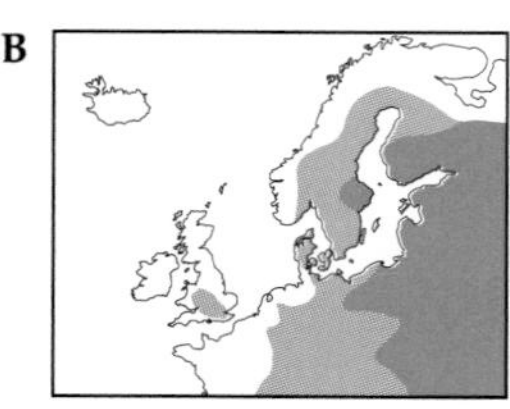

C

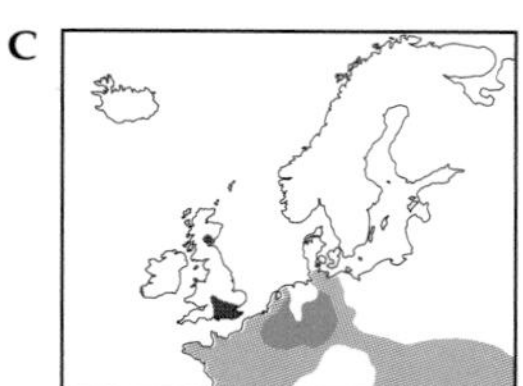

D

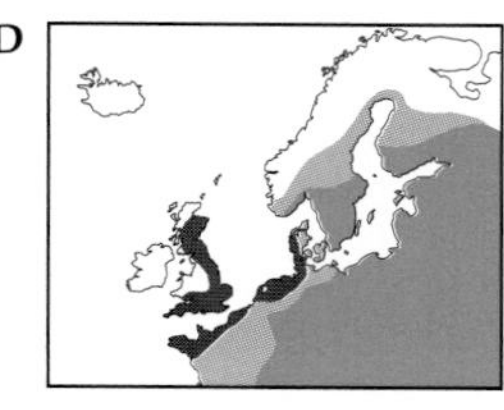

J

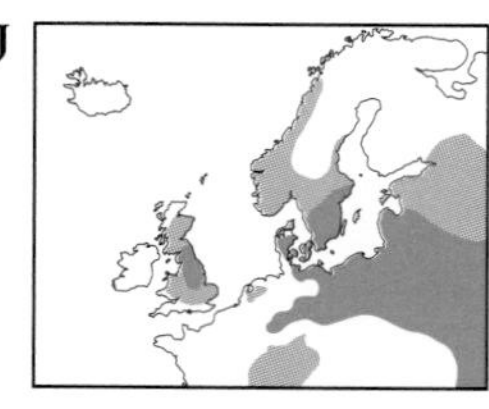

K

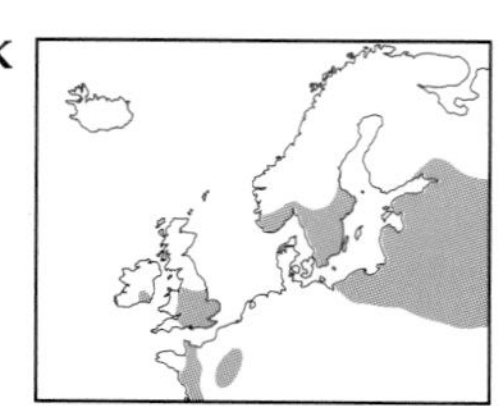

L

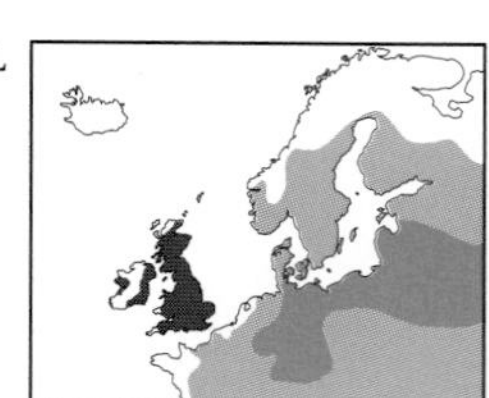

Bellflower Family
Campanulaceae

Herbs, with alternate undivided leaves without stipules. Corolla regular with 5 equal lobes.

A Arctic Bellflower *Campanula uniflora* Dwarf perennial herb, with erect unbranched stems to 15cm at most. Basal leaves spoon-shaped, to 20mm long, upper leaves linear. Flowers solitary, nodding, 7-10mm long, bell-shaped, blue. In calcareous grassy and stony places; Arctic Europe southwards to central Norway. **Fl** 7-8. **Br** Absent.

B Spreading Bellflower *Campanula patula* Slender erect perennial herb to 70cm, with rough stem and leaves. Basal leaves spoon-shaped, stalked, to 40mm, round-toothed; stem leaves smaller, narrower and unstalked. Inflorescence branched, open, with flowers erect on slender stalks; corolla bell-shaped, 20-25mm long, but usually much more open than other species, with lobes as long as tube, rosy purple to blue. In grassy places, through much of area, but largely absent from Scandinavia. **Fl** 7-9. **Br** Very local, mainly on the England-Wales border; declining.

C Rampion Bellflower *Campanula rapunculus* Variable biennial, with erect, hairless or slightly hairy stems to 1m. Basal leaves 8-10cm long, contracted abruptly into stalk; stem leaves linear-lanceolate. Flowers in a simple spike-like inflorescence, unstalked or short-stalked and *erect;* flower stalks have bracts at base; corolla 10-20mm long, lobes as long as tube, pale mauve-blue. On roadsides, field-margins and edges of woods; native north to Holland and Germany, naturalised elsewhere. **Fl** 6-8. **Br** Naturalised in a few localities, scattered throughout except the north.

D Peach-leaved Bellflower *Campanula persicifolia* Hairless, erect perennial to 70cm. Basal leaves lanceolate to ovate, 8-15cm long, with rounded teeth; stem leaves narrowly linear, with rounded teeth. Inflorescence few-flowered and terminal, with flowers stalked and spreading; corolla rather pale blue, large (30-40mm), bell-shaped but wide-spreading, with very short lobes; calyx teeth half the length of corolla. Meadows, woodland edges and roadsides; in mainland Europe except the extreme north. **Fl** 6-8. **Br** Introduced, locally naturalised, mainly in the south.

E *Campanula barbata* Has erect simple hairy stems to 30cm, with flowering and non-flowering leaf rosettes. Basal leaves lanceolate-oblong, roughly hairy; inflorescence few-flowered, pendent hairy blue bell-shaped flowers, 20-30mm long. Acid grassland rare in S Norway; common in Alps. **Fl** 6-8. **Br** Absent.

F *Campanula sibirica* Similar to *Campanula barbata,* but taller, with more branched inflorescence, and without non-flowering rosettes. NE Germany, and on eastern fringes of area. **Fl** 7-8. **Br** Absent.

G *Campanula thyrsoides* Erect, unbranched, bristly-hairy biennial to 60cm. Leaves unlobed, rather wavy, oblong to strap-shaped. Flowers bell-shaped, pale yellow, woolly, in dense cylindrical inflorescences, with long bracts – a distinctive plant. In meadows and pastures in mountain areas, from the Jura and Alps southwards. **Fl** 7-9. **Br** Absent.

H Clustered Bellflower *Campanula glomerata* Erect, downy perennial to 30cm, occasionally more. Basal leaves ovate, rounded or heart-shaped at base, long-stalked, with blunt teeth; upper stem leaves ovate-lanceolate, clasping. *Flowers mainly in dense terminal head,* with a few others lower down stem, erect and virtually unstalked; *corolla violet-blue,* narrowly bell-shaped, 15-20mm long, with lobes about equal to tube; calyx teeth narrowly triangular. Downs, meadows and other grassy habitats, on calcareous soils; throughout except the far north. **Fl** 6-10. **Br** Locally common in S and E England, rarer to the north; absent from Ireland.

I *Campanula cervicaria* Rather similar to Clustered Bellflower, but lower leaves more lanceolate, narrowed gradually into a winged stalk; *flowers paler blue,* with blunt sepals and a protruding style in more widely separated whorls. Northwards to S Scandinavia, in meadows and woods, local. **Br** Absent.

J Giant Bellflower *Campanula latifolia* Tall, erect, *hairless or downy herb* to 1m, with unbranched *bluntly angled stems.* Basal leaves to 20cm long, ovate, narrowed gradually into stalk, which is often winged, margins shallowly and irregularly toothed (**j**). Flowers in a leafy, usually unbranched, spike, individually on 20mm stalks, semi-erect; corolla blue (rarely white), bell-shaped, 40-55mm long, lobes slightly shorter than tube; calyx lobes narrowly triangular, to 25mm long. Semi-shaded habitats; widespread except far north, local in many lowland areas. **Fl** 7-8. **Br** Widespread, but very local in the south commoner to the north.

K Nettle-leaved Bellflower *Campanula trachelium* Similar to Giant Bellflower, but *more bristly-hairy,* with *sharply angled stems.* Basal leaves to 10cm, narrowed abruptly to the stalk, stem leaves short-stalked, coarsely toothed and rather *nettle-like* (**k**). Flowers darker blue, 30-40mm on 10mm stalks; calyx lobes triangular, to 1cm long. In woods, hedgerows and scrub; north to S Sweden, locally common. **Fl** 6-9. **Br** South and east, very local elsewhere.

L Creeping Bellflower *Campanula rapunculoides* Erect downy or hairless perennial to 1m, often forming clumps from creeping rootstock. Root leaves ovate, to 80mm, long-stalked, heart-shaped at base and toothed; stem leaves narrower and unstalked. Flowers in long racemes, *all drooping to one side,* on 5mm stalks; corolla bell- or funnel-shaped, blue-violet, 20-30mm long; calyx teeth narrowly triangular, *bent back at flower time.* Meadows, roadsides and wood-margins; native in most of N Europe except the Arctic. **Fl** 6-9. **Br** Locally naturalised, widespread.

M Harebell *Campanula rotundifolia* Slender erect or ascending herb to 40cm. Basal leaves long-stalked, rounded to ovate, heart-shaped at base, 5-15mm long and toothed; stem leaves narrowly linear, upper ones unstalked. Flowers few, drooping, on slender stalks, in loose, branched inflorescences; corolla pale blue and bell-shaped with short triangular teeth; calyx teeth very narrow and spreading. In dry grassy places, on acid or calcareous soils, common and widespread. **Fl** 7-9. **Br** Common and widespread, though rare in SW Britain.

N *Campanula baumgartenii* Similar to Harebell, but has angled not round stems; inflorescence many-flowered. Local in dry grassland, E France and S Germany only. **Fl** 6-8. **Br** Absent.

A	B	C	D
E	G	H	I
J	K	L	M

A Arctic Bellflower

B Spreading Bellflower

C Rampion Bellflower

D Peach-leaved Bellflower

E *Campanula barbata*

G *Campanula thyrsoides*

H Clustered Bellflower

I *Campanula cervicaria*

J Giant Bellflower

K Nettle-leaved Bellflower

L Creeping Bellflower

M Harebell

j

k

A

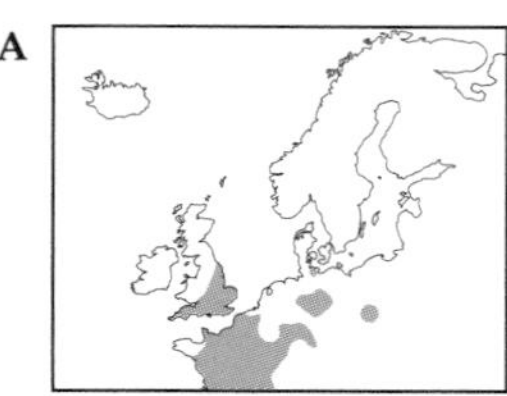

C

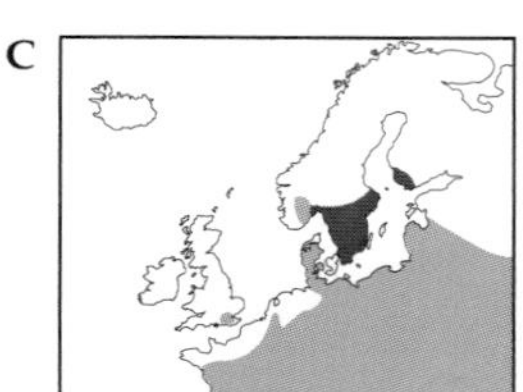

E

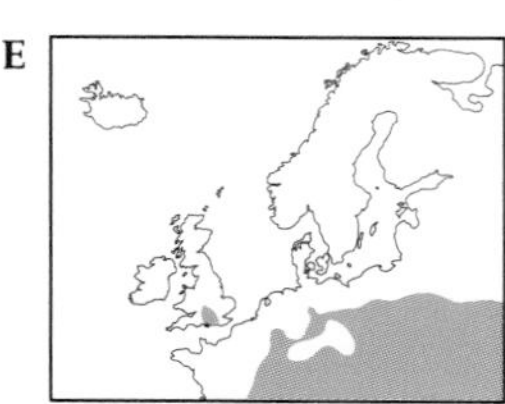

F

G

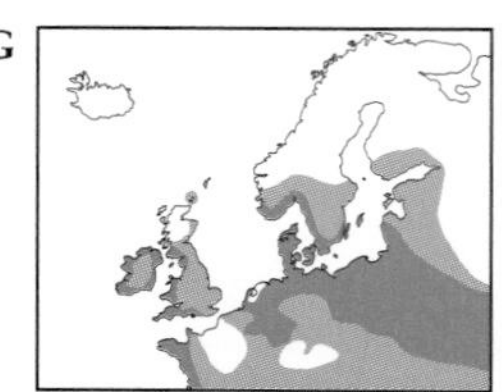

H

I

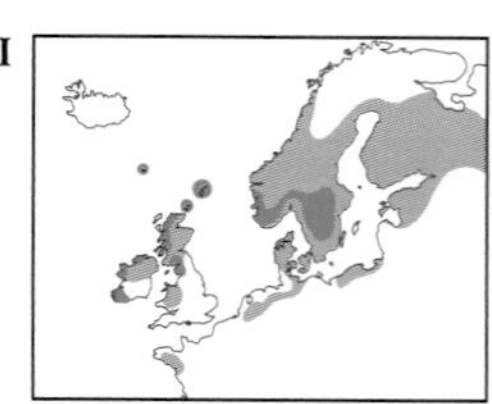

A Venus's-looking-glass *Legousia hybrida* Erect or straggling bristly annual to 40cm. Leaves oblong, to 30mm long, wavy, lower ones short-stalked, upper ones stalkless. Flowers rather few, erect and mainly in terminal cluster; corolla lilac to dull purple, 5-10mm in diameter, flat not bell-shaped, 5-lobed, with *lobes only as long as calyx teeth, opening in sunshine*. Differs from bellflowers in the long ovary, about 3 times as long as wide. In arable land, on free-draining soils; from Holland and Germany southwards, local and declining. **Fl** 5-8. **Br** Locally common only in S and E England; virtually absent elsewhere.

B Large Venus's-looking-glass *Legousia speculum-veneris* Rather similar to Venus's-looking-glass, but usually much-branched and spreading. Corolla red-purple to violet, *to 20mm in diameter, lobes at least as long as calyx teeth*, opening to star shape, *remaining open in dull weather*. In cultivated land, generally on dry soils; from Holland southwards; rare. **Fl** 5-7. **Br** Absent, except as rare introduction.

C Spiked Rampion *Phyteuma spicatum* Erect hairless perennial herb to 80cm. Basal and lower stem leaves oval, to 7cm long, with heart-shaped base, long-stalked and blunt-toothed; upper stem leaves narrower and unstalked. Flowers in a dense spike, egg-shaped but becoming cylindrical and longer (to 8cm); corolla creamy yellow, curved in bud, about 1cm long, lobes joined at tip at first, then eventually separating almost to base; stigmas 2. In meadows, woods and shady roadsides; from S Norway southwards, local, becoming commoner to south. **Fl** 5-7. **Br** Very rare and local, in E Sussex only.

D Black Rampion *Phyteuma nigrum* Similar in form to Spiked Rampion, but with broader basal leaves; corolla blue to blue-black (rarely white); bracts extending beyond base of inflorescence (not as long as width of inflorescence in Spiked Rampion); stigmas usually 3. In mountain meadows and wood-edges, usually calcareous; only from Belgium and S Germany southwards. **Fl** 5-6. **Br** Absent.

E Round-headed Rampion *Phyteuma orbiculare* (This name includes the form sometimes known as *P. tenerum*). Similar in form to other rampions, but generally smaller and more slender. Basal leaves narrower, not usually heart-shaped at base. Flowers blue in a dense *rounded head*, 10-25mm in diameter, with bracts much shorter than inflorescence. In dry grassland and rocky areas, often calcareous; from Belgium and S England southwards. **Fl** 6-8. **Br** Chalk downs, SE England west to Wiltshire only.

F Ivy-leaved Bellflower *Wahlenbergia hederacea* Slender hairless trailing perennial up to 30cm long. Leaves rounded to kidney-shaped, 5-10mm in diameter, toothed or lobed, sometimes ivy-like, all stalked, alternate, pale green. Flowers solitary or paired from leaf axils, with slender stalks to 40mm long; corolla pale blue, bell-shaped and somewhat nodding. In damp, humid and shady places, on acid soil; from Belgium and Scotland southwards but predominantly western, local. **Fl** 7-8. **Br** Local, commonest in SW England, but widespread in W Britain, and east to Kent.

G Sheep's-bit *Jasione montana* Downy, spreading or erect biennial or perennial herb to 30cm. Basal leaves in rosette, linear-lanceolate, to 50m long, wavy-edged and hairy; stem leaves shorter and narrower. Flowers in dense rounded scabious-like heads, to 35mm in diameter; corolla pale blue, 5mm long, with 2 broad stigmas. Differs from scabious in that the stamens do not protrude. In dry grassy places, usually avoiding lime-rich soils, commonest near coasts; almost throughout except the far north. **Fl** 5-8. **Br** Throughout, but local and predominantly coastal.

H Heath Lobelia *Lobelia urens* Erect, usually hairless, perennial herb to 60cm, with solid, angled stems. Leaves spoon-shaped or ovate, to 7cm, irregularly toothed, shiny dark green and barely stalked; upper stem leaves narrower. Flowers in a loose long inflorescence, with narrow bracts; corolla blue-purple, 10-15mm long, 2-lipped, with 2 upper and 3 lower lobes; calyx teeth long, narrow and spreading. On grassy heaths, open woods and acid grasslands; from Belgium and S England southwards. **Fl** 7-9. **Br** Very local and declining in SW England west of Sussex.

I Water Lobelia *Lobelia dortmanna* Has similar flower spikes to above, but differs in habit and habitat. Basal leaves in a rosette of numerous linear, blunt and untoothed leaves, producing leafless flower stems to 60cm. Corolla pale lilac, 15-20mm long. Grows with rosettes normally submerged in stony, acid still waters, usually in upland areas, to a depth of 3m, with flower spikes emerging above water level. A distinctive plant. Locally common southwards to NW France. **Fl** 7-9. **Br** A northern and western plant, becoming more common from S Wales northwards.

A	B	C
D	E	F
G	H	I

A Venus's-looking-glass
B Large Venus's-looking-glass
C Spiked Rampion
D Black Rampion
E Round-headed Rampion
F Ivy-leaved Bellflower
G Sheep's-bit
H Heath Lobelia
I Water Lobelia

A

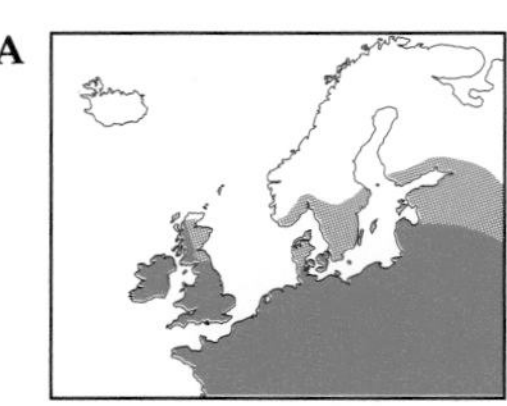

C

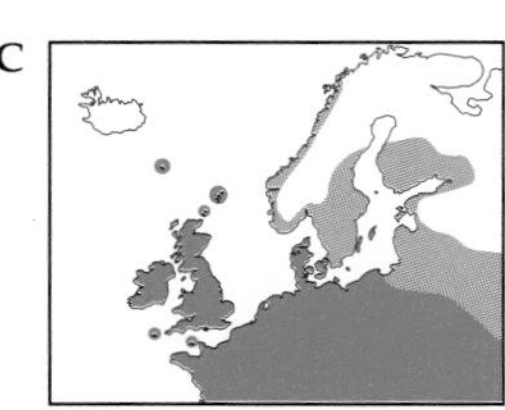

D

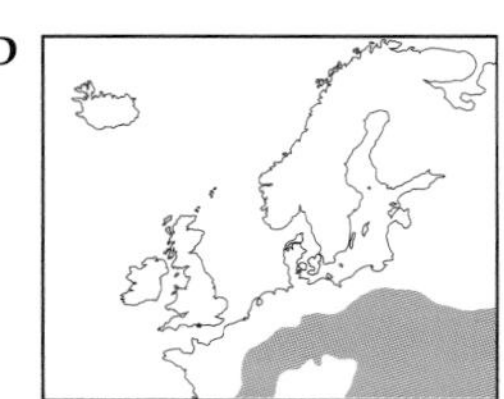

F

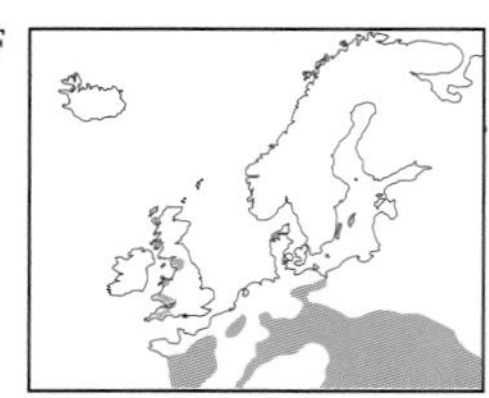

H

Daisy Family Compositae

Mainly herbs, with flowers in distinctive compound heads, the florets seated on a disc surrounded by a whorl of bracts, often like sepals. The form of the florets varies, and those in a head may be either all the same, or of 2 clearly different types, producing the typical daisy-flower type (known as 'ray' and 'disc' florets). The calyx varies: it may be a parachute-like pappus of hairs; or small and scale-like; or wholly absent. The stamens are joined into a tube attached to the inside of the corolla; the style forks into 2 stigmas. Some groups of *Compositae* are particularly difficult, with many very similar species; in some genera, such as *Hieracium*, only a few examples have been described as characteristic of the genus in view of the difficulty of providing enough information for certain identification.

A **Hemp Agrimony** *Eupatorium cannabinum* Large erect perennial, to 1.75m tall. Basal leaves roughly ovate and stalked; stem leaves trifoliate or 5-lobed, pointed toothed lobes, opposite and more or less unstalked. Flowers in numerous small heads, 2-5mm across, each with 5-6 florets, making up extensive, lax, rounded, branched terminal inflorescences; florets reddish mauve, or pale pink, with purple-tipped bracts; seeds with hairy pappus. Throughout most of N Europe except the far north, in damp grassy places and fens; common. **Fl** 7-9. **Br** Common in England, Wales and parts of Ireland; rare or absent elsewhere.

B **Goldenrod** *Solidago virgaurea* Variable, erect perennial, with stems to 1m in height. Basal leaves narrowly spoon-shaped, to 10cm long, stalked and usually weakly toothed; stem leaves narrowly lanceolate and unstalked. Flower heads numerous, in long, leafy, branched or unbranched heads; individual heads 6-10mm in diameter, made up of yellow ray and disc florets. Pappus dirty brown and hairy. Almost throughout the area, common in dry grassy and rocky places on most soil types. **Fl** 6-9. **Br** Widespread and generally common throughout, rarest in the south-east.

C **Daisy** *Bellis perennis* Familiar perennial herb, with a rosette of leaves and erect flower stems to 15cm. Leaves oblong to spoon-shaped, to 60mm, downy when young, 1-veined, narrowed to stalk. Flowers in clearly defined heads on slender leafless stalks, thickened below the flower head; flower head 15-30mm in diameter, with a yellow disc and numerous slender outer white rays, often purplish-red below. Involucral bracts 3-5mm long and blunt. Widespread and common in grassy places from S Scandinavia southwards (naturalised further north). **Fl** 3-10. **Br** Abundant everywhere.

D *Aster amellus* Erect perennial to 70cm, slightly hairy but not glandular. Basal and lower leaves spoon-shaped to lanceolate, narrowed into a stalk, variably hairy; upper leaves narrower, untoothed and stalkless. Flower heads few, occasionally solitary, 30-50mm in diameter, with blue ray florets (occasionally white), and yellow disc. Involucral bracts in 3 rows, spreading. In scrub, wood-edges and rocky places, usually on lime-rich soil; local, from N central France and S Germany southwards. **Fl** 7-10. **Br** Absent.

E **Sea Aster** *Aster tripolium* Rather similar to above, often taller, to 1m, and with fleshy leaves to 12cm; ray florets usually mauve (occasionally completely absent), heads 10-20mm in diameter; involucral bracts blunt, appressed and membranous at tips. In salt-marshes, coastal mud and cliffs, occasionally inland on saline soils, throughout where suitable habitats exist. **Fl** 7-10. **Br** All round the coast, very rare inland, in English Midlands.

F **Goldilocks Aster** *Aster linosyris* Superficially different to other asters. Erect or ascending stems to 60cm, with numerous leaves. Leaves narrowly linear, to 50mm long, pointed, alternate, 1-veined, untoothed but with rough edges. Flower heads in dense terminal inflorescence of several heads, each 10-20mm in diameter, with florets all disc type and yellow; bracts very narrow, outer ones spreading. On limestone rocks and dry grassland, very local from S Sweden southwards, often coastal. **Fl** 7-9. **Br** Very local and rare in a few western coastal localities.

G **Blue Fleabane** *Erigeron acer* Aannual or biennial herb, with erect hairy flower stem to 40cm, often branched in upper part. Basal leaves stalked and spoon-shaped, to 80mm; stem leaves lanceolate and unstalked. Flower heads 12-18mm in diameter, varying from 1 (rarely) to numerous in an erect, loose inflorescence; ray florets short, pale purple, barely exceeding yellow disc florets, erect not spreading; flower bracts often purplish. In dry grassy and rocky places, sand-dunes; almost throughout, locally common. **Fl** 6-8. **Br** Widespread in England and Wales; rare elsewhere.

H **Alpine Fleabane** *Erigeron borealis* Perennial herb with basal rosettes of leaves and erect flower stems to 30cm. Leaves lanceolate, to 30mm, with a winged stalk; upper ones narrower and unstalked; all hairy. Flower heads solitary, rarely 2-3, 20mm in diameter, with purple ray florets much longer than yellow disc florets, more spreading than in Blue Fleabane; flower bracts very hairy. In mountain pastures and stony ground, on lime-rich soils, from N Scotland northwards; mainly an Arctic plant. **Fl** 7-8. **Br** Very rare, in a small area of E Highlands, Scotland, only.

I *Erigeron uniflorus* Very similar to Alpine Fleabane, but usually smaller, to 15cm only; basal leaves only slightly hairy, stem leaves few in number. Flower heads always solitary, slightly smaller (10-15mm in diameter), *held well above leaves*, bracts moderately downy, purplish-tipped, ray florets white or pale lilac darkening with age. Local in mountain habitats in N Scandinavian mountains (and the Alps). **Fl** 7-9. **Br** Absent.

J *Erigeron humilis* Similar to *E. uniflorus*, but *very dwarf*, rarely above 10cm, with flower stems barely exceeding leaves. Leaves sparsely downy when young; *upper flower stem and bracts with long purplish hairs*; flower heads solitary, ray florets white to purple, *bracts purple*. Arctic Europe only, in mountains. **Fl** 7-9. **Br** Absent.

K **Canadian Fleabane** *Conyza canadensis* Variable erect, hairy annual up to 1.5m (usually 60-100cm). Leaves numerous, narrow, usually broader and more noticeably stalked towards the base of the stem. Flower heads small, 5-9mm, white or pinkish ray florets, in long, loose, many-flowered inflorescence. Native of N America, but widely naturalised in waste places and dunes except extreme north. **Fl** 7-10. **Br** Abundant in south, spreading northwards.

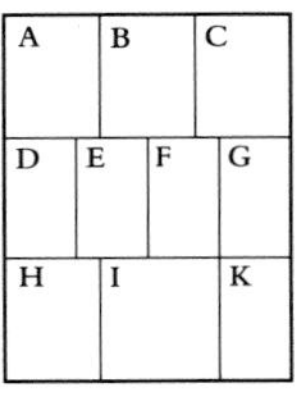

A **Hemp Agrimony**

B **Goldenrod**

C **Daisy**

D *Aster amellus*

E **Sea Aster**

F **Goldilocks Aster**

G **Blue Fleabane** arctic form

H **Alpine Fleabane**

I *Erigeron uniflorus*

K **Canadian Fleabane**

A
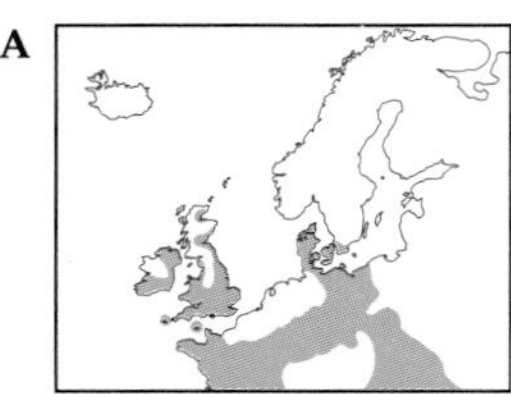

E
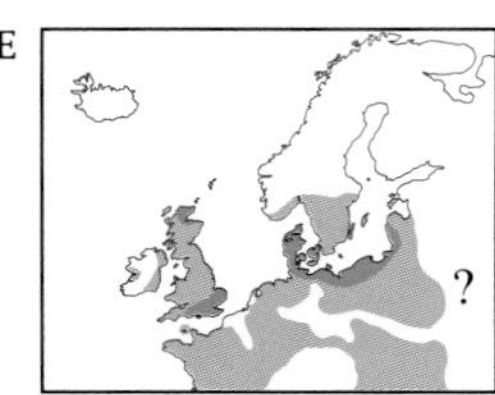

H
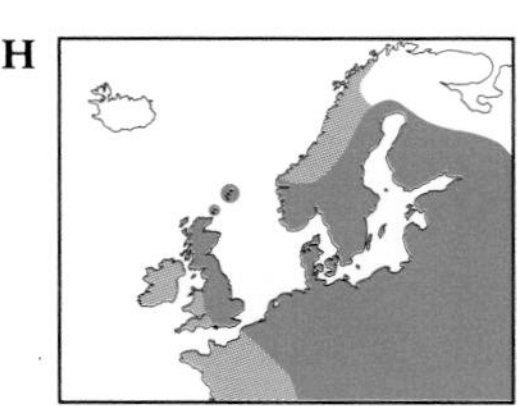

I
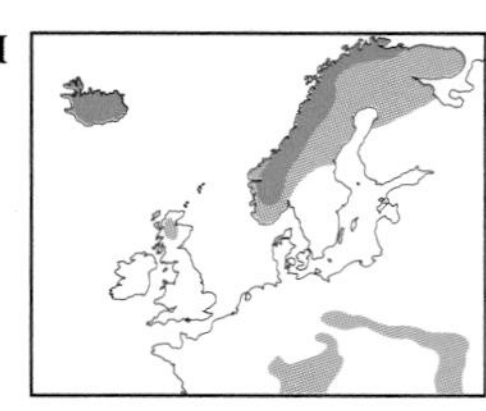

K
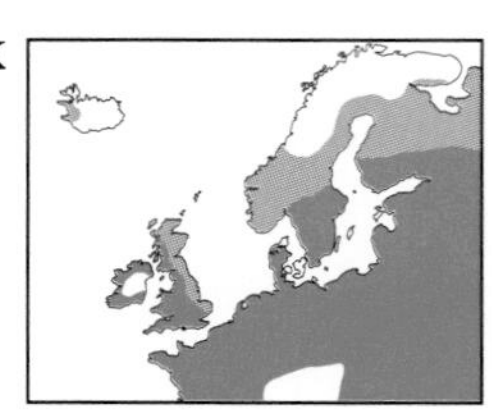

L
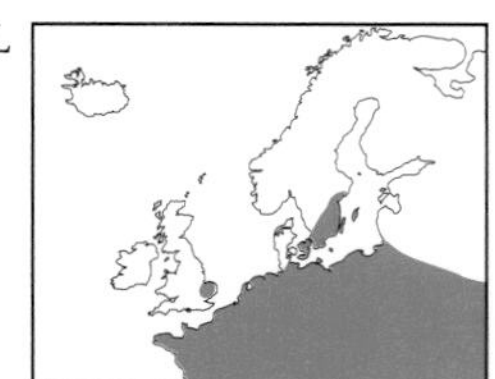

CUDWEEDS *Filago, Logfia* and *Omalothecia, Filaginella* and *Gnaphalium* A difficult group of small, usually woolly, plants with inconspicuous flowers, needing close examination of bracts, flower heads and leaves for identification.

A **Common Cudweed** *Filago vulgaris* Erect annual, with white-woolly stems and leaves, to 30cm, branched or unbranched at base, but always branching above into 2-3 forks. Leaves erect, strap-shaped, 10-20mm long, wavy-edged, untoothed and woolly. Flower heads in dense rounded clusters in branch axils and terminal, each made up of 20-35 heads, 10-12mm in diameter, not exceeded by the leaves immediately below them; bracts of flower heads narrow, straight, outer ones woolly, inner ones bristle-tipped, erect; florets yellow. From S Sweden southwards in dry grasslands and open habitats on sandy and acid soils; locally common. **Fl** 7-8. **Br** Locally common in S Britain, rare in the north, but generally decreasing.

B **Red-tipped Cudweed** *Filago lutescens* Similar to Common Cudweed, but with erect *yellow-woolly* stems; leaves broader, not wavy, bristle-tipped; flower heads 10-20 per cluster, overtopped by a few leaves; *bracts with bright red, erect bristle-points*. From S Sweden and Denmark southwards in disturbed sandy ground; local. **Fl** 7-8. **Br** Rare, in S and E England only.

C **Broad-leaved Cudweed** *Filago pyramidata* Rather similar to Common Cudweed, but spreading and branched from the base. Leaves ovate and bristle-tipped; flower heads in clusters along stems and at tips, 6-12mm in diameter, exceeded by their surrounding leaves; *outer flower bracts have yellow points*, curving outwards when in fruit. In sandy and chalky fields and open habitats; from Holland and England southwards; local. **Fl** 7-8. **Br** Rare, in S England only, decreasing.

D *Logfia arvensis* Annual, to 40cm, occasionally to 70cm, unbranched below, but with short side-branches above, all white woolly. Leaves lanceolate, woolly. Flower heads ovoid, to 6mm long, overtopped by leaves below them; *bracts linear, woolly right to their tips*, spreading out when in fruit. In cultivated fields and wasteland; from Denmark southwards. **Fl** 7-9. **Br** Casual only.

E **Small Cudweed** *Logfia mimima* Slender grey-woolly annual to 30cm, (usually less), with ascending branches from above the middle. Leaves linear-lanceolate, to 10mm long. Flower heads ovoid to pyramidal, to 3.5mm long, 5-angled, in clusters of 3 to 6 in angles of stem and at tips, exceeding their basal leaves; overall appearance yellowish; *outer bracts woolly at base, but with hairless yellow chaffy tips*, spreading when in fruit. In sandy fields, on heaths and other acid open areas, from S Scandinavia southwards. **Fl** 7-9. **Br** Widespread and locally common, though rare in Ireland, and absent from N Scotland.

F **Narrow-leaved Cudweed** *Logfia gallica* Similar to Small Cudweed, but all leaves narrower; *flower heads greatly exceeded by the leaves at their bases*; flower-head bracts sharp-tipped. From Holland southwards in gravelly places. **Fl** 7-9. **Br** Casual, probably extinct except on Sark.

G *Logfia neglecta* Similar to Narrow-leaved Cudweed, but with cylindrical flower heads, with flower-head bracts all the same, and brownish. Belgium and France only, in similar habitats. **Fl** 7-9. **Br** Absent.

H **Heath Cudweed** *Omalothecia sylvatica* Perennial herb to 50cm, with short leafy non-flower shoots, and erect leafy flower shoots. Rosette and lower stem leaves lanceolate-linear, to 80mm long, pointed, *1-veined (or indistinctly 3-veined)*, stalked, becoming smaller and less stalked up the stem; *all leaves green and hairless above, white-woolly below*. Heads 5-7mm long, in small clusters in axils of upper stem leaves forming a long leafy spike, interrupted below; florets pale brown, bracts with central green stripe, brown towards the margin. In open woods, heaths and dry grasslands on acid soils; widespread throughout. **Fl** 7-9. **Br** Scattered, but widespread and locally common; rare in Ireland.

I **Highland Cudweed** *Omalothecia norvegica* Resembles Heath Cudweed, but differs in that the *leaves are 3-veined*, not decreasing so clearly up stem, and are *white woolly on both sides*. Inflorescence shorter, rarely more than a quarter of the length of stem, with leaves below it exceeding it. Widespread in N Scandinavia, increasingly confined to mountains further south, and therefore absent from large areas. **Fl** 7-8. **Br** Scottish Highlands only, on acid rocks.

J **Dwarf Cudweed** *Omalothecia supina* Dwarf, tufted plant, with many non-flower stems, and flower stems to 12cm, all grey downy. Leaves lanceolate, 1-veined and woolly both sides. Flower clusters 3-4mm long, with only 2-10 heads, in short terminal spike; outermost bracts more than as long as head. In mountain habitats and tundra, usually damp and acid; N Scandinavia (and the Alps). **Fl** 7-8. **Br** Scottish Highlands only.

K **Marsh Cudweed** *Filaginella uliginosa* Spreading or ascending woolly annual, *much-branched from the base*, to 20cm. Leaves linear-lanceolate to oblong, up to 50mm long, woolly on both sides. Flower heads individually ovoid, 3-4mm long, clustered in terminal inflorescences of 3-10, well exceeded by the leaves at their base (which give the impression of green ray florets); florets yellowish-brown, flower-head bracts woolly at base, darker and hairless at tip. Widespread and common in damp, often disturbed places; almost throughout. **Fl** 7-9. **Br** Common throughout.

L **Jersey Cudweed** *Gnaphalium luteo-album* Annual herb, with erect stems to 45cm high from a creeping base, densely woolly; *stems unbranched below*, branched in inflorescence. Leaves woolly, broadly oblong below, narrower higher up stem. Flower heads ovoid, about 3mm long, in dense terminal clusters of 4-12, without overtopping leaves; *bracts pale yellow, florets bright yellow*, stigmas red. In damp sandy places from S Sweden southwards, but local. **Fl** 6-8. **Br** Very rare, in Norfolk and the Channel Islands only.

A	B	C
E	H	I
J	K	L

A Common Cudweed
B Red-tipped Cudweed
C Broad-leaved Cudweed
E Small Cudweed
H Heath Cudweed
I Highland Cudweed
J Dwarf Cudweed
K Marsh Cudweed
L Jersey Cudweed

A

C
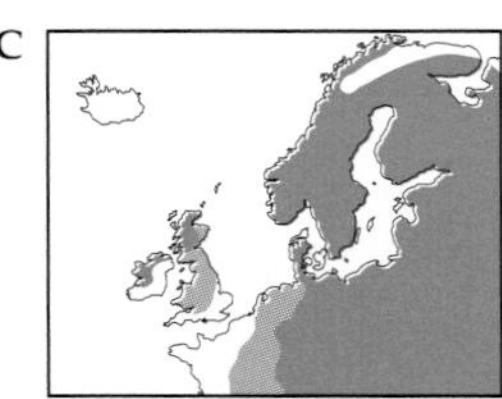

J
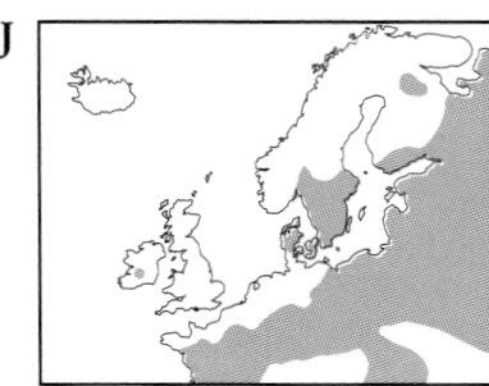

L
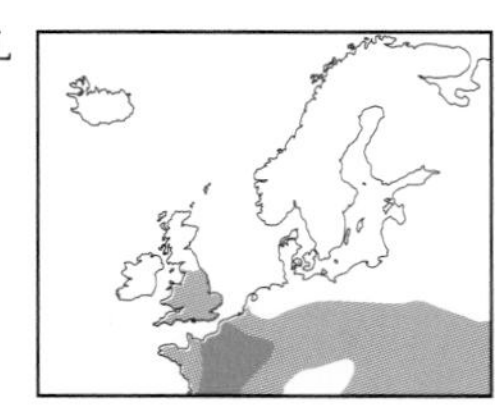

M

A Immortelle *Helichrysum arenarium* Erect white-downy perennial to 40cm. Leaves ovate-oblong, woolly on both sides, *flat*, to 70mm long and 1-veined; upper leaves much narrower. Flower heads individually 3-4mm in diameter, grouped together in a loose, branching inflorescence of 20-50mm in diameter; flowers bright yellow to orange, with yellow, blunt bracts that spread widely when in fruit. In dry sandy places from S Sweden and Denmark southwards; local. **Fl** 6-8. **Br** Absent.

B *Helichrysum stoechas* Similar to Immortelle, but leaves all linear *with rolled-under margins*; plant very aromatic; *outer bracts papery white*. In sandy, mainly coastal, habitats; France only. **Fl** 5-8. **Br** Absent.

C Mountain Everlasting, Cat's Foot *Antennaria dioica* Creeping, downy, perennial herb, with woody stems and leafy runners with rosettes, producing erect unbranched flower stems to 20cm. Basal leaves spoon-shaped and rather blunt, up to 35mm long; stem leaves narrower and erect; all leaves green and virtually hairless above, downy below. Flower heads white woolly in a dense umbel-like head of 2-8 flower clusters. Male and female plants separate: female flowers with larger heads, to 12mm in diameter, with pink-tipped bracts; male heads to 6mm in diameter, with white-tipped bracts, spreading outwards; all florets pink. Widespread and generally common, though local in lowland areas; on heaths, upland habitats and moors. **Fl** 6-8. **Br** Common in N Britain, increasingly uncommon southwards.

D *Antennaria nordhageniana* Similar to above, but less downy, *with purplish stems, underleaves, and bracts*. Very rare and local in Arctic Norway only. **Br** Absent.

E Alpine Cat's-foot *Antennaria alpina* Very similar to Mountain Everlasting, but the upper stem leaves have a *wide papery apex*, and the flower bracts are *narrower lanceolate* (not oblong to spoon-shaped) and *dark green-brown*. Most plants are female. In lime-rich mountain habitats, N Scandinavia only. **Fl** 7-8. **Br** Absent.

F Edelweiss *Leontopodium alpinum* Low, tufted, greyish white, wooly perennial to 25cm. Leaves oblong to strap-shaped, untoothed. Flower heads distinctive, yellowish, with a ruff of narrow white-wooly bracts. Dry grassy and rocky places in mountains, usually on limestone; from S Germany and E France southwards. **Fl** 6-9. **Br** Absent.

INULAS *Inula* A group of perennial herbs with undivided alternate leaves. Flower heads solitary or in small groups, yellow, large, and with separate disc and ray florets, though rays sometimes very short.

G Elecampane *Inula helenium* Robust, erect, hairy perennial to 2m, occasionally more. Leaves roughly ovate, up to 40cm long, basal ones long-stalked, stem leaves unstalked (**g**); all leaves virtually hairless above, softly downy below. Flower heads large, 6-8cm across, 1-3 together, with deep yellow disc and paler yellow, long, narrow rays. On roadsides, waste ground, plantations and other habitats; naturalised throughout except the far north, originally from central Asia. **Fl** 7-8. **Br** Naturalised throughout, but never common.

H *Inula helvetica* Erect, downy perennial with stems to 1.5m. Leaves lanceolate, to 12cm, toothed or untoothed, downy below, upper ones unstalked, but *not clasping*. *Flower heads large, 30-45mm in diameter*, solitary or in small groups; ray florets 15-20mm long, *much longer than bracts below them*; outer flower bracts have recurved tips. In woods and by streams; only in SW Germany and central France, then southwards. **Fl** 7-8. **Br** Absent.

I German Inula *Inula germanica* Erect moderately downy perennial to 60cm. Leaves ovate, to 10cm long, upper ones with heart-shaped bases *clasping the stem* (**i**). *Flower heads small, 7-11mm in diameter* with *short rays that barely exceed the bracts*. In grassy places; from central Germany south-eastwards. **Fl** 6-8. **Br** Absent.

J Irish Fleabane *Inula salicina* Erect hairless or slightly hairy perennial to 75cm. Leaves linear-lanceolate to ovate, up to 60mm, prominently net-veined above, usually hairy only on the veins below, upper stem leaves clasping with heart-shaped bases (**j**). Heads 25-40mm in diameter, usually solitary, or 2-5 together; *ray florets about twice as long as bracts*; outer bracts leaf-like, lanceolate, with somewhat spreading tips, hairy only on the margins. In fens, stony limestone areas and damp grassland; widespread but local through most of N Europe except the extreme north. **Fl** 7-8. **Br** Very rare, only in 1 area of W Ireland.

K *Inula britannica* Rather similar to Irish Fleabane, but leaves *more narrowly lanceolate*, softly hairy below; *outer flower bracts linear* and softly hairy. From S Scandinavia southwards, in damp meadows, streamsides and wet woods. **Fl** 7-8. **Br** Formerly in Leicestershire, now extinct.

L Ploughman's-spikenard *Inula conyza* Erect, downy, often reddish biennial or perennial herb to 1m. Lower leaves oval to oblong, to 15cm long, narrowed into a flattened stalk (rather similar to foxglove leaves); upper leaves stalkless, wedge-shaped at base and narrower. Flower heads ovoid, about 1cm long, numerous in tight, branched heads; florets dark yellow, ray florets very short or absent; inner bracts purplish, outer ones green and spreading. From Denmark southwards, in dry or calcareous grasslands and banks. **Fl** 7-9. **Br** Locally common in England and Wales only.

M Golden Samphire *Inula crithmoides* Fleshy, tufted, erect perennial herb, or small shrub to 1m. Leaves linear, to 50mm, numerous, fleshy, untoothed or with a 3-toothed tip. Flower heads 20-30mm in diameter, in a loose roughly flat-topped inflorescence; ray florets to 25mm, much longer than bracts; outer flower-head bracts linear and erect. From S Britain and N France southwards, coastal only, in salt-marshes, on cliffs or shingle. **Fl** 7-9. **Br** Coasts of S and W Britain only; local.

A	B	C
F	H	J
K	G	L	M

A **Immortelle**

B *Helichrysum stoechas*

C **Mountain Everlasting**

F **Edelweiss**

H *Inula helvetica*

J **Irish Fleabane**

K *Inula brittanica*

G **Elecampane**

L **Ploughman's-spikenard**

M **Golden Samphire**

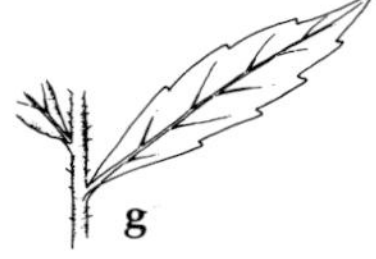

A

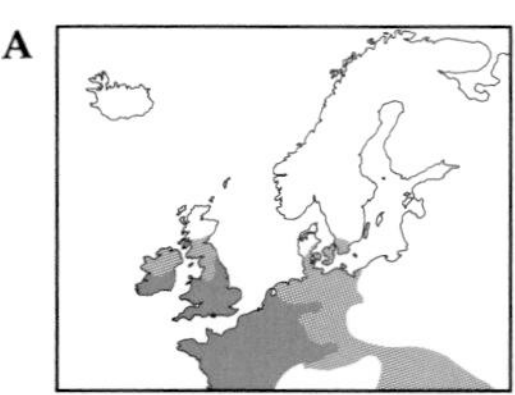

B

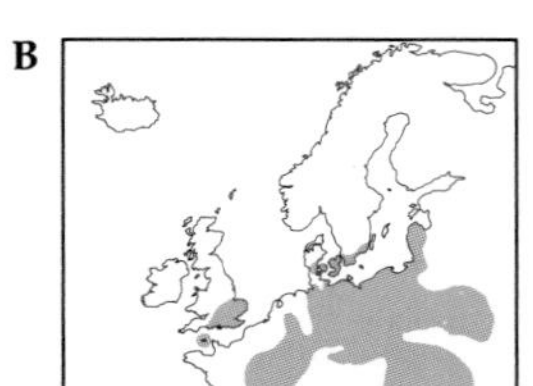

C

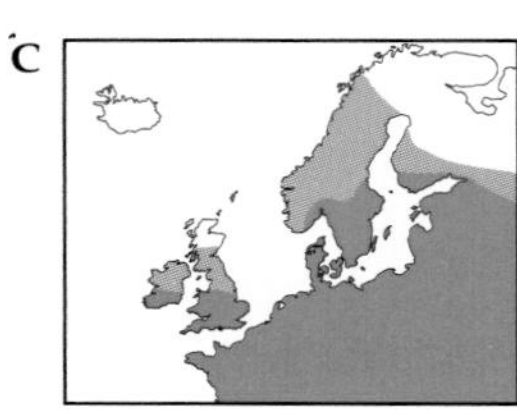

J

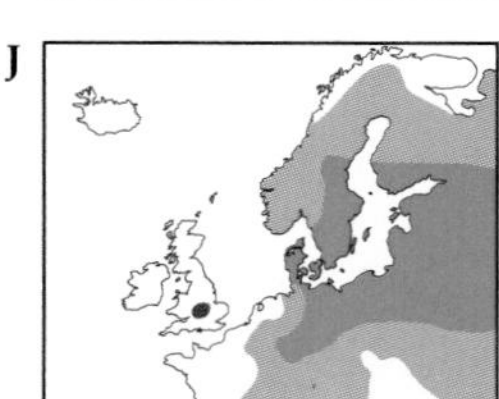

A Common Fleabane *Pulicaria dysenterica* Creeping, perennial herb, with downy or woolly, erect, branched stems to 60cm. Basal leaves oblong, withered by flowering time; stem leaves alternate, downy, heart-shaped at base and clasping. Flower heads 15-30mm in diameter, numerous in loose inflorescences, orange-yellow; ray florets numerous, much longer than disc florets; bracts below head narrow, sticky and hairy, with long fine tips. In damp grasslands and roadsides, on heavy soils; common generally as far north as Denmark. **Fl** 7-9. **Br** Common and widespread north to S Scotland.

B Small Fleabane *Pulicaria vulgaris* Rather similar to Common Fleabane, but annual, much-branched, to 40cm; *stem leaves round-based* not heart-shaped. *Flower heads smaller, 10mm in diameter*, numerous, *with short ray florets* and spreading outer bracts; all florets pale yellow. From S Sweden southwards, very local and declining, mainly in winter-wet grasslands and grazed hollows. **Fl** 8-10. **Br** Very rare in S England only (mostly New Forest); on grazed commons.

C Trifid Bur-marigold *Bidens tripartita* Hairless or slightly hairy annual to 60cm. Leaves 3-lobed (occasionally 5-lobed), coarsely toothed, with a short, winged stalk. Flower heads yellow, erect, 10-25mm in diameter, in branched clusters, *usually without ray florets, with 5-8 leaf-like spreading bracts below heads*. In damp places, especially where winter-flooded; widespread throughout but absent from the far north. **Fl** 7-10. **Br** Locally common in S Britain, much rarer to the north.

D *Bidens radiata* Very similar to Trifid Bur-marigold, but with *10-12 outer bracts*. In similar habitats, very local, from Denmark southwards. **Br** Absent.

E Nodding Bur-marigold *Bidens cernua* Similar to Trifid Bur-marigold, except that the leaves are in opposite *undivided lanceolate pairs; flower heads drooping;* occasionally short, broad, yellow ray florets present. In similar habitats, widespread except in the far north. **Fl** 7-10. **Br** Locally common in the south, much rarer to the north.

F Gallant Soldier *Galinsoga parviflora* Much-branched annual herb, with erect more or less *hairless stems*, to 75cm. Leaves ovate, in opposite pairs, stalked, few-toothed, pointed, up to 50mm long. Flower heads small, 3-5mm in diameter, in much-forked inflorescences; disc florets yellow, ray florets usually 5 only, about 1mm long and 1mm wide, 3-lobed at tip, white; bracts few. Originally from S America, but now widely naturalised in waste places and cultivated land, almost throughout. **Fl** 5-10. **Br** Widespread, though uncommon except in the south-east. Absent from Ireland.

G Shaggy Soldier *Galinsoga ciliata* Very similar to above, but at least the upper parts of plant *clothed with spreading hairs;* 4 or 5 ray florets, narrower than 1mm. In similar habitats; widespread but local, naturalised from S America. **Fl** 5- 10. **Br** Mainly south-eastern, very local elsewhere.

H Corn Chamomile *Anthemis arvensis Aromatic* annual herb, with spreading or ascending branched downy stems to 50cm. Leaves up to 50mm long, roughly oval in outline, but very divided, up to 3-pinnate with narrow pointed segments, *hairy or woolly below* especially when young. Flower heads solitary, long-stalked, 20-30mm in diameter, with yellow disc florets in a cone shape, and white rays with styles. Widespread throughout except the far north; in cultivated and waste ground, on calcareous soils. **Fl** 6-7. **Br** Frequent in England, but rare elsewhere and absent from Ireland.

I Stinking Chamomile *Anthemis cotula* Very similar to Corn Chamomile, except that the plant is *unpleasant-smelling and hairless;* ray florets have no styles. Similar habitats; absent from the far north. **Fl** 7-9. **Br** Locally common in the south, rare further north.

J Yellow Chamomile *Anthemis tinctoria* Similar in form to Corn Chamomile. Leaves have broader segments, less divided. *Flowers all yellow*, large (25-40mm in diameter). Resembles Corn Marigold superficially, but leaves very different. In cultivated ground and roadsides etc.; from S Sweden southwards; local. **Fl** 7-9. **Br** Introduced; locally naturalised except in N Scotland.

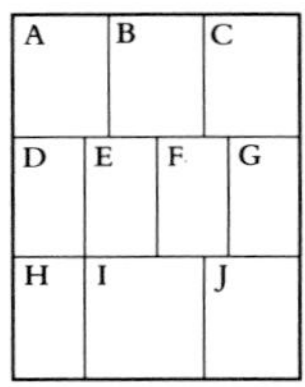

A Common Fleabane

B Small Fleabane

C Trifid Bur-marigold

D *Bidens radicata*

E Nodding Bur-marigold

F Gallant Soldier

G Shaggy Soldier

H Corn Chamomile

I Stinking Chamomile

J Yellow Chamomile

A
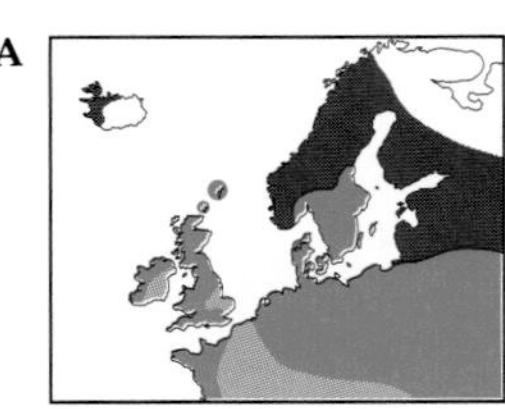
C

H

I
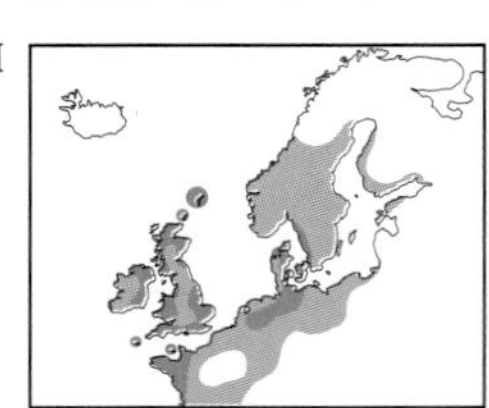

A Sneezewort *Achillea ptarmica* Erect, tufted, branched or unbranched perennial, normally to 75cm, but occasionally more, downy on upper parts. Leaves lanceolate, to 70mm, *undivided but finely and sharply toothed*, unstalked. Flower heads 10-20mm in diameter, with central greenish-white disc florets, and white oval rays borne in a loose few-flowered branched cluster. Throughout in wet meadows, marshy areas and damp woods, usually on acid soils. **Fl** 7-8. **Br** Locally common throughout, rare in calcareous areas.

B Yarrow *Achillea millefolium* Strong-smelling, creeping perennial producing erect, downy, furrowed, unbranched stems to 60cm. Leaves lanceolate in outline, but *highly divided, feathery*, 2-3 times pinnate, to 15cm long, lower ones stalked, upper ones unstalked. Flower heads numerous but small, 4-6mm in diameter, aggregated into dense rounded inflorescences; ray florets white or pink, 5 per head; disc florets yellowish white. Widespread and common throughout in grassy places, waste ground and hedgerows. **Fl** 6-9. **Br** Common throughout.

C Chamomile *Chamaemelum nobile* Creeping, downy, *greyish* perennial herb to 30cm, *strongly aromatic*. Leaves finely divided, 2-3 times pinnate, to 50mm long, with narrow bristle-tipped lobes. Flower heads solitary on erect hairy stems, 18-25mm in diameter, with white rays and yellow disc florets; on the disc florets, the base of each corolla tube is swollen, covering the fruit; bracts of flower head blunt, with brown papery margins. Very local, from S England and Belgium southwards (though locally naturalised elsewhere); in dry sandy grasslands. **Fl** 6-8. **Br** Very local, in S England and S Wales only.

D Scentless Mayweed *Matricaria perforata* Annual to perennial herbs, *odourless*, hairless, much-branched and spreading, to a height of 80cm. Leaves alternate, hairless, much-divided (2-3 times pinnate) into very narrow fine-pointed segments. Flower heads solitary, long-stalked, 20-40mm in diameter, in loose clusters, with white rays and yellow disc florets; *receptacle solid* and dome-shaped; achenes have black oil-glands near tips. In cultivated land and waste places almost throughout; common. **Fl** 7-9. **Br** Common throughout.

E Sea Mayweed *Matricaria maritima* Very similar to above, and both were formerly subspecies of *Tripleurospermum maritimum*. Differs in that it is generally more branched and spreading and the *leaf segments are blunt, fleshy and narrowly cylindrical*. In coastal habitats; throughout except the far north. **Br** Widespread, though commonest in the north.

F Scented Mayweed *Chamomilla recutita* Very similar to Scentless Mayweed, but *pleasantly scented; receptacle of flower head is conical and hollow*, and the *ray florets bend back early* (**f**); no black oil-glands on fruit. Widespread and generally common, except in the far north; on cultivated and waste land. **Fl** 6- 8. **Br** Widespread in the south, though rare or local in Scotland and Ireland.

G Pineappleweed *Chamomilla suaveolens* Annual, with similar structure to Scentless Mayweed, but *whole plant smells strongly of pineapple when crushed*; flower heads with conical hollow receptacle covered with greenish-yellow disc florets, *ray florets absent*. Widespread throughout in waste places, tracks and cultivated ground; probably an ancient introduction. **Fl** 5-11. **Br** Throughout.

H Cottonweed *Otanthus maritimus* Erect or ascending perennial with white-woolly stems to 50cm. Leaves oblong-lanceolate, to 20mm long, toothed or untoothed, white woolly, fleshy and unstalked. Flower heads in dense terminal clusters, individual heads globose, 6-9mm in diameter, with woolly bracts; florets yellow, ray florets absent. A distinctive plant. On sand and shingle shores; only in W Ireland and W France southwards; local. **Fl** 8-10. **Br** Now extinct, except 1 locality in Ireland.

I Corn Marigold *Chrysanthemum segetum* Erect or ascending hairless annual to 60cm, unbranched or branched, rather greyish green. *Leaves oblong, but deeply lobed or toothed and slightly fleshy*; upper leaves barely toothed and clasping. Flowers solitary, 35-60mm in diameter, with both ray and disc florets golden yellow, disc flat. Widespread and locally common, though decreasing, in cultivated ground, usually on acid soil, but absent from the far north. Probably an ancient introduction. **Fl** 6-10. **Br** Widespread and locally common.

J Tansy *Tanacetum vulgare* Erect or ascending aromatic perennial, to 1m or more. Leaves alternate, oblong, to 20cm, but pinnately divided, with segments further divided, sparsely hairy. *Inflorescence a dense umbel-like head*, up to 15cm in diameter, made up of 10-70 heads each 7-12mm in diameter, golden yellow; ray florets absent. Roadsides and waste places; common throughout. **Fl** 7-10. **Br** Common and widespread.

K Feverfew *Tanacetum parthenium* Erect or ascending, downy, strongly aromatic herb, branched above, reaching 60cm. *Leaves oblong, pinnately lobed, yellowish green*, lower ones long-stalked, upper ones unstalked. Flower heads 12-20mm in diameter, with short, broad white rays and yellow disc, clustered into a loose inflorescence. Widespread from S Sweden southwards; naturalised on walls, roadsides and near buildings. Origin SE Europe. **Fl** 7-9. **Br** Common throughout except the far north.

L Oxeye Daisy *Leucanthemum vulgare* Erect perennial to 70cm, hairless or slightly hairy. *Basal leaves spoon-shaped*, to 10cm, long-stalked, with rounded teeth (**l**); stem leaves variable, becoming stalkless up stem, oblong and toothed. Flowers solitary or several together, 25-40mm in diameter, with white rays and yellow disc florets; involucral bracts variable in shape, overlapping, with dark purplish edges. Widespread and generally common in meadows, pastures, roadsides and, less frequently, in disturbed sites. **Fl** 5-9. **Br** Common throughout.

A	B	C
D	E	F
G	H	I
J	K	L

A **Sneezewort**
B **Yarrow**
C **Chamomile**
D **Scentless Mayweed**
E **Sea Mayweed**
F **Scented Mayweed**
G **Pineappleweed**
H **Cottonweed**
I **Corn Marigold**
J **Tansy**
K **Feverfew**
L **Oxeye Daisy**

f

l

B

C

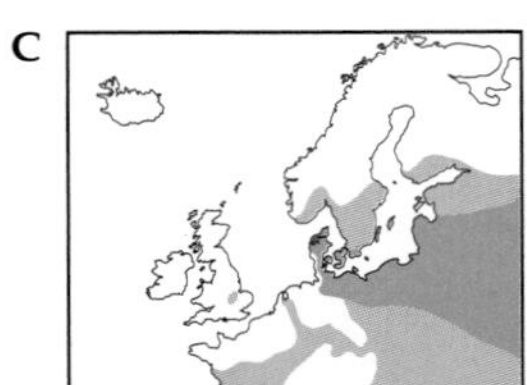

F

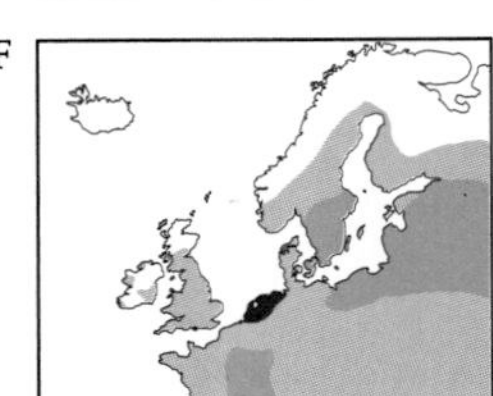

MUGWORTS AND WORMWOODS *Artemisia*
A small group of tall herbaceous or slightly woody plants, unlike other *Compositae* superficially. Leaves alternate and divided pinnately to a greater or lesser degree. Inflorescences normally made up of numerous small flower heads in long branching spike-like masses, without ray florets.

(1) Plants tiny, less than 20cm tall, with few flower heads.

A Norwegian Mugwort *Artemisia norvegica* Very dwarf, tufted, perennial Alpine plant, usually only to 10cm. Leaves mostly basal, 2-pinnate or palmate, stalked; stem leaves unstalked, all silky grey. Flower heads hemispherical, about 10mm in diameter, nodding, in few-flowered cluster; florets yellow. In gravelly and peaty places in mountains, and lichen heaths; central Norway and NW Scotland only. **Fl** 7-9. **Br** Mountains of W Ross only, very rare; only discovered in 1950.

(2) Taller plants, with terminal lobes of leaves very narrow, less than 1mm.

B Sea Wormwood *Artemisia maritima* *Strongly aromatic* perennial, with clusters of spreading to erect, partly woody stems to 60cm, *grey or white downy*. Lower leaves 2-pinnate with very narrow blunt segments (**b**), white woolly on both sides, withering at flowering time; upper leaves similar but smaller and short-stalked. Flower heads individually 1-2mm in diameter, ovoid, numerous in long leafy branched inflorescences, florets yellow-orange. Mainly coastal habitats from SE Norway and S Sweden southwards (rare inland on saline soils in central Germany). **Fl** 8-10. **Br** Frequent around most coastal areas, rare in the north and in Ireland.

C Field Wormwood *Artemisia campestris* Similar to Sea Wormwood, but *unscented and virtually hairless* or slightly silky hairy when young; leaf segments pointed (**c**). Ssp *maritima* has leaf lobes shorter and fleshy. Widespread but local in dry, often heathy, places, except the far north. Ssp *maritima* occurs on coastal sands from Holland southwards. **Fl** 8-9. **Br** E Anglian Brecklands only; rare.

D *Artemisia rupestris* Numerous non-flowering stems, to 45cm; leaves hairless or downy, unstalked; flower heads yellowish, nodding. Only around Baltic. **Fl** 8-9. **Br** Absent.

(3) Taller plants, but with terminal lobes of leaves flat, linear-lanceolate, more than 2mm wide.

E Mugwort *Artemisia vulgaris* Erect perennial, tufted, aromatic, to 1.2m, hairless or downy, usually with *reddish stems* that have a large area of white pith inside. Leaves to 80mm long, pinnately lobed, with deeply cut lobes, *dark green and hairless above, white downy below* (**e**); lower leaves stalked, upper ones smaller and unstalked. Flower heads oval, 2-3mm in diameter, erect, red-brown, in dense branched inflorescences; bracts woolly, with chaffy margins. Throughout, though rare in the far north, in disturbed ground, roadsides and waste places. **Fl** 7-9. **Br** Common throughout.

F Wormwood *Artemisia absinthium* Perennial, aromatic plant with erect, silkily hairy stems to 90cm. Similar to Mugwort, but *leaf segments blunter, silky hairy on both surfaces* (**f**). Flower heads bell-shaped, hanging, with yellow florets. Widespread but local throughout; often naturalised from cultivation, on waste ground, roadsides and coastal habitats. **Fl** 7-8. **Br** Not uncommon in England and Wales, rarer and more coastal elsewhere.

G Colt's-foot *Tussilago farfara* Creeping perennial with runners producing erect scaly leafless flower stems to 15cm tall. Leaves appear separately, after flowers are over, and are roughly triangular, with heart-shaped base, shallowly and irregularly toothed, up to 20cm long, stalked, slightly downy above and very downy below. Flower heads 1 per stem, in clumps, 15-35mm in diameter, with very narrow yellow rays, and yellow disc; flower stems elongate when in fruit, which is a white 'clock'. Common and widespread throughout, usually on damp and clayey soils, especially where bare. **Fl** 2-4. **Br** Common throughout.

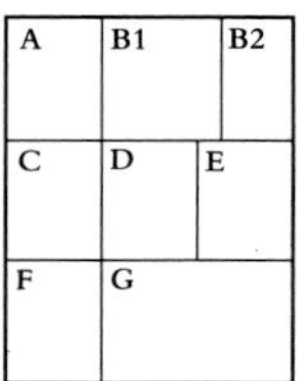

A **Norwegian Mugwort**

B **1 Sea Wormwood** showing habitat

B **2 Sea Wormwood** close-up

C **Field Wormwood**

D *Artemisia rupestris*

E **Mugwort**

F **Wormwood**

G **Colt's-foot**

b

c

e

f

A

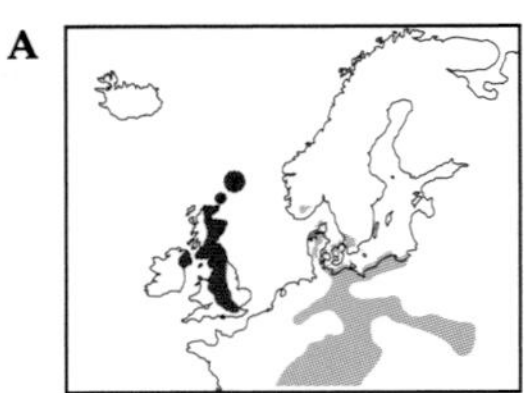

B

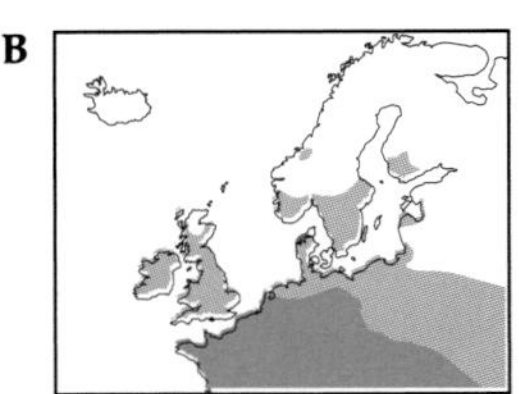

F

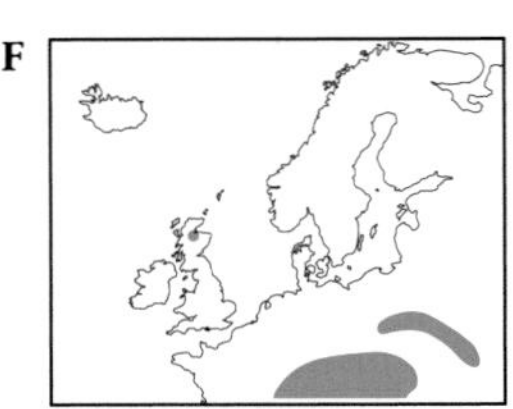

H

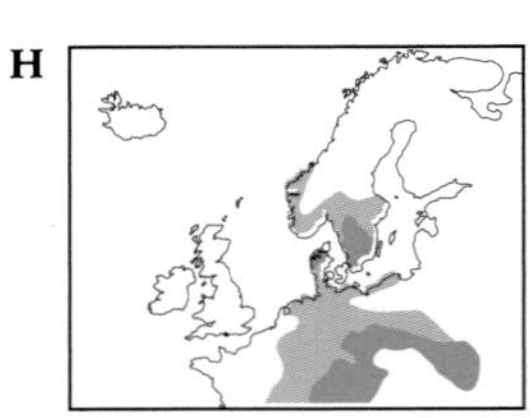

J

BUTTERBURS *Petasites* A small group of distinctive plants, with large basal leaves, erect cylindrical flower spikes with scale-leaves on the stems, and separate male and female plants.

A **White Butterbur** *Petasites albus* Creeping patch-forming perennial. Leaves rounded, heart-shaped, to 30cm across, long-stalked, woolly below, more or less hairless above, with margin noticeably lobed or toothed. Flower spikes to 30cm (much longer when in fruit), with dense rather broad spike of *whitish flowers* (male heads larger and more crowded). In damp and shady places, mainly in mountain areas; from S Norway and Sweden southwards, local. **Fl** 3-5. **Br** Introduced only; locally naturalised.

B **Butterbur** *Petasites hybridus* Perennial herb with creeping rhizome, producing erect flower spikes to 40cm (reaching 80cm when female spikes are in fruit), and large rounded heart-shaped leaves to 90cm in diameter, stalked, distantly toothed, downy below. Flowers in cylindrical spikes on stout stems with reddish or green scale-leaves; *heads pinkish red*. Female flowers individually 3-6mm, males 7-12mm; female spikes lengthen greatly as fruit matures. Widespread and common from N Scotland and N Germany southwards (naturalised in S Scandinavia); on riverbanks, damp woods and grasslands. **Fl** 3-5. **Br** Common and widespread except in N Scotland; female plants very local.

C *Petasites spurius* Very similar to Butterbur but with *leaves between triangular- and arrow-shaped; flowers yellowish or white*; tips of bracts below flower heads minutely fringed and hairy. Similar habitats, and also coastal areas, east from N Germany and Sweden. **Fl** 3-5. **Br** Absent.

D *Petasites frigidus* Similar to *P. spurius*, but has leaves between triangular- and heart-shaped; very few flower heads, with a few ray florets present (absent in other species). N Scandinavia only. **Fl** 4-6. **Br** Absent.

E **Winter Heliotrope** *Petasites fragrans* Smaller, slenderer plant than Butterbur. Leaves long-stalked, rounded, to 20cm, with even teeth, appearing with flowers, green on both surfaces. Flower spikes to 25cm, with *few lilac-pink flower heads, scented*, with short ray florets. Male plants only occur. Introduced from W Mediterranean region, but widely naturalised from Britain and Denmark southwards; in damp or shady places. **Fl** 11-3. **Br** Widely naturalised.

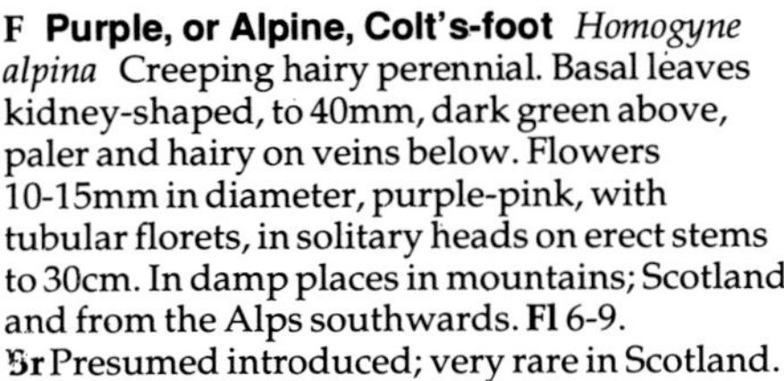

F **Purple, or Alpine, Colt's-foot** *Homogyne alpina* Creeping hairy perennial. Basal leaves kidney-shaped, to 40mm, dark green above, paler and hairy on veins below. Flowers 10-15mm in diameter, purple-pink, with tubular florets, in solitary heads on erect stems to 30cm. In damp places in mountains; Scotland and from the Alps southwards. **Fl** 6-9. **Br** Presumed introduced; very rare in Scotland.

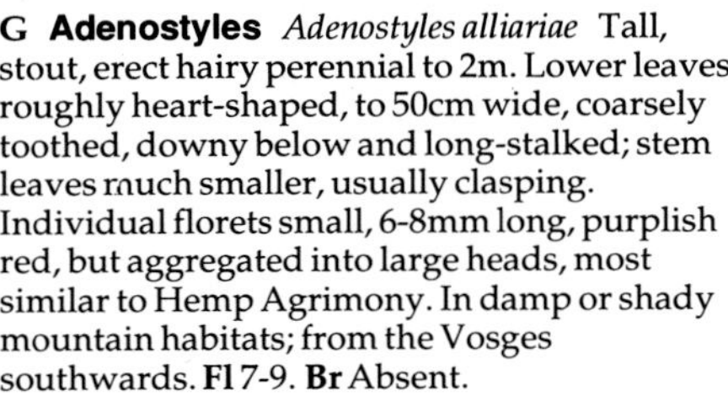

G **Adenostyles** *Adenostyles alliariae* Tall, stout, erect hairy perennial to 2m. Lower leaves roughly heart-shaped, to 50cm wide, coarsely toothed, downy below and long-stalked; stem leaves much smaller, usually clasping. Individual florets small, 6-8mm long, purplish red, but aggregated into large heads, most similar to Hemp Agrimony. In damp or shady mountain habitats; from the Vosges southwards. **Fl** 7-9. **Br** Absent.

H **Arnica** *Arnica montana* Hairy or downy erect perennial to 60cm. Basal and lower leaves elliptical to spoon-shaped, to 17cm, downy, with strongly marked, almost parallel, veins; stems leaves narrow, unstalked, in few opposite pairs. Flowers large, 5-8cm in diameter, with both yellow disc and ray florets, usually solitary on robust hairy stalks. In meadows, heaths and pastures, usually in mountain areas, avoiding lime-rich soil; from S Scandinavia southwards; local. **Fl** 5-9. **Br** Absent.

I *Arnica angustifolia ssp alpina* Similar to Arnica, with *leaves less than 20mm wide*, and *flower heads smaller (35-45mm in diameter)*. Grassland in N Scandinavia only. **Br** Absent.

J **Leopard's-bane** *Doronicum pardalianches* Erect, hairy perennial to 90cm. *Basal leaves heart-shaped* to ovate, long-stalked, to 12cm long (**j**); stem leaves alternate, becoming narrower and less stalked upwards. Flower heads 3-5cm in diameter, with bright yellow rays and disc florets, in loose, branching inflorescence of 2-6 heads; bracts below flower heads narrowly triangular with hairy margins. Southwards from Holland and Belgium; in woodland areas or as a naturalised plant, rare in the north of range. **Fl** 5-7. **Br** Scattered almost throughout, as naturalised introduction.

K **Plantain-leaved Leopard's-bane** *Doronicum plantagineum* Similar to Leopard's-bane, but basal leaves ovate-elliptical, narrowed gradually into a stalk (**k**); uppermost leaves narrow; *flower heads 5-8cm in diameter, usually solitary*. Woods, grasslands and heathy areas; from N France southwards, naturalised elsewhere. **Fl** 6-7. **Br** Often planted, occasionally naturalised.

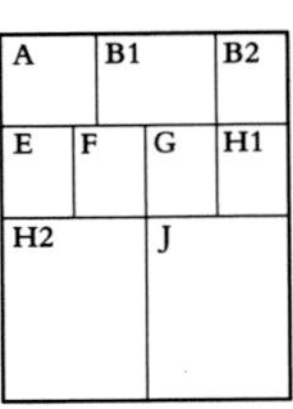

A **White Butterbur**

B **1 Butterbur** male plants in flower

B **2 Butterbur** female plants in seed

E **Winter Heliotrope**

F **Purple Coltsfoot**

G **Adenostyles**

H **1 Arnica**

H **2 Arnica** in mountain habitat

J **Leopard's-bane**

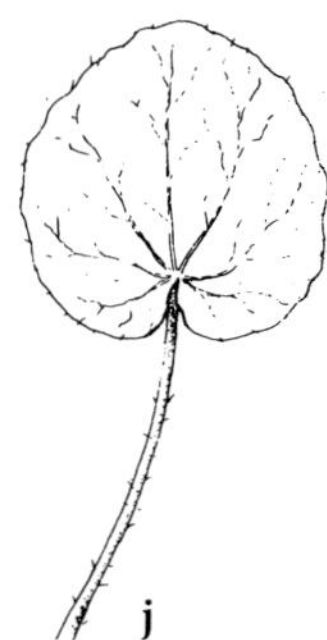

j

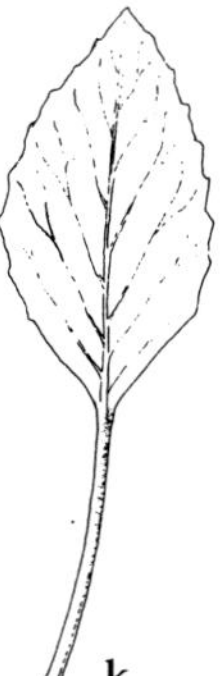

k

A
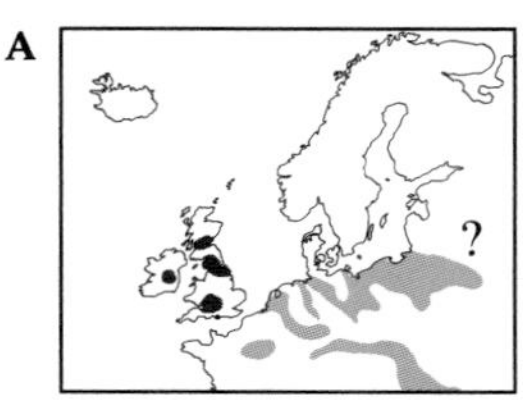

C
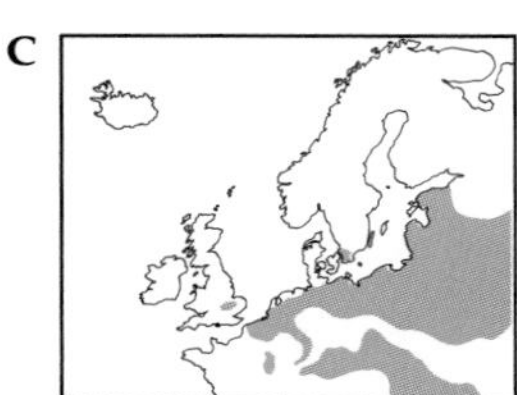

D
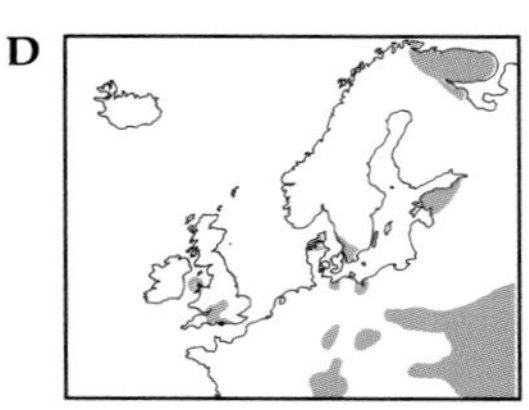

I
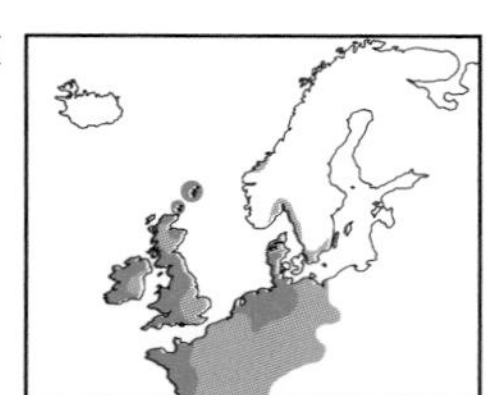

J
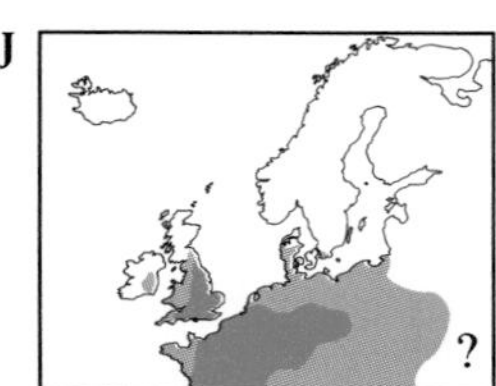

RAGWORTS AND GROUNDSELS *Senecio*
Annual or perennial herbs (including shrubs, trees and climbers elsewhere), usually downy, with alternate spirally arranged leaves, and flower heads aggregated into flattish-topped umbel-like clusters, always yellow; bracts below flower head in 1 row, with a few short outer bracts at base of head; ray florets almost always present.

(1) All leaves unlobed, usually oval to lanceolate.

A **Broad-leaved Ragwort** *Senecio fluviatilis* Creeping perennial with long stolons, and erect stems to 2m, densely leafy, hairy near top, hairless below. Leaves elliptical to linear-lanceolate, to 20cm, *hairless*, pointed, toothed, and unstalked (**a**). Flower heads numerous, 15-30mm in diameter, ray florets few (6-8 only). In damp meadows, fens and woods; native from Holland southwards, though naturalised elsewhere. **Fl** 7-9. **Br** Introduced; locally naturalised throughout.

B **Wood Ragwort** *Senecio nemorensis* Very similar to Broad-leaved Ragwort, differing in that the *leaves are often hairy below; teeth on leaf have outer margin straight or concave* – convex in above species (**b**), leaves decrease markedly in size up the stems. In damp woods and grasslands; from Germany southwards. **Fl** 7-9. **Br** Absent.

C **Fen Ragwort** *Senecio paludosus* Tall erect perennial, with *cottony-downy stems* to 2m. Leaves narrowly lanceolate, to 20cm, shiny above, *cottony below*, and toothed (**c**), lower ones short-stalked, upper ones stalkless. Flower heads 30-40mm in diameter, with 10-20 bright yellow ray florets, in large clusters. In damp places, especially fens, from S Sweden southwards, though absent from some areas. **Fl** 7-8. **Br** Very rare, in E England fens only.

D **Field Fleawort** *Senecio integrifolius* Erect perennial to 70cm, usually less, with more or less downy stems. *Basal leaves in a flat rosette*, rounded-ovate, 5-10cm long, short-stalked and untoothed; *stem leaves few*, narrower, unstalked and rather clasping. Flower heads 15-25mm in diameter, orange-yellow, with about 13 ray florets, solitary or in few-flowered inflorescence of up to 12 flowers; involucral bracts with tuft of hairs at tip. In dry close-grazed grassland, usually on calcareous soils; throughout except the far north, but local. **Fl** 5-7. **Br** Local, mainly on downland in S and E England. Plants from Anglesey have toothed basal leaves and more stem leaves, and are described as ssp *maritimus*.

E *Senecio helenitis* Very similar to Field Fleawort, but *basal rosette not pressed closely to ground, usually withered by flowering time, stalk longer than blade*. In grassland; from Belgium and S Germany southwards. In ssp *candidus*, flowers have 13-26 ray florets. Grassy coastal places, N France only. **Fl** 6-7. **Br** Absent.

F *Senecio rivularis* Similar to *S. helenitis*, but with coarsely toothed leaves, a long, winged leaf stalk, and leaves with roughly heart-shaped bases. Damp grassland in mountains; central and S Germany south-eastwards. **Fl** 6-8. **Br** Absent.

G **Marsh Fleawort** *Senecio congestus* Tall, erect, woolly perennial to 1m or more, with stout, *hollow*, very leafy stems. Leaves variable, usually roughly ovate, 5-15cm long, toothed or untoothed (rarely deeply divided), *woolly and pale green*. Flower heads *pale yellow*, 20-30mm in diameter, with about 20 ray florets, in dense umbel-like heads. In damp meadows, fens and marshes; very local, from Denmark southwards. **Fl** 6-7. **Br** Extinct.

(2) Plants with at least some leaves pinnately lobed. (N.B. Marsh Fleawort in group (1) may occasionally have pinnately lobed leaves.

H **Common Ragwort** *Senecio jacobaea* Biennial or perennial herb. Highly poisonous. Hairless or slightly hairy, with stout, erect, leafy, *furrowed stems* to 1.5m (usually less), not creeping. Basal and lower stem leaves 10-20cm long, *pinnately lobed with large blunt end-lobe*; upper stem leaves often more divided, with smaller end-lobe; all slightly hairy below. Flower heads 15-25mm in diameter, yellow, in much-branched *flat-topped clusters*; ray florets 12-15, rarely absent altogether (var. *flosculosus*). A common weed of pastures, waste ground and other places, on almost any soil; widespread except in the extreme north. **Fl** 6-10. **Br** Abundant throughout.

I **Marsh Ragwort** *Senecio aquaticus* Similar to Common Ragwort, differing in that it has *undivided or little-divided basal leaves*, with much larger end-lobe; stem leaves with large oval end-lobes. *Inflorescence spreading*, not dense and flat-topped; individual heads 20-30mm in diameter; bracts never black-tipped. Poisonous. In marshy places and damp grassland; from S Scandinavia southwards. **Fl** 7-8. **Br** Widespread and moderately common throughout.

J **Hoary Ragwort** *Senecio erucifolius* Rather similar in form to Common Ragwort, but stem and at least *undersides of leaves cottony-downy; leaf lobes all narrow and pointed*, with curled-under margins. Flower heads 15-20mm in diameter, *pale yellow*, in dense heads; outer flower bracts same length as inner long ones. In neutral or calcareous grasslands, including dunes; from S Sweden southwards, but rarer in the north of range. **Fl** 7-9. **Br** Locally common in England and Wales; rare in Ireland; absent from most of Scotland.

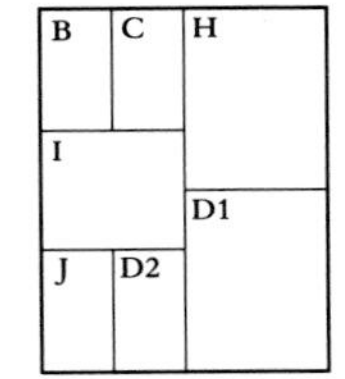

B **Wood Ragwort**

C **Fen Ragwort**

H **Common Ragwort**

I **Marsh Ragwort**

J **Hoary Ragwort**

D **1 Field Fleawort** normal form with Adonis Blue Butterfly

D **2 Field Fleawort** spp *maritimus*

a

b

c

E

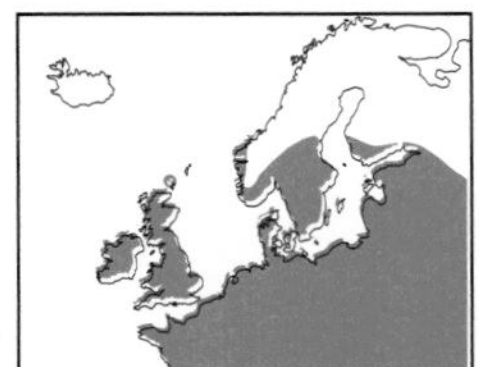

F

G

A Oxford Ragwort *Senecio squalidus* Annual, biennial or perennial plant, *usually branched at the base to form a spreading bushy plant*. Leaves 1-2 times pinnately lobed, with narrow, pointed leaflets, lower ones with a winged stalk, upper ones clasping. Flower heads 15-25mm in diameter, bright yellow, with all *bracts black-tipped*. Native to S Europe as far north as S Germany, but widely naturalised, especially in France and Britain; on walls, waste ground, railway lines, etc. **Fl** 5-12. **Br** Widely naturalised and common in England and Wales; rare in Scotland and Ireland.

B Welsh Ragwort *Senecio cambrensis* Natural hybrid between Oxford Ragwort and Groundsel, intermediate between the 2. More robust than either; flower heads 6-10mm in diameter, rays at first spreading then curling back. Fertility very low. N Wales and S Scotland only. **Fl** 5-10. **Br** Only occurs in a few places in N Wales and S Scotland; very rare.

C *Senecio vernalis* Erect annual to 50cm, rather like Oxford Ragwort, but with *young stems and leaves cottony-downy*; inflorescence branches more erect. Waste ground and bare stony habitats, as a naturalised plant, north to S Scandinavia. **Fl** 5-7. **Br** Casual only.

D Groundsel *Senecio vulgaris* Familiar annual weed, with erect or spreading, branched, rather fleshy stems to 45cm. Leaves pinnately lobed with short blunt lobes, usually downy below, shiny above, lower leaves stalked, upper leaves clasping the stem. *Flower heads much smaller than above species*, cylindrical, roughly 4mm in diameter, 10mm long, in dense clusters at first; florets yellow, *ray florets absent or few*, curling back; short outer flower-head *bracts black-tipped*. Abundant throughout except the far north, in cultivated and bare areas. **Fl** 1-12. **Br** Abundant throughout.

E Heath, or Wood, Groundsel *Senecio sylvaticus* Rather similar to Groundsel, but usually taller, to 70cm, with stiffer more erect branches. Lower leaves more deeply cut, downy when young. Inflorescence more lax, with flower heads long-stalked; flower heads more conical, *ray florets short and recurved; bracts not black-tipped*, stickily hairy. On heaths, woodland edges, disturbed ground, usually on sandy soils; throughout except the far north. **Fl** 6-9. **Br** Throughout, though local.

F Sticky Groundsel *Senecio viscosus* Similar in form to Heath Groundsel, to 60cm, but *stickily hairy all over*, and *strong-smelling*. Flower heads larger, to 12mm in diameter, long-stalked, with about 13 longer, rather curled, pale yellow ray florets. Locally common from S Scandinavia southwards on waste ground, railway lines, sand-dunes and other dry, open habitats. **Fl** 7-9. **Br** Common throughout, except the far north.

G Carline Thistle *Carlina vulgaris* Erect, spiny, biennial plant, branched or unbranched, hairless or cottony-downy, to 70cm. Leaves ovate to oblong, to 15cm, wavy and spinily lobed, cottony below, the lower ones with a short stalk, upper ones clasping stem. Flower heads solitary or 2-3 together, 15-40mm in diameter; florets yellowish brown, all disc, but surrounded by long yellowish bracts, spreading out like ray florets, with outer green spiny bracts – a distinctive combination. Throughout except the extreme north, locally common in dry grasslands, usually calcareous. **Fl** 7-10. **Br** Locally common throughout except N Scotland.

BURDOCKS *Arctium* Robust, erect, downy, branched biennial plants. Leaves large, alternate, roughly heart-shaped, downy, not spiny. Flower heads globose, solitary in lax clusters; florets red-purple, bracts numerous, with hooked spiny tips, forming the familiar burs in fruit, aiding dispersal by animals. Much hybridisation and overlap can occur in the group.

H Lesser Burdock *Arctium minus* Up to 1.5m tall. Basal leaves broadly ovate, to 50cm, *longer than wide*, heart-shaped at base (**h**), *with hollow stalks*. Flower heads 15-20mm wide, to 35mm when in fruit, globose, narrowed at top in fruit; cottony-downy at first, but becoming hairless later, short-stalked, with petals usually longer than bracts. Widespread throughout except in the Arctic; common in scrub, open woods, waste ground and roadsides. **Fl** 7-9. **Br** Common throughout.

I *Arctium pubens* (often described as a subspecies of Lesser Burdock) Has larger flower heads (20-25mm wide), on longer stalks (to 40mm), with florets equalling bracts in length. Similar habitats and flowering time; common from Holland southwards. **Br** Common in lowland England, especially the Midlands.

J *Arctium nemorosum* (also described as a subspecies of Lesser Burdock) Taller than the above 2 species, to 2.5m, with flower heads 25-35mm wide; florets equalling bracts, which are green to purple (yellowish in *A. pubens*). Similar habitats and flowering time. **Br** Widespread, commonest in the north.

K *Arctium tomentosum* Similar in form to Lesser Burdock, but the *leaf stalks are not hollow*. Flower heads smaller (12-20mm wide when in flower), *bracts covered with cobweb-like hairs*; tips of broad innermost bracts not hooked. Roadsides, wood-margins, scrub and waste places; throughout mainland Europe except the far north. **Fl** 7-9. **Br** Casual only.

L Greater Burdock *Arctium lappa* Similar in form to other species. Basal leaves *as wide as long* (**l**), *leaf stalks solid*. Flower heads large, 30-40mm in diameter, in very few-flowered inflorescence, becoming opened widely when in fruit; bracts greenish yellow. Widespread and fairly common throughout except the far north; in open woods, scrub and roadsides, on heavy soils. **Fl** 7-9. **Br** Common in much of England and Wales, but rare or absent further north.

h

l

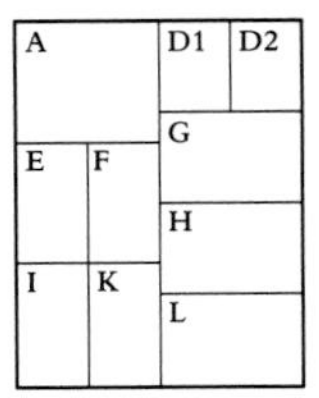

A **Oxford Ragwort**

D **1 Groundsel** showing common rayless form

D **2 Groundsel** showing rayed and rayless forms

E **Heath Groundsel**

F **Sticky Groundsel**

G **Carline Thistle**

H **Lesser Burdock**

I *Arctium pubens*

K *Arctium tomentosum*

L **Greater Burdock**

A

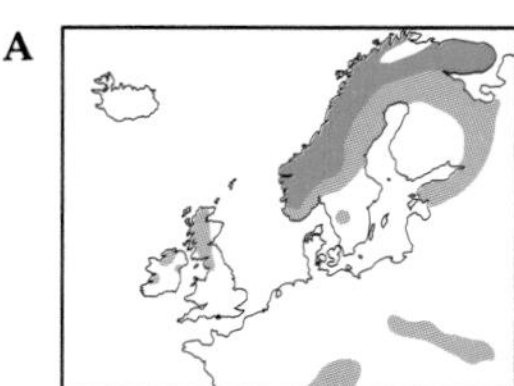

B

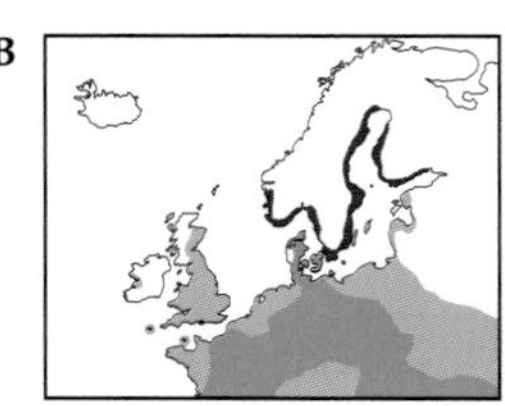

C

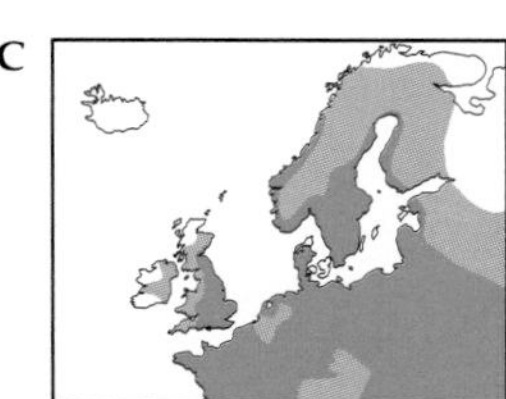

E

F

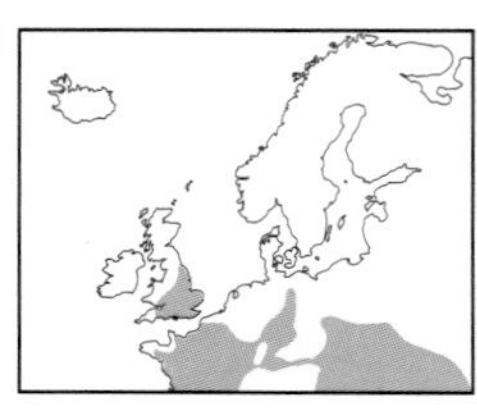

H

A Alpine Saw-wort *Saussurea alpina* Creeping perennial producing erect grooved rather downy flower stems to 50cm. Basal leaves ovate to lanceolate, to 18cm long, untoothed or slightly toothed, with narrowly winged stalk; upper leaves narrower and unstalked; all leaves more or less hairless above, white downy below. Flower heads egg-shaped, to 2cm long, more or less unstalked in a tight terminal inflorescence; florets all tubular, purplish at top, yellow-white below, greatly exceeding bracts; inner bracts grey hairy. In grassland, open woods, rocky places, cliffs, mainly in mountains, though widespread in the Arctic. **Fl** 7-9. **Br** Very local in mountain areas from N Wales and central Ireland northwards.

THISTLES *Carduus* Annual to perennial herbs with spiny-winged stems, and spine-edged leaves that are usually green above and cottony below. Flower heads solitary or in clusters, with masses of overlapping spine-tipped bracts. Florets all tubular, usually red to purple in colour.

B Musk, or Nodding, Thistle *Carduus nutans* Erect biennial plant up to 1.2m, with cottony spiny-winged stems, branched above, and *spine-free for a section below the flower heads*. Leaves pinnately lobed, with segments lobed and spine-tipped, cottony below, especially along veins. Flower heads rounded-cylindrical, large (4-6cm in diameter when fully opened), *drooping, solitary on long spineless stalks*; florets deep red-purple, surrounded by an involucre of long, narrow, recurved, spiny-tipped, often reddish bracts; flowers fragrant. From Denmark southwards, frequent (except in the north of range) in dry grasslands, dunes and roadsides. **Fl** 5-8. **Br** Common in England and Wales; much less common in Scotland; rare in Ireland.

C Welted Thistle *Carduus acanthoides* Erect, branched biennial up to 1.2m, with *virtually continuous narrow spiny wings on all stems, except for a very short section below flower heads*; stems cottony. Lower leaves elliptical in outline, deeply pinnately lobed, 3-lobed and spiny; upper leaves narrower, stalkless, with base running down stem. Flower heads roughly 2-3cm long, globose to cylindrical, usually *in small clusters*; florets red-purple; involucre of bracts roughly oval, with numerous narrow cottony spreading bracts, with weak spine-tips. From S Sweden southwards; in waste places, scrub, grassland and open woodland; common. **Fl** 6-8. **Br** Common throughout except N Scotland.

D *Carduus crispus* ssp *multiflorus* Similar to Welted Thistle, but more spiny, with *wings extending right up to flower heads*; leaves narrower, with raised veins, hardly hairy below; flower-head bracts slightly curved at tips. In waste places, roadsides and streamsides of mainland Europe, north to Arctic Sweden. **Fl** 6-8. **Br** Absent.

E Slender Thistle *Carduus tenuiflorus* Similar to Welted Thistle, to 1m tall. Differs in that it is more erect and narrowly branched, with *stems broadly winged right up to flower heads, very cottony* and greyish. Flower heads more slender, to 20mm long but only 5-10mm wide, in dense terminal clusters; *florets pale pinky red.* In dry grassy and open habitats, often near the sea. Native from Holland southwards, naturalised locally further north. **Fl** 5-8. **Br** Widespread, except in N Scotland; mainly coastal.

THISTLES *Cirsium* Very similar to *Carduus* thistles, differing mainly in that the flowers have a feathery-hairy pappus.

F Woolly Thistle *Cirsium eriophorum* Stout erect biennial plant, with *unwinged, cottony furrowed stems to 1.5m*, branched in upper part. Basal leaves large, to 60cm long, pinnately divided into narrow 2-forked segments, *usually with 1 segment pointing upwards, the other downwards* (giving a distinctive 2-rowed effect); stem leaves smaller and stalkless; *all white cottony below*, all lobes spine-tipped. Flower heads solitary, very large, globular, up to 7cm in diameter, with very *cottony bracts*; florets red-purple. From Holland and N England southwards on calcareous grassland and scrub. **Fl** 7-9. **Br** England and Wales only, north to Durham; local.

G Spear Thistle *Cirsium vulgare* Erect biennial, with cottony stems with interrupted spiny wings; branched in upper part, to 1.5m tall. Basal leaves to 30cm long, deeply pinnately lobed, with lobes forked and spiny, and a *single, long, stout, pointed end-lobe* (the spear); upper leaves smaller; all leaves bristly-prickly above, matt. Flower heads ovoid, 3-5cm long, with more or less cottony bracts; florets red-purple; *outer bracts with long yellowish spine-tips*. Very common and widespread almost throughout, in waste places, grassland and disturbed ground, as a persistent weed. **Fl** 7-10. **Br** Common throughout.

H Meadow Thistle *Cirsium dissectum* Perennial, with *creeping stolons* producing simple, erect, unwinged downy, ridged stems to 80cm. Basal leaves elliptical to lanceolate, to 25cm long, either pinnately lobed, or with widely separated teeth, *green and hairy above, white cottony below*, with soft marginal prickles; stem leaves similar, but narrower, and barely clasping stem. *Flower heads solitary* (rarely more) on *long, spineless stalks*, roughly 3cm long; florets red-purple; bracts of head narrow lanceolate, pressed close to head, outer ones spine-tipped. From Holland and N Germany southwards, rare in the north; in damp peaty meadows and bogs. **Fl** 6-8. **Br** Locally common northwards to N England; frequent in Ireland.

I Tuberous Thistle *Cirsium tuberosum* Similar to Meadow Thistle, but has *tuberous roots without runners; leaves much more divided*, usually twice pinnately lobed, *all green on both sides*, slightly cottony below; margins bristly, not spiny. In calcareous grassland; from Belgium and S England southwards; uncommon, declining. **Fl** 6-7. **Br** Rare and declining in a few southern localities. Hybridisation with Dwarf Thistle (*see* page 274) is contributing to the loss of this species.

J Brook Thistle *Cirsium rivulare* Similar in form to Tuberous Thistle, but with fibrous roots. Upper parts of stem leafless or with spiny bracts. Flower heads solitary or in small clusters; *florets purple, bracts reddish purple*. In wet meadows and streamsides; E France and S Germany only. **Fl** 6-9. **Br** Absent.

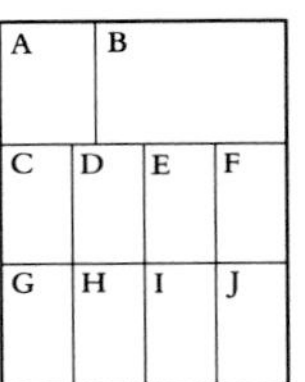

A Alpine Saw-wort
B Musk Thistle
C Welted Thistle
D *Carduus crispus ssp multiflorus*
E Slender Thistle
F Woolly Thistle
G Spear Thistle
H Meadow Thistle
I Tuberous Thistle
J Brook Thistle

A 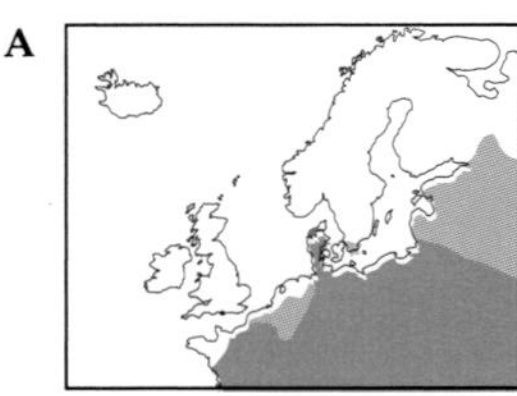

B 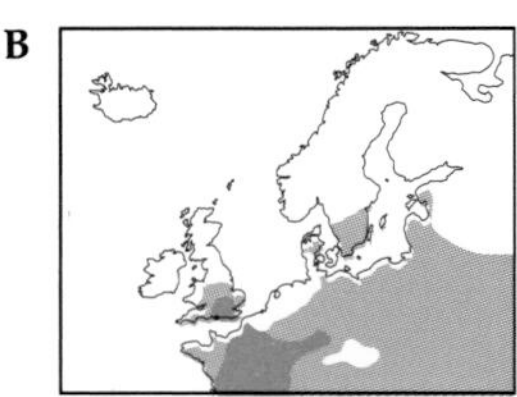

C 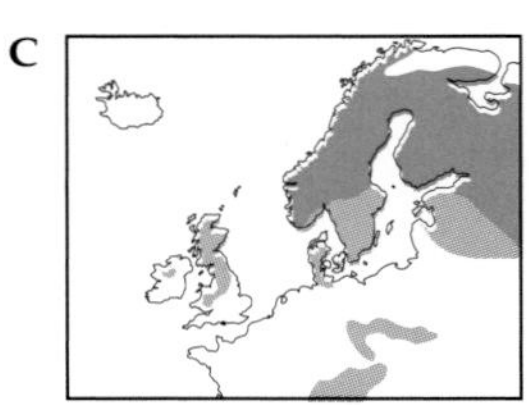

F 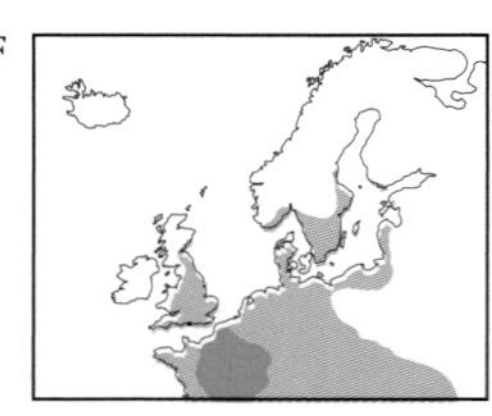

H 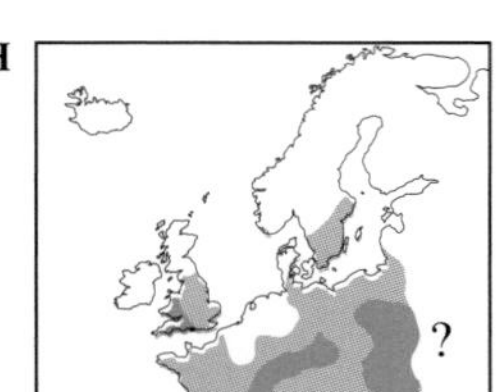

A Cabbage Thistle *Cirsium oleraceum* Erect perennial to 1.2m, with unwinged, almost hairless, furrowed stems. Basal leaves to 40cm, elliptical in outline, but usually toothed or pinnately divided; upper leaves undivided, clasping the stem with heart-shaped bases; all leaves weakly spiny, pale green. Flower heads oval, 25-40mm in diameter, erect and in clusters exceeded by soft leaf-like bracts; *florets pale yellow*. On roadsides, fens and damp woods; from S Scandinavia southwards; locally common. **Fl** 7-9. **Br** An occasional introduction only.

B Dwarf, or Stemless, Thistle *Cirsium acaule* Perennial with a basal rosette of leaves, and *stemless or short-stemmed flower heads* from the centre. Leaves oblong, to 15cm long, deeply pinnately divided, with divided, wavy, very spiny lobes. Flower heads usually stalkless and solitary, but sometimes several together, sometimes stalked to 30cm; heads oval, 3-4cm long, florets red-purple. In dry calcareous grasslands; from Denmark southwards, rare in the north of range. **Fl** 6-9. **Br** Locally common in S and E England and S Wales; absent from Scotland and Ireland.

C Melancholy Thistle *Cirsium helenioides* Rather like a large version of Meadow Thistle. Tall perennial to 1.2m, with cottony, unwinged spineless stems. Leaves roughly oblong, 10-25cm long, unlobed to pinnately lobed, flat, with softly prickly teeth, *green and hairless above*, but *thickly felted below*; upper leaves similar, but smaller, with rounded clasping bases. Flower heads solitary, or (rarely) in clusters of 2-4 on long stems; up to 5cm long, 3-5cm wide; florets red-purple. Widespread in damp pastures, open woods and roadsides; common in the north, more confined to mountain areas in the south. **Fl** 6-8. **Br** Absent from S England and S Wales; locally common from N England northwards.

D Marsh Thistle *Cirsium palustre* Erect biennial, with stems to 1.5m, often branched above the middle, *all stems continuously spiny-winged; whole plant often reddish-tinged*. Leaves linear-lanceolate, pinnately divided, wavy, *very lobed and spiny*, hairy above but shiny green. Flower heads in crowded leafy clusters both on main stem and branches; flowers 15-20mm long, with *dark red-purple* (occasionally white) florets, and purplish-green bracts. The reddish colour of the plant, and the dark small florets, make identification easy. Very common in damp grassy places; throughout except the extreme north. **Fl** 7-9. **Br** Common throughout.

E Creeping Thistle *Cirsium arvense* Far-creeping perennial herb, with erect leafy stems to 1m, *unwinged*. Leaves not in distinct basal rosette, oblong, deeply pinnately divided, with triangular spiny lobes, very wavy, hairless above; upper leaves similar, but clasping, sometimes running a short way down stems as a spiny wing. Flower heads in open clusters, narrowly cylindrical, 20mm long, 10-15mm wide; *florets pale pinkish purple or whitish, involucral bracts purplish*. Very common throughout in grasslands, cultivated land and waste places; a persistent weed. **Fl** 6-9. **Br** Very common throughout.

F Cotton, or Scotch, Thistle *Onopordum acanthium* Erect, robust biennial to 3m, with *white-cottony continuously broad-winged stems*, branched in upper parts. Leaves oblong to ovate, unstalked, toothed or wavy lobed, with strong spines, white-cottony on both surfaces. Flower heads solitary or in clusters of 2-5, roughly globose, 3-5 × 3-5cm; florets purplish pink, bracts narrow, green and tipped with strong yellowish spines. From S Sweden southwards in waste places, roadsides and dry banks, but probably not native in the north part of range. **Fl** 7-9. **Br** Reasonably common in S and E England, becoming rarer to the north and west. Probably not native.

G Milk Thistle *Silybum marianum* Erect, robust annual or biennial to 1m, hairless or cottony, often branched, stems unwinged. Basal leaves to 50cm, pinnately lobed or wavy-edged, spiny, hairless and *shiny green, marked with conspicuous whitish network of veins above*. Flower heads large, 4-5cm long, with red-purple florets and *surrounded by long, triangular, spiny-toothed bracts*. In waste places, roadsides and on coastal cliffs; native from France southwards, but naturalised further north. **Fl** 6-8. **Br** Possibly native on S coast, naturalised locally elsewhere.

H Saw-wort *Serratula tinctoria* Hairless perennial, *without prickles*, with erect wiry grooved stems to 1m, usually less. Leaves to 20cm, very variable in shape from undivided to deeply pinnately lobed, with finely toothed margins; lower leaves stalked, upper leaves clasping. Flower heads small, 15-20mm long in lax inflorescences; florets reddish purple, involucre of bracts narrowly cylindrical in shape, with *closely pressed purplish bracts*. From S Scandinavia southwards in permanent pastures, heaths and open heathy woods, on mildly acid or calcareous soils. **Fl** 7-9. **Br** Locally common north to S Scotland, rare in N Scotland and Ireland.

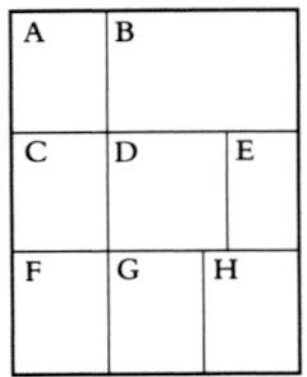

A Cabbage Thistle
B Dwarf Thistle
C Melancholy Thistle
D Marsh Thistle
E Creeping Thistle
F Cotton Thistle
G Milk Thistle
H Saw-wort

D
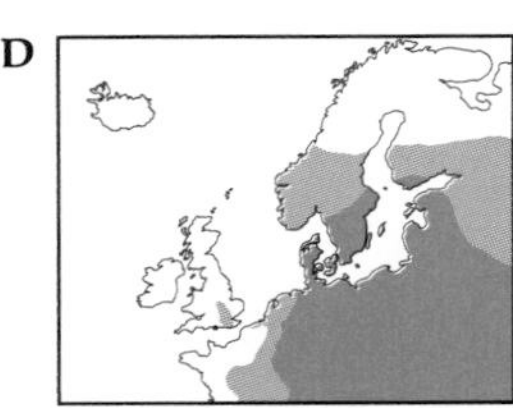

G

H
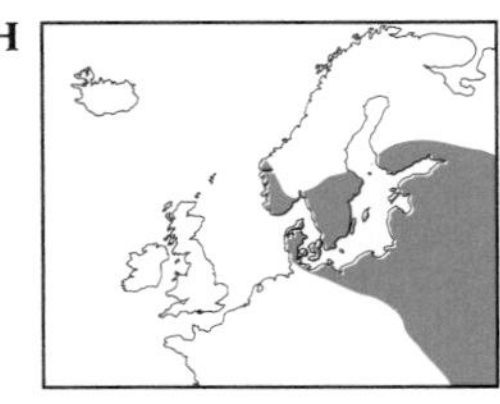

I
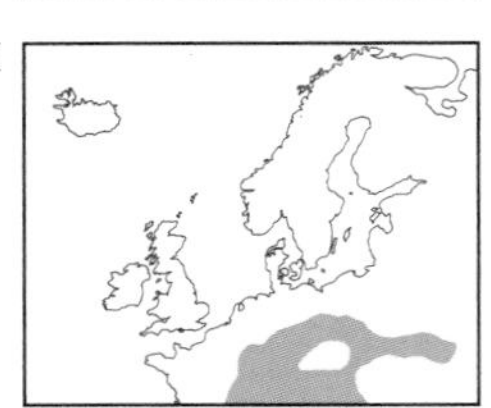

J
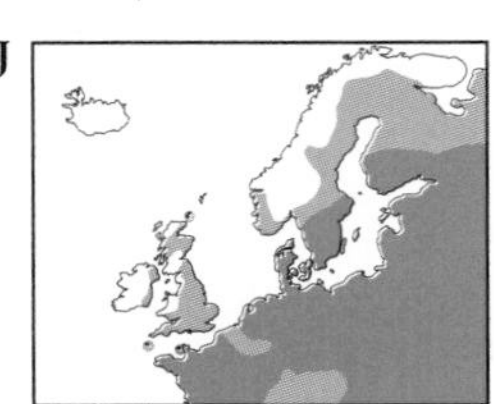

KNAPWEEDS AND CORNFLOWERS

Centaurea Annual or perennial plants, with alternate bristly (but not spiny) leaves. Flower heads rather thistle-like, but surrounded by distinctive head of bracts, each consisting of a normal bract topped by an appendage that is frequently bristly or toothed; the shape of these appendages is often diagnostic. Florets all tubular, but outer ones sometimes greatly enlarged.

A **Greater Knapweed** *Centaurea scabiosa* Erect downy perennial to 1m, with grooved stems, usually branched above the middle. Basal leaves to 25cm, stalked, oblong, *usually deeply pinnately lobed*, with lobes toothed; stem leaves similar, but stalkless. Flower heads large, 3-6cm in diameter, solitary; florets red-purple, *outer ones greatly enlarged forming a spreading outer ring*; bracts green with dark brown, horseshoe-shaped, fringed appendages (**a**). In grassy places and scrub, usually on calcareous soils; throughout except the far north. **Fl** 6-8. **Br** Throughout in lowland areas, rarer to the north.

B **Red Star-thistle** *Centaurea calcitrapa* Biennial herb, with branched erect or ascending hairless stems to 70cm. Lower leaves deeply pinnately divided, with narrow lobes; upper leaves toothed. Flower heads 8-10mm in diameter, reddish purple, but surrounded by a ring of long-spined, yellowish, spreading bracts, each about 20-30mm long. Native in S Europe, but naturalised locally throughout N Europe as far north as Holland and Germany; in grassland and waste habitats, especially on chalky soils. **Fl** 7-9. **Br** Well established on chalk on the Sussex coast; casual elsewhere.

C **Rough Star-thistle** *Centaurea aspera* Erect plant to 50cm, downy. Leaves pinnate. Flower heads pink-purple, but distinctive by the appendages which consist of *3-5 chaffy palmately arranged recurved spiny teeth* (**c**). Sand-dunes and dry habitats; W France and Channel Islands, naturalised elsewhere. **Fl** 7-9. **Br** Channel Islands, naturalised in S Wales.

D **Brown Knapweed** *Centaurea jacea* Downy perennial to 1m, with slender, rough stem, sometimes thickened below flower head, unbranched or branched from middle. Leaves oval to lanceolate, usually unlobed, but occasionally pinnately lobed. Flower heads solitary, 10-20mm across, with red-purple florets, outermost ring larger; bracts have *pale brown, rounded, untoothed or shallowly toothed appendages* (**d**). In grassland and open woods; throughout mainland N Europe. **Fl** 7-9. **Br** Not native, occasional as casual or hybrid.

E *Centaurea decipiens* Similar to Brown Knapweed, but usually smaller, with *markedly fringed oval-triangular bract appendages* (**e**). Pastures; mainland Europe from Norway southwards. **Fl** 7-9. **Br** Absent.

F *Centaurea microptilon* Similar to above 2 species, with smaller florets; *appendages lanceolate-triangular, blackish, curving back or erect, markedly fringed* (**f**). Grasslands; mainland Europe from Holland southwards. **Fl** 7-9. **Br** Absent.

G **Common Knapweed, Hardheads** *Centaurea nigra* ssp *nigra* Erect, roughly hairy perennial to 1m, with grooved stems, branched in upper part. Leaves oblong to linear-lanceolate, unlobed or slightly lobed but *not pinnate*; upper leaves narrow and unlobed. Flower heads solitary or few together, 2-4cm in diameter; florets red-purple, *outer florets usually not enlarged*; bracts of head have brown to black, *triangular, deeply fringed appendages with bristly, often forked, teeth* (**g1**). Very common in grassy areas north to S Sweden. **Fl** 6-9. **Br** Common almost throughout.
Ssp *nemoralis* differs in being very slender, often more branched, with stem not swollen below flower heads; florets paler pink-purple, commonly with enlarged outer ray florets; *teeth of bract appendage longer than undivided portion* (**g2**) (equal or shorter in ssp *nigra*, above). **Fl** 6-9. **Br** Local in England and Wales, mainly on lighter, calcareous soils

H **Wig Knapweed** *Centaurea phrygia* Similar in form to other knapweeds, but with *stout cottony stems, thickened below the flower heads*; leaves downy, generally undivided and narrow. Flower heads solitary, *large, 3-5cm in diameter*, with long spreading outer florets (like Greater Knapweed); *bracts have long narrow feathery-fringed blackish appendages* (**h**). In grassland and open woods; in S Scandinavia and N Germany. **Fl** 7-9. **Br** Absent.

I **Perennial Cornflower** *Centaurea montana* Creeping downy perennial, with erect stems to 80cm, winged where leaf stalks run down. Leaves ovate to oblong, unlobed or occasionally somewhat toothed or lobed, cottony below. *Flower heads large, 6-8cm in diameter, blue or pinkish blue*, inner florets usually redder than outer, with long, spreading outer florets; bracts with black fringes (**i**). In open woods and meadows, especially in mountain areas; from the Ardennes southwards. Often cultivated. **Fl** 6-8. **Br** Casual introduction only.

J **Cornflower** *Centaurea cyanus* Superficially similar to Perennial Cornflower, but *annual*, with an erect, wiry, grooved stem to 90cm. Lower leaves undivided or pinnately divided and narrow; upper leaves linear and unlobed. *Flower heads smaller, 15-30mm in diameter, with bright blue outer florets* and reddish inner ones; bracts with brown or silvery fringes. A weed of cultivated ground and disturbed areas; occurring almost throughout, but not native in the region, and generally declining. **Fl** 6-8. **Br** Once a common arable weed, now virtually extinct.

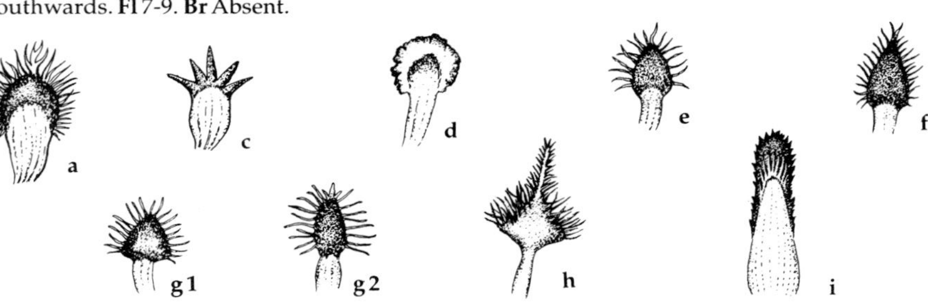

A	C	B
D	G1	G2
H	I	J

A **Greater Knapweed**

C **Rough Star-thistle**

B **Red Star-thistle**

D **Brown Knapweed**

G **1 Common Knapweed** rayed form

G **2 Common Knapweed** normal form

H **Wig Knapweed**

I **Perennial Cornflower**

J **Cornflower**

D

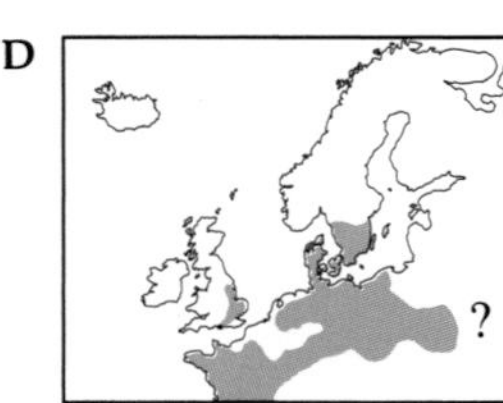

E

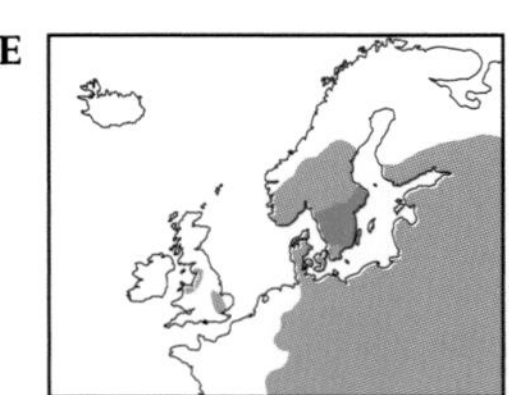

F

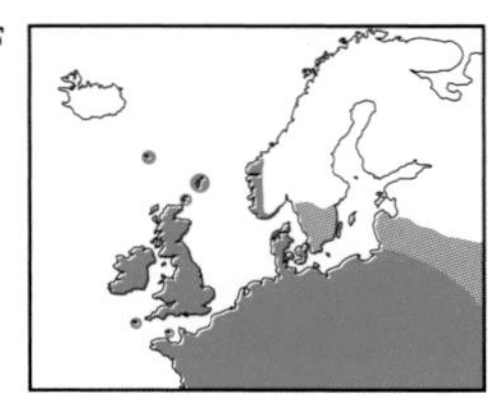

G

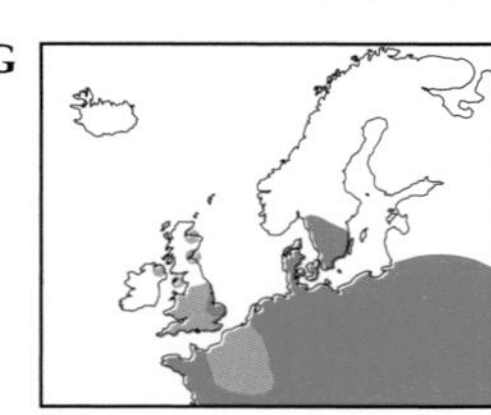

J

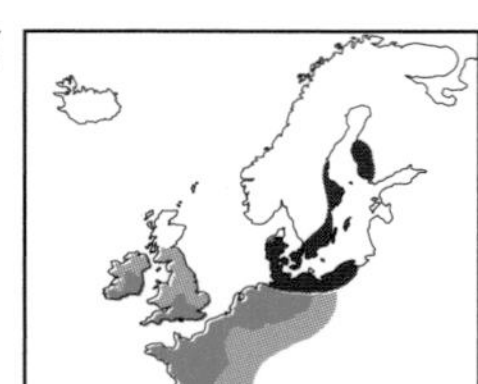

A Carthamus *Carthamus lanatus* Distinctive, prickly, cottony-downy annual to 1m. Leaves pinnately lobed and spiny. Flower heads yellow, 20-30mm across, surrounded by long, narrow, spiny bracts. In dry open habitats; N France southwards. **Fl** 6-8. **Br** Absent.

B Spanish Oysterplant *Scolymus hispanicus* Biennial or perennial plant to 1m, stems with interrupted spiny wings. Basal leaves long-stalked, pinnately lobed, few-spined; upper leaves narrower and spinier. Flower heads thistle-like, deep yellow, 20-30mm in diameter, all florets with rays. Rough grassy places; primarily S Europe, extending into N France. **Fl** 6-8. **Br** Absent.

C Chicory *Cichorium intybus* Erect perennial herb to 1m, with tough, grooved, branched stems, hairless or bristly. Basal leaves roughly spoon-shaped in outline, but usually deeply pinnately lobed or toothed; upper leaves becoming narrower and less toothed, more or less clasping the stem. Flower heads 25-40mm in diameter, in clusters of 2-3 on thickened stalks; *florets clear pale blue, all rayed, opening in morning*. Widespread and common throughout, except the far north, but local and only naturalised in much of the north; on roadsides, waste places and dry banks. **Fl** 7-10. **Br** Common in most of England, less common elsewhere.

D Lamb's Succory *Arnoseris minima* Distinctive plant to 30cm, resembling cat's-ears (*see* below), but easily recognised in flower by the hollow flower stalks strongly swollen at the top. Leaves in rosette, pinnately lobed. Flowers yellow, 7-10mm across, and solitary. In cultivated land, usually sandy; from S Sweden southwards; local. **Fl** 6-8. **Br** Formerly in S and E England, but probably extinct.

CAT'S-EARS *Hypochoeris* Annuals or perennials with basal leaf rosettes, erect unbranched or somewhat branched stems, and yellow flowers, with ray florets. Very similar to hawkbits (*see* below) differing in having membranous scales between the florets (absent in hawkbits).

E Spotted Cat's-ear *Hypochoeris maculata* Perennial herb with all leaves in basal rosette, roughly ovate, bristly, wavy-toothed, distinctive by *blotching of dark red-purple spots* (but *see* also Spotted Hawkweed, page 286). Flower stems bristly, usually unbranched, with scale-leaves only (or none); flower heads solitary, 30-50mm in diameter, *lemon yellow*; bracts narrow, blackish. In grasslands, open woodland and cliffs; widespread except in the far north, though local, mainly on calcareous soils. **Fl** 6-8. **Br** Rare and declining, in scattered localities throughout England and Wales.

F Common Cat's-ear *Hypochoeris radicata* Perennial, with basal rosette of lanceolate to oblong, bristly, wavy-edged leaves to 25cm long; stems to 60cm, almost hairless, *usually 1-2 times branched, thickened below flower heads*, with few scale-like dark-tipped leaves along them. Flower heads 25-40mm in diameter, solitary, with bright yellow florets; bracts in bell shape, narrowed abruptly to stem, with numerous hairless, purple-tipped, individual bracts. Widespread and common generally throughout, except the far north; in grasslands, dunes and roadsides, usually avoiding strongly calcareous soils. **Fl** 6-9. **Br** Common throughout.

G Smooth Cat's-ear *Hypochoeris glabra* Rather similar to Common Cat's-ear, but smaller, to 20cm; leaves shorter, hairless or slightly bristly, and glossy. *Flower heads small, 10-15mm, with the yellow florets barely longer than the bracts*; rays about twice as long as broad, opening fully only in sunshine. From S Norway southwards; in sandy grasslands. **Fl** 6-10. **Br** Frequent only in S and E England; rare or absent elsewhere.

HAWKBITS *Leontodon* Very similar to cat's-ears, but lacking the scales between the florets.

H Autumn Hawkbit *Leontodon autumnalis* Hairless or slightly hairy (*with unforked hairs*), perennial herb, with basal rosette of leaves and *2-3 times branched, erect flower stems*. Basal leaves variable, oblong-lanceolate, usually deeply pinnately lobed, sometimes wavy-edged, with few simple hairs, or hairless; stems bear *numerous small scale-leaves just below heads*. Flower heads 12-35mm in diameter, erect in bud, yellow, with *involucre gradually tapering into stem*. In dry grasslands, throughout, usually on more acid soils, common. **Fl** 6-10. **Br** Common throughout.
Ssp *pratensis* has the bracts covered in long dark hairs; it occurs mainly in mountain pastures, including Britain.

I Rough Hawkbit *Leontodon hispidus* Perennial herb, *covered with rough white hairs*. Basal rosette has oblong-lanceolate leaves, narrowing to base, wavy-toothed, *very hairy*. Flower stems to 40cm, hairy throughout with forked hairs, unbranched; flower heads 25-40mm in diameter, *solitary*, with golden yellow florets much longer than bracts; involucre narrows abruptly into stalk. In dry grasslands, usually calcareous; throughout the area except the extreme north. **Fl** 6-9. **Br** Widespread and common except in N Scotland.

J Lesser Hawkbit *Leontodon taraxacoides* Somewhat intermediate between the above 2 species. Stems bristly below, hairless above. Leaves variable, wavy-toothed to pinnately lobed, *sparsely bristly* with forked *bristles. Flowers solitary on unbranched leafless stalks*, drooping in bud; heads 20-25mm across; bracts hairless except for midribs. From Holland southwards (and naturalised further north); in dry grassy areas, especially sandy or calcareous. **Fl** 6-10. **Br** Common and widespread, except in the extreme north.

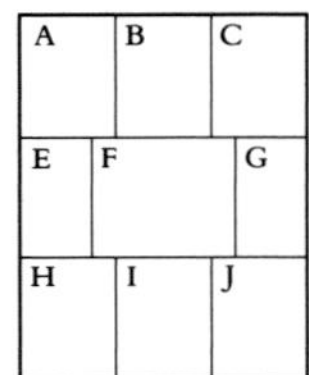

A **Carthamus**

B **Spanish Oysterplant**

C **Chicory**

E **Spotted Cat's-ear**

F **Common Cat's-ear**

G **Smooth Cat's-ear**

H **Autumn Hawkbit**

I **Rough Hawkbit**

J **Lesser Hawkbit**

A
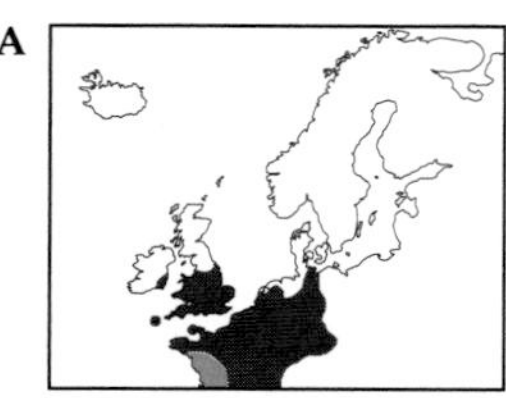

B
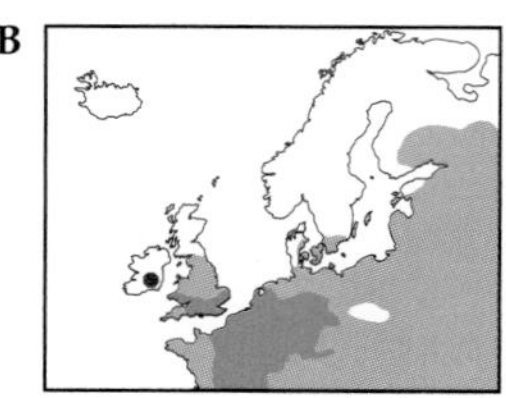

C
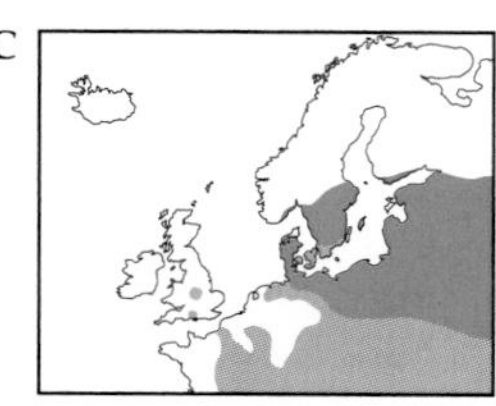

F
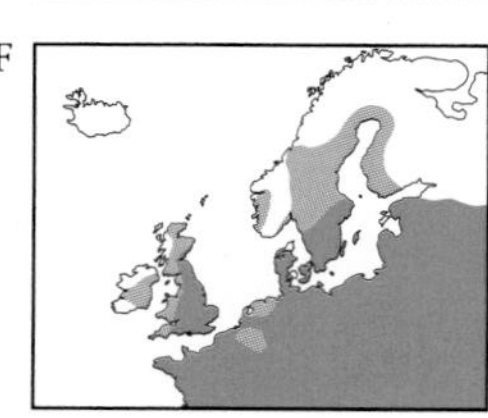

K

A Bristly Oxtongue *Picris echioides* Erect annual or biennial, with furrowed bristly branched stems, to 90cm. Basal leaves oblong, narrowing into stalk; upper leaves narrower, with clasping basal leaves *covered with robust swollen-based bristles* (**a**) (only Teasel leaves look at all similar, *see* page 248). Flower heads 20-25mm in diameter, in loose groups, florets yellow; outermost 3-5 bracts leaf-like, triangular, much broader than, but not as long as, inner bracts. Locally common from Denmark southwards, though not native over northern part of range; in grassy areas, disturbed ground and drier coastal habitats, usually on heavy soils. **Fl** 6-10. **Br** Locally common in S Britain, especially near coasts, but rare further north.

B Hawkweed Oxtongue *Picris hieracioides* Similar in form to Bristly Oxtongue, but *bristles not so swollen-based; lower leaves lanceolate* and wavy-edged (**b**). *Outer flower bracts small and spreading*, not large and erect. In rough grassy places, especially near the coast, but absent from much of NW Scandinavia. **Fl** 7-10. **Br** Common only in SE England, increasingly rare to the north and west; absent from Scotland.

C Viper's-grass *Scorzonera humilis* Perennial herb, with erect or ascending, usually unbranched, downy stems, from a black, scaly rootstock. Basal leaves elliptical to lanceolate, up to 30cm long, untoothed, long-pointed, and narrowing to base which is covered by sheath; stem leaves narrow, but with broader clasping bases. Flower heads solitary, 25-30mm in diameter, florets yellow; bracts have woolly bases, and are arranged in many overlapping rows (compare with *Tragopogon* species, *see* below). Widespread, but absent from N Scandinavia; in damp meadows and marshy areas. **Fl** 5-7. **Br** Very rare, now in Dorset only.

D *Scorzonera laciniata* Rather similar to Viper's Grass, with *pinnately divided leaves*, and smaller flowers. Mainland Europe from Belgium southwards; in dry grasslands. **Fl** 5-6. **Br** Absent.

E *Sorzonera purpurea* Very narrow leaves, and *lilac to purple flowers*. Mainland Europe, from central Germany southwards; in dry grassy places. **Fl** 5-7. **Br** Absent.

F Goat's-beard, Jack-go-to-bed-at-noon *Tragopogon pratensis* Variable annual to perennial, with erect, simple or slightly branched, stems to 70cm or more, downy when young, hairless and rather grey-green later. Lower leaves narrow linear-lanceolate, to 30cm, with distinct keel, broadened and slightly clasping at base; stem leaves similar but smaller, with long fine point. Flower heads solitary, long-stalked, to 5cm in diameter, with yellow florets. Bracts 8-10, in 1 row only (compare with *Scorzonera, see* above). Fruit is a large white 'clock', to 8cm in diameter.
Two subspecies occur in N Europe.
Ssp *pratensis* has *involucral bracts as long as or shorter than florets*, and the flowers remain open in dull weather. Throughout most of Europe in grassland. Ssp *minor* has *flower bracts much longer than florets*, and flowers close in dull weather and at midday. Similar habitats; W Europe only. **Fl** 5-7. **Br** Ssp *minor* is the widespread subspecies, frequent throughout England and Wales; rare elsewhere.
Ssp *pratensis* is not native.

G *Tragopogon dubius* Similar to the other *Tragopogon* species, but smaller, and with flower stalks markedly inflated below flower heads. Grassy places and wood-margins; from N France southwards. **Fl** 6-7. **Br** Absent.

H Salsify *Tragopopon porrifolius* Similar in general structure to Goat's-beard, but with purple to lilac flower heads subtended by 8 bracts. Native to the Mediterranean region, but widely cultivated and occasionally naturalised as far north as S Scandinavia; in grassy places. **Fl** 5-8. **Br** Casual, or very locally naturalised, mainly in the south and west.

SOW-THISTLES *Sonchus* Annual or perennial herbs with stout, hollow, milk-containing stems. Leaves pinnately lobed or with wavy, spiny margins; stem leaves clasping. Flower heads in umbel-like clusters.

I Prickly Sow-thistle *Sonchus asper* Erect, hairless annual or biennial (except for inflorescence, which may be glandular hairy), to 1m, with simple or branched stem. Lower leaves roughly spoon-shaped in outline, sometimes pinnately lobed, with triangular, toothed lobes, and *rounded auricles at base*, deeply toothed all round margins, *glossy green above*; upper leaves narrower, firmly clasping stem with rounded bases (**i**). Flower heads 20-25mm in diameter, golden yellow. Very common in cultivated ground and waste places; throughout. **Fl** 6-10. **Br** Common throughout.

J Smooth Sow-thistle *Sonchus oleraceus* Rather similar to above, but leaves are usually pinnately lobed, with triangular lobes, and end-lobe distinctly wider than next pair of leaflets down; *auricles at base of leaves pointed*, not rounded. *Leaves matt*, not glossy, on upper surface (**j**). Flowers pale yellow. In similar habitats; throughout. **Fl** 6-10. **Br** Common throughout.

K Marsh Sow-thistle *Sonchus palustris* Tall robust perennial to 2.5m (occasionally even taller), with stout erect 4-angled hollow stems, glandular hairy above and hairless below. Basal leaves oblong, with *arrow-shaped bases*, pinnately lobed blade, and a long pointed terminal lobe; margins finely spiny-toothed, leaves hairless; upper leaves narrow, with long, pointed, clasping basal lobes. Flower heads large, 3-4cm in diameter, and pale yellow; involucral bracts covered with *blackish sticky glandular hairs*. In marshes, fens, and uppermost parts of salt-marshes; from S Scandinavia southwards; local. **Fl** 7-9. **Br** Only in S and E England, from E Anglia to Hampshire; very local.

L *Sonchus maritimus* Similar to Marsh Sow-thistle, but shorter, to 60cm; leaves less deeply divided; base of flowers and upper part of stalks *covered with white down*. Damp coastal habitats, NW France southwards. **Fl** 6-8. **Br** Absent.

M Perennial Sow-thistle *Sonchus arvensis* Similar in form to Marsh Sow-thistle. Differs in that the leaves have *rounded bases*, and are pinnately lobed with round short lobes. Florets deep yellow; bracts and inflorescence branches all covered with long, *yellowish, glandular hairs*. Widespread and common throughout on arable and disturbed land, and coastal sands. **Fl** 7-10. **Br** Common throughout.

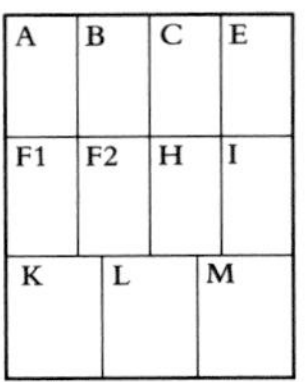

A Bristly Oxtongue

B Hawkweed Oxtongue

C Viper's-grass

E *Scorzonera purpurea*

F 1 Goat's-beard ssp *minor*

F 2 Goat's-beard ssp *pratensis*

H Salsify

I Prickly Sow-thistle

K Marsh Sow-thistle

L *Sonchus maritimus*

M Perennial Sow-thistle

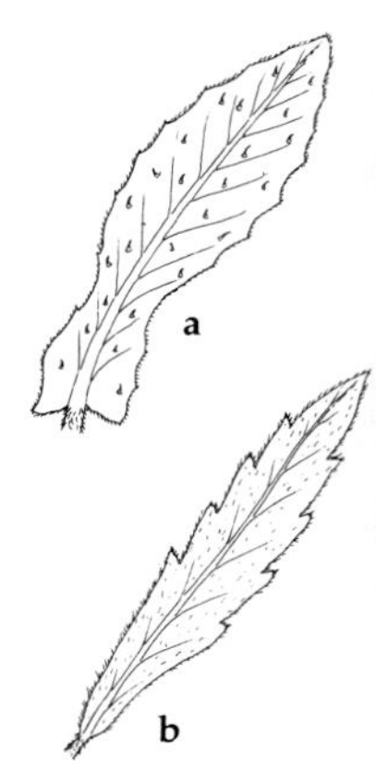

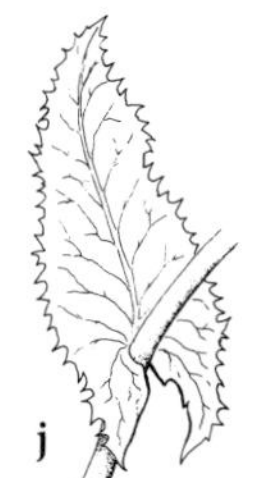

B

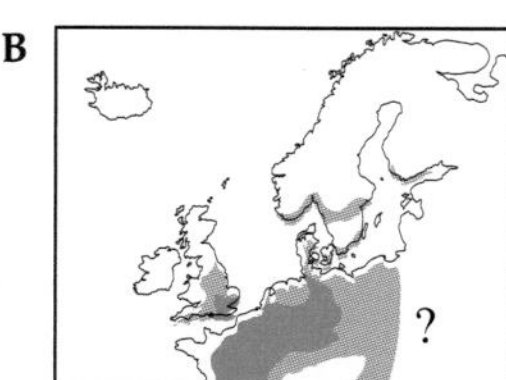

E

F

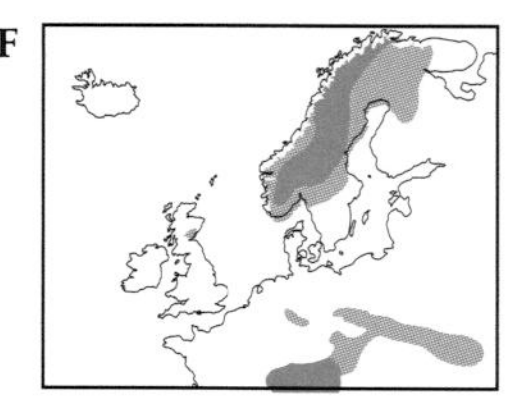

G

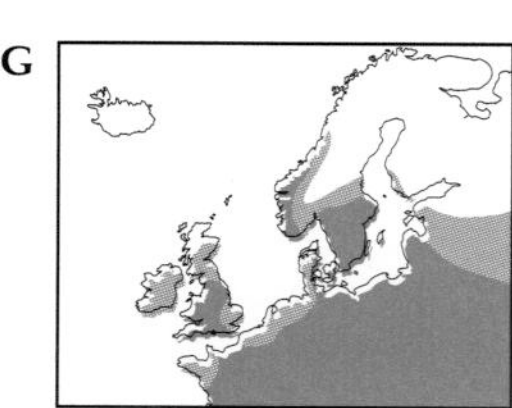

LETTUCES *Lactuca* Annual or perennial erect herbs, with milky latex. Flower heads with all ray florets; involucre cylindrical.

A *Lactuca sibirica* Hairless erect perennial, to 1m, with unbranched leafy stems. Leaves lanceolate, usually with distant teeth or lobed, with clasping bases, or short stalks. Flower heads large, to 30mm, lilac-blue. In open woods and scrub, especially on river-gravels; in N and E Scandinavia. **Fl** 7-9. **Br** Absent.

B **Prickly Lettuce** *Lactuca serriola* Stiffly erect hairless annual or perennial to 1.8m, branched above. *Leaves stiffly erect*, oblong-lanceolate, lower ones usually pinnately divided, with narrow, well-separated lobes, hairless but spiny on pale midrib underneath, and on margins; upper leaves less deeply divided, with clasping bases; all thick and waxy grey-green. Flower heads in loose inflorescence, with branches at acute angle to main stem; individual heads 11-13mm in diameter, with 7-12 yellow florets. On waste ground, roadsides and railways; widespread except in much of Scandinavia. **Fl** 7-9. **Br** Common in the south and east, but rare or absent elsewhere.

C **Least Lettuce** *Lactuca saligna* Slender annual to 1m. Leaves linear-lanceolate, bases arrow-shaped and clasping untoothed, *held vertically. Flower heads in a narrow spike-like inflorescence with short branches;* florets pale yellow, 10-15mm long, reddish below. From S England and central Germany southwards; dry banks near the sea; very local. **Fl** 7-8. **Br** Very rare and decreasing; near coasts in SE England.

D **Great Lettuce** *Lactuca virosa* Similar to Prickly Lettuce, but differs in that it is taller, to 2m, and stouter, often purple-flushed; *leaves spreading* not erect, with rounded clasping lobes at base, pressed to stem; *leaf lobes broad*. On waste ground, roadsides and dry sandy places; from Belgium and Germany southwards. **Fl** 7-9. **Br** Frequent in SE England, increasingly local to the north and west, absent from Ireland.

E **Blue Lettuce** *Lactuca perennis* Erect hairless perennial to 80cm, branched above. Leaves grey-green, pinnately lobed with very narrow, pointed segments. Flower heads few, in a branched inflorescence, long-stalked, 3-4cm in diameter, with bluish-purple florets. In rocky and dry places, on lime-rich soils, from Belgium southwards. **Fl** 5-8. **Br** Absent.

F **Alpine Sow-thistle** *Cicerbita alpina* Tall perennial herb with erect, furrowed stems to 2m, reddish-glandular above. Lower leaves pinnately divided, with large, triangular, end-lobe; upper leaves narrower, with winged stalks broadening out into heart-shaped clasping base. Flower heads 2cm in diameter, pale violet-blue, in long raceme, with sticky hairy bracts and stalks. Widespread in N Scandinavia in moist shady and grassy habitats; confined to mountains further south. **Fl** 7-9. **Br** Very rare, in Scottish Highlands only.

G **Wall Lettuce** *Mycelis muralis* Erect hairless perennial to 1m. Lower leaves pinnately lobed, lyre-shaped, with a large end-lobe, and winged stalks; upper leaves smaller, less divided, with clasping bases; all leaves thin in texture, often red-tinged. Flower heads small, 7-10mm in diameter, in a large open inflorescence with branches at right angles to main stem; florets yellow, usually with 5 rays; involucre of bracts narrowly cylindrical. In woods, on old walls and rocks, often on lime-rich soil; throughout except the far north. **Fl** 6-9. **Br** Throughout, though less common in Scotland and Ireland.

DANDELIONS *Taraxacum* Perennial herbs with tap root, a basal rosette of leaves, and *solitary flower heads on leafless hollow stems with abundant milky latex;* florets bright yellow, all rayed. Although easy to recognise as a group, dandelions are extremely difficult to recognise individually – over 1,200 species are recorded from Europe altogether. The description below is that of *T. officinale*, the Common Dandelion, but this name includes numerous microspecies within it. Readers should refer to specialist texts for more details. There are 7 more or less clearly defined groups that occur in N Europe:

Section: *Taraxacum*

H **Common Dandelion** *Taraxacum officinale* Variable perennial, with a basal rosette of pinnately lobed leaves, roughly spoon-shaped in outline, with winged stalks. Flower heads 2-6cm in diameter, on stalks to 40cm, rays usually having a brown or grey stripe below. Outer flower bracts curved back. Widespread and common throughout in grasslands. **Fl** 3-10. **Br** Common throughout.

Section: *Arctica* A very small group, with a few Arctic representatives. Flower heads small, outer bracts pressed to involucre, achenes blackish.

Section: *Ceratophora* A very small group. Leaves dark green; *outer flower bracts erect, with a distinct horn* (**h1**); achenes brownish. Scandinavia and Alpine areas.

Section: *Spectabilia* A large group of usually robust plants, *leaves often dark-spotted*, with *reddish midribs;* outer bracts erect or appressed, usually without a horn (**h2**). Mainly in hill and mountain areas.

Section: *Palustria* *Leaves often narrow*, lobed or unlobed. *Outer bracts often purplish, with distinct pale margins*, no horns, appressed. Common in wet places generally.

Section: *Obliqua* A group of 2 species only. *Flower heads often darker yellow, with red-purple stripes on rays* often curved inwards. Bracts horned, appressed (**h3**). In sandy coastal areas.

Section: *Erythrosperma* A large group. Generally small plants. Leaves often deeply divided. *Outer bracts often greyish, with paler margins*, usually appressed, with distinct horn. (**h4**) Common; widespread in dry grasslands.

I **Chondrilla** *Chondrilla juncea* Erect greyish plant to 1m, with ascending branches. Basal leaves deeply toothed, soon dying; upper leaves lanceolate. Flower heads numerous, with 9-12 florets, about 10mm in diameter, yellow. In dry open habitats, local, in France and Germany. **Fl** 7-9. **Br** Absent.

J **Nipplewort** *Lapsana communis* Erect annual to 1m, with leafy much-branched stems lacking latex. Basal leaves oval, often pinnately lobed with large oval end-lobe; upper leaves oval to diamond-shaped. Flower heads small, 1-2cm in diameter, much-branched loose inflorescence; florets all rayed, 8-15, yellow, short; involucre narrowly cylindrical, with 1 row of equal bracts and a few shorter ones, nipple-like in bud. Widespread and common throughout; in waste and cultivated ground, woodland margins, etc. **Fl** 7-10. **Br** Common throughout.

A	B	C	D
F	G	I	
E	H1		
H2	H3		

A *Lactuca sibirica*

B **Prickly Lettuce**

C **Least Lettuce**

D **Great Lettuce**

F **Alpine Sow-thistle**

G **Wall Lettuce**

I **Chondrilla**

E **Blue Lettuce**

H **1 Common Dandelion**

H **2** *Taraxacum* section: *Ceratophora* Arctic Sweden

H **3** *Taraxacum* section: *Taraxacum*

h1

h2

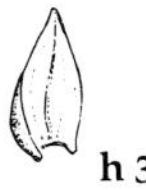

h3

h4

A
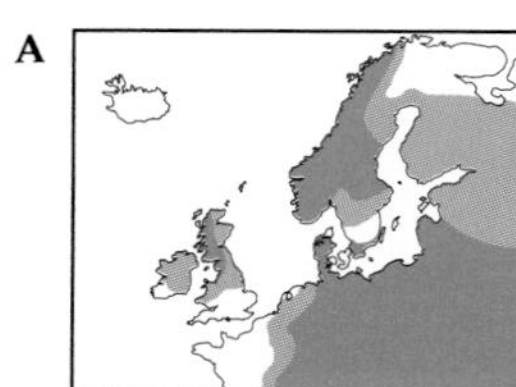

B
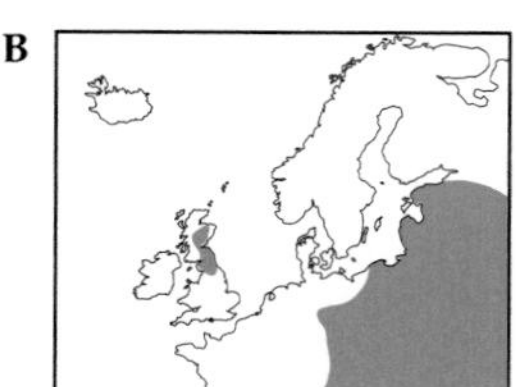

E
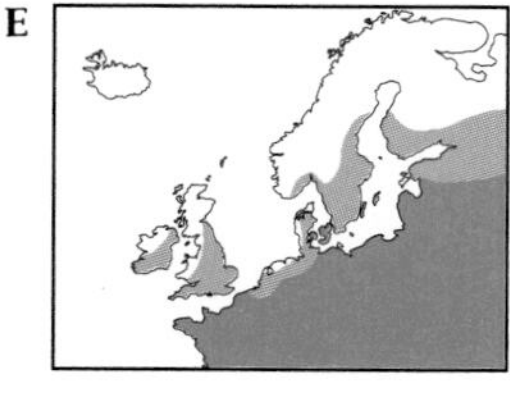

F
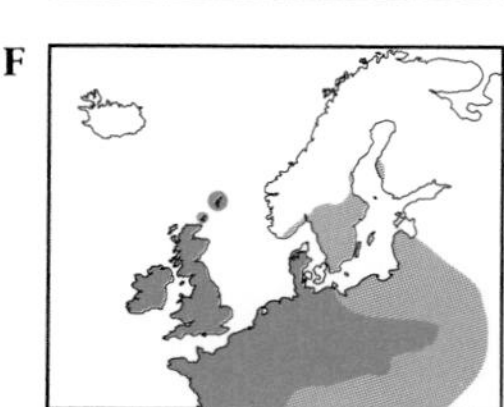

HAWK'S-BEARDS *Crepis* A small group of erect plants, annual to perennial, with branched stems. Leaves alternate, lobed or pinnately divided with backward-pointing lobes. Florets all rayed, yellow, strap-shaped; flower bracts in 2 rows, with outer ones shorter, often spreading.

(1) Plants with leaves toothed but not lobed.

A **Marsh Hawk's-beard** *Crepis paludosa* Perennial herb with erect *hairless stem* to 90cm, branched above. Basal and lower stem leaves lanceolate to ovate, narrowed into a *short*, winged stalk (**a**); upper leaves narrower, clasping, with *arrow-shaped bases*; all leaves shiny, hairless and wavy-toothed. Flower heads 15-25mm in diameter, in few-flowered clusters; florets yellow, bracts woolly with black glandular hairs. Throughout N Europe, though local; in wet meadows and woods. **Fl** 7-9. **Br** N Britain only, from N England and Wales northwards.

B **Northern Hawk's-beard** *Crepis mollis* Similar to Marsh Hawk's-beard, differing in that its basal leaves are narrowed into a *long*, winged stalk (**b**); middle and upper leaves clasping stem with *rounded bases*; bracts of flower heads sparsely hairy. In damp and shady places, from Denmark southwards, very local. **Fl** 7-8. **Br** A northern species, from N England northwards only.

C *Crepis praemorsa* Rather similar to Northern Hawk's-beard, but *leaves all basal, spoon-shaped*, stalked, *with margins rolled under*. Flower bracts with short pale hairs, or nearly hairless. Scattered, mainly NE Europe. **Fl** 5-7. **Br** Absent.

D *Crepis tectorum* Annual or biennial to 1m. Basal leaves lanceolate, toothed and sometimes lobed; upper leaves lanceolate and unstalked. *Flower bracts hairy, especially with appressed hairs on inner faces*. Widespread in mainland Europe in sandy disturbed ground. **Fl** 6-7. **Br** Absent.

(2) Plants with leaves pinnately lobed to some extent.

E **Rough Hawk's-beard** *Crepis biennis* Biennial herb with an erect *roughly hairy stem* to 1.2m, often purplish towards base. Basal leaves stalked, to 30cm, irregularly pinnately lobed with large end-lobe; stem leaves similar but smaller, semi-clasping, *without markedly arrow-shaped bases*. Flower heads 25-30mm in diameter, in loose groups, florets yellow; inner flower bracts dark hairy outside, downy inside; outer bracts narrow, spreading, without membranous margins. Widespread, though absent or obviously introduced in the north, in grasslands, roadsides and waste ground. **Fl** 6-7. **Br** Common, and probably native, in SE England; rare, and probably introduced elsewhere.

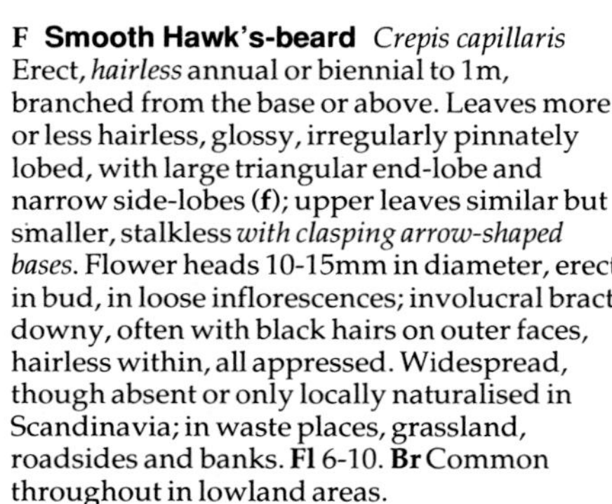

F **Smooth Hawk's-beard** *Crepis capillaris* Erect, *hairless* annual or biennial to 1m, branched from the base or above. Leaves more or less hairless, glossy, irregularly pinnately lobed, with large triangular end-lobe and narrow side-lobes (**f**); upper leaves similar but smaller, stalkless *with clasping arrow-shaped bases*. Flower heads 10-15mm in diameter, erect in bud, in loose inflorescences; involucral bracts downy, often with black hairs on outer faces, hairless within, all appressed. Widespread, though absent or only locally naturalised in Scandinavia; in waste places, grassland, roadsides and banks. **Fl** 6-10. **Br** Common throughout in lowland areas.

G **Beaked Hawk's-beard** *Crepis vesicaria* Similar to Smooth Hawk's-beard, but *downier*; leaves have broader lobes (**g**), *downy all over*. Flower heads 15-25mm in diameter, *florets orange-yellow*, outer ones striped reddish outside; outer involucral bracts spreading. Fruit have long beaks. From Holland southwards, in grasslands, waste ground and roadsides; common. **Fl** 5-7. **Br** Probably not native; common and widespread in England, except in the north; absent from Scotland; rare in Ireland.

H **Stinking Hawk's-beard** *Crepis foetida* Similar to above 2 species, but a shorter plant to 50cm, *smelling strongly of bitter almonds when bruised*. Rosette leaves very hairy, *flower heads drooping in bud*. From Belgium and S England southwards, on shingle beaches and waste ground; very local. **Fl** 6-8. **Br** Very rare, now in Kent only.

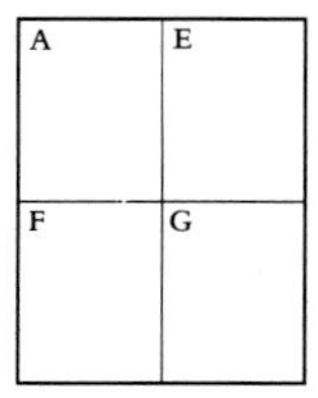

A **Marsh Hawk's-beard**

E **Rough Hawk's-beard**

F **Smooth Hawk's-beard**

G **Beaked Hawk's-beard**

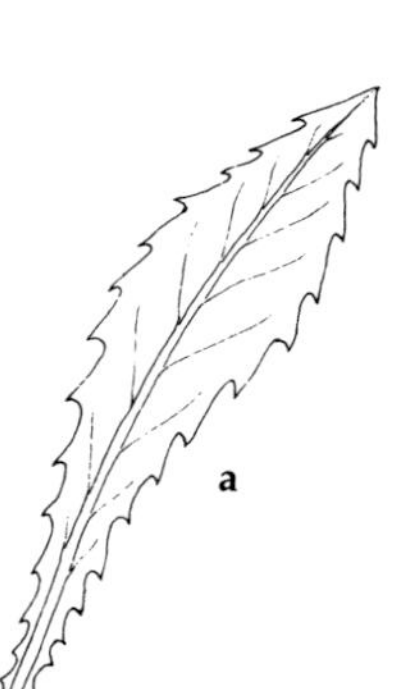

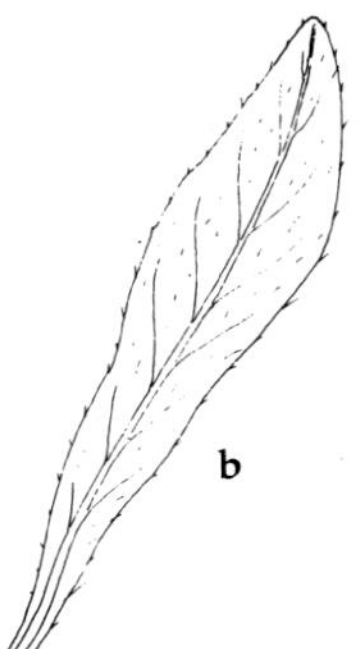

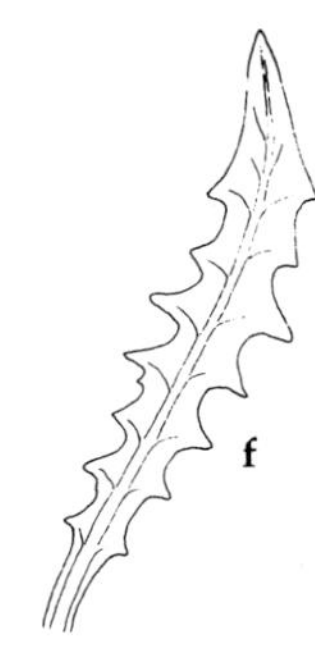

g

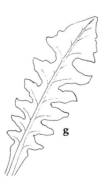

A

?

F

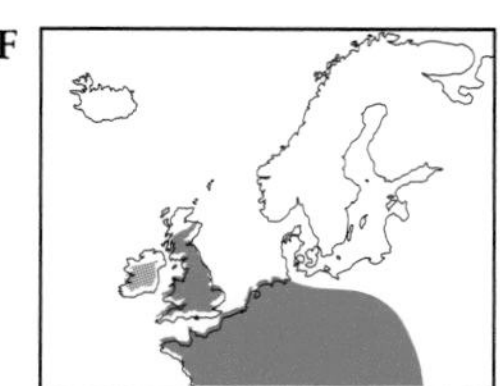

HAWKWEEDS *Hieracium* A large and highly complex group of plants, with several hundred very similar species. Perennials, without stolons (except in subgenus *Pilosella*), with erect, usually leafy, stems. Leaves toothed but not pinnately lobed. Flower heads with rays only, strap-shaped, usually yellow; flower bracts narrow, unequal, in overlapping rows. Identification is exceptionally difficult, and those interested in a more detailed treatment are referred to *Flora Europaea Vol. 4*. A very small selection of the more recognisable species is given.

Hieracium Subgenus: *Pilosella*

A **Mouse-ear Hawkweed** *Hieracium pilosella* Distinctive perennial herb *with leafy runners*, forming extensive patches, and erect leafless stems to 30cm. Leaves in rosettes, spoon-shaped, to 80mm long, *green and hairy above, but white-downy below*. Flower heads solitary, 15-25mm wide, *florets lemon yellow*, red-striped below. Throughout, except the extreme north; in dry grassy places, banks and heaths. **Fl** 5-8. **Br** Common throughout.

B **Orange Hawkweed, Fox and Cubs** *Hieracium aurantiacum* Similar to Mouse-ear Hawkweed, except the stem is taller, to 40cm, with *blackish hairs*, and bears several leaves. Flowers in clusters of 2-12 heads; *florets orange-red*, bracts covered with dark hairs. Widespread through N Europe, though probably not native in many western areas; local in grasslands, on banks, roadsides and often in mountains. **Fl** 6-7. **Br** Not native, but widely naturalised.

Hieracium Subgenus: *Hieracium*

Section: *Alpina*

C *Hieracium alpinum* Distinctive species, with numerous *rosette leaves covered with shaggy hairs*; stem leaves few or none. *Flower heads solitary, large, to 4cm*, on stalks up to 20cm; florets yellow, often hairy at tip and on the back; bracts silky-downy with white and black hairs (**c**). Grassy and rocky mountain habitats; mainly Scandinavian, but also in scattered mountain areas further south. **Fl** 7-9. **Br** Rare, in Scottish Highlands.

Section: *Umbellata*

D **Leafy Hawkweed** *Hieracium umbellatum* Tall erect perennial plant to 80cm, softly hairy. *Leaves all on stem*, numerous, stalkless, narrowly linear-lanceolate, barely toothed, sometimes with rolled-under margins. Flower heads clustered in an *umbel-like inflorescence*, roughly flat-topped; bracts hairless, with recurved tips, blackish green (**d**). Widespread almost throughout; in woods, roadsides, heaths and banks, on dry soil. **Fl** 6-10. **Br** Throughout, except the extreme north.

Section: *Vulgata*

E **Common Hawkweed** *Hieracium vulgatum* Erect perennial to 80cm, with lower part of stem hairy. Basal leaves ovate, toothed, stalked, in a loose rosette; stem leaves 1-3, unstalked. Inflorescence made up of up to 20 yellow heads, not all at the same height, with woolly but not glandular stalks. Involucral bracts glandular, sparsely hairy (**e**). In woods, banks, shady rocks, walls and heaths; throughout except the extreme north. **Fl** 7-9. **Br** Rather common in N Britain, rarer in the south, and absent from the extreme south.

F **Spotted Hawkweed** *Hieracium maculatum* Perennial, with stems to 50cm, reddish. Leaves oblong, long-stalked, *with numerous dark purplish spots* or blotches, usually toothed, stiffly hairy. Flower heads in loose inflorescence, bracts hairy and glandular (**f**). Spotted leaves are distinctive (together with some related species), though Spotted Cat's-ear (*see* page 278) is similar. In grassy and rocky habitats, often calcareous; absent from the north. **Fl** 6-8. **Br** Scattered through England and Wales.

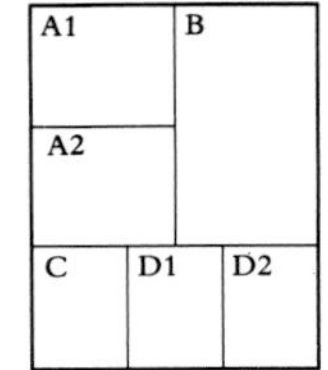

A **1 Mouse-ear Hawkweed**

B **Orange Hawkweed**

A **2** *Hieracium peleterianum*

C *Hieracium alpinum*

D **1** *Hieracium Sabauda* section

D **2** *Hieracium umbellatum*

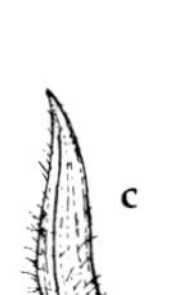

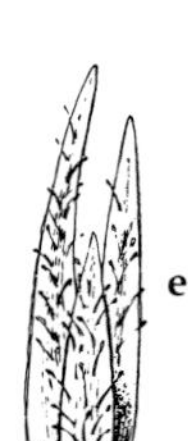

B

C

D

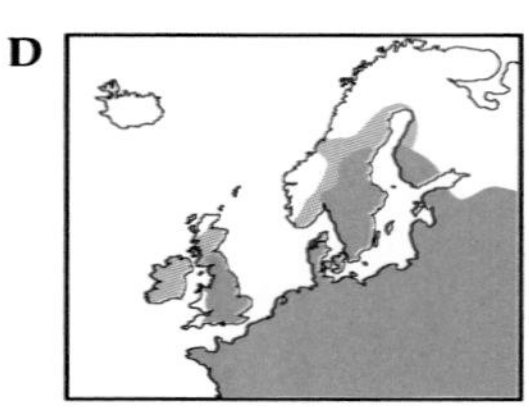

F

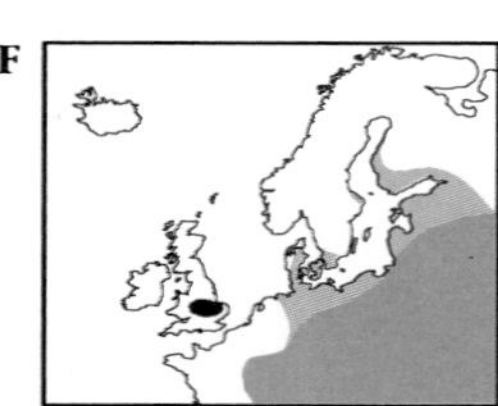

Order Monocotyledons

The second major group of flowering plants, generally easy to distinguish from Dicotyledons by the presence of only 1 seed-leaf in the developing seedling; flowers with parts in multiples of 3, most commonly 3 or 6; and leaves with veins that are roughly parallel. The order includes many familiar bulbous plants, especially in the lily family.

Water-plantain Family
Alismataceae

A small family of aquatic herbs. Leaves usually mainly basal and untoothed. Flowers have 3 separate petals and sepals, distinct from each other, and numerous carpels ripening into single-seeded achenes.

A **Arrowhead** *Sagittaria sagittifolia* Erect hairless aquatic perennial to 90cm. Aerial leaves distinctive, broadly arrow-shaped, long-stalked, erect, to 20cm long; submerged leaves linear and translucent; floating leaves, if present, oval to lanceolate. Flowers in a whorled raceme, individual flowers white, with purple blotch at base of petals, 20-25mm in diameter; lower flowers female with numerous carpels, upper flowers male. Widespread and generally common, though rare in the north; in still or slow-flowing water with muddy substrates. **Fl** 7-8. **Br** Locally common in lowlands of England and Wales; absent from Scotland; rare in Ireland.

B **Lesser Water-plantain** *Baldellia ranunculoides* Variable plant, erect, ascending or spreading, though rarely taller than 20cm. Leaves mostly basal, linear-lanceolate, to 10cm long, tapered at both ends, with long stalks. *Flowers solitary* (especially in creeping plants) or in few-flowered clusters, *petals pale pink*, flowers 12-16mm wide, with numerous carpels. From S Scandinavia southwards, widespread though local; in fens, ponds, ditches and dune-slacks, etc., often calcareous. **Fl** 6-8. **Br** Locally common in the south, becoming rarer in the north, absent from the far north.

C **Floating Water-plantain** *Luronium natans* *Aquatic*, with horizontal stems, floating or submerged, rooting at nodes. Floating leaves are elliptical, blunt, to 40mm long on long stalks; submerged leaves linear, very narrow, to 10cm. Flowers normally solitary, long-stalked, 12-15mm in diameter, *white with yellow central spot*. From S Scandinavia southwards, local; in lakes and canals with rather acid water. **Fl** 7-8. **Br** Very local, mainly in Wales and NW England; introduced elsewhere.

D **Common Water-plantain** *Alisma plantago-aquatica* Erect hairless aquatic perennial to 1m. Leaves elliptical to ovate, up to 20cm, long-stalked, with rounded or wedge-shaped base, emergent (**d**). *Flowers in much-branched whorled inflorescence*, small (to 1cm in diameter), white to pale lilac, with yellow centre; carpels numerous, *with style arising from below the middle of each*. Common in water and on mud; throughout except the far north. **Fl** 6-8. **Br** Common generally, though rarer to the north, absent from the far north.

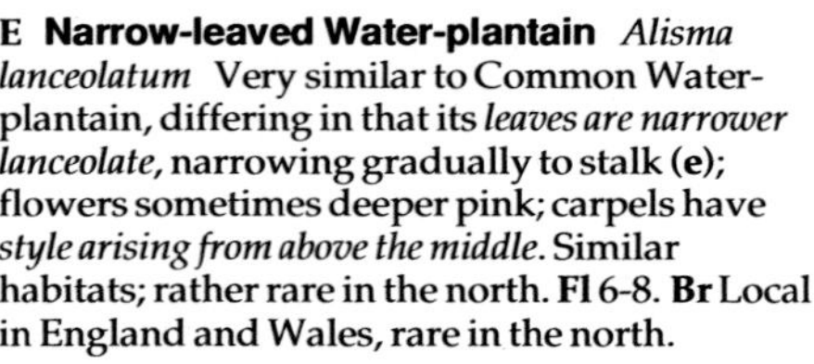

E **Narrow-leaved Water-plantain** *Alisma lanceolatum* Very similar to Common Water-plantain, differing in that its *leaves are narrower lanceolate*, narrowing gradually to stalk (**e**); flowers sometimes deeper pink; carpels have *style arising from above the middle*. Similar habitats; rather rare in the north. **Fl** 6-8. **Br** Local in England and Wales, rare in the north.

F **Ribbon-leaved Water-plantain** *Alisma gramineum* Similar to above, but a smaller plant, with *narrow ribbon-like leaves* (**f**) (occasionally with expanded blade). Flowers smaller, about 6mm in diameter; carpels broadest near top, with a *spirally coiled style*. From Denmark southwards in ponds and wet places; local. **Fl** 7-9. **Br** Very rare and declining.

G *Caldesia parnassifolia* Similar to the water-plantains, but leaves ovate (**g**) with heart-shaped base (like Grass-of-Parnassus, *see* page 94). Flowers white, 8-12mm in diameter, in whorls. From Germany and N France southwards; similar habitats. **Fl** 7-9. **Br** Absent.

H **Starfruit** *Damasonium alisma* Annual plant to 30cm. Leaves long-stalked, floating, blunt-tipped, heart-shaped at base, to 50mm long. Flowers white, about 6mm in diameter, in 1 to several whorls at top of stem. *Fruit distinctive*, with 6-10 carpels *spreading in a star-like whorl*. From S England and W France southwards; in ponds, especially where grazed and muddy. **Fl** 6-8. **Br** Very rare in a few localities in SE England only.

Flowering Rush Family
Butomaceae

Perennial aquatic herbs, with leaves all linear, basal only. Flowers in terminal umbels, with 3 petals, 3 sepals and 9 stamens.

I **Flowering Rush** *Butomus umbellatus* Very distinctive plant when in flower. Erect hairless aquatic perennial to 1.5m. Leaves all basal, linear, pointed, 3-angled, almost as tall as flower stems. Flowers pink, 15-27mm in diameter, in terminal umbel with brownish bracts, on tall rounded stems. In still and slow-moving fresh or slightly brackish water; throughout, except the far north. **Fl** 7-9. **Br** Locally common in lowland England and Wales; rare or absent elsewhere.

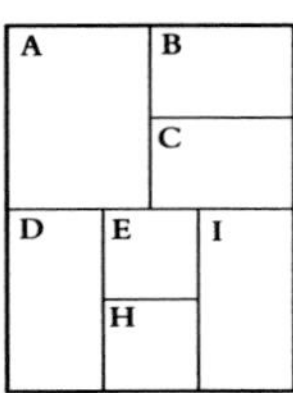

A **Arrowhead**

B **Lesser Water-plantain**

C **Floating Water-plantain**

D **Common Water-plantain**

E **Narrow-leaved Water-plantain**

I **Flowering Rush**

H **Starfruit** showing fruit and leaves

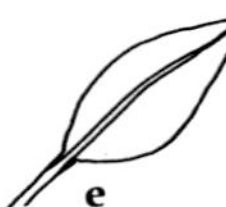

A

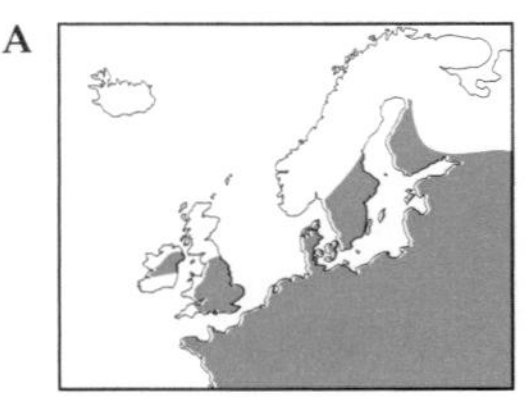

B

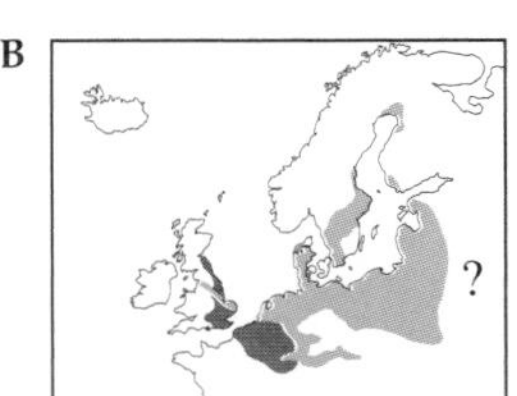

C

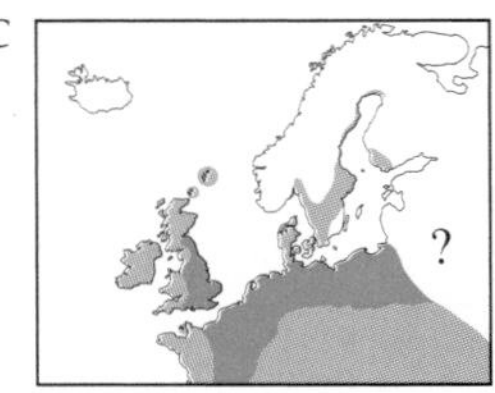

F

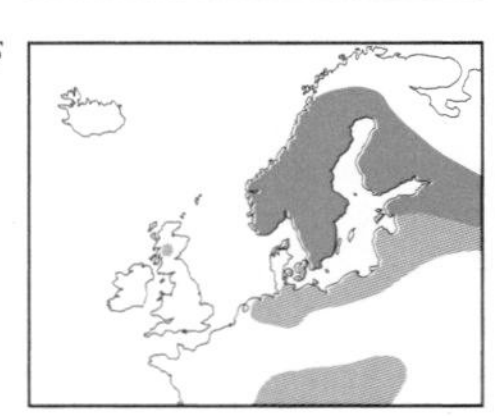

H

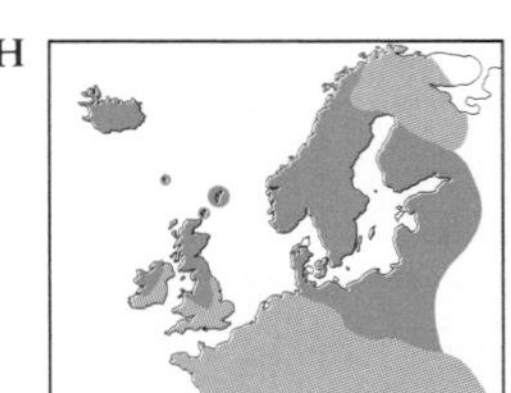

Frogbit Family
Hydrocharitaceae

Submerged or floating aquatic herbs. Flowers with 3 sepals, 3 petals and a variable number of stamens.

A **Frogbit** *Hydrocharis morsus-ranae* Hairless floating plant with runners producing tufts of leaves. Leaves rounded and kidney-shaped, 2-3cm in diameter, often bronze-green, long-stalked, with large stipules. Flowers long-stalked, 2cm in diameter, white with crumpled petals, and yellow spot near base of each; female flowers solitary, male flowers 2-3 together. Widespread throughout except the far north; in ditches, ponds and other still waters. **Fl** 6-8. **Br** Local in England, rare or absent elsewhere.

B **Water-soldier** *Stratiotes aloides* Stoloniferous aquatic perennial, submerged for much of year but rising to the surface to flower. Leaves in a coarse rosette, like a pineapple top, numerous lanceolate, to 40cm, rigid, spine-edged, slightly brownish green. Flowers erect, females solitary, males clustered 2-3 together, 3-4cm in diameter, 3-petalled, white. Widespread though absent from the far north and parts of the west, occasionally naturalised outside its range; occurs in ponds, canals and ditches. **Fl** 6-8. **Br** Probably native, and locally abundant, only in E England; rare and naturalised elsewhere. British native plants are all female.

C **Canadian Pondweed** *Elodea canadensis* Submerged perennial aquatic herb, with brittle stems to 3m long (usually much less). Leaves translucent green, up to 10mm long (occasionally more), *blunt*, oblong to linear (**c**), unstalked, in whorls of 3. Male and female plants separate, males very rare: female flowers 5mm in diameter, with 3 tiny white to purplish petals floating on long thin stalks. Naturalised in still and slow-moving waters throughout N Europe except for Arctic areas, originally from N America. **Fl** 5-10. **Br** Naturalised throughout.

D *Elodea nuttallii* Differs from Canadian Pondweed in having longer leaves to 18mm, *tapered to a point* (**d**), more recurved, *with a pair of brownish, fringed scales on the upper surface* near the base. Naturalised, from N America, in similar habitats to Canadian Pondweed, in W Europe, still spreading. **Fl** 5-9. **Br** Mainly southern, but still spreading.

E **Hydrilla** *Hydrilla verticillata* Very similar to the above pondweeds. *Leaves in whorls of 3-8, linear* and faintly toothed at the tips. Flowers very rare. Naturalised locally from N Germany southwards (tropical in origin). **Br** Lake District and W Ireland only; very rare.

Scheuzeriaceae

Perennial herbs with creeping rhizomes. Flowers bisexual with 6 sepal-like segments. Only 1 European representive.

F **Rannoch-rush** *Scheuzeria palustris* Erect perennial to 40cm from creeping rhizomes. Leaves alternate, up to 40cm long, linear, blunt, with conspicuous hole at tip. Flowers 4-5mm in diameter, greenish yellow, in clusters of 3-10 on a stalk that is shorter than leaves. Fruit distinctive with 3 fused, inflated carpels. Throughout N Europe in wet bogs, though local and absent from some areas. **Fl** 6-8. **Br** Very rare, Rannoch Moor only.

Arrowgrass Family
Juncaginaceae

Aquatic or marsh plants. Leaves all basal. Flowers in long spikes.

G **Sea Arrowgrass** *Triglochin maritima* Stout erect tufted hairless perennial to 60cm. Leaves erect, narrow, to 3-4mm, semicircular in section, *not furrowed*, all basal. Flowers green, 3-4mm in diameter, with 6 stamens, in long narrow spikes; *fruit egg-shaped*, with 6 compartments all containing seeds. In salt-marshes, mainly coastal; throughout. **Fl** 6-8. **Br** In suitable habitats all round the coasts.

H **Marsh Arrowgrass** *Triglochin palustris* Similar in general appearance to Sea Arrowgrass, except that the *leaves are deeply furrowed on upper surface near base*; the flowers smaller, (2-3mm); the fruit club-shaped, opening from base when ripe into 3 sections (only 3 compartments are fertile) *to form distinctive arrow shape*. In marshes and wet meadows, often near coasts; throughout. **Fl** 6-8. **Br** Throughout, but local in the south.

I *Triglochin bulbosa* Similar to Marsh Arrowgrass, except for the *bulbous* (not stoloniferous) base; leaves to 4mm wide. S Europe mainly, extending just to N France; in damp saline habitats. **Fl** 3-5 or 9-11. **Br** Absent.

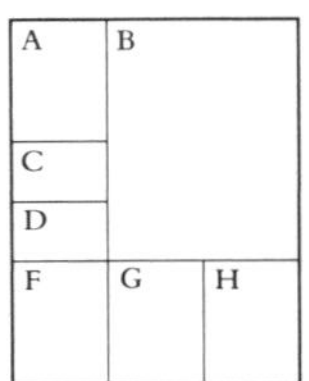

A **Frogbit**
B **Water-soldier**
C **Canadian Pondweed**
D *Elodea nuttallii*
F **Rannock-rush** in fruit
G **Sea Arrowgrass**
H **Marsh Arrowgrass**

B

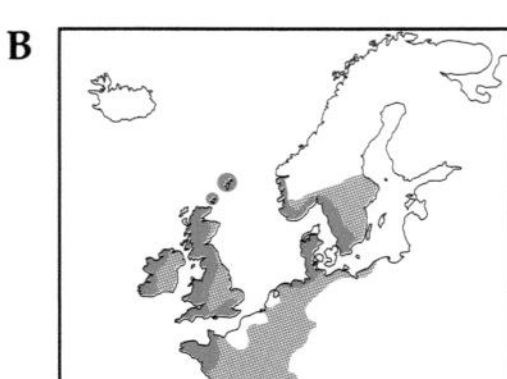

C

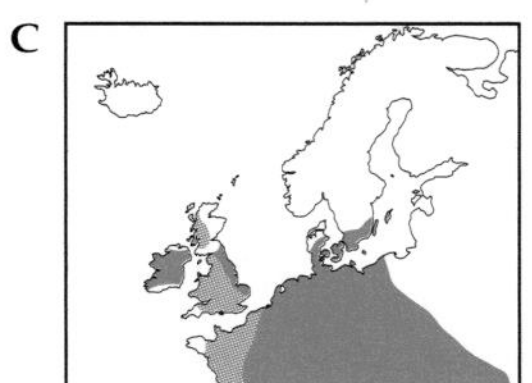

D

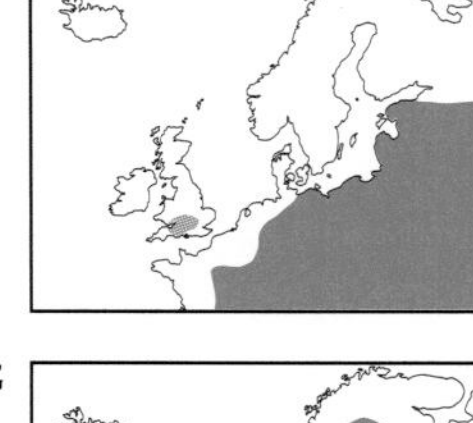

G

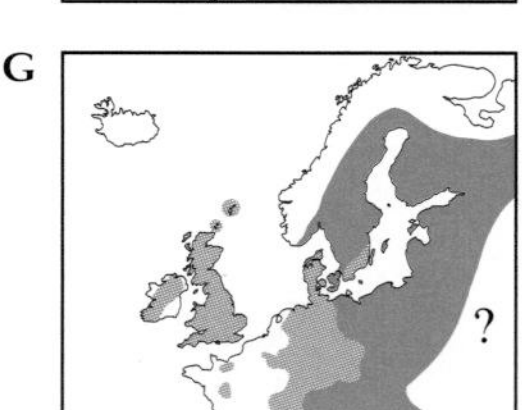

Pondweed Family
Potamogetonaceae

Aquatic herbs with opposite or alternate leaves, usually with stipules. Flowers in stalked spikes from the leaf axils. Individual flowers small, numerous, 4-parted with only 1 perianth whorl, usually greenish. Some species are difficult to identify, and many hybrids occur, complicating matters further.

(1)Plants with upper leaves relatively broad (more than 1cm), lanceolate to oval in shape.

A **Broad-leaved Pondweed** *Potamogeton natans* Submerged and floating leaves both present, stems cylindrical to 2m. Floating leaves dark green, opaque, blade length up to 12cm, *with a discoloured flexible joint* (**a**) *close to where the stalk and blade meet* (the only species with this); submerged leaves long, narrow, linear, to 30cm; stipules 5-15cm long, persistent, with close-set veins. Flower spikes cylindrical, dense, to 8cm long, emerging from water on stout stalk. Fruits greenish. Common throughout in still or slow-moving fresh water. **Fl** 5-9. **Br** Widespread and common.

B **Bog Pondweed** *Potamogeton polygonifolius* Similar to Broad-leaved Pondweed; *often reddish in colour. Floating leaves lacking flexible joint* (**b**), stipules 2-4cm, membranous, with well-separated slender veins. Flower spikes cylindrical, to 4cm, with stalk much longer than spike. Fruits brownish. Widespread and common, except in the far north; in bogs and acid waters. though absent from large areas. **Fl** 5-10. **Br** Widespread throughout, generally common except in more calcareous or highly farmed lowlands.

C **Fen Pondweed** *Potamogeton coloratus* Similar to above 2 species, but all leaf stalks shorter than blades (**c**); floating leaves ovate, reddish, translucent, with a *fine network of both parallel and cross-veins*, tapering into stalk, with no flexible joint. Fruits greenish. From S Sweden southwards; in calcareous waters and fens. **Fl** 6-7. **Br** Throughout, but local.

D **Loddon Pondweed** *Potamogeton nodosus* Similar in form to Bog Pondweed, but easily recognised by the *elliptical-lanceolate submerged leaves* (**d1**), narrowed at each end, thin and translucent, with *beautiful net-veining pattern*, all long-stalked; and the opaque net-veined floating leaves (**d2**). Stipules large. From Holland and Germany southwards, local; in still or slow-flowing waters, usually calcareous. **Fl** 6-9. **Br** Rare; in S England rivers only.

E **Shining Pondweed** *Potamogeton lucens* Wholly submerged aquatic. *Leaves all of similar type*, translucent, oblong-lanceolate, short-stalked, but with *blade running down stalk* (**e**); wavy-edged, to 20cm long, with minutely toothed margins. In lime-rich still or slow-flowing water; throughout, except the far north. **Fl** 6-9. **Br** Mainly southern and eastern; rare elsewhere.

F **Various-leaved Pondweed** *Potamogeton gramineus* Variable plant, much-branched at the base with numerous short non-flowering branches. Floating leaves ovate-elliptical, up to 7cm long (but often absent), opaque and long-stalked (**f**); submerged leaves unstalked, narrowly elliptical to linear, pointed, with *regular ascending transverse veins; stipules large and pointed*, to 5cm. Throughout; in still or flowing water, usually acidic. **Fl** 6-9. **Br** Widespread but local, mainly northern and eastern.

G **Red Pondweed** *Potamogeton alpinus Plant often tinged red.* Floating leaves (often absent), elliptical, opaque, to 8cm, wedge-shaped at base and short-stalked (**g**); submerged leaves unstalked, variable in shape, narrowed at each end, blunt and translucent, *conspicuously net-veined with a distinct midrib.* All margins untoothed. Stipules large, leafy, ovate and blunt, to 6cm. Widespread throughout; in still and slow-flowing waters, usually rather acidic. **Fl** 6-8. **Br** Widespread and locally common, especially in the north.

H **Long-stalked Pondweed** *Potamogeton praelongus* All leaves submerged. *Leaves strap-shaped to oblong*, much longer than wide (up to 20cm long × 4cm wide), rounded and semi-clasping at base (**h**), hooded at tip, translucent, *not net-veined*; stipules large, to 6cm, oval and persistent. Widespread throughout, though local; in still and slow-flowing waters, usually not calcareous. **Fl** 5-9. **Br** Local, and absent from S England.

I **Perfoliate Pondweed** *Potamogeton perfoliatus* Distinctive species. Leaves all submerged, *unstalked*, roughly oval, dark green and translucent, *clasping the stem with heart-shaped bases* (**i**). Widespread throughout; in freshwater habitats. **Fl** 6-9. **Br** Widespread, locally common.

J **Leafy Pondweed** *Potamogeton epihydrus* Floating and submerged leaves present; stem flattened. Submerged leaves *ribbon-like, less than 8mm wide*, unstalked, *with conspicuous band of air-cells on either side of midrib* (**j**); floating leaves oblong-elliptical, blunt, stalked and opaque. In lakes and ponds; rare; native only in Outer Hebrides, though introduced in N England. **Fl** 6-8. **Br** As above.

K **Curled Pondweed** *Potamogeton crispus* Wholly submerged. Distinctive by its *4-angled furrowed stems*, and dark green, translucent, linear to oblong, blunt leaves with *strongly wavy or crinkly margins* (**k**); 3-5 main veins only; margins minutely toothed. Throughout except the far north; in still or slow-flowing waters. **Fl** 5-10. **Br** Widespread and common throughout.

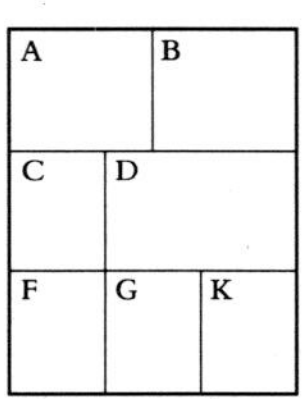

A **Broad-leaved Pondweed**

B **Bog Pondweed**

C **Fen Pondweed**

D **Loddon Pondweed**

F **Various-leaved Pondweed**

G **Red Pondweed**

K **Curled Pondweed**

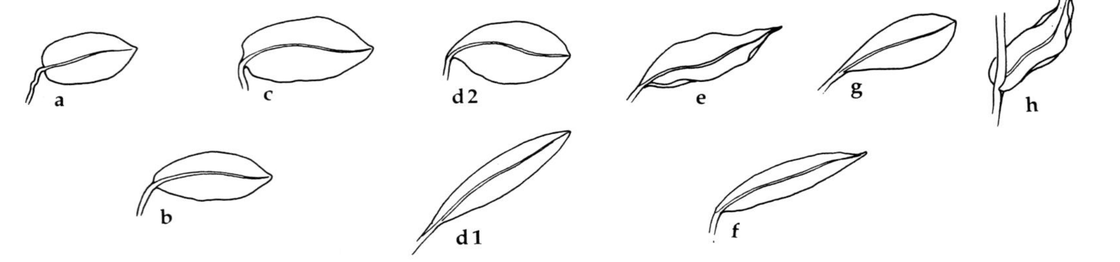

F

K

(2) Plants with all leaves narrow, less than 6mm wide, often thread-like.

A Flat-stalked Pondweed *Potamogeton friesii* *All leaves submerged*; linear, unstalked, to 7cm, blunt but with *small bristle-point*, *5-veined* with outer 2 veins close together near margins on each side (**a**); *stipules fused to form a tubular sheath*. Flower spike short, with several separated whorls of flowers. Widespread throughout in still and slow-moving waters, usually with muddy bottoms. **Fl** 6-9. **Br** Throughout lowland areas, except SW England; local in Ireland.

B Shetland Pondweed *Potamogeton rutilus* Rather similar to Flat-stalked Pondweed, but *leaves tapered to a fine point*, *usually 3-veined* (**b**). In lakes; from N Scotland and Denmark eastwards; very local. **Fl** 7-9. **Br** Shetlands and Hebrides only.

C Lesser Pondweed *Potamogeton pusillus* Similar to Shetland Pondweed, but *leaves narrow gradually to a long but blunt tip* (**c**); stipules tubular for most of length (not just at base). Throughout in calcareous or brackish still or slow-flowing waters. **Fl** 6-9. **Br** Widespread and locally common; rarer in N Scotland and Ireland.

D Blunt-leaved Pondweed *Potamogeton obtusifolius* Stem slender and flattened; floating leaves absent. *Leaves 2-4mm wide*, up to 90mm long, rounded at tip (**d**) (though sometimes with small bristle-point); *stipules forming an open sheath*, to 20mm, blunt. Widespread throughout, though local; in ponds and streams. **Fl** 6-9. **Br** Widespread, though absent from a few areas.

E Small Pondweed *Potamogeton berchtoldii* All leaves submerged. Slender plant. *Leaves very narrow*, less than 2mm, up to 50mm long, blunt at tip with *small bristle-point*, almost always *3-veined*, with lateral veins curving to meet midrib at right angles; *midrib bordered by air-spaces*. Widespread throughout, except the extreme north; in still and slow-moving fresh water. **Fl** 6-9. **Br** Common throughout.

F Hairlike Pondweed *Potamogeton trichoides* Similar to Small Pondweed, *but leaves very fine, less than 1mm wide*, flattened, tapered to a fine point, *apparently 1-veined* (with 2 indistinct lateral veins), lacking air-space bands. Stipules not tubular; leafy, shiny green. From S Sweden southwards; in still or very slow-flowing waters. **Fl** 6-9. **Br** Local in England; rare in Scotland and Wales; absent from Ireland.

G Grass-wrack Pondweed *Potamogeton compressus* Stems flattened; leaves all submerged, 2-4mm wide, to 20cm long, *grass-like*, with *rounded but bristle-tipped points* (**g**), *5-veined* (but with many additional fine vein-like thickening strands), with air-spaces bordering midrib; *stipules open*, *very blunt*, to 30mm. Throughout except the far north; in still and slow-flowing fresh waters. **Fl** 6-9. **Br** Widespread, though very local and only common in central and E England.

H Sharp-leaved Pondweed *Potamogeton acutifolius* Similar to Grass-wrack Pondweed, but with leaves *finely tapered to a sharp point*, 3-veined (**h**). Flower spikes very short and few-flowered (many-flowered, to 30mm long in Grass-wrack Pondweed). From S Sweden southwards; in still and flowing waters, usually calcareous. **Fl** 6-8. **Br** Local, only in S and E England.

I Slender-leaved Pondweed *Potamogeton filiformis* Leaves all submerged, very narrow and linear (usually less than 1mm), numerous, *blunt or rounded at tip*, unstalked, *made up of 2 hollow tubes, 1 either side of midrib; stipules form a closed tube, at least at base*. Throughout, though absent from many areas; particularly in fresh or brackish water, often near the coast. **Fl** 5-9. **Br** Mainly northern; absent from England.

J Fennel Pondweed *Potamogeton pectinatus* Very similar to Slender-leaved Pondweed, but *leaf tips pointed; stipule sheaths open down 1 side*, not tubular at base, white-edged. In similar habitats; throughout. **Br** Common throughout lowland and coastal areas.

K Opposite-leaved Pondweed *Groenlandia densa* Differs from *Potamogeton* species in the *opposite leaves* (occasionally in 3s). All leaves submerged, in opposite pairs, *without stipules*, oval-triangular, to 4cm, blunt or pointed, translucent, margins minutely toothed; often folded lengthwise, and curled back. Flowers in tiny short-stalked clusters, curving back when in fruit. In still or flowing fresh water, from Denmark southwards, rare in the north of range. **Fl** 5-9. **Br** Locally common in England, though decreasing; rare elsewhere.

D	G
K	J

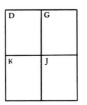

D Blunt-leaved Pondweed

G Grass-wrack Pondweed

K Opposite-leaved Pondweed

J Fennel Pondweed

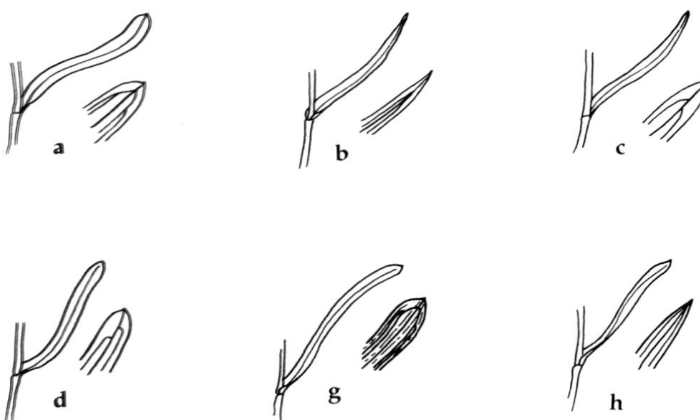

A
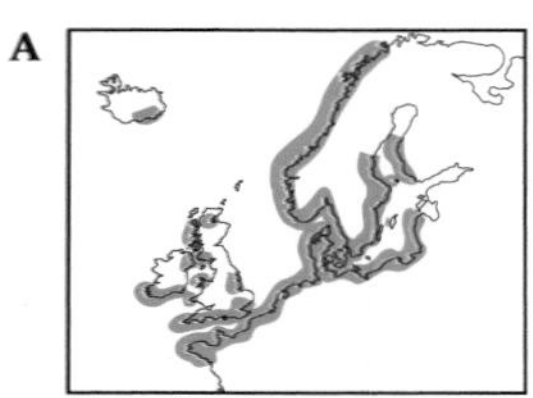

C
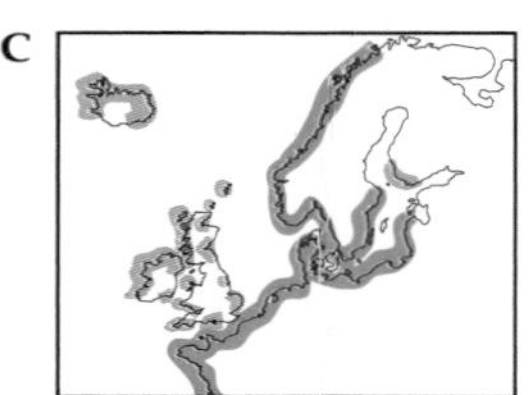

G
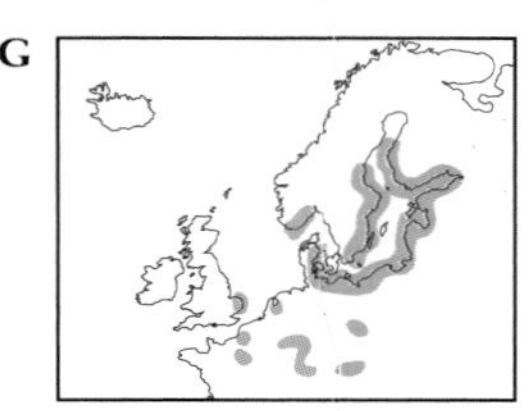

H
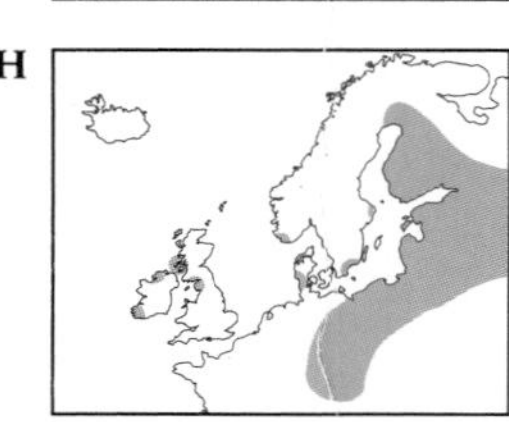

Tasselweed Family
Ruppiaceae

A small family of submerged aquatic herbs of saline or brackish waters. Flowers hermaphrodite, lacking petals or sepals, in pairs on long stalks.

A **Beaked Tasselweed** *Ruppia maritima* Slender aquatic perennial, wholly submerged, with hair-like stems. Leaves very fine, less than 1mm wide, light green, alternate or opposite, pointed. Flowers in umbel-like heads (actually several close-set pairs), with the common *stalk less than 60mm long*, less than twice the length of individual flower stalks; petals absent, 2 stamens to 0.7mm long. In saline or brackish water, usually coastal; throughout. **Fl** 7-9. **Br** Widespread around coasts, very local in the north, commoner in the south.

B **Spiral Tasselweed** *Ruppia cirrhosa* Very similar to Beaked Tasselweed, but leaves darker green, *inflorescence stalk is 10cm or more, much longer than individual flower stalks, becoming coiled in fruit*. Stamens to 1.7mm long. Similar habitats and distribution. **Fl** 7-9. **Br** Widespread around the coasts, but rare.

Eelgrass Family Zosteraceae

A small family of perennial grass-like herbs, unusual in being wholly marine in habitat. Flowers reduced to bare necessity of 1 stamen and 1 style, in separate male and female flowers.

C **Common Eelgrass** *Zostera marina* Submerged perennial herbaceous marine plant. Leaves to 50cm long (occasionally much longer), and *1cm wide, 3- (to 9-) veined*, with broad, rounded, *bristle-tipped points*; basal sheaths entire, not split; leaves on flower shoots similar but smaller. Flowers greenish, in terminal much-branched inflorescences, enclosed in base of a sheath; stigma twice the length of style. Locally common around all coasts, on fine sand or silt substrates, from low water down to 10m depth. Varies in abundance through disease. **Fl** 6-9. **Br** Widespread though local.

D **Narrow-leaved Eelgrass** *Zostera angustifolia* Similar in form to Common Eelgrass, but *leaves ribbon-like, 2-3mm wide*, up to 30cm long, *1- to 3-veined, usually notched at tip*. Inflorescence similar to above species, style and stigma of equal length. In similar habitats, though occurring higher up shore; throughout. **Fl** 6-11. **Br** Local, all around the coast.

E **Dwarf Eelgrass** *Zostera noltii* Similar to Narrow-leaved Eelgrass (and often confused with it), but smaller, slenderer, with leaves to 12cm long, *less than 1.5mm wide, 1-veined; leaf sheaths open down 1 side*. Inflorescence unbranched. Similar habitats; from S Scandinavia southwards. **Fl** 6-10. **Br** Local, all around the coasts, except the far north; rare in Ireland.

Zannichelliaceae

A small family, with only 1 genus in N Europe. Leaves very narrow. Flowers inconspicuous, with petals tiny or absent.

F **Horned Pondweed** *Zannichellia palustris* Slender, submerged, aquatic perennial herb. Leaves more or less opposite, linear, very narrow, usually under 1.5mm wide, up to 50mm long, fine-pointed, translucent, with few parallel veins. Differs from similar hair-leaved *Potamogeton* species in the inflorescence, which consists of *small unstalked clusters of flowers in the leaf axils*, with 1 male flower and several females in a cup-like sheath. In still or slow-moving fresh or brackish water; common almost throughout. **Fl** 5-8. **Br** Widespread but local.

Naiad Family Najadaceae

A very small family with 1 genus. Leaves virtually opposite. Male and female flowers separate.

G **Holly-leaved Naiad** *Najas marina* Distinctive submerged aquatic, with opposite pairs, or whorls, of narrowly lanceolate leaves (to 6mm wide), *with strongly spiny margins*, and scattered teeth on the stems (**g**); leaf sheaths without hairs. Flowers tiny, in leaf axils. In clear fresh or brackish water; widespread except in the north, though local. **Fl** 7-8. **Br** Rare and declining, in Norfolk Broads only.

H **Slender Naiad** *Najas flexilis* Similar in form to above, leaves in 2s or 3s, *very minutely toothed* (**h**), narrower (to 1mm wide), with few-haired leaf sheaths. From Britain and Germany northwards, in acid still waters, but very local. **Fl** 7-9. **Br** From N England northwards, and in W Ireland; very local.

I *Najas minor* Very like Slender Naiad, but with even narrower leaves, fewer teeth, and *leaf sheaths that have rounded auricles at base*. Still waters, Belgium and Germany southwards; local. **Fl** 7-9. **Br** Absent.

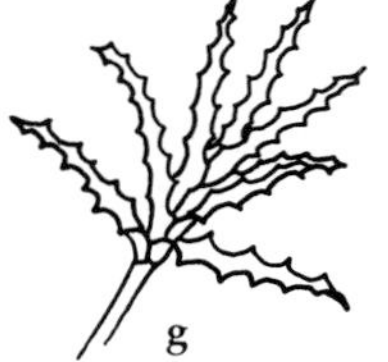

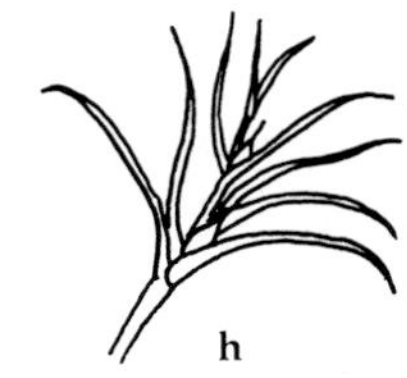

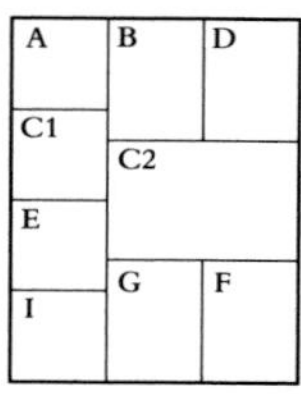

A **Beaked Tasselweed**

B **Spiral Tasselweed**

D **Narrow-leaved Eelgrass**

C **1 Common Eelgrass**

C **2 Common Eel-grass** in habitat

E **Dwarf Eelgrass**

I *Najas minor*

G **Holly-leaved Naiad**

F **Horned Pondweed**

A

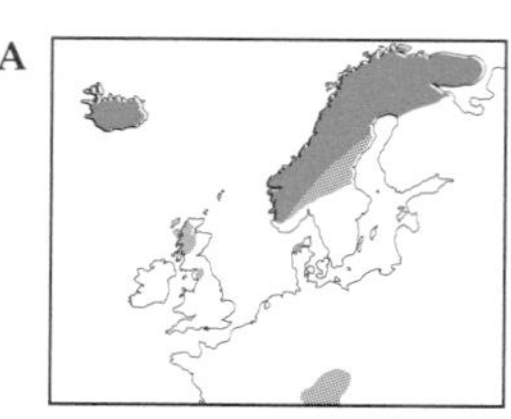

B

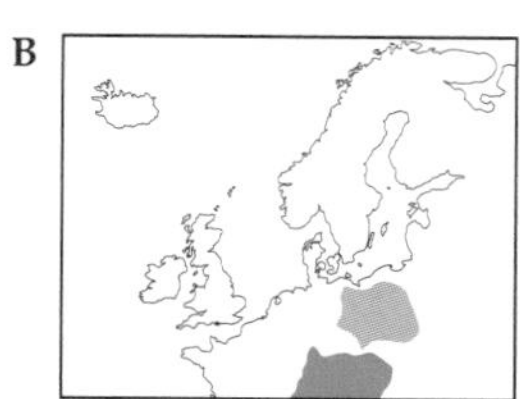

C

D

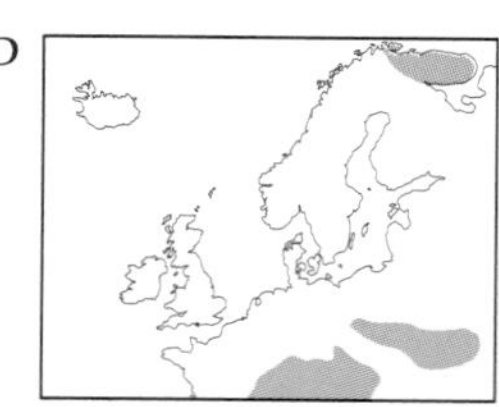

F

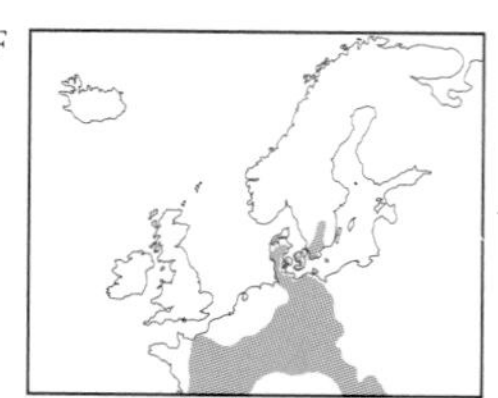

H

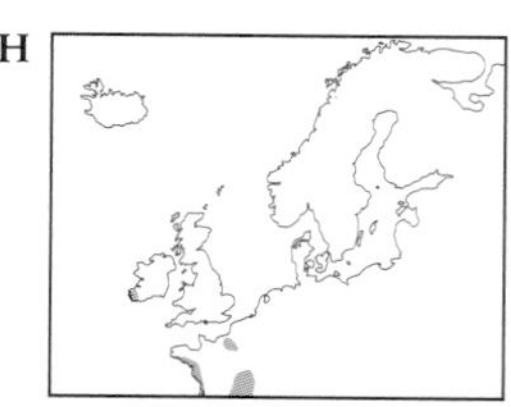

I

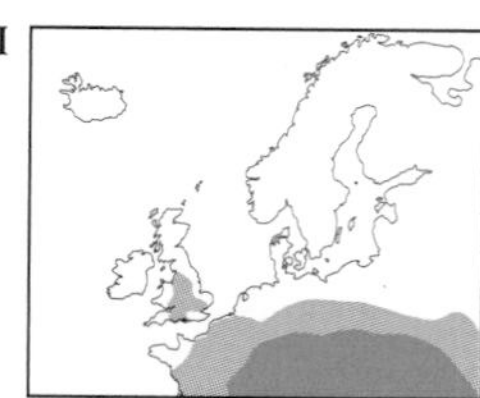

Lily Family Liliaceae

A very large family of herbaceous plants (at least, in N Europe), usually with bulbs or tubers. Leaves normally narrow, linear, untoothed and parallel-veined. Flowers normally with 6 roughly equal and similar perianth segments, in 2 whorls (equivalent to petals and sepals), except for May Lily, which is 4-parted. Stamens normally 6, ovary 3-celled and superior.

A **Scottish Asphodel** *Tofieldia pusilla* Erect hairless perennial herb to 20cm. Leaves mainly basal in flattened fan, like miniature iris leaves, to 80mm long. Inflorescence is a dense short-stalked spike, with 5-10 flowers; *flowers greenish or whitish*, about 2mm in diameter, with a 3-lobed bract at base. In damp flushes and boggy areas, mainly in mountains; throughout but very local and confined to mountains in the south. **Fl** 6-8. **Br** Upper Teesdale and Scottish Highlands only, locally common.

B **German Asphodel** *Tofieldia calyculata* Similar to Scottish Asphodel, but a larger plant to 35cm, with a longer spike of up to 30 *yellowish flowers*. In wet places, usually calcareous, in S Sweden and Alpine areas. **Fl** 6-8. **Br** Absent.

C **Bog Asphodel** *Narthecium ossifragum* Similar in form to the above asphodels, but with erect spikes of *larger (to 15mm in diameter) starry orange-yellow flowers* in a spike up to 10cm long; anthers orange-red, with conspicuously orange-woolly filaments. Leaves and fruits all become orange-red in late summer. In bogs, flushes and on wet heaths; from S Scandinavia southwards, locally common. **Fl** 6-8. **Br** Widespread but local, and absent from many lowland areas.

D **White False Helleborine** *Veratrum album* Variable, stout, erect, clump-forming perennial to 1.5m. Leaves crowded, alternate, oval to elliptical, hairless above but downy below, to 25cm long near base, upper leaves shorter, all with deeply marked veins. Flowers white to greenish, 15-25mm in diameter, in long inflorescences, branched in lower part. In damp grassy places, mainly in hill or mountain areas, in Finland, Norway, France and Germany only. **Fl** 6-8. **Br** Absent.

E **Asphodel** *Asphodelus albus* Robust perennial with a basal cluster of leaves. Leaves linear, flat, to 60cm, greyish green, pointed and ascending. Inflorescence stalk stout, solid, usually unbranched, to 1m, with terminal raceme; flowers white with brown midribs, 40-60mm in diameter, with dark brown bracts. In meadows, heaths and open woods; from NW France southwards. **Fl** 5-8. **Br** Absent.

F **St Bernard's Lily** *Anthericum liliago* Slender hairless perennial to 70cm, with leaves in basal cluster. Leaves linear, narrow, up to 40cm long, but only 3-7mm wide, flat or channelled. Inflorescence is a *few-flowered, usually unbranched, raceme*; petals white, flowers 25-50mm in diameter, flower bracts 10mm long; *style curved*, and ascending. In dry grassland, rocky banks and open woods; from S Sweden southwards, though local. **Fl** 5-7. **Br** Absent.

G *Anthericum ramosum* Similar to above, but with *inflorescence stems much-branched*, flowers smaller (20-30mm in diameter), bracts 5mm long, and *style straight*. Similar distribution, though more lowland generally. **Fl** 6-7. **Br** Absent.

H **Kerry Lily** *Simethis planifolia* Slender, erect, hairless perennial to 40cm. Leaves mainly basal, to 60cm long, and up to 7mm wide, over-topping flower spikes. Inflorescence a lax panicle, with 3-7 flowers; flowers white inside, pink-purple outside; stamens with white-woolly stalks, style undivided. On heaths, rocky ground and open pinewoods; very local in SW Ireland and W France (and further south in Europe). **Fl** 5-7. **Br** Local only in Kerry, SW Ireland.

I **Meadow Saffron, Autumn Crocus** *Colchicum autumnale* Hairless perennial herb, with an underground corm producing leaves in spring and flowers in autumn. Leaves oblong-lanceolate, bright glossy green, to 30cm long × 4cm wide, erect in spring, dying well before flower. Flowers arise directly from ground in autumn, without leaves, with long stalk-like perianth tube and 6 pink-purple perianth lobes, very like *Crocus* species (*see* page 310) but with 6 (not 3) stamens. Fruits appear with leaves in following spring. In meadows and open woods; north to Holland and Germany, local, naturalised further north. **Fl** 8-10. **Br** Mainly in the Midlands, rare elsewhere.

J **Snowdon Lily** *Lloydia serotina* Hairless bulbous perennial to 15cm (rarely more). Basal leaves thread-like, green, usually only 2, up to 20cm long; 2-4 lanceolate stem leaves are also present. Flowers solitary, white with purplish veins, erect, roughly cup-shaped, 15-20mm in diameter. Rock-ledges and mountain grasslands; in Wales and the Alps, local. **Fl** 5-7. **Br** Very rare, in Snowdonia only.

A	B	C
D	E	F
H	I	J

A **Scottish Asphodel**
B **German Asphodel**
C **Bog Asphodel**
D **White False Helleborine**
E **Asphodel**
F **St Bernard's Lily**
H **Kerry Lily**
I **Meadow Saffron**
J **Snowdon Lily**

A

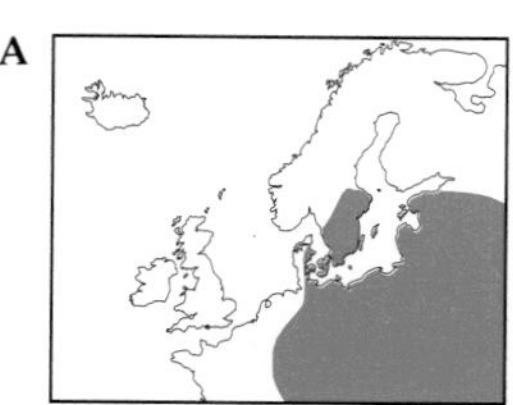

B

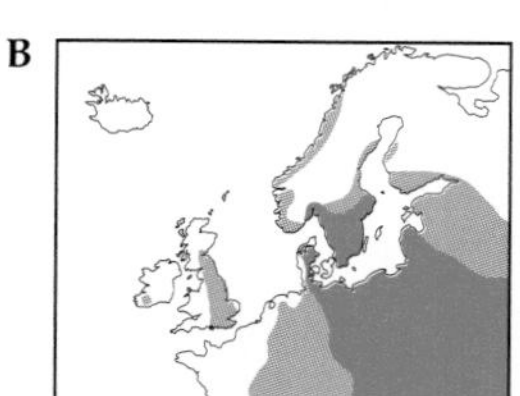

E

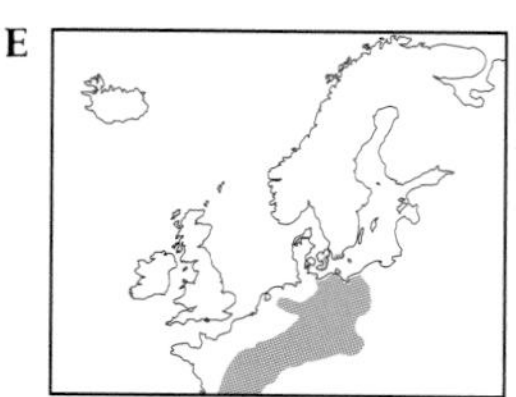

G

H

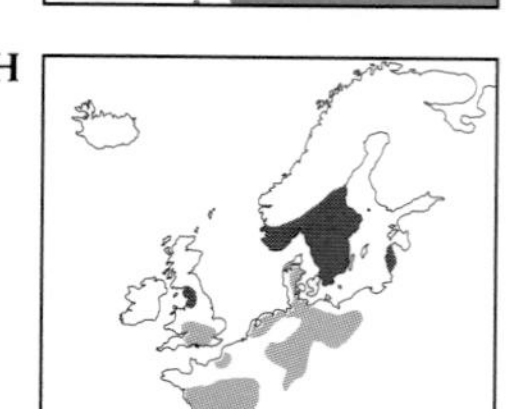

GAGEAS, STARS-OF-BETHLEHEM *Gagea* Small bulbous perennials with erect unbranched stems; leaves basal and on stem. Flowers erect, yellow (with a green stripe down back of each perianth segment), in umbel-like clusters (or solitary), with leaf-like spathe at base of inflorescence.

(1) Plants with only 1 basal leaf.

A **Meadow Gagea** *Gagea pratensis* Basal leaf up to 6mm wide, flat; stem leaves in 1 opposite pair. Flowers large (20-30mm in diameter), greenish yellow, in groups of 2-6; *stigmas 3, yellow.* In meadows and disturbed ground; from S Sweden southwards, though local. **Fl** 3-5. **Br** Absent.

B **Yellow Star-of-Bethlehem** *Gagea lutea* Very similar to Meadow Gagea, but basal leaf wider, to 15mm, with hooded tips. Flowers in groups of 1-7, sometimes with hairy flower stalks; *only 1 stigma, green.* In damp grassland and open woods, often on basic and heavy soils; local. **Fl** 3-4. **Br** Widespread north to S Scotland, but very local and absent from many areas.

C *Gagea minima* Has *basal leaf only 1-2mm wide, not keeled* like above 2 species. Flowers in groups of 1-7, with *pointed (not blunt) perianth segments,* becoming reflexed. Widespread almost throughout in similar habitats, but local. **Fl** 3-5. **Br** Absent.

(2) Plants with 2 or more basal leaves.

D *Gagea spathacea* All parts of plant *hairless.* Basal leaves 2, narrowly linear, to 4mm wide. Flowers in groups of 2-4, *with single spathe-like bract at base of inflorescence;* flowers 18-20mm in diameter, yellow. From S Sweden south to N France; local; in open woods, scrub and damp grassland. **Fl** 4-5. **Br** Absent.

E *Gagea arvensis* Greyish, slightly hairy plant. Basal leaves 2, narrowly linear, channelled; *stem leaves 2, in an opposite pair.* Flowers numerous, *5-12 together,* with narrow, *pointed perianth segments.* From Holland and S Sweden southwards in dry open habitats, arable land. **Fl** 4-5. **Br** Absent.

F **Early Star-of-Bethleham** *Gagea bohemica* *Very small plant,* with stems less than 20mm normally. Basal leaves 2, very narrow, long and wavy; stem leaves shorter and wider, 2-4, alternate. Flowers solitary or 2-3 together, with *blunt perianth segments,* wider towards tip. In dry grassy and rocky places, occasionally woods; Germany, Wales, and W France only; very local. **Fl** 1-3 (and therefore easily overlooked). **Br** Quite recently discovered in 1 locality in Wales.

G **Wild Tulip** *Tulipa sylvestris* Distinctive bulbous perennial, with erect stems to 45cm. Leaves linear-lanceolate, up to 30cm long, greyish green on upper surface, channelled. Flowers normally solitary (or 2), nodding in bud, erect when open, 3-5cm long, yellow, often greenish outside; stigmas 3. In meadows and grassy places; probably native only in NW France (and further south), but widely naturalised north to S Scandinavia. **Fl** 4-5. **Br** Introduced, naturalised locally; northwards to S Scotland, declining.

H **Snake's-head Fritillary** *Fritillaria meleagris* Erect hairless rather grey-green perennial to 30cm. Leaves alternate, not basal, narrow-linear. Flowers very distinctive within N Europe, large drooping lantern shape, 3-5cm long, chequered pink and brownish purple (less commonly all white), solitary or paired, with a nectary at the base of each segment inside. From Holland southwards (naturalised further north) in damp alluvial meadows, especially if winter-flooded. **Fl** 4-5. **Br** Very local, though often abundant where it grows, in a band across S and E England, mainly in Thames Valley.

I **Martagon Lily** *Lilium martagon* Robust erect perennial to 1.8m, with rough stems. Leaves oval-lanceolate, up to 16cm long (usually less), mainly in *separated whorls up stem.* Flowers large, 4-5cm in diameter, *reddish purple with darker spots, with perianth segments strongly recurved,* in a loose terminal raceme. In woods, scrub and grassy places; native from NE France southwards, but widely naturalised further north. **Fl** 6-7. **Br** Naturalised widely, possibly native in a few southern localities. Very local.

J **Pyrenean Lily** *Lilium pyrenaicum* Readily separated from Martagon Lily by the *narrow alternate leaves,* and *yellow, black-streaked, flowers.* Native of Pyrenees, but locally naturalised. **Fl** 5-7. **Br** Naturalised in a few places, especially in W Ireland and Wales.

B	E	F
G	H1	
I		
	H2	J

B **Yellow Star-of-Bethlehem**

E *Gagea arvensis*

F **Early Star-of-Bethlehem**

G **Wild Tulip**

H **1 Snake's-head Fritillary** in habitat

I **Maragon Lily**

H **2 Snake's-head Fritillary** showing normal and white forms

J **Pyrenean Lily**

A

C

D

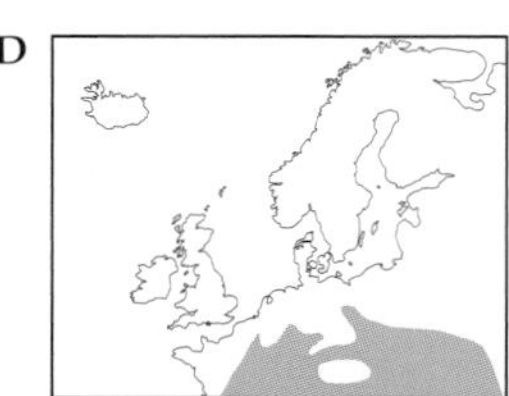

F

G

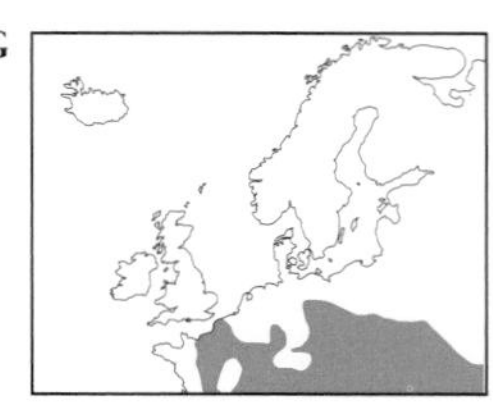

H

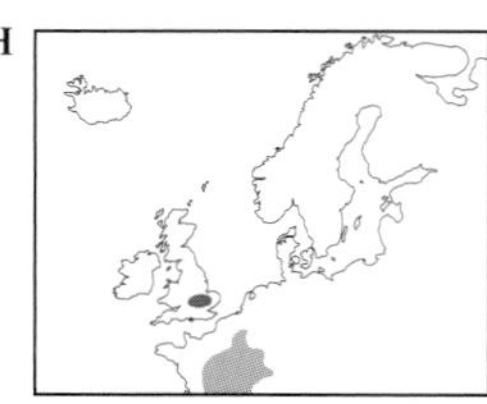

A Bath Asparagus *Ornithogalum pyrenaicum* Erect hairless perennial, with stout stems to 1m. Leaves linear, to 60cm, grey-green, all basal, withering early. *Flowers pale greenish yellow* to greenish white, starry, to 2cm in diameter, in long terminal raceme with short whitish bracts to each flower. Developing inflorescence resembles Asparagus, and is eaten locally (hence the name). Meadows, scrub and roadsides; from Belgium and S England southwards; local. **Fl** 5-7. **Br** Very locally common in a small area from Bath eastwards to Bedfordshire.

B Star-of-Bethlehem *Ornithogalum umbellatum* Low hairless bulbous perennial to 30cm tall. Leaves narrowly linear, to 30cm, with white stripe down central channel. *Flowers in an umbel-like terminal raceme*, with lower flowers on longer stalks than upper so that inflorescence is almost flat-topped; *perianth segments white*, with green stripe on back, in starry flowers 3-4cm in diameter. In dry grassland, roadsides and cultivated ground; from Holland southwards, though naturalised further north. **Fl** 4-5. **Br** Widespread, local, probably native only in E Anglia.

C Spring Squill *Scilla verna* Small hairless bulbous perennial to 15cm. Has from 3 to 6 linear leaves, to 4mm wide and 20cm long, curly, produced before flowers. Flowers in a 2- to 12-flowered terminal erect cluster; perianth segments pale blue or violet-blue, pointed; *each flower has 1 bluish-purple bract, usually longer than flower stalk*. In dry rocky grassy coastal sites; mainly western; local. **Fl** 4-5. **Br** Locally common on the coasts of W Britain, rare in the east.

D *Scilla bifolia* Similar to Spring Squill, but has *only 2 leaves*, wider (to 12mm), appearing with flowers; flowers bright blue, *without bracts*. In meadows and woods, not particularly coastal; from Belgium and Germany southwards. **Fl** 3-4. **Br** Absent.

E Autumn Squill *Scilla autumnalis* Very similar to Spring Squill, most readily distinguished by flowering time. Leaves produced in autumn, with or after flowers; *flowers dull purple, bracts absent*. In dry grassy and rocky places, mainly coastal; from S England and France southwards. **Fl** 7-9. **Br** Coastal sites in S England only.

F Bluebell *Hyacinthoides non-scripta* Familiar hairless bulbous perennial to 50cm. Leaves all basal, linear, to 15mm wide, glossy green, hooded at tip. Inflorescence a 1-sided raceme, with up to 16 drooping narrowly bell-shaped flowers; perianth segments blue or blue-violet (rarely pink or white), joined at base, with 6 lobes curled back at tips; anthers cream. In woods, scrub, grassland and coastal cliffs; from Scotland and Holland southwards, but predominantly western. **Fl** 4-6. **Br** Common throughout except on higher mountains and in the extreme north.

G Tassel Hyacinth *Muscari comosum* Distinctive plant; an erect bulbous perennial to 50cm, usually less. Leaves linear, to 40cm long, 15mm wide and channelled. Flowers in a long loose spike, with lower flowers pale brownish green, flask-shaped, closed at mouth; *upper flowers sterile, purplish, in an erect tuft; all flowers long-stalked*. In dry grassland and disturbed ground, from N France and S Germany southwards, naturalised further north. **Fl** 4-6. **Br** Introduced; occasionally naturalised in the south.

H Grape Hyacinth *Muscari neglectum* Variable, erect, hairless, bulbous perennial to 30cm. Leaves linear, semicircular in section, channelled, bright green, and up to 30cm long, *to 6mm wide*, all basal. Flowers in a dense cylindrical terminal spike, 20-30mm long; flowers dark blue, oval, inflated, 3-5mm long, constricted at mouth, with 6 small white teeth at opening; uppermost flowers smaller, paler and sterile. In dry, often calcareous, grassland areas; from Britain and N France southwards, naturalised to the north of range. **Fl** 4-5. **Br** Probably native in E Anglia; naturalised elsewhere.

I Small Grape Hyacinth *Muscari botryoides* Similar to Grape Hyacinth, *but leaves wider (to 12mm), hooded or wider at tip*; flowers pale violet, globular, 2-4mm long, in loose conical heads. In dry grasslands; from Belgium and Germany southwards, though possibly not native in the north of range. **Fl** 3-6. **Br** Absent.

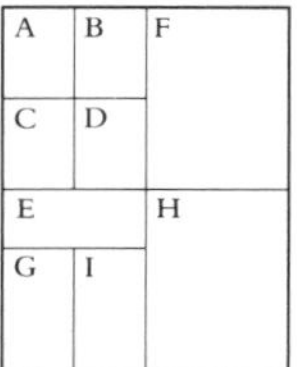

A **Bath Aspargus**
B **Star-of-Bethlehem**

F **Bluebell**
C **Spring Squill**
D *Scilla bifolia*
E **Autumn Squill**
H **Grape Hyacinth**
G **Tassel Hyacinth**
I **Small Grape Hyacinth**

A

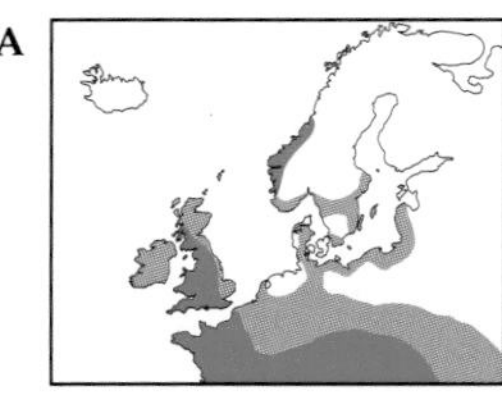

F

H

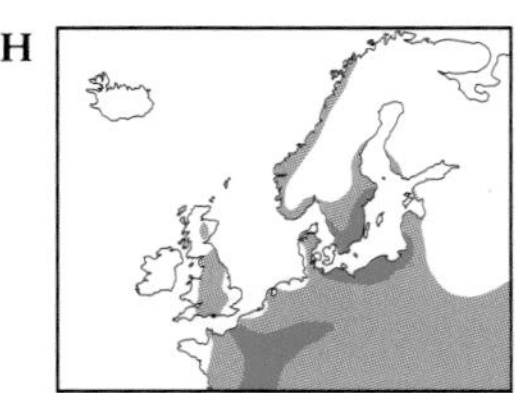

J

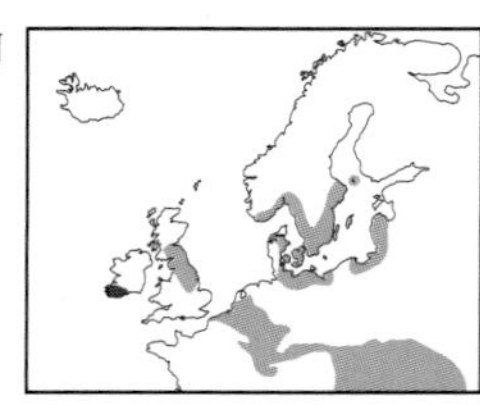

K

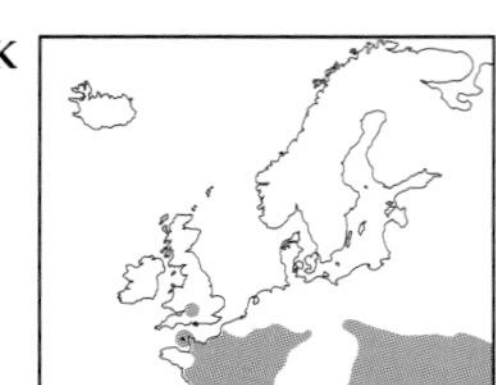

GARLICS, LEEKS AND ONIONS *Allium*
Perennial bulbous herbs, smelling of garlic or onion when bruised. Leaves variable, flat or cylindrical, sheathing at base. Flowers in terminal umbels, with 1 or more papery bracts below head. Flowers small with 6 similar perianth segments; bulbils are often mixed in with flowers in some species. A difficult group, with 13 species in the area.

(1) Plants with broadly ovate-elliptical leaves, to 7cm wide.

A **Ramsons** *Allium ursinum* Distinctive erect bulbous perennial. Leaves basal, stalked, ovate to elliptical, up to 25cm long and *7cm at broadest*, pointed. Flower stalk to 45cm, with spathe of 2 papery bracts, shorter than flower stalks, and globular head of up to 20 white flowers; individual flowers to 2cm in diameter; bulbils absent. Locally abundant in woods, especially on damp or calcareous soils; from S Scandinavia southwards. **Fl** 4-6. **Br** Locally abundant throughout except NE Scotland; rare in Ireland.

(2) Plants with distinctly 3-angled inflorescence stalks.

B **Three-cornered Leek** *Allium triquetrum* Perennial to 45cm. *Leaves 2-3*, linear, flat or keeled, to 40cm long, 15mm wide. Stem erect, strongly 3-angled, bearing spathe of 2 papery bracts to 25mm, shorter than flower stalks; flowers drooping in an umbel, perianth white with green stripe outside, to 20mm long, *without bulbils*. Few-flowered. Naturalised, from SW Europe; in hedgerows, roadsides, cultivated ground, etc., in Britain and W France. **Fl** 3-6. **Br** Naturalised, and locally common in SW England; rare elsewhere.

C **Few-flowered Leek** *Allium paradoxum* Similar to Three-cornered Leek, but differs in having *only 1 leaf*, bright green, to 30cm; *inflorescence usually consisting of 1 flower (or very few), and numerous bulbils*. Locally naturalised from Denmark southwards, originally from W Asia. **Fl** 4-5. **Br** Very local, mainly in the north.

(3) Plants with rounded or barely 2- to 3-angled inflorescence stalks.

D *Allium angulosum* Stem erect, to 45cm, angular. Leaves 4-6, all basal, linear, to 25cm long, 6mm wide, *keeled below*. Spathe 2- to 5-lobed. Umbel of flowers up to 45mm in diameter, with numerous pale purple cup-shaped flowers; stamens yellow at first, later purple, *slightly longer than perianth*. Damp riverside meadows, E France and S Germany only (and further south). **Fl** 6-7. **Br** Absent.

E *Allium senescens* Very similar to *A. angulosum*, but *leaves not keeled below; stamens distinctly protruding*; habitat quite different – dry rocky places; from S Sweden southwards; local. **Fl** 6-8. **Br** Absent.

F **Chives** *Allium schoenoprasum* Tufted plant to 40cm. Leaves cylindrical, *hollow*, greyish green, to 25cm long. Inflorescence stalks up to 40cm, cylindrical, with small dense umbel, 20-40mm in diameter, with 8-30 lilac-purple flowers; bulbils absent; *anthers yellow, not protruding; spathe made up of 2 bracts*, less than 15mm, shorter than umbel. In rocky and grassy habitats, or damper sites in mountains; throughout except the far north, often naturalised. **Fl** 6-8. **Br** Very local as native, on limestone; mainly western.

G *Allium paniculatum* Tall perennial, bracts 2, very much longer than flower.stalks (to 14cm); flowers pink or white. From N France southwards; in rocky or grassy places. **Fl** 5-6. **Br** Absent.

H **Field Garlic** *Allium oleraceum* Tall perennial to 1m. Leaves linear, to 4mm wide, up to 25cm long, sheathing stem in lower half, channelled above, strongly ribbed on underside. *Spathe consists of 2 long pointed bracts, with longer one up to 20cm long*. Inflorescence has a mixture of bulbils and long-stalked flowers, with whitish bell-shaped flowers, sometimes pink or green-tinged, *stamens not protruding*. Throughout except the far north; in rocky, grassy and disturbed situations. **Fl** 7-8. **Br** Local, widespread but mainly eastern; absent from N Scotland; rare in Ireland.

I **Keeled Garlic** *Allium carinatum* Similar to Field Garlic, with very long narrow uneven bracts; flowers purple to pink, *with stamens protruding*. Meadows and heathy areas, from S Sweden southwards, but very local; naturalised elsewhere. **Fl** 7-8. **Br** Very locally naturalised.

J **Sand Leek** *Allium scorodoprasum* Similar to above, with flat, solid, keeled, rough-edged leaves. Spathe with *2 bracts, shorter than flower stalks (to 15mm)*; umbel 10-50mm in diameter; perianth ovoid, reddish purple, with *stamens not protruding; purple bulbils present*. In dry grasslands, roadsides and sandy habitats; from S Scandinavia southwards, though local. **Fl** 5-8. **Br** N England to central Scotland only.

K **Round-headed Leek** *Allium sphaerocephalon* Tall plant to 90cm. *Leaves semicircular in section, but grooved on upper side*, up to 60cm long, but very narrow (1-2mm). Umbel dense, small (20-30mm in diameter, rarely more), spherical, *without bulbils; spathe of 2 bracts, short, less than 20mm*; perianth segments pink to reddish purple, *stamens protruding*. From Belgium and England southwards; in dry open habitats, such as limestone rocks and sand-dunes. **Fl** 6-8. **Br** Avon Gorge and Jersey only.

L **Crow Garlic** *Allium vineale* *Leaves semicircular in section, hollow, channelled*, to 60cm long, to 4mm wide. Spathe of a *single papery bract, not longer than flowers*, falling early. Umbel variable, usually with few long-stalked pink, red, or white flowers, and *numerous greenish-red bulbils*; may also be all bulbils, or almost all flowers; *stamens protruding*. Throughout in dry grasslands and disturbed habitats, except the far north. **Fl** 6-7. **Br** Common in the south, becoming rarer to the north.

M **Wild Leek** *Allium ampeloprasum* Tall robust plant, with cylindrical stem up to 2m. Leaves linear, grey-green, waxy, to 50cm long by 40mm wide, flat, channelled, with rough margins. *Spathe a single papery bract*, falling as flowers open. *Umbel large, to 90mm in diameter*, globose, with hundreds of flowers; perianth segments pale purplish, 6-8mm long, stamens slightly protruding; bulbils normally absent. Var. *babingtonii* (Babington's Leek) has *numerous large bulbils, and few flowers*. In disturbed, open, and rocky places, especially coastal; from S Britain and N France southwards. **Fl** 6-8. **Br** The type is rare in SW Britain; var. *babingtonii* is rare in Cornwall and W Ireland.

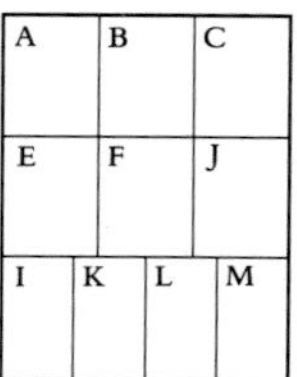

A **Ramsons**

B **Three-cornered Leek**

C **Few-flowered Leek**

E *Allium senescens*

F **Chives**

J **Sand Leek**

I **Keeled Garlic**

K **Round-headed Leek**

L **Crow Garlic**

M **Wild Leek** var. *babingtonii* **(Babington's Leek)**

D

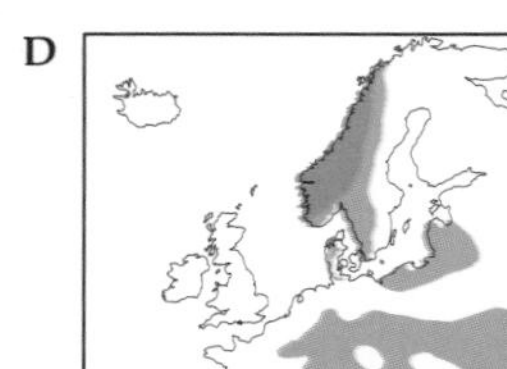

E

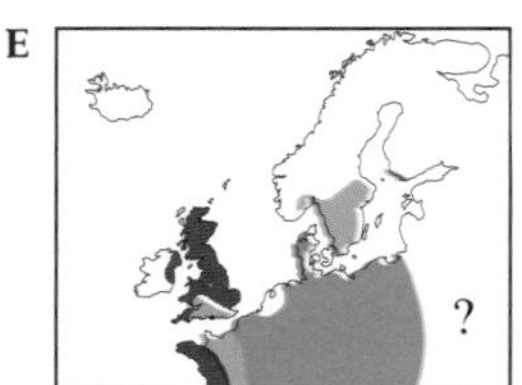

G

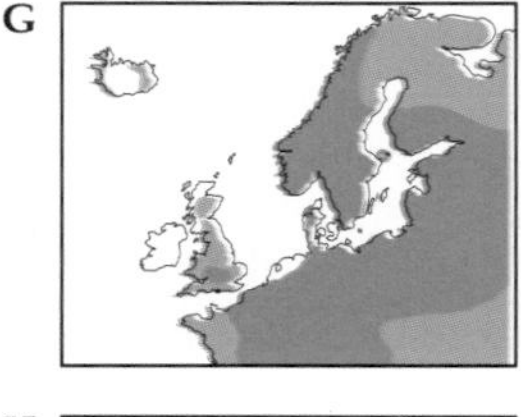

H

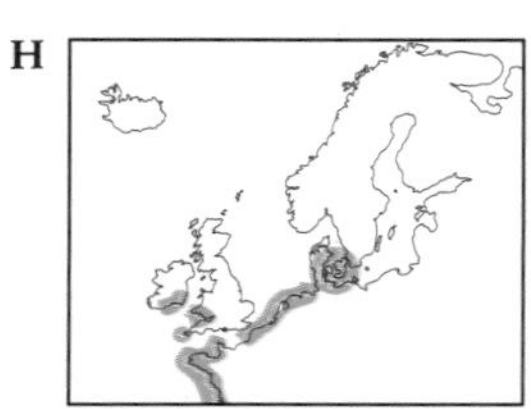

I

A Lily-of-the-valley *Convallaria majalis* Creeping hairless perennial with rhizomes. Leaves arise in pairs or in 3s, direct from rhizome, with green or reddish-purple scales at base; blade ovate to lanceolate, pointed, to 20cm long, 60mm wide. Flowers produced in 1-sided nodding racemes on leafless stalks, to 30cm; perianth bell-shaped, white (rarely pink), fragrant; fruit a globose red berry, 8-10mm in diameter. In woods, scrub, mountain meadows and limestone rocks; throughout except the far north. **Fl** 5-7. **Br** Local in England; rare elsewhere. Widely cultivated and naturalised.

B May Lily *Maianthemum bifolium* Perennial with creeping rhizome, and erect stems to 20cm, hairless except at top. Leaves deeply heart-shaped at base, alternate, stalked, pointed, 30-60mm long, usually both basal and on stem. Flowers in short, erect, cylindrical spike to 40mm, with up to 20 small white 4-parted flowers, 2-5mm in diameter. Fruit a red berry about 5mm in diameter. Widespread almost throughout in woods, often rather acid or humus-rich; local. **Fl** 5-6. **Br** Very local in woods in a few localities in England; absent elsewhere.

C Streptopus *Streptopus amplexicaulis* Creeping perennial, with leafy ascending stems to 1m. Leaves alternate, *heart-shaped, clasping*. Flowers singly or in 2s, from leaf axils on arching stalks; perianth greenish white, to 10mm long, bell-shaped; fruit a red berry, 6-8mm in diameter. From central Germany southwards; mainly in mountains. **Fl** 6-7. **Br** Absent.

SOLOMON'S-SEAL *Polygonatum* Three species (in this area) of creeping perennials with arching or erect stems bearing whorled or alternate leaves, with clusters of white tubular flowers from the axils.

D Whorled Solomon's-seal *Polygonatum verticillatum* Erect perennial, with angled stems to 80cm. Leaves linear-lanceolate, to 15cm long, *in whorls of 3-6*. Flowers in pendulous clusters in leaf axils, bell-shaped, constricted in middle, greenish white, to 10mm long. Throughout, though local; in woods and rocky ground, especially in mountains. **Fl** 6-7. **Br** Rare, only in N England and S Scotland.

E Common Solomon's-seal *Polygonatum multiflorum* Hairless clump-forming perennial, with *arching round stems* to 80cm. *Leaves alternate*, ovate to lanceolate, to 15cm long, stalkless or short-stalked, tending to spread out on each side of the stem. Flowers stalked, *in clusters of 2-6*, pendulous, from leaf axils; perianth greenish white, tubular bell-shaped, somewhat contracted in middle of tube. Widespread almost throughout; in dry woods and scrub, often on lime-rich soils. **Fl** 5-6. **Br** Curiously localised, mainly in central S and NW England, and S Wales.

F Angular Solomon's-seal *Polygonatum odoratum* Similar to Common Solomon's-seal, but shorter, to 60cm, with *stem distinctly angled; flowers 1 or 2 together*, longer, to 20mm, cylindrical, not constricted in middle. In woods and rocky places, usually on limestone; throughout except the extreme north. **Fl** 5-7. **Br** Local, in N and W England south to the Cotswolds; rare in Wales; absent elsewhere.

G Herb-paris *Paris quadrifolia* Highly distinctive plant. Perennial, with erect stems to 40cm, bearing a single whorl of 4 (or more) net-veined, roughly diamond-shaped leaves at the top. Flowers solitary, with 4 or more narrow green sepals, and 4 or more very narrow petals, topped by a conspicuous purple ovary, and 6-10 yellow stamens. Widespread almost throughout in woods, often on damp or calcareous soils. **Fl** 5-7. **Br** Widespread almost throughout, but local.

H Wild Asparagus *Asparagus officinalis* Hairless perennial, either with erect stems to 2m (usually less), or spreading. Leaves reduced to tiny membranous bracts, which may have clusters of short green cladodes (much-reduced stems) in their axils, producing the overall effect of a feathery much-divided leaf. Flowers tiny, 4-6mm long, in axils of leaves, greenish yellow, bell-shaped, separate male and female. Fruit a red globose berry, 6-10mm in diameter. In grassy habitats, waste places and dunes; northwards to Denmark and S Sweden, but widely naturalised elsewhere and within this range. **Fl** 6-9. **Br** Normal form is locally native or naturalised in England and Wales; prostrate form is rare in S England, Wales and Ireland only.
Ssp *prostratus* is a procumbent form with very short internodes, occurring on grassy sea-cliffs in SW Britain and W France.

I Butcher's-broom *Ruscus aculeatus* Highly distinctive plant. A hairless, much-branched shrubby erect plant to 1m, with separate male and female plants. Leaves are reduced to tiny membranous scales, with leaf-like cladodes in their axils; these are ovate-lanceolate, dark green, tough, spiny-pointed, to 40mm long. Flowers are produced, usually solitary, on the upper side of the cladodes; about 5mm in diameter, greenish, with 6 perianth segments. Fruit a globose red berry, 10-12mm in diameter. In woods, hedgebanks, normally on dry calcareous soils; from central England and N France southwards. **Fl** 1-4. **Br** Locally common in S England, rarer northwards, naturalised in Scotland.

A	B	C
D	E	F
	H1	H2
G	I1	I2

A **Lily-of-the-valley**

B **May Lily**

C **Streptopus** in fruit

D **Whorled Solomon's-seal**

E **Common Solomon's-seal**

F **Angular Solomon's-seal**

H **1 Wild Asparagus** prostrate form

H **2 Wild Asparagus** normal form

G **Herb-paris**

I **1 Butcher's-broom** showing habitat

I **2 Butcher's-broom** in fruit

A

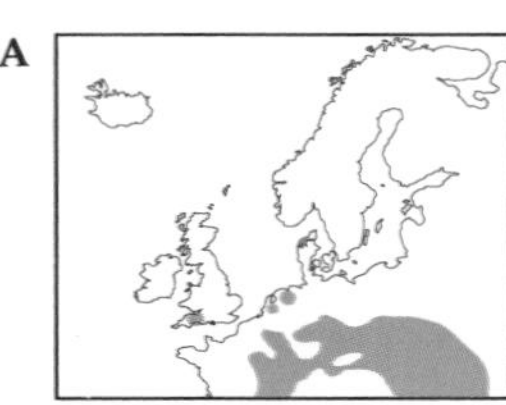

B

D

E

G

J

Daffodil Family
Amaryllidaceae

Hairless, bulbous perennials with basal, usually linear leaves, and leafless flower stems. Very close to lily family, differing in having ovary inferior, and flowers always enclosed in a spathe. Stamens 6, style single. In *Narcissus*, the flowers have a conspicuous cup, the corona, inside the petals.

A **Spring Snowflake** *Leucojum vernum* Bulbous perennial to 35cm. Leaves strap-shaped, bright green, to 25cm long, to 20mm wide. *Flowers usually solitary, rarely 2 together*, nodding at tip of stem; spathe green with papery border, up to 40mm long, usually forked at tip; flowers with 6 perianth segments all alike, in bell shape, white with greenish patch near the tip of each, 20-25mm long. In damp shady places or meadows; native from Belgium and S England southwards, though naturalised elsewhere. **Fl** 2-4. **Br** Possibly native in 2 localities, Dorset and Somerset only.

B **Summer Snowflake** *Leucojum aestivum* Rather similar to Spring Snowflake, but a taller more robust plant to 60cm. Leaves similar but longer, equalling the flower stem. *Flowers in an umbel of 2-5*, with a 40-50mm spathe, green at apex, undivided; perianth segments white, with green tip, 14-18mm long. In marshes and wet woods, including tidal ones; from Holland and S Ireland southwards; local. Also widely cultivated. **Fl** 4-6. **Br** Very local as native in S England and S Ireland; absent elsewhere except if naturalised.

C **Snowdrop** *Galanthus nivalis* Small bulbous herb to 30cm, often confused with *Leucojum* species. Differs in the *greyish-green linear leaves*, to 6mm wide. Flowers 1 per stem, drooping, with 3 outer segments to 25mm long, white, and 3 inner segments to 11mm long, white with green patch near the tip. In damp broad-leaved woodland; from N France and Germany southwards; naturalised elsewhere. **Fl** 1-3. **Br** Locally naturalised almost throughout, possibly native in SW England and Welsh borders.

D **Wild Daffodil** *Narcissus pseudonarcissus* Hairless perennial, with erect flat linear grey-green leaves to 50cm. Flowers solitary (rarely more), turned sideways, at tip of stems up to 50cm. Flowers 50-60mm in diameter, consisting of outer whorl of 6 pale yellow perianth segments, and an inner, deeper yellow cup, 25-30mm long (the corona). From N England, Holland and W Germany southwards; in woods and meadows. **Fl** 4-5. **Br** Locally common in England and Wales, though absent as native from large areas.

Yam Family Dioscoreaceae

Twining climbers, with leaves that look more like those of dicots than monocots. Flowers unisexual, in small spikes.

E **Black Bryony** *Tamus communis* Climbing herbaceous hairless perennial, twining clockwise, lacking tendrils. Leaves heart-shaped, 8-15cm long, bright glossy green, net-veined. Male and female plants separate; flowers greenish yellow, open bell-shaped, small (4-5mm in diameter), with males in cylindrical long racemes, females in small clusters. Fruit a red globose poisonous berry, 10-12mm across. From England and Germany southwards; in hedgerows, wood-margins, scrub and commons. **Fl** 5-7. **Br** Common in lowland areas of England and Wales; absent elsewhere.

Iris Family Iridaceae

Bulbous, rhizomatous or cormous plants. Similar to daffodil family, though with 3 stamens (not 6), 3-lobed style, and petals joined into a tube at base.

F **Blue-eyed Grass** *Sisyrinchium bermudiana* Hairless perennial with erect or ascending, flattened, winged stems from short rhizome. Leaves all basal, linear, to 5mm wide, 15cm long. Flowers in 2 (occasionally 1 or 3) terminal inflorescences, 2-4 in each, with leaf-like bracts below each; perianth light blue, 15-20mm in diameter, lobes ovate with distinct bristle-point. In damp grassland and lake-margins; native only in N and W Ireland; naturalised elsewhere. **Fl** 7-8. **Br** As above.

G **Stinking Iris, Roast Beef Plant** *Iris foetidissima* Tufted perennial herb, with erect stems from slender rhizomes. Leaves sword-shaped, dark green, evergreen, up to 70cm long and 2cm wide, about as long as flower stems. *Plant smells strongly of meat when crushed*. Flowers 6-8cm in diameter, *dull purplish with brownish yellow towards centre*, unbearded, with purple veins, in characteristic iris shape. Brown capsule splits into 3 segments when ripe, exposing large orange seeds. From N France and N England southwards; in woods, hedgebanks and scrub. **Fl** 5-7. **Br** Common on calcareous soils in S England and Wales, becoming rarer to the north; absent from Scotland and far N England.

H **Yellow Iris, Yellow Flag** *Iris pseudacorus* Perennial hairless herb, with erect stems to 1.2m, from rhizomes. Leaves sword-shaped, to 90cm long and 3cm wide, rather greyish-green. Flowers in clusters of 2-3, each with a spathe below, green with papery margins towards the tip. Flowers large, to 10cm in diameter, *bright yellow with red-purple veins*, unbearded. Capsule similar to Stinking Iris, but seeds duller brown. Throughout, except the extreme north; in marshes, riversides and other wet places. **Fl** 5-7. **Br** Common throughout.

I *Iris sibirica* Has narrow grass-like leaves to 1cm wide, *flowers violet-blue with yellow*, 6-8cm across, on stalks to 1.2m. In damp grassland; mainly eastern, but reaching Germany and E France and 1 place in W France. **Fl** 6-7. **Br** Absent.

J **Blue, or Butterfly, Iris** *Iris spuria* Perennial herb, with erect stems to 60cm, unpleasant-smelling. Leaves linear, to 2cm wide, usually shorter than inflorescence. Flowers to 5cm in diameter; *falls have almost round blue-violet tip, contracted abruptly to yellowish, winged stalk*; standards shorter, violet and erect. In damp places on calcareous or saline soils; from S Sweden southwards, but very local. **Fl** 5-6. **Br** Probably introduced, but long-established in Lincolnshire and Dorset.

K *Iris aphylla* Low perennial to 30cm, leafless in winter. Flowers in groups of 3-5, violet-purple, to 7cm across; *falls with yellowish beard*. An eastern species, extending into Germany; in dry rocky grasslands. **Fl** 5-6. **Br** Absent.

A	B	C
D	E1 / E2	F / G
H	J	K

A **Spring Snowflake**

B **Summer Snowflake**

C **Snowdrop**

D **Wild Daffodil**

E **1 Black Bryony** in fruit

F **Blue-eyed Grass**

E **2 Black Bryony** in flower

G **Stinking Iris**

H **Yellow Iris**

J **Blue Iris**

K *Iris aphylla*

A

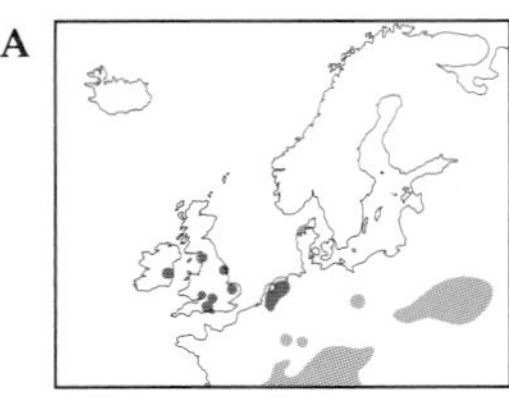

C

I

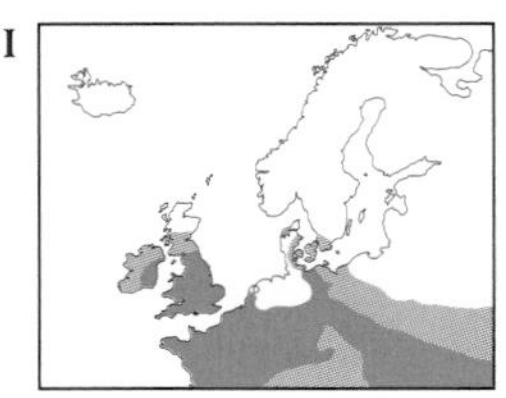

J

A **Spring Crocus** *Crocus vernus* Familiar crocus-type flower. Leaves linear, 2-4 from corm, 4-8mm wide, with central white stripe, still short at flowering time. Flowers goblet-shaped, up to 20cm tall, opening more widely in bright sunshine, purple, white or striped; style branched, orange. In grassland and open woods, commonest in mountain pastures; from Jura and S Germany southwards, though widely naturalised elsewhere. **Fl** 3-5. **Br** Naturalised locally in grasslands; declining.

B **Autumnal Crocus** *Crocus nudiflorus* Similar to above, but *flowers appear in autumn*, without leaves, up to 28cm tall, purplish, on long white tubes. More likely to be confused with Meadow Saffron (*see* page 298), which differs in having pinker flowers, 6 stamens (not 3), and an unbranched whitish style. Naturalised in scattered localities, originally from SW Europe. **Fl** 8-10. **Br** Locally naturalised in England.

C **Sand Crocus** *Romulea columnae* Very small cormous perennial. Leaves 3-6, narrowly cylindrical, curly, to 2mm wide and 10cm long, all basal. Flowers solitary or 2-3, 7-10mm in diameter, shorter than leaves, opening only in sun; perianth starry, purplish white inside, yellow towards the base, dark-veined, greenish outside, all equal in size and shape. In sandy and rocky coastal turf; from SW England and N France southwards. **Fl** 3-5. **Br** In Devon and the Channel Islands only; locally common.

D **Wild Gladiolus** *Gladiolus illyricus* Slender erect hairless perennial to 90cm, from corms. Leaves to 30cm long and 1cm wide, long-pointed, grey-green, all flattened in the same plane. Flowers in long loose rather 1-sided raceme of 3-10 flowers, with alternate ones pointing in different directions, each with a spathe of 2 green, often purple-tipped, bracts. Perianth bright rosy purple, with 6 unequal segments, 3-4cm long, the upper 3 forming a loose hood, all more or less streaked with white and red. On heaths, scrub and open woodland, mainly on acid soils; from S England and W France southwards, very local. **Fl** 6-7. **Br** Now only in the New Forest; locally common under bracken.

E *Gladiolus palustris* Similar to Wild Gladiolus, but has spikes very *strongly 1-sided, with 6 or less flowers*. In wet meadows and scrub; just extending westwards into S Germany and E France. **Fl** 6-7. **Br** Absent.

Pipewort Family Eriocaulaceae

A small family of herbs with rosettes of leaves and tight heads of mixed male and female flowers.

F **Pipewort** *Eriocaulon aquaticum* Distinctive rather slender aquatic herb, with erect tufts of leaves produced at intervals from creeping rootstock. Leaves narrow, 3-5mm wide, to 10cm long, somewhat flattened and tapering gradually to a fine point. Flower stems erect, angled, to 60cm, emerging above water surface. Flowers in dense flattened sphere, to 20mm in diameter, surrounded by a whorl of tiny grey bracts, described as resembling 'whitish-headed knitting needles'. In shallow peaty lakes and pools; only in W Ireland and W Scotland; very local. **Fl** 7-9. **Br** As above.

Arum Family Araceae

A distinctive family with leaves broader than most monocots, often lobed, sometimes net-veined. Flowers tiny, crowded into a spadix (short, dense spike), wholly or partly enclosed by a large fleshy bract, the spathe.

G **Sweet-flag** *Acorus calamus* Large, rhizomatous, aquatic perennial. Leaves long, linear, to 1.2m, 1-2cm wide, pointed, with margins wavy in parts, and with an off-centre pronounced midrib. Flower stem 3-angled, as tall or taller than leaves, with a long spathe and an apparently lateral cylindrical greenish-yellow spadix of flowers, to 9cm long. Naturalised in shallow water and wet places; throughout N Europe except the extreme north; originating from SE Asia. **Fl** 6-7. **Br** Locally naturalised.

H **Bog Arum** *Calla palustris* Aquatic perennial with a stout rhizome and stout stems to 30cm. Leaves rounded to oval, up to 12cm long, heart-shaped at base, with long stalks. Spathe broad, white on upper surface, not enfolding spadix, spadix short and squat, to 30mm long, flowers yellowish green. Fruit a red berry, about 5mm across. In swamps, marshes and lake-margins; central Europe, extending westwards to Belgium, Denmark and France. **Fl** 6-8. **Br** Very locally naturalised.

I **Lords-and-ladies, Cuckoo-pint** *Arum maculatum* Erect, hairless, tuberous perennial to 50cm. Leaves basal, arrow-shaped, shiny green, often purplish-spotted, with long petiole 15-25cm, *appearing in spring before flowers*. Spathe consists of rolled basal section, and unfurled cowl-shaped erect upper part, to 25cm high, pale green-yellow; spadix enclosed in spathe, with *purple-brown (rarely yellow)* club-shaped upper part visible in cowl. Fruit a red berry in a dense spike. Common as far north as Scotland and N Germany, in woods and hedgerows, often rather damp. **Fl** 4-5. **Br** Common in S Britain, increasingly rare to the north.

J **Large Lords-and-ladies** *Arum italicum* ssp *neglectum* Similar to Lords-and-ladies, differing in that *some leaves appear in autumn*; leaves are less pointed, more leathery, not spotted, less wrinkled. Spathe up to 40cm high, *with tip hanging forwards over spadix when fully open; spadix always yellow*. In woods and shady places, mainly coastal; from S England southwards. **Fl** 5-6. **Br** S England and Wales only, mainly near coasts. Locally common.

A	D	C
B		H
F	G	J
I1	I2	

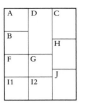

A **Spring Crocus**
D **Wild Gladiolus**
C **Sand Crocus**
B **Autumnal Crocus**
F **Pipewort**
G **Sweet-flag**
H **Bog Arum**
I **1 Lords and Ladies** in flower
I **2 Lords-and-ladies** in fruit
J **Large Lords-and-ladies**

A

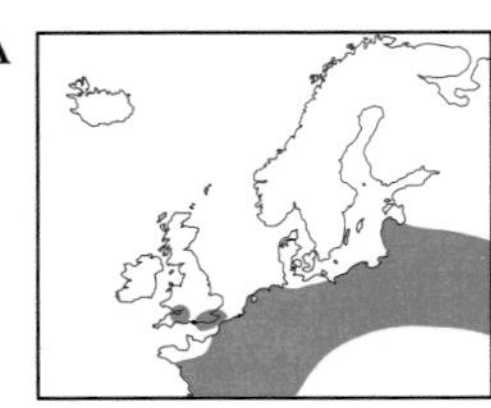

H

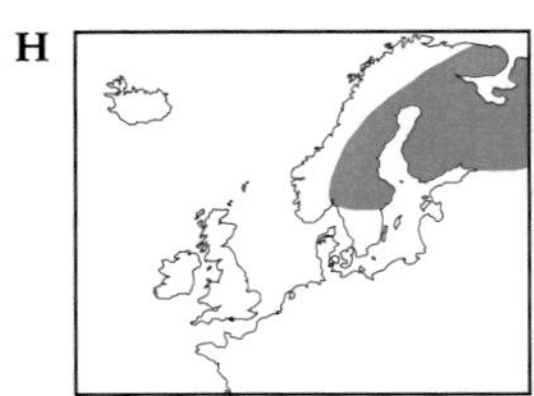

I

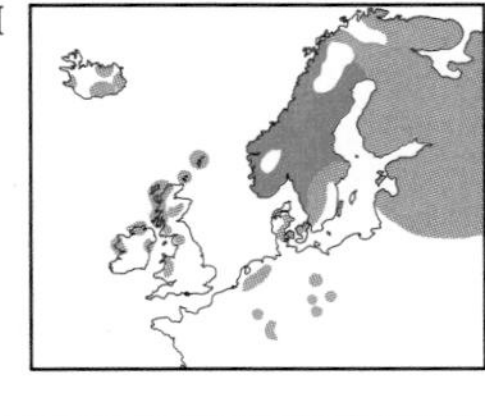

N

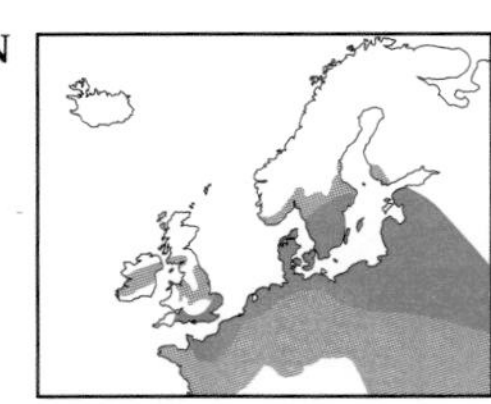

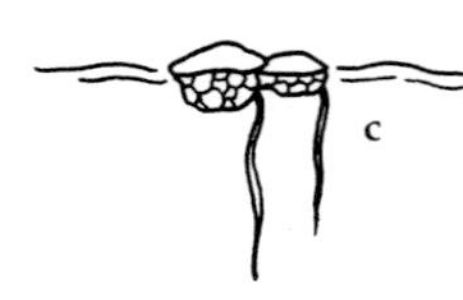

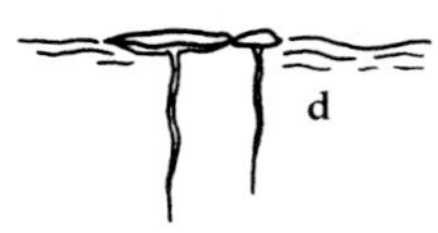

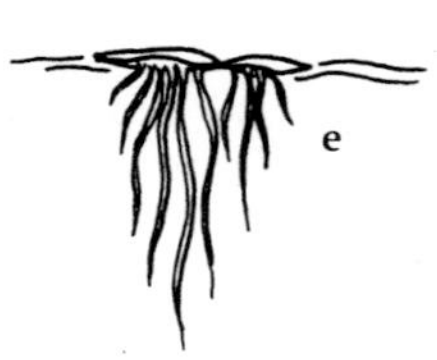

Duckweed Family Lemnaceae

A family of floating or submerged perennial herbs, often forming carpets on surface. No clear division into stem and leaves, merely a thallus with or without roots. All species small. Flowers tiny, reduced to stamens or ovary only.

A **Rootless Duckweed** *Wolffia arrhiza* One of the smallest flowering plants in N Europe. Consists of tiny ovoid green thallus, to 1mm long, without roots. Flowers in cavity on surface of frond, never produced in Europe. Local, from Holland and Germany southwards; in still fresh water. **Br** Very local (though easily overlooked!) in S England only.

B **Ivy-leaved Duckweed** *Lemna trisulca* Occurs slightly below surface of water. Consists of thin translucent elliptical leaves, 5-15mm long, tapering into short stalks and *joined into colonies, with terminal trio of leaves looking rather like miniature ivy leaves*. Flower leaves smaller and floating. Widespread and generally common in still fresh water, except in the extreme north. **Fl** 5-7. **Br** Common in the south, rare in the north.

C **Fat Duckweed** *Lemna gibba* Thallus oval, opaque, up to 5mm, green and convex above, usually *strongly swollen and white spongy below*, each with *1 root* (**c**). Widespread except in N Scandinavia; in still fresh water. **Fl** 6-7, rarely produced. **Br** Local in S Britain; absent from Scotland.

D **Common Duckweed** *Lemna minor* Thalli elliptical to rounded, symmetrical, *flat on both surfaces*, up to 5mm across, floating, with a *single long root* hanging below (**d**). Common almost throughout, except the extreme north; in still or slow-moving fresh water. **Fl** 6-7. **Br** Common throughout, except the extreme north.

E **Greater Duckweed** *Spirodela polyrhiza* Thalli to 10mm, rounded ovate, opaque, *flat on both sides*, often purplish below, *with several roots* (**e**) (up to 15 per thallus). Widespread throughout except the extreme north, locally common; in still fresh water. **Fl** 6-7, but rarely produced. **Br** Locally common in the south, rare or absent in the north.

Bur-reed Family Sparganiaceae

Perennial aquatic herbs, with leafy stems. Flowers unisexual, in dense spherical heads.

F **Branched Bur-reed** *Sparganium erectum* Erect hairless perennial to 1.5m. Leaves usually all erect, occasionally floating, triangular in section, *keeled* and linear. *Inflorescence branched*, with the globular yellow male heads borne above the female on each branch; flower clusters individually unstalked; perianth segments thick, with dark tip. In water and marshy places, not tolerant of grazing; throughout. **Fl** 6-8. **Br** Common almost throughout.

G **Unbranched Bur-reed** *Sparganium emersum* Rather similar to Branched Bur-reed. Leaves erect or floating, *triangular but not keeled*. *Inflorescence unbranched*, with several female clusters at base, and 3-10 separated male clusters on the main axis above them; style straight. In fresh water, still or slow-flowing; throughout. **Fl** 6-8. **Br** Locally common throughout.

H *Sparganium gramineum* Very similar to Unbranched Bur-reed, but *always floating*, with *very long leaves*. Inflorescence usually with branches at base; styles bent at base. Similar habitats, Scandinavia only. **Fl** 7-8. **Br** Absent.

I **Floating Bur-reed** *Sparganium angustifolium* Perennial with long slender, normally floating, stems to 1m. Leaves *flat in section, not keeled, inflated and sheathing at base*. *Inflorescence simple* with 1-3 male heads on the main axis, and very close together; style straight. Widespread throughout N Europe; in acid pools and ditches, though absent from many calcareous lowland areas. **Fl** 8-9. **Br** Mainly northern or in mountains; rare elsewhere.

J *Sparganium glomeratum* Stems always erect, *leaves sharply keeled, not inflated at base*, and a dense inflorescence. Similar habitats; Scandinavia only. **Fl** 7-9. **Br** Absent.

K **Least Bur-reed** *Sparganium minimum* Small, floating plant to 80cm long, with narrow leaves to 6mm wide, *translucent*, and only *slightly inflated at base*. Inflorescence small, with 1 male head, and 2-3 unstalked female heads, with bract of lowest head not exceeding inflorescence. In peaty acid still waters; throughout but local. **Fl** 6-7. **Br** Rare or absent in much of the south, locally common in the north.

L *Sparganium hyperboreum* Rather similar to above, but *leaves oval in section and opaque*; lowest bract distinctly longer than inflorescence. Similar habitats; N Scandinavia only. **Fl** 7-8. **Br** Absent.

Reedmace Family Typhaceae

A small family with 1 genus. Mainly aquatic, with flowers crowded into dense cylindrical inflorescence, with female flowers towards base.

M **Common Reedmace** *Typha latifolia* Stout robust perennial to 2.5m. Leaves mainly basal, 1-2cm wide, very long, often overtopping flower spike, grey-green, set in 2 distinct opposite rows. Inflorescence is the familiar dense cylindrical spike, with the *lower part very stout (up to 15cm long and 3cm in diameter)*, deep brown, made up of female flowers, topped by *immediately adjacent narrower yellowish male section*. In still water and wet places; widespread and common throughout. **Fl** 6-8. **Br** Common throughout.

N **Lesser Reedmace** *Typha angustifolia* Similar to above, but slenderer; leaves only 3-6mm wide, darker green; male and female parts of inflorescence *distinctly separated by a stalk of 10-90mm long*, whole inflorescence more slender. In similar habitats, though more local; absent from the north. **Fl** 6- 7. **Br** Locally common in England and Wales; rare or absent further north.

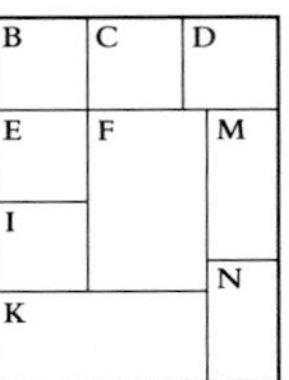

B **Ivy-leaved Duckweed**
C **Fat Duckweed**
D **Common Duckweed**
E **Greater Duckweed**
F **Branched Bur-reed**
M **Common Reedmace**
I **Floating Bur-reed**
N **Lesser Reedmace**
K **Least Bur-reed**

A

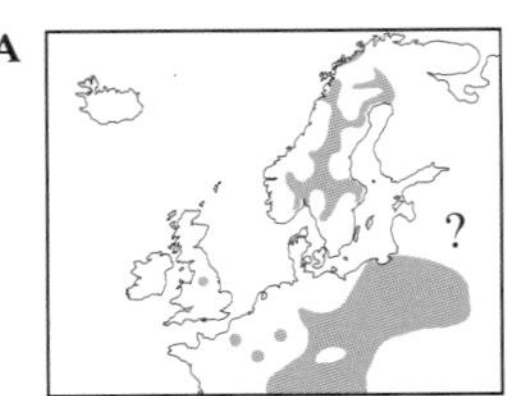

B

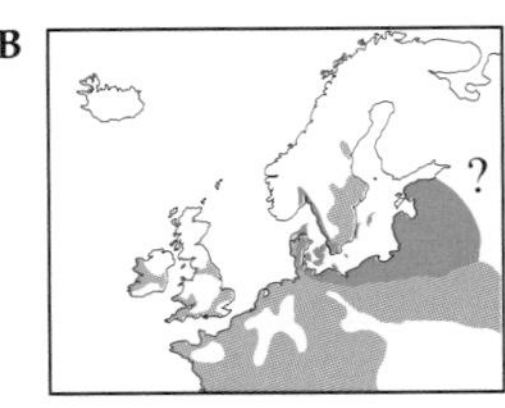

D

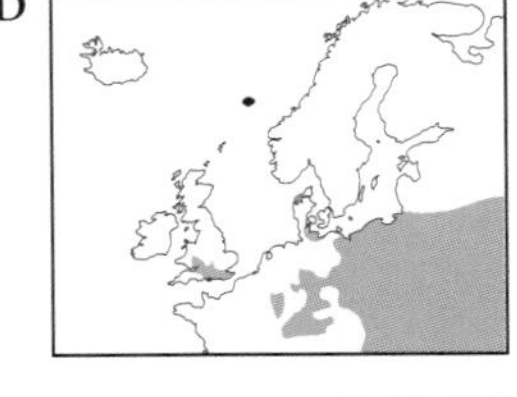

F

G

I

J

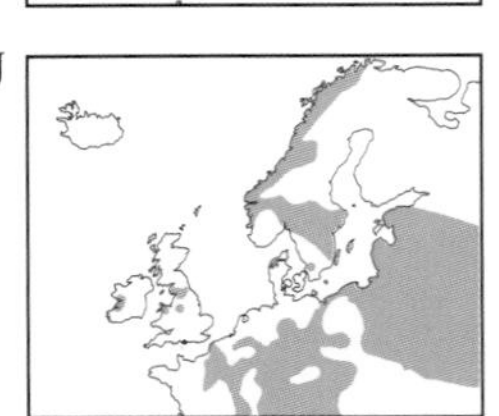

Orchid Family Orchidaceae

A huge mainly tropical family, with about 30,000 species worldwide. Perennial herbs, usually with rhizomes or tubers. Many have unusual modes of life, especially as saprophytes, living without green pigment (chlorophyll) and therefore dependent on rotting vegetation which they utilise with the aid of a fungus; many tropical species are epiphytes, growing on trees, but all N European species are terrestrial. Flowers are produced in spikes or racemes; they have the perianth in 2 whorls of 3, of which the outer 3 are usually all similar, while the inner 3 have 1 much larger than the other 2, known as the lip or labellum; this is usually on the lower part of the flower, and is often quite different from the other segments, which may themselves be modified greatly. The ovary is inferior, generally forming part of the flower stalk. The anthers and stigma are borne on a distinctive central column.

A **Lady's-slipper Orchid** *Cypripedium calceolus* Very distinctive plant, unlikely to be confused with any other N European native. Stems to 50cm, rather downy. Leaves oval to elliptical, pointed, sheathing, strongly veined. Flowers usually solitary (rarely 2) per stem, with large leaf-like bract at base; outer perianth segments narrow, maroon, to 9cm long; lip is shorter, but greatly inflated and yellow with red spots in hollow interior. In woods and grassy places, mainly on limestone soils; from central Scandinavia southwards, but very local and declining. **Fl** 5-6. **Br** Very rare in N England only.

HELLEBORINES *Epipactis* Plants without basal rosette, but numerous stem leaves. Flowers stalked in loose cylindrical racemes, usually twisted so that all face in roughly the same direction. Flowers have inner perianth whorl of 2 similar upper segments, and a 2-part lip, consisting of the inner hypochile and outer, roughly triangular, epichile; ovary straight, not twisted.

(1) Plants with all leaves spirally arranged.

B **Marsh Helleborine** *Epipactis palustris* Erect plant to 50cm, downy near top. Leaves oblong-oval to lanceolate, pointed, largest ones at base of stem, upper ones held erect. Flowers in loose raceme with up to 14 flowers; outer perianth segments ovate-lanceolate, brownish or purplish green; inner upper 2 shorter, whitish with red-purple streaks; lip has *heart-shaped white epichile, with frilly edges* and yellow spot at base; flowers open widely. In marshes and fens; widespread but absent from the far north. **Fl** 7-8. **Br** Local in England and Wales; rare or absent further north.

C **Broad-leaved Helleborine** *Epipactis helleborine* Erect plant to 80cm, with 1-3 stems in clump. Lowest leaves scale-like, largest leaves around centre of stem, ovate-elliptical, to 17cm long, strongly veined, dull green on both sides, all leaves spirally arranged. Raceme 7-30cm long, with up to 100 flowers; flowers (**c**) open wide, held horizontally or slightly drooping; outer perianth segments ovate-elliptical, green tinged purple; hypochile cup-shaped, dark red-brown, unspotted inside; epichile heart-shaped, broader than long, with curved-back tip, varying from green to red-purple; ovary hairless. Widespread in woods, shady banks and dune-hollows; throughout except the extreme north. **Fl** 7-9. **Br** Locally fequent throughout except N Scotland.

c

D **Violet Helleborine** *Epipactis purpurata* Rather similar to Broad-leaved Helleborine, but usually with more stems in cluster, *all strongly purple-tinged.* Leaves narrower, grey-green above, purplish below. Flowers (**d**) with *outer perianth segments whitish inside;* inner perianth segments similar, sometimes purplish-tinged; epichile triangular heart-shaped, with recurved tip, dull white with purple streak in centre. In woods, frequently of beech, usually on lime-rich soils. **Fl** 8-9. **Br** Uncommon in S England; rare or absent elsewhere.

E **Small-leaved Helleborine** *Epipactis microphylla* Similar to Broad-leaved Helleborine, but has *few short leaves, less than 30mm long and 10mm wide,* pale green. Flowers pale whitish green. In woods on lime-rich soils, often in mountain areas; from Belgium and S Germany southwards; uncommon. **Fl** 6-8. **Br** Absent.

(2) Plants with leaves distinctly in 2 ranks up stem, though not paired.

F **Narrow-lipped Helleborine** *Epipactis leptochila* Tall slender plant to 70cm. Leaves oval-lanceolate, to 10cm long, often yellow-green. Flowers (**f**) wide open, yellow-green, outer perianth segments pointed, with *epichile very narrowly heart-shaped* with flat tip, long-pointed, *yellowish green with white margin.* In woods and scrub, often very shady, usually on calcareous soils; rare or local from Denmark southwards. **Fl** 6-7. **Br** S England only; very local.

G **Mueller's Helleborine** *Epipactis muelleri* Very similar to Narrow-lipped Helleborine, but *epichile broadly heart-shaped,* broader than long, recurved at tip; outer perianth segments blunt (**g**). Rare, in open woods and scrub on calcareous soils; from Holland and Germany southwards. **Fl** 7-8. **Br** Absent.

H **Dune Helleborine** *Epipactis dunensis* Similar to Narrow-lipped Helleborine, but *flowers open less widely; epichile broadly triangular* (**h**), as long as broad, *with tip curled under,* often reddish-tinged in centre. In open and shady places on sand-dunes; N England, Anglesey and possibly Denmark only. **Fl** 6-7. **Br** Very local in N England and Anglesey only.

I **Green-flowered Helleborine** *Epipactis phyllanthes* Small slender downy erect plant to 45cm. Leaves light green, ovate-lanceolate, not strongly veined, up to 7cm long. *Flowers pendent, normally not fully open; all perianth segments yellowish green,* except hypochile which is white inside, and epichile which is greenish white. Very local from S Sweden southwards, but absent from many areas; in woods and on dunes on calcareous soils. **Fl** 7-9. **Br** Local in England and Wales; rare in Ireland; absent elsewhere.

J **Dark-red Helleborine** *Epipactis atrorubens* Stems usually solitary, downy, erect, to 60cm. Flowers all *reddish purple to brick-red,* hypochile spotted inside with red. A distinctive species. In woods, scrub and rocky slopes on chalk and limestone; throughout, except the far north. **Fl** 6-8. **Br** Very local, mainly in N England and N Wales, also W Ireland and NW Scotland.

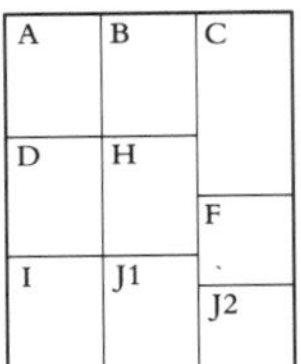

A **Lady's-slipper Orchid**

B **Marsh Helleborine** var. *ochroleuca* (left) and normal form

C **Broad-leaved Helleborine**

D **Violet Helleborine**

H **Dune Helleborine**

F **Narrow-lipped Helleborine**

I **Green-flowered Helleborine**

J **1 Dark-red Helleborine**

J **2 Dark-red Helleborine** flowers

d

f

g

h

A

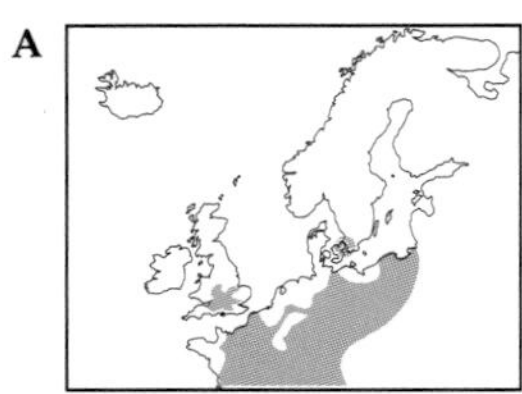

C

D

E

F

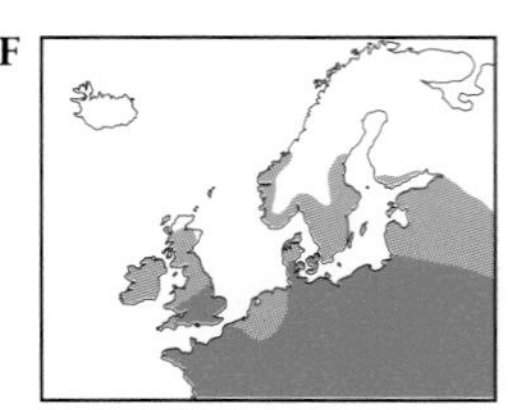

H

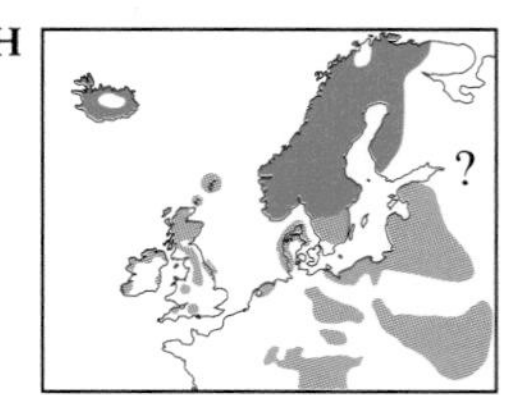

HELLEBORINES *Cephalanthera* These differ from *Epipactis* species in the flowers, which have less marked separation of the lip into 2 parts, and the folding forward of the perianth segments to form a bell shape.

A **White Helleborine** *Cephalanthera damasonium* Erect hairless perennial, with angled stems to 60cm. Leaves oblong-lanceolate to lanceolate at top, up to 10cm long. Flowers 3-12 in a spike up to 12cm long, each with a leaf-like bract at base; perianth *creamy white*, about 2cm long, *partially open*, erect, segments blunt; hypochile has an orange blotch, and epichile has orange ridges along it. Widespread from S Sweden southwards, in woods and scrub; commoner in the south. **Fl** 5-7. **Br** Local in southern half of England only, mainly in beechwoods on chalk and limestone.

B **Sword-leaved Helleborine** *Cephalanthera longifolia* Similar to White Helleborine, but stems less angled, with whitish (not brown) scales below; leaves long, narrow, linear, with tips slightly drooping. *Flowers purer white*, in a denser spike with shorter bracts, *opening more widely*; perianth segments pointed. Widespread except in the extreme north; in woods and other shady places. **Fl** 5-6. **Br** Widespread in scattered localities, but very local, and absent from many areas; declining.. Least rare in central southern England.

C **Red Helleborine** *Cephalanthera rubra* Rather like Sword-leaved Helleborine in form, with shorter straight leaves, few in number. Flowers all *reddish pink*, opening widely, with whitish lip marked with red and yellow; ovary and upper parts of stem sticky and hairy. In open woods and scrub; from S Scandinavia southwards, rare in the north of range, commoner in the far south. **Fl** 6-7. **Br** Very rare, in a few S England localities only.

D **Violet Limodore** *Limodorum abortivum* Highly distinctive plant. Erect, rather cane-like stems to 80cm, lacking green leaves (saprophytic, or possibly partially parasitic). Flower spike lax, with 4 to 25 flowers; perianth segments long, to 2cm, all violet or whitish; lip triangular, wavy, yellowish and violet. Woods and shady areas, often associated with pine; mainly S Europe but extending into N France, Belgium and S Germany. **Fl** 5-6. Appearance and timing very variable according to spring rainfall. **Br** Absent.

E **Ghost Orchid** *Epipogium aphyllum* Saprophytic plant with erect pinkish-yellow leafless stems to 20cm, rarely more. Leaves reduced to brownish scales. Flowers in loose raceme of 1-5 flowers; these are pendent, 15-30mm across, relatively large for size of plant, with linear, pale yellow perianth segments, and a 3-lobed white to pinkish, red-spotted lip. Throughout, extending inside the Arctic circle; in woods and shady places, but always very local. **Fl** 5-9. **Br** Very local, rare and sporadic in appearance, in a few S England beechwood localities.

F **Bird's-nest Orchid** *Neottia nidus-avis* Erect plant to 45cm, with pale brown stems, lacking chlorophyll. Leaves reduced to brownish sheathing scales. Inflorescence moderately dense, 5-21cm long, with numerous flowers; bracts shorter than ovaries; perianth segments all brown, 4-6mm long, curled together to form a hood over the flower; the lip is 8-12mm long, divided into 2 lobes. Widespread in shady woodland, especially on humus-rich soils; throughout except the extreme north. **Fl** 5-7. **Br** Local throughout except N Scotland, but rare in the north of range.

G **Common Twayblade** *Listera ovata* Erect plant to 60cm. There is a *single unstalked pair of broad ovate leaves*, up to 18cm long, *near the base of the stem*, forming a distinctive feature (hence the English name). Inflorescence is a dense or lax raceme, with numerous green flowers with short bracts; perianth segments form a hood, lip hangs down below, yellowish green, 10-15mm long, forked to half-way. Occurs in a wide range of habitats; throughout except the extreme north; generally common. **Fl** 6-7. **Br** Throughout, except in high mountain areas.

H **Lesser Twayblade** *Listera cordata* Similar in form to Common Twayblade, though quite obviously different. Plant much smaller, to 20cm at most, with *a reddish stem*. Leaves ovate to heart-shaped, up to 40mm long, in a single, opposite pair near base of stem, dark green and shiny above. Flowers *in short loose raceme of 4-12, much smaller than those of Common Twayblade;* perianth segments 2-2.5mm long, reddish, not in such a distinct hood; lip reddish, with 2 diverging lobes. Widespread; on moorland, in pinewoods and boggy areas, but local, and surprisingly inconspicuous, often growing under heather. **Fl** 6-9. **Br** Mainly N England and Scotland, becoming more frequent northwards; also on Exmoor, but very rare there.

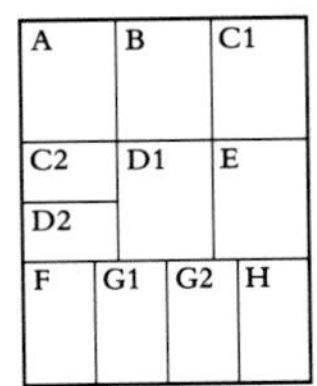

A **White Helleborine**

B **Sword-leaved Helleborine**

C **1 Red Helleborine**

C **2 Red Helleborine** flower

D **1 Violet Limodore**

E **Ghost Orchid**

D **2 Violet Limodore** flowers

F **Bird's-nest Orchid**

G **1 Common Twayblade**

G **2 Common Twayblade** flowers

H **Lesser Twayblade**

A
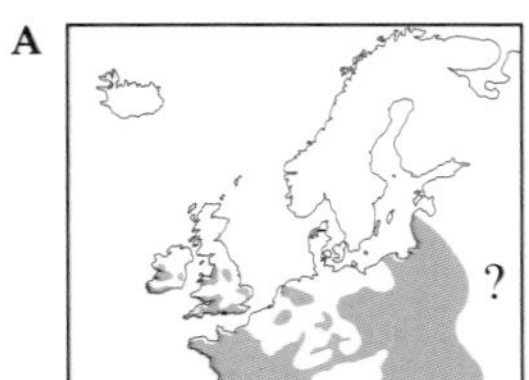

B
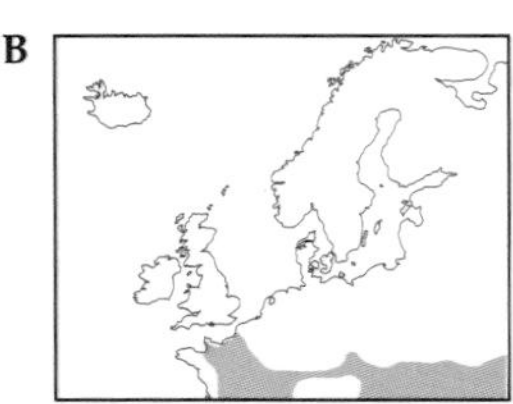

D
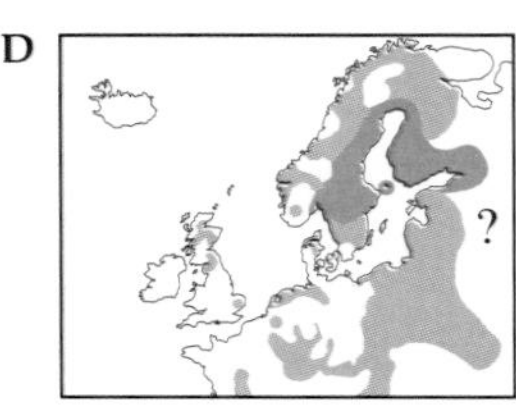

E
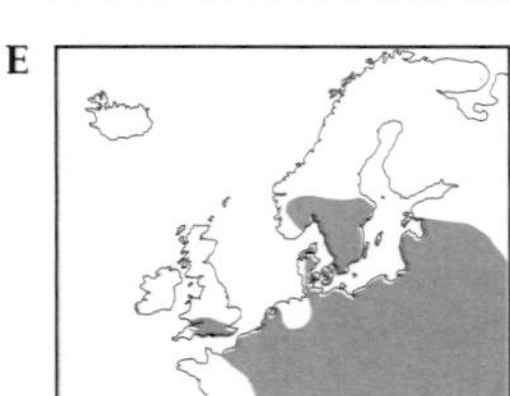

A Autumn Lady's-tresses *Spiranthes spiralis* Erect plant with flower stems to 20cm, bearing only small green scale-leaves; rosette of leaves withers long before flowering time, and the rosette for following year's flower spike is produced near base of spike. Inflorescence is in the form of a *tight single spiral* of 6-25 flowers, each small (6-7mm), barely open, and white; lip has green centre and frilly edges, curved downwards. From E Denmark southwards; in dry grasslands, stabilised dunes and coastal turf; local. *Fl* 8-9. **Br** Local in S England, Wales and S Ireland; rare in N England.

B Summer Lady's-tresses *Spiranthes aestivalis* Rather like Autumn Lady's-tresses, but taller, with longer flower spike (to 10cm), and *several lanceolate leaves on stem below.* Flowers slightly larger, purer white. In bogs, wet heaths and damp grassland; absent from Scandinavia and generally rare in the north of its range; declining. **Fl** 7-8. **Br** Formerly in the New Forest, almost certainly extinct.

C Irish Lady's-tresses *Spiranthes romanzoffiana* Rather stouter plant than above, to 25cm tall, with basal rosette and linear-lanceolate leaves on stem. Inflorescence consists of a *triple spiral of flowers,* forming a *thicker-set spike than other species;* flowers white to greenish, with perianth segments converging to form a tube-like structure, deflexed at tip. In moist meadows and cut bogs; only in SW England, W Ireland and NW Scotland (also in east N America); very local. **Fl** 7-8. **Br** As above.

D Creeping Lady's-tresses *Goodyera repens* Differs from *Spiranthes* in having *creeping stems,* and *evergreen leaves with conspicuous cross-veins* between the longitudinal ones. Stem to 25cm, with narrow, slightly twisted spike of dull white, barely opened flowers; perianth segments blunt, sticky-hairy, in tight hood; lip short and narrow. In mossy coniferous or mixed woods; throughout N Europe, though local. **Fl** 7-8. **Br** In coniferous woods, mainly old pinewoods, in N England and Scotland, and 1 colony in Norfolk.

E Musk Orchid *Herminium monorchis* Erect plant to 25cm, from tubers. Leaves 2-3, close to base of stem, yellow-green, lanceolate to oblong, with bract-like leaves higher up stem.

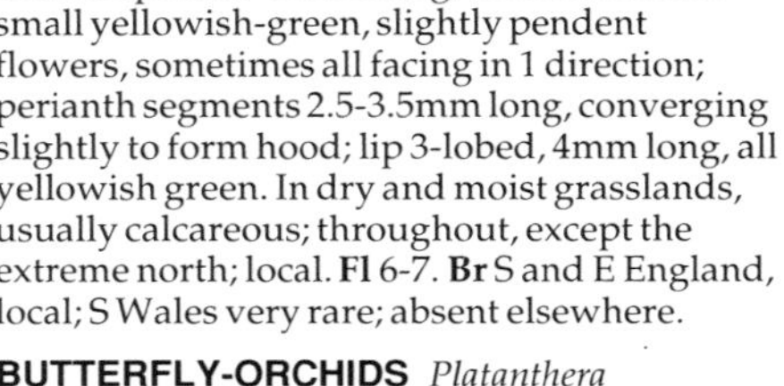

Flower spike 20-60mm long, with numerous small yellowish-green, slightly pendent flowers, sometimes all facing in 1 direction; perianth segments 2.5-3.5mm long, converging slightly to form hood; lip 3-lobed, 4mm long, all yellowish green. In dry and moist grasslands, usually calcareous; throughout, except the extreme north; local. **Fl** 6-7. **Br** S and E England, local; S Wales very rare; absent elsewhere.

BUTTERFLY-ORCHIDS *Platanthera*
Tuberous plants, with paired or few leaves near base of stem. Flowers white or greenish, with lateral lobes spreading, lip long and strap-like, and a spur.

F Lesser Butterfly-orchid *Platanthera bifolia* Erect stems to 45cm, with 2, almost-opposite, oval leaves near base of stem, up to 8cm long. Stem has only scale-leaves up it. Flowers (**f**) in dense or loose cylindrical spikes, up to 20cm long; perianth segments white, and 2 inner segments form a hood with upper outer segment; lip 6-10mm long, broadly strap-shaped; *the anther lobes run parallel*; the spur is long (25-30mm), slender and *horizontal.* Widespread almost throughout in open woods, moors, heaths, bogs and grassland, with little soil preference. **Fl** 5-7. **Br** Throughout, but local.

G Greater Butterfly-orchid *Platanthera chlorantha* Similar to Lesser Butterfly-orchid, but taller, to 50cm. Flowers (**g**) larger, in larger spike, usually more greenish-white in colour; the *anther lobes diverge downwards,* the spur is shorter (18-25mm long), thicker, and swelling towards tip, usually held pointing downwards; lip broader and shorter, more triangular in shape. In woods, scrub and grasslands, usually on calcareous soils; throughout, except the far north. **Fl** 5-7. **Br** Local, throughout.

H *Platanthera hyperborea* Stems arise from a large encircling basal leaf, with several smaller stem leaves; flowers small (perianth segments 3-4mm long), greenish yellow. Open habitats; Iceland only. **Fl** 7-8. **Br** Absent.

I *Platanthera obtusata* ssp *oligantha* Small plant to 20cm, with a *single basal leaf* and *another just below flowers.* Spike few-flowered, with yellowish-white small flowers. Calcareous heaths and woods; Arctic Scandinavia only; rare. **Fl** 7-8. **Br** Absent.

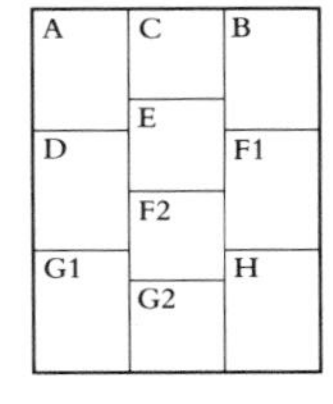

A **Autumn Lady's-tresses**

C **Irish Lady's-tresses**

B **Summer Lady's-tresses**

D **Creeping Lady's-tresses**

E **Musk Orchid**

F **1 Lesser Butterfly-orchid**

F **2 Lesser Butterfly-orchid** flower

G **1 Greater Butterfly-orchid**

G **2 Greater Butterfly-orchid** flower

H *Platanthera hyperborea*

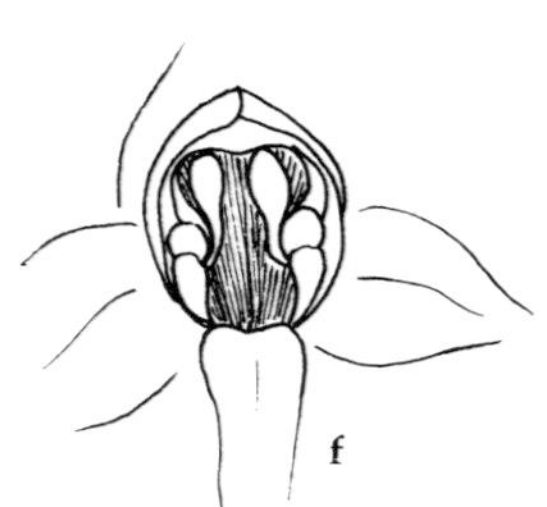

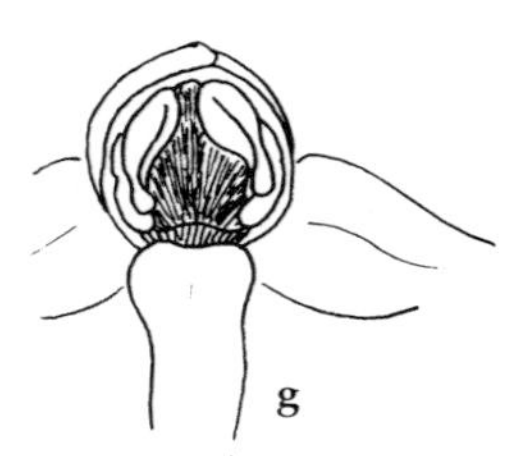

A

D

E
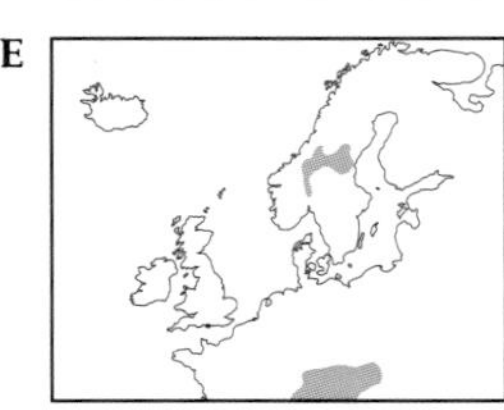
H

A *Chamorchis alpina* Small plant, rarely more than 12cm tall, with erect flower stems. There are *4-8 narrow grass-like leaves arising from the base of the stem* (a distinctive feature). Flowers in a short, few-flowered spike, with slender bracts that exceed the flowers; perianth segments greenish yellow, tinged red, only 3-4mm long; lip varies from 3-lobed to unlobed. In mountain pastures and tundra, usually on calcareous soils; locally common in Arctic Europe, otherwise only in the Alps. **Fl** 7-8. **Br** Absent.

B Fragrant Orchid *Gymnadenia conopsea* Erect plant to 45cm, with 4-8 linear, glossy green unspotted leaves near the base, and a few small narrow leaves up the stem. Flowers numerous in a *dense cylindrical spike*, up to 16cm long; *flowers all pink to reddish lilac* (rarely white); lateral outer segments spread out horizontally, while remaining 3 curve up to form a hood; the *lip has 3 blunt equal lobes*, and there is a *long slender downward-pointing spur*, almost twice the length of ovary. Widespread almost throughout in damp or dry grassy places, fens, etc., usually calcareous; plants of more acid sites may be slenderer and with longer, barely lobed lip, these plants are sometimes distinguished as *G. boreale*. **Fl** 6-7. **Br** Locally frequent throughout,

C *Gymnadenia odoratissima* Similar to Fragrant Orchid, but generally smaller (to 30cm), with smaller flowers with short spurs (4-5mm, no longer than ovary), and *lateral lobes of lip shorter than central lobe*. From S Sweden southwards; in grassland, especially in hilly areas; local. **Fl** 6-7. **Br** Probably absent.

D Small-white Orchid *Pseudorchis albida* Slender erect plant to 35cm. Leaves 3-5, broadly lanceolate, becoming narrower up stem, up to 80mm long. Inflorescence a dense cylindrical spike, up to 70mm long, with numerous tiny greenish-white flowers; flowers 2-3mm, with perianth segments curving in to form a hood, and lip markedly 3-lobed; spur about as long as ovary, curved down. In pastures, heaths and mountain areas; throughout, but very local and absent from many lowland areas. **Fl** 6-8. **Br** Increasingly frequent from N England northwards and westwards; probably extinct in S England.

E Vanilla Orchid *Nigritella nigra* Slender, erect plant to 25cm, with angled stem. Leaves linear-lanceolate, channelled and pointed. Flower spike dense, conical becoming ovoid, with numerous *blackish-crimson* (rarely paler) *tiny flowers*; perianth segments spread widely, and unlobed lip is at top of flower. In meadows and pastures, mainly in mountains, but at lower altitudes in N Scandinavia. Absent from most of area. **Fl** 6-8. **Br** Absent.

F Frog Orchid *Coeloglossum viride* Erect, small plant to 30cm. There are 2-6 leaves, broadly lanceolate at base, narrower higher up. Inflorescence loosely cylindrical, with 5-25 flowers, with lower bracts exceeding flowers; the 5 upper perianth segments converge to form a hood; the lip hangs down, 6-8mm long, with 2 long marginal lobes and a very short central lobe; all segments yellowish green to reddish (can be distinguished from *Chamorchis alpina* by its broader leaves and more deeply lobed lip). Widespread almost throughout, locally common in calcareous grasslands, including hilly areas. **Fl** 5-8. **Br** Throughout, though rare, except in a few areas such as chalk downs in S England, and hill pastures in N Britain.

G Dense-flowered Orchid *Neotinea maculata* Small plant to 30cm. Lower leaves broad-oblong, upper ones becoming narrower, often with small brown spots. Inflorescence 2-6cm long, cylindrical, very narrow, with numerous small flowers; *flowers white or pinkish*, with perianth segments forming a hood, and pendent lip *divided into 3 lobes, with lower lobe divided, forming a man shape*. On calcareous rocky or sandy sites; very local, only in W Ireland and Isle of Man (otherwise mainly S Europe). **Fl** 4-5. **Br** W Ireland and Isle of Man only.

H Globe, or Round-headed, Orchid *Traunsteinera globosa* Distinctive species. Stems to 60cm carry a *globose head of pinkish-lilac flowers* (looking like an *Allium* from a distance); perianth segments pink, with small red spots, all spreading and slightly enlarged towards tip. In mountain meadows, southwards from E France, S Germany and Poland. **Fl** 5-8. **Br** Absent.

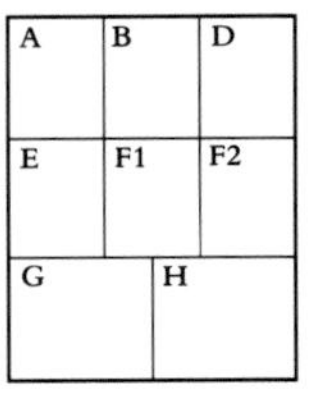

A *Chamorchis alpina*
B Fragrant Orchid
D Small-white Orchid
E Vanilla Orchid
F 1 Frog Orchid flowers
F 2 Frog Orchid
G Dense-flowered Orchid
H Globe Orchid

A

D

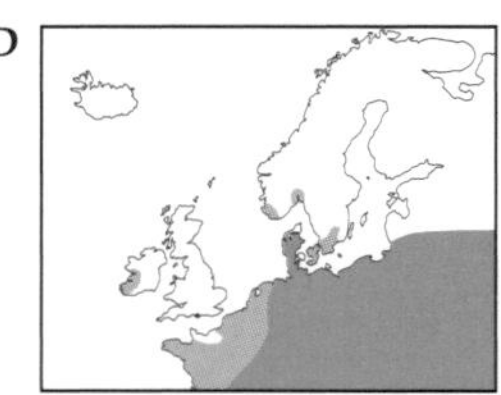

E

F

G

MARSH-ORCHIDS *Dactylorhiza* An extremely difficult group of plants, which appear still to be evolving. The boundaries between species are very blurred, and numerous fertile hybrids occur. The main characteristics are: tubers palmately lobed; leaves plain or often spotted; flowers have perianth segments all separate, equal or with inner lobes smaller; lip generally 3-lobed; spur present. Differs from the closely related *Orchis* species in the tuber shape, the leaf-like bracts that are as long as, or longer than, flowers; and in *Orchis* species, the developing flower spike is sheathed by the leaves.

(1) Plants with flowers wholly or partly yellow.

A **Elder-flowered Orchid** *Dactylorhiza sambucina* Distinctive amongst N European marsh-orchids in that it *frequently has yellow flowers*. Erect plant to 30cm, with several lanceolate pale green unspotted leaves. Flower spike cylindrical, dense; flowers commonly pale yellow, but also purple or mixed, usually retaining some yellow at mouth of spur (all forms can grow in 1 locality); lip shortly 3-lobed. Meadows, scrub and open woods, mainly in mountains, but at low altitudes in Scandinavia; widespread, but very scattered. **Fl** 4-7. **Br** Absent.

(2) Flowers purple or pink; stems hollow (can be tested by gentle finger-pressure); leaves spotted or not.

B **Early Marsh-orchid** *Dactylorhiza incarnata* Very variable species, with several named subspecies. Stem *very hollow*, erect, to 70cm. Leaves lanceolate, *yellowish green, unspotted*, keeled and *usually hooded at tip*. Inflorescence cylindrical, dense, with lower bracts much longer than flowers; the lip is small, entire or shallowly 3-lobed, but *strongly reflexed on either side*, making it appear very narrow from the front, and with a U- shaped line on either side in most forms; colour variable, from cream to deep purple, normally flesh pink. Ssp *cruenta* is pale purple, with leaves spotted both sides; ssp *coccinea* is brick-red, leaves unspotted; ssp *pulchella* has flowers deep purple, streaked red; ssp *ochroleuca* has cream or yellow unmarked flowers. Widespread throughout, except the far north; in a range of wet habitats, from acid to alkaline. **Fl** 5-7. **Br** Local throughout.

C *Dactylorhiza pseudocordigera* Similar, but *no more than 20cm high*; lower leaves elliptical, spreading; few-flowered, with flowers small, and purplish red. In calcareous damp places; Norway and N Sweden only. **Fl** 6-7. **Br** Absent.

D **Broad-leaved Marsh-orchid** *Dactylorhiza majalis* Up to 75cm. *Lower leaves elliptical*, not more than 4 times as long as wide, spotted or unspotted; upper ones narrower, reaching or exceeding base of inflorescence; bracts long, often exceeding flowers. *Flowers deep magenta* to pinkish purple, with spreading side-lobes, and a broad 3-lobed lip, broader than long, with side-lobes broader than central lobe; sometimes barely lobed at all. In damp meadows, marshes and fens, often calcareous; from S Sweden southwards. **Fl** 5-7. **Br** Ssp *majalis* (above) is absent, but ssp *occidentalis*, a shorter plant with deeper purple flowers, occurs in NW Scotland and W Ireland.

E **Northern Marsh-orchid** *Dactylorhiza purpurella* Often listed as a subspecies of Broad-leaved Marsh-orchid, but differs from it in the *lanceolate lower leaves*, unspotted or spotted towards the tip; *lip small* (5-9mm long), *almost entire, broadly diamond-shaped*, with regular deep crimson streaks all over. Local from S Scandinavia southwards; in fens and wet meadows. **Fl** 6-7. **Br** N Wales and N England northwards, except for 1 site in S England.

F **Southern Marsh-orchid** *Dactylorhiza praetermissa* Taller plant up to 75cm. Lower leaves lanceolate, unspotted (or ring-spotted in the var. *pardalina*), in 2 roughly opposite ranks up stem. Flowers pale pink-red to purplish; lip 10-14mm long, broader than long, *3-lobed with side-lobes very shallow and mid-lobe short and blunt*; centre of lip marked with light crimson dots and streaks. In fens, wet meadows and dune-slacks, etc., often calcareous; from Denmark to N France, commonest in the south. **Fl** 6-7. **Br** The southern equivalent of Northern Marsh-orchid; widespread in the south, rare in N England; absent elsewhere.

G **Narrow-leaved Marsh-orchid** *Dactylorhiza traunsteineri* Short plant to 40 cm, with a slender, *barely hollow stem. Leaves few, very narrow* (to 15mm wide), *lanceolate*, keeled, unspotted or with small spots near tip. Inflorescence *short and few-flowered*; flowers red-purple, lip 8-10mm wide, roughly diamond-shaped, but 3-lobed, with *mid-lobe longer than side* 2, and margin of lip slightly deflexed; lip marked with strong pattern of lines and dots; spur short and slender. An uncommon plant of fens and marshes; from S Scandinavia southwards. **Fl** 5-6. **Br** Very local, but scattered through England, N Wales and Ireland.

(3) Flowers purple or pink, stem solid; leaves always with transversely elongated blotches; bracts narrow, no longer than flowers.

H **Heath Spotted-orchid** *Dactylorhiza maculata* Differs from similar marsh-orchids as described above. An erect plant to 60cm. Leaves lanceolate and dark-spotted. Flowers (**h**) in dense slightly pyramidal spike, varying from whitish to pale purple; *lip broad, triangular, shallowly 3-lobed*, with *central lobe small and not longer than lateral lobes*; lip marked with streaks and loops. Throughout, on heaths, moors, and damp, usually acidic, habitats. **Fl** 5-8. **Br** Locally common throughout.

I **Common Spotted-orchid** *Dactylorhiza fuchsii* Similar to Heath Spotted-orchid, except that basal leaves tend to be broader, elliptical and blunt. Flower spike generally more evenly cylindrical when flowers open; flowers (**i**) pale pink, with numerous darker streaks and spots; *lip more deeply and evenly 3-lobed*, with lobes rather pointed, and *central lobe at least as long as lateral lobes*. Widespread and common throughout, except the extreme north; in neutral to calcareous damp or dry grasslands, scrub and woods. **Fl** 6-8. **Br** Locally common throughout.

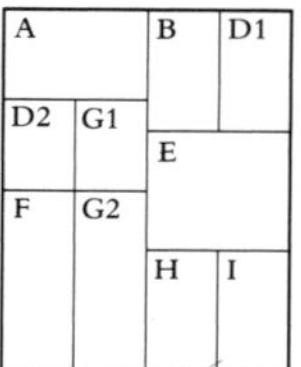

A **Elder-flowered Orchid** showing two colour forms

B **Early Marsh-orchid**

D **1 Broad-leaved Marsh-orchid** ssp *majalis*

D **2 Broad-leaved Marsh-orchid** ssp *majalis* flower

G **1 Narrow- leaved Marsh-orchid** flowers

E **Northern Marsh-orchid**

F **Southern Marsh-orchid**

G **2 Narrow-leaved Marsh-orchid**

H **Heath Spotted-orchid**

I **Common Spotted-orchid**

h

i

A

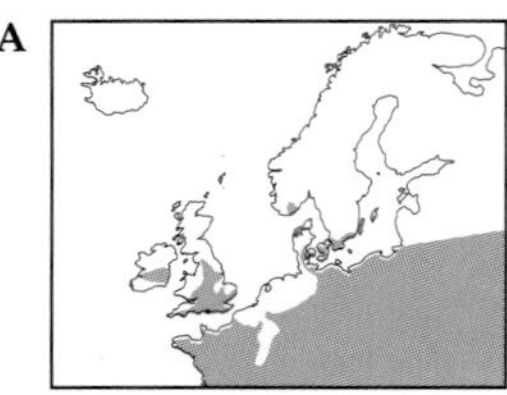

B

C

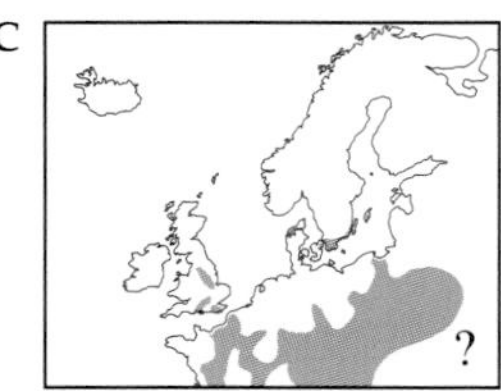

D

E

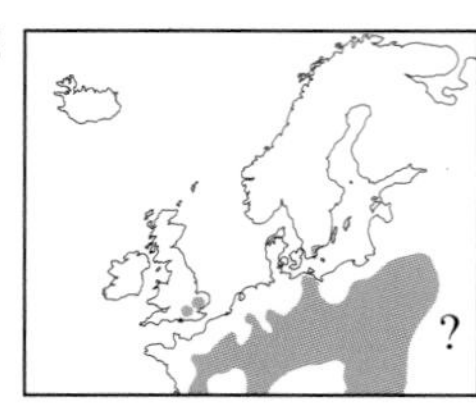

F

Orchis A large genus, rather similar to the marsh-orchids, but differing as described under marsh-orchids (*see* page 322).

(1) Plants with flowers that have the upper 5 perianth segments forming a tight helmet over the lip.

A Green-winged Orchid *Orchis morio* Erect plant to 50cm, but very variable in height according to conditions. Leaves in a rosette, glossy green, *unspotted,* and crowded up the stem. Flowers variable in colour, from reddish purple, through pink, to white, but always having *outer perianth segments strongly veined and suffused with green;* lip broad, bluntly 3-lobed, with central pale patch dotted with red; spur about length of ovary. Widespread and locally common, except in N Scandinavia; in pastures and other long-established grasslands. **Fl** 4-6. **Br** Locally frequent, though declining, in much of England and Wales, but rare or absent elsewhere.

B Bug Orchid *Orchis coriophora* Rather similar to Green-winged Orchid, but has *narrower leaves, lacks the green veins,* and has the lip longer than wide, deeper red-purple with greenish streaks, with long central lobe. In damp grasslands; from Belgium and S Germany southwards; rare. **Fl** 4-6. **Br** Absent.

C Burnt, or Burnt-tip, Orchid *Orchis ustulata* Small plant, usually to 20cm, occasionally more. Flower spike distinctive, with the *unopened flowers appearing very dark purple,* giving the burnt-tip in contrast to the white and red opened flowers; the lip is 4-8mm long, 3-lobed, man-shaped, white with red spots. In dry grasslands, usually calcareous; as far north as S Sweden. **Fl** 5-6, with a few populations flowering in 7. **Br** In England only, but rare except on S England chalk downs.

D Monkey Orchid *Orchis simia* Erect plant to 45cm. Lower leaves broadly lanceolate and unspotted. Flower spike cylindrical, with *flowers opening from top downwards* (the opposite to most *Orchis* species). Flowers whitish pink, with an upswept hood; lip distinctive, in shape of a man with white body (dotted with minute reddish tufts of hair), and crimson arms, legs and minute tail, with arms and legs narrow and curved; spur cylindrical, downward-pointing, as long as ovary. In grasslands, scrub and open woods, usually on calcareous soil; from S Sweden southwards, but rare in the north of its range. **Fl** 5- 6. **Br** Very rare in S England and Yorkshire only.

E Military Orchid *Orchis militaris* Rather similar to Monkey Orchid. *Hood greyish outside;* the labellum is similarly shaped to Monkey Orchid, but with *shorter, wider legs and arms,* less distinctly different in colour from the body, and the legs diverge widely; the *flowers open from the base of the spike first.* In grassland, scrub and open woods, often calcareous; from S Scandinavia southwards, though rare in the north of its range. **Fl** 5-6. **Br** Very rare, in a few protected sites in SE England only.

F Lady Orchid *Orchis purpurea* Close to Monkey Orchid and Military Orchid in general form, though often larger, to 80cm occasionally. Flower spike up to 15cm long, becoming cylindrical, flowers opening from bottom upwards. The helmet of the flower is deep reddish purple outside; the lip is much broader than in the above 2 species, with the *broad central lobe divided into 2 further broad lobes, resembling a Victorian lady in a wide skirt,* coloured pale pink-white with red dots and suffusions. In woods, scrub and grasslands, from Denmark southwards, becoming commoner in the south of its range. **Fl** 4-6. **Br** Virtually confined to Kent and adjacent areas, where it is locally abundant; very rare elsewhere.

(2) Plants with at least some of perianth segments spreading, not all forming a tight helmet.

G Early-purple Orchid *Orchis mascula* Medium-sized orchid to 40cm. Leaves oblong-lanceolate, to 10cm long, *glossy green with numerous dark purplish blotches,* extending lengthwise (compared with transversely on matt leaves of spotted orchids), occasionally unspotted. Flowers in loose cylindrical spikes, red-purple; the lip is 8-12mm long, shallowly 3-lobed, with the central lobe notched, and the sides of the lip folded back to a variable degree; the central part of the lip is whitish, speckled red; spur stout, curved upwards, as long as ovary. In grasslands, woods and scrub; throughout except the far north and east; probably the commonest orchid of the area. **Fl** 4-6. **Br** Throughout, locally common, in a wide range of habitats.

H *Orchis spitzelii* Resembles Early-purple Orchid, but has *dull green leaves, without spots;* the *upper perianth segments are brownish green inside,* and the spur is shorter than the ovary. In open woods on calcareous soils; only on Gotland, Sweden, in N Europe (though commoner in S Europe). **Fl** 6-7.

I Lax-flowered Orchid *Orchis laxiflora* Rather similar to Early-purple Orchid, but usually taller, up to 1m. *Leaves unspotted,* lanceolate, under 2cm wide. Flowers red-purple, lip with central lobe very short or absent; spur shorter than length of ovary, and flower bracts with 3-7 veins (usually 1 (-3) in Early-purple Orchid). In marshes and damp meadows; as far north as S Sweden (only as ssp *palustris*), though absent from Holland, Denmark and N Germany. **Fl** 4-6. **Br** Only in the Channel Islands, where it has declined considerably.
Ssp *palustris* (formerly distinguished as a separate species) differs in the paler flowers, tighter narrower inflorescence, and more distinctly 3-lobed lip, with central lobe as long as marginal lobes. Similar habitats and flowering time, in S Sweden and Germany. **Br** Absent.

A | B1 | B2 | C
D1 | D2 | E1
E2
G | F | H | I

A Green-winged Orchid showing colour variation

B 1 Bug Orchid

B 2 Bug Orchid flowers

C Burnt Orchid

D 1 Monkey Orchid

D 2 Monkey Orchid flower

E 1 Military Orchid

E 2 Military Orchid flower

G Early-purple Orchid

F Lady Orchid

H *Orchis spitzelii*

I Lax-flowered Orchid

A

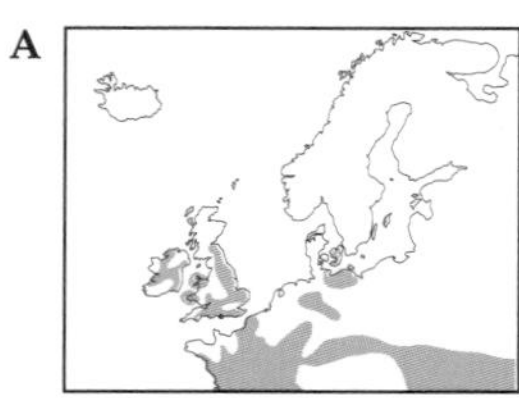

D

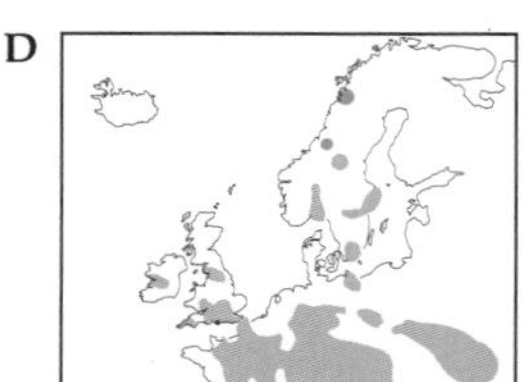

E

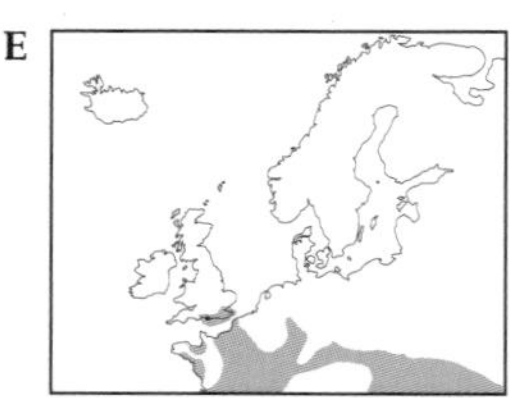

F

G

A Pyramidal Orchid *Anacamptis pyramidalis* Erect plant to 30cm. Leaves lanceolate, slightly greyish green, unspotted. Flowers in a short dense spike, up to 8cm long (usually less), *distinctly conical or dome-shaped*. Perianth and lip all deep pink; lip broad, deeply 3-lobed, with 2 ridges at its base; spur very long and slender, longer than ovary. Readily distinguished from Fragrant Orchid by the shape of the inflorescence. On dry, often calcareous, grasslands and stabilised dunes; from S Sweden southwards. **Fl** 6-8. **Br** Mainly southern, extending locally to NW Scotland.

B Heart-flowered Serapias, Heart-flowered Orchid *Serapias cordigera* Distinctive plant, unlikely to be confused with anything else in this area (though there are many other similar species in S Europe). Inflorescence few-flowered, each one large, with a pale greyish-pink helmet, and a large heart-shaped maroon to orange-red hairy lip. A S European species, extending into NW France; in grasslands and scrub. **Fl** 4-5. **Br** Absent.

C *Serapias parviflora* Recently discovered in various sites in north-west Europe (Brittany and SW England). It has much smaller flowers than Heart-flowered Serapias (about 15mm, compared to 25-35mm). Although occurring in suitable habitats (dry grassland), these sites are beyond its normal range in the Mediterranean and its exact status is uncertain. **Fl** 4-5. **Br** 1 site only, in Cornwall.

OPHRYS A distinctive group, with few-flowered inflorescences; flowers have greatly enlarged lip, furry, and often resembling an insect, with spreading outer perianth segments, and remaining 2 inner segments often reduced. In S Europe, there are many confusing species, but the 4 that occur in N Europe are reasonably distinctive.

D Fly Orchid *Ophrys insectifera* Tall slender plant to 60cm, with leaves both basal and on stem. Inflorescence open, with 2-14 well-spaced flowers; outer perianth segments greenish yellow and roughly equal; *inner 2 blackish purple, thin and short like an insect's antennae*; lip narrow, 6-7mm wide, 3-lobed with a notched central lobe, furry brown except for a central bluish patch (like a reflection on the 'fly's' wings), soon fading. In grasslands, open woods and scrub, occasionally in fens, on calcareous soils; widespread but absent from the far north. **Fl** 5-6. **Br** Local in England and Wales, mainly southern; rare in Ireland; absent from Scotland.

E Early Spider-orchid *Ophrys sphegodes* Leaves mainly in basal rosette. Stems to 40cm, usually less. Flowers larger and broader than Fly Orchid, with lip 8-12mm wide, in a loose 2- to 10-flowered spike. *Perianth segments all yellow-green*, with inner 2 not reduced to antennae-like structures; lip large, velvety brown, without appendages, *marked with bluish H- or X-shaped speculum mark*. From S England and central Germany southwards; in short turf and open rocky areas, usually on calcareous soils. **Fl** 4-5. **Br** In S England only; local and mainly coastal.

F Late Spider-orchid *Ophrys fuciflora (O. holoserica)* Usually taller, with longer inflorescence than Early Spider-orchid. *Flowers have pink outer perianth segments*, with inner 2 segments shorter, triangular, pink with green; lip large, broader than long (up to 12mm long and 15mm broad), velvety brown, barely 3-lobed, but with a forward-pointing, heart-shaped, green appendage at tip; *speculum variable, roughly H-shaped*, with symmetrical side-lobes. In dry calcareous grasslands and scrub; from Belgium and S England southwards. **Fl** 5-7. **Br** Rare and local, in E Kent only.

G Bee Orchid *Ophrys apifera* Rather similar to Late Spider-orchid. Flowers differ mainly in that the *2 inner perianth segments are narrow, greenish* (or reddish); the lip is narrower and smaller, with 2 distinct, but small, furry side-lobes; *centre of lip marked with a rough U-shape*; lip appendage present, but curved back underneath. From Holland and N Ireland southwards; in dry grasslands, dunes and old quarries, usually on calcareous soils. **Fl** 6-7. **Br** Local throughout England, Wales and Ireland, but rare or absent in the north.

H Wasp Orchid *Ophrys apifera* var *trollii* Distinctive variety of the Bee Orchid, similar except for the flowers, which have a narrower, more pointed lip, marbled with yellow and brown. Similar habitats and flowering time to the type, but very local. **Fl** 6-7. **Br** Very local, in parts of SW England only.

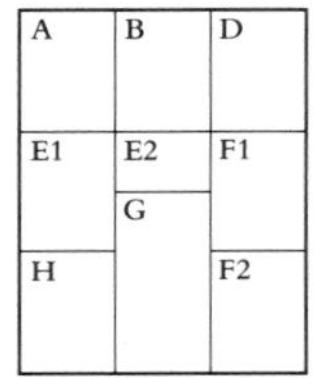

A **Pyramidal Orchid**

B **Heart-flowered Serapias**

D **Fly Orchid**

E **1 Early Spider-orchid**

E **2 Early Spider-orchid** flowers

F **1 Late Spider-orchid**

G **Bee Orchid**

H **Wasp Orchid**

F **Late Spider-orchid** flowers

A

B

D

E

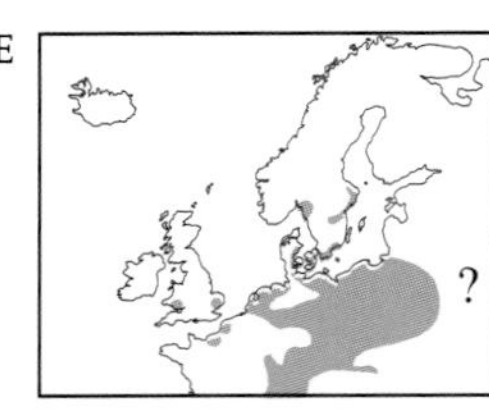

G

?

A Man Orchid *Aceras anthropophorum* Rather yellowish-green plant to 30cm. Leaves oblong-lanceolate, glossy green and unspotted. Inflorescence is long, narrow and cylindrical, with as many as 90 flowers. All perianth segments greenish-yellow, streaked and edged with red-brown; lip pendent, 12-15mm long, of similar colour, with very *distinctive, narrow, man shape; no spur*. From Holland southwards; in calcareous grasslands and scrub. **Fl** 5-6. **Br** Rare, only in S and E England., most frequent on the North Downs.

B Lizard Orchid *Himantoglossum hircinum* Tall, stout, highly distinctive plant to 1m. Basal leaves roughly oval, withered by flowering time, stem leaves narrower. Inflorescence long, up to 30cm, cylindrical, with numerous large flowers. Flowers have 5 perianth segments forming a hood that is greenish grey outside, striped red inside; the lip is unlike that of any other N European orchid, with the central lobe prolonged into a ribbon-like tongue, up to 5cm long, twisted and forked at the tip. In grassland, scrub, wood-margins and stabilised dunes; from Holland and England southwards. **Fl** 5-7. **Br** Only in S England in a few scattered sites, where it often appears and persists for a few years only.

C Coralroot *Corallorhiza trifida* Small erect saprophytic orchid to 30cm, lacking normal green leaves. Stem yellowish green, often clustered, with brownish scales. Inflorescence is lax, with 2-12 pendent flowers. Perianth segments greenish yellow, lip pendent, white with red lines, unlobed or with 2 small side-lobes. Widespread, though local, throughout, commoner in the north or in mountain areas further south; mainly in damp boggy woods, wet moorland and dune-slacks. **Fl** 5-7. **Br** Northern, mainly in N England and E Scotland.

D Calypso *Calypso bulbosa* Beautiful and very distinctive orchid. It has 1 stalked, oblong, basal leaf, and a single stem bearing a solitary large flower, up to 5cm across. This has 5 long narrow pink-purple sepals held erect, and a large inflated pink- or whitish-speckled lip. In damp woods and boggy areas; N Scandinavia only. **Fl** 5-6. **Br** Absent.

E Fen Orchid *Liparis loeselii* Small erect perennial, with roughly triangular stems to 20cm, from a bulb-like structure. Leaves normally 2, basal, in opposite pair; oblong in shape, yellowish green, greasy in appearance. Flowers in a loose spike with 2-10 flowers; perianth segments yellow-green, narrow, linear, 5-8mm long, and spreading but curving inwards; lip broader, at top of flower, since the ovary is not rotated at all; no spur. In fens, bogs, dune-slacks and other wet places; from central Scandinavia southwards. **Fl** 6-7. **Br** Rare, in scattered localities in E Anglia, SW England and Wales.

F Single-leaved Bog-orchid *Microstylis monophyllos* Relatively tall slender orchid to 30cm, with a single broad leaf at base of stem. Flowers green in a cylindrical raceme, with lip on upper side. In fens and wet woods; rare; from central Scandinavia southwards, but absent from most areas. **Fl** 7. **Br** Absent.

G Bog-orchid *Hammarbya paludosa* Differs from the above species in its much smaller size, rarely exceeding 12cm, though often only 6-8cm high, with 3-5 leaves. The inflorescence is a small narrow spike, up to 6cm long, with numerous tiny yellow-green flowers; the ovary twists through 360°, so that the ovate lip faces upwards; perianth segments narrow and spreading; spur absent. In acidic marshes, bogs and flushed areas; throughout, though very local and absent from many areas. **Fl** 7-9. **Br** Scattered, mainly northern, though locally common in the New Forest and Purbeck area.

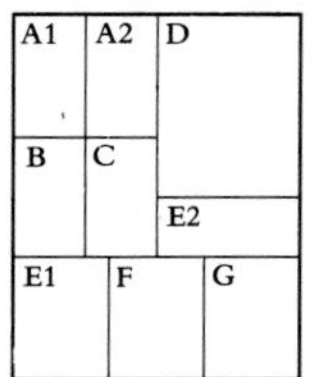

A **1 Man Orchid**

A **2 Man Orchid** flowers

D **Calypso**

B **Lizard Orchid**

C **Coralroot**

E **1 Fen Orchid** flowers

E **2 Fen Orchid**

F **Single-leaved Bog-orchid**

G **Bog-orchid**

INDEX

Acknowledgements

Photographs

Peter Brough 11I, 23A, 31O, 33J, 35A, 37H, 37J, 41M, 43F, 47D, 49L, 53A, 55O, 59D, 71O, 71Q, 81D, 91D, 93A, 93G, 101G, 105H, 121J, 125F, 125N, 163A, 175A, 175K, 183J, 191E, 191F, 203B, 205F, 213D, 225N, 239B, 251D, 259G, 265A, 281C, 307B, 319C, 321F2, 325F; **Paul Harcourt Davies** 315F, 321H, 323D1, 323D2, 323G1, 325H; **Trevor Dolby** front cover centre; **Xaver Finkenzeller** 35B, 47E, 57F, 57O, 63E, 63K, 73F, 73G, 81G, 87J2, 89G, 103D, 103O, 107E2, 279A; **Ron & Christine Foord** 11C, 27D, 27G, 29F, 31A, 33H, 37M, 37N, 49F, 51E, 59A, 73P, 105I, 109J, 115M, 117A, 117H, 131B, 139D, 299H;

Bob Gibbons endpapers, title page, 6, 7, 11A, 11E, 11G, 13B, 13C, 13E, 13F, 13G, 15H, 15N, 17H, 17J, 17K, 19K, 21B, 21D, 21H, 23B, 23I, 23L, 23N, 25A, 25C, 25I, 27B, 27H, 27K, 27M, 29D, 29I, 29J, 29M, 29O, 33K, 33L, 35G, 35I, 35K, 37D, 37I, 37O, 37P, 39B, 39K, 39M, 41A, 41B, 41F, 41H, 43A, 43I, 45A, 45B, 45D, 45J, 45M, 45N, 47B, 47G, 47H, 47J, 47K, 47L, 49A, 49E, 49I, 51C, 53D, 53F, 53K, 53M, 53N, 55C, 55E, 57E, 57L, 57M, 59G, 59J, 59N, 61H1, 61H2, 63A, 63B, 63D, 63H, 63M, 65A, 65F, 65G, 65J, 65K, 67B, 67C, 67D, 67H1, 67H2, 67O, 69K, 69O, 71A, 71H, 71I, 71J, 73A, 73C, 73D, 73M, 75C, 75I, 75K, 75L, 75N, 75Q, 77D, 77G, 77K, 79B, 79D, 81C, 81E, 83E, 85D, 85G, 87D, 89A, 89C, 89H, 89M, 91J, 91K, 91M, 93K, 95B, 95F, 95G, 95H, 95I, 97A, 97B, 97D, 97F, 97G, 99G2, 101E, 101F, 101H, 103B, 103F, 103L, 105B, 105G, 105L, 107E1, 107E7, 107E8, 107E9, 109A, 109C, 109D, 109F, 109G, 111A, 111I, 111R, 111T, 113A, 113G, 113I, 113L, 115A, 115C, 115F, 115K, 115N, 117F, 119B, 119C, 119G, 121A, 121D, 121F, 121L, 123D, 123H, 123K, 125B, 125L, 125M, 125P, 127C, 127F, 127L, 127O, 127P, 129E, 129I, 129J, 129L, 131A, 131E, 131F, 131H, 131L, 133A, 133B, 133D, 133E, 133H, 133J, 133L, 135A, 135B, 135D, 135F, 135H, 135N, 137A, 137D, 137G, 139C, 139F, 139G, 139J, 139L, 141A, 141D, 141E, 141I, 141J, 143C, 143D, 143E2, 143G, 143H, 143J, 145G, 145H, 145J, 147A, 147D1, 149B, 149C, 149D, 149F, 149I, 151A, 151G, 151H, 151I, 151J, 153A, 153D, 153G, 153H, 153J, 153K, 153L, 155B, 155I, 155J, 155L, 157B, 157D, 157I, 159B, 159D, 159H, 159L, 159M, 159N, 159O, 161B, 161D, 161F1, 161F2, 161G1, 161G2, 161H, 163C, 163F, 163I, 165A, 165F, 165G, 165I, 167A, 167E, 167F, 169C, 169D, 169E, 169H, 171B, 171K, 173B, 173J, 175G, 175H, 177I, 179B, 179C, 179D, 179G, 181D, 181F, 183A, 183B, 183N, 185A, 185C, 185E, 185F, 185G1, 185G2, 187D, 187F, 187H, 187O, 189C, 189H, 189J, 189K, 191A, 191D, 193A, 193K, 193L, 193M, 193N, 195C, 195D, 195I, 195L, 197E, 197F, 197J, 199A, 199D, 199H, 199K, 201C, 201D, 201E, 201K, 203A, 203C, 203F, 203H, 205B, 205D, 205E, 205J, 205K, 207E, 207G, 209A, 209D, 209E, 209G, 209J, 209O, 211A, 211F, 213B, 213C, 213F, 213G, 213H, 213I, 215C, 215E, 215F, 215I, 215M, 217A, 217B, 217C, 217E, 217F, 217G, 217I, 217J, 217L, 219A, 219D, 219E, 219F, 219G, 219J, 219M, 221B, 221D, 221F, 221K, 221L, 221M, 223A, 223G, 225A, 225D, 225E, 225F, 225G, 225K, 225L, 227F, 227I, 227L, 229E, 229F, 229H, 229I, 229K, 231A, 231E, 231G, 231H, 231J, 231K, 231L, 233A, 233F, 233J, 233L, 235F, 235G, 235H, 237F, 237G, 237J, 239A, 239E, 239F, 239H, 241B, 241E, 241I, 241J, 241K, 243A, 243C, 243E, 245A, 245B1, 245C1, 245C2, 245E, 245G, 247A, 247F, 249A, 249F, 249G, 249H, 251A, 251C, 251E, 251G, 251H, 251L, 253A, 253C, 253D, 255A, 255F, 255G, 255K, 257H, 257I, 257J, 259B, 259K, 261B, 261E, 261J, 263C, 263E, 263F, 263G, 263H, 263I, 263K, 265B1, 265D, 265E, 265F, 267A, 267B2, 267E, 267F, 267H2, 267J, 269B, 271E, 271F, 271K, 273A, 273B, 273C, 273D, 273F, 273G, 273I, 273J, 275C, 275F, 275G, 275H, 277A, 277D, 277G1, 277I, 279B,279E, 281A, 281F2, 281I, 281M 283A, 283D, 283F, 283G, 283H2, 285E, 285F, 287B, 287C, 287D2, 289B, 289D, 289E, 289I, 291B, 291C1, 291H, 295J, 299A, 299B, 299E, 301H, 301I, 301J, 303B, 303C, 303D, 303F, 303I, 305E, 305F, 305I, 305K, 305L, 305M, 307A, 307C, 307D, 307E, 307F, 307H2, 307I1, 309B, 309D, 309E2, 309G, 311C, 311J, 313B, 313D, 313I, 313K, 313N, 315C, 315D, 315I, 315J1, 317A, 317C1, 317H, 319A, 319B, 319F1, 319G1, 321A, 321E, 323A, 323B, 323F, 323H, 323I, 325A, 325C, 325D1, 325E1, 325I, 327A, 327B, 327E2, 329B, 329G; **D Goodfellow** 321B; **Bill Helyar** 97H; **N H T Holmes** 293G; **Ann Horsfall** 101I, 135K; **Peter Lawson** 99B, 119E, 123J; **A R G Mundell** 43L, 253H, 257L, 271D2, 279C, 279G, 281B, 281K, 283E, 287A1, 315B; **Natural Image**/***Bob Davies*** 213E/***Paul Davies*** 315A, 317D2, 317E, 319F1, 325B2, 325D2, 327F1, 327F2, 327H, 329D/***Robin Fletcher*** 63L, 183K/***J Howard*** 111M/***P R Perfect*** 227K/***E Rowlands*** 99A1, 229A/***Peter Wilson*** 17M, 33N, 145A, 165B, 195F, 197B, 223D, 237E, 243F, 291F, 305A, 311H, 315H;

Nature Photographers/***S C Bisserot*** 19C, 137F, 175J, 245B2, 261A, 261I, 271I/***Frank V Blackburn*** 11F, 11H, 19B, 23M, 25B, 71G, 181C, 223B, 271H/***Derick Bonsall*** 99C, 99G3, 111G, 301B, 309J/***Idris Bowen*** 87J1, 189G/***Brinsley Burbidge*** 11B, 13J, 17L, 25H, 39D, 49G, 53I, 55B, 55K, 55M, 55R, 59B, 73I, 77N, 79O, 81A, 81F, 93D, 93L, 99E, 101J, 101K, 101L1, 105N, 107A, 111F, 113J, 115D, 121B, 137B, 141G, 147C, 151N, 153E, 167J, 169G, 179A, 179J, 183I, 189E, 189I, 191K, 197A, 223H, 233E, 235M, 237A3, 243I, 255C, 255D, 255I, 259F, 263B, 271A, 271D1, 271L, 275D, 283H1, 287A, 299F, 309F, 317C2, 317D1, 317G1/***Robin Bush*** 37A, 37L, 39E, 39G, 41L, 45K, 53J, 53L, 57J, 59K, 65C, 69A, 69B, 69C, 75O, 79Q, 83M, 85M, 89B, 89I, 91B, 91I, 93C, 93I, 105A, 107E10, 107E3, 111C, 115L, 117K, 135C, 151K, 153B, 167I, 169A, 169I, 179E, 183M, 187B, 201G, 205C, 207J, 209B, 209L, 227G, 233H, 233I, 235C, 237H, 239C, 239D, 239G, 241D, 245D2, 255H, 259C, 261H, 279I, 289H, 305C, 307H1, 311D, 311F, 315J2, 319G2, 321G, 325E2/***A A Butcher*** 47I, 125D, 181G, 235I/N A Callow 55I, 183D, 329E2/***Kevin Carlson*** 159A, 227B, 235N, 325B1/***Bob Chapman*** 91F, 253I/***Hugh Clark*** 45C/***Andrew Cleave*** 21C, 23C, 25G, 31D, 33D, 33M, 45E, 45O, 53G, 55L, 61B, 61E, 69J, 83A, 83H, 85L, 87B, 91N, 97C, 103A, 103R, 107E4, 107E5, 111O, 113F, 125I, 127E, 127G, 131K, 137C, 147B, 147D2, 149E, 149G, 155A, 155D, 157C, 157J, 157K, 163B, 165H, 171C, 171E, 171G, 171H, 173A, 177E, 183C, 183L, 191B, 193E, 193G, 193J, 207H, 215A, 223C, 227C, 255A, 259L, 265B2, 267G, 271G, 273E, 275A, 279F, 279J, 291G, 303G, 305B, 309A, 317B, 319H, 329F/***A K Davies*** 187A, 313M/DOE 77A, 111S, 175I, 207D, 269D2, 321D/***Thomas Ennis*** 297C2, 323G2/***Geoff du Feu*** 199C, 263D, 311B, 329E1/***C H Gomersall*** 75A/***Christopher Grey-Wilson*** 55D, 83I, 85I, 119I, 123A, 251B, 277J, 309K/***Jean Hall*** 21M, 45L, 103M, 127B, 195J, 211G, 213J, 253G, 267B1, 267H1, 299D, 311A/***James Hyett*** 53B, 187C, 195A, 213A, 241G, 253B, 329A2, /***E A Janes*** 19J1, 165C, 243B, 245D1, 245I, 251K, 311I2/***L G Jesssup*** 73H, 155H, 207A, 207C, 265G, 289A/***Owen Newman*** 215K/***D Osborn*** 319D, 327E1/***Charles Palmer*** 89E/***William S Paton*** 229D/***David Rae*** 19I, 59L, 263A/***J Russell*** 109I, 109K, 141B, 143A, 151C, 203I, 215H, 217D, 251J, 255B, 263J/***Tony Schilling*** 11D/***D Smith*** 27C/***Robert T Smith*** 19J2 /***Paul Sterry*** 15B, 17E, 19A, 21F, 23J, 25F, 27F, 29C, 29G, 31G, 37G, 39H, 41E, 41I, 41K, 43D, 43E, 43P, 45I, 49C, 49D, 49K, 49N, 51A, 53C, 55A, 55F, 57A, 59H, 59I, 61A, 61G, 63F, 65I, 67A, 67G, 79H, 87A, 87C, 89N, 91L, 93F, 93H, 95A, 97E2, 105F, 111K, 113E, 113K, 117C, 117I, 117J, 119A, 119D, 121E, 121K, 125K, 125O, 127M, 127N, 129A, 129H, 131D, 131G, 133C, 133I, 133M, 135O, 139H, 141F, 143E1, 145C, 145I, 149H, 149K, 151F, 155C, 157A, 161E, 163D, 165D, 165J, 167B, 169J, 169L, 171A, 173F, 173H, 177J, 181A, 185H, 187G, 187N, 187P, 191C, 193C, 193D, 193F, 195G, 197G, 199F, 201H, 201I, 203D, 207K, 213K, 215B, 215J, 217H, 219C, 219H, 219K, 221A, 221C, 223F, 225B, 229C, 229G, 235A, 235D, 237A2, 237C, 243K, 247B, 249C, 251M, 253E, 253F, 255E, 257A, 257B, 257C, 257E, 257K, 259M, 261C, 261F, 265C, 269D1, 269H, 269I, 275B, 275E, 277B, 277G2, 281F1, 281H, 283C, 289C, 293B, 299C, 299I, 301G, 301H, 303A, 303H, 307G, 307I2, 309C, 309H, 313F, 317G2, 319E, 323E, 325G, 327G, 329A1, 329C/***R Tidman*** 47A, 87I, 99A2, 123C, 179H, 245F/***Derek Washington*** 97E, 317F, 327D/***Anthony Wharton*** 33I, 127H, 181B, 203G, 283H3/***Jon B Wilson*** 301F; **Octopus Illustrated Books**/***Adrian Davies*** 19D, 19E, 19F, 19G, 21A, 43J, 43K, 61I, 65B, 79C, 83J, 83K, 93M, 93N, 101A, 101L2, 105E, 123G, 125A, 125H, 143F, 147E, 147G, 191J, 197C, 197D, 199E, 205H, 227A, 245J, 273H, 291C, 293A, 309E1/***Geoff du Feu*** 25E, 57C, 59C, 71F, 85O, 85P, 85Q, 95J, 129C, 149A, 157E, 247G, 247I/***Peter Loughran*** 17F, 17G, 75F, 87E, 103C, 103H, 107E6, 111H, 115H, 127I, 141H, 143B, 163K, 189A, 219L, 227H, 231I, 233K, 263L, 311I1; **Photo Flora**/***A N Gagg*** 13A, 13D, 13L, 15C, 15D1, 15D2, 17C, 25D, 25J, 25L, 27I, 27J, 27L, 33A, 33E, 33G, 33O, 37K, 39I, 39J, 39L, 47F, 47M, 49J, 65D, 65E, 69G, 69P, 71N, 71P, 73R, 77L, 818, 81Q, 83C, 83F, 83G, 83O, 91O, 99G1, 109L, 121C, 139A, 149J, 163G, 171F, 181E, 199L, 201J, 209H, 227D, 227E, 231M, 243G, 243H, 249D, 249E, 261G, 269J, 277C, 277H, 279H, 283B, 285A, 285G, 287D1, 291D, 295D, 295G, 297B, 297C, 297E, 313E;**Derek Ratcliffe** 39F, 91H; **Tim Rich** 85A, 85B;

Heinz Schrempp 15A, 15G, 15Q, 17A, 21G, 23D, 31K, 31P, 31Q, 31R, 35E, 39A, 51D1, 51D2, 57H, 69F, 69H, 69L, 73O, 75D, 75J, 79I, 79K, 79N, 79P, 79R, 79S, 81K, 81M, 81P, 85J, 85K, 89F, 89K, 101D, 105M, 109H, 115B, 123M, 145D, 155M, 159C, 159J, 167G, 167K, 167L, 173C, 173D, 173E, 177B, 177D, 177F, 177G, 179I, 183H, 187K, 187L, 189B, 199G, 201A, 205A, 207F, 207I, 211J, 215L, 219B, 221H, 221I, 225I, 225J, 233B, 235L, 237A1, 237A4, 237I, 247D, 247H, 249B, 249I, 251I, 259A, 259H, 259J, 261D, 269C, 281E, 281L, 283I, 291A, 293C, 293D, 293F, 293K, 295K, 297A, 297F, 297G, 297I, 299J, 301E, 305J, 311G, 313C

Artworks

Chris D Orr 10-110; Robin Somes 112-286; Tiffany Passmore 288-328;

Maps

Research by Martin Walters and John Akeroyd; artwork and production by Carte Blanche